The Realities of Witchcraft and Popular Magic in Early Modern Europe

Palgrave Historical Studies in Witchcraft and Magic

Series Editors: **Jonathan Barry, Willem de Blécourt and Owen Davies**

Titles include:

Edward Bever
THE REALITIES OF WITCHCRAFT AND POPULAR MAGIC IN EARLY MODERN EUROPE
Culture, Cognition, and Everyday Life

Julian Goodare, Lauren Martin and Joyce Miller
WITCHCRAFT AND BELIEF IN EARLY MODERN SCOTLAND

Forthcoming:

Johannes Dillinger
MAGICAL TREASURE HUNTING IN EUROPE AND NORTH AMERICA
A History

Soili-Maria Olli
TALKING TO DEVILS AND ANGELS IN SCANDINAVIA, 1500–1800

Alison Rowlands
WITCHCRAFT AND MASCULINITIES IN EARLY MODERN EUROPE

Rolf Schulte
MAN AS WITCH
Male Witches in Central Europe

Laura Stokes
THE DEMONS OF URBAN REFORM
The Rise of Witchcraft Prosecution, 1430–1530

Wanda Wyporska
WITCHCRAFT IN EARLY MODERN POLAND, 1500–1800

Palgrave Historical Studies in Witchcraft and Magic
Series Standing Order ISBN 978-1-4039-9566-7 Hardback 978-1-4039-9567-4 Paperback
(*outside North America only*)

You can receive future titles in this series as they are published by placing a standing order. Please contact your bookseller or, in case of difficulty, write to us at the address below with your name and address, the title of the series and the ISBN quoted above.

Customer Services Department, Macmillan Distribution Ltd, Houndmills, Basingstoke, Hampshire RG21 6XS, England

The Realities of Witchcraft and Popular Magic in Early Modern Europe

Culture, Cognition, and Everyday Life

Edward Bever

© Edward Bever 2008
Softcover reprint of the hardcover 1st edition 2008 978-1-4039-9781-4

All rights reserved. No reproduction, copy or transmission of this publication may be made without written permission.

No paragraph of this publication may be reproduced, copied or transmitted save with written permission or in accordance with the provisions of the Copyright, Designs and Patents Act 1988, or under the terms of any licence permitting limited copying issued by the Copyright Licensing Agency, 90 Tottenham Court Road, London W1T 4LP.

Any person who does any unauthorised act in relation to this publication may be liable to criminal prosecution and civil claims for damages.

The author has asserted his right to be identified as the author of this work in accordance with the Copyright, Designs and Patents Act 1988.

First published 2008 by
PALGRAVE MACMILLAN
Houndmills, Basingstoke, Hampshire RG21 6XS and
175 Fifth Avenue, New York, N.Y. 10010
Companies and representatives throughout the world

PALGRAVE MACMILLAN is the global academic imprint of the Palgrave Macmillan division of St. Martin's Press, LLC and of Palgrave Macmillan Ltd. Macmillan® is a registered trademark in the United States, United Kingdom and other countries. Palgrave is a registered trademark in the European Union and other countries.

ISBN 978-1-349-54664-0   ISBN 978-0-230-58211-8 (eBook)
DOI 10.1057/9780230582118

This book is printed on paper suitable for recycling and made from fully managed and sustained forest sources. Logging, pulping and manufacturing processes are expected to conform to the environmental regulations of the country of origin.

A catalogue record for this book is available from the British Library.

Library of Congress Cataloging-in-Publication Data

Bever, Edward Watts Morton.
 The realities of witchcraft and popular magic in early modern Europe: culture, cognition, and everyday life / Edward Bever.
   p. cm. — (Palgrave historical studies in witchcraft and magic)
 Includes bibliographical references and index.

1. Witchcraft—Europe—History. 2. Magic—Europe—History. I. Title.

BF1584.E9B48 2008
133.4'3094—dc22
                                                                    2008000163

10 9 8 7 6 5 4 3 2 1
17 16 15 14 13 12 11 10 09 08

Transferred to digital printing in 2009.

For Patricia

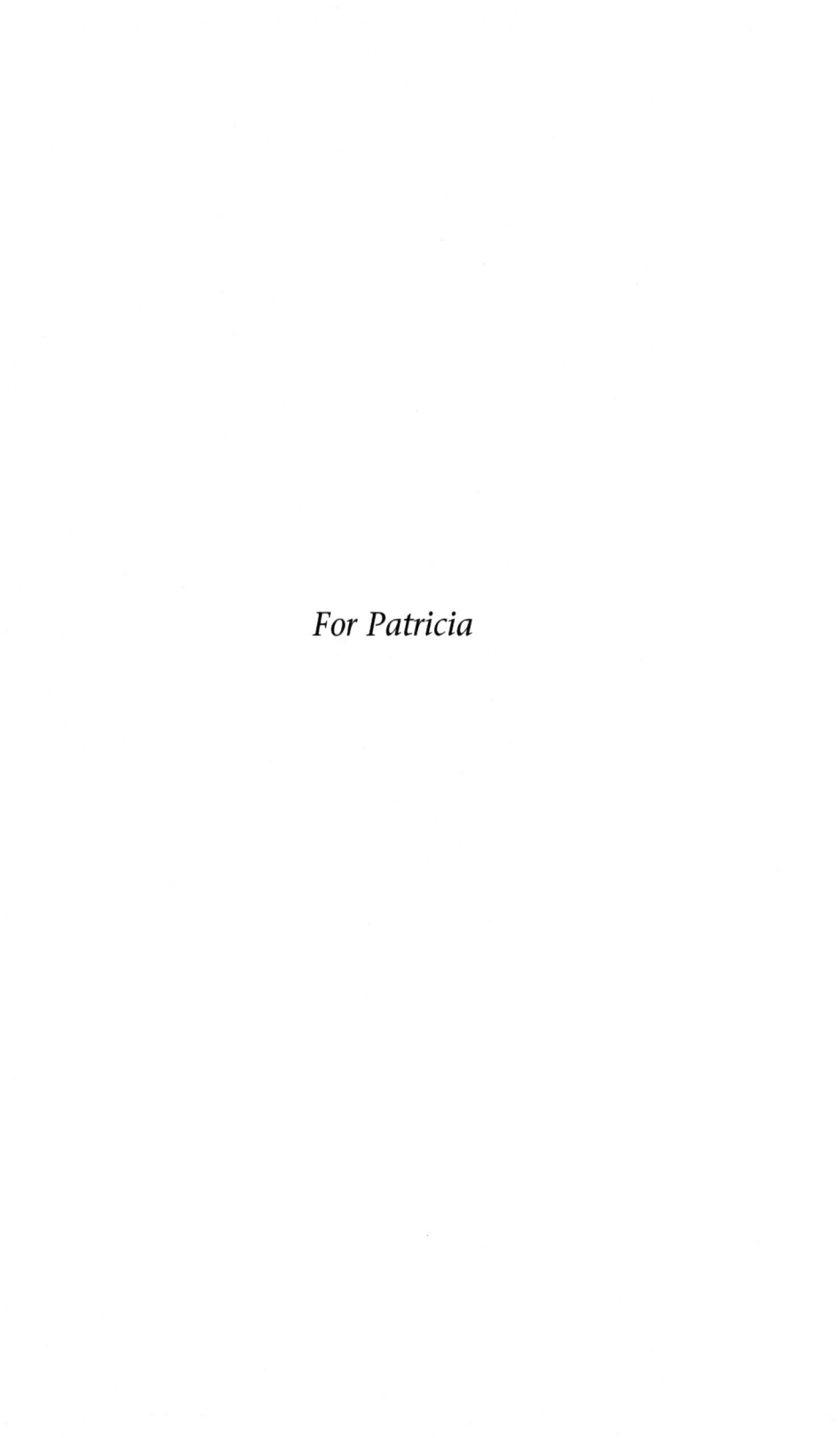

Contents

List of Figures	ix
List of Tables	x
Acknowledgments	xi
Introduction	xiv

Part I The Reality of *Maleficium*   1

1 The Varieties of *Maleficium*   5
    Poison and assault   8
    Occult injury and psychosocial factors in disease   11
    Ill will and interpersonal communications   20
    Harm to animals   37
    Conclusion   39

2 *Maleficium* and Society   40
    Maleficium and intracommunal conflict   40
    Gender, age, and interpersonal power   47
    Hard times and hard hearts   60

Part II The Realities of Diabolism   65

3 The Devil in the Duchy of Württemberg   67
    Origin and diffusion of the diabolic stereotype   67
    The Devil made me do it   73
    Dealing with the Devil   79

4 Witch Dances and Witch Salves   93
    Rumors of witch dances   97
    Dreams of dances   106
    Dances and trances   118
    Scopolamine dreams   129

5 Sorcery, Satanism, and Shamanism   151
    The realities of sorcery in early modern Europe   154
    Sorcery and satanism   168
    Witchcraft and shamanism   185
    Conclusion   212

Part III The Realities of Beneficent Magic — 215

6 Divination and Prophesy — 219
   The varieties of divinatory activity — 219
   Divination and guilt — 221
   Locating hidden things — 230
   Fortune-telling and prognostication — 250
   Prophesy — 258
   Conclusion — 269

7 Beneficent Manipulative Magic — 271
   Magical healing — 273
      The varieties of healing practices — 274
      The efficacy of magical healing — 287
   Magical countermeasures — 303
   Magical enhancements — 312
   Supernatural powers and anomalous events — 318
   Conclusion — 334

Part IV Repression and Reality — 337

8 Magic and Society — 339
   Practitioners of beneficent magic — 339
   The mechanisms of repression — 349
      The judicial system — 350
      The church — 356
      Local communities — 362
      Individual psychophysiology — 372
   Repression and the marginalization of magic — 378
      The roots and rise of judicial repression — 381
      The prosecutions falter — 389
      Second surge and the decline of witchcraft — 399
      Enlightenment and repression — 415
   Conclusion — 429

Conclusion — 433

Appendix — 441

Notes — 444

Bibliography — 504

Index — 558

Figures

Figure 8.1	Witchcraft and magic trials	379
Figure 8.2	Witchcraft and magic trials per 100,000 inhabitants	380
Figure 8.3	Witchcraft and poison cases	395
Figure 8.4	Witchcraft, magic, and poison trials	403
Figure 8.5	Witchcraft, magic, and poison trials per 100,000 inhabitants	404
Figure 8.6	All trials for magic, healing, and treasure-hunting	421
Figure 8.7	All trials for magic, healing, and treasure-hunting per 100,000 inhabitants	424

Tables

Table 1.1	Accusations of *maleficium*	6
Table 3.1	Geographic distribution of witch publication over time	69
Table 6.1	Sampled uses of divination by trial type	221
Table 7.1	Purposes of sampled beneficent magic by trial type	272
Table 8.1	Sources of accusations over time	389
Table 8.2	Torture in sampled cases	393
Table 8.3	Executions for witchcraft in Württemberg	393
Table 8.4	Terminology used by Tübingen law faculty for witchcraft	393
Table 8.5	Theological examinations	396
Table 8.6	Characterizations of magic in trial documents over time	425

Acknowledgments

I would like to start by thanking the people who contributed most directly to this book getting done: my old friend Allan Malz, who read and corrected drafts of all the chapters; Richard Golden, historian and editor extraordinaire, who read and critiqued the entire book as well; Michael Winkelmann, who generously agreed to look over the manuscript with an anthropologist's eye even though I contacted him out of the blue; and Matthew Rizzo, who took time from his teaching, research, and practice to review the neurocognitive sections for me. I also owe a debt of gratitude to Willem de Blécourt, who invited me to submit a proposal for the book as part of the "Palgrave Historical Studies in Witchcraft and Magic" series, and who also spent a long evening discussing it with me when the first draft was done. Finally, I have to thank Anita Raith, now Bendner, who encouraged me to emphasize the interdisciplinary aspects of my research, and took the time to discuss with me at length cases in my study that she is familiar with. All of these peoples' help has been invaluable; responsibility for any failings is, of course, mine alone.

Next, I would like to thank the scholars who have helped me in various ways with the efforts that led to this book. First and foremost, I want to thank Theodore K. Rabb, who was my advisor when I wrote the thesis which forms the core of this study, and has been very helpful and supportive since. I also want to thank Natalie Z. Davis, Erik Midelfort, James Vann, Inge Schöck, Michael Harner, Peter Stearns, Carlo Ginzberg, and Brian Levack, whose support and encouragement contributed to this study in a variety of ways. Additionally, I would like to thank the members of the *Arbeitskreis Interdisciplinäre Hexenforschung* for a number of stimulating sessions and evenings in the "Trinkstube," and also express my appreciation to Dieter Bauer of the Academy of the Diocese of Rottenburg-Stuttgart and Jurgen Michael Schmidt at the University of Tübingen, the participants in several faculty development sessions at SUNY Old Westbury, and the students in my course "Women and Witchcraft" in 1998, 1999, and 2004. I thanked the numerous people who helped with my dissertation in the acknowledgements there, but I feel I should reiterate my appreciation for the help and support of two in particular, Maureen Callahan and Christine Lunardini, who contributed in innumerable ways to that phase of this project.

I owe a debt of gratitude to the staffs of a number of research institutions. First and foremost is the staff of the *Haupstaatsarchiv* in Stuttgart, whose friendliness and helpfulness always made it a pleasure to work there. Secondly, I thank the circulation, reference, and interlibrary loan personnel at the Stony Brook University library for their unfailing courtesy and assistance; the helpful and friendly staff in Old Westbury's library; the staffs of the

Württemberg *Landesbibliotek* and the New York Public Library; and the Library of Congress, which is truly a temple of democratic knowledge. I appreciated the opportunity to use the New York University library once as well, and, finally, I want to thank Klaus Graf, who runs the Listserve "Hexenforschung," which has given me invaluable bibliographic leads and stimulating exchanges.

SUNY Old Westbury has been particularly supportive of my scholarly research, with a Presidential Grant, a number of faculty development grants, and a sabbatical last year that enabled me to bring this project close to completion. I appreciate this support greatly. I also thank Judith Walsh, who as chair of my department during a very tumultuous period respected the time I needed to complete this work after my sabbatical was over.

Next I want to acknowledge the kind permission I received to incorporate parts of articles of mine that were previously published in two journals and two books. Specifically, sections of Chapter 1 are reprinted, in part, from "Witchcraft Fears and Psychosocial Factors in Disease," *The Journal of Interdisciplinary History* 30 (2000), 576–81, with the permission of the editors of *The Journal of Interdisciplinary History* and the MIT Press, Cambridge, MA © 2000 by the Massachusetts Institute of Technology and *The Journal of Interdisciplinary History*, Inc. Similarly, sections of Chapter 2 are reprinted, in part, from "Women, Witchcraft, and Power in the Early Modern Community," *Journal of Social History*, 35/4 (Summer, 2002), 955–88, with the permission of the editors of *Journal of Social History* and George Mason University Press, Fairfax, Virginia © 2002 by Peter N. Stearns. Other sections of Chapter 2 are reprinted, in part, from "Old Age and Witchcraft," *Old Age in Preindustrial Society*, editor Peter N. Stearns (New York and London: Holmes and Meier, 1982), with the permission of Peter N. Stearns © 1982 by Peter N. Stearns. Finally, sections of Chapter 8 are reprinted, in part, from "The Crisis of Confidence in Witchcraft and the Crisis of Authority," in *Early Modern Europe: From Crisis to Stability*, editors Philip Benedict and Myron P. Gutmann (Newark, DE: University of Delaware Press, 2005), with the permission of Associated University Presses and Rosemont Publishing & Printing Corp © 2005 by Rosemont Publishing and Printing Corp.

On a more personal note, I want to thank my friends Volker and Christel Koehl and their family, who opened their home to me for extended periods a number of times over the past decades while I did my research in Stuttgart. Our chance meeting gave me the opportunity to get to know Württemberg in a way far beyond what can be gleaned from books and archives, and has blossomed into a life-long friendship. I am deeply grateful for all they have done for me from the beginning of my research through my final check of the archives, both personally and for the contribution it has made to my work.

Closer to home, I want to thank my brother, Christopher T. Bever, MD, for reading and critiquing a draft of my paper on psychosocial factors in disease, which gave me valuable insights into current medical thinking on this issue, and also for lending me a number of books on neurology that stimulated my thinking in this area enormously. I thank my sister Poppy for giving me the jar of peanut butter that started this all, and my sister Sarah, who agreed to take the peanut butter in exchange for the book. She was also my friend and confidante for decades, and I miss her. I owe an incalculable debt of gratitude to my parents, for without their loving support this project would not have been begun, resumed, or completed. I have appreciated the cheerful patience and enthusiastic encouragement of my two younger children, Tony and Celia, and I thank my older son, Noah, for being such a cool guy.

And, of course, I cannot hope to express my full gratitude for my wife Patricia, whose unflagging love, encouragement, support, and patience have kept me pointed toward this project, no matter how obliquely, even when I myself did not see how I would ever get it done. She has brought me books, told me of her dreams, kept me at it, made sacrifices, listened to me work through ideas, and suggested many herself. She has never doubted the need for me to write this, and never wavered in her commitment to helping me see it through. I love her immensely, and thank her profoundly. It is to her that I dedicate this book.

Introduction

The basic question this book seeks to answer is, "What basis did early modern beliefs about witchcraft and magic have in reality?" To answer this question, it focuses on a detailed study of trial records from the Duchy of Württemberg, a medium-size principality in southwestern Germany that conducted a moderate number of prosecutions, and evaluates the events and experiences reported in them in the context of Württemberg's judicial administration, socioeconomic development, and provincial culture; the findings of historical studies of other parts of Germany and Europe; and interdisciplinary investigations into the activities and phenomena they describe. The results of this investigation indicate that early modern Europeans' fears of malefic magic reflected both actual practices and potential harms more than previous accounts have suggested; that belief in the Devil and witch Sabbaths not only contributed to but also reflected the perceptual and cognitive processes by which people construct their experience of reality; that beneficent magic was both pervasive and more potent than heretofore appreciated; and that while the European elite's campaign to repress popular magic during the period did not succeed in eliminating it, the effort did succeed in marginalizing it and thereby contributed to the eventual triumph of disbelief in modern culture.

Determining what was real about early modern witchcraft and magic involves addressing three more specific questions. First, to what extent did people really engage in and experience the things contained in the beliefs? Second, to what extent did their activities have real effects, and their perceptions reflect objective events? Third, to the extent that their perceptions did not reflect external reality, what were the actual sources and nature of these subjective experiences? The book's purpose in answering these questions is both to help satisfy the curiosity many people have about the reality of the phenomena involved and also, by establishing that there was more to the beliefs than scholars have generally assumed, to enrich the discussion of the wider role and significance of witchcraft and magic in early modern society and culture, and of the reasons for and consequences of their eventual decline as well.

In seeking the answers to these questions, this study employs two basic methodologies. First of all, it is centered on a close reading of judicial records preserved in Württemberg's archives. The core of the study is a series of systematically sampled trials, supplemented by material drawn from an extensive reading in additional records. These are carefully examined to distinguish as far as possible what people actually did and what they experienced from what they later only claimed from fear, pain, perversity, expediency, or suggestibility. As a general rule, tortured testimony is excluded from consideration, and all other evidence is evaluated with a consciousness that not only can less blatant pressures and inducements influence what people say, but also that judicial records by their nature emphasize certain things and disregard others and, in the end, are written by one party in a contentious interaction. Nevertheless, a substantial amount of credible testimony is contained in the records, which generally helps answer the first question, the extent to which people really did and experienced things contained in their beliefs about witchcraft and magic, and it also helps answer the second question, the extent to which these activities had real effects (for example, by demonstrating the actual use of poisons) and were based on actual experiences (as when a partner in illicit sex was afterward understood to have been the Devil). The information thus gleaned is connected to the evidence of similar and related activities and experiences in other parts of Europe and discussed in relation to broader sociocultural trends so that the results of this intensive local study have a significance beyond the specific incidents and provincial culture involved.

The second methodology the book employs is to conduct interdisciplinary investigations into the types of activities and experiences revealed by the archival research. The specific disciplines involved vary depending on the nature of the activities and experiences in question, but include in particular recent work on psychosocial factors in health and disease and nonconscious interpersonal communication, new studies of cognition and perception, contemporary research into consciousness and alternate states of consciousness, and scientific investigations of fringe phenomena. These investigations contribute additional insight into which unusual perceptions could have been of objectively real physical phenomena (like when what appears to have been ball lightning, an unexplained but widely accepted physical phenomenon, was seen near the grave of a recently buried woman), which activities could have had real results, and what those results might have been (as when expressions of anger appear to have triggered stress-reactions contributing to illness, or when divination seems to have elicited unconscious knowledge through ideomotor activity). When the evidence suggests that an experience did not reflect an external event, interdisciplinary insights can help explain how such perceptions arose and why they were taken to be important sources of knowledge by the people who experienced them.

While these two methodologies address the basic questions the book seeks to answer, they are not sufficient to accomplish its larger purpose, which is to show how the answers they supply impact the broader historical understanding of witchcraft and magic and their relationship to early modern society and culture as a whole. Therefore, the book also draws liberally on approaches used in other, more standard historical studies. For example, it discusses intellectual and legal history, starting with the general European background and moving to the specific situations in southwestern Germany and Württemberg, to show the interplay of popular and official beliefs and their relationship to the legal system as background to the cases that are studied in detail. It includes statistical information about witch suspects, accusers, and beneficent magicians in systematically sampled trials to help determine their social positions in their communities, and it considers how magical beliefs and practices fit into the larger context of popular culture. By integrating interdisciplinary investigations involving the cognitive and other sciences and more traditional social and cultural approaches, the book develops a richer picture of the specific cases being investigated while conveying their implications for our broader understanding of early modern witchcraft and magic.

By focusing squarely on what was real about early modern witchcraft and magic, *The Realities of Witchcraft and Popular Magic in Early Modern Europe* adopts a significantly different perspective than most other scholarly historical treatments. A glance at some of the most notable recent English and American works on the subject highlights this difference. Alison Rowlands' *Witchcraft Narratives in Germany* (2003), for example, seeks to explain why one German city near Württemberg did not experience many witch trials, assuming that such trials were displaced expressions of "social and psychic tensions" in which the participants "pursued strategies, expressed emotions and negotiated conflicts" that were only obliquely manifested in accusations and confessions of witchcraft (p. 1). Walter Stephens' *Demon Lovers* (2002) interprets demonology as a desperate attempt to defend supernatural delusions, while Hans Peter Broedel's *The Malleus Maleficarum and the Construction of Witchcraft* (2003) traces the interplay of elite and popular beliefs in the creation of that seminal witch tract. Michael Bailey's *Battling Demons: Witchcraft, Heresy, and Reform in the Late Middle Ages* (2003) focuses on Johann Nider's earlier work in the context of late Medieval religious tensions, and Gary Waite's *Heresy, Magic and Witchcraft* (2003) offers a broader interpretation of the witch trials as manifestations of religious tensions and confessional conflict. Lyndal Roper's *Witch Craze: Terror and Fantasy in Baroque Germany* (2004) explains witchcraft accusations in terms of "passions ... derived from deeply rooted fantasies," while Stuart Clark's *Thinking with Demons* (1996) argues explicitly against attempts to discern reality in witchcraft beliefs. All of these works raise interesting issues and offer stimulating insights, but all work within well-established social, intellectual, and psychological traditions that focus on the elements of unreality rather than the aspects of reality in beliefs about witchcraft and magic.

The current study does not exist in isolation, however. Robin Briggs' *Witches and Neighbors* (1996), while it shares the basic assumptions of the works mentioned above, uses a focused study of witch trials in Lorraine, like Württemberg a center of widespread but not virulent prosecutions, as the basis for a generalized depiction of witchcraft beliefs in popular culture in the core areas of persecution: western and central Europe. Eva Pócs' *Between the Living and the Dead* (1999), which is more specialized but also more groundbreaking than Briggs, concentrates on an area peripheral to the main persecutions, Hungary, and is therefore able to bring to light popular beliefs and practices involving witches, healers, and other magical folk that were obscured by the prevalence of the witch stereotype and the use of torture in the core areas. In a sense, the present work seeks to combine the strengths of these two works, including elements of each that the other lacks – information about the core areas that is in Briggs but not Pócs, and insights about popular magic beyond witchcraft that are in Pócs but not Briggs – while going beyond them by undertaking explorations of the origins and nature of magical beliefs that neither attempts. The present work also has affinities with Carlo Ginzburg's *I benandanti* (1966, translated as *Night Battles* in 1985) and *Ecstasies* (1991) and Wolfgang Behringer's *Shaman of Oberstdorf* (1998), which are more narrowly focused but specifically treat elements in popular culture as actual experiences rather than simply folk beliefs.

One very recent book, Emma Wilby's *Cunning Folk and Familiar Spirits: Shamanistic Visionary Traditions in Early Modern British Witchcraft and Magic* (2005) appeared too late to be consulted for this study, but according to an online review by Moira Smith, it discusses witches' familiar spirits, a concept most characteristic of English witchcraft, as "remnants of pre-Christian belief and practice," an instance of a "transhistorical and transcultural" shamanism "that survived amongst the folk" in the form of "vision experiences of British cunning folk who regarded the fairy folk as sacred spirits." The review criticizes the book for some methodological flaws – specifically an oversimplified presentation of shamanism as a transcultural phenomenon, and assumptions that current folklore connects in some direct way to prehistoric religion, that popular and elite culture exist in substantial isolation from each other, and that contemporary tribal religions can be used in a straightforward way to illuminate prehistoric European religions – but whatever the merits of this critique, it sounds as if the book does present some additional evidence of shamanic activity in the British Isles and may find support in places from the interpretation developed here.

While looking at the relationship of the approach employed in the present work to other recent studies conveys something of its implications, these are most apparent in considering the relationship of its two methodologies to the larger tradition of scholarship on witchcraft and popular magic as a whole.

The first methodology, close reading of archival materials to determine what people actually did and experienced and what effects those actions and experiences had, is a basic historical practice that would be totally unremarkable in an investigation of almost any other topic. In the case of witchcraft and magic, though, while close reading of archival materials is not unusual, reading them to determine what was really going on is less common, for historians have traditionally started from the assumption that at bottom nothing real can have been going on, and therefore have focused on explaining why people would hold delusional beliefs and engage in inefficacious activities. Of course, they have always recognized that some real activities and experiences were involved, but traditional rationalists explicitly regarded them as superstitious nonsense, while the leading romantic scholar, Margaret Murray, constructed a credulous interpretation of witchcraft beliefs that, when it was debunked, effectively discredited attempts to discern aspects of reality in them for a generation. Social historians recognized that there was a certain amount of real activity recorded in the archival materials they analyzed, but they focused their attention on the evidence of mechanisms by which other, to them more significant, processes like class conflict or gender oppression were re-directed into witchcraft accusations, and tended to treat any actual activities as secondary by-products of these social forces. Postmodern historians have adopted the cultural relativism of anthropology and the epistemological relativism of semiotics, which have enabled them to make considerable progress in establishing people's actual beliefs and practices, but the implication of this approach (and frequently the explicit position as well) is that the beliefs are produced by the logic of narrative and the interdependence of cultural forms essentially independent of anything that might have actually happened.

In terms of discerning the aspects of reality in early modern witchcraft and magic, recent historical work, not only that of Pócs, Ginzburg, and Behringer mentioned above, but also of historians such as Keith Thomas, Willem de Blécourt, Owen Davies, Gábor Klaniczay, and the whole school of German historians who focus on witchcraft in the context of "everyday life," such as Reiner Walz in *Hexenglaube und Magische Kommunikation im Dorf der Frühen Neuzeit* and Eva Labouvie in *Verbotene Künste*, has been particularly fruitful in the area of popular magic, where the existence of beneficent practices and practitioners has been established with relatively little controversy. The existence and, more importantly, significance of malefic magic is a touchier subject, however, for there is an understandable reluctance to "blame the victims" of persecutions that have been recognized as misguided and unjust for centuries. The historians who have explored beneficent magic have done much to show how witchcraft fit into normal life, but their emphasis is still on explaining witchcraft fears rather than examining malefic practices. Nevertheless, evidence of actual malefic practices is scattered throughout the historical literature, and discussed more directly in Chadwick Hansen's *Witchcraft at Salem* and a few recent works like Giovanna Fiume's "The Old Vinegar Lady," Ingrid Ahrendt-Schulte's *Zauberinnen in der Stadt Horn*, Richard Kieckhefer's *Magic in the Middle Ages*, and Hans Sebald's "Justice by Magic." It is also, as we shall see, revealed by a dispassionate reading of the records of small trials. Therefore, the most notable contribution of the close archival readings to determine what people were really doing and experiencing conveyed in the following chapters is to show what *maleficium* actually involved and the extent to which it was a real factor in early modern peoples' individual and communal lives. Without in any sense attempting to justify the early modern persecutions, the book provides new insights into why the fear that fuelled them existed and what their consequences were.

The second methodology employed in this book, interdisciplinary investigations into the types of activities and experiences revealed by the archival research, sheds additional light on *maleficium*, because the research into psychological factors in disease and subliminal communication suggests that it was far more potent than is generally acknowledged, being rooted in the ability of threat displays, unconscious as well as conscious, to induce chronic stress, independent of the belief-system or psychological health of their target. Additional interdisciplinary investigations explore the nature and significance of the experiences related to diabolism; the efficacy of divination, healing, and other forms of beneficent magic; and the neurocognitive basis of disbelief. A number of historians have reported on examples of people who really had experiences they understood to be magical, but attempts to understand what these involved, how people could have experienced them, and what effects they could have had are few and far between. Traditional rationalists regarded such experiences as ephemeral, either fraudulent or manifestations of some pathology. Romantics portrayed the experiences as physical events as far as possible, explaining the demonology as a misunderstanding of their true nature (peasant rebelliousness or an underground, prehistoric pagan religion) and offered little insight into the roots and nature of the physically impossible features beyond the suggestion of the influence of hallucinogenic drugs. Social scientists have developed models of the psychological processes by which social conflicts could be sublimated into witchcraft accusations, but their explanations for magical experiences, to the extent that they attempted or implied them, have generally involved emphasizing the degree to which they were based on rationally intelligible misrepresentations such as fraud or therapeutic deception and then falling back on vague speculations about pathology or drugs. Postmodern scholars extend their agnostic approach from the external efficacy of magic beliefs to their internal psychology, treating belief as sufficient to account for reported experience, and paying little heed to the difference between construction of a narrative and the process of perception.

In recent times, a number of historians have evinced interest in understanding the roots and nature of experiences like, as opposed to beliefs about, demonic possession (Moshe Slutovsky in "A Divine Apparition or Demonic Possession," for example) and the "Old Hag" syndrome (particularly Owen Davies in "The Nightmare Experience, Sleep Paralysis, and Witchcraft Accusations"). However, so far these investigations have been relatively isolated and *ad hoc*, with some reviving psychoanalytic interpretations and others drawing eclectically on cognitive materials. *The Realities of Witchcraft and Popular Magic in Early Modern Europe* is intended to provide a broader, more cohesive theoretical framework for this latter approach, for, while the impetus for the various interdisciplinary investigations the book includes is the specific evidence found in the archival material, the investigations are not unrelated. Instead, research into the relationship of mind and body in disease, the workings of perception and cognition, and the effects of alternate states of consciousness like dreams, trance, and intoxication leads to an interconnected body of recent work by cognitive and cross-cultural psychologists, neuroscientists, psychological anthropologists, and even cognitively oriented scholars of religion that has changed our understanding of how humans think and experience the world so substantially that it has been labeled the "cognitive revolution." For a long time, this work in the cognitive sciences and the cultural approaches that currently dominate historical scholarship have been seen as antagonistic, but recently attempts have begun to bring them together, to show how cognitive structures, perceptual processes, and cultural constructs interact in shaping human understanding and experience. Some examples of this trend that proved particularly helpful for the present study include Brad Shore's *Culture in Mind: Cognition, Culture, and the Problem of Meaning*; Merlin Donald's *A Mind So Rare: The Evolution of Human Consciousness*; Michael Winkelman's *Shamanism: The Neural Ecology of Consciousness and Healing*; Charles Laughlin, John McManus, and Eugene d'Aquili's *Brain, Symbol, and Experience*, and Alexander Hinton's *Biocultural Approaches to the Emotions*. *The Realities of Witchcraft and Popular Magic in Early Modern Europe* seeks to contribute to this movement by drawing from and at the same time adding to the growing body of literature on the relationship between cognition and culture. Its final goal is to help open up an historical dimension to this interdisciplinary discussion while developing a fuller and richer "realist" understanding of witchcraft and magic.

Part I The Reality of *Maleficium*

Introduction

The Latin word *maleficium* originally meant "wrongdoing" or "mischief," but in Roman times it came to be specifically associated with harmful magic. Most agricultural peoples have believed that injury can be inflicted via occult means, and have tried to defend themselves against it by utilizing protective magic, appeasement, and various forms of counteraction including counter-magic, spontaneous physical retribution, and formal legal sanctions. Correspondingly, early Roman law outlawed harmful ritual magic, sorcery, because of the injury it was thought to inflict on individuals. Later, imperial Rome persecuted magical practitioners more generally as a threat to political stability, and the Judeo-Christian tradition regarded any ritual magic as a moral lapse, so when Rome adopted Christianity Theodosius' law code substituted *maleficium* in place of the more neutral word *magia*, categorizing all magic, whatever its intent or effect, as harmful. Medieval law codes and theology maintained the idea that all magic was to some degree harmful, but generally treated magic used to cause injury more seriously than magic used for benign purposes. Late medieval demonologists like Heinrich Kramer, the author of the *Malleus Maleficarum*, argued that all magic was equally harmful because it involved the agency of demons and at least an implicit pact with the Devil, and their arguments led to a strengthening of laws in this direction, but the moral equivalence of all forms of magic never won general acceptance in early modern Europe's elite, let alone its popular, culture. Most witch accusations made by commoners concerned harmful magic, and most witch trials included charges of *maleficium*, harms inflicted through occult means.[1]

There was no single law against witchcraft in early modern Europe, and, in fact, there was no single legal definition of the crime. Statutes varied enormously in their wording and significantly in the substantive importance they placed on different aspects of the generalized belief. However, there was no question of the crucial role of malefic acts, whether because of their inherent harmfulness or as evidence that the suspect was "given to Satan."[2] The example of the steps that led to the proscription of witchcraft in Württemberg illustrates the idiosyncratic process by which demonological theory influenced legal practice, while highlighting both the centrality of *maleficium* and continuing uncertainty about the role of the Devil. In 1532, Charles V promulgated the *Constitution Criminialis Carolina*, a model law code for the jurisdictions contained in the Holy Roman Empire. Dubbed the *Carolina*, the code stipulated that "when someone harms people or brings them trouble by magic, one should punish them with death, and one should use the punishment of death by fire. When, however, someone uses magic and yet does no one any harm with it, he should be punished otherwise, according to the custom of the case."[3] The *Carolina* thus proscribed harmful magic in clear and unequivocal terms, but sidestepped the issue of nonharmful magic. In 1667, the Duchy of Württemberg implemented the suggested reforms in its Sixth Provincial Ordinance, adopting the *Carolina's* prohibition of harmful magic "almost word for word," while creating a more complex compromise regarding magic without harm in which a pact with the Devil alone was to be prosecuted and punished as severely as *maleficium*, but magic involving neither a pact nor injury was to be dealt with more leniently.[4] Here again, the issue of *maleficium* seems to have been clear-cut, while the question of witchcraft without harm involved a compromise between those who held that any dealings with the Devil were equally bad and those who argued that beneficent magic was less bad than malevolent magic.

As in most jurisdictions, the Württemberg statute did not specify exactly what constituted harmful magic. Instead, commoners who suspected their neighbors, local officials investigating complaints, ducal officials supervising the trials, and the legal experts at the University of Tübingen who reviewed them at critical junctures all worked from a common fund of knowledge that mixed in different degrees local traditions, regional pamphlet literature, and the Europe-wide demonology. Witches were generally thought to use magic to influence the weather, interfere with smaller-scale domestic processes like churning butter and brewing beer, harm farm animals or prevent them from producing eggs or milk, cause impotence in men or frigidity in women, and injure people through illness or accidents.[5] The means by which they were thought to work their *maleficium* included secret spells and incantations; actions and gestures; potions, salves, and powders; magically potent objects; a look, breath, touch, or blow; public verbal curses; and the sheer power of their ill will. Some of these means involved deliberate rituals, which anthropologists and historians call sorcery, while others manifested an inherent power in the witch, referred to as witchcraft; but while early moderns recognized the potency of both means, they did not consider the distinction crucial. Evidence of sorcery would certainly strengthen an accusation, but it was by nature often not available, and was not necessary to sustain a charge of *maleficium*; the correspondence of an expression of ill will followed by some injury was the most typical basis for an allegation.

In the first chapter of this section, we will look at the variety of injuries and expressions of ill will that were connected to allegations of *maleficium* that precipitated small trials or came out during their course. In contrast to most previous historical discussions, however, we shall do this with an eye toward discovering what was really going on, both in terms of the extent to which suspects really did express ill will in various ways, and in terms of the extent to which these expressions of ill will really could have caused the harms intended. In the second chapter, we will look at the social context of these expressions and their consequences: how they fit into the larger constellation of interpersonal conflicts typical of village and small urban communities in early modern Europe; how they related to social characteristics like class, gender, and age; and how they related to the mass witch prosecutions that swept up dozens, and even hundreds, of victims at a time in a relentless cycle of denunciation and torture so horrifying that it came to dominate our understanding of witchcraft to the point that it has hindered for centuries our ability, our very willingness, to see the real activities and their real consequences that lay at the root of the phenomenon.

While both chapters draw upon a wide reading of materials in the archives of the Duchy of Württemberg, they center on a detailed analysis of a systematic sample of 29 trials labeled as witchcraft or a pact with the Devil in the archival index. The sample was drawn from the cases contained in the records of the Ducal High Council, "Malefizsachen," A209. The sample was stratified chronologically, with the specific cases chosen at random within three strata. One was chosen from the four before 1590 (25%), 20 of 132 between 1581 and 1669 (15%), and 6 of 49 after 1670 (12%). The reason for the stratification was to ensure representation of early and late trials; the reason for the slight overrepresentation of cases in the middle section is that examination of the index of *concilia* concerning witchcraft and related in the University of Tübingen's legal archive indicated that a number of cases from this period were contained there that were not contained in the High Council's archive, and so the actual number of trials in the duchy in this period is actually slightly underrepresented by a sample drawn from the High Council's records.[6] The sample was used as the basis for a considerable amount of quantitative analysis of judicial and social aspects of the trials in my dissertation "Witchcraft in Early Modern Wuerttemberg," but since these characteristics have been fairly well established since it was written (see especially Brian Levack, *The Witch Hunt in Early Modern Europe*), these analyses are drawn on here as appropriate to support the present inquiry and the sample is mainly used to give a general quantitative structure to the discussion in order to counteract the subtle biases that a lack of attention to quantities can introduce into analysis. The cases are listed in the appendix.

In addition to the witchcraft sample, a similar sample was taken of 21 out of 48 cases labeled *zauberei, magia*, or other general terms for magic in the archival index. Upon examination, about half were found to basically be late witch cases, but the government's changing terminology (discussed in Chapter 8) led the archival indexer to label them more vaguely as magic. The other half were a combination of beneficent magic cases generally designated by more specific labels like "blessing" and "treasure-hunting" and a miscellany of other magical practices and unusual occurrences. The latter group is utilized with the samples of specific beneficent practices in Part III, as explained in the introduction there, while the witch-like cases were not analyzed systematically, but instead are drawn upon like the numerous other cases read unsystematically to supplement the systematic sample.

1
The Varieties of *Maleficium*

Historians have long recognized that some people in early modern Europe did attempt to perpetrate *maleficium*, but have downplayed it both because their focus has generally been on the dysfunctions of early modern society that led to the widespread indiscriminate witch persecutions and because its has generally been regarded as essentially ineffectual, as strong at most as the weakness of the people against whom it was directed. Indeed, the main focus of their attention, as with other social scientists, has been on the reasons why people say that they are the victims of occult attack. Explanations have included fraudulent self-interest, the projection of anger or guilt onto the object of the anger or guilt, a way of accounting for inexplicable misfortune, the workings of a self-referencing symbol system, and "infantile fantasy."[1] Confessions of witchcraft are correspondingly treated as some sort of cognitive malfunction resulting from either some individual psychological or some more general cultural defect: the confession is either an ex-post-facto bid for attention or a narcissistic delusion of control to compensate for powerlessness.[2] To the extent that people did suffer misfortune related to perceived *maleficium*, this is explained as a result of their own weakness; "fears," it has been noted, "have genuine power against the suggestible."[3] Even postmodernist analysis tends to reinforce this basic view, for while it takes the position that "reality" is just a sociocultural construct, this ends up just being another way of explaining how the people involved in witchcraft cases didn't know what was really going on.[4]

Evidence contained in the stratified random sample of trials conducted in the Duchy of Württemberg between 1565 and 1701 considered in light of recent advances in cognitive and medical science, however, suggests that these various explanations, while they do a good job of explaining certain phenomena associated with witchcraft and magic beliefs, are seriously incomplete.[5] The reason is that they start from the basic assumptions that occult attack was uncommon, that it was usually ineffectual when it happened, and that when it was effective it was only as effective as the purported victims let it be. All three of these assumptions, however, are wrong. Occult attacks may not have been as common as some early moderns feared, but they were an integral part of early modern life; many of them had genuine physical or psychological power; and this power was to a significant degree independent of the beliefs, fears, or psychological weaknesses of the people on the receiving end.

Table 1.1 shows the various types of accusations that were made in the course of the 27 cases:

Table 1.1 Accusations of *maleficium*

Type of injury	Primary	Secondary	Total
Theft	2	2	4
Arson	0	1	1
Poison	7	6	13
Assault	5	5	10
Occult injury	6	18	24
Harm to animals	3	21	24
Total	23	53	76

Source: Sampled witchcraft cases (see the appendix).

Primary accusations refer to those which precipitated trials, while secondary accusations are older allegations that surfaced during the course of a trial.

Several things are immediately apparent from this table. First of all, some of the types of *maleficium* that were part of the general discourse about the crime are not here, specifically weather manipulation and interference with domestic production (there was one allegation involving impotence, which is included in the occult injury category). There were a couple of spectacular trials involving allegations of weather manipulation early on in the region, but their absence from the sample of trials, as well as the impression given by a less systematic reading of a much larger number of trial records in the ducal archive, suggests that trials involving this form of witchcraft were infrequent at most in Württemberg. In the case of Württemberg this might be attributable to a local theological tradition discounting witches' power over the weather, but a similar pattern of a few spectacular trials centering on weather magic seems to have obtained in some other parts of Europe like Scotland and Hungary, while the great majority of trials centered on other things.[6] Similarly, interference with domestic production was also reported in the pamphlet literature, particularly in England, but appears to have been no more frequent in actual trials there than in Württemberg.[7]

Secondly, the great majority of accusations were concerned with injury to people and animals, which is also consistent with patterns noted elsewhere.[8] Theft and arson were the only forms of damage to inanimate property reported, and there were only five reports of these among the sampled trials (and only another two mentions of witchcraft and theft and one of witchcraft and arson in the archival index cataloging Württemberg's judicial records from the time). Moreover, the specific circumstances of these accusations further reduce their apparent importance. The charge of arson was just a secondary accusation.[9] Both of the primary accusations linking theft and witchcraft (as well as the only other two mentions of the two crimes together in the archival index) occurred relatively early, before 1620. In the earlier of the sampled cases, a woman named Barbara Tolmayer was arrested in the town of Freudenstadt for theft; she was accused of witchcraft because her husband had recently been executed for the offense in the nearby town of Balingen, confessed to witchcraft under torture, but seduced her jailer and escaped.[10] In the second case, a young woman named Maria Braittingen was arrested for stealing in the village of Eberspach in 1619 and volunteered that she had had sex with the Devil.[11] In neither case does the theft appear to have been put forward as substantial evidence in support of the charge of witchcraft. In the first, it may have contributed to the impression of Tolmayer's bad character, but her husband's conviction and execution appear to have carried more weight, while in the second case the theft and the girl's refusal to admit it even when the missing items "were all found with her" led the constable (*Vogt*) of Blaubeuern, who was questioning her, to remark "that she appeared to be no Christian, but rather given to Satan himself," which precipitated her confession that she had already slept with him "in the form of her boyfriend."

The two secondary accusations involving theft did involve a crime often connected to witchcraft, stealing milk, but in one case the allegation appears to have concerned a physical rather than magical crime, while in the other it is ambiguous. In the first, the accuser said someone "broke in and took the milk" from his cow, while in the other the accuser, a 71-year-old woman named Agnes Fritz, said that another old woman, 73-year-old Agatha Stosser, must have stolen cream from her because she sold much more than she could have gotten from her own cow.[12] We shall see in Chapters 5 and 7 that other allegations of milk stealing came to light in other jurisdictions and during trials in Württemberg of beneficent magicians accused of using divination and counter-magic against it that clearly assumed that magical means had been used, but the contribution of such concerns to witch trials themselves appears to have been quite limited.

The third thing that is immediately apparent in Table 1.1 is that it includes a number of offenses that, like surreptitious milking, are not, to modern eyes anyway, particularly magical: in addition to theft and arson, poisoning, assault, and, depending on the circumstances, harming animals. We may wonder about allegations involving occult bewitchings, how they would work and if any significant number of people would attempt to perpetrate them, but poisoning and assault are concepts whose mechanisms we can understand, and whose occurrence we should be able to evaluate unclouded by uncertainty about what they entailed.

Poison and assault

Allegations of poisoning precipitated the greatest number of trials of any single accusation, and they also comprised a number of secondary denunciations. In about half the cases, including most which began trials, the victims did not actually die, but just became ill. In several cases, it appears that the "poison" was actually intended to benefit the victims. For example, this was the conclusion a young woman named Johanna Fehlen came to when she discovered a white powder at the bottom of a glass of wine given to her by an older woman, Barbara Schmied, at Barbara's nephew's wedding.[13] It was probably also the case when the suspect in another of the sampled cases, Anna Schnabel, brought a neighbor named Margretha Ruchhinbrodt some disgusting soup when Margretha was sick.[14]

In other instances, it is not clear whether the suspect actually gave the victim poison at all. In 1659, the pastor in Geradstetten, a village near Schondorf, Johannes Brand, accused a woman named Maria Laichlin, whom he thought his sister-in-law Susanna Catharina was spending too much time with, of poisoning the young woman with a piece of bread. She had become weak and disoriented while returning home after going to borrow some milk from Maria's one day, and later had seizures, became paralyzed, and suffered from pain and hallucinations. However, the case dissolved when witnesses could not agree whether Maria had given Susanna Catharina any bread, poisonous or otherwise.[15] Similarly, the charge made by Hans Rolf Kellern that Catharina Freyberger sold him poisoned cheese that made him and his wife sick collapsed in the face of both her apparently genuine surprise upon arrest and the testimony of a man who had eaten her cheese without ill effect.[16]

Sometimes it is difficult to judge what the suspect intended. In 1688, an old widow named Anna Serrin gave a teenage girl named Anna Maria, who lived nearby in the village of Wasserstetten, a piece of stale bread saying it was too hard for her to eat, after which the girl "was driven from inside to hop and jump bizarrely."[17] She then set out to collect a debt owed to her father by a man who lived in the village of Dottingen, an hour away, "without telling her father," and on the way she said she met a man with a "red beard and hair" who told her of a horse master she could go to, to get some money. She followed his instructions, but when she got there, she acted "as if she didn't know what she was doing." The man reappeared to her, but the horse master said it was "only an hallucination." Some people tried to get her to go home, but "out of the earlier compulsion to jump around, she sprang in the river named the Lauter, which fortunately wasn't deep." Her father finally caught up with her and brought her home, where she told him "she doesn't know why she was overcome by this desire to jump," and that he shouldn't worry about money since he would soon get more. She acted unusually secretively and somewhat wild for a number of days more, and "one could not anger her in the least, or else she'd become very abusive, which she was not like before."

While it is not possible to definitely diagnose Anna Maria's problem, her wild, compulsive behavior and hallucinations make it sound like she could have suffered from ergot poisoning. Ergot is a fungus that grows on grains containing several alkaloids related to LSD that cause similar, although weaker, effects.[18] When consumed in bread, it can cause either gangrenous ergotism, known as St. Anthony's Fire, or convulsive ergotism.[19] Both cause delirium and hallucinations, but the former goes on to cause a sensation of burning inside, dry gangrene, and the loss of fingers, toes, and even limbs, while the latter causes at most convulsions. At times entire communities in premodern Europe appear to have suffered from accidental ergot poisoning, which has led some scholars to suggest that this was the cause of the witch fears and trials.[20] While this claim seems overly ambitious, given that the great majority of trials clearly do not contain evidence of ergotism, it may well have been the cause of some witch panics and trials. In this case, it seems quite likely that ergot is what caused the girl's strange behavior and perceptions, but we cannot know whether Anna Serrin knew the bread was contaminated. She admitted she had given Anna Maria the bread, but insisted she "had put nothing bad in it." As is often the case with suspected poisoning, it is impossible to know for sure.[21]

In certain cases, however, the charge of malicious poisoning was credible, and in several of the sampled cases it was almost certainly true. To begin with, both naturally occurring and synthetic poisons were available, and there is no question that they were used.[22] In 1674 Anna Maria Schilling accused Barbara Gessler of giving her a poisoned apple, and two neighbors came forward with stories of earlier incidents when Barbara was suspected of poisoning people she was ostensibly nursing.[23] After Anna Maria died, the doctor who examined her body said that she had succumbed to poison, but it was impossible to determine where it had come from. Less mysterious was the source of the poison that afflicted a young boy, Jakob Endriss, in 1628. His step-grandmother, Maria Schneider, the mother of his father's second wife, had prepared a soup for him, and when he became ill, a doctor "found ... that something wrong had been given to him in his food."[24] Jakob told the investigating constable that Maria had earlier threatened to "feed him lye" and when the official questioned her, "at first she did not want to admit any knowledge of a soup," at all. Confronted by the testimony of other witnesses against this transparent lie, she "finally ... acknowledged her guilt."

We know that poisoning is possible and that it works through biochemical actions that are as a rule independent of the victim's state of mind, but the administration of poison is by its nature surreptitious and so, as the examples discussed above illustrate, is often difficult to verify.[25] Assault, on the other hand, is a more open form of attack which could also, as Table 1.1 shows, be linked to witchcraft. For example, in the earliest of the sampled cases, an elderly woman named Magdelena Horn confessed in 1565 to having struck a boy so hard that he died several days later, and when the magistrates of Cannstatt investigated, the mother said that he had complained of her assault, but when he died she did not pursue the matter.[26] Similarly, the one assault that precipitated a case was also confirmed. It occurred after Katharina Masten, a 71-year-old wife of a carter and citizen of the village of Metzingen, went to a neighbor's house to collect a debt he owed. When a servant girl in the household, Catharina Baitinger, told her that he was not home, Katharina barged into the kitchen and began to take food as compensation. The girl tried to stop her, insisting that she would have to pay for the food. The next day, when Catharina was walking alone on a secluded path in the woods, Katharina approached her, demanding the money once again. Catharina said that she would get it after her chores were done, but Katharina became angry and began to berate and hit her, knocking her down. When the magistrates investigated, Katharina denied that the incident had taken place, but witnesses placed her at the scene of both the argument and the subsequent assault, while a smith reported that "she had told him she had given the girl what she deserved."[27]

Most of the secondary allegations of assault seem to have involved relatively limited injuries. One of the secondary allegations against Catharina Ada, a woman accused in 1628 of bewitching a neighbor, was made by a servant girl who said simply that Catharina attacked her in the street for saying she was a witch, while another servant girl said that Catharina's daughter Margaretha slapped her three times on the arm for saying that all witches ought to be killed.[28] In 1681, a soldier's son claimed that Agnes Langjahr, a woman being investigated for poisoning an ox and killing a girl, hit him in the face.[29] In 1701, Barbara Dannenritter accused Anna Maria Rothin of grabbing her arm and causing it to hurt a lot, and another woman said she had hit her arm, which made it go lame.[30]

Two other assaults by Anna Maria Rothin were said to have caused the victims' deaths, though. George Klingen claimed that Rothin had stroked his wife's thigh, which caused her to become so crazy that she hanged herself, and Conrad Herwick testified that his wife became lame and eventually died because Anna Maria had smeared something on her. The doctor the magistrates consulted about the original charge informed them that "some doctors report of a powder which the witch spreads in her hand" before grabbing her victim, which, he observed, "the investigation makes not a little suspect."[31] Indeed, a suspect in an investigation three years later in Herrenberg, a woman named Agatha Weil, admitted to having committed 10 acts of *maleficium*, nine by smearing an ointment on people, mainly children, which caused them to become lame and some to die.[32] Three instances were so old that the magistrates could not check out her stories, in one case the person denied that anything had happened, but in the other five witnesses confirmed that the maladies Agatha claimed to have caused had in fact occurred.[33]

The use of a powder or ointment makes these cases seem more like poisonings than assaults, except for several considerations. First of all, it is hard to imagine that early modern commoners had access to a poison so potent that the small amount that might be absorbed through the skin would be fatal. Secondly, if there was such a poison, it is hard to see how it could have been used as described since that involved the suspect smearing it first on her own hand. And, third, the first suspect did not die from the direct effects of any sort of chemical agent, for she became crazed and then hung herself. All these considerations make it seem much more likely that the ointment was the same or similar to the ointments that, as we shall see in Chapter 4, some people in the region appear to have smeared on themselves to induce hallucinogenic experiences. The most commonly used ingredients, Solanaceous plants like datura, henbane, nightshade, and mandrake contain the alkaloids atropine, scopolamine, and hyoscyamine that mimic the neurotransmitter acetylcholine.[34] By occupying the receptor sites on neurons for acetylcholine, the chemicals in the witches' salves disrupt the flow of information in both the central and peripheral nervous systems. Applied locally they "have a paralyzing effect in small amounts," and if the chemical was carried into the bloodstream to the brain it could also have caused more generalized neurological disruptions resulting in disorientation and delusions.[35] Such an experience might well terrify an unknowing and fearful victim, accounting, for example, for George's wife's craziness and suicide, and quite possibly for Conrad's wife's lameness and death. It seems unlikely that such ointments account for all or even most of the maladies attributed to a witch's touch, but it seems probable that they were responsible for some.

Occult injury and psychosocial factors in disease

Thus, while assault with an ointment might be considered a type of poisoning, it would seem to have at least as much relation to another type of *maleficium* which is here referred to as occult injury. The category includes all references to harms inflicted without any physical medium of attack being specified, about one-third of all the sampled malefic accusations. In a few cases, so little information is given about the incident that it is possible that some physical mechanism may have been involved but was not mentioned, as when Wolf Körner said that Maria Rau was "not a little suspect" when he "lay sick for eight weeks" without specifying why he suspected her or what he thought she had done, and when Johann Koenbeckhen testified that Magdelena Kochen had made him lame after he refused to let her bake bread in his oven.[36] In most of the incidents in which no mechanism was specified, though, the wording suggests that injury was thought to have resulted from an occult power exerted by the suspect, as when, during a trial in Leonberg in 1701, a man named Michel Gansslen claimed that the suspect, Anna Maria Rothin, had once bewitched him, but then helped him to get better.[37] And in still other instances the allegations included specific details about the circumstances in which it originated and the nature of the malady, like the one that precipitated the trial of Agatha Sacher in Dornstetten in 1611. In this case, she had been jilted by a man named Ziegler, who then became engaged to another woman.[38] Agatha was said to have said that "she wanted to hurt Ziegler's fiancé," and when she attended the wedding festivities, "after some time Ziegler's bride became so crazed that finally she thought she must kill herself." She was taken to a doctor, who declared that "her spirit had been taken," and treated her with a potion.

Historians have come to recognize that psychological processes can have somatic effects; Joseph Klaits mentions how "belief in a witch's ability to do evil could give her real power" through "psychosomatically induced symptoms," while Robin Briggs similarly speaks of how "expressions of ill-will can have genuine power against the suggestible."[39] This effect is linked to the social explanations of witchcraft as one of the ways in which people project their own anger or guilt onto a scapegoat figure, and to the cultural approach to the topic as an artifact of a predisposing belief system. However, while a cultural predisposition certainly did contribute to some peoples' psychosomatic reaction to social conflicts, causing them to generate "accusatory symptoms" as a way of pushing culpability onto their opponent, the way in which these and other historians discuss psychosomatic processes indicates that their ideas are based on an older understanding of psychophysical processes which limits and distorts the role that they played in witchcraft beliefs. Classic psychosomatic theory was rooted in Freudian dynamics, and posited that a wide variety of ailments were symbolic somatizations of repressed psychological processes. However, in the 1970s and 1980s, this understanding of the relationship between the mind and body was recognized as having been applied far too indiscriminately, and it is now seen as just one, and far from the most important, of three ways in which psychological processes can cause or contribute to somatic complaints. Called "somatoform disorders," this class of psychophysical ailments include somatization disorder, conversion disorder, and pain disorder, which are all conditions in which somatic symptoms appear, but there is either no organic disorder or organic damage cannot account for the severity of the symptoms. Somatization disorder is a prolonged condition that includes multiple physical symptoms like gastrointestinal distress, vomiting, dysmenorrhea, and pain in the sex organs or the extremities, and until recently was linked to histrionic personality disorder, what used to be called hysteria. Conversion disorder, which involves an organically inexplicable malfunction in a motor or sensory system, also used to be thought of as a symptom of hysteria, but it is now understood to occur "in the context of virtually any character structure," including those that do "not manifest serious character pathology," in response to "unresolvable or inescapable stress." In an analogous way, pain disorder involves painful sensations either in the absence of an organic problem or in excess, considering the nature and extent of actual physical damage.[40]

The physiological processes that produce the somatic symptoms in somatization and conversion disorders are not known, but the physiology of pain is somewhat better understood. Whereas pain was once thought to be felt in direct response to (and in direct proportion to) a signal from a nerve ending, the current medical consensus assumes that these signals are mediated by "a spinal gate (SG) mechanism ... controlled by nerve impulses that descend from the brain" which can intensify or suppress them. A newer theory suggests that the involvement of the brain is even greater than in the SG model, positing that pain is actually a complex construct created by the brain, combining "psychological, neurochemical, and neurophysiologic influences functioning as systems and subsystems that interact to activate or modulate the pain experience." Whether the mechanism is mediation or construction, though, there is no question that "pain is ... a class of behaviors that can, by virtue of selective reinforcements, come under the control of the patient's social environment," reflecting a person's "learning history, socialization, social identity, and cultural predisposition to behave in certain ways in particular circumstances" as well as any "disturbed biological process."[41]

In a similar way, whatever the physiological mechanism underlying conversion disorders, they are generally understood to be a "response to an intrapsychic conflict which is engendered by certain social stresses and expressed in particular cultural contexts." They occur "across generations, classes, and cultures," but their "form ... reflects local cultural ideas about acceptable and credible ways to express distress." Somatoform disorders have been called "a nondiscursive protolanguage," for they manifest a "psychosocial need or conflict" in order to "express ... emotions or ... evoke nurturance ... [or] punish or blame others."[42]

The sampled trials include a number of accusations that appear to have been based on somatoform disorders, in particular conversion symptoms and pain disorder. For example, in a case from Sindelfingen in 1628, Anna Rueff, a cow herder's wife, accused Catharina Ada, a pig herder's wife who was already strongly suspected of witchcraft, of coming to an annual event in which the cow herders' wives divided up a gift of bread from the people whose animals their husbands tended, "where she did not belong," and "without an invitation stood to her right and helped to divide the bread."[43] Anna, who clearly resented this intrusion and also knew of Catharina's malign reputation, said that this action caused her "head to hurt somewhat and the next day" she "became lame on her right side," the side where Catharina had stood. In another case, during an investigation precipitated by allegations that Magdelena Kochen had harmed a neighbor's cow after a dispute, another neighbor, Georg Seeger's wife, said that some time previously Magdelena had caused her leg to hurt, and then made it worse with an attempted cure.[44] Further, a former resident of Sulz, Johann Koenbeckhen, sent a letter testifying that Magdelena had made him lame after he refused to let her bake bread in his oven.[45] In a third case, 72 years later, a woman named Anna Kliegstein accused Anna Maria Rothin, who, as we have already seen, was suspected of injuring several women with her touch or a salve, of having caused her arm to go lame 15 years previously, and a soldier reported that she had once placed a curse on him that caused him to go lame.[46] Finally, a year before Agatha Sacher was said to have bewitched her ex-boyfriend's bride, an old man had claimed that "during harvest-time" Agatha, whose father had been burned as a witch and whose grandmother had died in jail while awaiting trial, and who had claimed to be able to work magic as a girl, had "put a sheaf [of grain] from a wagon on his head to carry," but he "immediately felt such a pain in his thigh that he could not walk, and had to put the sheaf down."[47] He became bedridden and maintained that she had caused it until he died.

Given that somatoform disorders involve not only symptoms that occur when there is no organic problem, but also symptoms that are excessive considering the nature and extent of actual physical damage, it seems significant that in all of the other sampled allegations of assault except the servant girl's report that Catharina Ada attacked her in the street involved paralysis or intense pain. In some cases, particularly when the suspects were young adults, the reported effect may have reflected purely mechanical trauma, as when a young woman named Margaretha Stuertzen accused a 25-year-old man named Hans Rueff, who had recently married someone else, of grabbing her by the arm and causing it to hurt terribly and become lame.[48] Physical trauma may also have been the cause of an injury that Christoph Schweickhlen said his neighbor Agatha Stosser inflicted on his son Hans Conrad when she grabbed his arm, although Stosser was 73, and, furthermore, Schweickhlen said that Stosser accompanied her physical action with the words "Hans Conrad, go in and tell your father this woman is a witch!" so the boy's psychological reaction very likely intensified the perceived pain.[49] The psychological element seems particularly likely since the pain went away later when Stosser was induced to stroke it while saying, "little boy, it's nothing and, God willing, won't hurt you." Similarly, in all of the other instances the assault was said to have caused notable pain or paralysis that appears "in excess considering the nature and extent of" the attack, and therefore probably involved a significant psychological component. The girl who said Catharina Ada's daughter Margaretha slapped her three times on the arm said that this "caused the whole arm to hurt and become lame, and ultimately her entire side began to hurt."[50] Catharina Baitinger, the servant girl who tried to keep Katharina Masten from collecting the debt owed by her master, said that the older woman's blows had caused her to become "so limp that she could only crawl away."[51] The boy, who said Agnes Langjahr hit him in the face, said that it caused him to become lame, but then he became better when she rebuked him for accusing her.[52]

We have already seen that the salves some suspects appear to have smeared on their victims probably worked at least as much through their psychological as their chemical effect, and some of the more conventional poisonings seem to have worked at least partly in this way as well. Certainly the ergot-laced bread that Anna Serrin appears to have given the teenage girl Anna Maria, whatever her motive, presented more of a psychological than a physiological danger to her. In the case in which the pastor Johann Brand alleged that Maria Laichlin had poisoned his sister-in-law Susanna Catharina by giving her a piece of bread, as we have seen, witnesses denied that the woman had given the girl any bread at all, and the malady may have resulted from the young woman's distress at being the object of a power struggle between her sister's husband, in whose house she lived and to whose authority she was therefore subordinated, and Maria Laichlin, whom she liked to visit despite her brother-in-law's opposition.[53] Similarly, when Rolf Kellern and his wife became ill after eating the cheese given to them by Catharina Freyberger, their discomfort probably resulted from their own suspicions about it, since another man ate some with no ill effects. In some cases, like when Maria Schneider put poison in her step-grandson's soup and when Anna Maria Schelling succumbed to poison that may or may not have been in the apple Barbara Gessler gave her, the poisons involved appear to have been potent in-and-of themselves, but in other cases, like Susanna Catharina's and the Kellerns', psychological forces rather than biochemical ones appear more likely to have caused the symptoms attributed to poisoning.

While somatoform disorders clearly played a significant part in generating witchcraft suspicions, they are not the only way that psychological and psychosocial factors influence health, and were not the only source of accusations or the root of belief in witchcraft.[54] While "psychosomatic" is often used for somatoform disorders, the term is generally reserved in medical usage for the second form of somatic distress influenced by psychological processes: "disorders which, although of an unquestioned organic physical nature, are also strongly influenced by emotional and psychosocial factors." The term "psychophysical" is used interchangeably for these disorders, and "examples include bronchial asthma, peptic ulcer, migraine, hypertension, colitis, menstrual disorders, sexual dysfunction, skin diseases ... and very many more." The physiological ways through which psychological processes contribute to these somatic ailments vary from case to case, but in general they are thought to be byproducts of the direct physiological effects of stress. The word "stress" is commonly used loosely to indicate psychological pressure or tension, but in medical terms the stress response is "a nonspecific automatic biological response to demands made upon an individual" involving a series of changes in the nervous and endocrine systems that prepare the body for strenuous activity. These changes have great value when dealing with intense physical challenges, but they can have negative side effects when they are too acute or chronic, and as a consequence stress "is considered to play the key role in the psychological etiology of disease."

Many of the changes that make up the stress response are related to specific maladies. Stress causes the back muscles to tense, for example, which is thought to cause as many as 95 percent of backaches. A similar process causes tension headaches. Stress causes the heart rate to increase and blood vessels to contract, so chronic stress can contribute to hypertension and other forms of heart disease. Acute stress can trigger cardiac arrhythmias, which can cause "sudden death" in people with coronary artery disease. Stress also increases the amount of immunoglobulin E in the bloodstream, which is associated with allergies. Changes in saliva as part of the stress response can even contribute to tooth decay. Stress effect on the gastrointestinal system can cause or contribute to a variety of ailments ranging from diarrhea to ulcers. Stress curtails the body's production of testosterone, which can result in sexual dysfunction in men and women. There is still debate among medical researchers over the exact roles that genetic predisposition, physiological weakness, and psychological distress play in these and other psychophysical disorders, but there is no question that while "biological factors are important, ... psychological variables, are also crucial."

Research has shown that people across cultures and social groups have a physiological susceptibility to stress-related somatic disorders, but there is variation in what events are stressful, to what degree they are stressful, and what somatic symptoms they generate.[55] The existence of culture-specific diseases suggests that cultural labels can "influence the perception of experience and shape the somatic experience and symptomology of illness," but few strong correlations between specific stressors and specific disorders have been found. The process by which the psychosocial stresses cause or contribute to somatic disorders is clearly not straightforward; it involves a complex interplay between cultural, psychological, and physiological factors. On the one hand, the importance attached to different stressors varies from person to person, reflecting a combination of individual psychology, social pressures, and cultural expectations. On the other hand, the bodily systems most susceptible to damage from stress also vary from person to person, reflecting some combination of individual physiological and psychocultural predispositions.[56]

While psychological influences on bodily health can be generated by purely internal psychological processes, they can also be triggered by environmental factors, including interpersonal and social ones. In fact, a great deal of research on the influence of psychological stress on somatic health is based on correlating incidence of disease with stressful life situations. It has revealed that people are more likely to suffer from physical disease if they have recently experienced some significant disruption in their life. Furthermore, while much attention has been focused on major life events, "research into stress shows that it's not always the major events, but sometimes the minor hassles, that can accumulate and cause problems ... Various studies have showed that hassles are strongly related to episodes of illness, even when there are no major life events to consider." Furthermore, "one group of researchers found that hassles have a greater impact on health than do major life events – and that the influence of major life changes may actually be ... because they cause an increased number of minor hassles." There is no question that psychosocial stressors can cause and contribute to physiological maladies, and these psychosocial stressors include not only major life events, but also incidental hassles in day-to-day living.[57]

In an example of psychosocial influence on health of particular interest in relation to witchcraft beliefs, one of the early researchers working on the correlation between life stress and illness noticed that "a person often catches cold when a mother-in-law comes to visit." He went on to say, only partially tongue in cheek, that "patients mentioned mothers-in-law so often that we came to consider them a common cause of disease in the United States."[58]

While symptoms typical of somatoform disorders predominated among those discussed in the sampled cases, some of the ailments ascribed to witchcraft sound more like psychophysical complaints. For example, the pain in her head that Anna Rueff said Catharina Ada caused by barging in where she was not invited and standing right next to her may have started as a psychophysical tension headache, with the intense pain and paralysis conversion symptoms built upon it. More clear-cut is a case from Ebingen in 1622. During the wedding festivities of Konrad Streich and Ursula Wahnhaasen, when Konrad walked past Anna Gebhard on his way to lunch, she grabbed his trousers and made some bawdy comments.[59] He laughed at her horseplay along with the other guests, but when he passed by later, she slapped him on the back and made more suggestive remarks, and "suddenly such a fright came over him," that "he lost his manhood and thereby became impotent." While the evidence suggests that Anna Gebhard meant no harm with her ribald horseplay, it is perfectly possible that it contributed to, and may have even caused, Konrad Streich's impotence, for, as we have seen, "sexual problems ... have been reported ... to be associated with personal distress." More specifically, in men, "erectile problems tend to be associated with fear," fear of failure, fear of inadequacy, or, in Konrad's case, the fear that came over him as a result of Anna's harassment.[60] However, impotence is now understood not to be a conversion reaction, but rather to be a psychophysical problem, a result of hormonal changes brought on by the stress reaction.

Even more dramatic evidence for the probable effects of psychophysical processes is provided by some of the instances in which the cause of death was attributed to witchcraft. In the case in which Anna Rueff "insisted that the swine herder's wife" Catharina Ada "had inflicted" on her headache, lameness, and pain when she intruded on the cow herders' wives' ceremony and stood "hard on" her right "side," for example, the woman's "suffering increased day by day ... so that the following Thursday evening she became crazed, would not eat, talk, or listen, but shouted and bellowed, until she died on Saturday."[61] While it is impossible to know for certain what killed the woman, the timing of the onset and course of her ailment and the combination of her clear anger toward Ada and her fear of her certainly make it possible that the stress induced by their encounter caused or contributed to her "miserable and pitiable" demise. The phenomenon of "voodoo death" in which a person put under a curse does die has long been recognized. It is not "uncommon in villages of Western countries," while "what has puzzled Western observers ... is its relative frequency among primitive people."[62] Early medical explanations for it tended to focus on psychodynamics, treating it either as some sort of conversion reaction or a result of autosuggestion, more recent work suggests that it is related to severe disruption of the autonomic nervous system. Current medical opinion now attributes "sudden death" to ventricular arrhythmia, a heart attack induced by "an electrical accident" that causes "chaotic ventricular activity that does not effectively pump blood throughout the body and thus quickly produces collapse and then death."[63] While such arrhythmias most frequently result from ischemic heart damage due to atherosclerosis, "central nervous system activation of a cognitive type could produce lethal arrhythmias in people without organic heart disease." Our popular image is that heart attacks occur at a moment of severe emotional shock, but the background to cardiac arrhythmias is generally a debilitating demoralization: "'giving up' is a prominent premonitory finding in people with emotional correlates of sudden death."

It is possible that Anna Rueff's symptoms, her refusal to "eat, talk or listen" and her shouting and bellowing were purely manifestations of psychological distress leading to a cardiac arrhythmia; it is also possible that she was suffering from some debilitating and painful organic disease. However, this possibility does not preclude an important role for her encounter with Catharina Ada in the onset and course of her ailment, for the stress response is also responsible for the third way in which psychological processes can directly influence physical health. In addition to triggering the various changes in the autonomic nervous and endocrine systems responsible for the psychophysical disorders discussed above, the stress response also suppresses the immune system, which may make the body more susceptible to a wide range of diseases including "cancers, infectious diseases, allergies, and autoimmune disorders." Furthermore, while much attention has been focused on the impact of chronic stress, "stress doesn't have to be chronic to compromise the immune system," for the vulnerability lasts many hours even when the stress response is brief. This link between stress and immunosuppression is one of the main reasons why "psychological factors are potentially important in all disorders." And interestingly from the point of view of witchcraft beliefs, sources of stress vary in their effects on immunity, and "stressful events that are interpersonal in nature ... are more likely to depress the immune system."[64]

Historians have noted that witches were commonly blamed for a wide variety of ailments that could not be readily explained, particularly when their onset seemed connected to some interpersonal altercation.[65] Among the sampled cases, for example, during the investigation of Maria Laichlin for poisoning Johannes Brand's sister-in-law, Laichlin's friend Maria Rau was also investigated, and Michael Brien testified that some months after he quarreled with her his wife became so sick she was bedridden, and "the doctor and barber he consulted told him that it was caused by magic."[66] While Brien's wife apparently recovered, in other cases suspects were blamed for people's deaths, and the circumstances suggest that this third form of interpersonal psychological influence on health, compromised immune function, may well have been a factor. For example, another charge against Catharina Ada was that she had put a curse on a refugee from Freiburg who became severely ill, swelled up, and died. Since swelling is neither a typical conversion symptom nor associated with heart problems, it seems most likely that Catharina's curse contributed to the man's vulnerability to some other disease.[67] Similarly, Andrea Leichten said that Agnes Langjahr's harassment of his family so disturbed his daughter that she refused to go outside, and eventually died.[68] It is possible that the girl suffered a fatal cardiac arrhythmia, but since it is most common when there is predisposing heart disease that is more strongly associated with older males than female children, it is at least as likely that Agnes' hostility contributed to the girl's death by inducing stress that reduced her immune competence and made her vulnerable to some form of infectious disease.

In addition to these direct effects of psychological processes on bodily functions, there are other, indirect ways in which the psyche influences somatic health. "Personality traits or copying style" and "maladaptive health behaviors" are among the "psychological factors affecting medical conditions;" the latter may be at least partially responsible for the process of "wasting away" to the point of death that is observed in some objects of curses.[69] Suicide is another cause of death that obviously stems from psychological problems, and we have seen that Georg Klingen said that his wife became distraught and hanged herself after Anna Maria Rothin stroked down her thigh.[70] Even accidents can be a means by which psychological processes influence health. Recent research has shown that stress makes them much more likely. Researchers in one study, for example, successfully predicted from information about nurses' emotional circumstances which ones "would be involved in a rash of accidents or job-related errors."[71] An example of this in relation to witchcraft was contained in an incident that took place in 1673 in the village of Hörterichshof, near Bottwar. A young woman named Anna Barbara complained that a "useless, uncouth fellow" named Viet Grossman had been following her and had grabbed her, which she said caused her hands, arms, and face to hurt and swell. The healers she consulted, however, pointed out that she had reddish, yellow, and bluish spots on her arms, "and thought it could easily have been caused by ... a cut by something unclean," since she worked "in a filthy vineyard." While it is possible that Anna Barbara's symptoms resulted directly from her distress over Viet's assault, it is also possible that they resulted indirectly from it, that she was involved in a "job related" error, as the healers suggested, because of her emotional circumstances.[72]

It is clear that psychological factors have a wide and pervasive influence on health, causing some disorders and contributing to a broad range of others. Recent estimates of the proportion of diseases with significant psychological roots go as high as 90 percent. Psychological problems not only make people think they are sick, they actually make them sick, sometimes alone and often in combination with other agents. Sometimes maladies are symbolic expressions of these psychological problems, but more often they are manifestations of the effects of stress, either the direct manifestation of the physiological changes it engenders or a byproduct of its suppression of the immune system.

Furthermore it is equally clear that interpersonal relations can be an important source of physiological stress.[73] As we have seen, numerous modern studies point to a correlation between disruptions in social relations and psychophysical problems. The emotional triggers of stress stimulated by social influences are many and varied. Fear is the most obvious one in connection with witchcraft, but it is by no means the only psychological state that causes stress. Less focused feelings of anxiety, anger, loneliness, depression, despondency, resentment, and frustration at a lack of social, economic, or political power have also been linked to increased susceptibility to stress-related disorders. A person does not have to believe in magic or fear witchcraft in order to be physically affected by another person's hostility. On the contrary, fear of malefic magic reflects the fact that any strong negative emotion provoked by another person's attitude or actions can cause or contribute to any one of an extremely wide range of physical disorders.[74] Early modern people were being neither cynical nor credulous in insisting that disrupted social relations could affect them in ways that were physically detrimental. Nor were they simply enacting some sort of self-fulfilling cultural expectation. In a variety of ways, only some of which depend on any sort of cultural predisposition, psychosocial conflicts can cause or contribute to illness, accidents, and reproductive problems, the very problems most commonly attributed to *maleficium*.

Ill will and interpersonal communications

However, the concept of *maleficium* involves both less and more than social influences on health and disease. It involves less because it involves only a subset of the possible social situations that potentially generate stress: the social stresses generated by interpersonal conflict. And it involves more because it involves the idea that the illness, accident, or reproductive problem results from the projection of ill will by the opponent in an interpersonal conflict. Modern studies connecting psychosphysical maladies to social relations tend to deal with statistical correlations because it has been axiomatic among educated Westerners since the end of the witch hunts that people are physiologically isolated from each other and that psychological problems are necessarily a manifestation of the pathology or cultural predisposition of the person experiencing them. But it also used to be axiomatic among educated Westerners that psychological influences on health were limited to a small number of hysterical pseudo-illnesses, and only recently has educated Western opinion regained awareness of the pervasive interaction between mind and body in normal human life. This reversal should make us chary of discounting out-of-hand premodern ideas about the projection of ill will, and, indeed, there are several reasons to believe that there is more to this notion than historians and other social scientists have traditionally allowed for.

To begin with, some of the activities ascribed to accused witches were obvious expressions of ill will and a desire to inflict harm, especially assault, poisoning, ritual spell casting, and curses. Poisoning is generally intended to be surreptitious, of course, but in one case, at any rate, a poisoner was said to have told her victim what she had done afterwards: in 1628 Catharina Bertschen testified that four years earlier her husband had "come home very sick" one day and "said he was going to die" because Catharina Ada had insisted that he eat some food she had prepared and then "had assailed him saying he would die," which he did.[75] Furthermore, if the method of delivery was smearing an ointment on the skin, as Anna Maria Rothin was accused of doing, then, as we have seen, the awareness that one had been poisoned would probably have been the most potent contributor to any subsequent illness. Similarly, if the "poison" was an hallucinogen in a food, as the bread Anna Serrin gave the teenage girl appears to have been, and the bread Johannes Brand said Maria Laichlin gave his sister-in-law Susanna Catharina most likely would have been, given her symptoms, if the older woman gave her anything at all, then any illness that resulted would have been the result of the fear and dismay experienced by the recipient upon realizing that she had been given something irregular to eat, as well as any fear caused by the unusual sensations, perceptions, and thoughts it engendered.[76]

Assault, on the other hand, is by nature overt, and while we tend to assume that the physical contact is the essential element and any psychological effects are inherently secondary, even more than with poisonings, the sampled cases suggest that there was actually a spectrum of possible relationships between the physical and psychological dimensions of an assault, and between the psychological predisposition of the victim of the assault and the intentions of the perpetrator. At one end were incidents like when Magdelena Horn hit Peich Elsa's boy so hard it killed him, where it seems probable that the main force of the attack was in the physical blow, and the "occult" (hidden) element that made it an instance of *maleficium*, rather than just a physical assault was the fact that it was delivered surreptitiously against a child. In the middle were incidents where physical force and psychological forces would seem to have both contributed substantially, like when Hans Rueff was said to have grabbed Margaretha Stuertzen so hard her arm became lame, or when young Margaretha Ada paralyzed the arm of the servant girl who said that all witches should be killed by hitting it three times. Here the emotional relationship between the attacker and the victim seems to have been at least as important as the physical force; while we traditionally focus on the psychological characteristics of the victim as the source of the attack's emotional power, in the circumstances described, and given what we now know about the power of disturbed interpersonal relations on health, we need to recognize the role of the emotional message being sent by the attacker in these incidents. This effect is conveyed even more strongly by the cases at the end of the spectrum in which the physical effect of the attack and the emotional culpability of the victim appear to have been substantially overshadowed by the attack's psychological effects, as when the servant girl 71-year-old Katharina Masten hit for refusing to let her collect the debt her master owed became "so limp that she could only crawl away."[77] While it is always possible that the woman got in a lucky punch that stunned the girl, it is hard to see how a woman of Masten's age could have so overpowered a teenage girl through physical means alone. For her part, the girl had had the gumption to stand up to the older woman on two occasions, so she does not seem to have been a fearful or weak-willed person; the fact that the older woman was not reputed to be a witch makes it even more unlikely that the girl was simply succumbing to her own superstitious preconceptions. Instead, it appears to have been the ferocity of the woman's assault, the raw emotional pressure it exerted, which reduced the girl from a determined defender of her masters' interests into a helpless wreck.

Overt spell casting was another form of attack associated with *maleficium* that was an explicit expression of dislike, although in there was no physical mechanism associated with it. One of the sampled cases included allegations that involved an explicit magical ritual, an incident that was a secondary accusation against Agnes Langjahr, who was being investigated in 1681 for killing a girl, as we have seen, and also for poisoning an ox.[78] While the officials investigated, they found that one of the allegations against her came from Christian Cammer, a judge in her village, who said that the year before she had come into his house, ignoring their warnings to stay out, gone to the room where a woman who had given birth three days before lay, and "placed three eggs in her lap." In German folklore witches were thought to use eggs to transmit their spells, and placing noxious items in bed was a common way to cause people to become ill.[79] New mothers and newborn babies were thought to be particularly vulnerable to magical as well as physical dangers, and, indeed, the woman did sicken and die after flying into an uncontrollable rage and verbally and physically attacking her husband, who also "fell into a painful and miserable sickness."

The other explicit form of attack involved the use of language: uttering curses and making threats.[80] The association of witches and curses has been a staple of historical interpretation at least since MacFarlane (working from Reginald Scot and George Gifford) pointed to the "classic" situation in which a poor old woman was refused charity and uttered a curse in retaliation, which led to a denunciation when some misfortune followed.[81] In this view, the curse was the overt connection between the original incident and the purported consequence, but only in the subsequent interpretation of the events. We have seen, however, that interpersonal conflict can, in fact, cause and contribute to a variety of maladies, and while one "goal of cursing" is "to bully or threaten," another "is to [cause] harm."[82] Curses are "the product of cortical, subcortical, and autonomic nervous system interaction" that is "closely associated with anger" arising in the limbic system of the person uttering them, and they can correspondingly serve to "escalate the listeners' arousal" by triggering the fight/flight response, otherwise known as the stress response. Some of the examples from the sampled cases in Württemberg contain evidence of the power that words can have on the mind, and through it on the body. One was the case precipitated by Anna Gebhard's harassment of Konrad Streich at his wedding feast and his subsequent impotence. In this case, the words do not seem to have been intended to harm him, but in another case, that of the malady suffered by Agatha Sacher's rival at her wedding after Sacher was said to have said she "she wanted to hurt Ziegler's fiancé," the hostility was clear from both the circumstances and the content of the remark, and they appear to have had a pronounced impact on the bride.[83] Even more dramatically, Catharina Ada was said to have cursed both the refugee from Freiburg who became ill, swelled, and died and another person, who became paralyzed and died.[84] Exactly what role Catharina's curses played in the refugees' illness cannot be determined, given the limited information available to us; but given the variety of ways and extent to which psychological factors influence health, it is quite possible that they caused or contributed to the peoples' maladies, just as Catharina appears to have intended.

The tongue was widely regarded at the time as a powerful source of evil because of its power to curse, but Paracelsus was closer to the mark when he observed that "a common curse commonly comes true" because "it comes from the heart."[85] Modern people tend to concentrate on the ideas conveyed by the words used in verbal expression, both because of our cultural orientation toward language and because, in the case of early modern witchcraft, words are mostly what the documents record, but there is another dimension of verbal expression, including (and perhaps especially) cursing, which is actually more important than the content of the words: the tone of voice, or what linguists and psychologists call the prosody.[86] Prosody, the timing, pitch, and stress of an utterance, is a normal and inevitable part of verbalization, and it conveys a great deal of emotional information that supplements, and sometimes contradicts, the meaning of the speaker's words.[87] Prosody sometimes contradicts the explicit message because it is often encoded unconsciously, or at most semiconsciously, as the person formulates the words. Similarly, the listener generally decodes the prosodic elements of speech unconsciously or semiconsciously, while attending to the explicit meaning of the words. Despite the focusing of attention on the explicit meaning, however, modern experiments have shown that people's attitudes about other people are far more strongly affected by tone of voice than by the content of what is said.[88] And interestingly, from the point of view of witchcraft and curses, anger is one of the two emotions that people recognize most readily from tone of voice (the other is fear).

It is clear from the situations and interactions recounted in the records that many of the interactions involved raised voices, but in general the documents seldom pay much attention to prosody accompanying a curse or threat. Partly this lacuna reflects the nature of the documents as legal records, in which explicit meanings conveyed by words play the leading role, and partly it reflects the fact that while a curse might be uttered in some sort of dramatic way that would cause people to note its delivery, such drama is not necessary for nonverbal cues to affect their recipient strongly.[89] In fact, stimuli that are perceived and processed implicitly (unconsciously or semiconsciously) have been found to exert a stronger influence than those which are processed consciously.[90] An angry tone of voice need not be loud or otherwise exaggerated to powerfully convey the speaker's anger.

The prosodic dimension of speech is actually only one of several forms of nonverbal communication that take place along with, or sometimes instead of, verbalization.[91] In addition to prosody, facial expression, bodily contact, gestures (including posture), and spatial behavior all contribute as well to any face-to-face interpersonal exchange.[92] These nonverbal signals are sent and decoded simultaneously with each other and with the explicit content of speech, and together play a far greater role in expressing emotions and communicating interpersonal attitudes than does the meaning of the words. "Up to two-thirds of human behavior in dyadic interaction is nonverbal" overall, and experiments suggest that nonverbal cues are five time stronger than verbal ones in conveying emotions and interpersonal attitudes.[93]

The same studies that showed that tone of voice carries more weight in affecting interpersonal attitudes than the content of the words showed that facial expression is even more important than tone of voice, including in the communication of anger.[94] In fact, facial expression is the single most important channel of nonverbal communication. Furthermore, the eyes are the most important area of the face, which is particularly significant for the issue of the transmission of hostility associated with *maleficium* because of the widespread belief in the "evil eye."[95] The idea that a hostile power can be projected through the eyes is not universal, but exists in many areas of the world, and while it is not clear if it played a role in the trials in Württemberg, there is evidence of it in connection with witchcraft beliefs there as in many other parts of Europe.[96] Animals, including primates, use gaze to signal threat, and while people generally use gaze as a sign of interest, the existence of phrases like "looking daggers" and "if looks could kill" suggests that this is not the only use.[97] When a person becomes angry both the eye as a whole and the pupil narrow, and supporting changes in the surrounding face, like a wrinkling of the brow inward toward the center of the face, occur.[98] Experiments have shown that the eyes are the most accurately decoded part of the face. People can articulate the meaning of gaze patterns, and they react unconsciously to them as well.[99] Not only can "changes in attitude ... be detected by ... changes in pupil size," but also "enlarged or constricted pupils can ... affect the attitudes and responses of the person who observes them."[100] For example, not only will people looking at pictures rate someone whose pupils are dilated as more attractive than the same person in another copy of the same picture with constricted pupils without being able to specify why they find the one preferable to the other, but also the viewer will unconsciously adjust their own pupils to match the dilation or constriction of the pupils of the person in the photograph. The reason dilated pupils are more attractive than constricted ones is that widened pupils are an autonomic expression of a favorable interpersonal attitude, while constricted ones express reserve or hostility. In other words, an interpersonal attitude can be expressed and cause both an autonomic adjustment and an emotional reaction in another person without either party being aware that any sort of communication has taken place. This transmission of emotion, both the expression of the sender's feelings and the reception and reaction by the receiver, happens spontaneously and unconsciously as a matter of course in all face-to-face interactions. In cultures that recognize it through an explicit belief in the evil eye, a person can direct their angry gaze at another person in the reasonable expectation that it will cause them injury, and, even more importantly, even when neither party believes in, or even has ever heard of, the "evil eye," an angry stare would still seem to have the potential to trigger the stress response in its recipient, and thereby to cause or contribute to a wide variety of psychophysical disorders.[101]

The eyes do not exist in isolation from the rest of the face, of course, and part of peoples' ability to recognize the meaning of a gaze comes from cues conveyed by other parts.[102] In particular, the face displays anger through "frowning, raised upper lid, wrinkled lower lid, dilated nostrils, open lips, lower teeth exposed, and depressed lower lips," and flushing.[103] This combination of facial movements is recognized across cultures, and is one of seven expressions that are widely seen as manifestations of seven universal human emotions (along with happiness, surprise, fear, disgust, sadness, and interest).[104] While the existence of these universal emotions, the recognizability of facial expressions, and their connection to each other is subject to some debate, evidence for them has come not only from cross-cultural studies suggesting that people from widely different backgrounds are able to recognize the emotional meaning or situational precipitant of different expressions, but also from studies of infants and neurology.[105] Babies and children who have been blind since birth, for example, not only make faces that express their emotions, but also make faces that generally resemble the cross-cultural norms, and, furthermore, show variations from the norms that resemble those of other members of their families, even when they have been separated from them since birth.[106] Sighted babies demonstrate an attraction to face patterns within ten minutes of birth, and there is evidence that they exhibit an innate fear of negative faces.[107] There is a specific portion of the cerebral cortex "responsible for dealing with facial features such as eyes and mouth" in order to identify a face, and the amygdala, the limbic organ that plays a central role in anger and fear, has "neurons which respond only to specific stimuli," including "neurons, which are sensitive to different facial expressions."[108] The latter is particularly significant from the point of view of malefic witchcraft and the psychosocial causes of disease because the amygdala is the part of the brain that also triggers the "fight or flight mechanism" (the physiological expression of anger or fear) that is responsible for so much of the psychological influence on health. Since "stimuli from the sensory systems are sent directly to the limbic structures, and ... under certain circumstances, emotional responses remain unimpaired even when higher cortical functions have been lost," and, further, people produce a neurophysical reaction indicating recognition of a face even when they do not consciously recognize it, it would seem that the processing of a sensory impression of a hostile face into an autonomic response preparing the viewer to fight or flee is possible without conscious mediation or cultural expectation.[109]

Of course, the various parts of the brain are highly interconnected, and in practice conscious cognition and other input from higher cortical functions play a significant role in the coding and the decoding of nonverbal signals.[110] In the decoding process, both the immediate context and cultural traditions provide guidance in what meaning to attach to facial expressions.[111] For example, research suggests that recognition of the intensity of the expression of the basic emotions is also universal, but that consciousness of that recognition and overt behavior based on it is "a function of learned cultural decoding rules."[112] Furthermore, culture provides the knowledge needed to decode a wide variety of additional nonverbal cues for other emotional and interpersonal information that are culture-specific. Correspondingly, culture influences the coding process by providing these conventional nonverbal cues and also establishing "display rules" which modulate the innate expression of the universal emotions.[113]

While nonverbal expression is less subject to conscious control than verbal, it too can fall under conscious control as well as the influence of cultural shaping.[114] The face, for example, is more subject to conscious control than other nonverbal channels, and is therefore particularly difficult to decode, although tone of voice and the other channels can also be manipulated.[115] The reason to do this, of course, is to modify the emotional or interpersonal information being transmitted, or, put more simply, to lie, for "emotional deception" can be "a very effective social weapon."[116] Lying is a universal human behavior, and because of the importance of trust in peoples' interdependent social life, detecting lies is a critical skill.[117] Fortunately, it is difficult or impossible to control all the channels of nonverbal communication. For example, the smile displayed by the mouth is easy to fake, and therefore is often used to mask less friendly feelings, but "the external eye muscle involved" in smiling "is not under voluntary control, which makes it possible for an observer to distinguish genuine from fake smiles."[118] In a related phenomenon in one of the sampled cases, Agatha Stosser was said to have "laughed too loud" as she denied having caused Hans Conrad's pain by grabbing his arm.[119] People have proved in experimental situations to be quite good at detecting these sorts of discrepancies (although they may consciously or habitually ignore them to maintain superficial social harmony), and will disregard the friendly signals and act on the hostile ones.[120] This effect may be why some witchcraft suspicions, like that of Stosser, were supported, and in some cases even triggered, by seemingly innocuous comments or friendly gestures. Historians have tended to regard them as evidence of the perversity of the accuser or the irrationality of their beliefs, but without knowing the tone of voice in which they were expressed and the nonverbal cues which accompanied them we should not be too quick to rule out the possibility that in some cases, at least, the accusation was well-founded, that the illness following on an ostensibly friendly remark may, in fact, have resulted from subtle signals that betrayed the suspect's true feelings.[121] Such incongruities undoubtedly reflected the accused witch's sincere attempts to maintain social peace despite harboring antagonistic feelings sometimes, but other times it is possible that friendly words were, as the accusers suspected, deliberately used as a cover to convey a hostile subtext.

Touch is considered to be another form of nonverbal communication, and, indeed, is thought to be the most powerful of all.[122] It is an area with strong cultural rules and meanings, and we have already considered the effect of physical contact in relationship to early modern *maleficium* in discussing assaults, including the dramatic results that followed from what in some cases was no more than a stroke. Gesture is another form of nonverbal communication that some cultures strongly associate with witchcraft.[123] In early modern records it does not feature as prominently, although, again, this may reflect a lack of conscious recognition and, even if noticed, legal weight as evidence, for it is hard to imagine some of the angry interchanges in the exchanges discussed without some form of head-rocking, arm-waving, or fist-shaking.

Bodily posture and orientation are two other forms of nonverbal communication that do not generally figure prominently in witch beliefs, although they may have played a role in specific incidents, but the records convey more substantial information about the final form of nonverbal communication we will consider here: spatial communication.[124] This category includes both peoples' immediate "personal space," their personal territory, and temporary "home territories" that they establish in public space. While different cultural tradition may define personal space differently, a zone of personal space immediately around the body seems to be a human universal (and, indeed, is shared by other primates and other large mammals), and the creation of temporary personal territory is widespread. Undesired intrusions into personal spaces are disturbing psychologically, and have been shown to have a physiological effect as well.[125] Three of the cases from Württemberg involved this sort of activity. The first was the one in which Anna Rueff said that she became ill after Catharina Ada came uninvited and inappropriately to the cow herders' wives' gathering, and then, as Hans Rueff deposed, "stood hard on his wife's side."[126] The second case involved Agnes Langjahr, who was accused of causing a girl's despondency and death. One of the things her father, Andrea Leichten, cited as evidence of the woman's harassment was the fact that she repeatedly "came in the house," violating the family's space, which greatly upset the girl.[127] The third case involved Agatha Sacher, the young woman whose romantic rival became weak and despondent during her own wedding festivities. We have seen that Agatha had used words, saying "she wanted to hurt Zigler's wife," but she also attended the wedding celebration, in a sense invading the bride's temporary home space.[128] Whether any of these women added other forms of nonverbal expression during their invasions is not known, but the simple fact of their intrusion was a statement in itself that appears strongly to have been the cause of the victim's malady in the third case, and at least a contributing factor in the first and the second.

In addition to these physical, verbal, and nonverbal means by which people accused of witchcraft manifested their ill will, there was one other channel of communication that witches were accused of using to inflict harm – what we would consider to be truly supernatural means. However, such cases were quite rare, at least in trials, since accusations generally needed some explicit evidence, at least an expression of hostility followed by some misfortune, and secret magic was by definition generally known only to the perpetrator. Still, some people did confess to performing sorcery designed to punish their enemies supernaturally, and in some cases sorceress' paraphernalia was found during trials. For example, in the Vorarlberg region of Germany a suspect's home was searched and the authorities found, among other things, a variety of herbs, powders, and salves; "an old sealed case with an old communion Host in it;" a "horseshoe nail bound in a handkerchief;" a small "locket" in which was "a lump of wax in the middle of which a piece of wood was stuck;" a small pillow with various things sewn into it, including "human skin;" and "a small wooden horse, whose hindquarters were bound together with string."[129]

For the most part sorcery probably worked through the psychological mechanisms already discussed. To begin with, in most instances an ugly interpersonal altercation had already taken place, so any psychophysical response leading to illness would already have been triggered before the "witch" returned to her home and mobilized her familiars.[130] Even when the witch hid her anger from its object, third parties would have been an alternative channel of communication, and the knowledge that a reputed sorcerer is casting a harmful spell has been shown to be sufficient to cause some people to become ill.[131] Finally, as we shall see in Chapter 5, rituals performed in real secrecy could have an effect in subsequent face-to-face encounters by intensifying the witch's feelings and expression of anger and creating a certainty of the other's doom which would then be conveyed through nonverbal signs.[132]

Such processes may have been implied in the secondary accusations that alleged that the suspect had caused an illness or bewitched a victim without specifying the means, but only one accusation in the entire sample specified an explicitly supernatural bewitching. In 1663, the preacher and district superintendent in Cannstatt reported to the chancellery that during their spring visitation, an annual rite in which they inquired into the activities of their parishioners, they heard rumors of several people who practiced magic.[133] Several witnesses testified that Anna Schnabal had exhibited or talked of a number of nonmalefic powers, like overturning a water glass without spilling any water and knowing an incantation that would make you invisible to the ducal forest rangers, and one witness, Michael Klein's wife, said that "one time in her kitchen" as she was "preparing lunch, she suddenly saw something like a shadow that went through the kitchen, perched on the windowsill, turned its back to her, looked around ... [and then] slipped off the sill" outside. Klein was so "shocked she couldn't speak, but she went to the window, and saw Schnabel, in her old clothes, leaving her yard." Almost immediately, Klein began to feel ill, and her children became ill as well.

Schnabel's apparent intrusion functioned much like the invasions of territory we have seen in the cases of Agnes Langjahr and Agatha Sacher, except that it seems that Schnabel did not actually enter the room: Klein said that it was "something like a shadow" and did not recognize it as Schnabel even when she saw its face.[134] She only decided it was Schnabel when she saw the old woman leaving her yard, and then seems to have based the identification more on her distinctive "old clothes" than anything else. What she actually saw, if anything, in her kitchen and garden is unclear; it may have been physically possible for the elderly woman to have flitted through the kitchen, climbed through the window, and scuttled out of the yard, but given that Schnabel was about 60 it seems highly unlikely. It seems more plausible that Schnabel was in the yard for some reason, and after being startled by something, some effect of lighting, or simply a feeling, Klein went to the window, saw Schnabel, and unconsciously revised her memory to fit it to the realization that her neighbor, who was already said to have magical powers which at least some people thought were malign, was nearby. The most likely possibility, though, seems to be that Schnabel was not physically present at all, that Klein saw, or merely felt, something strange, which she perceived at first as a nebulous shadow, then, frightened, a contorted face, and, finally, struggling to make sense of her perceptions (and to make her perceptions make sense), she "saw" a retreating figure who she "recognized" as her already-suspect neighbor. In other words, she experienced a hallucination, accepting it as real because her culture told her it could be real, and perceiving it as her neighbor Schnabel for some mix of cultural prompting about the powers of magical people and her own psychological orientation toward her neighbor.

The existence of this process of self-delusion or hallucination has long been recognized, of course. It was an important component of the Enlightenment's rejection of magic and is a staple of rationalist interpretations of witchcraft and magic.[135] However, how this effect is achieved, what happens in the brain to make it perceive things that are not there, has been something of a mystery. It is still imperfectly understood, but in the last several decades physiologists and psychologists have clarified important aspects of the process as part of their larger investigations into perception and cognition.

To begin with, there are several different phenomena that have loosely been discussed as hallucinations.[136] In true hallucinations, the person is convinced he or she perceives something that is not there at all. In illusions, in contrast, the person misperceives features of something that is there. In pseudohallucinations the person perceives something that is not there, but is aware that the perception is not real. Finally, hypnagogic and hypnopompic experiences are the dreamy images that occur while falling asleep and waking up.

Psychologists used to regard hallucinations and illusions as pathological or at least malfunctions of the perceptual system, but they have come to see them as part of a continuum of perceptual experiences that are experienced with some regularity by otherwise normal people, and result from the same perceptual processes that produce our normal waking perceptions.[137] Our eyes, for example, do not work like television cameras, passively taking in whole images that are then interpreted and given meaning by the mind.[138] Instead, visual perception is an active process of synthesis of percepts, memories, and expectations through which the brain constructs a model of external reality in its neural circuitry. Visual perception involves the synthesis of various components of the visual field, the synthesis of this visual information with information from other perceptual modes, and the integration of this newly acquired information about the world with the memory of the last construction of the outside world (to fill in portions of the visual field that were not perceived anew, since the eyes focus on only a portion of it at any one time, and compensate by shifting focus rapidly), and older memories and expectations (to resolve ambiguities and anticipate the progress of situations in process).[139] The other sensory systems have not been studied in as great detail, but they are generally thought to work in a similar fashion.

Furthermore, at times this neural circuitry is entirely given over to constructing scenes from memory and expectations, for our imagination appears to utilize much of the same neural circuitry as our perceptions.[140] As a result, we have no intrinsic way of knowing if our perceptions are real, illusory, or hallucinatory.[141] Instead, we use a process known as "reality testing" or "reality discrimination" to constantly check the validity of the model of the external world in our heads by contrasting information from various sensory modalities against each other and against our "common sense" knowledge of how the world works, which appears to mix innate cognitive structures, individually learned lessons, and cultural rules.[142]

There is evidence that culture influences the frequency and modality of hallucinations in different populations.[143] Surveys of modern people have revealed that the frequency of hallucinatory experiences among adults ranges from 10 percent among English people to 40 percent among some groups of Hawaiians. Modality varies from mostly auditory among Westerners to an equal mix of auditory and visual hallucinations in at least some non-Western cultures. Culture also plays an important role in providing the content of hallucinations, directing to some degree as well as "clothing" with specific details the individual's psychological fears and preoccupations.[144] However, it is the individual's psychology (and probably also physiology) which plays the critical role in determining whether he or she will experience hallucinations, and exactly what these will be.[145] In general, it is accepted that hallucinations, like dreams, manifest the fears, preoccupations, and expectations of the person, a process we saw illustrated by Michael Klein's wife's gradual "realization" that the apparition she saw in her kitchen was her magically inclined neighbor.

Unfortunately, we do not know much about Klein's reasons for fearing a magical attack by Schnabel since she insisted that she was not aware of enmity between them, but another case from Württemberg provides some additional insight into this aspect of the hallucinatory experience.[146] It took place in Tuttlingen in 1606 and came to light during a trial against Anna Rechlin.[147] A scabbard maker named Jörg Ganßer testified that as he and his friend, a hatter named Michael Droll, were walking outside the town, Droll told him that he and his master had had an ugly exchange that very morning with a woman named Ursula Schmidt. At the end of the argument

Schmidt cursed the men in the Devil's name. Just as Ganßer heard this story, "a wind came as if a bird flew by" which caused him to fall. As he stood back up, he "clearly saw the faces of both" Schmidt and Rechlin. What exactly caused Ganßer to fall over is unclear, but he clearly associated it with the curse, because he immediately hallucinated the faces of the two women.

Traditional historical interpretations would emphasize that Ganßer's "hallucination" served to "confirm" his suspicions that Schmidt's curse was causing his misfortune; rationalist historians might question whether the whole thing was a fabrication, while cultural relativists might say that he constructed his own reality as part of a cultural script victimizing stereotypical scapegoats for inexplicable misfortune. However, the research on hallucinations suggests that while hallucinations are often associated with heightened emotions, they are not simply manufactured to order by emotional distress.[148] Instead, psychologists consider five elements to contribute to hallucinatory experiences: predisposing psychological or physiological factors like emotional distress, environmental stimulation, reinforcement, expectancy, and, most significant for this discussion, stress-induced arousal, the stress response. Studies of modern hallucinating people show physiological changes "indicative of high internal arousal," and hallucinatory episodes are associated with traumatic life changes, life-threatening situations, and protracted, moderate stress.[149] The stress reaction does not automatically bring on hallucinations, of course, but it produces specific changes in bodily functioning that make them more probable. Specifically, "abnormally high arousal levels bias the individual's information search towards readily accessible forms of information, increase the selection of information pertaining to physical characteristics of stimuli and decrease the processing of semantic information."[150] The result of "this more superficial style of information processing will decrease the efficiency of reality discrimination by limiting the ability of the subject to access and use appropriate cognitive cues." When we remember that the purpose of the stress response is to prepare the body to fight or flee, these effects make sense: a focus on physical rather than linguistic information is more useful in dealing with a physical situation, and a readiness to act on incomplete information rather than waiting for more accurate analysis is useful in the kind of situation in which the danger of acting too late is generally greater than that of acting too quickly. Even more significantly for the specific relationship between witchcraft fears and hallucinations, clinical evidence suggests that schizophrenic patients are "particularly vulnerable to stress associated with face-to-face contact with hostile or over-involved family members."[151]

Since modern studies of hallucination concentrate on psychiatric patients, any conclusions from them must necessarily be tentative, but the current view of their hallucinatory experiences as extremes on a continuum of mental functioning rather than a qualitatively different functioning means that some insights may be gained from them. Particularly, the connection of hallucinations with the stress response, which, we have seen, is also responsible for psychophysical ailments, suggests that some hallucinations may have functioned somewhat like the "accusatory" conversion reactions that people suffered, as a kind of "early-warning system" manifesting psychological distress related to interpersonal tensions that had the potential to cause the kind of "real" psychophysical and immune-related problems associated with chronic stress if they continued unabated.

The connection between hallucinatory experiences and interpersonal tension is suggested even more strongly by the final means of inflicting interpersonal harm: incidents in which a witch's attempt to inflict harm without any physical or interpersonal contact corresponded quite closely with the victim's experience of being attacked by the witch. The sampled "magic" cases contained two instances of this phenomenon.[152] One case was that of Agatha Weil, the elderly woman in the almshouse in Herrenberg, who, we have seen, confessed to having smeared salve on enemies to lame and kill them. She also said that she flew magically to an old friend, who lived nearby, two weeks before and touched her.[153] Similarly, in 1740 a young girl, Margaretha Wagner, who was being investigated for a variety of magical practices, confessed to having used magic to "push some people at night."[154] In both cases, purported victims said they felt these magical attacks. One of the people Margaretha claimed to have "pushed," Jacob Wolff, said that he could only remember a vague incident like that, but a 45-year-old man named Johann Michael Rolle said he had felt a push at night like "a millstone on his heart," and a 30-year-old widow, Juliana Herber, said that she had felt a pressure at night also. A fourth witness, 66-year-old Johann Georg Hoch, said he never felt a pressing, but said that Margaretha had threatened him and he had been sick for a long time thereafter.[155] Similarly, Agatha's friend reported that once many years before, an incubus had come to her and pushed her, and that some days before she had felt something similar, although it "did not push her," but instead brushed across her face, feeling like a hand.[156]

The experiences of the people at the receiving end in these stories are instances of what one study has called the "Old Hag" phenomenon. This is an experience that was widely connected to witchcraft in Württemberg, other parts of Germany, and across Europe, and has been reported across a variety of cultures.[157] In it, a person either wakes up at night or is just falling asleep, perceives some sort of intruding presence, feels a pressure pinning them to their bed or strangling them, and remains trapped, unable to move or speak, until someone intervenes or they force themselves awake. Physiologically, the experience appears to be some sort of hypnagogic (while falling asleep) or hypnopompic (while waking) dream state, perhaps related to the common perception of "faces in the dark" during these transitions. However, hypnagogic and hypnopompic experiences are different from the true dreams of full sleep, and the "Old Hag" experience is not completely like either. Hypnagogic and hypnopompic images and sounds tend to be vivid and realistic, but brief. The "Old Hag" could be a vivid tactile hallucination, but it is not brief, and the experience includes some sort of muscular or neurological paralysis unrelated or only partially related to more typical experiences during the transitions between waking and sleeping.[158]

If the roots of the sensations associated with the "Old Hag" experience are elusive, the roots of the manifest content are even more perplexing, for it seems to be explained by neither psychology nor anthropology. On the one hand, "a thorough search of relevant psychological literature has demonstrated that no ... explanation is available" from that discipline.[159] On the other hand, "although the occurrence of identifiable "Old Hag" experience is associated with knowledge of models for the experience ... such models are not necessary," for "recognizable "Old Hag" attacks of great complexity can and do occur in the absence of explicit models."[160]

Instead, the most substantial explanation that has been given is the "experiential model." If physiology can only account for sensation, and cultural beliefs reflect rather than create the generalized content of the experience, the "experiential model" looks for the roots in common human experiences that recreate similar experiences from similar circumstances. More specifically, "the emotion of fear or the idea of attack do not by themselves require a cultural link," and "may be considered universals."[161] Fear is one of the seven universal emotions that has been identified and appears to be innate, but "the idea of an attack" is not a universal in the same sense. The debate over "nature" versus "nurture," or, in its current incarnation, between sociobiological and cultural anthropological approaches to human knowledge and behavior, has tended to focus attention on their sources being either instinctual or culturally determined, but there is another source that lies in between: common situations and experiences that recur from culture to culture and life to life that are learned and acted on over and over again, starting with the same basic biological endowment, moving through a unique set of specific circumstances that nevertheless conform to a generalized pattern, and ending with a common understanding. In the case of "the idea of an attack," the experience of being overpowered is more-or-less universal, because all people start as infants and move through childhood subject to the physical dominance of adults and older children. In the "Old Hag" experience, the person appears to start with hypnopompic paralysis, associates it with common memories of infantile or childhood experiences of being restrained, generally reacts with fear (the usual trigger of the stress response), and imagines through hallucinations and related bodily sensations details (not unusually although not necessarily manifesting cultural expectations and/or more current relationships) that support the hypothesis of being pressed down by some agent.[162] This process seems to be pretty much what the people Margaretha Wagner claimed to have "pressed" reported and the woman Agatha Weil "visited" said she experienced long before, with the woman's more recent experience being a variant in which she associated her hypnopompic sensations with a more benign experience of being stroked by a hand.

The foregoing analysis accounts at least provisionally for the experiences of the people who felt the pressure or stroke, but both of these cases present the additional twist that our knowledge of them comes not from reports initiated by the people who experienced them, but from the people who claimed to have caused them. There are four possible explanations: (1) the people who "confirmed" the original statements were claiming to have experienced something they had not, either as a conscious fraud or an unconscious re-configuration of their memories; (2) Wagner and Weil heard the people speak of their experiences and claimed to have tried to cause them when they did not, either as a conscious fraud or an unconscious re-configuration of their memories; (3) both sets of people did and experienced what they said they did and experienced, and the correspondence between the action of the "sender" and experience of the "receiver" was a coincidence; and (4) the "senders" influenced the "receivers" through some sort of parapsychological process.

The first possibility, that the "confirmers" either consciously or unconsciously misrepresented their actual experiences, is, given the nature of the phenomenon and the evidence, impossible to substantiate or to rule out. However, while the people Wagner said she "pressed" may have had some beef with her, it was the man who *denied* having felt the pressure who said she had threatened him, and three different people said that they experienced what she said she caused. Even more perplexing was the fact that the woman who confirmed Weil's story was not an enemy, but a friend, and she described the experience in a relatively benign way, both of which undercut the idea that she was trying to get Weil in trouble. While it is impossible to rule out some sort of misrepresentation by the "receivers," the number of people involved and the different ways in which they confirmed and corrected the original accounts cast doubt on this possibility.

Similarly, given the nature of the evidence, there is no way to substantiate or rule out the second possibility, that Wagner and Weil heard their acquaintances talk about their experiences and then claimed to have caused them afterward, but it seems even less likely than the first. For one thing, the experience, while more common than "common knowledge" might suggest, is not particularly frequent, and it seems unlikely that three different people would have had similar experiences and by chance happened to talk about them to Margaretha. Furthermore, one man claimed not to have had such an experience, but instead became ill after Margaretha threatened him, and it is unclear why she would have changed a perfectly good curse story into an unfounded "Old Hag" story when she already had three others. Finally, if Weil was taking retroactive credit for what her friend experienced and presumably related to her, it's unclear why she would have misreported one of the most significant details, the nature of the sensation. Again, while it is impossible to rule out this sort of information leakage entirely, there are problems with both interpretations.

At the other extreme, the possibility that Wagner and Weil influenced the "receivers'" psyches or bodies through some sort of paranormal process, stands on weak, but not inconsiderable, scientific grounds which, given the thrust of this inquiry, need to be considered. Scientific investigations of "paranormal" phenomenon have been going on for over 100 years, with increasing methodological and technological sophistication, and have produced a substantial body of evidence suggesting that there are natural processes which are not adequately explained by current scientific understanding.[163] There are currently researchers attempting to create a theoretical explanation for these, and most scientists today accept the possibility of such phenomena, but few regard them as proven.[164] The magical attacks claimed by Wagner and Weil would be explained in this way as some sort of telepathy, by which the "senders" influenced the minds of the "receivers," or psychokinesis, by which they actually exerted some sort of physical pressure on them. However, there is a dedicated cadre of skeptics who resolutely dispute the claims of parapsychologists; no single demonstration has been performed and replicated which establishes the existence of the phenomena beyond all possible doubt; the validity of statistical analyses of series of trials has been called into question; meta-analyses of numerous studies that attempt to get beyond this objection are currently being debated; no theoretical structure integrating the phenomena into current physical understanding has been established; and, overall, there is no scientific consensus that parapsychological phenomenon can occur at all.[165] At the moment, the scientific situation seems to be at a stalemate, and 300-year-old depositions from a judicial inquiry cannot resolve the current controversy one way or the other. Instead, at the present time the parapsychological possibility has to be judged unlikely on a priori grounds.

The remaining possibility is that Wagner and Weil did think they "pressed" or "flew to" the people they said they did, and those people coincidentally experienced the "Old Hag" phenomenon around the same time. The possibility of this happening completely by chance seems remote, but co-incidence need not occur randomly. Instead, it can result from two things beginning from the same cause occurring in a coordinated fashion independently. For example, Carlo Ginzburg has shown that the *benandanti* routinely experienced coordinated dreams in which a number of people in the Friuli region of northern Italy imagined they flew to battle against witches to protect the harvest on regular evenings during the year.[166] These dreams appear to have been culturally determined: people born with their caul were assumed to be new *benandanti*, and learned from their culture what was expected from them. What may have been happening here is some variant of these dreams. Wagner, in particular, seems to have threatened her enemies, which could have predisposed them to have the "Old Hag" experience at night, around the very times she imagined herself to be causing it. In Weil's case, a similar sort of parallel processing, but in this instance of friendly feelings, could have been at work, producing complementary halves of a shared experience, whose possibility both of them took for granted. In a sense, the issue of a paranormal connection is irrelevant; in these closely bound communities, where people dealt with the same small set of individuals day in and day out, the degree of interpersonal psychic integration may have made a direct physical connection unnecessary. Early modern peasants' thoughts and dreams, emotions and health appear to have been tightly intertwined with those of the other members of their community, producing the marked degree of psychological interdependence that we have already seen in relation to implicit nonverbal communication of emotions and psychophysical influences on health and well-being.

Harm to animals

If allegations of truly supernatural attacks on people's health – attacks, that is, that did not involve some physical or immediate, face-to-face interpersonal medium – were few and far between, accusations involving the last category of *maleficium*, harm to animals, were among the most frequent. The most common complaint against witch suspects was that they harmed farm animals.[167] The means by which they were said to have inflicted the damage varied. In most cases, the accusers did not specify the means by which the injury was supposed to have been caused. In some instances, though, accusers said the suspects with exercising unnatural power over with exercising unnatural power over animals.[168] The one previous suspicion of Maria Schneider before she poisoned her step grandson was that she had once caused a horse to throw its rider "through her witchcraft."[169] Margaretha Rettnier reported how she had once seen Catharina Ada first cure and then kill a cow. After many people had tried and failed to help the sick animal, Catharina "took it by the horns and cried 'up, up' and then it stood up." Within three weeks the cow had completely recovered, but sometime later Catharina "threw a bucket of water on it," whereupon the cow "sat down, refused to stand up, and in two days died."[170]

Recent laboratory studies have demonstrated that animals' attempts to survive are strongly influenced by their learned expectation of survival, and a huge number of investigations of psychosomatic factors in disease use animals as subjects.[171] Mice, rats, ferrets, dogs, monkeys, and pigs have all been used, for example, to study the influence of stress on the development of ulcers, thyroid function and the development of Graves' disease, and rheumatoid arthritis and immune responses.[172] The health of both monkeys and mice has been shown to be affected by the dynamics of their social groups, while submissive rats, shrews, and some zoo animals have been shown to be vulnerable to sudden death through cardiac arrhythmias if harassed by a dominant animal.[173] Even cockroaches establish hierarchies of dominance and submission, and excessive harassment by a dominant insect has been shown to result in the paralysis and death of the subordinate one, with "no sign of external damage."[174] There is no question that animals' health is subject to psychosomatic influences, and there is no question that these psychosomatic influences include social relationships.

The extent of human influence over animals' health and behavior is not as well studied, but there is a growing body of evidence that indicates "that farm animals may be very fearful of humans, with adverse consequences for the animals."[175] Excessive handling apparently causes stress in chickens that reduces their output of eggs, while fear of humans affects the growth and reproduction of pigs. "Significant associations" have been reported "between the personality of the stockperson and milk production of cows," which suggests that the "underlying psychological factor of the stockperson, by affecting the stockperson's behavior, may affect the cow's level of fear."

Other allegations that specified the means by which the injury was inflicted alleged physical contact or proximity, which allowed for poison or mechanical injury. For example, Jakob Thoma saw Barbara Gessler, the woman accused of giving her neighbor a poisoned apple, enter a neighbor's pigsty just before the pigs became ill, and the preacher of Fellbach had observed her sneaking into a barn where a calf was later found sick, with blood on its hindquarters.[176] Maria Mayer testified that her cow became sick and dried up after Agatha Stosser, the woman accused of injuring Hans Conrad Schweickhlen, fed and milked it, and Johannes Fuehrman's horse became crazy, stumbled, and died after he saw Agatha put something in its fodder.[177]

Magdelena Horn, the suspect from the earliest sampled trial, which took place in 1562, spontaneously confessed that she had injured her neighbor Albrecht Kerber's pigs and her neighbor Konrad Schmettlin's cow.[178] While she did not specify the means by which she had hurt them, when the magistrates investigated, both men confirmed that their animals had sickened at the time Magdelena said that she had harmed them. Some attributions of animal maladies to suspects were undoubtedly baseless, but others were undoubtedly true. Farmsteads in Württemberg's' villages, as in many other agricultural societies, were crowded together, and it was impossible to lock the animals away or keep them under constant supervision. Most peasants could afford to support at most a few animals, so the death or injury of one was a major economic blow. Harming a person's livestock was an obvious way to inflict punishing damage, and has been well documented in the nineteenth century as a manifestation of rural social conflict.[179] While it may not have been as widespread as some sixteenth- and seventeenth-century villagers feared, there can be no question that it did happen.

Conclusion

If harming livestock was not as common as some early modern peasants feared, it and other forms of *maleficium* were more common, and more important, than historical accounts of early modern witchcraft have generally allowed. We have seen in this chapter why they were more important than has generally been recognized. Both the projection of hostility and the infliction of harm could be carried out not only through physical means, like poisoning and surreptitious battery of children and animals, but also, and more centrally, through psychological means. These psychological means included both explicit and subliminal forms of communication – verbalizations, body language, and symbolic actions – that could cause or contribute to a wide variety of ailments ranging from symbolic somaticizations through psychophysical disorders to purely organic diseases. Furthermore, while culturally defined symbols could be used to express hostility and culturally defined beliefs could promote vulnerability to it, neither was critical for the interpersonal effect to occur. Instead, the expression of anger through prosody and body language appears to have a visceral, limbic component that is not a cultural artifact but either an incidental manifestation of the physiological preparation to act or a vestige of our prehuman evolution as social primates. Similarly, our vulnerability to expressions of anger is primarily a product of the physiological effects of the stress reaction, which can be triggered by interpersonal threat displays as well as by environmental dangers, and can become chronic and debilitating in the context of crowded, small-scale communities like those that made up early modern Württemberg and much of the rest of Europe.

Having seen (in this chapter) the reasons why *maleficium* was more important than is commonly appreciated, in the next chapters we will see how common it was in early modern Europe, and how it related to larger developments in early modern society and culture.

2
Maleficium and Society

If harming livestock was not as common as some early modern peasants feared, it and other forms of *maleficium* were more common, and more important, than historical accounts of early modern witchcraft have generally allowed. In the last chapter we saw that the great majority of hostile actions encompassed by the concept of *maleficium*, from physical acts like poisoning and surreptitious battery of children and animals through ailments caused or contributed to by overt manifestations of anger like assault and cursing and subliminal forms of communication like eye contact and bodily posture, were really practiced and could have real consequences. In this chapter, we shall examine how these actions and behaviors fit into the overall framework of social relations in the early modern period: how they connected to other forms of conflict; who used them, how extensively, and why; and how and why they contributed to the great upsurge in witch prosecutions in the late sixteenth and early seventeenth centuries.

Maleficium and intracommunal conflict

To begin with, *maleficium* appears to have been just one of the forms of conflict that early modern Württembergers, like villagers and townspeople elsewhere in Europe, engaged in with their neighbors. We tend to have an image of premodern communities that combines a nostalgia for simpler, rustic times with assumptions about the naturalness of social and personal self-restraint and autonomy that are actually the highly specific product of enculturation into modern, urban society. The milieu in which people like Magdelena Horn and Catharina Ada lived was radically different from that we are used to, one in which people were far more tightly connected to the other members of their local community, which gave rise to both the sense of belonging for which we sometimes long and an intensity of enmity which we have difficulty imagining.

While communities in early modern Europe ranged from the scattered farmsteads of Scandinavia and the Alpine uplands to teeming metropolises like Paris and Rome, Württemberg was a more typical mixture of villages and small towns, typical particularly of the areas in which most witch trials took place.[1] Most of its territory comprised the open farmland and terraced slopes of the upper Neckar Valley, which lay in the southwestern corner of Germany, separated from the larger Rhine and Danube valleys by the relatively wild and isolated forested hill country of the Black Forest in the west and the upland pastures of the Swabian Alb in the southeast. Its economy was based, like most parts of Europe, on cereal cultivation supplemented by horticulture and animal husbandry, although a thriving viticulture supported a significant proportion of the population before the Thirty Years' War, and a growing manufacturing sector supplemented it and then replaced it after most of the vines were destroyed in the war.[2] The duchy's agriculture produced sufficient food for only about 85 percent of its prewar population, but export of wine, along with textiles and some forestry products, enabled the population to grow beyond the limits of subsistence, to the point that Württemberg became one of the most densely populated parts of Germany.[3] While parts of the Black Forest and the Alb had fewer than 20 inhabitants per square kilometer, the farming districts of the central plateau averaged 60–70, and the wine-producing regions like the northern river valleys supported 100 or more since the vines could be grown on steep valley slopes as well as in the flatlands, were labor-intensive, and produced a relatively handsome reward from a small amount of soil.[4] Somewhere between a quarter and a third of the population lived in towns of 5,000–10,000 people, with most of the rest in substantial villages, for single farms and small hamlets were rare outside the Black Forest and forested parts of the Alb.[5]

The differences between the towns and villages were less significant than the terms suggest, however. To begin with, in the sixteenth century the ducal government forbade the villagers from building beyond the hedges that surrounded them, ostensibly to preserve the land for crops but perhaps also to facilitate the collection of rents and taxes. Consequently, houses were packed together, subdivided into two or even more residences, and outbuildings of all descriptions were constructed in the intervening spaces.[6] Furthermore, the ducal government refused to support guild monopolies during the sixteenth century, so villages contained a significant number of part-time and even full-time artisans, and in some regions large numbers of people in town and country supported themselves in part or completely doing piecework in their homes for the textile industry.[7] While the towns undoubtedly contained most of the duchy's limited number of merchants (most in the region lived in the independent "imperial cities" that neighbored, and in some cases were surrounded by, the duchy's territory) and a larger proportion of artisans and wageworkers, in most cases the majority of their inhabitants worked in agriculture, particularly viticulture, and a steady flow of migrants from villages to towns ensured that the towns had many similarities to the overcrowded villages.[8]

The inhabitants of these towns and villages ranged from a small upper stratum of prosperous merchants, artisans, and farmers down to impoverished laborers. In Württemberg, about 5 percent of the commoners belonged to the upper stratum (with 750 Reichstaler or more of property), about 20 percent owned substantial farms (225–750 R), 25 percent were smallholders (75–225 R), 20 percent were cotters with a minimal amount of property (30–75 R), and about 30 percent comprised propertyless servants, farm hands, and laborers (who generally owned less than 30 R worth of possessions and enjoyed no rights of commons).[9] This relatively smooth gradation reflected the duchy's system of partible inheritance, but while there were important differences between areas that used this system and areas that kept property intact from one generation to the next, these do not appear to have been particularly significant in terms of *maleficium*, because the functional unit of importance for this was the neighborhood, "the everyday realities of the proximity of human beings to one another."[10] Whether they lived in towns of 5,000 or villages of 500, and whether they were sharply divided between farmers and cotters or comprised a more graduated community of smallholders, most early modern commoners lived, like Württembergers, in proximity to a small community of neighbors that included both well-to-do and impoverished members, but with most falling somewhere in between.

These small communities were held together by a variety of formal and informal institutions. These included town or village governments, which in Württemberg were structured fairly similarly, and represented to a significant degree the interests of the community, for over the course of the early modern period the right to participate fully in village government was gradually expanded from the top 25 percent of substantial peasants to the smallholders and cotters, so that by the late seventeenth century about 75 percent of the heads of households had a say in the community's affairs.[11] The communal councilors or elders were elected by them; judges, mayors, and other functionaries were generally selected from among these; and local government's chief responsibility was to coordinate the commoners' activities to minimize conflict and mediate disputes either informally or in the familiar setting of the communal court.[12] In addition, towns and villages and the neighborhoods that made them up were held together by social networks of kinship, church membership, patronage, and the cultural ties of collective festivities and "good neighborliness." Neighbors were often related by ties of blood or marriage, and, in Württemberg anyway, this tendency was pronounced because the crowded towns and villages supplied sufficient marriage partners within a short distance, and over time marriages between communities became less common than marriages within them. In Württemberg, as in most localities in Europe, everyone attended the same church, socializing and worshipping together, confessing publicly, and absorbing a common creed.[13] Religious controversy was not unknown, of course, and some people held back from religious observances because of personal differences with the local clergyman or congregation or because of more general doctrinal disagreements, but Lutheranism was genuinely popular in the duchy, and this seems to have been fairly typical; while there certainly were parts of Europe where neighborhoods were split between confessions, the great majority of Europeans appear to have embraced whatever religion prevailed in their area.[14] Beyond regular services, church included cycles of common festivities, including both yearly holidays and celebrations of the significant life passages of each member. These celebrations combined devotional activities, which served not just to mark the event but also to secure the spiritual fortunes of the participants, and revelry, which brought the members of the community together and reinforced their solidarity. Solidarity was further reinforced by loans and patronage; lending between neighbors was common, and well-to-do commoners also served as godparents, hired neighbors in preference to strangers, and cosigned mortgages. Finally, "neighborliness" involved a readiness to help out with occasional large tasks like raising a barn, participation in routine gatherings like sewing circles, and a willingness to aid a neighbor in an emergency situation like an accident, illness, or fire. Württembergers, like people across Europe, interacted with and depended on the small circle of people within their immediate geographic compass to a degree that modern people can scarcely imagine, and the formal and informal institutions that bound them together actually did a remarkable job of coordinating their efforts and managing their conflicts.

However, "rustic community spirit was not a manifestation of utopia but rather the product of common need." Communities were held together by both "reciprocity and fear," and when the former failed, the latter was called into play.[15] In Württemberg as elsewhere, village courts met periodically, and had the power to hear complaints, determine guilt, and levy fines or incarcerate offenders for short periods. On a more informal level, neighbors considered it their right, and indeed their duty, to keep an eye on each other. Gossip quickly spread the word of any violations of communal norms that were noticed, and spontaneous forms of public censure like charivaris, festivals of harassment by boisterous youths, were used to punish offenders.

Of course, the line between communal sanctions and individual or factional vengeance was not always clear, for the very intimacy that bound neighbors together put them under tremendous psychological pressure that led to sharp interpersonal conflicts, entrenched animosities, and bitter feuds.[16] Most people undoubtedly enjoyed warm friendships with some of their neighbors and peaceful coexistence with most others, but at the same time most people were at odds with some of the people who lived nearby and some people were in conflict with most.[17] "Everyday life was a continual struggle with reputation, respect, and material well-being at issue," so "the notions of 'enemy' (*Feind*) and 'quarrel' (*Spar*)" were "fundamental" aspects of early modern communal life.[18] "Neighbors and enemies are intimately related terms," for "enemies were mostly people to be found in the village or town where the particular person lived." Neighborhoods were "always faction ridden," and hatreds built up to an intensity "appalling to us" in which estranged neighbors "showed an astounding cruelty," "an almost unbelievable lack of empathy," a "wish for the utter annihilation of the opponent," a readiness "to pursue personal quarrels with a ... persistence and ruthlessness which" might "harass an enemy even unto death."[19]

In this "community of terror," as one historian has described it, "nothing could be more natural than to expect persecution from the other side," and so "aggression was critical for survival."[20] "Conflict was an accepted part of local competitive strategies," and people employed a range of means that included malicious gossip, verbal abuse, legal action, and physical violence.[21] Communal life was often characterized by "insults and even ... violence," and local courts were generally dominated by complaints about "assault or verbal attack."[22] Some people "distinguished themselves by the volume of their voices and general combativeness" and used the implied or stated threats to cow their neighbors and get their way.[23] Such bluster was not necessarily bluff since "violence within the village was routine," and an exchange of words could easily lead to physical combat. Men fought without restraint, hitting, biting, and pulling hair "as today only children" fight, and there was only concern if someone was maimed or killed.[24]

Maiming and killing crossed a certain threshold and took the fight beyond the routine backbiting, bickering, and boxing of communal life to a higher level in which bitter anger and vicious threats became lethal deeds. When this happened, the resultant judicial process would involve the government beyond the commune, for by the sixteenth century, capital cases in Württemberg came under the jurisdiction of the district constable, the ducal official who resided in one of the 58 towns that served as district capitals, and who managed the duchy's administrative, financial, and judicial affairs.[25] However, even if a criminal prosecution resulted in the punishment of the perpetrator, it could not undo the damage that had been done. The death or crippling of a villager would almost certainly be a disaster for the domestic unit he was part of, for most Württembergers, like most early modern Europeans, lived on the margins of subsistence, just one step away from destitution.[26] The loss of a productive member of the household could be just such a blow, and even if it did not lead to disaster, it would almost certainly cost dearly.

Homicide was not the only extension of communal conflict into the mortal realm, as we have seen. Arson was also a way of carrying disputes to the level of mortal combat, for it would lead to the economic ruin and possibly even death of the opponent. Injuring livestock was another way of dealing an enemy a severe economic blow. If it took the form of cattle maiming, while the act was covert, the injury was overt and the mechanism by which it was caused clear. If the intent was to send a message, this would be desirable, but it could draw unwanted attention and spark legal or extralegal retaliation. Therefore, harming an animal by poison, or some sort of physical blow or threat display that left no mark, kept both the act and the injury covert. The injured party might have a pretty good idea of what had happened, who had done it, and why, but would have far less evidence to support any allegation, and we have seen cases, like Magdelena Horn's, where the perpetrator was less concerned that a message be sent than that the damage be done. Similarly, poison was another form of attack that could inflict fatal damage while possibly leaving suspicions but generally no overt evidence. Not surprisingly, commoners in Württembergers, as elsewhere, routinely fed bits of food they borrowed or received as a gift from a neighbor to the chickens before consuming it themselves.[27] Secret rituals and hidden magical objects, of course, left even less evidence, and children's complaints that they had been battered by a neighbor appear to have carried little weight. Verbal threats, curses, gestures, sharp glances, and bodily contact like touching, grabbing, slapping, and hitting were all overt acts that were routinely employed in normal interpersonal conflicts; but when they were followed by ailments, or, in the case of bodily contact, ailments that seemed disproportionate to the physical power they involved, then they were recognized as a manifestation of the malefic influence some people seemed to be able to exert on others.

Many communal conflicts centered on economic issues, and anger and violence between prosperous commoners and their less well-to-do neighbors were certainly frequent. This relationship underlay the by-now classic "charity denial" model of witchcraft, in which a prosperous yeoman refused charity to an impoverished widow, who responded by cursing him as she went away, and was then blamed when misfortune struck the household sometime later. Among the sampled cases, the one involving Magdelena Kochen fits this model well, for she was the very poor, 55-year-old widow of a swineherd with three children who was accused of causing Anna Schollen's cow to die when the relatively well-to-do woman refused to buy something she didn't need from Magdelena, whereupon other neighbors came forward to say that their cows had dried up or they became lame after they refused to do her favors like let her bake bread in their oven or lend her milk.[28] However, studies of general patterns of communal conflicts suggest that they were most frequent between people who were relatively equal in station, and the sampled witch trials from Württemberg conform to this model.[29] Most accusers were local notables (local officials and their families) or established commoners, while some suspects were either clearly marginal or not distinguished, but analysis of the individual relationships involved in the sampled cases indicates that the aggregate statistics are somewhat misleading. Of the 65 accusers whose status relative to their suspect is known, a plurality (26) were indeed higher, but a majority were roughly equal to or even lower than the suspect.[30] To give one example, Johannes Brand, who accused Maria Laichlin of poisoning his sister-in-law Susanna Catharine, was the preacher of Geradstetten, while Laichlin was the village mayor's wife.[31] In another example, Anna Maria Rothin, who grabbed Barbara Dannenritter's arm and caused it to become lame, was worth 600 R, making her a wealthy widow indeed, while Dannenritter's husband was the village scribe.[32] Many accusers denounced their poorer neighbors, but more denounced people of equal or even higher status.

Relatively few of the sampled cases involved conflicts within families, either among close kin or extended families.[33] Most of these accusations involved diabolism, and were mainly made by children who accused their older relatives of being at witch dances with them, and marital partners who saw their spouses' sexual misbehavior to be a kind of devilishness.[34] Nevertheless, cases like Maria Schneider's attempt to poison her stepgrandson Jakob Endriss indicate that there was no categorical imperative that prevented people from utilizing *maleficium* against their relatives.[35] Indeed, it was not uncommon for men in bad marriages to fear being poisoned by their wives, and several other cases from Württemberg involved spousal fears of *maleficium*. For example, Stoffel Hezler denounced his wife Anna in 1620 and asked for a divorce because, among other things, she took two knives to bed with her; kept a store of herbs, roots, and a white powder; and had hit his son on the head, which he said had caused it to swell and bleed.[36] While Anna denied having done anything wrong, saying that the knives were to protect her when he was drunk, it is clear that there was nothing unusual about the idea that *maleficium* might be utilized within a dysfunctional family.

The *Malleus Maleficarum* claimed that "the most powerful cause which contributes to the increase of witches is the woeful rivalry between married folk and unmarried men and women"; the case of Agatha Sacher, who caused her ex-boyfriend's bride to become ill at her wedding, is an example.[37] Several other incidents occurred at weddings, and older suspicions of widows by married people formed a notable minority of secondary accusations.[38] However, a majority of the sampled primary accusations occurred between people with the same marital status, and this relationship occurred in precisely half the 64 accusations of all types for which the relationship is known.[39] Of the other half, seven occurred between widows and spinsters, so at most 40 percent could have involved "the woeful rivalry between married folk and unmarried men and women."

Generational differences, on the other hand, figured in a significant majority of the 27 relationships for which the relative ages are known, two-thirds. This proportion held for both primary and secondary accusers.[40] The social relationships involved in witchcraft accusations point to generational tensions between middle-aged adults and elderly women. But, on the other hand, many suspects were not elderly women, and all suspects except children ran about the same risk of punishment. Nor were all accusers middle-aged adults. In fact, elderly people themselves appear to have made a disproportionate number of accusations. Conflicts between the generations were the most frequent occasion for the manifestation of witchcraft fears, but they were not their source.

Gender, age, and interpersonal power

As almost everywhere else, women in Württemberg made up the great majority of suspects, about 80 percent, and men tended to be treated less harshly when denounced.[41] Conversely, analysis of the constellations of accusers around the suspects in the sampled trials suggests that men dominated most trials.[42] Most groups of accusers were at least two-thirds male, and all or even predominantly female groups were rare. Nevertheless, as was true elsewhere, almost half the accusers were women, and common women actually precipitated more of the sampled trials than common men.[43] Therefore, the trials were hardly a straightforward victimization of women by men. Only certain women were suspected of witchcraft, and the social attribute most strongly associated with suspicion was not age, not marital status, not class, but reputation.[44] Eighty percent of the suspects had bad reputations or had manifested attributes held to be bad, which was as high a percentage as gender and significantly higher than any other social attribute. Furthermore, a suspect who had an existing reputation as a witch or as a bad person generally was much more likely to be punished than someone who had a good reputation. Most of the suspects in the sampled trials had bad reputations already, and those who had no prior record at all stood little chance of being punished. Ordinary criminals ran a somewhat higher risk of being punished, especially if they were associated with magic, but disagreeable personality traits, particularly aggressiveness, brought an even greater risk. Suspects with a generally bad reputation ran about a 50 percent chance of being punished, and all three of the sampled suspects who were executed and both of the ones who were tortured and then banished had bad reputations.

Most of these women who were so ill regarded had already been suspected of, and in some cases prosecuted for, witchcraft. The magistrates recorded prior suspicions about 15 of the 25 women in the sampled cases whose reputations were noted. These women ran the greatest risk of punishment. The rate of punishment was significantly higher than that for either ordinary crimes or disreputable behaviors. Two-thirds of the women with prior suspicions were punished, and they included all three of the executed and one of the two banished suspects. Prior suspicions did not automatically bring punishment, but they did make it more likely.

However, while a bad reputation, particularly prior suspicion as a witch, clearly made both accusation and punishment more likely, too much should not be made of this characteristic by itself for three reasons. First of all, going to court was often a last resort for early modern commoners, and prosecutions for other crimes like theft and assault generally came only after a series of incidents that had been ignored or handled informally. Secondly, the magistrates routinely looked into suspects' reputations and allegations of past incidents in criminal investigations because their forensic powers were limited, and in making their judgments they, like the village courts and in contrast to courts in our day, weighed the suspect's general pattern of life and evidence of similar past wrongdoing along with testimony and any physical evidence available about the current charge in assessing the probability of guilt and determining the harshness of any punishment. Thirdly, to a considerable degree, the reputation that mattered was the reputation for being a witch. While witch suspects, especially those punished, were generally poorly regarded, the sampled cases suggest that there was less continuity between other forms of disreputable or criminal behavior and witchcraft suspicions than has often been assumed; for the most part, witch suspects were simply people who were suspected of being witches.

This finding is consistent with that of Reiner Walz, who has studied witch accusations in the context of all judicial activity in a set of German villages in Lippe.[45] While he found that women played as important a role as men in the combative village culture, far more men ended up in court as a result of verbal exchanges, and he further found that eventual witch suspects were seldom among the women.[46] Most accounts have assumed that women specialized in verbal combat and have treated witch accusations as the culmination of an escalating series of interactions in which the woman moved from scolding to threats to curses, and was denounced when one of these was coincidentally followed by some harm supposedly associated with witchcraft. What seems to have been the case, however, is that women were suspected of witchcraft, and accused of *maleficium*, simply because they seemed to have a special propensity for projecting ill will in occult ways that caused injury to their neighbors.

Walz, like most other historians, assumes that women predominated among suspects so heavily because of sociocultural traditions scapegoating women by linking them to witchcraft, so that when misfortune occurred and a suspect was identified, people retroactively interpreted incidents to support the new accusation.[47] However, while some people undoubtedly did alter their memories and stories as Walz suggests, his focus on this process reflects the assumption that suspicions of *maleficium* were essentially baseless, and therefore need to be explained on the basis of some sort of cognitive malfunction. However, we have seen that charges of *maleficium* reflected real practices and behaviors with real consequences, and even if they were not necessarily valid in a particular case they were not inherently unreasonable, so there is no more or less reason to believe that old stories were retroactive falsifications than stored-up stories about thefts or slander (which is to say, it did happen, but was not their main source).

Furthermore, many of the prior incidents and suspicions mentioned had left some public record or involved some explicit comment at the time.[48] For example, Agatha Stosser, the woman tried for causing Hans Conrad Schweickhlen great pain by grabbing him, had been tried 14 years earlier, and the documents were included in the same dossier in the archive.[49] Similarly, Agatha Sacher, the young woman who caused her ex-boyfriend's bride to become ill, had been investigated a year earlier for laming an old man who had lodged a complaint about her before a preacher and two judges, and witnesses in another jurisdiction attested to her boasts about her magical abilities when she was a child.[50] In other cases there was no official record of the suspicions, but several witnesses testified about the same incident, as when Georg Krieger testified that Barbara Gessler, the woman accused of giving Anna Marie Schilling a poisoned apple, had given her own first husband a poison in the guise of a remedy when he was sick that did not make him better but instead did him in, and Ursula Schlosser testified that on his deathbed the man had rebuked Gessler for giving him a soup that was killing him.[51] In another case, Christian Cammer testified that a year before the trial of Agnes Langjahr for causing Andrea Leichten's daughter to sicken and die, she had left three eggs in his wife's lap as she lay recovering from childbirth. In both these cases, while the validity of the accusations may be in doubt, the correspondence of testimony in the first and the physical presence of the eggs in the second make retroactive misrepresentation seem less likely than that the suspicions did exist at the time. While some of the secondary accusations were vague charges that were undoubtedly concocted consciously or unconsciously to support the current suspicion, some were definitely and others appear most likely to have been based on genuine memories of events in which injury seemed to have followed from ill will at the time they took place.

If witchcraft accusations were not necessarily the outcome of some scapegoating process, but rather reflected, at least in part, real behaviors and practices that inflicted injury, then the predominance of female suspects can be interpreted in two ways. Either men and women were equally likely to have engaged in the practices and manifested the behaviors of *maleficium*, but because of social processes and/or cultural expectations only women were accused of it, or women really were more likely to employ *maleficium* in their interpersonal disputes, and the cultural expectations and social processes reflected that tendency.

Based on the evidence from Württemberg, there is no question that men could and did exert the kind of interpersonal influences associated with *maleficium*. Among the sampled cases, we have seen that one stemmed from an accusation by a young woman, Margaretha Stuertzen, that a young man, Hans Rueff, caused her to become lame by grabbing her right arm, and seven witnesses supported her claim.[52] In a similar case in the duchy that was also discussed in chapter 1, a young woman named Anna Beyler complained that a young man named Viet Grossman had stalked her and eventually grabbed her by the arms.[53] Her hands began to hurt and swell shortly thereafter, and her face became so swollen she had trouble seeing, so she consulted three different healers. When none could cure her, she went to the magistrate, "completely convinced that this condition resulted from" a magic spell. Whether her symptoms resulted from a "workplace accident," as the healer who mentioned the possibility of "a cut by something unclean ... in" her "filthy vineyard" or some sort of conversion reaction that more directly manifested her distress, it seems very likely that his harassment played a significant role.

However, Hans Rueff was the only sampled male suspect accused of *maleficium*; all the others involved were either men said to have been at witch dances or otherwise involved in diabolism and "cunning men," magical healers who had been consulted before the magistrates arrived and were investigated for using illicit incantations, ceremonies, and medicines to help their clients rather than for malefic or diabolic witchcraft. Similarly, Viet Grossman was one of only two men in the sampled "magic" trials accused of *maleficium*. Furthermore, neither Rueff nor Grossman was punished. Grossman was let off because by 1673, when the incident took place, the ducal government was clearly skeptical about witch allegations and required clear evidence. Since none of the three healers would confirm that Anna Beyler's malady was unnatural and Grossman had not made any explicit threat or curse during their encounters, there was no manifest evidence that he had cast a spell. Hans Rueff's case occurred earlier, in 1631, when the government was still quite willing to prosecute witches, but in his case the chancellery found that despite the testimony on Margaretha's behalf there was insufficient evidence.

One thing that did count against Rueff was that his mother and grandmother were reputed to be witches, and what started as an investigation of him ended up being an investigation of his mother. While she was also released, she was forced to pay the costs of her confinement while he was able to just walk away. An even more dramatic example of the disparity with which men and women were treated in regard to malefic activities was provided by the other of the sampled magic trials. In 1653, in the village of Schmier near Cloister Maulbronn, Michael Ellwein, a shepherd around 30 years old, was suspected of attempting to murder his wife and children by mixing poison with their salt. The magistrates took the salt to the apothecary of Vaihingen, and he found "the strongest fly poison" in it.[54] The magistrates reported that his "reputation is indeed bad ... because he associates with notoriously loathsome men," and "was seen by his assistant, a young boy, performing different types of evil magic." His wife and neighbors said he often went out at night and never went to church. One quoted him as saying his wife "was such a pitifully unhealthy person, afflicted by epilepsy, that he had no desire to stay home with her." Indeed, he had taken up with another woman, Catharina Seeger, who lived with her parents in a neighboring village. She confessed that she had encouraged Ellwein to poison his wife, and said she was her enemy "in order to win his love." Over several weeks of questioning, she admitted bringing him "poisonous drinks and apples," although she denied bringing him the poison he actually used, and during a "special" interrogation that lasted three hours she broke down and confessed to having "denied God" and a whole list of offenses ascribed to witches. Seeger recanted afterwards, but the magistrates obtained permission to torture her, and under torture she reconfirmed her earlier confessions. Both Seeger and Ellwein were beheaded, but he was convicted simply of attempted poisoning, while she was convicted of being a devil-worshipping witch, even though he was a dissolute man who reputedly dabbled in magic and had attempted to kill his own family, while she was at most an accessory to his crime. Adding insult to injury, he obtained a mitigation of his sentence – his body was not put on public display as originally stipulated – because of her supposed diabolic influence over him.

Clearly, there was a cultural bias regarding gender at work in the government's handling of cases that could be construed as *maleficium*. However, in looking at the statistics for the duchy overall, women were also accused of simple poisoning at rates comparable to those for men except, significantly, for the 1660s and 1670s, when, as we shall see in Chapter 8, the government chose to handle an increasing number of witch accusations as poisonings. Moreover, even if all the accusations of witchcraft and poisoning against males are added together, they do not come near to equaling the number of women accused of both, so it seems clear that the government was not just calling the same crime different things for the different genders. Furthermore, ordinary Württembergers showed themselves so concerned about *maleficium* that they denounced numerous women for whom the government found insufficient evidence to convict, even during the early period when it was not particularly skeptical, while the witch literature left a clear opening for men to be implicated. Traditionally, the emphasis on women has been assumed to be part of the cognitive malfunction that makes people believe in *maleficium* to begin with; in fact, reducing the range of the misperception to one gender would have helped protect it from countervailing evidence from reality. Since, however, as we have seen, *maleficium* really occurred, both as conscious practices and as an unconscious interpersonal effect, it is hard to see why people who were clearly so concerned about it that they denounced numerous female suspects of dubious guilt would have restricted themselves to only recognizing it when it came from one gender and not from the other, and overlooked clear cases when it came from men. There is no question that cultural expectations steered witchcraft suspicions toward women, but before we conclude that the preponderance of women among people accused of *maleficium* was simply the result of cultural expectations about women, we should consider whether it also reflected (and, in fact, the cultural expectation reflected) a real tendency for women to engage in the practices and exhibit the behaviors associated with *maleficium* more often than men.

Women in early modern Württemberg, like women generally, were involved in far fewer violent crimes than men, but this leaves open the question of whether they were simply less aggressive, or whether they acted out their aggression in different ways, in ways associated with witchcraft.[55] Early cross-cultural psychological studies of female aggression concluded that women are less aggressive than men, a conclusion that fit comfortably with the prevailing Western notion of "natural" female character at the time.[56] Critics, however, have suggested that the studies' definition of aggression was biased toward male forms, and more recent studies suggest that both genders have similar capacities for aggression, but that they manifest them rather differently.[57] Across cultures, males are more likely than females to use direct physical aggression; the two genders tend to be roughly equal in their propensity toward verbal aggression; and females are more likely than males to use indirect aggression: spreading gossip, manipulating surrogates, and other forms of covert attack.[58] When women do commit acts of direct aggression, like murder, they tend to use surreptitious means that minimize the actual violence, like poison or battery against a sleeping foe, although when they have power and think they are unobserved (as when they care for children and aged people) they are less reticent about resorting to direct physical violence.[59] While the correspondence between these modern findings and early modern suspicions about witches are not exact – the witches were thought to, and in some trials were shown to, use more direct violence (poisons, ritual magic, and battery) than the females in the modern study, the parallels are certainly suggestive.[60] Furthermore, on the other side of the gender equation, the propensity for direct physical violence of early modern men documented by Württemberg's court records is strikingly consistent with the general patterns observed for men, not only in modern Western society, but cross-culturally and through history.[61] On balance, the cross-cultural evidence seems to support the conclusion that early modern witch fears did reflect a real tendency for women to engage in witch-related practices and exhibit witch-like behaviors more often than men.[62]

The reasons for these different styles of aggression are discussed in many of the cross-cultural studies, and there is general agreement that sociocultural forces play a strong role.[63] Modern studies emphasize modern women's greater degree of social integration to account for both their reluctance to openly aggress and their reliance on indirect means, while early modern historians discuss the importance of women's social space as the arena in which witch-related activities took place.[64] However, it is becoming clearer that the either-or division between sociocultural influences and biology, nature and nurture, is an oversimplification; sociocultural and biological factors interact in complex ways to influence human behavior, including gendered behavior.[65] And while they sometimes exist in tension or conflict, sociocultural structures "commonly" reinforce or exaggerate biological differences.[66] This seems to be the case in regard to the aggressive behaviors, for while women tend to utilize indirect and covert aggression in part because they have internalized sociocultural images of appropriate female behavior, they also do this because of a conscious or unconscious recognition that they are at a disadvantage physiologically in confrontations with men, because men on average are larger and heavier and have more muscle-mass in their upper bodies.[67] On the one hand, this difference in biology to some degree underlies the difference in sociocultural images, for males have specialized in hunting and physical combat since Paleolithic times, and have augmented this basic biological difference with individual training in fighting, the use of increasingly complex and lethal weapons, and an expanding scale of group cooperation, further magnifying the differential physical coercive power of men and women.[68] It seems significant that in many simple societies men and women are thought to have similar, if not always the same, propensities to use magical powers, while in Western civilization, dominated by male violence, male government, and male religion, females have come to be seen as particularly likely to rely on occult forms of power. On the other hand, the difference in biology is itself in part a product of social forces, for it was the existence of effective social groups that enabled human beings to evolve specialized physiologies to this degree.[69]

The role of gross anatomical differences between women and men in predisposing them to certain modes of aggression, both directly, through conscious or unconscious calculation of optimum conflict strategies, and indirectly, through sociocultural expectations and restrictions, would seem relatively unproblematic. Other, subtler, biological differences are more controversial, but also seem to play a role. The best-known gender difference in behavior directly linked to physiological differences is the effect of male sex hormones (androgens) in stimulating aggression in men.[70] While recent research has challenged the simplistic notion that surges of testosterone cause uncontrollable fits of aggression in males, it is well established that prenatal exposure to androgens produced in response to the presence of the Y chromosome causes the hypothalamus to develop differently in males than females.[71] Because of these differences, testosterone affects males' brains differently than females' brains, and while some researchers argue that it simply makes men capable of violence rather than compelling them to it, in either case this difference does appear to be a biological contributor to the differential levels of direct aggression observed across cultures.[72] The absolute levels of violence manifested by both sexes vary widely from one culture to the next, but the relatively greater readiness of males to resort to overt violence appears to be a constant, and appears to be attributable to this genetic and hormonal difference as well as to gross anatomical differences and differences in social roles and acculturation.[73]

While the different prenatal development of females makes them less responsive to the influence of androgens, it would be a mistake to conclude that their behavior is simply a reflection of their lack of something males have. In the first place, the presence of estrogen has been shown to promote composure, even in men, so women's greater restraint also reflects their possession of something men lack (or at least have far less of).[74] Furthermore, the evidence suggests that the forms of aggression women do tend to favor are positive adaptations that maximize their natural strengths. Specifically, across cultures women have been shown to be on average more emotionally responsive, more socially attuned, and more verbally gifted than men.[75] While socialization undoubtedly accounts for much of that difference, both because girls are encouraged to foster these skills in order to take on their role as nurturers and because subordinate groups in society generally cultivate a greater awareness of the nuances of behavior and expression than dominant groups, the evidence suggests that the tendency has biological roots as well.[76] One study, for example, has shown newborn girls to be more responsive to sounds of other peoples' distress than newborn boys, while another has shown that at four months girls are already better at recognizing faces than boys.[77] Furthermore, women appear to be biologically equipped to hear better, see better in the dark, have better visual memories, differentiate tastes better, and smell more acutely than men.[78] Women's brains are structurally different from men's: they are 15 percent smaller (even accounting for differences in body size), with proportionately the same number of neurons, but more tightly packed.[79] There is some evidence that the corpus callosum, the nerve bundle that connects the right and left hemispheres, is bigger in women than men, and it has been suggested that this enables women to integrate the cognitive activities of the two hemispheres more quickly than men.[80] More solidly established is the fact that women process emotion in more regions of the brain than men; both hemispheres of women's brains recognize the emotional content of visual messages, whereas only the right hemisphere of men's brains do.[81] As a consequence, some of women's emotional processing is located in the same hemisphere as the areas responsible for verbal activity, which suggests a reason why women may express emotions more readily than men, in whom emotional processing and verbal activity occur in different halves of the brain.[82] Furthermore, women's verbal dexterity may be further enhanced by the fact that their language centers are consolidated in one region of the brain, while men's are scattered.[83] Finally, there is some evidence that estrogen plays a role in the full development of verbal fluency, memory, and the recognition of emotion in faces.[84] Indirect aggression (the infliction of harm through the manipulation of third parties) and the infliction of harm through verbal or gestural emotional signaling are thus conflict strategies that exploit abilities that women tend to be good at while, like covert violence, they avoid contests women tend to be less well equipped for.[85]

None of these physiological attributes impels women to behaviors associated with witchcraft, of course; what the cross-cultural and biological evidence suggests is not that some or all women have some innate drive to act like witches, but instead that they have innate as well as learned characteristics that make them more likely than men to adopt conflict strategies in violent cultures or moments of anger that are characterized as *maleficium*.[86] Women in early modern Württemberg, like women throughout early modern Europe, lived in a society permeated by violence, and the cross-cultural and biological evidence suggests that it is no wonder that some of them acted in ways that made them seem like witches to their neighbors. Most women, like most men, lived either nonviolently or within socially acceptable bounds of aggressiveness, but some early modern women, like some early modern men, aggressed beyond acceptable limits. The difference was, the men tended to aggress with fists or knives, while the women tended to aggress with poisons, rituals, or raw expressions of anger.[87] In so doing, they were manifesting both their culture's expectations and their own psychophysical endowments.[88]

Of course, not every woman accused of witchcraft had engaged in practices or manifested behaviors associated with *maleficium*. The great majority of people caught up in mass panics, in particular, were implicated through tortured testimony of suspects who were prompted to provide the names of their supposed accomplices. The first few people accused in these trials were often stereotypical suspects, some of whom may have engaged in *maleficium*, but they were rapidly outnumbered by people named simply to produce the required list. In southwest Germany as a whole, larger trials involving six or more suspects constituted about 15 percent of all trials between 1300 and 1700 while accounting for about 70 percent of both known suspects and known executions.[89] In the duchy of Württemberg, such trials amounted to about 10 percent of the prosecutions, but contributed only about 40 percent of the suspects, and 50 percent of known deaths. The sample of cases studied intensively from the duchy deliberately excluded mass panics in order to focus on trials in which actual practices and behaviors were most likely to be revealed, so it is representative of about half the suspects (the 40 percent in the small trials themselves plus the stereotypical suspects typically caught up in the beginnings of mass panics), and we have seen a number of cases in which *maleficium* was alleged but the magistrate's investigation either cast doubt that anything had happened at all or suggested that the injury was not the result of ill will.[90] For example, Rolf Kellern's accusation that Catharina Freyberger sold him poisoned cheese dissolved in the face of her apparently genuine surprise, her generally good reputation, and the fact that another man said he ate some of the same cheese without ill effect. Johanna Fehlen's illness at her wedding seems to have resulted from the white powder Barbara Schmied put into her wine, but both she and the magistrates were satisfied both that it was a benign rather than malign substance and that putting it there had been a friendly rather than hostile gesture. Similarly, Anna Gebhard's bawdy joking with Konrad Streich at his wedding seems to have been a significant factor in his subsequent impotence, but despite the woman's reputation for witchcraft her actions were not deemed hostile, and she was acquitted.

Nevertheless, other allegations of *maleficium* appear to have been better founded. Of the 44 suspects in the 27 cases, there was significant evidence that about 11, or 25 percent, consciously engaged in practices or unconsciously manifested hostile behaviors associated with *maleficium*. Specifically, Magdelena Horn confessed to injuring animals and hitting a child, and Maria Schneider was caught in a lie when she denied giving her stepgrandson soup that made him ill.[91] Catharina Ada assaulted and cursed a number of people, and appears to have poisoned another.[92] Anna Maria Rothin grabbed Barbara Dannenritter which caused her great pain, smeared something on a woman that caused her to become lame and possibly caused her death, stroked a woman on the thigh who subsequently became so distraught she hung herself, and hit and lamed the arm of yet another woman.[93] Barbara Gessler gave Anna Maria Schelling an apple shortly before she died of a poison, and also gave several other people potions from which they apparently died.[94] All five of these examples seem to have involved deliberate attempts to inflict harm, as did the incident in which Agnes Langjahr placed eggs in Christian Cammer's wife's lap.[95]

Langjahr also appears to have at least inadvertently caused or contributed to the death of Andrea Leichten's daughter by her obtrusiveness and hostility, the paralysis of another child when she hit him in the face, and was suspected of having harmed several farm animals. Similarly, Agatha Stosser caused or contributed to Christoph Schweickhlen's son's severe pain in his arm when she grabbed it, and she was suspected of having poisoned a woman and caused a number of animals to sicken and die when she hit them or put things in their fodder.[96] Magdelena Kochen was accused of causing several people to become lame and was suspected of having injured several animals in retaliation for refusals to help her in various ways.[97] Agatha Sacher made it known that she wanted to harm her rival and attended her wedding, although it is not clear if she did anything more overt in the other woman's presence to precipitate her malady, just as it is unclear if she intended to lame the old man she worked with the previous year.[98] Similarly, Katharina Masten clearly assaulted Catharina Baitinger because she was angry that the servant girl had delayed her repayment for her master's debt, and Hans Rueff appears to have grabbed Margaretha Stuertzen, but in both of these cases, while the suspects acted in overtly hostile ways, their actions appear to have been more spontaneous and the source of any effects beyond the physical force of their grip or blows was unconscious or unintended.[99]

These suspects amounted to 25 percent of the accused in the sample of small trials, which suggests that similar suspects must have made up at most about 15 percent of all suspects since the great majority of suspects in mass trials were implicated as part of the terrible "chain reactions" of accusations produced by torture and therefore were presumably innocent of any significant behaviors associated with *maleficium*.[100] While this makes the social significance of these suspects seem limited, their full importance in the early modern community is suggested by the fact that this 25 percent of the sampled suspects were charged with 54, or over 70 percent, of the 75 reported acts of *maleficium* that started or came to light during trials. Studies of modern crime have found that a small number of repeat offenders are responsible for most crimes, and the same pattern appears to have occurred in the case of early modern *maleficium*.[101]

The fact that ten of these eleven suspects who appear likely to have actually engaged in the practices or exhibited the behaviors associated with *maleficium* were women supports the idea that women did tend to utilize them more than men, but they also shared another significant social characteristic: most of them were old. Magdelena Horn was described in the documents as "old," Agatha Stosser was 73, Maria Schneider was 65, Magdelena Kochen was 55, Katharina Masten was over 70, Anna Maria Rothin was 80, and Agnes Langjahr was 50. Catharina Ada had a 15-year-old daughter, so, given the tendency of women in early modern Württemberg to marry in their early 20s, she was probably in her late 30s at least, while the fact that Barbara Gessler was married to her second husband and some of the secondary accusations went back a decade or more suggests that she, too, was probably at least around the same age. Only Hans Rueff and Agatha Sacher were definitely less than 30 years old.

This age profile is roughly consistent with information about ages of suspects elsewhere in Europe, and the proportion of elderly suspects in the sampled cases definitely constitutes an overrepresentation of older people relative to their proportion of the overall population.[102] Of course, trials often culminated years and even decades of suspicions, and, indeed, charges against Magdelena Kochen dated back almost 5 years; those against Agnes Langjahr about 10; the ones against Agatha Stosser almost 20 years, and those against Anna Maria Rothin at least 30. However, subtracting these spans from the suspects' ages at trial indicates that the suspect incidents began when the suspects were between 40 and 50 years old.

This age seems particularly significant since it was the time when people in early modern Europe generally began to be considered old. While old age clearly and unambiguously ends with death, when it begins is not so clear. However, while early modern notions ranged from 40 to 65, the earlier end of that range seems appropriate when considering the relationship of *maleficium* and older women for several reasons. First of all, it is the time when women generally went through menopause, the end of reproductive potency, and a woman's reproductive potential was more central to her status then than it is now. Secondly, because of the rigors of childbirth and motherhood, women often appeared old early, and thirdly, it was the time when people were generally perceived to begin to exhibit "undesirable changes in personality" that seem related to those associated with *maleficium*. One typical early modern commentator observed that "in our old age ... we may see ... sin and lusts ... which we saw not before."[103] He described the elderly as "covetous ... fearful ... touchy, peevish, angry, and forward ... unteachable ... hard to please ... full of complaints ... suspicious ... and apt to surmise, suspect, and fear the worst." Humoral theory linked old age and melancholy, which made people "easy prey for the Devil."[104] These "distinctly negative undertones" were even found "in the attitudes of the elderly toward their own aging," which often created in them "a continuing anxiety."[105]

Similarly, in our culture "emotional liability, lack of stability ... short-circuit reactions ... fanaticism and querulous tendencies ... occur ... frequently toward the fiftieth year and during the fifties."[106] Members of both sexes suffer frequently from depression during these years, and "needs stemming from insecurity and threat" increase in importance. The attendant "anxiety ... is especially important as a generator of defensive and handicapping behavior patterns."[107] Inevitable "differences in what time has taught lead to perennial clashes ... between youth and age." Many people begin to show "a lack of concern about the social situation, a lessened influence of everyday social controls, and a dominance of self-concern."[108]

The basis of the negative personality changes which often develop early in old age in women have traditionally been linked to the menopause, the deactivation of the reproductive system. During this transition, which occurs around age 50 in modern women, but happened about a decade earlier in early modern women, the ovaries cease producing some hormones and the production of others is reduced.[109] Since the body's functioning depends on a delicate hormonal balance, "their removal requires considerable readjustment." In particular, the loss of the estrogen–pituitary gonadotropic hormone balance affects a woman's "whole physical mechanism on all levels of control." Most significant from the point of view of *maleficium*, perhaps, is the declining levels of estrogen, which, as we have seen, may be linked to the self-restraint shown by younger women relative to the levels of aggressiveness of men within the same culture.

Contrary to the old view of menopause as the cause of "morbid irrationality ... hysteria ... melancholy and the impulses to drink spirits, steal, and, purchase, to murder," though, it is now known that the great majority of women have at most minor problems during the physiological adjustments, and most of these "are culturally induced."[110] Estrogen replacement therapy has shown that "the only symptoms ... uniquely characteristic of the menopausal period are hot flashes ... and genital atrophy."[111] However, "the menopause ... can and frequently does serve as a stimulus for emotional distress," for it "is only one part" of a "transition made during a period of fifteen to twenty years" referred to as the climacteric.[112] In modern men and women "midlife stresses are a result of a combination of personal, family, social, and biological variables." In women, the climacteric begins a few years before the end of menstruation, and in both sexes it tapers off slowly as adjustments are made not only to the end of reproductive potency, but also to the start of physical and mental decay, the loss or modification of social status, and the nearing of inevitable death. This combination of changes, affecting a person's self definition at all levels, from the biological to the metaphysical, causes the intensification of negative personality traits in modern elderly people discussed previously.

Among elderly modern people the climacteric is a temporary transitional period followed by a time of greater adjustment and relative calm. Yet the sampled suspects showed a steady level of suspicion and rate of accusation from age 50 all the way to, in one case, 80, which amounts to a steadily greater disproportion as women got older. What this suggests is that it was not the menopause or even the climacteric per se that were responsible for the women performing the practices and manifesting the behaviors associated with *maleficium*, but instead that it simply intensified preexisting dispositions, dispositions that were similar to those of some women who began manifesting them far earlier in their lives, and which were maintained once started not because of some hormonal adjustment but because they worked. The towns and villages of early modern Württemberg and elsewhere in Europe were, as we have seen, rough-and-tumble places, where power, status, and resources were often gained and secured only through verbal, physical, legal, and in some cases magical combativeness. Women operated at a distinct disadvantage in many ways, and elderly women were particularly disadvantaged. Most elderly women were legal wards and economic dependents of younger male relatives, living in their household or under their supervision nearby. If they were independent, it was usually the precarious independence of the impoverished widow, who depended on the kindness of neighbors, particularly if she, like Magdelena Kochen, had dependent children. Relatively well-to-do widows had the mirror-image problem to the poor ones: they had to defend their property and prerogatives from encroachment by younger relatives and neighbors, some of whom not only resented but contested the power and influence of their elders, despite cultural admonishments that the old were to rule and the young were to obey. All of these situations had strong potential to generate conflicts, and elderly women were particularly likely to react with the "hostile, vengeful, grasping or aggressive" behaviors associated with *maleficium*, reactions that could become habitual or even chronic since "events in the outside world, including social interactions, have lasting effects on ... neurobiological processes" so that "negative interactions ... develop into a 'vicious circle'" in which hostile encounters and successful belligerence create "subtle and widespread changes in monoamine transmitter systems" amounting to a "progressive reconfiguration of ... critical sensory-filtering and mood-setting pathways" in ways that entrench angry feelings and aggressive reactions.[113] Women at any age could resort to the practices or exhibit the behaviors associated with *maleficium*, but elderly women were particularly likely to do so because both their psychophysical predisposition and the sociocultural pressures on them compounded the psychophysical attributes that characterized and the sociocultural challenges that faced women of all ages at the time.

Hard times and hard hearts

Significantly, the circumstances contributing to the kind of interpersonal conflicts that formed the context of *maleficium* intensified at the very time when concern about, and prosecutions for, witchcraft rose dramatically. By the late sixteenth century, the beginning of the period of intense witch prosecutions, Württemberg was seriously overpopulated, with a rate of increase of 6–7 per thousand per year until 1598, and 5.5 per thousand per year from then until the 1630s, when its population reached about 450,000.[114] By the eve of the Thirty Years' War, the duchy's economy could not provide work for about 15 percent of the workforce, even with the import-export sector that had enabled the population to grow beyond its base subsistence capacity, and the problem of providing for destitute paupers and beggars, vagrants, and tramps had become completely unmanageable.[115] The effects of the economic underperformance were felt much more widely than the problem of the destitute, though; it took the form more of a widespread underemployment and a growing indebtedness that affected smallholders, cotters, and laborers as well as the indigent. While all were affected, farm hands and boarders were the hardest hit, for they enjoyed no communal rights and could be evicted at the discretion of the head of the household they resided in. Before the Thirty Years' War "these rural poor posed ... the greatest social problem."[116] When they could not find work, "they either had to be charitably taken in indefinitely by one household, or passed around the community from farm to farm." Even as the smallholders and cotters struggled with the substantial farmers for established rights in the village commune, they made common cause with them against this swelling underclass.[117]

As the ranks of the destitute grew they strained both the resources and the generosity of the productive community. The small number of almshouses, known as *Spitalen*, that had been created during the fifteenth and sixteenth centuries proved totally inadequate, and their numbers were not increased until the eighteenth century. Cloister districts, which provided generous alms to their poorer inhabitants, were swamped by impoverished immigrants.[118] Ordinary towns and villages had always had a certain number of poor residents, and had established procedures for soliciting alms from the prosperous commoners for their support.[119] During the second half of the sixteenth century their charity came to be strained to the limit. In 1562, the nearby Imperial City of Ulm began refusing relief to new residents who had not lived there for at least five years.[120] Around the same time it proposed to the Swabian League that member states "forbid that beggars be given money, in order to discourage young people from becoming idlers."[121] The League did not adopt this draconian policy, but member states did routinely confine vagrants to workhouses to discourage them. The League organized a force to police the countryside, to which Württemberg contributed beginning in 1585, but "despite the … police patrols, the League never got control of this problem." Nor could individual communities solve the problem posed by resident paupers. The proportion of the population in dire straits rose steadily as the population increased, until almost a quarter of the duchy's inhabitants lived at or below the margin of subsistence, and those above them had to scramble ever harder to secure property, positions, and patronage.[122]

We have seen that the sampled cases provide graphic examples of the kinds of problems these general trends caused, like the widow Magdelena Kochen, who had conflicts with her neighbors over their reluctance to help support her, and Katharina Masten, who fought the servant girl Catharina Baitinger when she came to collect a debt from the girl's master.[123] However, we have seen that most conflicts took place between people of roughly equal station, and many were not directly over material goods. The period from 1550 to 1650 has been called the "Iron Century" not just because of the economic crisis that took place during that period, but because of the cumulative effects of overpopulation, depression, confessional conflict, political struggles, and open warfare on the overall quality of life.[124] Just as the 15 percent deficit in Württemberg's productive capacity was manifested as a much wider underemployment and an even broader competition for limited resources, the economic crisis created a cultural climate of competition, suspicion, lack of charity, struggle, and hatred.[125] Confessional conflicts and political struggles and the wars that grew out of them contributed as well, with the net result that this period was particularly hard, a time of hard hearts, hard words, hard feelings, hard bargaining, and, when it came to it, hard fighting.

The Thirty Years' War climaxed the period, both in that the problems reached their maximum intensity and the foundations for better times were put in place. At first it intensified the preexisting difficulties, fueling inflation, disrupting trade, and pushing up the burden of taxes.[126] In Württemberg the war brought unprecedented suffering and destruction after the Battle of Nordlingen, when Catholic soldiers were let loose in the duchy to rape, pillage, and kill in retribution for its support of the Protestant cause.[127] Moreover, the marauding soldiers brought plagues and famines in their wake that further devastated the population. Estimates vary, but at least half the duchy's people died from the violence, disease, and hunger, or fled.[128]

The murderous occupation threw society into upheaval as farmers left the land, artisans lost their tools, and the vintners' vines fueled the soldiers' watch fires. The disorders continued until the end of the 1630s, when "one-third of arable land" lay "uncultivated and overgrown," and, according to one estimate, the population reached its nadir at 100,000, less than a quarter of what it had been on the eve of war.[129]

The number bounced back to about 225,000 by 1652, undoubtedly because many refugees returned as conditions improved, and the duchy adopted a deliberate policy of encouraging immigration. In a perverse way, the very brutality of the events laid the foundations for later improvement, but the progress was very uneven. Murder, disease, and flight left the duchy's population at only about 50 percent of its prewar total at the end of the war, a level that the economy was better able to sustain with the resources available in the seventeenth century; but in the decades after the war, agricultural depression, periodic wars, and endemic poverty meant that widespread misery continued to be a problem beneath the *ancien regime*'s glittering facade.[130] Social and economic conflicts continued, and the interpersonal interactions that underlay the concept of *maleficium* remained in play. The great majority of Württembergers continued to believe in malefic witchcraft and were ready to denounce their neighbors when they felt that they had been injured by them, so the per capita number of witch accusations actually peaked during the 1660s. However, despite the difficulties, the favorable ratio of people to resources meant that desperation was not as widespread or intense, and when the provincial elite began to back away from prosecuting witchcraft for reasons we shall see in Chapter 8, the pace of prosecutions declined steeply as the century came to an end. By the time population growth began to challenge the duchy's productive capacity again in the eighteenth century, both magical aggression and the fear of it would, as we shall see, play a very limited part in peoples' response.

One of the occupational hazards of studying witchcraft is that it can lead to an overestimation of the role of witchcraft fears and the witch persecutions in early modern society and culture. While some places were overwhelmed by mass panics that consigned scores of people to the pyre within a matter of months, and others experienced a steady stream of denunciations and trials over the course of years, or even decades, for most Europeans witchcraft was a secondary issue: one or a few surly neighbors might be suspected of perpetrating harm through occult means, but their unpleasantness was taken in stride, avoided or appeased for the most part, and endured or cured when inescapable. Witch trials mostly happened sporadically or in small wavelets, with years or even decades between them in any particular locale, and some regions saw few or even no trials at all. It is therefore ironic that the role of *maleficium*, the actual infliction of harm through conscious practices and unconscious behaviors associated with witchcraft, remains significantly underestimated in accounts and analyses of witchcraft fears and the witchcraft persecutions. While historians have come to routinely acknowledge that some suspects did engage in various practices associated with it, they just as routinely dismiss these as secondary to the belief in and fear of witchcraft, the primary phenomena which they regard as a cognitive malfunction requiring explanation in terms of some combination of errant social, cultural, and psychological processes. However, we have seen in this chapter and the one before that *maleficium* involved a range of practices and behaviors that not only were really engaged in by some people, but also could have real consequences for the people who were their targets. As with every crime, of course, not every allegation was valid, but the belief that *maleficium* might be perpetrated and fear that it might cause harm were not irrational. Nor was the conviction that certain people consciously or unconsciously engaged in these behaviors and practices occasionally or even habitually, or the understanding that they were most likely to be manifested by women, and particularly elderly women. Instead, belief in and fear of witches and witchcraft were rooted in the fact that malefic behaviors and practices constituted a set of actions and activities that enabled some people, mostly women, and most frequently elderly women, to exert power in their communities, to defend or assert a claim to material and social resources coveted or controlled by others. Similarly, while the mass panics and judicial abuses of "the burning time" require the kind of social, cultural, and psychological explanations that historical accounts have traditionally focused on, the surge of trials in the late sixteenth and early seventeenth century itself does not. Witchcraft trials became more frequent in the late sixteenth and early seventeenth centuries because the conditions leading to the interpersonal conflicts that precipitated the malefic behaviors and inspired the malefic practices associated with witchcraft became more common at the time.

Of course, as has long been known, the fundamental reason why the trials spun out of control, why commoners' conviction that certain of their neighbors had harmed them through occult means led to wanton torture and wholesale slaughter, had to do with the connection that was posited between *maleficium* and diabolism, the fear that individuals' inclination and ability to inflict harm through magical means was symptomatic of membership in a widespread antisocial conspiracy. As long as *maleficium* was regarded as illusory, that connection could be explained relatively easily, as one unfounded set of beliefs connected more or less arbitrarily to another. However, if *maleficium* was not illusory, as we have seen here, then its connection to diabolism becomes more problematic. Who was this Devil, and what, if anything, did he have to do with the ability to cause harm magically in reality? It is to this question that we will turn in the following chapters.

Part II The Realities of Diabolism

Introduction

To a very considerable extent, early modern commoners' fear of witchcraft reflected their real vulnerability to their neighbors' hostility. Angry people in villages and towns could and did resort to occult means to harm their enemies, and thereby could inflict real damage through both physical and psychological mechanisms. People who feared that they might be the objects of such an attack could and did resort to a variety of protective and countermeasures, up to and including recourse to the law. This interplay of occult attack, defense, and counterattack was typical of agricultural peoples, including medieval Europeans, but early modern witchcraft was distinguished by the fact that such occult attacks, *maleficium*, were taken to be signs of diabolism, allegiance to the Devil.[1] It conceived of witches not simply as isolated old women aggressively advancing their interests through magical attacks, but as Satan's servants, members of a malevolent underground heretical sect recruited and led by the Devil himself. Unlike fear of *maleficium*, which was the main concern of commoners and generally manifested local beliefs and activities, diabolism was the primary concern of the elite and reflected a cosmopolitan concept contained in and disseminated by written works.[2] These works were composed over the course of several centuries and in different parts of Europe, so each had its own particular take on the topic, but by the mid-1500s, when the period of greatest concern about witchcraft began, a fairly standard composite depiction of diabolic witchcraft had emerged.[3] In it, the Devil seduced witches with sex or money in moments of weakness, magically transported them to a witches' Sabbath at which they renounced God, signed a pact with the Devil, and engaged in various sacrilegious, perverted, and obscene activities; and finally transported them back home armed with the powers and potions needed to perpetrate *maleficium* and return periodically to additional Sabbaths.[4] The three chapters in this section examine each of the three main elements of this diabolism – contact with the Devil, attendance at Sabbaths, and acquisition thereby of the power to perform harmful magic – in relation to the actual practices and experiences for which there is evidence in the archives in Württemberg.

Before we begin, two things should probably be noted. First, whereas Part I focused on investigating the physical reality of many forms of *maleficium* that have previously been discounted as purely psychological, in this section "reality" is understood to include perceived experiences regardless of whether the source of the perceptions appears to us to have been internal or external, both because in at least some cases it is clear that the people involved really did experience the things they described, which means that the experiences were real even if we think they did not correspond to any external physical events, and also because even imagined experiences have a physical dimension in the neurological processes that make them manifest. Second, it should probably be noted upfront that the evidence does not vindicate the demonologists' fear that there was a cohesive, widespread underground movement of Devil-worshipping witches. However, it also does not support the idea that this fear was based only on scholastic reasoning and clerical misogyny, displaced social tensions, or even a compendium of popular beliefs. Instead, it indicates that not only its details but also its overall structure reflected actual experiences and practices as well as thoughts, beliefs, and stories and were created, sustained, and developed through a dynamic interaction between learned theories, popular beliefs, and some peoples' real activities and perceptual experiences.

3
The Devil in the Duchy of Württemberg

In this chapter, we will look at the realities of the first element in the diabolic stereotype, the idea that the Devil was an active, direct agent in the world, a palpable spiritual force, or even a distinct physical entity, that people could perceive and even interact with much like a normal person. We will start by considering where this idea came from, then look at how it connected to existing beliefs and practices in the region including Württemberg, how it evolved in the interaction between learned theories and popular culture, and finally consider what role it played in the development of popular mentalities and collective experiences during the early modern period.

Origin and diffusion of the diabolic stereotype

The diabolic stereotype originated in the late fourteenth and early fifteenth centuries in the Alps when inquisitors and magistrates discovered what they took to be a "new form of sorcery" involving Devil worship and profanation of the Christian sacraments.[1] It included ideas from learned traditions of scandalous allegations against heretics, lepers, and Jews and the necessity of demonic involvement in magic, but it also included popular traditions of malefic magic, animal metamorphosis, and magical flight that combined collective fears and individual experiences.[2] In fact, recent scholarship has revealed that virtually every feature of the diabolic stereotype was rooted in such popular traditions. First of all, there is plenty of evidence that some people did practice malefic magic, and some forms of that magic, necromancy, involved the deliberate invocation of demons.[3] Such sorcery sometimes involved appropriations or perversions of Christian rituals, and might include promises of obedience and devotion to the demon's service.[4] Secondly, magical practitioners, like most people, formed networks of mentors, protégés, and associates, and some forms of magic, like weather magic, were at least sometimes performed by groups.[5] Further, popular traditions involving magical flight were widespread, and some people actually thought they experienced them.[6] While most of the people who did so appear to have been asleep or in a naturally induced trance, some used hallucinogenic drugs. Some of the people who thought they flew at night thought that they did so to get to babies that they could kill and eat, while others went to gatherings including both people and spirits, where they feasted and made merry.[7] At those festivities, there was often a leader spirit to whom the others paid court, and in at least one case the leader made it clear that she ruled, if not in opposition to Christ, at least outside the bounds of Christianity.[8] In the same case, the participants reported that they learned magic skills at the gatherings that they retained for use in their everyday roles as wise women, and similar cults also involved popular magical practitioners, although any connection between their participation in the cult and their magical powers is not made clear.[9] The sin of the men who created the diabolic stereotype was not so much that they made up the practices they reported, but rather that they interpreted them in the most negative way possible, added in a few elements from purely literary traditions, and amalgamated them willy-nilly into a composite that distorted the individual elements as it assimilated them into an illusory whole.[10] Consequently, whenever evidence of one element was found, the others were assumed, and torture confirmed the suspicion with fair reliability, which further solidified the stereotype. There was thus a kind of "ratchet effect" in which isolated elements that really existed were added to the composite stereotype as they were discovered in one context and their existence in other contexts later appeared to be confirmed through tortured testimony.

Even as it solidified, the stereotype diffused, slowly at first, by word of mouth and manuscript, but then faster, in print, for it came of age in the same century as the printing press. The revolutionary impact of this invention was first shown by its decisive role in spreading the Reformation, which also taught printers that division, debate, scandal, and unbridled invective sell.[11] The Protestants thundered against the Catholics and the Catholics thundered back, with both employing rhetorical weapons ranging from subtle learned treatises to scurrilous broadsides that drew stark, simplified contrasts based on exaggeration, distortion, and flagrant lies. They conveyed an image of the world as the battleground in a monumental confrontation between good and evil in which the stakes were the salvation of humankind.[12] The diabolic stereotype, with its flattened and diabolized message and its call for violent countermeasures, fit right in, and perhaps even took up slack in the Holy Roman Empire when confessional conflict abated after the Peace of Augsburg.[13] In any case, the number of German works proliferated in the second half of the sixteenth century, and their places of publication appear to have shifted gradually from the south and west to the north and east, bringing the "shocking news" that the "loathsome Devil" was recruiting a "fanatical army" of "witches and fiends" who "came together in an assembly" to do their "horrible deeds and activities (see Table 3.1).[14]

Table 3.1 Geographic distribution of witch publication over time

Direction	Place	Pre-1560	1560s	1570s	1580s	1590s	1600s	1610s	1620s	1630s
SW	Basel	2								
SW	Zurich		1							
SW	Freiburg					1				
W	Strasburg		1		1					
NW	Frankfurt	2	1	1	4		1	1		
	Tübingen		1	1	2		4	1		
	Stuttgart							1		
SE	Ulm									
SE	Lauingen						1			
SE	Augsburg		1							
SE	Nürnburg	1						1		
NE	Hof			1	1					
NE	Dresden					1				
NE	Erfurt							1		
NE	Leipzig						1	2	1	

Source: Bever, "Wuerttemberg," Table 2.1.
Note: Directions are relative to Württemberg.

Württemberg was fully open to the new intellectual currents. The number of printing establishments in southwestern Germany increased steadily over the late fifteenth and early sixteenth centuries, and Württemberg itself had several before the turn of the century.[15] In addition to these local and regional presses, the duchy lay near numerous German and Swiss cities of international importance.[16] The University of Tübingen, founded in 1477, became a flourishing intellectual center and, over the course of the sixteenth century, young upper-class men, particularly members of the urban notability, came to routinely spend several years studying there before moving into posts of public responsibility.[17]

However, the diabolic stereotype did encounter significant local resistance from theologians and lawyers who worked in the tradition of the medieval *Canon Episcopi*, which asserted that women who thought they flew at night with the Goddess Diana or Holda were victims of diabolical illusions (the word "*Unhold*," a common term for witches in the region, appears to be connected to this tradition).[18] As early as the 1480s, at the same time the Dominican Heinrich Kramer was writing his notorious contribution to the diabolical stereotype, the *Malleus Maleficarum*, and drawing on the same set of trials that Kramer based his work on, the legal scholar Ulrich Molitor composed an alternative perspective arguing that the witches' crimes were illusory. His point of view was first expressed at Tübingen by Martin Plantsch in 1505, and the tradition was given its definitive formulation in the 1520s and 30s when the religious reformer Johann Brenz extended its logic to say that witches who believed they could cause storms and other misfortunes were also deluded by the Devil. Brenz advanced the argument with telling effect in a debate with Johann Spreter, who took the hard-line position of the *Malleus Maleficarum*, forcing Spreter to concede the point, and the *Episcopi* tradition remained "dominant and unmodified" at Tübingen "until the start of the Thirty Years' War."[19]

Nevertheless, while the *Episcopi* tradition won the intellectual battle, the *Malleus* tradition won the cultural war. The *Canon Episcopi*, after all, asserted that the Devil caused the illusion of flight, and Brenz argued that the Devil deluded weather magicians by letting them know when a storm was coming so that they would do their rituals and then think they had caused it.[20] The provincial "moderates" thus accepted that the Devil is an active agent in the world, that some people did practice magic, and most conceded that anyone who truly worshipped the Devil deserved to die. Their theoretical distinctions came to mean less and less as cautious tomes and sensationalist pamphlets alike depicted society as rife with malevolent women who worshipped the Devil and practiced harmful magic. They reported on witch hunts in which dozens of suspects were implicated and executed, and so great did the Devil's legions seem that one pamphleteer observed, "if one wanted to burn all such malevolent women, one would not have enough wood and fire."[21]

Awareness of and concern about the Devil's conspiracy diffused into society in the second half of the century through a variety of channels that both drew from and contributed to the printed discourse. In 1546, for example, Duke Ulrich instructed preachers in the duchy to denounce magical practices in their sermons, and the Provincial Law Code of 1567 obliged them to warn their parishioners of the Devil's activity in their midst.[22] Many preachers read verbatim from written texts in their sermons, and drew heavily on the stories and moralizing of the witch literature.[23] The court preachers Matthew Alber and Wilhelm Bidembadr, in turn, published their own sermons, feeding back from the oral into the printed discourse.[24] Other, less formal, channels also spread word of the Devil's conspiracy: letters; travelers' eyewitness accounts of trials; and stories transmitted across the countryside during work breaks and business socializing, over dinner tables in towns and taverns, and during the evening discussion and storytelling sessions that spread news and ideas from household to household in the countryside. Even the counter-magical activities of cunning folk, healers and diviners who themselves stood accused by many demonologists of congress with demons and thus at least an implicit pact with the Satan, contributed to the general raising of concern about witchcraft and hence awareness of the Devil's alleged role in it, although they, not surprisingly, tended to focus on the malefic aspects of witchcraft, which were in any case their clients' chief concern.[25] Some of the letters, like some sermons, were published and distributed, and some trial documents recorded the involvement of cunning folk, but most of these forms of communication left few traces and their influence can only be surmised.[26] Nevertheless, by the end of the sixteenth century it is clear that the idea that some people had given themselves over to the Devil in order to enjoy illicit pleasures and inflict occult harms was firmly embedded in elite culture in Württemberg and was exerting a growing influence on popular culture as well.

Popular culture in Württemberg, like popular culture in many parts of Europe, was particularly open to the idea that the Devil was recruiting adherents to an anti-Christian sect because it came at a time of growing concern about the Devil's involvement in human affairs in general. The Devil had been around for a long time, of course, with precursors in the malign or chaotic spirits of animist religions and an ancestor in the god of evil in Zoroastrianism, and he had served as God's chief antagonist in the Judeo-Christian tradition since biblical times.[27] He was blamed for everything from storms and disease to tempting Eve to eat the apple.[28] Conceptions of him varied from enduring traditions in folklore that depicted him as a semicomic trickster or mundane demon who could be duped and bested to elite notions that he was a spiritual analogue to a feudal high lord, ruling over a hierarchy of subordinate malign spirits and sinful humans.[29] In the early Middle Ages he was often understood to be a "non-anthropomorphic power of destruction," and was relatively seldom perceived in person except by hermits and monks, to whom he appeared as a hideous monster.[30] In the High Middle Ages his direct role in human affairs seemed to increase, as some clerics came to "recognize the Devil's hand" in every misfortune, and he also took on a stronger and stronger anthropomorphic physical character. He could appear in a wide variety of animal forms, but his most characteristic presentation was a semi-human body with shaggy hair, cloven feet, and horns.[31] His increased involvement in human affairs and physical characteristics were conveyed through mystery plays and works of literature and art, and by the later Middle Ages his palpable presence and powerful role in the world were widely recognized.[32]

In the early sixteenth century, the Devil got a particular boost from Martin Luther, who experienced him as "a real, living power, a concrete personality" who, "in an increasingly personalized form ... persecuted" Luther as he got older.[33] Luther himself did not emphasize the Devil's role in his theology as much as his personal obsession might have suggested, but he influenced other Protestant writers who did.[34] As the first round of confessional conflict died down in the middle of the sixteenth century, they began to produce a series of "Devil books" that proliferated rapidly.[35] The books grew out of a tradition that assigned each human sin or vice, from pride to fornication to suicide, its own devil, so each book concentrated on a specific human failing, which made them the perfect product for the rapidly expanding book market.[36] The first "Devil book" appeared in 1552 and seven first editions and 17 reprints were published before the end of the decade.[37] The next decade saw 14 new editions and 70 reprints totaling 100,000 volumes, while the two following saw many more new editions and a total of 100,000 additional books. In all, over a quarter million copies were printed, a figure that was "strikingly significant for the period."[38] They made a major contribution to the "demonization of the world," the growing conviction in the German, and indeed European elite, that life was a dramatic struggle "of good with evil, of angelic with diabolical."[39]

The Devil books did not simply describe human failings and demonstrate their relationship to the demonic, but exhorted their readers to rise to a higher moral level.[40] They, along with the works on witchcraft, were part of an even larger body of literature that aimed to improve moral standards, which was itself just one front in a broad campaign by religious reformers – including Johann Brenz, the reformer of Württemberg – to improve the standards of human conduct.[41] "Probably the most sustained attempt there has ever been by clerics to standardize ordinary peoples' cultural habits," this was an internal missionary mission in two senses: it was internal to the Christian commonwealth, aimed at people who were already Christian, and it aimed not just at their outward behavior, but at their internal lives.[42] The sixteenth century reformers did not initiate this impulse in Christianity, of course, for the religion had been concerned with faith and sin since its inception, and the introduction of penance in the twelfth century had manifested a new focus on intention in the High Middle Ages.[43] The late Middle Ages saw a blossoming of lay piety and mysticism, and in the fifteenth century "the single most important method of authorizing and conditioning ... belief and behavior" was introduced: the catechism.[44] Consisting of simple statements about the faith designed to be repeated and memorized, the catechisms were first intended as moral guides for priests to use to help parishioners prepare for confession, but the printing press made it possible for them to be disseminated to the laity. By 1600, a "prodigious number were in circulation in Germany, and most school ordinances made catechism the only form of instruction."[45] Lutheran leaders called for parishioners of all ages to go to catechism classes three times a week, and while this proved to be somewhat ambitious – in Württemberg only children actually attended regularly, and teenagers attended sporadically – in the long run generations influenced by this instruction began to come of age.[46] The catechisms did not focus on the Devil, but he had his place in them, which directly impressed on people his role in their inner lives.[47] Furthermore, by fostering an awareness of moral issues in an environment pervaded by concern about diabolic influences they contributed indirectly to heightened awareness of his baleful influence on humanity as well.

Of course, reformers had other means of communication through which to work, and these increased awareness of the Devil too. Sermons, as we have seen, were used in Lutheran areas like Württemberg to disseminate the diabolic witch stereotype, and many preachers featured the Devil in a wide range of other contexts. Moreover, confession had long imposed an "analysis of behavior" and "moral being," and it became far more intrusive in the sixteenth century.[48] Lutherans were expected to attend church frequently – several times a week in theory, and weekly at least – and to take communion regularly, and pastors kept track of their parishioners' performance of these obligations. In order to take communion, though, parishioners had to apply the day before, and confess publicly, which both upped the costs of transgression in this honor-conscious society and made it more difficult to avoid owning up to misconduct that others might know about.[49] Failure to attend, while not uncommon, brought the shirker into conflict with the civil as well as religious authorities, and on the whole attendance at the basic Sunday morning service tended to be good, in Württemberg at least.

The result of these various forms of enculturation was, over the course of the late sixteenth century, to establish the Devil as an active and immediate presence in the world for commoners as well as the elite. The old folk traditions of the Devil as a somewhat hapless trickster remained, but it was paralleled, and for a time overshadowed, by the more ominous role of the Devil as the instigator of evil, ever lurking in the shadows, waiting for the opportunity to lead the weak or unwary astray.[50] The success of the Devil books in the retail market was one sign of this development; the frequency with which people used his name in aphorisms, insults, and curses was another; and the rise of demonic possession cases at the time was yet another.[51] However, they are not all signs of exactly the same thing. The success of the Devil books and the use of his name in common discourse shows that many people accepted the idea of the Devil as an influence on their lives, but the rise of demonic possession cases indicates that some people had internalized this idea to the point that it was no longer simply an idea, or a way of talking, but had become an active part of their psyches.

The Devil made me do it

One of the earliest cases in Württemberg, which took place in 1565, only a decade after the publication of "Devil books" began and at the tail end of the first small wave of witch trials in the Duchy, gives insight into the process by which this transition took place.[52] It involved Magdelena Horn, who, as we have seen in Chapter 1, confessed to having killed a child and injured several farm animals, and she also said that she had tried to poison one of her husbands, although that could not be confirmed.[53] In their first letter to the ducal High Council, on May 3, the magistrates of Cannstatt reported that Magdelena said the "evil Satan" vexed her "day and night" because "at the urging of evil she had done so many bad things in her time to people and animals that she could not describe them all," and now it was "her overwhelming regret ... that she had honored the evil."[54] In their second report, sent two days later, they reported that Magdelena had elaborated considerably on her contact with the Devil during intensive conversations with the preacher. Satan had "come to her ... and he was black and wore black clothes," and she had often participated in the dances on the Feuerbach meadow ... at times with her daughter ... and others, whom she could not or would not name."[55] The preacher's attempts to lead her back to God, they reported, were "without effect," but his attempts to "bring the truth to light" had apparently influenced her conception of the Devil. The first letter describes Magdelena talking of him as a source of temptation and distress, a disembodied presence, not a physically defined being. The second letter recounts how after her lengthy conversations with the preacher, she talked of the Devil as a human-like being, giving stock details of his appearance and clothes, and adding a story about attending witch dances.

Clearly, prompted the preacher, Magdelena had added elements drawn from folklore and the diabolic stereotype.[56] Her motivation is easy to guess: she was a widowed old woman in the poor house, and suddenly she was the center of the local notables' attention. What she was actually thinking is harder to imagine. It is quite possible that she was self-consciously lying, of course, deliberately making up a story to satisfy her audience; for, like a modern person who claims to have experienced Satanic ritual abuse or alien abduction, her story catapulted her "to a special social status" that brought "a certain degree of comfort and a sense of belonging and identity," but required that she "please the authority figure" with a satisfactory narrative.[57] Narratives are performative social transactions in which the narrator of even an ostensibly factual account can be led to embellish the story to fulfill the expectations of the audience, and at least one *donna di fiora* in Italy confessed "that sometimes to please her listeners she had told them things that she had neither seen nor had any knowledge of."[58] However, it is also quite possible that in the process of constructing her narrative for the preacher, Magdelena, again like some modern people in therapy, was constructing memories for herself; for, the neurophysiological process of remembering appears to involve a more active process of reconstruction than traditional notions of memory suggested. We do not have some sort of "memory-bank" in our brains where we store entire memories as units; instead, it seems that what we "remember" is how to (re)assemble a neurological configuration (or, more accurately, trigger a series of neurological events) that will recreate – reconstruct – the experience or information.[59] This is a "fallible, quirky" process at best, particularly in old people, and "when memory is absent or impoverished, people fill in the gaps with imaginative constructions ... based on what could have plausibly occurred."[60] The sort of intense counseling situation that Magdelena was in can be a particularly fertile environment for the creation of "imaginative constructions," with "what could have plausibly occurred ... suggested by" cultural "stereotypes, schemas, and scripts."[61] Such "social scripts" thereby come to "serve as powerful organizers of memory."

While we can't know how Magdelena understood the embellishments she added to her story, she does seem to have accepted the basic premise that her past bad behavior was prompted by an evil spirit, the Devil, and that he was the cause of her current distress. Similarly, another of the sampled cases, one from the town of Besigheim during the next century, shows how strongly internalized the intimate connection between sin and the Devil became, in some peoples' minds at least. It began in 1678, when 74-year-old Dorothea Richter, "crying hard," announced from her sickbed that "the Devil used her sins," and now "tormented her so much she could not bear it any longer."[62] Specifically, she claimed to have committed adultery on numerous occasions over the years, and named as partners a number of local men, including a *Bürgermeister*. She also claimed to have sacrificed a bastard she had borne long before to the Devil by plucking out its eyes and tongue, and that she had a Devil's mark as well. She said that "she wanted to stab herself, if one would only give her a knife," and "that she did not deserve a Christian burial, but rather 'belonged'" in a dishonorable gravesite "under the gallows."[63]

Nor surprisingly, Dorothea's claims made quite a stir in town, and there was considerable resistance to them. The magistrates pointed out that the *Bürgermeister* she had implicated was in such good standing that he had recently served on the judicial council, she had "never been the least suspected of witchcraft," and her condition was referred to as "ill- and weak-mindedness."[64] Witnesses pointed out that she had denounced another woman for witchcraft but the charge didn't hold up, and said that she had recently declared "that she wanted to shame the town."[65] However, Dorothea had once done penance for adultery with a servant, and a letter from the village of Winterbach, where she had lived before moving to Besigheim 28 years before, said that she had committed prostitution with soldiers who occupied the area during the Thirty Years' War, and that she had borne a bastard who died. It denied that she had mutilated the child, though, saying "rather it ... had given itself a stab in the neck, from which it died."[66] Similarly, when confronted by the men, Dorothea repeated her accusations firmly, and only faltered when talking about signing a pact with Satan in blood and other diabolic activities, at which point "she cast her eyes down, [and] either gave muted answers or said didn't know anymore."[67] The men "appeared to be somewhat warm," and "argued only her infamy against her, and that she wanted to make herself respectable." Another woman "contradicted them firmly," however, and testimony that the *Bürgermeister* had been seen leaving Dorothea's house at four o'clock in the morning convinced the government that her charges were credible.

Dorothea died a few days later, swearing on her deathbed that her claims were true, and the controversy shifted to the question of her burial. Since she had renounced the Devil, repented her sins, and begged for forgiveness on her deathbed, the government decided that she should be buried at night, a mild form of dishonor.[68] The populace, however, demanded that "as a reputed and known witch" she should be burned, or at least buried outside the graveyard, which were much stronger symbols of disgrace that removed the body from the community of the faithful and, in the case of burning, insured that the soul would not remain in the vicinity.[69] They argued that "places where such people were buried in God's acre, were hit with hailstorms for many years in a row," and claimed that "some days before a shepherd saw a fiery ball fall from heaven, which is already a bad omen." Some people threatened to give up their citizenship, and on the night Dorothea was to be buried about 30 men armed with guns and clubs gathered and threatened to prevent it. The minister was able to calm them down and she was buried as planned, but when he preached a sermon on fornication and witchcraft that defended the government's decision, the controversy intensified and in the end he was forced out.[70]

The evidence from Winterbach suggests that Dorothea did not mutilate her bastard in some sort of diabolic ritual as she had claimed, and her evasiveness about other elements of diabolism she had mentioned suggests that she had neither done nor even constructed compelling memories of them. However, the Devil clearly played an important role in her understanding of the transgressions she had committed. She did not voice any guilt about the wives she had betrayed; nor did she say anything about her relationship to God or Christ. Instead, she focused on the contribution that her sins made to the cause of evil, and how this threatened to alienate her from the community. Her concern for her relationship to the community was traditional; this was the villagers' customary moral frame of reference.[71] The Devil served to put her behavior in a new, larger context, to help her see it in terms of broader issues of morality and the struggle between good and evil.[72] David Sabean, in a wider study of early modern consciousness based on records in Württemberg, has argued that early modern peasants lacked "what we might call a 'superego,'" or "conscience ... as a steering mechanism of behavior."[73] Instead, as both Magdelena Horn and Dorothea Richter's stories suggest, it was "retroactive rather than proactive," "more a sense of guilt about wrongs done than a mechanism of prior control or restraint."[74] However, Sabean proposes that by the eighteenth century, conscience had begun to act as "an active device" undergirded by "fear," and the two women's stories suggest that the Devil played an important role in this process by providing a rubric within which the moral value of their actions and its larger implications could be conceptualized. Modern psychologists, and historians who attempt to apply their theories whole cloth, tend to regard belief in the Devil as a way of pushing off responsibility for negative thoughts and behaviors, but this is because they are working within a culture in which thoughts and actions are assumed to be generated by individuals steeped in Christian/humanist morality.[75] Sabean's theory and the experiences described in these two cases suggest, on the contrary, that early modern belief in the Devil as an immanent presence was a stage in the development of this culture, a way of getting people to recognize the nature and significance of their actions beyond the bounds of their local community.[76] The Devil, of course, did not play the role of the superego; instead, his wicked temptations and the torments they could bring made it necessary to develop one.

Another sampled case, which took place 15 years earlier in the town of Schondorf, shows that the Devil was not necessarily just a way of making sense of a person's actions in retrospect, but instead could be understood to be the instigator of bad thoughts and behavior at the time they happened. It began when Johann Philip Bebion, a citizen and cobbler in the village of Endersbach, complained to the town government that his wife "generally acknowledges she is driven by the evil enemy."[77] She had long been melancholy in character and had occasionally spoken of suicide, but recently she had become much worse. Satan urged her to "strangle her husband and child in their sleep," and stimulated "such wanton and weak thoughts" that she had slept with her husband's apprentice. She rejected God's word, and claimed that the Devil had sex with her every night. She said that it all seemed like a dream when she did these things. The magistrates noted in their report that "it really seems at times as if she is filled with" the Devil, and "thus it is indeed possible ... Satan ... practices his damned wickedness through her." Fortunately for the woman, though, by 1663 the ducal government was readier to see her as melancholic than demonic, and so they instructed that she be committed to an almshouse that took care of the aged and infirm.

For Frau Bebion, the Devil was clearly more than a way of understanding past transgressions; he was an ongoing influence in her mental life, a source of current motivations. Again, a modern psychologist would be inclined to see the ascription of motivation to him as a way of shifting responsibility from the self, but this assumes that a unified, autonomous self is the default way by which humans understand their minds and the moral responsibility for their contents and their consequences. Starting with Clifford Geertz's observation that "the Western conception of the person as a bounded, unique, more or less integrated motivational and cognitive universe ... is, however incorrigible it may seem to us, a rather peculiar idea within the context of the world's cultures," Sabean argues that this conception is not really "Western," but historically and socially contingent, for in the sixteenth- and seventeenth-century peasantry, "there was as yet no notion of the person as a single, integrated center of awareness."[78] Sabean (and Geertz) may exaggerate the degree of fragmentation cultures can define for the "self," since the concept is affected by peoples' primary (immediate and personal) experience of the world as well as by their secondary (enculturated) understanding of it, and they may also overestimate the degree of consistency and cohesion that characterizes modern personalities in actuality.

Nevertheless, the fact is that a great deal of cognitive processing takes place outside conscious awareness, some of which impinges directly on conscious experience, yet there is no compelling reason in experience to assume that these mysterious inputs – sudden fears and irrational compulsions – are generated by a separate part of the mind that is bound to the conscious part and isolated from the rest of the world.[79] The psychoanalytic tradition, of course, was founded on the notion of an unconscious mind separate from yet connected to our conscious experience, and it has remained influential in the humanities and "soft" social sciences ever since, but through much of the twentieth century the mainstream of academic psychology rejected the notion under the influence of behaviorism, and the neurosciences pretty much ignored it as irrelevant to their interests.[80] However, "direct experimental evidence" in cognitive psychology has demonstrated that not only low-level homeostatic regulation, but also "cognitive and emotional processes," and even "abstract problem-solving processes," can "guide behavior even when we are unaware of them."[81]

Particularly important for the early modern conceptualization of the Devil as the source of at least some of these nonconscious inputs is the influence of evolutionarily older brain centers and vestigial cognitive structures, which "remain quite powerful and exert almost continual streams of influence that affect many different aspects of our lives."[82] During the last stages of physical evolution, the interconnections between the cortex and other, older brain centers increased significantly, giving the human cortex much more influence over these organs than in apes or other animals, thereby reducing the role of instinctive reactions, but it is still a two-way street, with the cortex strongly influenced by the other centers as well.[83] Cognition still involves a great deal of input from the lower, older centers, as well as from vestigial structures in the cortex itself. To take one example, the hypothalamus is "an exceedingly ancient structure" that "has maintained a somewhat similar structure throughout phylogeny and apparently over the course of evolution" that mainly "serves the body ... by attempting to maintain internal homeostasis" with little direct contact with the outside world, yet it "mediates or exerts significant or controlling influences on eating, drinking, sleeping and the experience of pleasure, rage, and aversion," generally in concert with, and moderated by other limbic and cortical structures, but in some circumstances it can itself "give rise to seemingly complex, higher order behavioral-emotional reactions."[84] Another example is how "the same hormonal impulses" that induce the physiological event of ovulation, also induce "the psychological state of sexual desire," and while this is obviously not the only reason for arousal, it is one that arises inexplicably, without relation to anything that can be perceived by consciousness.[85] This is not to suggest something as simplistic as that Frau Bebion's behaviors were just by-products of the activation of the hypothalamus or ovulation, but instead to illustrate how a myriad of physiological, deep neurological, and nonconscious emotional and cognitive processes generate feelings, thoughts, and desires that can influence behavior without their source being apparent. In fact, Frau Bebion's problem may not have been so much that she felt sexual and violent urges, but that she was unable to either suppress them or indulge them in a way that would not call attention to herself, as Dorothea Richter had done with her sexual desire through most of her life and Magdelena Horn apparently did with her desire to kill her husband.[86] This lack of inhibition on Frau Bebion's part resulted in behaviors generated by impulses and thoughts her culture identified as the Devil's promptings, impulses and thoughts shared by many, or perhaps all, people, but ordinarily kept in check or denied. Such impulses and thoughts can pose a physical danger to others and a challenge to social relations, and linking them to the Devil not only made sense of ones urges in the past, but indicated how they should be regarded when they appeared.[87] If, as Sabean suggests, early modern commoners did not have a proactive conscience to act as "a mechanism of prior control or restraint," then recognizing bad urges as the Devil's promptings at least partially made good the lack. Once again, ironically, the king of bad was working to promote the good.

Dealing with the Devil

In one way Frau Bebion's Devil was more than just the instigator of her transgressive thoughts and impulses: she said that he had sex with her every night. This statement suggests that she experienced him as a palpable presence, but what exactly she perceived is unclear. However, her statement is reminiscent of another sampled case, which took place in 1614 in the town of Bottwar, that provides more insight into what such a claim might mean. It began when a young woman named Katharina Miembler brought a complaint "against her husband," Endriss, saying "that he engaged in indecency with the evil spirit," while lying next to her in bed.[88] Apparently, after their wedding he had disappeared for "several hours," until his bride "found him in a cow stall." Later, when they went to bed, Katharina "felt that next to her ... he was having marital relations with somebody," and on subsequent nights she "noticed from him motions ... just like coitus." Her parents "whose bedroom was under theirs, also noticed the movement of the bed." She asked for the marriage to be dissolved and for permission to remarry.

The magistrates' investigation revealed that Endriss had been orphaned and raised by a kindly woman "as if [he were] a relative." He was an industrious and well-regarded young man who earned his living diligently tending a vineyard, but he was withdrawn and seemed somewhat simple. His brother, on the other hand, went bad, and was arrested for stealing, and was imprisoned, and beaten with a rod. This development depressed Endriss, and his brother's punishment made a particular impression that would have a significant impact on the investigation into his marriage; for, when

Endriss was first taken into custody he was so scared, he later claimed, that he said "yes" to everything asked of him. Consequently, he said that "he had indeed known that it was the evil spirit with whom he was committing indecency," that the Devil had first appeared to him a month before his wedding when he was in the hut in the vineyard, that he had taken coins from the Devil (which "turned to pottery shards when the spirit disappeared"), that he had let the Devil open a vein and take blood from him as a token of his allegiance, that he had seen a dance from the vineyard, that the Devil had come to him on his wedding night and counseled him to "abandon his bride," and that the Devil had given him a pot of witch salve while he was in prison. However, the local officials cast doubt on whether he really could have seen a dance as he claimed, and he mixed up the time of day in later testimony. Similarly, he changed the number of coins he supposedly got several times, and when the constable was unable to locate the pot of salve where he said he had hidden it, he admitted that he had made the story up. Ironically, since the common assumption is that torture was used to confirm the diabolic stereotype, Endriss was tortured into retracting the story about opening his vein, denying that he had pledged himself to the Devil in any way, and saying that he had not realized he was having sex with the Devil, but "blinded and deceived by the evil spirit," had thought it was his wife. Later, he told the magistrates that the "the evil spirit prevented him from taking communion," but that twice when it approached him in prison he had "driven it away with strong prayers." Furthermore, he told them that right after his wedding ... not only his wife, but also her mother and father" had become "hateful" toward him, "held him for a fool," and "often threw his brother" in his face. His wife refused to have sex "with anybody who had anything to do with the Devil," and said that "he had such a family, that she didn't want to have his children."

Given all the confessions and retractions and hidden agendas, what was really going on? We can't know for certain, but we can consider the possibilities. One is that the whole thing was a setup by Katharina and her parents; between his brother's dishonor and Endriss' squirreliness at the wedding, they decided that she had gotten a bad deal, and decided to get out of it by making up a story that it wasn't really Katharina Endriss he had been having sex with, but the Devil, and figuring that Endriss was such a simpleton that he wouldn't see through the deception. The idea that demons could manifest themselves in male and female forms as "incubi" and "succubi" to copulate with humans was well established by the end of the Middle Ages, and while Protestants tended to treat such spirit manifestations as the Devil himself rather than as part of a complex (and Catholic) demonology, the basic idea was current in the culture.[89] If Katharina's family was playing a trick, then they struck gold, because he was scared into confessing not only that he had fornicated with the Devil, but also anything else the magistrates asked him about, at least at first. However, there are several problems with this interpretation. First of all, succubi were generally portrayed as having a bodily presence, and Katharina did not mention actually seeing or feeling anyone else in bed. Secondly, once Endriss began retracting his false confessions, why didn't he retract them all? Thirdly, even if he was too intimidated by Katharina and her parents' testimony to insist that it had been her he made love to, he still could have retracted the stories about the Devil appearing to him at the vineyard, while he was in the cow stall on his wedding day, and at the prison. The fact that he let these stand, and that he felt unable to take communion, suggests that, at the very least, he accepted in retrospect the idea that his doubts about the marriage were the Devil's prompting, and appears to have constructed detailed visual and auditory memories based on it, just as Magdelena Horn did in regard to her transgression. Furthermore, he recognized the Devil's active attempts to influence him in prison, as he would actively influence Johann Bebion's wife a half century later. If Katharina and her parents duped Endriss, it was because he was primed to believe them; their lie crystallized a whole set of doubts and guilty feelings in him that locked into place around their charge as if they belonged there.

However, while it is possible that Katharina had sex with her husband and lied about it, and Endriss was simple enough to believe it, Lyndal Roper has found that in a case in Augsburg in the early eighteenth century children's masturbatory activity was called "indecency ... with the Devil," which suggests another possibility in Endriss' case. Not only did he accept that he had not made love to Katharina on their wedding night or the nights thereafter without a significant argument to the contrary, even when he was freely retracting other confessions, but also he explained that he did not want to because "he did not feel conjugal love" from her. For her part, Katharina was not happy about his brother's troubles with the law or Endriss' disappearance after the wedding, so it seems quite possible that they did not, in fact, make love, but instead Endriss relieved himself, making "motions ... just like coitus," while imagining a woman, or even his wife. The faculty of the University of Tübingen said in a consilium that the Devil's approaches to Endriss when he was in jail made plausible the "acts of indecency" he was accused of, suggesting that what Endriss was experiencing there was the urge to masturbate. Similarly, it seems likely that when Johann Bebion's wife said she had sex with the Devil every night, this is what she meant. We don't know who or what she was thinking about when she masturbated, but it seems more than likely that in this situation the Devil was not just the urges impelling her actions, but, as with Endriss Miembler's fantasy bride, a presence with a face and a body, at least as long as her eyes were closed.

A sampled case in the district of Blaubeuern that took place a few years later (in 1619) shows that the Devil could take more concrete form, though. When the mayor of the village of Ebersbach caught a 17-year-old girl named Maria Braittingen with stolen goods and she refused to acknowledge her guilt, he remarked, "that she appeared to be no Christian, but given over to the loathsome Satan."[90] She, apparently much to his surprise, agreed, saying that "when she went in the grass, the abominable Satan came to her and ... had dishonorable relations with her." She elaborated that "the evil enemy appeared ... in the form of her boyfriend," with whom she admitted she had wanted to have sex so that he would be more committed to her, and she only saw who he really was afterwards.[91]

As far as we can tell, Maria had intercourse with a real man, but because she saw what she had done as sinful, she felt afterward that she had been seduced by the Devil "in the form" of her boyfriend. Similarly, the authorities, in discussing the case, said "it was quite certainly her lover," and yet attributed her seduction to "the evil enemy's vexed tricks and deceptions."[92] Their conception of the relationship between the Devil and her boyfriend was reminiscent of Luther's doctrine of consubstantiation – a spiritual presence coexistent with an ordinary physical being. Their understanding of the world "blended the evidence of their senses with a firm conviction about the presence and power of unseen creation;" and they experienced "both aspects of reality ... as existing simultaneously, present at the same time and in the same place."[93] The Devil was like a spiritual chameleon, able not only to simulate the form of a person or animal, but also to take over and meld himself with a real one.[94]

It is not clear what "signs" Maria perceived that indicated to her that her boyfriend was really the Devil, but a woman who had a similar encounter with the Devil in 1660 described what she saw, and her description conveys how powerfully the realization that a person was dealing with the Devil could affect them, how it could influence their actual perceptions of the world around them. The case took place in the district of Urach, and started when Anna Eberlin, a young widow from the village of Bempfingen, complained of a "headache and dizziness ... threw up repeatedly," lay "with chattering teeth" and "her eyes reversed," and "acted as if she were possessed."[95] When the preacher asked her about the cause of her disturbing malady, she replied "with genuine and good understanding ... that she had consorted with the evil spirit and abominable Devil." More specifically, she said that "the evil enemy must have had relations with her."[96] She said that a few days earlier a boarder came to clean out the stalls in her barn. When she took him to the barn, he turned to her and said, "he had no wife and she had no husband, whereupon [he] grabbed her by the neck, which hurt her greatly." He threatened to beat her and "had his way with her in the cow's stall." Afterward, as they were leaving the barn he turned and said, "come, come, you wanted it too." He chased her back into the barn, and she saw a "fiery" glow "around him, and he blew, which made a great stink." As he left, she noticed "that he had not real feet," but "goat's feet." When the preacher pressed her to continue, she admitted that when she first "saw him through her window," she could not help noticing "what a man he was." As she thought this, "something flew in her mouth" that was "very blue, like a fly." She pulled it out with her fingers, and then saw "something like a mouse on the wall that said 'don't pray,'" while overhead she saw two beautiful birds that said 'pray, pray.'"

While traditionalists would be inclined to dismiss the supernatural details in Anna's story as either imaginative fabrications or evidence of some sort of pathology, and postmodernists would regard them as narrative elements in a story she constructed either in her dialogue with the preacher or in her thoughts beforehand, recent developments in cognitive science suggest that she may well have experienced the episode substantially as she described it. We have seen in Chapter 1 how visual perception is built in part from internal inputs that can create fleeting "overlays" on ambiguous percepts, and Anna's experience indicates that this effect can be much more powerful, involving sustained and self-standing images and multiple sensory inputs to create extraordinary perceptions of an incredible scene. To begin with, the eyes move rapidly and process information before sending it to the brain, and in some circumstances this can lead to the halo effect that Anna saw as a glow around the man.[97] Next, as sensory input is processed, the brain unconsciously amplifies and dampens it according to its current concerns; experimental evidence shows that sounds can be increased by up to 500 percent if attention is focused on them, and similar effects could account for both the fact that she saw his glow as "fiery" (the "aura" that can be perceived around people is usually rather muted) and that his breath, which she surely had been smelling all along, suddenly "made a great stink."[98] Finally, the process which most likely accounts for her seeing his feet as "goat's feet" (and actually could easily account for all the different elements of her hallucinations about him) was the actual creation of her perception of the scene. As we have seen, "our 'normal' vision is a reproduction of reality," an "abstraction," a "hypothesis," an "abstract cognitive achievement."[99] In fact, only 20 percent of the nerves feeding into the LNG, the part of the thalamus where the optic nerve connects to the brain, come from the retina; the other 80 percent come from other centers within the brain.[100] This integration of fresh sensory data and internal inputs occurs throughout the process of creating our perceptual field, so that, in the end, "we do not see what we sense. We see what we think we sense."[101]

This constructive nature of perception enables culture to influence people's perceptions, their experience of reality, profoundly.[102] In the first place, as Anna's account shows, cultural expectations can directly affect the content of perceptions: a fiery glow, a great stink, and goat's feet were stock elements in contemporary descriptions of the Devil, and other people across Western Europe reported similar perceptual experiences in the early modern period.[103] Secondly, cultural expectations can affect not just the content of perceptions, but also the relative proportions of sensory and internal inputs, in other words, the extent to which they incorporate hallucination.

Individuals vary in their "illusion susceptibility," (or, to put it another way, ability to hallucinate), and so do cultures.[104] For example, seeing ghosts was far more common in Victorian England that today, and four times as many Hawaiians experience hallucinations as mainland Americans.[105]

While the fact that perception has proven to be a physical process of construction strongly influenced by culture reinforces the postmodern position that our "reality" is a social construct, it undercuts the common postmodern position that that reality is a narrative construct. The devilish features Anna noticed about the man may have come from a cultural stock of visual imagery, and may even have been conveyed to her linguistically, but she did not appropriate them to be parts of a narrative, a story to be told. Instead, she used them to manifest an ongoing cognitive process in which she evaluated the events that were transpiring in terms of her culture's values and beliefs and brought her conclusion to consciousness in the strongest possible way, in a way that embodied its reality rather than just formulating it in words. Charles Zilka has complained that the "primary failing" of modern interpretations of early modern religious experience "is that they have largely ignored the tangible immediacy, the almost corporeal and physical nature of the religious world which gave shape to that experience."[106] The analysis of Anna Eberlin's visual and olfactory perceptions of her attacker as the Devil, as well as Maria Braittingen's encounter with him "in the form" of her boyfriend, suggests that an appreciation of the full cognitive dimension of human experience, and not just its linguistic aspects, can help us understand, and perhaps even gain some empathy for, the "corporeal and physical nature of the religious world" that early moderns experienced.

The mouse and the birds were probably visual hallucinations as well (although both might have been real animals, the birds in particular seem unlikely since she was indoors), but they were different from the hallucinations Anna had about her attacker in three ways. First of all, the birds, and probably the mouse as well, were freestanding visual images, not additions or modifications to existing figures. Second, they talked. Third, they acted as autonomous centers of consciousness. They are related to, and in fact are scaled down versions of, hallucinations that Endriss Miembler said that he had while he was in the vineyard shelter and later when on his wedding day: he reported that the Devil approached him, seeming to be a fully physical presence with "form and clothing," and "spoke to him."[107] Freestanding figures are less common than features added on to existing forms, but they are not uncommon, as hallucinations go. Clinical studies have been done of people who are able to envision a freestanding figure and then place it in their visual field, and one found that when the subject was imagining the character normally, as in image in her head, her retina registered flashes of light aimed at her eyes, but when she was "projecting" the imagined character into her visual field, flashes of light did not register, showing that this form of "perception" is different from more regular forms of daydreaming or visualizing, that it involves a more profound alteration of the functioning of the nervous system.[108]

The physicality of this sort of experience can go beyond even 3-D projection into the visual field to an actual experience of physical contact, as an experience of Maria Braittingen showed. After confessing to having had sex with the Devil "in the form of her boyfriend," she said that the Devil came to her one other time, but this time he appeared "white: and hit her: and wanted her to kill herself."[109] While she did not say she was bruised by the blow, Lyndal Roper reported on a case in Augsburg where a girl who was supposed to have been beaten by the Devil was covered with bruises, and Fernando Cervantes describes an instance in Latin America when the Devil bit a possessed woman and left visible bite marks.[110] While in both cases it is possible that the injuries were inflicted physically, it is also quite possible that their perceived injuries manifested somatically, for the mind can have a profound effect on the body. In one modern instance, for example, "a sailor who had been shipwrecked … relived the traumatic event in a hypnotic trance" and "as he went on through the experience of hanging onto a rope, severe marks, real burns or weals, appeared on the skin."[111] The early modern religious world could have a "corporeal and physical nature" indeed!

The auditory hallucinations that Endriss and Anna had are not particularly unusual; in fact auditory hallucinations are the most common form of hallucination people experience.[112] Most modern people generally experience aural hallucinations almost continually, when they imagine they hear their own voice talking in their head.[113] Modern people understand this imagined voice to be something generated by their brains, and generally have it under volitional control (in fact, it is as much a part of our "self" as our body awareness and our experience of perceiving our visual field), but there is some controversy about when human beings began subvocalizing and the way people at different points in the past have experienced it, and it has been suggested that such subvocalizations were originally perceived coming from outside the self.[114] Be that as it may, there is no question that even some modern people experience aural hallucinations as generated by some consciousness outside the "self." These voices can give people orders, even telling them to kill themselves and such "hallucinations can dominate the entire thinking, feeling, and action of the patient."[115] As this last passage suggests, when modern people experience this, they are considered to be sick, and, indeed, premodern people generally also recognized some such experiences as a form of pathology, when they seemed to take long-term control of the person and cause them to act in antisocial, self-destructive, or culturally unintelligible ways.[116] However, they also generally regarded other, similar experiences as nonpathological, socially useful, or at least culturally intelligible, forms of communication from outside the "self." Whether they were considered to be gods or spirits, angels or demons, God or the Devil, varied from culture to culture and situation to situation, and sometimes their meaning was contested via controversy over their presumed origins. For example, the voices that spoke to Joan of Arc were considered angelic by her and the French, but demonic by the English, but in Maria Braittingen's and Endriss Miembler's cases there was general agreement that the voices which spoke to them were the Devil's, and in Anna Eberlin's case the nature of the apparitions that spoke to her were so anomalous and yet so obvious that there seems to have been little discussion of them.

In some circumstances, such voices can be seen as an aural extension of the inchoate urges which were ascribed to the Devil by Magdelena Horn, Dorothea Richter, and Johann Bebion's wife and their communities, a "bubbling up" of urges in the form of a subvocalization rather than just an impulse, analogous to when we think to ourselves "Time for a snack!" in addition to feeling or instead of being conscious of feeling the physical sensation of hunger. However, in the in the cases at hand here, and particularly in the case of Endriss Miembler, something more was going on, for the solid form, talking images were more than the "bubbling up" of a simple urge; they had the character of autonomous centers of consciousness that engaged in extended deliberative action and even interaction.

To understand how these people could have these experiences, it is necessary to consider in somewhat more detail how the human brain works. In particular, it is now generally understood that it is organized modularly: groups of neurons work together in "functionally distinct circuits" that perform basic "cognitive and emotional processes" like recognizing our place in space and anticipating rewards.[117] There is currently a great deal of controversy about whether (or the extent to which) high-order cognitive skills like language are hardwired through genetic programming or created "on the fly" through interaction with the environment after birth, but what is clear is that both processes contribute to human cognitive development.[118] There is no question that huge amounts of our brain structure that we have in common with other primates, other mammals, and even more distantly related animals, which enable us to do things like construct visual scenes and experience emotion, are inherited, and some more advanced skills facilitating things like face recognition, toolmaking, and sophisticated verbal communication may well be also, but it is equally certain that "vast parts of" the cerebral cortex "have no clear function," and are thus free to be organized as "functional networks."[119] These networks are organized both hierarchically and laterally, so that manifest behaviors like writing involve the activation of a whole set of modules, which themselves consist of submodules, which consist of even lower-level modules, and so on, and at the same time these submodules may also be tied into other networks (like speaking and listening, in this case).[120]

Furthermore, and more important from our point of view, many modules are at work simultaneously and, to a significant extent, separately in the brain in what is called "parallel distributed processing."[121] While there are cross-connections between modules and their output is integrated with that from other modules as it is delivered to higher-order modules, the modules work in substantial isolation from each other. Even the modules that feed directly into our consciousness don't know about much of the activity in the others, or in other processes not involved with creating consciousness, and consciousness works serially, only focusing on one thing at a time, so, as noted earlier, much of our ongoing cognition takes place beyond our awareness.[122]

Not only does much cognition take place outside of conscious awareness, but also complex behaviors can be executed unconsciously, as when a musician plays without thinking, or a person drives while conversing with a friend. Called "dissociation," this "splitting off of certain mental processes from the main body of consciousness" creates "highly developed automatisms" whose "behavior is so intricate, and even creative, that it almost seems as if some separate personality makes the fingers move" or the car ease to a stop.[123] Indeed, "subordinate cognitive systems" can develop such a "degree of unity, persistence, and autonomy" that they become "self-like and intentionally motivated."[124] Since consciousness itself is produced by a module "organized hierarchically, dynamically, and temporarily," the boundary between it and "the unconscious ... part of the mind often seems fluid and permeable," and "complex other-self configurations in potential or actual conflict with one another" can develop.[125] A sense of self is not only a human universal, but also a characteristic of animals, which are aware of their own bodies, their extensions, and the boundary between themselves and the world, but it is clear that, while not infinitely divisible, the "self" as understood in modern terms, the physical body plus all mentation produced by it, is "not a seamless, unfractured whole, but rather the end product of a complicated series of feedforward and feedback loops," some of which may intrude into awareness as autonomous consciousnesses and even take control of volitional activity.[126]

There seem to be three basic ways in which autonomous consciousnesses are manifested: as apparently external entities perceived by the person's normal conscious "self" through one or more of the five sense modalities; as an alien presence or force within the body that influences the person's normal conscious self through urges or urgings that are felt, sensed and understood, or perceived even when the eyes or ears are consciously covered to block them out; or as a foreign consciousness that actually takes control of the body while the person's regular "self" is either entirely unconscious or looks on impotently, powerless to intervene. The first category includes the kind of visual and aural hallucinations experienced by Anna Eberlin, Endris Miembler, and Maria Braittingen. The second involves the kind of inchoate urges and wrenching realizations reported by Johann Bebion's wife, Magdelena Horn, and Dorothea Richter. The third includes multiple personality disorder and possession.

While there may have been instances of multiple personality disorder in earlier times, the phenomenon was seldom noted until recently.[127] Possession in contrast – the state in which an external spirit (as opposed to an alternative internal "self") appears to have taken control of the body – has been observed since biblical times, and is a normal means of communication with the spirit world in a large number of societies around the globe.[128] There was, as we have seen, a wave of possession cases in Protestant Germany in the late sixteenth century, and the phenomenon was certainly known in Württemberg at the time. It was mentioned in a number of cases, like that of Anna Eberlin who, as we have seen, was said to have lain "with chattering teeth" and "her eyes reversed ... as if she were possessed," and some cases involved exaggerated symptoms reminiscent of it, like when a young man named Johann Jakob Wagner thought an elderly woman named Christina Nethen had bewitched him and then "howled like a dog," dreamed he had sex with her that "created horrible progeny," and tried to kill himself with a knife. However, the magistrates only said that Anna acted "as if ... possessed," while Johann Jakob Wagner never appeared to have been taken over by any sort of autonomous consciousness.[129]

Only two cases are known from the Duchy that came close to involving possession in the etic sense. One, which took place in Stuttgart in 1695, centered on a 43-year-old crippled woman who had apparently been regularly seized by convulsions in her sleep since she was orphaned at the age of three, and whose condition had been variously ascribed to "the loathsome Satan" or "malevolent people."[130] However, when the constable and others observed her, while she did lose consciousness, convulse, hold her breath for "a quarter hour," was insensate to blows with a staff on her "hands ... head ... [and] chest," and evinced no memory of the episode when she awoke, she does not appear to have manifested any sort of alternative consciousness while in this state. Similarly, when she was later observed by the head of a hospital where she was placed, she seems to have walked about in a dissociated state, a kind of waking-sleepwalking, exhibited pronounced mood swings, and mumbled incoherently, but the symptoms do not seem to have come together in a way that suggested actual possession.[131] The High Council summarized her behavior as acting "*as if* she were possessed by the loathsome Satan," and when the court physician examined here he "could find nothing in the least which would lead us to believe that she has been possessed by the Devil."[132] She seems from our point of view to have been sort of half possessed, experiencing dissociation and some of the somatic symptoms typical of the state (contortions, insensibility), but not manifesting an alternative consciousness in place of her own.

The other case comes closer to being a full-blown case of possession, but even that did not involve the full-blown diabolic possession that was prevalent in other parts of Europe. It took place in Klein Ingersheim, near Bietigheim, in 1642, toward the end of the Thirty Years' War, when the preacher heard that Maria Wurster, a cooper's wife who had recently given birth, was suffering from "various afflictions" which she said resulted from an encounter on a path with Anna Schwendel, the widow of a forest ranger, whom she called "a witch."[133] Shortly after the encounter Maria suffered from a headache and bad dreams, and her condition worsened to the point that she felt that an evil spirit had entered her and was causing uncontrollable movements in her stomach, she inexplicably ate "a whole handful of feathers and other filth," emitted an "unbearable stink ... complained that baptism and the Eucharist had been taken from her ... several times pursed her mouth and wrinkled her nose at the name of Jesus, and said that she could not believe in her heart what was said of him," and "had said several words several times in a foreign language." The latter, in particular, was a standard feature of possession cases – in fact, the Catholic Church considered being able to converse in an unknown language an important sign of true possession – as were her sense that her stomach convulsions were caused "by an evil spirit" that had entered her "imperceptibly" and her aversion to Christian symbols and sacraments. Maria may have been influenced by things she learned outside the Duchy, for her husband was a drummer and soldier from Switzerland and they moved a lot, but at no point was the "evil spirit" that invaded her identified as the Devil, and her affliction seems to have had at least as much to do with the belief that a witch could inflict injury by dispatching malign spirits into their victims as with diabolic possession.

While these cases were not particularly typical of either diabolic possession cases elsewhere in Europe or of the incidents that led to investigations of witchcraft and diabolism in Württemberg, it seems worth considering possession in some more detail both because there is a body of recent historical literature on it that deals with many of the issues raised here and because by contrasting it with the more typical cases of encounters with the Devil more insight can be gained into them as well.

To begin with, as stated above, possession involves an altered state of consciousness, a state of dissociation in which control of the body is temporarily lost by the person's everyday consciousness and is taken over by an autonomous alternate consciousness. This is worth repeating because older historical accounts tend to approach it as psychopathology, while more recent ones treat it as a form of "culturally specific ... deviant behaviors" in which the possessed are "acting out roles in a piece of theatre."[134] While the latter position avoids the ethnocentrism of the former by emphasizing that in most societies possession is seen as, if not normal, at least as not pathological, and has opened up a way of gaining greater understanding of the cultural role of (and in) possession, it loses sight of a dimension that the older approach at least attempted to grapple with. The subjective reports of people who were possessed, the impressions of skeptical observers, and the fact that possession was difficult to fake – all indicate that there really was an altered psychological, and beneath that neurological, state involved.[135]

Next, cross-culturally, young women are particularly prone to possession, while in early modern Europe pious young people of both sexes were.[136] Similarly, in the cases we have examined, the people who experienced strong visualizations of the Devil were the younger ones (Maria Braittingen and Endriss Miembler were around 20; Anna Eberlin was in her mid-30s, and Johann Bebion's wife appears to have been somewhere between 20 and 40), while the two older women, Dorothea Richter and Magdelena Horn, appear to have experienced the Devil as, at most, a more amorphous presence. In contrast to possession cases (including the two from Württemberg), though, most of the people who encountered the Devil as an external being or as inchoate urges were not pious but the opposite: all the women had bad reputations, and Endriss, while he was reasonably well regarded, was more neutral than especially good, and he was at that time involved in behavior that was considered indecent.

The reason for this difference in characters undoubtedly has to do with the nature of the contact with the Devil. In the cases we have seen, contact with the Devil was a private experience (except, inadvertently, for Endriss) and had to do with him influencing the person involved to do bad things. In the case of diabolic possession, in contrast, the experience of the Devil was a public display, the purpose of which was generally to expose other peoples' individual and collective sins and otherwise make public "unknowable, suppressed, or repressed knowledge about a community."[137] This is probably why possession generally involved young women more than young men, for in most societies their opportunities for self-expression are more limited while the pressures on them to behave properly, especially sexually, are stronger. This latter point may also help explain why women were more likely to meet the Devil in general. It seems noteworthy that almost all of the encounter cases discussed here started because of sexual transgressions, and of the two that didn't, sexual misconduct still played a major role in one (Frau Bebion's). Women were held to standards, and were increasingly holding themselves to standards, that were stricter than the ones for men.

In both the encounters discussed here and in early modern diabolic possession sex often played a prominent role.[138] Moshe Slutovsky has noted that possessed young women often were at the age of first menstruation, when they lost their virginity, or when they were just married. Among the encounter cases we have examined here Anna Eberlin was a relatively young widow who had just had sex with a man she admitted she was physically attracted to (she could not help noticing, she said, "what a man he was."); Endriss Miembler was a newlywed with a clear problem in marital relations, at least with the woman he married; and when Maria Braittingen saw her boyfriend as the Devil it seems likely that she had not had sex much, for while she admitted to having had it with her boyfriend before, the report from the village where she had lived until recently said that "no one had seen her as loose."[139]

Slutovsky goes on to develop a theory of these possession cases as manifesting the women's' "sexual anxieties" and equating "their personal notions of sexual impurity with parallel familial and/or communal dangers."[140]

Others have developed similar psychological explanations involving psychodynamic theories positing some sort of symbolic transference.[141]

While this approach may have some merit, Stuart Clark has questioned "the assumption that there is something universal in mental disorder lying beyond culturally relative accounts of the causes and symptoms."[142] Since psychodynamic explanations conceive of psychology in terms of symbolic processes, it is reasonable to for him to assert that "the question of whether the symptoms ... since they can only be expressed in cultural idioms, are not in greater need of interpretation than of clinical diagnosis is ... an open one."[143] On the other hand, his solution, an "accounting for possession as a phenomenon with a basis in culture rather than nature" which, he asserts, will free us "once and for all from the problem of reference to a 'real' world" is neither necessary nor helpful.[144] It is not necessary because, while it may not be reasonable to assume a universal psychodynamics, it is reasonable to assume a universal neurophysiology, for anatomically modern humans emerged about 200,000 years ago, and while there is some evidence that two changes to genes related to brain size have occurred since then that may have had some impact on cognitive abilities, the long, broad, and continuous historical record of possession cases makes it reasonable to assume that human beings share the same basic neural hardware, at least as far as that involved in this phenomenon is concerned.[145] It is not helpful because, while semiotic analysis in his hands and others' sheds a great deal of light on how psychological experiences are shaped by culture and the role they play in culture, his hegemonic claims for semiotics would, if they were paid heed, cut off other approaches to the phenomena which offer independent insights that would not and could not be revealed by analysis of symbol systems.

Specifically, in the case of the dissociation leading to possession and hallucinations, it is not a particular psychodynamic or cultural situation that precipitates this state, but rather the stress that any one of a number of psychological situations can create that triggers it.[146] Naturally, cultural factors play a strong role in creating situations of stress, but they are not the only factor. Sex, for example, is a strong biological urge that early modern society tried to restrict, and we cannot understand how this tension could build to a physiological crisis point, or what could be unleashed by that crisis, purely by reference to a system of symbols. Furthermore, even if the antagonistic psychodynamics are completely cultural, like, say, a person torn between loyalty to community and a commitment to the truth, whether the tension between them builds to a crisis resulting in dissociation or not, and what range of things can happen in that state, is as much a function of physiology and the individual's psychology as of culture. In both cases, the state of dissociation precipitated by the stress is not a symbol. It is not a cry for help, a protest against disempowerment, a dialogue, an act, a form of theatre, or any form of symbolization or statement at all.[147] Like a fever, it is what it is: a direct manifestation of a physiological process going on inside the body.

Of course, once the person enters the dissociated state of consciousness, the autonomous consciousness that comes out, like the hallucinated being in an external Devil encounter, will be strongly shaped by culture, just as a person's normal dream content is strongly shaped by culture.[148] Both the person experiencing the dissociation and, in the case of possession, members of the community will have general cultural concerns and values as well as specific expectations of what a person going through a crisis should experience and act like that will contribute to its character, course, and outcome. Furthermore, like a fever, the dissociation itself can and will be construed as a sign, and the culture will attach any number of meanings to it, treating it as a good or a bad thing, a sign of spiritual depravity or of spiritual progress, an exalted state of consciousness or a form of mental illness, and so on. However, it is important to keep in mind that dissociation, like a fever, or smoke, or anything else that directly manifests a natural process, is a particular kind of sign, a natural sign, whose basic meaning is not arbitrary and does not come from its relationship to other signs. People can assign all sorts of more or less arbitrary secondary meanings to this class of sign, but their essential meaning comes from their practical relationship to reality. To enter a dissociated state was not a form of communication, with others or with the self; it was a direct experience in which ordinarily latent modules in the brain gained control of awareness, and possibly behavior, as a consequence of the physiological state of stress.

The point of all this is not simply to joust with semioticians or prove that the influence of, encounters with, and possession by the Devil had physiological roots as an academic exercise, but, to get back to Charles Zilka's lament about historians' failure to convey "the tangible immediacy" of early modern religion, to show that what we are dealing with is not just beliefs, strings of words describing ideas about reality, but lived experiences: old women tormented by "the evil spirit" for the wrongs they had done at its behest; young women aghast that their illicit desires had opened them to the Devil's snare; a friendless young man debating with the Devil whether to get into his loveless marriage bed or head out of town. For these people, the Devil was not just a prop, an idea, or a symbol, a way of explaining things, but a purposive player in their situations, a manifestation of cognitive processes in their own brains perhaps, but no less real even if so. Furthermore, the stronger their emotions, the more real he became, taking on more tangible form as visible features on a human figure, or even appearing as a walking, talking figure himself. This development, too, was not just window dressing, and its meaning was not that it symbolized something else, or related to other symbols. It was what it was, the breakdown of the "self's" control of the nervous system, and the breakthrough of realizations that would not establish themselves in consciousness otherwise, and which manifested much more power over the person's understanding of the world and his or her place in it for being full 3-D experiences rather than mere words, the fullest expression of unconscious knowing rather than the diluted messages that usually filter up.

4
Witch Dances and Witch Salves

The idea that witches flew to Sabbaths to worship the Devil through a variety of obscene rites, including perversions of the Christian sacraments, came to play an increasingly prominent role in learned theories of witchcraft over the course of the fifteenth century, and became a crucial element in the early modern witch persecutions.[1] It transformed an individual's sinful behavior into evidence of participation in an underground counterreligion, which both made the threat posed by witchcraft seem much greater and implied that one witch must know the identity of others. Combating a subversive conspiracy justified more extreme measures to defend the community than dealing with individual malefactors, and the perceived need to root out entire groups led to the chain-reaction mass panics in which suspects were tortured into denouncing others, who in turn were tortured into denouncing still others, that most distinguished European witchcraft in the early modern period.

Of course, there was no underground counterreligion spread across Europe, diabolic or otherwise. "No careful researcher has discovered even a trace of a true witch cult with Sabbaths, orgies, black masses, and Devil worship," and virtually no historians have seriously argued that, as Montague Summers insisted, "witches ... were, in fact ... the active members of a vast revolutionary body, a conspiracy against civilization."[2] Margaret Murray's more influential thesis that witches were members of a widespread, organized underground pagan religion demonized by their Christian rivals was widely accepted during the early twentieth century, but her reading of the evidence was discredited by a series of historians in the 1960s and 1970s, and is no longer taken seriously by scholars.[3]

The discrediting of Murray's thesis did not, however, result in the vindication of the traditional alternative, the argument that the witch cult was nothing more than a figment of clerics' imaginations, an amalgam of classical references, scholastic syllogisms, and misogynist fantasies, for at almost the same time that scholars were discrediting Murray's reading of the evidence, the historian Carlo Ginzburg discovered a remarkable set of inquisitorial documents in the Fruili region of northern Italy that showed clearly the existence of a network of self-proclaimed magical fertility warriors, who operated in a tradition that involved a complex of beliefs about soul travel and contact with the dead that had little connection to either the Christian God or the Christian Devil.[4] Traditional rationalists pointed out that these *benandanti* only traveled, assembled, and fought in their dreams rather than, as Murray's thesis would suggest, physically, and, since they also seemed to be a rather isolated phenomenon, historians at first treated them as interesting but of only limited relevance to understanding the broader contours of European witchcraft.[5] However, research by Ginzburg and others has shown that the *benandanti* were related to a range of practitioners and beliefs in Eastern Europe from the Baltic to the Balkans, other parts of Italy, across the Alps in Central Europe, in the Celtic parts of Britain, and Scandinavia.[6] Magical flight and festive assemblies including both people and spirits were just part of a larger set of beliefs and experiences that made up an alternative "fairy" or spirit world thought in large parts of Europe to exist parallel to the ordinary world of everyday experience.[7] Some of the denizens of this world were good, some were evil, but most were morally ambiguous, capable of doing either good or bad depending on circumstances.[8]

In addition to discovering this complex of non-Christian beliefs, Ginzburg's research also showed that the self-definition of the *benandanti* gradually changed over the course of a century from benign to diabolical under the pressure of inquisitors who could only understand their activities as a form of witchcraft. This process of redefinition has become a paradigm for how the diabolic stereotype arose in the first place, through the interaction of the Christian elite's understanding of the world and the popular heterodox beliefs and practices they encountered among the populace in various regions of the Alps.[9] Christianity and popular traditions rooted in paganism had coexisted uneasily throughout the Middle Ages all over Europe, until inquisitors looking for heretics who had withdrawn into remote Alpine valleys encountered far stranger beliefs that the clerics could only understand as evidence of a diabolic cult.[10] As word of their discovery spread, other inquisitors and secular magistrates used it to make sense of similar beliefs and practices they encountered, using torture to fit increasingly diverse phenomena into this Procrustean bed until many came to assume that all forms of magical practice and occult power were connected to it.[11]

The broad diffusion and acceptance of the fear that some members of society were secretly members of an underground diabolic sect, who flew to meetings to perform obscene forms of worship and revelry, clearly reflected the ability of torture to confirm suspicions to order, as well as the persuasive power of authoritative pronouncements and texts, the belief's congruence with the larger system of learned knowledge, and the perverse attractions of both its paranoid and its sexual features.[12] However, it seemed plausible also because it had important points of contact with the realities of late Medieval and early modern life.[13] To begin with, popular festivities were ubiquitous; peasants and townspeople congregated to feast and drink in celebration of weddings, baptisms, and a wide range of seasonal holidays.[14] Fueled by alcohol, such gatherings could become extremely boisterous, spin off semi-furtive sexual assignations, and last long into the night. Most of them were connected with formal religious rituals, and many were imbued with or involved rites with magico-religious significance themselves.[15] Similarly, popular religious sites, festivities, and movements like the "Drummer of Niklashausen" could draw people from a wide area and involve them in activities combining popular amusements and popular spirituality.[16]

These popular celebrations and rites often involved activities and beliefs whose relationship to Christian orthodoxy was questionable at best, and popular culture contained a significant current of explicit anticlericalism as well.[17] Most of the time this was confined to jokes and resistance to financial exactions, but in much of Europe it boiled over into open rebellion during the Reformation, and even in areas that went Protestant it reappeared within a generation or two as a new clerical caste entrenched itself. Furthermore, tension between the religious establishments and local communities increased in both Protestant and Catholic lands as the churches strove to impose stricter standards of conduct and belief on their flocks. Small wonder that people found it believable that some people might renounce their ties to the established church and join an opposing organization.

In fact, such a development was more than a theoretical possibility. A variety of underground religious movements did, in fact, exist in Medieval and early modern Europe. Various cults "of natural and other than Christian supernatural powers … surfaced not only in the early Middle Ages, but throughout the centuries," and in the face of repression, the Cathars, Waldensians, Hussites, and Anabaptists all went underground, as did some Jews and Muslims after their forced conversions in Spain.[18] The undoubted existence of these underground sects was positive proof that such movements could and did exist within the Christian community. While the early modern belief in an underground diabolical cult is often dismissed as if the idea of a secret underground sect was absurd, if it did not in fact exist it was not because a widespread and persistent underground heterodox movement was prima facie impossible.

Nor was the idea that a heretical movement might be linked to magic entirely without foundation. In antiquity, "Simon Magus was the prototype of the heretical magician" who had used magic "to win a following," and while there was controversy in the Medieval church about whether all magic involved heresy, there was general agreement that some forms did.[19] In popular culture, belief in some peoples' magical ability to fly, either in spirit or body, unassisted or on an animal, was extremely widespread.[20] The Cathars believed that they had spirit doubles that could fly, and had specialists who were "charged with establishing and maintaining contact with the dead."

The Waldensians in the Alps, the persecutions of whom are currently thought to be the source of the idea of the Sabbath, were said to use a magic potion supplied by a "Mistress of Ceremonies," an idea far more likely derived from popular practices related to the "good company" that were current in the region than classical models or scholastic reasoning.[21] The Bible told of Jewish priests who performed miracles to demonstrate the power of their god, Christ himself had performed miracles that validated his teachings, and Christian missionaries had used them to impress the heathens they were trying to convert, so it was far from unreasonable for Christian leaders to think that heretics might use magic.[22]

Beyond these general points of congruence between the idea of a witch Sabbath and early modern social and cultural realities, there were specific connections in the case of Württemberg's popular culture. In Swäbisch-Gmünd witch dances were said to take place at the same location that served in "1529 as the secret meeting place of Gmünd's Anabaptists," while in the neighborhood of Stuttgart, the first mass witch trial, in which 11 people were executed, took place in the same year, 1562, that a mass trial of 21 Anabaptists took place in nearby Esslingen.[23] As far as the notion that witches flew to their Sabbath goes, there were several traditions current in Swabia during the late Middle Ages involving night flying spirits. One, current in the Alemanni areas of Germany and which appears to be related to the "good company" traditions to the south, was the idea of "night people" who traveled to festive nocturnal gatherings at which they feasted and drank, listened to beautiful music and danced.[24] Another, variants of which were widely shared by Celtic as well as Germanic peoples, was the more ominous "Wild Hunt" or "Wild Ride."[25] In one version known in southern Germany, the souls of the dead were led by the god Wotan in a great procession through the night.[26] In others, the leader was the goddess Holda (also known popularly as Pechta or Bertha and identified with Diana, the classical hunting goddess, by medieval churchmen) who led a retinue of spirits and/or female followers.[27] Originally Holda was a benign goddess, helping women in labor and making the soil fertile, but she also punished the lazy, and the host she led on the "Wild Ride" so scared people that "in the fifteenth and sixteenth centuries it was customary in much of southern Germany to put out food and drink" on the four ember nights to appease them.[28] The original term for "witches" in south Germany, which was often used in tandem with the Swiss-derived "Hexen" in Württemberg's legal documents, was "Unholden," a negative derivative of Holda's name.[29] These "Unholden" were said to congregate on the Heuberg, a mountain in the Swabian Alb region, near the Württemberg district seat of Balingen.[30] The poet Heinrich von Wittenweiler mentioned it as the place to which witches flew at the beginning of the fifteenth century; Johann Nider similarly identified it in 1435; and so did Johann Geiler von Kaisersberg, the cathedral preacher in Strasburg, in 1508. A woman condemned to death in the area, in 1520 said she rode on a broomstick to it, a young woman told a friend that she wanted to take her there in 1663, and a young girl told her friends that she went there with her mother in 1678.[31] Thus, while the idea that witches worshiped the Devil might have been imported from the Swiss trials, the notions that witches could fly through the air and would congregate with spirits for nocturnal festivities were not imports at all; Swabians clearly shared with the people of the Fruili, southern Italy, Eastern Europe, and the Celtic regions of Britain the belief in a parallel spirit world in which some people could participate. This evidence does not show whether there were people who actually experienced the phenomena contained in the beliefs, as the *benandanti* and similar people in other regions did, but it does show that the beliefs themselves were current in the region including Württemberg.

The myth of the witches' Sabbath occupied a central place in learned theories of witchcraft, and magistrates routinely tortured suspects into describing the lurid details of obscene rites by which the Devil's disciples supposedly worshiped their evil master. But, as was true elsewhere, these illicit festivities did not much concern the commoners in Württemberg, who referred to them by the less portentous name of "witch dances."[32] Among the sampled cases, no accusations about them were made before the 1660s, and both that involved them were started by children. In other cases, adult suspects confessed participating in witch dances, mostly under torture, but occasionally of their own free will. Their descriptions were seldom very lurid, though; they reported that the participants were content to feast, drink, and dance, and the Devil, when he appeared, was just a "black man," or a man with a "red beard."[33] In some cases people testified that the participants had sex with each other or with the Devil, but the sexual acts described were fairly tame, little different from the illicit couplings that went on in the bushes and sheds in real life.[34]

Rumors of witch dances

Both of the two sampled cases that started with accusations about witch dances took place in 1663. One began in early June when the magistrates of Wildbad learned of a rumor going around town that a number of women were "suspected of witchcraft" because four weeks earlier they had "been seen an hour before dawn" returning to their homes in and around the town, or even, according to some accounts, actually holding "a dance outside the [town] gates."[35] Four had been "identified by name," and were attracting increasing public attention. All of them were "citizens' wives," and one was the wife of a judge while another was the wife of the *Bürgermeister* Jacob Dengler.[36]

When the magistrates began investigating the rumor, they found that the immediate source of the names was Anna Gärtnerin, a servant girl who worked for the Denglers. She said that she had "heard from people that Hans

Jacob Kettener had seen these women, but no longer knew from whom."[37] Because she "did not want to admit anything more" and also had "repeated several times in secret such [slanders] against her own employer," the magistrates decided to hold her in the women's jail while they followed up on her story.

Anna's sister Burga, who was a servant in the household of another *Bürgermeister*, Hanß Jacob Franckhen, testified that the she and her sister had heard the story about the dance one evening when they slipped out a town gate to where "a number of men were standing and talking about the women." She, however, "could not name any" of the men either. Judith Dengler, Jacob's stepdaughter, told a different story, though, and did name a source. She said that when they were "by her barn Burga said that Jacob Kettner had watched from a window as the women held a dance" and then dispersed to return home. She also reported that Burga said she had learned of this from Hanß Wolff Mayer from Neuenburg when he was in the Frankhens' house. Frankhen's daughter Sabina also testified that when he was in their house, Hanß Wolff had said that Jacob Kettener "drunkenly" told him and the district church supervisor in Calmbach about seeing the witches dance and then disperse." Frankhen's son, young Hanß Jacob, further corroborated this account.

When the magistrates interviewed Hanß Jacob Kettener, he denied "that he had seen or spoken of anything improper." He admitted that he had stayed at a tavern named the Kettlemoth House when he went to Calw on business, and that a number of men discussed the women from Wildbad, but that it was Jerg Woltz who said they had held a dance, and the mayor (Schultheiss) of Neuweyler claimed to have heard about it from the district supervisor of Wildbad while he was in Neuweyler to celebrate the ordination of two new pastors. The magistrates in Wildbad therefore had officials in Neuenburg take a deposition from Hanß Wolff Mayer.[38] He testified that four weeks earlier, he was with the supervisor when they were approached by Hanß Jacob Kettener, who "was pretty drunk on wine." According to Hanß Wolff Kettener said that he "knew well" that the supervisor had gone to Neuenburg as part of an investigation of some women there. When the supervisor asked Kettener who he had heard this from, "Kettener answered from the old miller and the new miller in Neuenburg," and that people were also talking of "the same business" in Wildbad. He told Hanß Wolff he had heard that the night watchman "had seen with his own eyes ... the witches going home." Finally, Hanß Wolff said, Kettener claimed, "there was a married couple in Wildbad, and the man said to the woman that he wished he didn't know what he knew, to which the woman responded that she also wished he didn't know what he knew." Hanß Wolff said he did not know who the two were since Kettener did not identify them.

Faced with Hanß Wolff's deposition, Kettener said he had told him and the district supervisor someone escaped from jail in Calw through magic, "which the constable of Calw had told him himself," but he denied having said "the slightest thing about the women from Wildbad or the married couple," and he went on to accuse Hanß Wolff of being the one spreading rumors.[39] Hanß Wolff, in turn, denied Kettener's allegations and asserted that the supervisor would confirm his version.[40] The supervisor, however, contradicted both men, denying everything Kettener said "except the Neuenburger business," while confirming "nothing Hanß Wolff said beyond that something was said about Wildburg." When Kettener and Hanß Wolff were placed in confrontation, "each hardened his insistence that he had said nothing about anyone from Wildbad ... wanted to attest to his version with an oath on the Bible," and demanded that the other "be punished by the government as a liar."

The magistrates of Wildbad gave up their attempt to determine source of the alleged witches' names since they were at an impasse with the two men, and the investigation was causing an uproar "to the great consternation of the visitors to the baths and disgrace of the town."[41] However, they had managed to uncover the source of the rumor that had given rise to the specific allegations. They interviewed Jacob Spör, the night watchman who supposedly "had seen with his own eyes ... the witches going home," and he "explained the basis of the affair." Between 1 and 2 in the night of Thursday, May 12, while he was sitting on a bench near the lower gate, he heard "something come down the chapel path and on the pavement as if it were three horses."[42] Two of them seemed to continue on across a bridge, but "the third on the other hand came ... through the gate" where he was. He "could not say, though, what it was, if it was a man, woman, or something else, because it was very dark and completely black, and once it was through the gate he could not hear or see it any more. More he did not know."

This incident in Wildbad is a good example of some of the processes by which a general belief in the witches' conspiracy could become a more focused conviction that a branch of that conspiracy was operating locally, and then an even more focused set of allegations about specific people in the community. The role of inquisitorial trial procedures and torture in particular in generating testimony about witch dances is well known, as is the importance of reputation in the community in generating and sustaining accusations of *maleficium*, but here we can see the forces of rumor and gossip at work transforming the abstract concerns of the elite into an active component of popular belief.[43] One man's hazy perceptions in the dark of the night became grist for a rumor mill that interpreted them in light of the prevailing belief in the reality of diabolic witchcraft, and the resultant story fed the raw material of individual accusations into a network of gossip.[44] While it seems unlikely that there was anything "real" underlying the rumors, or at least anything that resembled what was rumored, the rumor took on a reality of its own, becoming a real influence in the life of the community despite its illusory foundations.[45] Consequently, it is worth considering how it came into being and developed in light of what is known about how rumors and gossip work.

To begin with, rumors and gossip, while often closely connected, are not the same thing. "Gossip is internal news and the small community or primary group is its locus ... whereas rumor is more impersonal" and "comes from the larger society."[46] Since the allegations that began the magistrates of Wildbad's investigation appear to have begun as a rumor that only later became the gossip that triggered the magistrates' investigation, we will begin by examining how the rumor got started and developed, and then look at its later life as an item of gossip.

Rumor is defined as unsubstantiated information generally passed by word of mouth, and in modern culture is sharply distinguished from news, which is gathered and disseminated by formal organizations tasked with verifying it through investigative reporting or official corroboration. Consequently, much early social scientific interest in rumors focused on how the information in them becomes distorted and why people believe them in the first place.[47] In early modern Württemberg, as in most premodern societies, however, news in the modern sense scarcely existed. The only formal sources of information were church sermons, occasional public readings of government decrees, governmental and business correspondence (available only to a tiny minority), and a nascent press that drew most of its "news" uncritically from the traditional rumor mill.[48] The great bulk of information people got therefore came from informal oral sources. "Oral narrative" has been characterized "a means of communication characterized more than any other by uncritical acceptance of what is said," but this assessment seems somewhat anachronistic.[49] Information, and particularly information from competing sources, was by modern standards a very scarce commodity, and modern critical appraisal depends more than anything on comparing multiple sources. Premodern people paid attention to the character of the teller and the plausibility of the information judged against their general knowledge of the world, but they often had little reason not to accept what they were offered in deciding what to believe or not believe.

Among the earliest systematic investigators of rumors were Allport and Postman, who formulated a "basic law of rumor" which states that the intensity of a rumor is the product of the importance of the information to the people involved and the ambiguity of the evidence ("R ~ i X a").[50] They went on to argue that rumors tend to be simplified by three standard processes: leveling, in which details are left out; shaping, in which they are edited down to concrete and easily remembered form; and assimilation, in which they are connected to peoples' interests.[51] Some of their specific mechanisms have been challenged by subsequent research – indeed, we have seen a rumor that became more complex and detailed rather than less so as it was passed on (although it did evolve to connect to peoples' interests and expectations as Allport and Postman predict) – and the difficulty of quantifying importance and ambiguity has been pointed out, but the "basic law" is still frequently used as the starting point for discussions of rumor because it sets out the two most important features driving the circulation and modification of rumors.[52]

While some research has suggested that people are more likely to spread rumors about things that aren't important to them than about things that are, on balance it seems that rumors do tend to be about things people find significant.[53] The importance can come from the explicit intellectual content of the information, but its emotional resonance, and particularly negative emotional resonance, seems to be more important.[54] In the case at hand, the rumor clearly had a negative valence, but its importance seemed to vary from transmitter to transmitter. For Anna Gärtnerin, it involved a person who played a crucial role in her life, her mistress, and so the suggestion that the woman was a witch was of prime importance to her. For her sister Burga, the information was not as crucial; but since it involved her sister and her sister's employer, who was part of the same social circle as her own mistress, it was still highly charged. Hanß Wolff, on the other hand, lived in another town, and was related only to Burga's employers, not Anna's, so far as we can tell. Hanß Jacob Kettener lived in the same town as the suspects, who, as the wives of notables, occupied a higher place in local society than he did, but he does not appear to have had a direct relationship with any of the other people besides Hanß Wolff. While spreading the rumor may have had served some immediate psychological purpose for Anna and Burga – Allport and Postman pointed out that rumor spreading is used "often to protect and justify the existence of emotions which, if faced directly, might be unacceptable" – for Hanß Wolff and Kettener the most likely explanation is simpler: spreading the rumor was a form of "attention getting," a way of boosting their own sense of importance by being the bearers of provocative news.[55] Certainly Kettener's drunken encounter with the supervisor in which he volunteered that he "knew well" why he had been in Neuenburg suggests that he felt that he was in possession of inside information that gave him a special status.

The witch dance rumor in Wildbad certainly started with ambiguity – the ambiguity of what the night watchman Jacob Spör perceived and reported. The study of rumor was one of the early practical areas that recognized and explored the ways in which perception, cognition, memory, and description are shaped by the forces we saw at work in the encounters with the Devil in the last chapter; the case at hand began when Spör heard "something" that sounded like "three horses."[56] Like him, we can never know what, if anything, actually made the noises he heard that night, and what he "saw" that went through the gate. Perhaps there were one or more animals or people moving outside the gate, or the wind made sounds he heard as horses and inspired his mind to generate the shadowy figure moving through the gate, or perhaps there was nothing at all; his brain could have generated the entire experience of hearing the sounds along with the hint of a figure while he was dozing, or as a waking hallucination.

While it seems unlikely that what Spör heard was actually three horses, since it was pitch dark and the one that went through the gate disappeared immediately without further sound, it is important to keep in mind that Spör did not actually say that there were three horses, he just said it sounded "*as if* it were three horses" (emphasis added). In fact, Spör's testimony is notable as much for its restraint as for his imagination: he recounted only what he experienced without speculation what it "really" was, and he readily admitted that his knowledge was very incomplete. His testimony may have provided the kernel from which the rumor about the witches' dance grew, but it contributed far more by its vagueness than by any speculation on his part.

The disjunction between Spör's original experience and report and the rumor that grew from it is actually fairly typical of the relationship between individual and social memory. While a few individuals will radically alter their memories to suit their current interests and everyone tailors their memories to some extent, "to a considerable degree the original perception constrains the individual to keep his transformations in bounds," while "social memory ... has no comparable anchorage."[57] As a result, the social process of rumor transmission can lead to a cascading series of modifications that end with a story that, as in this case, bears almost no resemblance to the original report. In the case in Wildbad, what sounded like horses became witches, the number of individuals supposedly involved grew, Hanß Jacob Kettener replaced the watchman as the purported witness, he was said to have actually seen the witch dance and the witches returning, and, finally, the witches were identified as specific individuals in the community.

The reason for this sort of transformation is that, on an individual basis, each person in the chain of transmission inevitably filters and alters what they perceive, retain, and report as they strive to find "meaning and good closure" in (or, more precisely, impose it on) ambiguous information they receive.[58] However, each individual is constrained to some degree by what they have been told, so rumors can only be fully understood as collective constructions, the products of a series of transactions. Sociological explanations tend to focus on rumors not as some sort of cumulative pathology, but instead as "in integral part of the process whereby men develop more adequate ways of coping with new circumstances;" as "a way of promulgating new schemes of coordination when we undergo a derangement in our way of life."[59] However, while such an approach may help explain the origins and function of rumors during wars and other large-scale upheavals, it does not seem to have much relevance to the situation in Wildbad, which was not engulfed by any sudden catastrophe or abrupt change in life. More promising is a culturally oriented, more broadly social-constructionist approach that treats rumors as "symbolic realities."[60] On an individual level, rumors act as a "cue for the subconscious," while on a collective level they are shared fantasies that "express what cannot be formulated in other ways." In this view, the rumor in Wildbad can be seen not only as a possible expression of generalized socioeconomic resentments and jealousies held by commoners against members of the local elite and gender tensions between ordinary men and important women, but also as a culturally specific way of conceptualizing anxieties about the nebulous dangers that surrounded seventeenth-century people living in small towns and villages on the edge of the Black Forest.

The rumor about the witch dance had been circulating for four weeks before the magistrates at Wildbad began investigating it, and their official interest was only aroused when specific names, and specifically the names of some of their wives, were mentioned. To understand this dimension of the situation, the transition to and circulation of the names of particular individuals in the community, we must move from consideration of rumors to an examination of the related but distinct practice of gossip. The testimony of Judith Dengler and the two Frankhen children indicates that Hanß Wolff transmitted the rumor that Hans Jacob Kettener had seen witches dancing and returning to town to them and the Gärtnerin sisters, but not that he mentioned any names. Instead, the specific accusations appear to have arisen after the rumor was introduced into the immediate circle of the accused, and in particular that of *Bürgermeister* Jacob Dengler's wife.

The evidence suggests that Anna Gärtnerin, Dengler's servant, was the ultimate source, possibly in concert with her sister, for neither could identify who they had heard the names from, and the other children's' testimony about Hanß Wolff, which Anna confirmed, suggests that Burga fabricated her story about having overheard a conversation outside the town gate.[61] Furthermore, the magistrates uncovered evidence that Anna had a grudge against the Denglers. At one point she had been heard to comment that Jacob Dengler "acts like he's the Devil's" after he rebuked her and some others in his employ, and she had earlier been accused of stealing an apron. While she claimed that she had said that "it was *not* possible" Dengler "followed the Devil," and said that she had returned the apron after she found it, it seems clear that her relationship with her employers was strained, and that she conceptualized their antagonism in terms of allegiance to the Devil.

How Anna transformed the report about the unidentified women Hans Jacob Kettener was supposed to have observed into an allegation against her mistress and three other women is not clear. It may have involved some of the purely internal mental processes explored in the previous chapter, but her sister Burga's inclusion of herself in her lie about overhearing the names outside the town gate suggests that the process involved some degree of interplay between the two girls, a speculative leap made collaboratively as they discussed the scandalous story Burga heard from Hanß Wolff. The accusations themselves may thus have originated in gossip, and, in any case, they became socially important because they became gossip, information circulated within a small group about members of that group.

Because gossip involves the flow of information within small groups, it has attracted the particular attention of anthropologists. Their earliest theories about gossip were rooted in functionalism, and emphasized the way that gossip contributes to social equilibrium.[62] For one thing, as early human groups grew from around 50 to around 150 individuals, the exchange of information about other members of the group probably replaced mutual grooming as a way of cementing interpersonal bonds, since the growth of group size made the time-cost of the older primate practice impractical.[63] In aggregate, gossip thus helps structure social relationships as a whole by defining who is included in an "in-group" and who is not.[64] Furthermore, the actual content of gossip reinforces group norms by disseminating examples of positive and negative behavior, and by rewarding the former and punishing the latter with public exposure.[65] And viewed from another perspective, this functionalist understanding has allowed anthropologists to use gossip as a source of insight into the structure and values of a society; they map the channels of gossip and analyze its contents to help discern networks of relationships and systems of values.[66]

While this interpretation of gossip undoubtedly has merit, it does not seem to be very helpful in understanding the case at hand, for Anna seems to have been the one who contravened social values more than the Denglers, and her gossiping served more to undercut than bolster the established social structure. Indeed, the functionalist interpretation has been criticized more generally on precisely these grounds, that gossip can be used to undermine as well as reinforce the social order, and functionalist arguments do not do justice to the individual, asocial, and even antisocial motivations that stimulate many gossipers.[67] An alternative, transactionalist perspective has therefore been developed which sees gossip as a form of power projection in which individuals use information management to promote their own interests and undermine those of antagonists.[68] This is why gossip is often both feared and disparaged: it is feared because it can undermine a person's standing in the community, often without providing an opportunity for rebuttal, and it is disparaged because in the process it weakens social cohesion generally. Gossip is widely regarded as a negative practice, in theory at least; even people who engage in it in practice disparage it in the abstract.[69] Medieval and early modern Europeans condemned it on both practical and biblical grounds, for both the Old and the New Testaments spoke against it, equating it with malice, envy, and deceit.[70] At the same time, Medieval and early modern Europeans feared gossip, because honor and reputation played a critical role in their small scale, geographically circumscribed communities.[71] In these conditions, gossip had a direct coercive power, as people would adjust their behavior to avoid being its object, and it had indirect power because it could mobilize other social agents like the courts.[72] However, because gossip could cause substantial damage, it could also be "a dangerous weapon to use" because "some pursued with a vengeance those who were said to have spoken ill of them."[73] Thus, in the case in Wildbad, Anna's words first drew public scorn onto the women she implicated and then mobilized the power of the government, but instead of advancing her interests the latter process turned against her and she rather than the women she incriminated ended up in jail.

Another issue that the role of gossip in the Wildbad case relates to is the connection between gender and gossip. This issue actually involves two separate questions: whether women are particularly prone to gossip, as a widespread popular image holds, and whether women gossip differently than men. As far as the amount of gossiping goes, while there is a strong contrast between the image that women are particularly prone to gossip and the reality that both sexes actually gossip extensively, and in some societies and circumstances men actually gossip more than women, on balance it seems that women do gossip more than men.[74] The reason for this tendency is related to the explanation for women's stronger association with malefic magic: "faced with limited opportunities to exercise real power [sic]" women "ridicule, gossip, and use other intrigues to gain their ends."[75] As far as the nature of men's and women's gossip goes, men tend to talk more about themselves, range across a relatively wider social field when discussing others, and converse by taking turns proclaiming complete thoughts, while women's gossip tends to be more other-directed, is more focused on their immediate social circle, and is conducted as an interplay of partial statements.[76] This last point, the tendency of women to "speak in short sections and allow others to speak, so conversation is a collaborative build-up," supports the idea that Anna and Burga generated the specific names in the course of gossiping, rather than one generating them in her head and then telling the other. On the other hand, the substance of the girls' discussion, the generation of witch accusations, undercuts the rather idealistic assertion that "it is the aim of" women's' gossip "to create and maintain good social relationships."[77] To the extent that a person, male or female, uses gossip to promote his or her own interests while undercutting antagonists, as Anna Gärtnerin did, the net effect on social relationships will be negative. Early modern towns and villages, as we have seen, were rife with rivalries and quarrels, a milieu in which "what were considered 'appropriate' female virtues, such as harmony and conciliation, often played little part."[78]

A final point to be made about this case is how it shows the way that popular culture was assimilating elite concern about the Devil's conspiracy. The night watchman does not seem to have thought of witches initially, since he reported that the sounds he heard were like horses' hooves. At some point, though, either he or someone else reinterpreted his perceptions as evidence of witchcraft activity, and his hazy impression of movement toward the gate became someone else's observation of witches dancing. Then, as the rumor circulated, it linked up with a servant girl's conflict with her employers, and without alleging that her mistress had engaged in any *maleficum* at all she was able to tar her with the brush of witch accusation. This appropriation may have been a self-conscious fraud, but Anna's earlier comments about Dengler being given to the Devil suggest that it was instead the result of the girl's internalization of the idea that the Devil was a real presence in the world, directly responsible for one's misfortunes and conflicts with others. Unlike the people discussed in the last chapter, Anna did not perceive the Devil herself, but she did think that she could perceive his influence on others.

Dreams of dances

The second of the two sampled cases, involving accusations of attendance at a witch dance, took place in the same year as the rumor in Wildbad in a small town that lay about 40 miles to the east, just northeast of Stuttgart. In late January, the magistrates of Winnenden reported that an eight-year-old boy named Hanß Ferner claimed to have seen his mother, grandmother, many other women, and a local musician at a witch dance that the Devil had taken him to.[79] Apparently the Devil, whom Hanß described as a black man with horns, had been after the boy for some time, appearing to him both day and night, scaring and threatening him. Eventually Hanß told some schoolmates about the "black man" who was bothering him, and they told the schoolmaster. Hanß was put into confinement and watched by a guard, who reported that he seemed particularly agitated at the beginning of the night and early in the morning. Indeed, early on the previous Tuesday morning, Hanß had cried out that the "black man" had stabbed him in the foot, and when a barber-surgeon, the town scribe, and two other men examined the foot they saw that it did in fact have a cut on it where Hanß claimed the Devil had stabbed him. Hanß explained that earlier that night he had finally agreed to give himself to the Devil, who thereupon carried him to the "merry and happy" festivities where he saw the women and the musician. At the dance, the Devil fussed over him, carried him on his shoulders, brought him bread and meat, "told him to call him father, and called him his son," and eventually carried him back home. Hanß worried, though, that he would not be able to go to heaven because of his decision, and that is what provoked the Devil to stab his foot.

The magistrates' investigation revealed that Hanß was a bastard who had been cared for as an infant by his grandmother, a poor "old, angry, abusive woman."[80] Despite his mother's promiscuity, her reputation was "not among the worst," though, so when Hanß was four she married an honorable citizen and took Hanß back. Unfortunately, the stepfather died before long, which was when Hanß began to show increasing signs of being "disturbed and fearful." He himself testified that this was when the Devil had begun to "frighten and threaten" him, starting the process that had culminated in his trip to the witches' dance.

Hanß' mother and grandmother tearfully denied that they had attended any such festivities, and the musician denied any part in them either.[81] When confronted by his mother and grandmother, Hanß wavered in his testimony, retracting his accusations, but then partially reiterating them when alone (saying they were there, but didn't dance). Hanß also accused a woman of having told him on the day of his dream that the "black man" would come to him that night and also of attending the dance. In confrontation, though, she denied both accusations vehemently and there was evidence that his family had had a dispute with her, further undermining his testimony. Hanß discredited himself even more by asking his guard's daughter, who often accompanied her father at his post, to lay with him. The ducal government concluded that he was "a very bad boy" who had denounced innocent people, and instructed the magistrates to have him beaten to impress upon him "the wicked depravity of magic," scold him for his slanders, see that the town preacher visited him regularly to lead him in earnest prayer, and watch his mother and grandmother for any further signs of trouble.[82]

The first question this case raises is what, so far as can be determined, really happened. Was this really a report about a tormented child's imaginary struggles to resist the Devil's blandishments? Or was it an example of a child's opportunistic exploitation of a common cultural construct to victimize people he was angry with?[83] Or perhaps it was nothing more than a fantastic schoolyard story that snowballed out of control.[84] The inconsistencies in some of Hanß' statements suggest that he did consciously or unconsciously improvise some points in response to the pressures or opportunities of the situation, but several things suggest that Hanß' story is more or less what it purports to be, the record of a boy's struggles to resist the Devil. First of all, his mother and grandmother reported that he had been behaving strangely since his stepfather's death several years before, which is when he said the Devil first approached him.[85] Secondly, his guard observed him to sleep restlessly in general, and he cried out in his sleep on the very morning he claimed to have traveled to the witch dance and been injured by the Devil. Hanß may not have really flown to a witch dance, but it appears that he really dreamed he did.

If Hanß Ferner really dreamed that he gave himself to the Devil and flew with him to a witch Sabbath, the next question that presents itself is what, if anything, that experience meant. Dreams have been interpreted since antiquity and before by virtually every human society, and the interpretations range from treating dream experiences as real supernatural events to regarding them as meaningless neural noise, with intermediate positions conceiving them to be unreal but sources of important truths accessible through one of any number of interpretive schemes.[86] Hanß himself clearly understood his experience to have been a real event, and the magistrates of Winnenden were clearly prepared to believe it was.[87] As the investigation proceeded, though, their openness to his claims declined until the government concluded that his report about the witch dance was false, a change of heart that constituted one small step in the larger process of cultural evolution by which Europe's elite gradually came to the conclusion that magical flights to diabolic dances, like magic generally, only take place in the mind, in dreams and fantasy. This position became the basis for modern interpretations of dreams, which have ranged from rationalist dismissals of them as ephemeral nonsense to psychological treatments of them as coded expressions of unconscious thoughts and feelings.

The most prominent modern theory of dreams, of course, is Freud's theory that dreams are a mechanism by which the brain maintains sleep in the face of disturbing thoughts that well-up from the unconscious, mechanisms that involve distorting repressed desires into symbolic forms that embody them in a manner that keeps them from waking the sleeper up.[88] However, just as Luther was followed by waves of Protestant reformers who disagreed with each other almost as vehemently as they disagreed with the Pope, Freud was followed by waves of clinically oriented psychologists who developed their own dream theories, none of which was able to establish itself as clearly superior to the others, or to Freud's.[89] Furthermore, recent physiological studies of sleep utilizing technologies such as electroencephalography (EEG) and positron emission tomography (PET) combined with systematic laboratory studies of dreaming conducted by interrupting and interviewing people at various stages of sleep have substantially superseded, to the extent that they have not simply discredited, older, clinically based theories.[90]

In this void, the most promising approach might seem to be to apply the general methods of postmodernism, to understand historical dreams, like other past mental experiences, as elements of distinct cultural systems that can best be understood in terms of their place within those systems rather than as manifestations of some common human cognitive process. From this point of view, Hanß' dream itself was as inaccessible as any other aspect of purported reality; all we have is the narrative he constructed about it, which itself is contained in the narrative constructed by the magistrates. Like any text, it can be deconstructed both to expose the way that it reflected the structural imperatives of narrative and to show how its elements embodied various aspects of its cultural milieu. In this analysis, the meaning of Hanß' dream for us comes not from what he experienced, but from what he said he experienced, and from what others then said about what he said.

However, this approach rests on certain assumptions that call its applicability to understanding dream experiences into question. In particular, it privileges linguistic modes of thought, assuming either that dreams are essentially narratives themselves, or that because narrative texts are our only evidence of them, we can only understand them as linguistic artifacts. However, the second position is rather like saying that because our only knowledge of, say, Roman siege engines is written descriptions of them, we can only understand them as literary artifacts, without reference to the properties of the materials they were constructed of or to the physical laws governing ballistics. Clearly, while it is vital to treat the texts containing our knowledge of past things like catapults with the caution due to any historical sources, it would be absurd to ignore the fact that they once really existed, and were subject to forces and constraints beyond the laws of semiotics. The fact that our knowledge of something comes from texts does not necessarily mean that the only way we can gain understanding of it is from those texts.

Of course, if the first position is true, and dreams themselves are merely a form of narrative, then this objection to the second point is, in the case of dreams, moot, and they can indeed best, or only, be understood in terms of the rules governing, or derived from the study of, language. On its face, this is not an unreasonable position, for dreams often do contain some verbalizations, they generally involve significant narrative sequences, they are generally recalled in a narrative format, and these dream narratives take their place within the larger narratives through which people organize their waking consciousness. In fact, one of the current theories of dreams argues precisely that they are a form of "inner speech" and are therefore governed by linguistic principles.[91] It notes that "the most striking feature of dreaming is its narrative cohesion," infers that dreaming must be "generated by the same cognitive systems that produce the ordinary speech of waking life," and concludes that since "the core of dream formation" is "its narrative structure ... a useful focus for recovering the 'essence' of the dream would lie in applying linguistic analytical schemes."

It must be recognized, though, that this approach rests on an inference, that dreams are generated by the same systems that produce speech, which is based on observations about the reported content of dreams rather than direct evidence of brain functioning. More recent research into the neurophysiology of sleep and dreaming undercuts this assumption, and so the most promising approach to Hanß' dream would seem to be first to explore the current state of knowledge about the physiology of sleep and dreaming, and then to evaluate Hanß' case in light of this.

To begin with, it has been found that sleep consists of four different phases: the hypnagogic phase at sleep's onset, long periods of what is called nREM, or "Not REM," sleep, which alternate with shorter periods of REM, or "rapid eye movement" sleep, and finally the hypnopompic phase at the end of sleep.

NREM sleep is the oldest form of sleep, occurring in reptiles, birds, and mammals, and is very different from wakefulness.[92] Brain waves change dramatically, mentation (in people at least) tends to be either absent or simple and repetitive, and the body replenishes and restores itself in a variety of ways, repairing damage, growing new tissues, and resupplying itself with chemicals depleted during wakefulness. The limbic system is active but "forebrain activity is low," and the left cerebral hemisphere tends to be more active than the right.[93] Some dreaming does take place, but it is usually brief, closely connected to waking concerns, and verbal and conceptual rather than visual and emotional.[94]

The hypnagogic and hypnopompic phases are relatively short periods of transition into and out of nREM. They are characterized by brain waves between the waking and nREM patterns and mentation that can include "rapidly changing, jumbled images and thoughts, often related to what was last seen, heard, or thought of before nodding off."[95] Visualizations are "more vivid than dreams," and proceed in accelerated rather than real time.[96]

REM sleep is not quite as old as nREM, being found only in most birds and mammals, and is not only dramatically different from nREM, but also is in many ways much like being awake.[97] To begin with, in REM the eyes dart back and forth just as they do during wakefulness. In terms of brain waves, REM's "EEG profile is virtually the same as ... in an awake person," while in terms of most brain systems, "activation levels during REM are comparable to those in waking."[98] However, in other ways REM sleep is radically different from being awake.[99] For one thing, the motor output systems are deactivated, so the body is effectively paralyzed, and sensory input systems are muted. For another, the higher executive systems "which normally imbue human thought ... with logical coherence, [and] propositional structure" and "constrain perceptual possibilities on the basis of established knowledge of the world" are also switched off.[100] Thirdly, production of aminergic neurotransmitters, which play a role in maintaining focused attention, stops, while large amounts of cholinergic neurotransmitters, which promote diffuse associations, are produced.[101] Fourth, the right cerebral hemisphere, which "is organized principally to process novel challenges" through non-verbal, gestalt-oriented, and emotive cognition, is more active than the left, which specializes in established, "sequential-temporal" processing, like language.[102] Fifth, the limbic system and associated areas which play a central role in emotion, memory, and visual and auditory associations are, if anything, more active than during waking.[103] Finally, mentation during REM takes the form of complex, episodic, vivid, emotionally-charged, multisensory experiences, in other words, what we think of as dreams.

When the close association of REM and dreaming was first discovered, researchers assumed that dreams are a part of REM sleep. However, further research has revealed that dreams indistinguishable from dreams in REM can occur during nREM sleep.[104] Therefore, it appears that dreaming is an autonomous process that occurs when the network of brain centers producing them is stimulated in the absence of external stimuli or activity in the executive centers that would otherwise hinder them.[105] Nevertheless, dreams do seem to relate to the neural activity that stimulates them, and since they most frequently occur during REM sleep, a greater understanding of them, or at least the great majority of them, can be gained through a greater understanding of what the brain is doing during REM.[106]

Clues to the function of REM sleep are provided by studies of changes in REM activity during maturation and experiments on animals and people during REM. In most species, young animals spend a greater percentage of their time asleep in REM than adults, and the proportion of time spent by the young is inversely related to the species' degree of maturity at birth.[107] REM has been detected in fetuses; human newborns spend 50% of their time asleep in REM while adults only spend about half that time in it; and human babies have been found to smile, frown, show anger, perplexity, and disdain, all among the universally recognizable facial expressions, during REM sleep before they exhibit them socially.[108] Animals and people whose brain centers that inhibit movement during REM have been incapacitated will get up and act out their dreams; for example, REMing cats will get up and stalk, kill, and even eat imaginary prey.[109] All mammals' brains produce theta waves during REM, the same rhythm the produce when engaged in critical survival activities while awake (cats when they're hunting, rats when they're exploring, rabbits when they're avoiding hunters).[110] In humans, REM deprivation has not been shown to produce great psychological damage, but people confronted with complicated learning tasks REM more afterwards. Furthermore, subjects deprived of REM learn complex material less well, recall "material of personal and emotional relevancy ... more poorly," show greater emotional brittleness, and exhibit a "rebound effect" of increased REM when allowed to sleep uninterrupted.[111]

Overall, the evidence suggests that REM sleep is a period of neurological "housekeeping" in which neural networks are wired or rewired.[112] Specifically, REM sleep seems to be when young animals complete the creation of neural circuits, and when animals of all ages do certain kinds of neural processing that relates to critical skills and experiences, particularly memory consolidation and storage.[113] This processing is not a passive transfer of information, but an active and creative procedure involving the creation of associations, elimination of unneeded material, generation of original interpretive elements, and transformation from short term to long term storage modalities.[114] It is also not quick, for analysis of dream content suggests that it involves forming and reforming connections relating to a common theme in increasingly complex patterns involving increasingly diverse older material over the course of a night, and there is evidence that full integration of new material into long-term memory may take repeated processing over many nights.[115] The result is more than just a storage process, but amounts to a form of learning, or even problem-solving, in which new experiences are evaluated in terms of established cognitive structures and established cognitive structures are updated in response to new experiences.[116] Since the brain's emotional systems are highly active while centers of conscious reasoning are shut off during REM, this processing seldom centers on intellectual, logical-procedural, or broad social problems, but instead is rooted in feelings about the self and the immediate social world.[117] However, because higher level cortical and subcortical centers, in particular those which "instigate goal-seeking behaviors" and those which handle "concrete spatial cognition ... [and] quasispatial (symbolic) operations" are also active, processing during REM does not involve purely visceral reactions to experiences, but instead involves a dynamic interplay between very basic "flight-fight" level responses and more sophisticated mentation.[118]

Sleep and dream researchers are currently divided on the question of whether the semi-conscious visualizations and verbalizations we think of as dreaming, as opposed to the neurological tasks that stimulate them, play an essential role in sleep, fulfilling some psychological purpose essential to our individual functioning and survival as a species, or are evolutionary spandrels, incidental byproducts of the interaction between somnambulant neurological housekeeping and coincidentally active systems connected with conscious awareness.[119] Fortunately, though, a resolution of this issue is not necessary to assess Hanß Ferner's dream, for what is important is that virtually all researchers agree that dreams do offer insights not only into the dreamer's concerns and preoccupations, but also into his or her mental structures and cognitive processes.[120] Furthermore, the weight of evidence suggests that dreams appear confusing not because the brain is actively censoring the material, as Freud believed, but because they are generated through the interaction of low-level emotional processing that proceeds according to its own, in REM sleep chemically enhanced, associative logic, and higher level conceptualizing that struggles to systemize it without the help, during REM sleep, of the brain centers responsible for logical coherence, propositional structure, and physical plausibility.[121] The effect can perhaps be thought of as like looking over the shoulder of a movie editor at work: one might see a coherent narrative episode, but then jump to a symbolically or thematically rather than chronologically or narrative-structurally related next sequence; then splice in a significant visual detail; and so on, as the editor follows the train of connections dictated by her own creative process. The succession of images and episodes appears arbitrary not because the editor is trying to either confuse or communicate with the observer, but because she is following her own train of associations and procedural efficiencies without regard to the coherence or lack of coherence of the series of images and sequences at the moment. Dreams are meaningful not because they present stories containing surreptitious messages, but because they reflect the process by which the brain constructs memory, and in the process generates new knowledge. They open "the door" to "direct evidence of ... social and psychological learning."[122]

Returning to Hanß Ferner's dream, to begin with, like about half of all dreams, it related directly to waking events from the previous day, both the fact that he was under supervision because of his reports of diabolic contacts and, if his claim was true, the neighbor woman's specific warning that the black man would visit him that night.[123] However, his dream also clearly manifested his longer-term concern about the Devil, and this, in turn, reflected a widespread preoccupation with witchcraft in Württemberg around 1660.[124] For example, the father of a four-year-old girl from Kirchheim who said she and her parents went to a witch dance the next year reported that "among the adults conversation ... turns constantly to the witch theme, 'which the child must have latched onto.'"[125] As the experience of the *benandanti* discussed by Carol Ginzburg in *Night Battles* shows, dreams can be inspired by precise cultural expectations and shaped by precise cultural scripts.[126]

Secondly, the first and central parts of Hanß' dream were certainly based on a cultural script: acceptance of the Devil and flight to a witch dance. His sense of giving in to the Devil, because his description lacks visual details, may have been either a hypnagogic experience or an nREM dream, more a diffuse rumination than an episodic visualization, while the dream of flying to the witches dance, given the amount of visual detail, was most likely a REM dream.[127] The imagery of the Devil as a black man with horns, the flight to the dance, and the festivities with a fiddler were all stock elements of the German peasant synthesis of learned demonology and their own folk culture that generally appear in popular reports of witch dances.[128] However, at the point that the "black man" began acting like a father, Hanß abandoned the cultural script, and the dream took off in an uncharted direction as he amalgamated his own experience, including his ongoing dream experience (his actual surrender to the Devil), with cultural symbols and meanings.[129] Specifically, his adoption of the Devil, the prince of evil who prayed on the defeated and disillusioned, as his father would seem to reflect his awareness of his own disreputable origins and his despondency at the loss of his stepfather. It may be an inspired inversion of the cultural view of God as a father figure, but it was an inversion that was Hanß' personal innovation, for such an association was not part of the pan-European demonology or the regional folk culture. The presence of his mother and grandmother at the dance may have just reflected the fact that children generally populate their dreams with relatives and other people close to them, but it also may have reflected his awareness of their disreputability, and his anger with them as well (seeing them as evil).[130] Upon returning home, Hanß departed even further from the witch script in what sounds like nREM agitated verbal mentation in which he mulled over the implications of the preceding developments, with little emphasis on what the Devil looked like or how he acted when he "struck" him. However, he does seem to have moved his body as part of that experience, for he was reported to have slept restlessly and, unlike during REM sleep, the body can and does move during most of nREM sleep, which is when sleepwalking occurs.[131] Of course, it could be said that he had just changed to his culture's repentance script, but that did not include the denouement, the Devil's attack, during nREM or the hypnopompic phase, that woke him up. While the Devil was known to threaten or even hit people, in this case the ending was more likely an interpretation backward from a coincidental somatic event cause by Hanß' agitated movement to dream content, for somatosensory stimulation "have the highest rate of incorporation" into dreams.[132] Coincidence can play a role as well as culture and cognition in forming dreams; in this case, it showed Hanß that the Devil would not be spurned so easily.

The central point is that Hanß's dream was not structured by a script, or even a narrative backbone; he was actively grappling with the implications of his situation as he became increasingly aware of its personal, social, and cultural meaning. There was no overarching storyline laid out in advance, and he was not sending himself a disguised message; instead his brain was figuring things out as it went along, advancing from association to association, experience to experience, and realization to realization in a series of ruminations, visualizations, and even bodily movements that directly manifested his cognitive processing. In the process he utilized plenty of cultural symbols and followed not one but several cultural scripts, but he only followed them so long as they worked for him, and he jumped to another or created his own original next step as the logic of his cognitive processing dictated.

Beyond its personal meaning, Hanß' dream is of historical interest because it enables us to literally watch enculturation in the seventeenth century at work. Clearly, Hanß was grappling with a difficult personal situation, and we can see in his dreams how he was integrating the concepts of the Devil and witchcraft with it, using them to make sense of it (and it to make sense of them).[133] He was the product of sin, "born to the world from the sinful disgrace of prostitution," and it was a legacy that he could not seem to escape.[134] He lost his best hope for social as well as psychological redemption when his stepfather died, and in his despondency he felt the temptation of the Devil, who was, in a sense, already his father. On the night of the dreams, he gave in, which he acknowledged by his acceptance of the Devil.[135] He then realized that the next step, according to the logic of his culture, would be flight to and participation in a witch dance, which he did. At that point, though, his personal issues came to dominate, and his dream took the unorthodox but personally satisfying turn of the Devil adopting him as his son. Hanß was thrilled to have a father while at the dance, but once he returned home he realized that the cost would be alienation from Christian society, signified by an inability to get into heaven. Again he deviated from the cultural script, and instead of returning home to practice harmful magic, he tried to take back his affiliation with the Devil. In the struggle he injured himself, which in the dream became his punishment for spurning his new father figure. In his dream we can thus observe the process by which he was internalizing the contemporary cultural values regarding bastardy, the Devil, witches, community, and heaven, associating them with aspects of his own life and making them part of his conceptual framework for understanding the world.

Hanß' experience has even larger significance for us when it is seen in the context of its time, for his was just one of many similar child-centered trials in the region during the mid-to-late seventeenth century. In fact, children were rarely involved in witchcraft except as victims of adult witches' magic before the late sixteenth century.[136] They first began to play a prominent role in trials in Germany in the 1580s, and their participation increased steadily, there and in many parts of Europe, over the decades.[137] Both because of their increasing involvement and because of the gradual decline of trials centered on adults (particularly middle-aged adults), child-centered trials became a characteristic feature of the last phase of the trials, with the children's dreams and fantasies often, as in the case we have just seen, playing a leading role.[138]

The increased role of children in late witch trials was quite pronounced in Württemberg. Only six child-centered trials took place prior to 1660, but there were 11 during the 1660s alone.[139] Thereafter, they tapered off slowly, with six in the 1670s, seven in the 1680s, and seven final ones spread over the first half of the eighteenth century. Some involved *maleficium* and others simple contact with the Devil, but many centered on children's reports of participation in witch dances.[140] Many resembled Hanß Ferner's case, involving children's dreams, although each had his or her own take on the experience. One boy said that he traveled on a boat with his girlfriend; several reported being abducted from their beds by women rather than traveling voluntarily with the Devil, stories that resemble "witch abductions" that were widely reported in Hungary.[141] Reports of the food, wine, and dancing were relatively similar from case to case, but some children's sabbaths involved sex, and a few included ritual homage to the Devil and acquisition of malefic materials.[142] In at least one case, a boy really did wander out of his house at night, but there were no known cases like the one reported in Augsburg, which lay only about 30 miles east of the duchy's enclave around Heidenheim, in which children actually conducted Sabbaths complete with diabolical pacts, desecration of the host, and sexual play.[143]

Contemporary observers noted the increasing prominence of children in witch trials in the latter part of the seventeenth century, and regarded it as something of a mystery since it did not fit into either learned or popular traditions regarding witchcraft.[144] Historians have also recently recognized this issue, and have advanced a number of explanations for, first, why children in particular might have gotten involved in witch allegations, and, second, why their involvement seems to have increased over the course of the seventeenth century.

To start with explanations for children's involvement in trials, one observation that has been put forward is that children spend a good deal of time imitating adults, and they may have spent an even greater proportion of their time doing so in the past because of the limited availability of toys and stories tailored to children.[145] A second explanation that has been put forward is simply the "wanton mischief of undisciplined youngsters, a callous readiness to make false allegations.[146] A somewhat more sophisticated version of this explanation is the concept of "mythomania," an "obsessive-compulsive myth-creating" psychopathology fueled by "unmitigated maliciousness, the need for attention, or precocious sexual appetites."[147] A third line of reasoning focuses on particular cognitive characteristics of children: the vividness of their imaginations and tendency to magical thinking because the frontal lobes don't fully develop until the late teens; the plasticity of their cognitive structures and their tendency to "spontaneously alter the truth" guilelessly between the ages of around seven and nine; and the development of their attribution of intentionality, whose roots were variously traced to internal mentation and the Devil's machinations during the early modern period, around the same age.[148] Added to this list can be an observation inspired by Hanß Ferner's case, that children do not begin to dream the kind of complex, episodic, vivid, emotionally charged, multisensory experiences adults do until they are around ten years of age.[149] Before that they dream far less frequently, and their dreams tend to be static and bland. Thus, when they first experience an emotionally charged, dynamic, and vivid dream like Hanß', they may have less ability to distinguish it from reality, and also to connect it to the dreams they are used to. That would seem to have been the case in another child-witch trial from 1665 in Möckmühl, for when the magistrates asked the boy it centered on if the witch dance he experienced might not have just been a dream, "and if he in fact knew and understood what a dream is, he answered, 'Yes, he dreamed once that he dug and found some money ... but when he woke up it wasn't real.' When, in contrast, he went out to a dance and traveled there by ship, 'he did not dream like that.'"[150] In all these ways, their accusations and stories took on a subjective authenticity that transformed malicious talk and idle imaginings into experiences and memories of compelling intensity.

Nevertheless, while some children undoubtedly indulged in "wanton mischief" or were driven by some pathological "mythomania," Hanß Ferner's case should caution us from assuming too easily that most of the children were driven by some sort of bizarre destructiveness, and encourage us to see how "the latching of children onto the witch mythology was motivated by their life history," how their dreams and stories "reflect ... the real experiences and the powerful feelings of the children."[151] In some cases, for example, their claims to have attended a dance were a device to get revenge on adults they were angry with, but in other cases, it reflected, as Hanß' did, their assessment of their own social situation or moral status.[152] In some cases, the issue was anger and aggression because they were "marginal, outcast children, whose lives presented an unbroken succession of rejections and disappointment."[153] In other cases, it was the children's precocious sexuality, and in many it was both.[154] They were using "the material of the witch beliefs ... to make sense of themselves and their circumstances."[155] Some may have identified with the Devil in anger, as "a revolt with explicitly anticlerical tendencies," but others, like Hanß, did so merely because it seemed to fit; it "symbolized and dramatized" their "inner state and experiences, feelings and wishes."[156] Like Scottish Presbyterian children going through conversion experiences at the time who felt terror, had visions of the Devil, were plagued by evil "thoughts and temptations," many witch children were struggling to reconcile their human urges and social conflicts with their culture's Manichean morality.[157]

As far as why children's role in witch trials seems to have grown over the course of the seventeenth century, several explanations have been put forward. To some extent the phenomenon can be explained by changes in the trials and witch beliefs themselves. To begin with, the start of children's involvement as participant/accusers came very near to the beginning of the period of mass hunts, when the concept of the Sabbath played a central role – the late sixteenth century – for it was the idea of the Sabbath that enabled them to take this dual part.[158] Secondly, some historians have pointed to the wider breakdown of stereotypes during mass trials, their tendency to start with typical suspects, old women, but gradually widen to include middle-aged adults and children.[159] Others point to the growth of skepticism about witchcraft as the seventeenth century wore on, and the way that children's innocent sincerity and vivid descriptions seemed to offer clear evidence of an otherwise increasingly murky phenomenon.[160] A final structural point is that children's trials, in which diabolism was introduced spontaneously by the child accusers, continued even as adult trials, which tended to be triggered by accusations of *maleficium* and depended on torture to extract evidence of diabolism, declined, since, as we shall see, torture was being abandoned and allegations of *maleficium* were being reclassified as poisoning or other material actions.[161]

On the other hand, contemporary observers who noted the phenomenon tended to focus on changes in children themselves and blame bad parenting.[162] They complained that parents set a bad example or used bad childrearing techniques. In taking this approach, they were linking the problem of witch children to a broader cultural concern about parenting that began to grow during the sixteenth century.[163] This concern, in turn, was part of the even broader campaign of confessionalized social discipline; concern about children's' morality was just one front of the wider push to reform popular behavior and recast popular culture.[164] On a social level it led to the late-seventeenth century drives to suppress the youth gangs, which made up a significant part of the problem of vagrants and beggars, through accusations of magic and witchcraft, while on an individual level, it brought children into sharper conflict with the elders in their household and community.[165]

The case of Hanß Ferner suggests that another process may have been at work as well. It provides further evidence that the sermons and pamphlets decrying witchcraft and magic were having an effect, that the ideas they contained about bad people banding together under the Devil's banner were not only disseminating into popular culture, tavern rumors, and village gossip, but also were working their way into peoples' consciousness, their concept of the social world and even their concept of themselves. Furthermore, the rash of child-centered trials in the mid-to-late seventeenth century would seem to be a measure of the success of this process: social discipline had moved beyond curbing adult behaviors to molding children's consciousness. Many older witches confessed to having entered the Devil's service as children, but they either did not make the connection between their actions and his cause until they were tried for witchcraft or they kept that realization secret for decades.[166] The wave of child confessions and accusations toward the end of the period of the trials suggests that this innocence, this inability to see or, having seen, to act on a realization of moral transgression, was coming to an end. It suggests that the cumulative effect of individuals' enculturation was society's acculturation.[167]

Dances and trances

While Hanß Ferner claimed to have attended a witch dance, his experience was pretty clearly an ordinary dream, and his mother and grandmother strongly denied his accusation that they had been there as well. In other cases, though, adults did confess to attendance at witch dances, and their stories are not so easily explained as simple dreams. We have already considered Magdelena Horn's confession in 1562 that she had gone to dances "on the Feuerbacher meadow," but since she mentioned them only after long talks with a clergyman they may well have been imaginative embellishments to her confession of evil thoughts and deeds.[168] On the other hand, in January 1667, the magistrates of the university town and district seat Tübingen reported that "for the past quarter year or so Hannß Walther's wife ... Apolonia ... has often been heard saying godless and magical, thoroughly shameful" things.[169] Specifically, she claimed that "at night she flew all over the countryside as far as Turkey." One night, she said, "her prince, understood to be the Devil, with a black mustache, had carried her out," and thereafter, "from time to time ... she and her husband traveled on a pitchfork, then on a cat, and when they came to their destination they met a group from Tübingen, Reütlingen, and also from her village" who "amused each other, drank red and white wine from golden cups." Afterward "her Hannß, understood to be the Devil, lay with her," and she "returned in a twinkling" to her home.

Apolonia claimed to have learned "this witchcraft from a butcher named 'Urbanle,' who had recently been burned in Reütlingen." In addition, she "often ridiculed the village preacher," and said that "her Hannß, the Devil, had threatened to beat her if she told the preacher everything, and if she prayed with" him. She stated that "her prince is the most powerful in the world, and therefore she must follow him." When the preacher, the village mayor and her husband brought her to the town hall, she engaged in "a vile Devil's game in which she said good and bad things, prayed and spoke lewdly, [and when] asked where she kept her salve," the ointment witches reputedly used to travel to their dances, "she answered, 'in a trough,' but when impartial men searched for it, nothing was found." Since she "threatened to set fire to the houses" in the village, "and seemed ready to do it" the magistrates in Tübingen decided to keep her in custody pending instructions from the High Council.

Apolonia's case occurred late in the period of witch trials (1667) and Tübingen was both the home of the provincial university, whose faculty had championed legal caution for decades already, and was peripherally involved in the last wave of a mass persecution in the neighboring Imperial City of Reutlingen, so it is not surprising that in their report to the High Council the town's magistrates said Apolonia "appears to be out of her wits," and that they "found nothing other than that ... this woman" suffered from "a great delirium."[170] Their diagnosis is not far from what a modern doctor or traditional historian might say, for Apolonia exhibited many symptoms associated with the current medical understanding of delirium: "impaired perception, delusions or hallucinations," mood swings that "may be rapid and unpredictable," "a dreamlike quality" to thought "with some merging of content from dreams with reality," and "other disruptions of thinking and behavior."[171] Older people like Apolonia are particularly prone to delirium because it is a symptom of "neurotransmitter abnormalities," including acetylcholine deficiencies, so the "reduced numbers of receptors for acetylcholine in older people predisposes them" to it.[172] Furthermore, delirium can result from a wide variety of problems ranging from "primary cerebral disorders" like stroke or trauma through bodily ailments like myocardial infarction and infections to metabolic disorders, intoxication, and substance withdrawal, and older people are particularly prone to many of these.[173] As in Apolonia's case, "an older person who has been functioning adequately" may suddenly develop symptoms "over a short period of time" that bring a "dramatic change" in the "person's level of functioning."[174] Which of these, or what combination, brought on Apolonia's disturbing behavior is not clear, but the magistrates had clear reason to regard her behavior as disturbed.

However, Apolonia's reported behavior does not include some characteristic features of delirium, which casts doubt on the easy characterization of her behavior as simply a manifestation of some acute organic brain disorder.

Some of the characteristics that were not noted in Apolonia's case, like "some degree of temporal dislocation," which is considered "necessary for the diagnosis of delirium" today, may be a culture-bound manifestations of the modern preoccupation with time, but others, like disorientation, "rambling, irrelevant, and incoherent speech," "a deficit in attention or conscious level," and "abnormally increased or reduced psychomotor activity," would seem to be more universal effects of the organic problems responsible for delirium, and the magistrates' report does not contain evidence of any of these.[175] Her speech, while belligerent and focused on mystical experiences, was not "rambling," "irrelevant," or "incoherent;" there is no suggestion of "a reduced ability to maintain and shift attention to external stimuli;" and she was not reported to have exhibited any abnormal physical activity. Furthermore, many of the "symptoms" that do seem to be present are, upon consideration, less clearly indications of delirium as medically understood than they first seem. For example, Apolonia's provocative statements to the preacher may have manifested a more general and normal cognitive decline involving deterioration of the "restraint function," which normally inhibits "strong responses ... whenever the most potent response is not the most appropriate and when alternative responses need to be considered."[176] This sort of decline is not uncommon as the brain ages, and Apolonia's anger and defiant identification with the Devil's cause may well have been connected to the fact that "this woman, along with her husband" had "a very bad reputation" since "they both consorted often with people in Reütlingen already burned for magic." The "Devil's game" Apolonia played, saying "good and bad things, praying and speaking lewdly" when she was taken to the Tübingen town hall could also have manifested this deteriorating restraint, and her struggle against it, since being brought in may have both incensed and alarmed her. Her imagining that she heard the Devil's voice, as we have seen, was in her culture not so much delusional as a form of unconscious sub-vocalization. Apolonia does seem to have been suffering from some cognitive decline reflecting neurological deterioration common in advanced age, but her behavior and utterances cannot simply be written off as the incoherent raving of a lunatic.[177]

In particular, while Apolonia's reports about her flights to the witch dances do appear to have merged dream content with reality, in her culture such mixing had traditionally been assumed, and the specific type of dreams she reported, dreams in which the dreamer was transported to another place to participate in magical events and which the dreamer experienced as real rather than as dreams, were, as we have seen, experienced in other parts of early modern Europe, and indeed, were recorded in other cases in Württemberg, by younger people whose cerebral integrity was not in question. The most famous example from elsewhere in Europe, mentioned earlier, were the north Italian *benandanti*, who four times a year found themselves magically transported to dreamy fields of combat to ward off witches' threat to the harvest.[178] To the south, in Sicily, *donni di fuora*, or "ladies from outside" said they "went out at night" in "companies" with each other and fairies (spirit beings) to party in other peoples' houses or the countryside, while Hungarian records contain numerous reports by people who said they had been abducted by witches and taken to their Sabbaths as well as, less frequently, confessions by witches who admitted to having attended voluntarily.[179] Among the sampled cases from Württemberg, one other suspect, Maria Braittingen, who we have seen confessed in 1619 to having had sex with the Devil, "in the form of her boyfriend," confessed freely to nocturnal experiences with some strong similarities to Apolonia's while once again in custody for theft in 1622, when she was 20.[180] Maria admitted to stealing some clothing to sell, reconfirmed her contact with the Devil three years before, and said that he now "gave her no peace, and wanted to have sex with her."[181] He appeared, she said, "in the form of a farm-hand" who appeared "to her outside the jail here, said that his name was Hanß, and that she should be his." He promised "he would get her out" of jail, but "when she prayed he was very angry at her." She went on to say that some time earlier "once she attended a night dance, which was held in an open field and a meadow at eleven o'clock." She said "the evil spirit woke her from sleep and transported her" there. During the trip she felt "as if she sat in a saddle; it went very fast and she quite soon came to the place, which she did not recognize, and at that point [she] realized that it was a goat" she had ridden on. "The dance lasted until after midnight, around 2 o'clock, [and] afterwards the evil spirit, in the form he had picked her up in, returned her to her master's house." She came in, she said, the same way she had left: "through the regular front-door." In addition to this "night dance," Maria said she had attended "two feasts that took place in a house at which wine was available and one drank out of glasses," and where "she played, and the cook gave her meat to eat." Furthermore, she "also indicated that she was at witch dances," at first saying it had been four, but later saying it was "so often that she couldn't count them." She said that she had persuaded "her lover, the evil spirit" to kill her master's cow when he had made her angry, but she insisted that she herself had never given in to the Devil's blandishments to "harm people or animals," and that "despite her relationship to Satan" and his protests and even blows, she "often attended church, sermons, and the holy sacraments." In their response to the magistrates' report the High Council instructed them to examine her again about whether she had harmed anyone, but she must have stuck to her story because that seems to have been the end of the trial.[182]

Maria and Apolonia's accounts correspond with each other and those from other parts of Europe in important ways, and they have some significant differences as well. To begin with, Maria explicitly stated that she woke up before traveling to the "night dance" while Apolonia does not specify whether she thought she was asleep or awake. The *benandanti* experienced "an almost dream-like" state which they entered in a state of "profound prostration, or catalepsy" quite distinct from normal sleep; one Sicilian *donna di fuora* spoke of her travels "taking place in a dream" but said that these experiences could occur "without going to sleep;" the Hungarians were seen to be "lying in a trance" rather than simply asleep.[183] Maria said that she was woken up at the beginning of her journey by the "Evil Spirit" while the *benandanti* were summoned by "a man," sometimes "with a drum" which presumably only they could hear; the Sicilian *donna* said her company "called her out;" and the Hungarian victims of witch abductions naturally reported being roused by the witches. Apolonia, in contrast, attributed the initiation of only her first experience to an external agency; after that she does not mention receiving any prompting. Once on her way, Apolonia seemed to be flying high and far, which some Hungarians and Sicilians also did, while Maria, felt that she traveled rapidly but close to the ground, which was also commonly reported in Hungary and other parts of Europe.[184] The *benandanti*, in contrast, do not seem to have paid so much attention to the journey by which they got to their destination; their descriptions tend to jump from summoning to the meeting place without much detail about the transition from the one to the other.[185] They, like all of the others, reported riding on animals during their journeys at least some of the time, though, and while the *benandanti* are best known for traveling to combat evil witches to determine the fate of the harvest (or in the case of female *benandanti*, to communicate with the dead), they also reported their meetings involved revelry as well.[186] The *donna di fuora* similarly mixed business and pleasure in their travels, for they traveled both to take part in festivities and to intervene on behalf of people made ill by the fairies.[187] The abducted Hungarians were generally forced to participate in the witches' revelry, while the two women from Württemberg voluntarily flew only to take part in festivities; neither reported engaging in or learning any sort of instrumental magic.[188]

In addition to their similarities and differences with experiences reported elsewhere in Europe, the two women's reports also have similarities and differences with the Sabbaths in the demonological literature. Apolonia's differed mainly in that, while she did have sex with the Devil, she did not note any unusual coldness, she did not mention that this was part of an orgy, and she did not gain any magical powers from the experience (significantly, her threat to cause harm involved arson rather than any sort of magical measures). Maria's report, which was the earlier one by half a century, diverged even more markedly: she called her first experience a "night dance" and distinguished it and the two "meals" she attended from the "witch dances" she also said she had participated in. At the night dance the only thing that she implied took place was dancing, and, similarly, at the two feasts the only things she spoke of were the "meat the [female] cook gave to eat," the wine "one drank from glasses," and that "she had played." She gave no details, in contrast, about how she got to or what she did at the "witch dances," which raises the question of whether she experienced them at all, or just said she did to satisfy her interrogators, particularly since she changed her story from saying that she had attended four to saying that she had attended "so many she couldn't count them."

In any case, though, what is important here is that both Apolonia's and at least some of Maria's reports seem to reflect their actual nocturnal experiences. The content, and perhaps the onset, of their dreams were clearly influenced by the demonological ideas about witchcraft that spread in the area in the seventeenth century, but the dream states in which their travels took place sound similar to those reported in other parts of Europe that were entered into prior to and independently of the spread of demonology. Given that ideas about magical flights of various sorts had existed, as we have seen, in the region for centuries, Apolonia and Maria's reported experiences would appear to have manifested long-standing local traditions of magical flight and mystical gatherings mixed with more recent imports from the pan-European witch demonology (which itself, of course, was an amalgamation of local traditions, including those of southwestern Germany, with an admixture of Christian theology).

One important feature in the cases from Württemberg is that neither Apolonia nor Maria made it clear whether they felt that they flew bodily or only in spirit. Whether all flights to the Sabbath took place in spirit only or some happened physically was a question that was hotly debated in the demonological literature at the time, and reports by confessed witches differed as well.[189] The *Canon Episcopi* insisted that women who thought that they flew at night with Diana were victims of illusion, which for centuries was the basis for a more general position of the Church that magic is illusory, but the *Malleus Maleficarum* argued that this did not mean bodily transportation could not happen sometimes, and other late Medieval demonologists similarly insisted that some witches flew to Sabbaths physically. To bolster its argument, the *Malleus* cited the testimony of one night-flying witch who claimed that both methods were practiced.[190] Hungarian abductions were usually understood to be in spirit but sometimes were described "as concrete physical acts."[191] Similarly, the *benandanti* mostly claimed to travel in spirit only, but there was at least one case in which a woman not only said people could travel either way, but claimed that she herself "always went ... physically."[192] The Sicilian *donnas*, in contrast, appear to have traveled in spirit only.[193] Perhaps, however, Apolonia and Maria did not know which way they had traveled, and did not care. While ordinary people seem to have been generally as aware as scholars that many of the people who experienced fantastic flight did so in fantasy because their bodies were observed at home in bed, the issue seems to have been less important for them than for theologians and officials, for whom it was important to establish that the Devil's conspiracy existed as a physical reality. For the participants, the important thing was the experiences themselves, and so it is often "impossible to determine precisely who interpreted a given narrative in what way."[194]

The question is important, however, for more than just establishing the comparability of the Württemberg cases with learned notions and popular experiences in other parts of Europe at the time, for in many ways Apolonia and Maria's experiences are reminiscent of what are currently called "out of body experiences," which have a rich history and have been the subject of considerable scientific inquiry over the past century.[195] The very term "out-of-body experience" suggests that experients perceive that they have left their bodies and many modern people indeed report "seeing" their own body during the experience.[196] Many others don't, however, and report merely that they felt "exteriorized."[197] Still others report that they feel as if their body is floating in space, and others "have vivid and realistic images of distant places without feeling exteriorized."[198] Some, like Apolonia and Maria, "have the feeling of traveling" to this "distant location."[199] As we shall see, there may be some differences in the underlying physiology that account for these different sensations, or the differences could reflect some combination of cultural and personal factors, but there is good reason to regard them all, including Apolonia and Maria's experiences, as "basically similar experiences."

Scientific studies of "out-of-body experiences" (OBE) stand at the juncture of psychology and parapsychology. For a long time researchers were preoccupied with the issue of whether something actually leaves the body, with the implication that it is a discrete experience of considerable metaphysical importance (the parapsychological position), or whether the experience is all in the head, with the implication that it is a psychophysical dysfunction secondary to some other, more reputable pathology (the psychological point of view). Recently, however, parapsychologists have moved to a more agnostic, phenomenological point of view (whatever the physical reality, people really have the experience, which makes it worthy of investigation in any case), while psychologists have begun to recognize that, whatever the physical reality, a significant portion of the population in modern Western countries have the experience and it is known to virtually every culture in the world, which makes it worthy of investigation in and of itself, and not just as a secondary feature of some psychopathology.[200] This convergence has begun to establish what OBEs are and, in the process and just as importantly, have come a long way in establishing what they are not.

To begin with what OBEs are not, they are not, as psychology traditionally assumed, a form of pathology, either symptomatic of some other pathology like schizophrenia or a pathological syndrome in themselves.[201] Nor are they manifestations of some form of personality disorder; personality tests have found that they are not associated, as has been suggested, with depersonalization, frustration concerning lack of self-worth or power, or a morbid need to "prove" the existence of the soul to overcome a fear of death.[202]

Neither, on the other hand, are OBEs cultural artifacts, simply stories people tell or scripts they enact. Cultural expectations can play a role in promoting or discouraging OBEs and they do influence the content of experiences; but the ubiquity of OBEs across cultures, the fact that people who do not believe in them or expect them to happen or even know that they could happen experience them nonetheless, and, as we shall see, the way they seem to be generated physiologically all indicate that OBEs are primarily artifacts of the way our brains operate, and only secondarily elements of culture. Because OBEs happen to people who exist within cultures, they have symbolic meanings as part of the system of symbols that make up culture, and those meanings can influence how often people experience them and what they experience during them, but at the bottom "out-of-body experiences" do not exist because they fit into some matrix of meaning. Instead, cultures weave them into their matrix of meanings because they exist.[203]

Another set of things that OBEs have proved not to be is forms of other experiences. To begin with, OBEs are not the same as regular dreams. A small number of the regular dreams that people report involve flying, but these are not the same as OBEs.[204] Most OBEs happen to modern people when they are resting but not asleep; sometimes they happen when people are immersed in frenetic activity; people undergoing them while sleeping do not exhibit REM; and "there are certain qualitative characteristics by which experients themselves confidently distinguish their OBEs from dreams."[205] Further, while many OBEs occur during the hypnogogic state, they are not the same as the hallucinatory images that characterize that state. Hypnogogic images are generally "bizarre, disconnected, inclined to rapid and frequent change, devoid of images of oneself, [and] little open to conscious manipulation," while "the OBE features completeness and continuity of awareness at least comparable to the waking state of consciousness" making them seem to experients "more real than a dream."[206] Finally, OBEs are not the same as autoscopy, the experience of being suddenly confronted with oneself "face-to-face" as an external being, or sleep paralysis. OBEs can occur during episodes of sleep paralysis, but researchers have found that they constitute "distinctive factors" from the fearful sense of bodily constriction and menacing presence more typical of sleep paralysis.[207]

What OBEs are, then, is a distinct form of experience in a discrete state of consciousness characterized by sensations of detachment from the body or floating in space and perceptions from an extracorporeal, elevated point of view.[208] They are experienced as distinct and more real than dreams and other fantasy mentation, they often include the visualization of the experient's own body, and they may include vivid, sustained, and coherent sensations and perceptions of traveling far and fast effortlessly, presence at apparently distant locales, and participation there in encounters and events.[209]

They are more often felt as beneficial than harmful, and some people attribute to them "a new perspective" on life, "positive attitudinal changes," and "imaginative and unexpected solutions" to their problems.[210]

While OBEs are not associated with any particular personality types, they are associated with certain cognitive attributes, in particular intraception (attentiveness to one's own mental processes), somatic dissociation, fantasy-proneness, suggestibility, and a propensity for lucid dreams (dreams in which the dreamer becomes aware of the fact that he or she is dreaming).[211] In some people, at least, they appear to be related to traumatic experiences in childhood, probably because children who experience trauma often cope by learning to disassociate themselves from their surroundings. They can be connected to epilepsy and migraine headaches, and may be more likely to occur during periods of personal upheaval or distress.[212]

An OBE can occur spontaneously or be induced deliberately, but "fundamental to the occurrence" is an "extreme" level of "cortical arousal," which can be either "very high or very low."[213] Thus, sometimes OBEs are triggered by situations of extreme danger or stress or amidst frenzied activity, but more often they begin in states of repose like the hypnogogic state or sleep. Whichever way they start, though, recent cognitive and neurological studies suggest that they involve disruption of the normal "integration of proprioceptive, tactile, and visual information of one's body (personal space)" that normally takes place at "the temporo-parietal junction" in the brain.[214] This can happen because, as we have seen, brain functioning involves parallel processing by separate specialized neural networks, whose results are then integrated at steadily higher levels, so that discrete sensory inputs are gradually integrated with each other and with emotional and cognitive inputs to create an awareness and assessment of the person's current condition and situation.[215] If any of the parallel neural networks are damaged or the process of integration is disrupted, the person's perceptions, understanding, and feelings about the world can be affected, as in the condition prosopagnosia, in which a person loses the ability to consciously recognize familiar faces but continues to evince the associated emotional response, and the converse affliction, in which a person can recognize faces but does not feel any corresponding emotion. In the latter case, the brain may not only fail to make the normal association, but also may create a rationalization for the disjunction, concluding that the other person, their spouse perhaps, is actually an impostor. In the case of OEBs, the disruption appears to take place at the temporo-parietal junction because the parietal lobes of the cerebral cortex focus "especially on touch sensations, body and joint orientation, and space-location relationships," the temporal lobes specialize in "hearing, smell, taste, language and music perception ... higher visual processing ... and memory," and the temporo-parietal junction therefore plays a "key role" in the "integration of multi-sensory bodily information, the visual perception of the body, the perception of biological motion, and the distinction between self and other."[216] Epileptic seizures, which can produce OBEs, involve electrical "storms" in this region, and deliberate electrical stimulation of the area has also been found to produce OBEs.[217] Thus, what is experienced phenomenologically as a dissociation of the self from the body and has been posited to be a form of psychological or cognitive dissociation appears to be literally a form of neurological dissociation, the accidental or deliberate failure to integrate normally bodily processing, self-processing, and visual processing.[218]

Neurological studies suggest OBEs in which there is a conscious sense of exteriorization and flight experiences, like those reported by Apolonia and Maria, are closely related although subtly distinct. In recent experimental studies, "vestibular illusions (of elevation, rotation, flying, lightness) and multisensory illusions ... could be evoked by electrical stimulation of the same cortical area where higher stimulation currents induced out-of-body experiences," suggesting that they "share similar functional and anatomical mechanisms."[219] Of course, the lack of reference to exteriorization in Apolonia and Maria's cases could simply reflect a lack of concern about the issue on their parts either during their experiences or in reporting on them, or it could stem from a lack of concern on the parts of the magistrates interrogating them and recording their stories, in either case reflecting the participants' different personal and/or cultural concerns, but on balance the evidence suggests that what Apolonia and Maria experienced were a variant form of OBE in which they had the sensation of floating and perceived themselves to fly to a remote location to participate in various activities there but did not experience the full sense of disembodiment that gives "out-of-body experiences" their name. Despite the discrepancy, though, the close resemblance of their experiences to OBEs both phenomenologically and, apparently, physiologically suggests that they should be considered a particular form of the more general phenomenon.

Connecting Apolonia and Maria's experiences to the general phenomenon of OBEs gives us a much richer appreciation of what was probably going on in their heads when they "flew all over the countryside as far as Turkey" and "attended a night dance." To begin with, knowing that OBEs are not uncommon, and are more frequent in some cultural settings than others, makes it seem more likely that their accounts were, in fact, based on their actual experiences than the traditional historical presumption of suggestive questioning or compulsive confessing would suggest.[220] Secondly, an understanding of OBEs indicates that their experiences were not evidence of pathological disorders, either organic or psychogenic. On the other hand, neither were they simply cultural artifacts, experiences manufactured to order by cultural expectations. The expectation that they could happen may have influenced the women's experiences, and expectations about what they would involve most certainly did, but the experiences themselves could only happen, and were distinct from other experiences like ordinary dreams, hypnogogic hallucinations, and sleep paralysis, because of the neurobiological processes underlying this particular form of dissociation. Apolonia and Maria's experiences indicate that some ordinary villagers in early modern Württemberg, like some otherwise ordinary people in Southern and Eastern Europe, and most likely all across Europe, entered a distinct state of consciousness in which they perceived themselves to fly to distant locations and participate in extraordinary activities.

The fact that beliefs in such flights were talked about in the region long before the diffusion of the witch demonology (and, indeed, contributed to it) suggests that such experiences continued a deeply rooted tradition rather than being the recent importation of some foreign ideology. However, the two women's stories do suggest that the diffusion of the demonology had an effect on what people experienced during OBEs. In 1622, Maria talked first of going to a "night dance" and then of two feasts held in a house and presided over by a female cook, and only mentioned going to "witch dances" after that, and without elaboration or details. Furthermore, while she spoke of being woken up by the "evil spirit" and magically traveling on a goat, she did not describe any diabolical ceremonies, sexual activity, or magical initiation. She also made it clear that, while the Devil came on strong to her, she was fully capable of fending him off and only involved herself in things she wanted to be part of. Fifty-five years later, in 1667, Apolonia spoke of going on a soaring flight "as far as Turkey," and seems to have assumed that her experience was a witch dance, and her description of the dance was more composite and stereotypical, including food, interactions with the others (Maria seems to have only played by herself at the feasts), and sex. Furthermore, Apolonia's relation to the Devil was more conventionally subordinate than Maria's. While it is not possible to draw any strong conclusions about change over time from just these two cases, the differences between them suggest that the witch demonology did influence Württembergers' expectations, and through them their experience, of the flight and festivities that could take place.

Not only can research on OBEs inform our understanding of early modern flight experiences, but research on early modern flight experiences can inform our understanding of OBEs. In particular, it highlights the impact that culture can have not only on the content but on the contours of the experiences.[221] To begin with, psychological research has found that most modern Westerners' OBEs are relatively short in duration, lasting between one and five minutes generally, while Maria said that her "night dance" lasted for three hours, from about 11 PM until about 2 AM, and observers who saw the bodies of people other early modern people who claimed to have flown to dances said that they were unconscious for hours.[222] Perhaps related is the fact that modern people tend to experience OBEs in a drowsy, hypnogogic state in which they are neither fully awake nor fully asleep, while early moderns reportedly entered a deep trance state in which they were thoroughly unconscious and virtually impossible to rouse. Also probably related is that most modern OBEs seem to involve short excursions to the corner of the ceiling or down the hall, whereas early modern people seem to have more commonly experienced flights to neighboring houses, the surrounding countryside, and points beyond. And, finally, early modern Württembergers, like early moderns elsewhere, seem to have participated in elaborate and relatively standardized activities once they reached their destination, whereas modern reports appear to be less involved and generally more idiosyncratic when elaborate. All of these differences would seem to reflect the fact that going into the early modern period, OBEs were supported by a collective belief in their normality, reality, and significance, and by a long and evolved cultural tradition of what they would involve, whereas in the centuries since the Enlightenment OBEs have been regarded as aberrant illusions, unimportant at best and pathological at worst. While numerous cultural scripts have been preserved in fairy tales and myths, these are diluted with literary elements unrelated to actual traditions of experience and are undercut by the general belief that they are merely imaginary. As a consequence, modern people, it would seem, often cut these experiences short rather than prolonging them, and they do not have any idea that anything of consequence can come from them.

Scopolamine dreams

Maria's OBEs appear to have occurred spontaneously, as a form of sudden false awakenings during sleep somewhat like entering lucid dreams. Like a lucid dreamer, Maria had the feeling of entering waking consciousness while still asleep, but instead of realizing that she was still dreaming and steering the subsequent dream experience, she understood her subsequent dreams to be physically real events experienced while awake.[223] Apolonia, in contrast, did not convey a clear idea of what occurred when "her prince" came to carry "her out," or, later, how "she and her husband" got started when they "traveled on a pitchfork, then on a cat," to their merry festivities. She did say that she "had learned this witchcraft from a butcher ... in Reütlingen" who was presumably one of the "people" there she consorted with who had been "burned for magic," and when asked she said that she kept a salve "in a trough." However, as the magistrates reported, the "impartial men" who went to look for it could not find anything, and so it remains unclear exactly what triggered Apolonia's nocturnal flights.

The magistrates asked Apolonia about the salve because the idea that witches smeared themselves and/or a stick with an ointment to fly to their Sabbaths was by the mid-seventeenth century a standard feature of the witch ideology. Both demonologists like Nider and Bodin and skeptics like Laguna and Della Porta claimed they or people they knew had observed people anoint themselves with witches' ointments, fall into a deep sleep, and awaken convinced that they had flown away and enjoyed all manner of marvelous pleasures, and such stories influenced local writers like August Lerchheimer and Abraham Saur.[224] However, the searchers' inability to find a salve was not unusual. In most cases, it was officials rather than suspects who brought up the salves, and they tended to confirm their suspicions through torture rather than an attempt to actually find the ointment.[225] Not infrequently, suspects said that they had thrown the container away.[226] When officials actually got their hands on tubs full of grease, they often decided that they were inert, and in some instances suspects admitted that they had confessed to having and had even concocted bogus salves in order to satisfy their interrogators.[227] These problems, plus evidence that many experiences like those of the *benandanti* did not involve drug use, have led many recent historians to downplay the significance of hallucinogenic drugs in early modern witchcraft to the point of denying that they played any significant role or even were used at all.[228]

Despite the examples of coerced testimony and dubious evidence, there is nevertheless strong evidence from the general European record and from specific cases in Württemberg that some early modern people did use "witch salves," that these and other such preparations could have a profound effect on their cognitive processes, and that they played an important role in early modern witchcraft.[229] The "use of salves, greases, lotions, and unguents" for medicinal purposes was "widespread" in "folk pharmacopoeia" at the time, and the psychoactive plants that most of the recipes given in the literature listed as ingredients – nightshade, henbane, mandrake, and thorn apple, all members of the *Solanaceae* family – were all well known, readily available, and used for a variety of more mundane purposes.[230] Nightshade was a four and a half foot high perennial native to northern Europe with distinctive flowers and berries that got its nickname "belladonna" from the fact that some Italian ladies put a few drops of juice from its berries in their eyes to dilate their pupils in order to make themselves more attractive, and got its ominous reputation from the fact that in large doses it was a deadly poison.[231] It was apparently common enough in Württemberg that in 1667, after an accidental poisoning, the government issued a "Decree Concerning the Partaking and Propagation of Nightshade" instructing that the people be "warned against the consumption" of it "and its eradication ordered."[232] Henbane was also native to northern Europe and, while only an annual or biennial, grew around three and a half feet high, had prominent yellow flowers, and gave off a "rank odor." It could "easily" be found "along trails and in the neighborhood of human settlements" and was offered for sale as well since it was widely used as a sedative and was added to beer to make it stronger. In fact, just as Coke originally contained coca leaves, "pilsner" beer originally contained henbane – *Bilsenkraut* – as part of its standard recipe, and the famous Bavarian "purity law" regulating the ingredients of beer has been called the first antidrug law since one of its purposes was to counter the common practice of adding henbane and other psychoactive adulterants to supplement the alcohol in beer (it is sobering to consider how many late Medieval people must have gone around in a state of not only alcohol intoxication, since beer and wine were routinely consumed throughout the day, but also low-level intoxication from hallucinogens in various adulterants as well).[233] Mandrake was not native to northern Europe, but was widely available from peddlers because it was used as an anesthetic as well as sedative, was added to wine to make a person "light-hearted and pleasant" (though it also induced "fantasies and images in the thoughts and mind"), and, because the roots look somewhat like little people, it had a wide range of uses in sympathetic magic.[234] Thorn apple was a more recent immigrant from southeastern Europe, but spread into the wild from the herb gardens where it was first cultivated, and was valued as an aphrodisiac.[235]

The fact that these plants were commonly available and their psychotropic effects were well known and exploited in more mundane ways makes their employment in hallucinogenic salves seem less improbable than consideration of their role in the demonological literature alone. Furthermore, the skeptical claim that none of the accounts in the literature "even pretends to come from an eyewitness" is, at best, based on a very circumscribed sample, and the argument that all such eyewitness accounts are simply literary borrowings traceable to Apuleius because "Renaissance intellectuals ... spent their days cribbing stories like this from one another's books" seems untenable given the wide variations in the accounts and the unique veridical details some of them contain.[236] Some writers openly recounted stories taken from others, as von Kaisersberg drew on Nider and was in turn cited by Luther, and some undoubtedly modeled their accounts on others, as Della Porta may have "used a model from ancient tradition," Apuleius' description of Pamphilë's transformation into a bird in *The Golden Ass*, "to report his experience ... that there actually were old sorceresses who anointed themselves with salves prepared from plants, and who then imagined that they flew through the forest by night." But contrasting three of the best known accounts, those of the demonologist Johann Nider and the skeptical physicians Andrés de Laguna and Giambattista Della Porta, shows that each differs substantially from the others and from their supposed classical source.[237] For example, Nider and Della Porta said their "witches" agreed to anoint themselves, while de Laguna said he got the unguent from the house of some suspects and used it on a patient suffering from insomnia; Apuleius' witch was observed unwittingly. Nider's subject sat in a large mixing bowl on a bench, while Della Porta's (like Apuleius') seems to have stood, and then fallen down (Apuleius' sprouted feathers and flew away). De Laguna described how his patient's eyes opened "wide like a rabbit, and soon ... looked like those of a cooked hare" before she fell asleep, a detail consistent with the drugs' effects but far beyond the beautifying effect for which it was generally known, and one that was not mentioned in the other reports, whose subjects fell asleep "at once." Della Porta and de

Laguna's subjects slept so deeply that they could not be woken up even when beaten, while Nider's thrashed about in her sleep and woke up when she fell off the bench she was seated on. Other, less well-known accounts diverge even more, like one about a woman from Strasburg who claimed to have been out eating and drinking with the very priest to whom she was demonstrating her arts, not flying to her lover or over the countryside, as in Apuleius or the famous demonologies.[238] A German pamphlet from 1580 reported that a woman described the "blue flowers and fruit" of one "Devil's weed" she used, and the "yellow leaves" of another, which match the appearance of nightshade and henbane.[239] Differences in ingredients, proportions, and, ultimately, knowledge and experiences would account for these divergences and details; literary imitation does not.

In addition to the demonological accounts and pamphlet literature, actual trial "records show that some of the accusations concerning pharmaceutical dabblings were based on fact."[240] In one case, a woman in Hesse testified in 1596 that "she and her companions" used a salve that included "tansy, hellebore, [and] ginger" which they rubbed on their feet. "Tansy (*Chrysanthemum vulgare*) contains an alkaloid" that can "cause paralysis and loss of consciousness" while "black hellebore (*Helleborus niger*)" is "a narcotic ranunculaceous plant" containing "two glucosides, helleboreine and hellebrine, which are similar to telocinobufagine, a skin-gland venom of the toad," a chemical similar to the active ingredients in henbane and nightshade (significantly, toads were also mentioned in some recipes, and some witch suspects were reported to keep, or found to keep, toads).[241] In another instance, in 1651, one woman said another gave her "bitter almonds," some of which "she was to eat" and "others she was to chew and spit out on a cloth" and "rub herself with." After doing this, the woman became "sick," experienced "seizures," and felt "as if asleep." Based on the symptoms, the 'bitter almonds'" would appear to have been "nightshade berries."[242]

This latter case appears somewhat reminiscent of the sampled case from Württemberg discussed in Chapter 1 in which Barbara Schmied was suspected of poisoning Johanna Fehlen on her wedding day.[243] In that instance, as Johanna finished drinking a glass of wine Barbara had gotten her from the kitchen, she noticed that there was "a white residue from a powder or herb" at the bottom of it. Shortly thereafter, she felt as if "everything in her whole body (as she put it) was turned around, and as she went home, could no longer stand up, but felt completely lame, and in her head became so confused that she no longer knew where she was." Johanna's symptoms may have manifested wedding-day jitters as much as anything, but there seems to have been no question that something was in her drink, and that Barbara had put it there. In the end, no trial ensued because Johanna felt that Barbara had meant well and intended the additive to be beneficial. What it was, and whether it was supposed to act as an aphrodisiac, a tranquilizer, or simply reinforcement to the alcohol we cannot know.

There were several other cases in Württemberg in which people ingested substances given by others and then felt or acted strangely that suggest somewhat more strongly that psychoactive drugs were known and used at the time. In 1623, for example, Gerg Geiler, a miller from Heidenheim charged with adultery, claimed that his partner, an elderly woman, had drugged him.[244] In another case, in 1685 a 16-year-old servant girl named Anna Maria Rippen in Bietigheim described how she had been given something "in a glass of wine" that gave her stomach pains so severe that she had to lie down, and which were followed by a series of strange experiences that she was not sure were real or a dream.[245] The magistrates called her story an "example of how simple women and girls are led astray into witchcraft." The sampled case we have seen in which Anna Serrin gave her neighbor Anna Maria the piece of bread that caused her to be "driven from inside to hop and jump bizarrely," and, less probably, the one in which Susanna Catharina, sister-in-law of the preacher Johannes Brand , said that Maria Laichlin gave her a piece of bread that caused her heart to pound, her limbs to become weak and eventually lame, and her to experience uncontrollable movements and hallucinations, may also have been attempted initiations, although we cannot know precisely what was intended.[246]

A clearer case took place in the village of Vöhringen near Rosenfeld in 1663, however. It began when "two unmarried women" found a 14- or 15-year-old servant girl named Margaretha "in a field in Haberösch" acting "completely crazy and wild, as if out of her senses."[247] Asked about it "after she dragged herself back to the village," she blamed "a servant girl ... named Magdelena" Schmid, who was "around 16 years old" and was the daughter of a Swiss immigrant who had died around 12 years before. The two girls, "with two others," had gone to a strawberry patch, and Magdelena "gave her, like the other two, although without her asking, a peculiar piece of bread from a sack to eat." After she ate it, she felt "as if she had swallowed a stone," things "swirled around," and "both her hands were completely lame and the fingers ... cramped." When Magdelena was brought in, Margaretha "accused her of being a witch," saying "that she had revealed to her that she could transform herself into a calf, and insisted that she ... should travel with her to the Heuberg."

Magdelena initially protested her innocence, saying Margaretha "must have only eaten something" bad, which "happened to her ... the same day," since she had seen "a spider crawl out of the sack, which made her sick." However, from the beginning she did "not particularly deny the calf and travel to the Heuberg," and, after agreeing to help Margaretha get better, she slipped away and was caught trying to flee to "the next village, where she had grown up." Once in custody in Rosenfeld, she "contradicted herself" when questioned, and "after a good long talking to, tearfully ... acknowledged ... that approximately five years earlier she had been led astray by Leonberger Hansen's deceased wife." She had "traveled with her to witch dances" near Sulz and on "the Heuberg," given herself to "the Devil," and "under pressure of the loathsome Devil brought harm to the injured Margaretha by using "as she had learned from her mistress, Leonberger Hansen's wife, two small grains she had given her, along with many others" to make "a peculiar piece of bread."

Considering Margaretha's symptoms and Magdelena's description of how she prepared the bread, it seems most likely that the special grains she put in it contained ergot (*Claviceps purpurea*), the fungus that, as we saw in Chapter 1, grows on grain and contains varying amounts of several lysergic acid alkaloids related to LSD.[248] These would account for Margaretha's sensation that things "swirled around" and that later she seemed to the two women who found her "completely crazy and wild, as if out of her senses," for they "can cause short-term or lasting psychosis, as well as other mental disturbances such as panic attacks, illusions, hallucinations, and frightening dreams."[249] The fungus also contains "alkaloids of the peptide type," which are known to produce constriction of peripheral vessels, would account for the fact that "both her hands were completely lame and the fingers ... cramped."[250] She may have gotten a stomachache, which is not typical of ergotism, because of some other contaminant in the bread, but it is also quite possible that it resulted from normal anxiety, amplified by the effects of the hallucinogens when she realized that she had eaten something "peculiar."

The government referred to the incident as a "magical poisoning" and the Tübingen law faculty recommended that Magdelena be executed "for the misdeeds she committed and acknowledged," but their focus was on the harm she caused Margaretha and her overall involvement with the Devil rather than determining why, exactly, she had given the other girl the bread, and what, exactly, the teenagers had gone to the strawberry patch to do. It is possible, of course, that they simply went there to pick strawberries or just while away the time, and Magdelena maliciously gave Margaretha alone some tainted bread because of some unstated animosity in order to injure her. However, the fact that instead of expressing any animosity, Magdelena had "insisted that" Margaretha "should travel with her to the Heuberg" suggests that she gave her the bread not to harm her but to start her on the journey. Furthermore, the fact that Magdelena also gave a piece of bread to at least one other girl who accompanied them to the strawberry patch at her request, and appears to have eaten one herself, suggests that they went to the patch with the intention of ingesting "peculiar" bread and Magdelena intended to initiate Margaretha into the practice without telling her. Margaretha, however, reacted badly to the surprise, with unpleasant consequences for her and fatal consequences for Magdelena.

Is it credible to suggest that a group of teenagers snuck off to a strawberry patch in the early summer of 1663 to eat ergot-laced bread in order to experience an LSD-like trip? There is no question that ergot was known and used in early modern Europe, for it was not hard to recognize and midwives employed it "medicinally ... as an aid in cases of difficult parturition throughout Europe in the Middle Ages," presumably because of its paroxysmal effect "on involuntary muscles" and its "ability to control post-partum hemorrhage" (it was also "widely used as an aborting agent").[251] Of course, ergot would be risky to use as an hallucinogen, for, depending on the concentrations of different alkaloids in it, which can vary greatly, it can cause "gangrenous ergotism ... leading to mummification and even to loss of the extremities" rather than "convulsive ergotism" which brings only "convulsions ... epilepiform states, delirium and hallucinations," but modern people in search of intoxication have been known to run great risks, like creating alcoholic drinks from industrial alcohol, which can cause blindness, or inhaling glue, paint thinner, and even gasoline, which cause severe neurological damage, so the risks of gangrenous ergotism cannot prima facie rule out the possibility. According to Ginzburg, a "wealth of mythical associations ... point to an ancient awareness of the potency of the plant" that could be tapped to "obtain states of loss or alteration of consciousness," and Gordon Wasson has hypothesized that it was "used to prepare the secret, allegedly hallucinogenic potion that played a fundamental role in the Mysteries of Eleusis in the Greece of antiquity."[252] More recently, "a late 17th century manuscript by district governor H. H. Lilienskiold" in Finnmark, northern Norway, has been found that provides other direct evidence of witch trials that involved ergotism, and in about a third of them the suspects testified explicitly that "witchcraft was 'learned' by consuming ... bread or other flour products ... milk or beer, or in a combination."[253] While many of the cases may have reflected accidental poisoning and suspects' testimony was coerced, "in several of the ... records, the wording may suggest that the witches were well aware of the effect of ergot." Since "entire groups of youngsters" in southern Germany "were implicated" in the early eighteenth century in "widespread abuse of pharmacopoeia, with its quack and black-magic lotions, lubricants, and powders," it is certainly plausible that Magdelena gave Margaretha the "peculiar" piece of bread not to poison her but to launch her on the trip she had said she wanted to take "with her to the Heuberg."[254]

Magdelena's case shows that one hallucinogen, ergot, was known and deliberately used, several others from Württemberg provide additional evidence of the intentional use of hallucinogens by people to deliberately alter their own state of consciousness. The first case was the investigation of Margaretha Wagner, the girl from Marbach in 1740 who, as we saw in Chapter 1, claimed to have "pressed" people at night. Her case changed from an investigation of illicit sex into one into magic because one of the young men she implicated as a partner protested that the cause "of the delinquency ... was her magical practices," which she "herself acknowledged."[255] She volunteered that she had learned love magic and other occult arts from her grandmother, with whom she had lived, "and denied that these were a fantasy or a dream." Among these arts was how to "ascend" by smearing a pitchfork or shovel with a salve. She added that to make it work best, "you also smear the temples and the veins of the hands," and described feeling "as if she sat in a wagon and her feet just scraped over the ground." When the magistrates searched her aunt's house, where she now lived, they "found a little tub with something like a salve in the corner by the oven," but they do not seem to have tested it. Furthermore, Margaretha later changed her testimony, saying she had "learned such only from hearsay, and indeed partly from a beggar girl, and partly ... where commonly such godless and superstitious things are brought up and discussed," so it may well have been based on what she heard others talk about rather than what she herself had experienced.[256] Nevertheless, the details about smearing the temples and the veins of the hand as well as the handle, and her non-stereotypical description of the sensations that resulted (elsewhere she said that she traveled "quick as the wind" but "not higher above the ground than a table, completely straight ahead") suggest, as we shall see, that if not she than someone she had overheard was familiar with the use as well as the effects of hallucinogenic salves.[257]

If the source of Margaretha's knowledge remains somewhat obscure, the second case presents clear first-hand evidence of deliberate use of hallucinogenic salves. It began about midday on January 6, the first Wednesday after New Year in 1631, when the surprised magistrates of Lauffen found young Hanß Jacob Langen locked up in a jail cell. They were surprised because the night before the cell had been empty, and no one knew "who had put him in there."[258] The shiftless son of a poor cobbler, he had been apprenticed to several tradesmen, but had shown himself to be lazy and dissolute, and had run away over a half a year earlier. Under the constable's questioning, he gradually revealed what he had been up to since he left, and what had led him to end up in the jail cell.

While on the road, Hanß Jacob said, he fell in with an itinerant charlatan from Regensburg named Egidins Schneeberger, who appears to have accepted him as a sort of assistant and apprentice for a time.[259] Schneeberger introduced him in turn to three women named Catharin, Margareth, and Lisa. After Hanß Jacob had known them for about two weeks, they asked him "if he wanted to learn the art of traveling on a pitchfork." Hanß Jacob agreed, and they showed him how to "smear ... a shaft ... with an ointment," which he then "sat on." For Hanß Jacob's first trip he "mounted in a beer brewer's house" around "twelve o'clock at night" and traveled with the women to "a beer cellar in Ingolstadt" where they "drank beer without bread" in company with others, "some young, some old."[260] He did not say much more about what happened during this or any of the subsequent trips he took with them, except that the "third time, when he traveled on the pitchfork from Donauworth" at another beer brewer's house, "a barber named Hannß ... opened a vein in his right hand, drew several drops of blood, [and] he had to renounce the Holy Trinity, and sign with his blood in a book, whereupon they promised him they would teach him how to make lice and fleas." He also noted that the barber was brightly dressed, with "red pants and deep blue jacket," and that "the vein ... quickly closed up and healed." He took two more trips thereafter with his companions, but then the charlatan sent Hanß Jacob away.

The young man returned to his hometown, but was afraid to return home and face his father. He had resolved "not to learn a trade," but "had the idea to go to Frankfurt, intending to beg as he went across the countryside." He lingered, though, for about a week. On the night of January 5, a Tuesday, with nowhere else to go, he took refuge under the town hall, "and from there traveled on a rod, which he had cut in Weidach, and smeared with an ointment that some women had given him." The rod took him, along "with several men and 20 women" who he said were "from Neuburg on the Danube ... into the jail cell." There the merry company partied with him, staying "from midnight until four in the morning," and then departed, leaving him asleep and "locked in."

The magistrates found his testimony somewhat "inconsistent" and noted that "it appeared almost impossible, that so many people from such distant places could sit and dance in the cell ... so that one doesn't know if this ... should be regarded as a fantasy or in fact true." They therefore pressed him to admit that "he brought himself into the jail on his own, because he could not go to his father's house, and nobody would take him in, in order to get out of the cold," or that "he was brought there by the women, and then left behind in the morning."[261] He insisted, however, that "no, he had traveled there on a rod" with 5 men and around 20 women and they had danced "until morning." Asked straight out if "it was an illusion, or a drunken dream" he "maintained that it was real and true and had in fact happened."

Pursuing the opposite tack, the magistrates probed to learn if Hanß Jacob was a witch as conventionally defined. They asked if "he had been taught the art of harming people and animals," but he said no, he only knew how to make fleas and lice. He admitted that he would create frost to harm the crops if he could in the coming Spring, but said he didn't yet know how. When asked "if during all this travel, carousing, and dancing a woman was ever offered him," he replied, "no, never." He confessed that he had been given to the Devil his whole life, and said "he considered the Devil to be his friend, and ... often conversed amicably with him," but he denied that he had taken money or any other reward from him. He also denied that the Devil had promised him any special help while he was in jail.

The ducal High Council instructed the constable of Lauffen to keep Hanß Jacob locked up for two or three weeks and have the minister work with him, but while he seemed repentant at first, the longer he was held in custody, the more resistant he became. He asked why they were "doing him the injustice" of keeping him locked up, and, encouraged by his mother, who was bringing him food, he demanded to know "what he was guilty of." He refused to pray with the minister, became "obdurate," and disregarded Sundays.[262] When he did pray, "it did not," in the estimation of the authorities, "come from his heart," and at one point he "said that if he prayed any more, hail would strike him dead." The magistrates examined him again to find the evidence of harm to people or animals, *maleficium*, but he stuck to his story, admitting to his "trips on the rod" and his allegiance to the Devil, but denying having harmed anyone. He said that he wanted to return to God, but the constable wondered "if this is a true, inner, and heartfelt recognition, or merely a pretense," while the minister lamented that "there is little hope for him."[263]

A week later, however, events took a dramatic turn, for Hanß Jacob confessed to the minister, "with tearful eyes, that shortly before Christmas, as he was coming back to Lauffen ... in the woods near Gunzenhausen, about an hour out of Nurnburg ... while drunk, he had murdered ... a twelve-year-old boy."[264] He "first knocked him down with a stick, and then stabbed him in the throat with a knife." Once the boy was dead he dragged his body away from the road and hid it under some leaves. His motive? To steal "a few florins and his hat."

Hanß Jacob confirmed his confession to the constable, while reiterating that he had "renounced God, ridden the rod ... [and] signed himself to the Devil in blood," and admitting that "if he had heretofore prayed ... it did not come from his heart." He also confessed that he had a knife hidden in his cell, "which the Devil advised him to use to kill himself." After a month of deliberation, the government sentenced Hanß Jacob to be severely beaten, banished him from Lauffen for three years, and warned him that if his behavior did not improve, and he gave the slightest indication of falling into his old ways, "he would without fail be disciplined with a stronger punishment to life and limb."[265]

Hanß Jacob's story provides strong evidence that psychoactive ointments were being used to induce hallucinogenic trips in early modern Europe. First of all, it was a direct statement of experiences he had initiated for himself, not something that was done to him or that he did to someone else. Secondly, it was not coerced, or even prompted. Not only was torture not threatened or used, but the magistrates were clearly inclined to see it as an excuse for getting out of the cold or for having used the jailhouse to carouse with a few women, and it was Hanß Jacob who stuck to it long after he had warmed up, and at the same time he was insisting that he should be released. Thirdly, it does not contain the stereotyped description of a witches' Sabbath that would be expected if it were simply drawn from stock elements of the witch demonology. He made no mention of flying to a gathering of devil-worshipping witches during his trips, and his renunciation of the Trinity and signing in blood was made after two flights but before beginning the third. His description of traveling to the beer cellar in Ingolstadt is clearly reminiscent of the folklore of night travelers and witches, who often stopped in to eat and drink on their way home, from a neighbor's stocks, but the complaint about there being no bread would seem to be his own. He admitted he had given himself to the Devil in the metaphorical sense of the pattern of his life and the literal sense of a friendship with him, and even said he had signed in blood in a book and renounced the Trinity, but he denied having received anything from him or having the contractual relationship that was supposed to be at the core of the relationship. He also denied having had sexual relations during any of his trips, another central element of the stereotyped witch beliefs.

The trip Hanß Jacob described in most detail, his last, followed the pattern of "waking delusions" – his "ride" into the cell – "followed by a deep sleep in which dreams on awakening become confused with objective reality" – the party – which is a typical product of "the ingredients in witches' ointments."[266] However, it relates far less to the stereotyped witch experience than to accounts by modern people who have experimented with the plants used in the ointments, generally without any knowledge or expectation of them beyond the fact that they are potent hallucinogens. The background and first part of Hanß Jacob's story, for example, has striking parallels with an account by a young man who used jimsonweed, an American species of *datura* closely related to thorn apple (they are both considered *datura stramonium*, and contain similar hallucinogenic alkaloids), and almost as closely related to the other solenaceous plants:

> When I was 18, I was in a strange place in the world. I was homeless, penniless and with no real ambition to pull myself out of the gutter. Although I was without ... food and shelter, I had ... drugs that were dispensed, I suppose, out of sympathy by many of my friends. ... One evening, ... a guy I barely knew gave me a large freezer bag full of ... Jimson Weed.
>
> I slept in a building gutted by a fire a few years before and the freezing November air woke me ... so I decided it was the right time to open the door of perception ... The heavy sense of inebriation was quickly followed by powerful, disorienting visuals. ... The sense of detachment was strong ... I felt very threatened ... I knew I needed a comfort zone, a place I could relax in. A friend lived nearby. I walked to his apartment complex and stood in front of the stairwell. ... There's a memory gap between the stairs and my friends apartment, but I ended up on his couch.[267]

The second part of Hanß Jacob's account also has significant parallels with another modern experience, this time one with belladonna:

> As the sun set I lay down ... The next thing I know there was a huge party being held in my bedroom. The people were quite nice. It was a real as real gets. Soon everyone left except for an old peasant man in worn work clothes. We chatted for a while. I must have started to come back to my senses, for when I reached over to touch him to see if he was real, I realized I was touching some of my dirty laundry piled on the floor. It was morning by then.[268]

Some (though not all) of the German witch researchers in the nineteenth and twentieth centuries who used hallucinogens listed in early modern salve recipes experienced flight and Sabbaths much like the demonological accounts, which shows that culturally derived expectations can certainly influence such experiences. But Hanß Jacob's and the modern accounts here, which diverge from the demonological stereotype in important ways, yet resemble each other despite the separation of centuries and the lack of cultural continuity, indicate that there is something more going on as well.

Most current historians acknowledge that hallucinogens have some inherent effects on the structure of users' experiences, like inducing a sensation of flight or producing the feeling of growing fur, but downplay their significance relative to the cultural influences on the manifest content of the perceptions.[269] However, flight and shapeshifting play little role in modern accounts of trips on these drugs, except for some of the nineteenth- and twentieth-century German researchers who took them to explore their relationship to witches' experiences.[270] These drugs do have inherent effects, but Hanß Jacob's and modern accounts suggest that they are somewhat different, and are rather more important, than they are usually depicted.

The first characteristic that almost every experient seems to comment on is the utter reality of the hallucinations and dreams that solanaceous hallucinogens produce. Hanß Jacob, as we have seen, insisted that his experiences were not "an illusion, or a drunken dream," but instead were "real and true and in fact happened," and the subjects of the experiments reported in the demonological literature similarly insisted that their experiences were real rather than fantasies.[271] Similarly, the author of the first modern account cited above observed that the "visuals ... seemed as clear as sunlight," while the second similarly noted that "it was as real as real gets." This verisimilitude has been noted before, but there is more to the reality of these experiences than simply the vividness of the visual experience. Modern experients often report initial nausea and disorientation, but then get to a point where, as one reported, "there doesn't seem to be a distinct difference in tripping and not tripping, you feel completely normal, yet you are in serious delirium." Whereas "with most ... drugs ... you are still aware that the plant or chemical are [sic] responsible for the effects," with these, as another modern experient noted, "I was hallucinating very heavily ... [but] it just seemed natural that the world should appear to me in this form."[272] Magdelena Schmid, who gave Margaretha the bread laced with ergot, which, like LSD, is a serontonic rather than anticholinergic drug, reported that her experience of turning into a calf "was nothing other than as if she was sleeping," while the German pharmacologist H. Führner noted after his own experience with the *datura*-based salves, "there can be no doubt that the narcotic witches salves not only deluded their victims, but also enabled them to palpably experience" their hallucinations and dreams, "so that ... they were certain of the reality" of what they had perceived.[273]

The second transcultural feature of the reported drug experiences is the fact the users always seem to populate the imagined world with numerous fully formed images of autonomous intelligences. The demonologists generally reported that their subjects were convinced they had interacted with other people, and, as we have seen, Hanß Jacob said he drank in the beer cellar in Ingolstadt with "some young, some old" people, and partied in the jail in Neuffen with "several men and 20 women." The modern German researchers similarly reported flying to festivities involving other participants, and the contemporary experients describe numerous such encounters. We have seen that one found that there was "a huge party" in his room, "the people were quite nice," and after they left he "chatted for a while" with the "old peasant man in worn work clothes." Another experient said he could "recall seeing and talking to friends ... whom I had not seen in years" and "having direct conversations with people, while hearing other people in the background having totally unrelated conversations."[274] These experiences can take place in drugged dreams, and may be related to the kind of social-emotional processing that goes on in normal dreams, but they can also happen while the person is apparently wide awake; this last experient said his "roommate was awakened a few times by my talking and he heard me open the front door numerous times and say 'Hello' and 'See you later' to people. ... He asked me who all I was talking to, ... said he didn't see anyone, and ... went back to bed." Since the users are absolutely certain they are interacting with people who others in the area cannot perceive, the net effect is to heighten the sense that there are differing dimensions of reality, that a world of spirits, autonomous intelligences that present themselves as physical forms that can be perceived and interacted with by some people but not others, exists in close proximity to the everyday world we normally experience.

The third inherent property of Solanaceae hallucinogens is the length of time for which their effects remain. While dosage naturally plays an important role, in general even a small amount will cause effects that last for several days.[275] Since experients generally are no longer feeling the disorienting and uncomfortable initial effects of the drugs, they may go about their business unaware that they are still substantially under their influence, and the people around them will have no idea anything is going on unless they see or hear them talking with an inanimate object or someone who can't be seen.[276] Furthermore, particularly after repeated use, the drugs can have lingering and even permanent aftereffects of a similar nature, especially if the person periodically ingests low levels as an adulterant to beer or wine, so that the experient gradually slides into a world containing autonomous intelligences only they can perceive and in which extraordinary physical events happen. As Della Porta observed, "they receive such impressions and steadfast imaginations into their minds, as even their spirits are altered thereby; not thinking upon any thing else, either by day or by night."[277]

These apparently inherent effects of the Solenaceae hallucinogens – the reality and perceived normality of the experiences under their influence, their long-lasting action and possible aftereffects, and the fact that they generally involve interaction with autonomous intelligences, are particularly important for understanding the significance of these hallucinogenics in early modern witchcraft because they not only made the specific experiences they involved seem utterly real, but they also powerfully validated entire magical world view. The people who used these drugs could say with complete certainty that it is possible to be transported bodily, that it is possible to get together with people from distant places or who were long dead not just in spirit but in physical reality, that nature is more malleable than it seems ordinarily. In short, culture did not have to suggest that extraordinary things can really happen, for people experienced that for themselves. On the contrary, what culture eventually did, at the end of the early modern period, was to persuade them, at least retrospectively, that what they felt they experienced was not, in fact, real, no matter how real it had felt.

The very realness of the early modern drug experiences, the conviction of at least some of the participants in magical events that they took place in physical rather than some alternate spiritual reality, contributed to both the seriousness with which they were persecuted and, later, to the extent to which they were discredited. The position that magical experiences can occur only in spirit, as the *Episcopi* tradition maintained, kept the focus on the spiritual problems they entailed, while belief in their physical reality made them seem both more urgent and more amenable to secular intervention and correction. Later, the insistence that the events described took place in physical reality set them up to be discredited when observers could see that the experients were not doing what they so vehemently insisted they were doing, a discrediting that contributed significantly to the wider discrediting of magical beliefs generally.

These phenomenological reports convey important insights into activities and beliefs related to witchcraft, but an even deeper understanding can be gained by considering the biochemical and neurological effects of these hallucinogens and the ways that they induce the altered states of consciousness in which the phenomena appear. Of course, the manifest content of hallucinogenic experience are influenced by factors such as the "set," or expectations, of the person having them, and the physical, social, and cultural "setting" in which it takes place.[278] Furthermore, factors such as dosage, method of consumption, interactions among psychoactive agents, and the specific physiology of the person involved also play important roles. However, the specific chemistry of the drugs involved and the way they impact the nervous system play a crucial role in structuring the overall experience and influence its manifest content as well.

Hallucinogenic drugs appear to act through a combination of general and specific effects on the nervous system. The specific effects are the more difficult to isolate, both because of the complexity of the nervous system and because of the interactions of the different chemicals contained in the various ingredients listed in the recipes.[279] Nevertheless, the psychoactive chemicals contained in the plants listed in the recipes are relatively well understood, and some of their specific effects on the nervous system are clearly connected to the specific experiences that result. We will therefore begin by considering the ways that the specific ingredients of the hallucinogenic salves appear to have related to specific elements of the experiences attributed to them, then consider some of the paradoxical effects they seem to have, and finally look at their more general effects, the commonalities of the influence that they and other psychoactive chemicals seems to have on the human nervous system.

As mentioned above, the hallucinogenic plants most commonly included in the early modern recipes were members of the Solonaceae family: belladonna or nightshade (*Atropa belladonna*), henbane (*Hyoscyamus niger*), mandrake (*Nandragora officinarum*), and thorn apple (*Datura strantimonium*).[280] They contain varying amounts of a variety of alkaloids, but the three most important are the anticholinergics hyoscaymine, scopolomine, and atropine.[281] Scopolamine is the most powerful, and atropine the least, but they all act on the nervous system in basically the same way, by mimicking the neurotransmitter acetylcholine and taking its place on nerve-end receptors, thereby preventing them from receiving the neurotransmitter.[282]

Acetylcholine is "utilized by practically every cell in the body for one purpose or another," and cholinergic neurons play an important role in both the central and peripheral nervous systems, but certain roles seem particularly relevant to the experiences associated with anticholinergic drugs.[283] Since acetylcholine is "the basis of skeletal muscle voluntary movement because of its role at the neuromuscular junction," blockage of these peripheral synapses may account for the lack of coordination and bodily torpor produced by the drugs.[284] Anticholinergics also interfere with its role in regulating salvation, heart rate, and dilation of the pupils, which would account for their ability to make Italian women more attractive and de Laguna's patient's eyes open "wide like a rabbit, and soon" look "like those of a cooked hare". Disruption of peripheral nerve transmissions may also be responsible for the sensation of "bodily dissolution" that is often felt, which could contribute to a sensation of flying.[285] However, similar sensations are sometimes caused by LSD and other nonanticholinergic hallucinogens (we have seen, for example, that Magdelena Schmid appears to have used ergot to "fly to the Heuberg"), this effect could also result from its influence on the central nervous system.[286] Or, most probably, it is a combination of both, for "it is ... probable that atropine has separate peripheral and central actions that can lead to the same result."[287]

Turning to the central nervous system, acetylcholine plays a crucial role in it, so the anticholinergic drugs have pronounced specific effects on it as well. In some cases, the relationship between the cholinergic system and the anticholinergics' effects appears to be relatively straightforward. The cholinergic system is involved in "alertness, arousal, and memory functions," contributes to learning, plays "an important role in cognitive processes," inhibits "incorrect responses," and is "intimately involved in attentional processes."[288] Disruption of these functions by anticholinergics would seem to contribute to the lethargy, disorganized thinking, and profound delirium characteristic of anticholinergic intoxication.[289] Paradoxically, though, cholinergic neurons deep in the pons are the usual triggers of REM sleep, and acetylcholine is the dominant neurotransmitter during this phase of sleep, which, as we have seen, is when most dreaming, and particularly most visual dreaming, takes place, yet anticholinergics, instead of inhibiting dreams, are known to "intensify the dream experience" and make them "more vivid and frightening."[290] What causes this paradoxical situation does not seem to be well understood, but it may be related to another paradoxical phenomenon, which is that acetylcholine also works with serotonin to regulate the trophotropic, or parapsympathetic, nervous system, the subset of the autonomic nervous system responsible for our relaxation response.[291] That the same chemical could be responsible for both activation and relaxation in different subsystems of the nervous system could simply be explained as differing functions in different systems, except that the experiences most strongly associated with the salves containing anticholinergics is for the experient to fall into a deep sleep with incredibly vivid dreams, exactly the opposite effect that would be expected from drugs that block the effects of a neurotransmitter that seems to play a predominant role in dreaming and rest.

The resolution of this paradox would seem to come from closer consideration of the known effects of anticholinergic drugs, how they were used, and their relationship to the more general process by which hallucinogens induce altered states of consciousness.

Before looking at these factors, however, the role of expectations and other cultural factors must also be taken into account, since there is no question that they can impact hallucinogenic experiences. First of all, it is clear that these influence their manifest content, for early modern people traveled to beer cellars and country dances, consorted with people who presumably spoke their language and dressed in familiar clothing, and encountered processions of the dead, demons, and the Devil, while modern American experients seem to attend parties that take place in living rooms and involve apparently normal modern Americans, distant friends and dead relatives.[292] It is also possible that expectations can influence the structure of the experience, so that early modern people promptly fell asleep after applying their salves while modern American psychonauts sit around waiting for the trip as if they had just swallowed LSD, which is in many ways our cultural model for hallucinogenic experience.[293]

However, there are clearly some drug effects that are independent of conditioning and expectations, and there are some physiological factors that may also help account for the paradoxical effects of the anticholinergics.[294] For one thing, the fact that they were taken transdermally, via salves absorbed through the skin, would mean that relatively large amounts would have entered the bloodstream quite suddenly compared with oral consumption, which is how modern experients generally report taking them, so there would not have been a period of gradually mounting agitation, but instead a sudden, overwhelming onrush of effects.[295] Significantly, the German researcher Gustav Shenk, who smoked henbane seeds, which is also a relatively quick way of introducing chemicals into the bloodstream, felt himself dissolve and fly away and observed vivid scenes below, but while his ability to move was "greatly curtailed" he "was not peacefully sleeping with limbs relaxed, but in motion" a report reminiscent of the somnambulant flailing of the woman Nider reported on.[296]

Other salves used by other subjects may have suppressed even these types of clumsy movements because the effects of the salves would have manifested not only the biochemistry of the anticholinergics, but also those of other ingredients that have other, albeit milder psychoactive properties. Tansy, for example, which was included in some recipes, can cause "paralysis and loss of consciousness" in large doses, while wild celery, whose seeds have been found to contain seeds contain limonene, "a mild tranquilizer," promotes "restfulness and sleep."[297] The balance of drugs contained in salves may thus have induced, or at least promoted, the soporific effects reported.

However, other ingredients, like parsley and hellebore, actually have stimulative properties, and so the most important chemical factor would seem to be the effects of the main hallucinogens and their relationship to the general nature of altered states of consciousness.[298] First of all, in addition to suppressing the parasympathetic nervous system, anticholinergics, as we have seen, also interfere with voluntary movement of skeletal muscles and often produce nausea and general discomfort, symptoms that would induce the experient to repose and, particularly under the influence of the cultural expectations and possibly other chemicals, fall into a subdued state with only sporadic, uncoordinated motion, as Shenk and Nider's subject did, or a completely supine state in which no overt movement took place even though internally the person was in a high state of arousal, as the women who seemed to fall into a deep sleep even as they were dreaming taking off and flying far and fast. Even modern experients who ingest relatively simple concoctions orally without any particular expectations about how it will affect them appear to become physically torpid even as they experience great mental agitation, and so the combination of the expectations created by their culture, the mix of chemicals in the salves, and the contradictory influences of the anticholinergics themselves would have put early modern users into a state of external inactivity and internal arousal.

This internal state of arousal seems particularly important if we turn to the general effects of hallucinogenic drugs on the nervous system, because it appears to be the critical element leading to the kind of cataleptic trance or alternate state of consciousness (ASC) in which flight and the other reported experiences generally seem to occur.[299] Entering an ASC, it has been observed, is a two-step process, with a "critical moment of flux" or transition between them. Normal consciousness must be disrupted to the point that it "becomes suspended or highly disorganized," and then consciousness can be repatterned into a relatively stable alternate state.[300] The disruptive influences can be stimulus overload, sensorimotor deprivation, intense alertness, or some specific stimulus that acts as a trigger.[301] Whatever the specific mechanism, at least for the first three, the crucial thing appears to be that the disruptive influence pushes the sympathetic or ergotropic nervous system into overload, which precipitates a rebound activation of the parasympathetic system.[302] In the transitional phase, since, as we have seen, "consciousness ... is a conglomerate of subsystems, functioning in many separate, but interacting, dynamic combinations," it is possible for some of the brain's "deeper functioning networks" to be "'jostled' temporarily out of phase," and then are "free to join ... into new physiological patterns," during the process of repatterning.[303] We have seen that OBEs appear to reflect this sort of creation of "new physiological patterns" among the brain's "deeper functioning networks," and lucid dreams have also been proposed as examples of how "if you dissociate brain states during transitional intervals, their substrates can reassemble in the form of some very curious hybrids."[304] There are many alternative configurations that the brain can shift into, but of particular interest here is when the "coactivation of processes ... derived from components of waking and dreaming modes of consciousness" results in a state of "consciousness akin to a 'waking dream,'" which can be manifested as the feeling of flight coordinated with vivid airborne visualizations and hyperrealistic constellations of tactile, visual, and auditory perceptions generated alongside or in the absence of all sensory input.[305] Furthermore, a common feature of ASCs that follow when "the normal state of balance within the autonomic nervous system breaks down under intense stimulation of the sympathetic system" is "parasympathetic dominance in which the frontal cortex is dominated by slow wave patterns originating in the limbic system and related projections into the frontal parts of the brain."[306] The result is "an overall synchronization of the cortex" under the influence of "the hippocampal-septal region," which is the "gateway between the limbic system," the "central processor of the brain, integrating emotion and memory, and interosceptive and exteroceptive information," and the neocortex, the seat of higher thought and conscious perception. In other words, the state of consciousness that results is not simply an alternative *state* of consciousness, but an integrative *mode* of consciousness, a neural configuration in which the two cerebral hemispheres and the cortex and limbic system are brought in to synchronization, and, apparently, both greater pleasure and greater psychosocial understanding result.[307]

In the case of anticholinergic drugs there has been some debate about whether the driving influence is the chemicals' specific effects on the nervous system or a general "emergency" reaction to their severe disruption of normal functioning, but the most likely answer is both, which would explain why they produce such a profound experience.[308] On the one hand, their disruptive influence on so many aspects of the body's functioning may well trigger the ergotropic, "flight-fight" system in reaction to what appears to be a mortal threat. On the other hand, as we have seen, anticholinergics directly interfere with cholinergic regulation of the parasympathetic system, apparently preventing it from alternating normally with the sympathetic system. The net result is a trajectory that seems to manifest both the disruption – repatterning and the ergotropic – trophotropic alternation, "an initial ... state of excitation," accompanied by "hallucinations, delirium" and then sleep involving vivid, fantastic dreams.[309]

Hanß Jacob's story, in particular, indicates several things about the role of hallucinogens in early modern witchcraft. First of all, it provides direct archival evidence that psychoactive substances were not simply used as poisons on others, and were not simply something that people talked about, but that they were used, as the demonological literature reported, deliberately by some people to induce radically altered states of consciousness in which the experient had the compelling sensation of flying and enjoying festivities of various sorts. Secondly, it provides rare insight into the social organization of these people. They do not seem to have formed anything like a religious or counterreligious sect, as the demonologists and, with a different twist, romantic historians, supposed, but there does seem to have been some collective activity, contrary to the rationalist historical tradition.[310] Instead, there seems to have existed, in seventeenth-century Southwestern Germany, anyway, a loose network of itinerants like charlatans and barbers, disreputable members of the settled community like brewers and tavern-keepers, and some regular tradespeople and peasants who gathered informally to "travel on the pitchfork" much as circles of friends and acquaintances get together to take drugs today. This is not to suggest that the majority of witch suspects, or even suspects who freely confessed to attending Sabbaths, used hallucinogens or were part of this network, but it does suggest that a few did and were; how many we cannot know due to the contamination of most evidence by torture and intimidation. Thirdly, these groups also seem to have taught each other petty magic (Hanß' companions "promised him they would teach him how to make lice and fleas," the lowest form of popular magic.), and apparently blacker arts as well (He indicated that he would have learned how to create a frost to harm the crops, another well-known form of popular malefic magic, if he had stayed longer.); we will take a closer look at the connection between altered states of consciousness and magical practices in the next chapter. Finally, Hanß' story suggests that the people who participated in these activities were well aware of where they stood on the moral spectrum, and whose interests they ultimately served. He himself said that he had been given to the Devil his whole life, and while his hallucinatory experiences did not involve any sort of Devil worship or diabolical intercourse, he did say that at his third trip "a barber named Hannß ... opened a vein in his right hand, drew several drops of blood, [and] he had to renounce the Holy Trinity, and sign with his blood in a book." He claimed that this happened before, not after, he rode the pitchfork, but the fact that "the vein ... quickly closed up and healed" makes it sound like the experience was hallucinatory.[311] Regardless, what mattered was what it signified about his understanding of his place in society and in God's universe.

Did Apolonia Walther, the elderly woman who claimed to have flown to dances with the Devil and later with her husband, use hallucinogenic ointments after all? The fact that she said she kept it in a "trough" but then the "trough" could not be found casts doubt on her claim, and, as we have seen, hallucinogenic salves were certainly not necessary for someone to experience vivid dreams and OBEs. Drugs are but one means of triggering these sorts of dissociative states: a variety of others like dancing, drumming, sex, sensory deprivation, and deep meditation can also used, and some "highly hypnotizable" people can even enter trance states in which they "perceive self-generated imagery of hallucinatory strength" like "a whole animal, embedded in a scene" that develops "into a vivid movie" spontaneously, "as if someone flipped a switch."[312] Drowsiness, the hypnogogic and hypnopompic states, and the transition between deep sleep and REM sleep can also trigger the onset of such alternative states of consciousness, and the spontaneous or deliberate use of such states to achieve ASCs is common.[313] However, the fact that she said she "had learned this witchcraft from a butcher ... in Reütlingen" suggests that she may have used hallucinogens, at least at one point, for it is hard to see how someone could have taught her how to fly to dances via dreaming, but easy to see how this could be done with a salve. If so, the anticholinergic drugs would have had a particularly strong effect on her since anticholinergics are known to affect older people, and especially older women, particularly strongly, and this, or the cumulative effect of use, might account for her persistent delirium.[314] However, this does not necessarily mean that she used a salve every time she flew to a witch dance, or even frequently; for once altered states of consciousness have been entered a number of times it becomes possible to return to them via "triggers," stimuli that induce the brain to return its neural circuitry to the configuration that produced it.[315] People who have used LSD, for example, sometimes experience "flashbacks" while awake or "high dreams" in their sleep, spontaneous recreations of the drug experience without having ingested the drugs recently, or even for years. Apolonia may have started out with a salve under the tutelage of the butcher in Reutlingen, but gone on to experience flights to the Sabbath spontaneously in her sleep, triggered by some sensation or image that came to her in a dream. Of course, she may have, as Maria Braittingen appears to have, experienced the flights and dances without ever having leaned to "travel on a pitchfork" via a hallucinogenic salve at all, or if she did use a salve, it could have been, as some recipes were, inert, a placebo, but, given Hanß Jacob's experiences, it is quite possible that she and her husband were tied into the loose network of people in the region who did do such things, and learned from them to do them as well.[316]

Whatever the source of her experiences, Apolonia, like Hanß Jacob, knew where they put her on the moral spectrum of her society. However, while both of them clearly felt considerable antipathy toward their society, in view of the literal demonization of their experiences it is interesting to consider what their actual content and effects were. In Apolonia's case, what she actually experienced was an exhilarating flight, an entertaining party, and satisfying sex. She did not say she learned any harmful magic, and does not appear to have done anyone any magical harm. Hanß Jacob did learn to make fleas and lice, he said, and committed the far more serious, although natural, crime of murder, but when he did it he was not under the influence of an illicit witch salve, but instead was under the influence of the legal demon rum. In fact, under the influence of the salve he not only attended a peaceful party, but actually locked himself in jail, beginning a relationship with the authorities that ended with his confession and punishment for the murder he committed while drunk. If Hanß Jacob and others were drawn to hallucinogens for their entertainment value, because they seemed to offer the ultimate virtual-reality experience, they found that they could bring far more than just an evening's diversion. Unlike externalized entertainments like novels, plays, movies, and television, hallucinogens do not follow a consciously sculpted script designed to edify or entertain. Instead, they are structured by the person's own subconscious and manifest his or her own deepest desires and fears.[317] It was this wild and uncontrollable power that so scared the religious and secular authorities and upright citizens. The magic of the witches' flights to the Sabbath was not that people were moved bodily from one place to another place, or even that their spirits went from here to there, but instead, as with modern psychonauts who "get high" on marijuana and "trip" on LSD without ever imagining that they have actually traveled in any geographic sense, the real magic of the witches' "flights" was that the contents of their unconscious minds were released as hallucinations, dreams, and unreflective actions. This is what made them seem so subversive: they were a flight from the sober consciousness of the rationalized order to the uncontrolled regions of the mind, from the mighty fortress of Christian prescription to the tumultuous waves and treacherous currents out upon the Devil's sea.

5
Sorcery, Satanism, and Shamanism

According to demonological theory, witches returned from their dances with the knowledge and tools to work harmful magic, or sorcery. According to anthropological reconstructions, sorcery arose out of shamanism, the altering of consciousness in order to interact with spirits for the benefit of the community.[1] In general, shamans enter a trance state in which they experience their spirit or soul journeying to a world of spirits where they can gain information about or effect actions to influence the normal world of humans, although they can also summon spirits to aid them in both the spirit and the normal worlds, and some people consider mediumship, in which practitioners in a trance are possessed by spirits, to be a form of shamanism as well.[2] Shamans proper, though, undergo an initiation in which they travel to the spirit world to gain experience, and then conduct public performances while in a trance to accomplish some communal purpose through interaction with the spirits. Shamans are found in hunter-gatherer, pastoral, and simple agricultural societies around the world, and their practices are generally held to be continuations of the oldest form of magico-religious practice, dating back to Paleolithic times. Their general orientation is to accomplish positive social purposes like healing the sick, but the spirits they interact with are not always benign, and some shamans specialize in working with the destructive ones.[3] Furthermore, the power to heal also confers the power to harm, and shamans sometimes use this to inflict illness on members of competing groups, or battle other clans' shamans in spirit in order to prevent them from doing this to their people or to gain some other advantage for their own group.[4]

So long as people lived in small, autonomous social units, the high level of interdependency discouraged the use of harmful magic on other members of their own group, although shamans, who acted as clan leaders, may have used their power to assert their authority by punishing malefactors.[5] However, the transitions to pastoralism and agriculture and more particularly the development of larger scale societies and polities loosened this restraint, and some shamanic practitioners began to use their power for their own private ends, whether as part of leadership struggles with rivals or for more personal reasons.[6] Some shamans also came to perform spiritual attacks on behalf of clients, either as part of a full-service practice or as a specialty.[7] Healing came to routinely include diagnosis and cure of such magical attacks, sometimes by retaliating to force the attacker to call off the spirit or simply pushing it back on him or her, along with curing other forms of disease, both natural and spiritual.[8] In some societies the spiritual sources of disease included magical harm caused by another person spontaneously, purely by force of ill will, what anthropologists call witchcraft.

Historically, records of sorcery go back to ancient Mesopotamia and Egypt, and continue through classical Greece and Rome through the Middle Ages. Physical remains of "voodoo dolls" used for image magic and innumerable cursing tablets have been found from ancient as well as classical civilizations, literary sources describe the use of verbal curses, ligature, incantations, necromancy, and the evil eye, not to mention magic potions, ointments, and poisons, and professional practitioners as well as amateurs are known to have used them.[9] The use of cursing tablets and much of the learned magic contained in books fell off in Europe at the beginning of the Middle Ages, but the Germanic invaders brought their own traditions of harmful as well as helpful magic which mixed with the popular survivals from antiquity.[10] These remained in use, gradually modified by their interaction with the Christian religion and each other, into the later Middle Ages, when they were supplemented by written traditions recovered from antiquity and imported from Byzantine and Arab civilizations to form a "common tradition" of magical assumptions and practices that was shared by almost all Europeans, from philosophers to peasants, popes to the poor, assumptions and practices that did not simply stoke peoples' fear of harmful magic, but also equipped them with an arsenal of magical weapons that some people most definitely used.[11]

Early medieval penitentials treated image magic and toxic potions as actual practices and engraved Norse runes were part of an extensive system of harmful as well as helpful magic.[12] Itinerant sorcerers in the ninth and tenth centuries extorted tribute from peasants by threatening to bring storms down on their crops, while Burchard of Worms tells of women who "remove a turf from their [enemy's] footprints and ... hope thereby to take away their health or life."[13] Accusers in late medieval sorcery trials brought forth "magical amulets that had been left under their thresholds or beds" that contained "noxious powders, human feces, wood from a gallows, or other such materials" like "the bodies of ... small ... animals."[14] Necromancers' manuals containing intricate rituals for summoning demons which were used by some learned magicians for various nefarious purposes survive from the late Middle Ages, and there is ample evidence that, just as in the classical world, professional sorcerers were available to work their baleful magic for a fee.[15]

Insight into the situation at the end of the Middle Ages is provided by court records from Florence and its rural environs. Between 1375 and 1450, without any "evidence of official pressure or popular agitation against sorcery, cases did crop up regularly" that "demonstrate ... the existence of a substantial group ... which engaged, actively or vicariously, in the practice of the black arts."[16] While some of their rituals were for harmless divination or treasure-seeking, many were love magic designed not for romantic but for sexually or materially exploitative ends, and some were intended to be homicidal.[17] A number of cases involved books of necromancy, while others stemmed from the use of simpler folk techniques. The populace at large and the government do not seem to have regarded these practices a grave threat to society, but there was clearly "a widespread fascination with the diabolic arts" and a readiness on some peoples' part to use them maliciously.[18]

Before turning to sorcery in the early modern period, it is worth noting that while there was clearly development in the theory and practice of magic over the centuries, the continuity in the practice of sorcery in Western Civilization is rather striking; evidence of ancient practices like image magic, cursing, and incantations seem little different from practices recorded in the late Middle Ages. However, there does seem to be a significant discontinuity between the Western tradition of harmful magic as a whole and the shamanistic practices that are supposed to have come before. Shamanistic sorcery operates mainly through personal action, the shaman's spiritual flight, and/or the direct action of his personal spirit helpers, whereas Western magic has a more impersonal, almost mechanistic character: the sorcerer inscribes curses on tablets, mutilates images, secretes potent objects under thresholds, invokes spirits or demons, with proper execution of the ritual and/or the mediation of demons as the active agent in the magic. There is clearly some overlap, for Western sorcerers were sometimes thought to fly at night to attack their enemies in their sleep, transform themselves into animals as some shamans were thought to, and employed familiar spirits reminiscent of shamans' spirit helpers.[19] It is possible that the more mechanistic forms of Western sorcery evolved out of shamanistic practices, with ritualized invocation of spirits replacing soul flight, ritualized expressions of anger replacing spiritual projections, and ritualized mutilation of images and secretion of objects replacing visualized attacks.[20] However, it is also possible that mechanistic sorcery developed from different roots, from a simple recognition of the coincidence of expressions of anger and harm suffered by the object of that anger, and the subsequent elaboration of techniques to express anger in order to deliberately inflict harm.

Whichever relationship obtained originally, though, it is clear that by the late Middle Ages European culture contained a wide and rich array of magical techniques for inflicting harm on others derived from a number of historical traditions, and that some people at all levels of society were more than ready to use them.

The realities of sorcery in early modern Europe

Evidence that knowledge and practice of this rich tradition of harmful magic survived into the early modern era in popular as well as learned culture comes from all across Europe.[21] In England, cursing tablets "in the ancient tradition" have been found from the seventeenth century, one buried along with "the skin and bones of a frog, which had been pierced by several large pins," and another at the bottom of a well along with a wax figure with a pin through it.[22] In 1590, a "Mrs. Dewse" was found to have "paid a conjurer 'two lemons a sugare lofe, and a capon' to make figurines of several leading statesmen who had contrived to eject her husband from office," hoping that "the suffering would be deemed divine retribution."[23] In Scotland, a sorcerer buried enchanted meat under doorways for a female client in a dispute with a man, and then made a wax image of him that they, together with her mother, roasted over a fire.[24] In Lorraine, sorceresses sought to cause hail by beating water with a stick.[25] Elsewhere in France, a pharmacist in Normandy "was arrested 'in possession of ... four pieces of virgin parchment containing invocations of evil spirits'" in 1605, while a priest in the same area "was caught red-handed in possession of magical recipes (in Latin) for ... seducing women."[26] In southern Italy, "such works frequently surfaced in trials," and in one case two charms were said to have been thrown into a well as part of a harmful spell were recovered.[27] In Spain, an "'impotence spell' was used to render "a man impotent, except when in the presence of the woman who bound him."[28] In Venice a woman placed "a wax statue punctured with needles under the altar in the local church" in the hope, she claimed when it was discovered, that this would force her husband to return to her. In the same city "various cursed things, or *fatture*," like "bones ... human nails ... seeds ... coals ... and the teeth of the dead" were found in a sick woman's mattress, while a mixture called *lazaro puzzolente* containing quicksilver, urine, and asafetida resin was known to be made to work a similar magic when placed under victims' thresholds.[29] In Istria "every clan had one *kresnik* who did good and one *kudlak* who harmed people" by attacking them in the shamanic style, in their dreams, while in Slovenia clan shamans who won trance battles against another clan's shaman for fertility "punished the region of the loser with hail."[30] This list could go on, but the point should be clear: sorcery was the hard edge to the world of magic in early modern Europe, and there were clearly people ready to use it. Those ready to dabble in sorcery appear to have been a distinct minority of the overall population, and those ready to specialize in it were certainly an even smaller minority.[31] Their exact numbers remain shrouded in even greater uncertainty than the notorious "black numbers" involved in all premodern crime due to the inherently surreptitious nature of most of their activities, but they appear to have been present in many small and most sizable communities, and the uncertainty about their identities, numbers, and activities and the recognized potential of these activities to cause harm made it understandable that people erred on the side of overestimating rather than underestimating the threat they posed to the population at large.

Germany was no exception to this general European pattern. The *Malleus Maleficarum* contains a report that "a wax image pierced with two needles, and little bags containing bones, seeds, and other things" were found under the threshold of a sick woman, placed there by a neighbor with whom she had quarreled, according to the neighbor's boyfriend, while in 1579 a diviner working for Hans Fugger found a "container of hair and bones ... under the lintel of the stable" that she thought had been placed to harm Fugger's gardener.[32] The learned magician Cornelius Agrippa "tells of seeing a man inscribe the name and sign of a spirit on paper and giving it to a frog while murmuring an incantation, all to arouse storms," while, lower on the social scale, a woman "threw worms and maggots into the air in order to cause a plague of vermin."[33] Rituals to make bugs and rodents, the lowest form of sorcery, sound trivial to us, but in an agricultural society they could have a ruinous effect on grain stores and other stocks of foodstuffs.[34] Similarly, the loss of a farm animal, as we have seen, could be calamitous, and attacks on them could take symbolic as well as subliminal form: "a note with magic formulas in the fodder" of one cow, or "a sack with poisonous insects" placed in the stall of a sheep. Whether the effect of this sack was expected to be chemical or magical is not clear, but the distinction was less important at the time than it is to us, for poisoning was closely related to sorcery since the effects of poisons were understood to be related to "the bad wishes" of the poisoner as well as the material composition of the toxin.[35] The same ambiguity exists in a case in which mandrake was used to cause illness in a person; the source does not make it clear whether it was used as a poison or as a magical prop.[36]

Not all cases, though, were so ambiguous: one young woman had been "observed practicing black magic rituals" that she confessed to in 1756, and books containing malevolent magic were found in Germany as well as elsewhere.[37] Other physical evidence included herbs used for love magic found in a man's mattress, and chests, or *Hexentöpfe*, discovered during trials containing things like "cursing tablets, ointments, charms," and "spells, herbs, roots ... and hair" that were thought to be able to "cause hailstorms and untimely frosts, sickness in man and beast; impotence; miscarriage and death."[38] These collections often included body parts, like the penis, fingernails, and toenails of a criminal who had been broken on the wheel that were found in one man's magic chest, and some executioners did a lively trade in pieces of cadavers for use in magic and sorcery.[39] And, finally, as elsewhere in Europe, the practice of sorcery in Germany was divided between a limited number of otherwise ordinary people who succumbed to the temptation to use it in an unusual moment of anger, curiosity, or need; a subset of the semiprofessional magical practitioners who might consent to help clients with it; and a small number of people who made use of it habitually for personal reasons and perhaps for clients as well.[40]

In Württemberg's archives there are records of several cases in which there is no doubt that an ordinary villager succumbed to the temptation to use sorcery against a personal enemy. In one, a teenage servant boy in Schondorf confessed in 1655 that he "cut a little patch of leather from the pants of" his master "in order that the master 'would slowly sicken and die,'" and "in fact, in investigating this assertion the magistrates found a hole in Hans Biener's pants."[41] In another, in the early summer of 1696 in the small town of Söhnstetten, outside of Waiblingen, Maria Magdalena Rauschenberger, the wife of the town warden saw from her window a woman named "Schöllhornin furtively clamber over the churchyard wall and bury three twigs in a child's grave" while incanting, "So as the twigs grow in the ground, so shall brother-in-law perish from the earth, in the name of the Father, the Son, and the Holy Spirit."[42] How did Rauschenberger, from her vantage point, know what Schöllhornin was doing, let alone saying? "Just a week before, Schöllhornin had told her what a bad relationship she had with her brother-in-law Finninger, and all that he had done to hurt her. Thereupon the warden's wife told Schöllhornin that her brother, who lived in Fellbach, had gotten revenge on a peasant he had a conflict with by burying three twigs in the churchyard while reciting a spell." When Rauschenberger told Finninger what his sister-in-law had done, he became "very sick ... felt 'infirmity in the limbs,' had to remain in bed, and stopped eating 'so that he became more like a skeleton than a man." He got better once Rauschenberger and a friend dug up the three twigs, which was lucky for Schöllhornin, because she ended up punished with four weeks imprisonment and penance for her sorcery rather than the much harsher penalty she would have faced had he died. She may have been set up, but there seems to have been no question that, in her lust for revenge, she fell for it hook, line, and sinker.

Among the sampled cases involving *maleficium*, as we have seen, there were a significant number of instances when poisons seem to have been used, and also a significant number of cases when curses were hurled, but evidence of, and even allegations of, the use of ritual magic to cause harm were relatively rare. Of course, curses were a form of sorcery when uttered with the premeditated intent of causing harm, but it is difficult to know what a suspect's intent and degree of mental preparation were, so it is difficult to tell when curses were uttered as premeditated spells, when they were spontaneous outbursts of anger spoken in the hopes that they would actually inflict injury the moment they were articulated, and when they were just part of the routine trading of insults, warnings, and threats that expressed anger without the hope or expectation that they would actually have physical consequences.[43] Similarly, poisoning is by nature surreptitious, and many other techniques of sorcery, like putting objects under thresholds or chanting incantations, were conducted secretly, and when a secreted object was innocuous in itself, like a bone buried in a stall or entryway of a barn, even if found it would be difficult to tell that it had been placed there deliberately. For example, when a man who suspected that Agatha Stoßer had bewitched his cow went to a wise woman for help, she told him to dig around the door and he'd find a bone that he should get rid of to make the cow better.[44] When he did as she said, he did find "such a bone ... from a rib," but whether Agatha, or anyone, had put it there on purpose is impossible to determine. Similarly, in 1682 a woman named Magdelena Oswald was accused of causing her husband's death by burning "three chickens so completely that their feet fell off their bodies, 'because she intended to cause the same injury to her husband's feet.' And in the event Magdelena's husband did suffer ... from an illness that made his feet and legs lame and the skin discolored, and eventually led to" his death.[45] At first Magdelena claimed that she burned the chickens in an attempt to cure her husband on the advice of a healer, and then changed her story to claim that she did it to get rid of them since people were saying she'd stolen them, so in the end we can't know whether her act was successful sorcery, unsuccessful healing, or, as she maintained in the end, just one of those weird coincidences.

The early modern approach to *maleficium* got around this problem by focusing on the inferred effects of a witch's hostility rather than worrying about the mechanism by which it was projected, so most testimony in trials simply recounted the harms attributed to the suspect without speculating about whether they had been induced deliberately or spontaneously, through sorcery or through the inherent power of the witch's ill will. The early modern concept of diabolism also shifted focus away from the mechanics of magic, for a pact with the Devil was assumed to bring magical powers, and once enough testimony alleging *maleficium* had been accumulated to justify torture, the focus of the trials shifted to eliciting confessions of participation in the Devil's conspiracy, seeking at most a simple affirmation of responsibility for harms suffered by other people. Tortured suspects might confess to details of their activities, but at that point it is impossible from our point of view to tell what might have been true and what they simply made up, undoubtedly drawing on popular notions about sorcery, to satisfy their inquisitors and end their torment.

However, the instances that were contained in the sampled trial records that do seem to reflect actual activities are worth careful examination, for they undoubtedly represent some "dark figure" of additional instances that were either undetected or ambiguous, and they shed some light on the shadowy workings of popular sorcery, suspicions of which did so much to feed peoples' fear of their neighbors.

We have seen some evidence of sorcery in previous chapters, like Hanß Jacob Langen's statement that his companions had offered to teach him to make fleas and lice, and that he wanted to learn how to cause hail.[46] The sampled case in which malefic sorcery was most clearly involved, though, was the trial in 1681 of Agnes Langjahr, the 50-year-old widow from Wittershaven, near Alpirsbach, who, it was said, had come into Christian Cammer's house over the family's protests, went to the room where a woman who had given birth three days before lay, "pulled the curtain back, and ... lay three eggs on the lap" of the woman laying there.[47] As noted in Chapter 1, in German folklore witches were thought to use eggs to transmit their spells, and placing noxious items in bed was a common way to cause people to become ill.[48] New mothers and newborn babies were thought to be particularly vulnerable to magical as well as physical dangers. In this instance, the woman flew into an uncontrollable rage, attacking her husband verbally and physically, whereupon "the man fell into a painful and miserable sickness," and the woman died.[49]

The impact of the eggs on the woman shows the powerful effect that an act of sorcery could have on people, but the source of that power is obscure, and the interpretive approaches currently used by historians offer only limited help in understanding it. A traditional sociological treatment of witchcraft focusing on community-level social tensions might point to the fact that the Cammers were part of the local notability and Agnes was just an elderly, widowed servant already long suspected of witchcraft to suggest that the accusation stemmed from some socioeconomically rooted conflict, treating the egg accusation as either a fabrication or a misinterpretation of a friendly gesture. Indeed, Agnes initially denied that she had gone into the room at all, but when a witness from Sulz submitted a written statement in support of the Cammers' story, she conceded that she had, but said that she had put the eggs "on the table."[50] However, "in confrontation," the part of an investigation when the accuser and suspect were placed face-to-face, she changed her story again, conceding that it had been "on the bed." While it is possible that Agnes brought the eggs as a gift, the fact that she put them on the woman in the bed but later lied and said that she had put them on the table make this seem unlikely, particularly since no one, not even Agnes, suggested that this was the case.[51]

Of course, it is possible that the woman was sick from other causes and the fact that she died shortly after Agnes deposited the eggs was a coincidence, but several things suggest this was not the case. First of all, it is clear that she did have a strong emotional reaction, and vented it on her husband, and we have seen that in general such stress can, in fact, cause or contribute to illness. Secondly, and more specifically, both Cammer and his son insisted that after she died, the woman's "thigh, where the eggs lay was quite black." While it is possible that blood just pooled there for some reason as she died, this was the top rather than the bottom of her body, and if, as we have seen, people under hypnosis can cause welts to appear on their skin, there is no reason to think that a person could not similarly cause discoloration to appear where the instruments of a spell that was killing her had been laid.

A more current, culturally oriented approach would recognize that Agnes did attempt an act of sorcery, playing out a socially ascribed role by suggesting that the eggs were placed in the bed as a symbolic statement to the Cammers, a sign drawn from the contemporary cultural complex of magic and employed as part of the shared understanding of the pervasive interplay of magical forces in everyday life. However, we have seen that because acts of *maleficium* could have real power, some people employed them occasionally and a few did so chronically not because they were maneuvered by their community into attempting impotent rituals as part of a self-destructive social role, but because they learned that the actions could be efficacious and that the power they bestowed compensated for the social stigma they brought. We have seen in Chapter 1 that interpersonal interactions could generate stress in people leading to a variety of ailments, up to and including death, and it should at this point be easy to see how subliminal communication or overtly threatening behaviors could generate such reaction. What is at issue here, though, is how a purely symbolic act, placing eggs on someone in bed, could have such dramatic emotional and physiological consequences.[52] While the woman would have to have understood the meaning of the eggs in order to trigger her response, the power of that understanding does not come from culture; knowledge of meaning does not in-and-of itself create the kinds of physiological effects seen here.

Traditional psychodynamic psychology suggests that the couple's reaction to the eggs exposed some weakness in their psyches, intraspsychic tension stemming from their personal histories or some culturally induced vulnerability caused by their belief in magic. However, we have far-too-little information about the woman to do the kind of in-depth analysis needed to understand her rage and despair in this way, and, as we have seen, psychodynamically rooted psychosomatic explanations, while they have become a kind of folk-psychology underlying social scientific and cultural accommodations of the manifest effects of magical attacks, have been largely abandoned by medical professionals in favor of a broader and more direct understanding of the interplay of psychological and physiological factors in health and disease. Vulnerability to psychophysical ailments can certainly be caused by personal psychodynamics and enculturation, but they are not necessary for them to occur. The woman had to understand the meaning of the eggs in order to react to them, but that reaction is not proof that she was psychologically impaired, nor, as we saw above, can it explain by itself the psychophysical reaction it provoked.

Fortunately, recent work in the neurophysiology of symbol processing offers a new way of exploring the power of the eggs in the bed by looking at them not in terms of how they related to social structures, other symbols, or psychodynamic theories, but rather in terms of how the perception of them was connected to other parts of the woman's nervous system in a way that elicited such a dramatic response. To begin with, as we saw in Chapter 3, the brain appears to work in important ways through neural networks, complex interconnections among neurons that work together as functional units. Entrainment is the process by which these connections are set up.[53] Some entrainments are created consciously, as a result of deliberate learning, but most are established without consciousness; some are generated genetically, while others are created in dynamic interaction with life experiences and cultural conditioning.[54] Penetration is the term for the way that systems of entrainments interconnect with other systems, interconnections that can be established between parts of the brain that are widely separated both physically and functionally.[55] Many systems of entrainments are created in response to perception; the core of these systems is the basis for recognition based on pattern-matching, but they also may include more or less extensive connections with other perceptual, cognitive, emotional, and even physiological centers with which they have become interpenetrated.[56] A "symbol is any stimulus that provides sufficient patterning for entrée into a model that contains more information than that provided by the stimulus," and "symbolic penetration" is "the effects exercised by the neural system mediating a symbolic percept (or the entire perceptual field) upon other neural, endocrine, and physiological systems."[57] Symbols thus have the "potential to evoke any neural network that becomes entrained to the network mediating the percept" which "may include lower autonomic and endocrine structures mediating arousal and metabolic functions; core brain and limbic structures mediating sentiment, emotion, or feeling; and cortical structures mediating conceptual organization, imaginal organization, logico-mathematical functions, cross-modal sensory transfer, and other functions."[58] A symbol can thereby "produce the experience of love or terror, voiding of the bladder, movement of the hands, salivation, increased blood pressure, fantasies and thoughts, and reminiscences."[59] A symbol can even "evoke intentionality ... via intentionality integrated with its meaning."[60] The symbolic process works through all sense modalities, not just sight and hearing, and the entrainments involved in symbolic penetration do not necessarily include the neural networks involved in consciousness, so it is possible for symbols to evoke emotional and even physiological reactions without the person being aware of the cause.[61] In this case, however, the woman was aware of the cause, and the symbol of the eggs appears to have been able to penetrate not only the "cortical structures mediating conceptual organization" of her life-situation and the "core brain and limbic structures mediating sentiment, emotion, or feeling," but also the "autonomic and endocrine structures mediating arousal and metabolic functions," and even, judging by the discoloration Cammer and his son noticed, the "physiological systems" regulating that specific portion of her upper leg. The eggs had, so to speak, struck a nerve.

The point here is that while sorcery makes great use of culturally defined symbols and belief in their power, it does not ultimately depend on them. Instead, sorcery depends ultimately on the personal meaning of the symbols it employs for the person it is used against, and on the ability of these personally meaningful symbols to penetrate deeply into that person's nervous system and disrupt his or her normal physiological functioning. The power of symbols does not come simply from their connection to a culture's overall system of symbols, but comes from how those meanings connect to the overall system of entrainments in the nervous systems of the people who understand them. In fact, it could be said that while the meaning of symbols comes in some abstract sense from their place in the system of symbols that make up the culture, in practical terms the meaning of symbols is the set of entrainments between the perceptual apparatuses that perceive them and the neural networks in the cortex, limbic structures, autonomic nervous and endocrine systems that react to them.

If Agnes' eggs show how a simple act of sorcery could have a profound influence on its object, two other examples shows how simple acts of sorcery could have important influences on the people who performed them. The first was the case of the girl Margaretha Wagner, who, as we saw in Chapter 1, claimed to have "pressed" people at night while they were asleep. In her testimony, she described this not as a spontaneous occurrence, or one occasioned merely by her desire to do it, but as one involving ritual preparation. Specifically, she said "one takes a salve, smears with it the lower threshold of the door and inhales such, without saying anything thereto."[62] Since the experience of the "presser," like that of people who experience being pressed, took place at night during sleep, this ritual would constitute a form of psychological priming, the process by which people can "seed" their dream experiences by symbolic preparation before nodding off. This technique is used by modern lucid dreamers to trigger the onset of lucidity in a way that is reminiscent of how Maria Braittingen said the Devil woke her at the onset of her "out-of-body" flights to night dances.[63] The physiological basis for it is the "interaction between the automatic state control system in the brain stem" that controls modes of consciousness "and the more voluntary upper stories of the brain."[64] This "top-down causation" is possible "because the cortical structures are so intimately linked to the more primitive functions of the limbic and autonomic systems" that, as with the woman Agnes put the eggs on, "symbolic and mental levels" can "cause physiological effects."[65] Conducting the ritual to "press" an enemy at night primes the sleeper to experience the expected event, much as the *benandanti* were primed by awareness of the date to experience their nocturnal flights and battles. As one modern scientist who practices lucid dreaming has observed, "autosuggestion is one of the most potent techniques for altering consciousness," or, more simply, "priming works."[66]

The second of the sampled cases contains a report of a verbal incantation that was used for prohibited, although not really malicious, purposes that shows not only how ritual could be used to affect the practitioner's nervous system, but also how that effect could affect the perceptions and cognition of another person. It came to light during the investigation of Anna Schnabel, whose spirit, we have seen, a neighbor said she saw flit across her kitchen.[67] Among the other incidents recounted to the investigators, another neighbor, Catharine Decker, said that once when they "went in the woods, in the grass" Anna "said to her she wanted to teach her an incantation so that no forest ranger should see or catch her."[68] In addition, a twelve-year-old girl in the neighborhood named Catharina Kramer had also been heard to brag that she knew a spell "whereby she cannot be seen," and when questioned she said she had learned it from Anna's granddaughter. The magistrates expressed concern that Anna was leading "a good number of young people astray," and they also declared that "any person who used such forbidden incantation should be punished."[69] They were concerned in part because the use of such magic was disobedient and sacrilegious, but also because it represented a real threat to the government's control over the duchy's forest resources, and over the population more generally. The purpose of this "grass spell," as the magistrates called it, was to avoid the ducal officials in charge of the forest land, which was criminal, and even subversive. Forests were subject to complex and overlapping concepts of ownership and usage, with local communities traditionally using them to pick berries and mushrooms, graze pigs, gather firewood, harvest lumber, and hunt game; the upper classes, and the dukes in particular, using them to hunt game; while merchants used them as a source of lumber for export. As the population grew, usage was subject to increasing regulation; at first by local communities, but in the fifteenth century the counts of Württemberg became more involved.[70] Forest regulation was part of the first ducal ordinance in 1495, and this was expanded and strengthened in a series of ordinances during the sixteenth and seventeenth centuries.[71] A system of administration was put into place with the woodlands divided into a series of districts overseen by foresters, and the districts were subdivided into wards that were managed by rangers.[72] While the main concern of the regulations were timber management and hunting, neither of which was likely to have been an activity an elderly woman like Anna Schnabel would have engaged in, virtually any use of the forest was subject to administrative supervision, at least theoretically, and, significantly, administrative concern with issues beyond hunting were increasing in the 1660s.[73] Furthermore, under the morals regulations put into place at the end of the Thirty Years' War, simply being outside the bounds of the village and fields was suspect, so even if a villager was not poaching resources from the forest, being caught there by a ranger could still lead to trouble. On the whole, it seems that the need for regulation of forest resources to avoid overuse and misuse had been generally accepted since the mid-sixteenth century, but individuals, and even communities, continued to make illicit use of the woodlands in a variety of ways, leading to chronic conflicts between them and the duke's forestry officials. Commoners resented and resisted this usurpation of their traditional rights, and poaching remained a common problem throughout the early modern period.

Use of the incantation was not just a symbolic issue, for it could have a practical effect. The words could not, of course, make people invisible in an objective sense, but they could help a trespasser remain unnoticed – become invisible in practical terms. In mottled light and tangled undergrowth, stillness is often the best camouflage. Small animals freeze when they become aware of a predator nearby, because even if they are in its field of vision, they may escape notice, whereas flight virtually guarantees pursuit.[74] For a poacher trying to avoid forest rangers, the greatest danger was overactivity, and an incantation could help avoid this in several ways. First of all, it would reassure her intellectually with the faith that she would not be seen or caught, so if one was nearby there would be no need to run; "intensifying self-confidence" is one way that such magic "can actually influence reality."[75] Secondly, it would give her something to do with her mind. Instead of anxiously miscalculating her chances of escape, she could preoccupy herself with remembering and reciting the incantation. Thirdly, the cadence of the words would itself produce a calming effect. Oral recitation imposes control over breathing, and experimental studies have demonstrated that even purely mental activities can produce physiological states of greater relaxation.[76] Spells can be thought of as a form of "psycholinguistic programming" that entrain cognitive and emotional neural networks in ways that "can provoke profound physiological changes."[77] During the Vietnam War, for example, some US Navy SEALs were taught that if a sentry approached them while they were lurking on the edge of an enemy camp at night they should lie still and tell themselves that they had become a log in order to achieve the same effect. Of course, the SEALs did not become logs in an objective sense any more than Anna and Catharina became objectively invisible, but the objective reality was not important; what mattered was that the person involved was not seen at a particular time by a particular person. In order for that to happen, it was just as important for the SEALs to believe in the power of their belief as it was for an early modern poacher to believe in that of hers, because the effective agent in both cases was the person taking control of their own nervous system, not only to manage their own behavior, but also thereby affecting the perceptions of others.[78] It is a commonplace by now to accept that magic can have real effects on a person who believes in it, but it is less widely appreciated that it can have effects on other people regardless of their beliefs. By controlling their own thoughts and behaviors, both the early modern poachers and the Navy SEALs were able to manipulate the patrolling watchmen's perceptions to keep them from seeing what was really there.

Another case from Württemberg, one that was contained in the sample of magic trials, involved a more direct manipulation of the practitioner's nervous system to affect that of the target. The case took place in Güglingen in 1740. It began when a 17-year-old servant girl named Maria Magdelena Geken bragged to a number of people that she could work magic and knew how to "travel ... to a witch feast."[79] She claimed that she had bewitched a horse so that it would not eat, a claim her previous employer later seconded. She had also demonstrated her ability to disturb animals to a young man by spooking his horse, and while he refused to tell on her, others who heard her boasts did. Before the magistrates took any action, though, her employer, who had also heard the rumors, asked her about them. She told him that to work her magic on horses "she had prayed a prayer all day, from morning to evening," and she added to her claims the ability to cause thunder and rain and to turn herself into an animal.[80] When the authorities investigated, Maria's employer testified that she said the incantation to keep a horse from eating went:

Dein Maul muß verbaut seyn
Dein Maul muß versteckt seyn,
Du bist des Teufels,
Du must verhext seyn,
Dem Teuffel must du seyn
Du must 24 Studen nimmer fresen konen.

(Your mouth must blocked be
Your mouth must stopped be,
You are the Devil's,
You must bewitched be,
You must the Devil's be
You won't eat for 24 hours.)

Maria later conceded that she could not really affect the weather, and said that she did not repeat her incantations *all* day, but she insisted that she did practice this simple sorcery and, as the witnesses had confirmed, she did seem to be able to spook horses. Maria's protracted, repetitive incantation could have had a strong effect on her own nervous system since epistrophe, the "rhetorical device" of ending successive phrases with the same word, is "a classical hypnotic induction" technique "effective for inducing trance."[81] With the cadence of the spell creating a trance state in the person incanting it, the linguistic message establishes its "set," the emotional tenor which molds the person's facial expression and body language. These, in turn, can reinforce the person's emotional experience and physiological reaction.[82] We saw in Chapter 1 that threatening displays can have profound effects on domesticated animals, triggering their stress response and thereby affecting their health, reproduction, growth, and, in the case of chickens and cows, production of eggs and milk. Since one of the effects of the stress response is to decrease digestive activity and suppress hunger, displaying threat to a horse and thereby inducing stress in it could well prevent it from eating for a time. For such communication to take place would not require that the animal in any sense understand the linguistic content of the spell, or even the specific intent of the person. Nor need the interaction be long or the person's behavior blatantly demonstrative; it would simply need to help generate a threatening expression of malign intent in the practitioner's expression and posture to trigger a generalized stress reaction that would affect the animal's appetite as one of its normal metabolic effects.[83]

While spooking horses may seem like a trivial form of sorcery, we have seen that harm to domesticated animals was the single-most common accusation of witchcraft, and for early modern peasants this could be a devastating form of damage. In Chapter 1 we saw that this was accomplished by poisons and physical blows in some cases and spontaneous displays of emotion in others, and this example shows a third approach, the use of a ritual incantation by a person to manipulate her own nervous system in such a way that it triggered corresponding changes in that of the animal. Maria only claimed to be able to bewitch horses with her incantations, but the same process could clearly be used to affect another person. Indeed, laboratory experiments have shown that, "an actor can manipulate elements of the stress response in another person through nonverbal signals" like eye contact, posture, gestures, and tone of voice.[84] We have seen that injuries to people were similarly caused by poisons and blows, on the one hand, and spontaneous expressions of anger, on the other, and we saw that the woman named Schöllhornin from Söhnstetten conducted a ritual involving an incantation as well as burying sticks on a grave with the explicit intention of injuring her estranged brother-in-law. The possibility of such ritual magical mobilization being used to amplify the effects of a person's anger lay behind not only the fear of threats, but also the use of threats as well, at least in some cases. Forms of sorcery like incantations not only express the desire to cause harm, they can cause the harm desired.

While historians have recently begun to recognize that given the wide variety of spells in use at the time for healing, protection, and divination, it was only natural that similar magic was used in attempts to cause harm, but they tend to ascribe whatever efficacy they had to peoples' belief in them.[85] What Maria's spell shows, however, is that while suggestion and fear certainly played an important part in making ritual magic effective, there could also be another form of communication at work as well: manipulation of the direct, visceral connection that exists between people (as well as between people and domesticated animals) to trigger the stress response. Human beings "are hybrids, half analogizers, with direct experience of the world, and half symbolizers, embedded in a cultural web."[86] Sorcery makes use of our ability to operate in both modes, manipulating both direct experience and cultural symbols. It can be used to manipulate the nervous system of its target via symbolic penetration, as Agnes Langjahr did by putting eggs in the woman's bed, or via the intricate subliminal interaction that takes place whenever two people come face-to-face.[87] In the first instance, the sorcery is purely mechanical; the person using it need only know the symbolic meaning of the object and its placement. In the second, though, the sorcery is expressive; the person doing it needs to manipulate his or her own nervous system, not to express their feelings as an end in itself, but in order to manipulate the nervous system of their target.[88]

Of course, the efficacy of some forms of sorcery, like weather magic, preventing butter from churning, spying on people at a distance, and causing harm through secret rituals would require paranormal processes whose existence has not been scientifically established.[89] As a consequence, at present we must therefore posit that for such magic to take effect some direct sensory communication must also take place, as when Margaretha Wagner "pushed" people in her community at night who reported that they had, in fact, felt the pressure. Otherwise, as has long been held about magic in general, the value of the procedure was simply that it made practitioners feel better by giving them the illusion that they were doing something, as would be the case with weather magic.[90] However, while purported paranormal processes garner a lot of attention in considerations of magic, in most sorcery "the sorcerer has come into some form of contact with the bewitched person, the bewitched animal or thing ... it was the person of the witch, her curses, her gestures and touch, her gifts or drinks, that made the spell work."[91] Not all sorcery can be reduced to psychophysical manipulation, of course, but it is clear that this plays a key, and somewhat underappreciated, role in much of it.[92] The object of most sorcery is to manipulate other peoples' nervous systems, but in order to do so a sorcerer first manipulates his or her own. As Cornelius Agrippa observed, "the affection of the fantasy, when it vehemently intends itself, doth not only affect its own proper body, but also another's. So also the desire of the witches to hurt, doth bewitch men most perniciously with steadfast looks."[93]

Where Maria learned the incantations is not clear. She claimed to her neighbors that an old widow for whom she had once worked, Catharina Alexen, had taught them to her, as well as taken her to witch dances.[94] However, when confronted with Catharina, Maria showed great reluctance to repeat the accusations. For her part, Catharina calmly denied the charges. At one point, Maria tried to implicate another woman, but recanted under further questioning. These variations discredited Maria's accusation, so we cannot tell where she really learned the spells. Certain aspects of her background and situation, however, suggest that she created the incantations herself, modeled on religious prayer and popular beliefs about how sorcery was practiced. Her parents were basically peaceful people, even though they attended church only irregularly and her father was a "blasphemer" with "little fear of God."[95] Her mother had never been accused of witchcraft or magic, although, significantly, it was rumored that she had once been dismissed from service at a palace for causing the animals to become disturbed. Maria was not known to have engaged in the "foolishness" before, but it was said that her father found that she had changed. The family had recently had to sell all their property except "half a bad house," and now lived in "great poverty." Maria's change in demeanor and boasts about magical powers may well have been an attempt to compensate for her family's loss of security and status. Drawing on popular beliefs about witchcraft and magic, she created her own incantations and, to give them authority, attributed them to a stereotypical old woman. Maria does not appear to have been connected to an active network of people practicing sorcery, but rather to have adopted an image from popular culture derived from folklore, religious practice, and, perhaps, popular images of learned magic.

In contrast, however, the case involving Anna Schnabel suggests that some more deliberate sharing of knowledge of illicit magic also took place among the villagers in Württemberg. Anna not only used the "grass spell," but also taught it to several younger women. Furthermore, a number of girls knew it, and they said that they had learned it from Anna's granddaughter. During the early modern period, a stereotyped assumption about witchcraft was that it ran in families. The fact that it was a stereotyped assumption has led historians to assume that it was inherently inaccurate, or, when suspects were from the same family, a product of the assumption itself. However, there are several reasons to think that there might have been some truth to the belief. First of all, the kinds of social pressure that alienate one generation and push it into an antagonistic relationship with the community would very likely exert at least as much pressure on the next. The sociologist Hans Sebald has described how in twentieth-century Franconia he "personally observed the transference of the evil role from a mother to a daughter in a village," with the result that the daughter "mirrored the attitudes and actions of her mother ... actively ... causing harm by meddling, corrupting, lying and sowing disharmony."[96] Secondly, and more importantly in the case of sorcery, in the close quarters of a peasant household children would likely be exposed to the activities of their elders in the normal course of daily life, who may have tried to keep them secret in some cases, but in others consciously passed them on. The testimony not of accusers but of young women who confessed suggests, in fact, that membership in the household may have been more important than family ties: Catharine Decker learned the spell from Anna Schnabel while she was a servant in her household; Maria Gekin claimed to have learned her spells from a woman she had worked for; and Magdelena, the girl who gave her friend the ergot-laced bread, said that she had learned this witchcraft "from her mistress, Leonberger Hansen's wife."[97]

Sorcery and satanism

One of the most basic features of sorcery is inversion, the use of socially unacceptable materials, or behaviors, or the misuse of socially valued items and rituals. These antisocial practices can both intensify dread in other people and increase the sorcerer's ability to express hostility effectively. Public perversity assaults other people's psyches; private perversity strengthens the sorcerer's own. Witches in small-scale societies are often said to urinate, defecate, or vomit in the presence or living space of their enemies, while "late medieval trials for sorcery" frequently involved "such materials as menstrual blood, excrement, or dead animals."[98] It has been suggested that "the use of human fat and blood, cat's brains and the like" in witch salves "must have helped to induce a marginal psychological state in the witches who involved themselves in these dark forms of sorcery. In one case in Württemberg, in 1626, a group of three young men and two women from Cannstatt broke into the grounds of a nobleman, spread human feces around the yard, and leaned a pitchfork that had been smeared with a noxious unguent and hung with a pot containing feces, human skin, and pubic hair from one of the women against the door, so that it would fall on whoever opened it.[99] While the incident appears to have been more of a malicious prank in retaliation for the man having recently accused local women of causing him to become lame through witchcraft than a serious attempt to inflict harm, and none of the sampled witch cases (or other known cases) from Württemberg involved the use of excrement or the smearing of an object with salve (as opposed to directly smearing a salve on a person), the perpetrators deliberately structured the vandalism to give the impression "that witches had been there," and it appears to have been inspired at least in part by "a witch book."[100]

In early modern Europe, one of the most powerful potential forms of inversion was the perversion of Christian symbols and rites. The strongest version of this, of course, was the full-blown parody of the mass involving desecration of the cross and indiscriminate sex that was supposed to have taken place at witches' Sabbaths.[101] Few suspects, in Württemberg or anywhere else, freely recounted experiences coming close to the lurid fantasies of early modern demonologists, though, and few accusers evinced any concern about them either. There were allegations of Black Masses involving Louis XIV's mistress and courtiers during the "Affair of the Poisons," and there is documentary evidence that a brother and sister who ran a brothel in Renaissance Florence "by divers methods and on several occasions, under the pretext of sorcery and incantations persuaded many women to commit sins and excesses," but whatever evidence there may have been in the first case was suppressed by Louis, and in the second the participants seem to have skipped the blasphemous rites and gone straight to the sex.[102]

In fact, religious objects and rites seem to have been used far less often for religious parody or inversion than for their straightforward spiritual power, disregarding more than exploiting the fact that this twisted their meaning 90 if not 180 degrees.[103] In England, for example, the priest and magician Roger Bolingbroke had a secret mass performed around 1440 to prepare "the instruments he needed for" divinatory "'nigromancie,'" and, in general, learned magic involved religious rituals to purify and protect the magician in preparation for the encounter with the dangerous spirits the ceremonies invoked.[104] In Italy, many instances of love magic are recorded in which the mass or prayers, the altar, blessed items, and psalms were utilized, and the host in particular was used for similar purposes elsewhere.[105] The host was probably the most commonly misappropriated sacred object because it was the sanctified item with which ordinary people routinely came into contact. In early modern Normandy, for example, a number of shepherds were "caught stealing hosts ... to make use of with certain words in order to seduce girls, and with other words to protect their flocks."[106] In Sweden it was used as a target to gain "free shot," or good aim in hunting, and it was used for other forms of magic as well.[107] In Württemberg, one of the sampled witchcraft cases included an allegation of stealing the host from mass; in 1631, during the investigation in Lauffen of Margaretha Stuertzen's complaint that Hans Rueff made her arm lame, Hanns Jerg Trall testified that he had seen Hans' mother, who was also suspected of witchcraft, take the host from her mouth during mass, and Joacherin Wedlin claimed that he had seen her take something from her mouth as well.[108] Two other cases from the duchy are known to have involved similar allegations. One, from 1594 in Schondorf, took place when Gorg Stockhenhäuser reported that Michel Kramer, a 20-year-old servant, told him "he had secretly taken" the host "out of his mouth ... and carried [it] home.[109] When Gorg told Michel that he thought it was a sin, Michel just laughed, and his mother said "she often had five or six such holy things" at home. The other incident took place in 1620 in Altensteig. Martin Nestle was suspected of burying a skull and bones in a nobleman's herb garden as part of "a healing magic" ritual, and several witnesses reported that he had said that he had used the host, which he slipped into his boot during mass, as well. Finally, in one of the sampled magic trials, Agatha Weil, the elderly woman in the public shelter in Herrenberg who, as we have seen, admitted in 1704 to a number of acts of *maleficium*, told the investigating magistrates that on occasion during mass she had drunk the wine but held the wafer in her mouth instead of swallowing it in order to sneak it to the Devil.[110] The first of these incidents in Württemberg rests only on what witnesses claimed they saw, but the second and third involved things the suspects were reported to have said, and the last involved an admission by the suspect to the magistrates. In two of the incidents the purpose of taking the host was not made clear, while in one it was benign, and in the last it was malign.

Another way in which sorcery was linked to illicit religious activity was the conjuring of demons, or necromancy. Technically, necromancy meant conjuring the spirits of the dead, but in the late Middle Ages it was used more broadly to refer to conjuring spirits in general. The practice may have been rooted in the archaic shamanic practice of flying to the spirit world, establishing contact with spirits, including those of the dead, and enlisting spirit allies who could later be summoned to accompany the shaman, or substitute for him, on subsequent spiritual quests. The tradition of contacting the spirits and the dead by traveling to or with them appears to have been continued by the contemporary fairy cults in southern and eastern Europe in which favored people were able to participate in mystical merriments with fairies and the spirits of the dead, and the cults of Diana or Holda and the "Furious Horde" in central Europe in which some women were thought to fly with processions of the dead. The tradition of summoning spirits to assign them tasks on behalf of the magician may be a similar continuation of this other part of shamanic practice, or it may be an independent development, but in any case the conjuring of spirits was practiced in the earliest civilizations in Southwest Asia and was a centerpiece of the learned magical tradition in classical Greece and Rome. Some knowledge of it was preserved in Europe through the early Middle Ages, and was supplemented by other strains of pagan magic introduced by the nomadic invaders. After 1000, it was infused with new elements from the Byzantine and Arab worlds, both ancient texts that had been lost to the West and more recent innovations in these sophisticated cultures, and elaborated in generations of learned and popular practice. Knowledge of these arcane rites and the complex hierarchy of obscure spirits they were supposed to contact were disseminated through face-to-face interactions of learned and popular magicians, and, particularly after the introduction of printing, through the dissemination of texts. By the late Middle Ages the idea, and practice, of conjuring demons through elaborate rituals was part of the common magical culture shared by Europe's learned elite and ordinary people.[111]

There is no question that some learned clerics and humanists practiced the complex rituals that were contained in books of necromancy, some of which have survived, and others of which were destroyed during trials or over time.[112] Similarly, there is no question that some people at lower levels of society all over Europe practiced such arts as well; magic books, images, and written incantations were found in their possession, and were supported by ritual actions and words. In Württemberg learned magic was known at the highest levels of society. Duke Ferdinand, in particular, during whose reign from 1593 to 1608 the witch persecutions really got under way, openly consulted astrologers and employed alchemists.[113] He also sponsored treasure-hunting activities, and both Duke Friedrich Karl and Duke Eberhard Ludwig more discreetely gave permission for them to be undertaken, in 1683 and 1711 respectively.[114] Officially treasure-hunting was only permitted if it did not involve magic, but the status of some techniques, like divining rods, was ambiguous, and the practice routinely involved ritual commerce with spirits. It enjoyed its greatest popularity among the duchy's commoners during the eighteenth century, but records of it in Württemberg go back to the beginning of the seventeenth century, and sources outside the duchy suggest that it was known far longer.[115] The practical basis for it was that, in a time with few banks, locks, or police, both nobles and well-to-do peasants really did bury valuables like coins and jewelry or hide them within buildings to protect them from robbers and marauding soldiers, and sometimes they remained hidden because their owner died, fled without revealing their whereabouts to others, or simply forgot where they were.[116] Consequently, such caches were occasionally discovered by accident, and probable hiding places could be deduced through common sense.[117] However, there were far more potential hiding places than actual treasures, and people hiding their valuables would try to avoid obvious places, so people hoping to find treasures generally sought supernatural aid.

The basis for this aid was thought to be two different spiritual sources: the spirits of the dead, and St. Christopher. The spirits of the dead were often connected with treasure because it was thought that if a person's fortune was tainted in some way, his or her spirit would be tied to it until it was dug up and used in some way that atoned for the transgression.[118] For this reason, spontaneous sightings of ghosts sometimes inspired treasure-hunting, and treasure-seeking often took on the character of a beneficent exorcism in which a damned soul would be liberated if the treasure was recovered and put to good purpose, either restored (at least in part) to some rightful owner or donated (at least in part) to a worthy cause.[119] St. Christopher's association with buried treasure came from the confluence of folk, Christian, and learned occult traditions.[120] Germanic folklore contributed the belief in water spirits whom men could contact for good or ill. Christianity contributed the namesake, who was long thought to be a helper of the needy and who also was said to have carried Christ across a stream, along with numerous elements of the ritual used throughout the region in treasure-finding known as "Christopher's Prayer" (*Christophelgebett*). Esoteric traditions supplied the rest of the ceremony.

The rituals involved elaborate ceremonies taken from or modeled on learned ceremonial magic. Books and manuscripts were often consulted.[121] Ritual circles were drawn in the soil with daggers, written spells were drawn up (in one case 43 pages long), and incantations were recited (in one case, all night).[122] Treasure-finding ceremonies often incorporated things like holy water, crucifixes, arcane symbols, and exotic objects like an iron stake that a criminal's head had been stuck on.[123] Treasure-finders used dowsing instruments like mirrors, crystal balls, and, most often, twigs and sticks of various sorts.[124] In at least one case incense were used, while another included "a powder" that the leader of the group "snorted like tobacco" and on another occasion one that he "smoked, so that his evil spirit would come to him."[125]

The purpose of the powder and ritual activity was to establish contact with the spirit associated with the treasure, which they would have done by inducing in the participants, or at least in their leader, who was generally a knowledgeable or even semi-professional specialist in the practice (when not an out-and-out charlatan), a trance state.[126] In the cases in which incense and powder were used, the chemicals would have contributed to this, but such aids were not necessary, since the central driving mechanism would have been the excitement generated by the undertaking combined with the often-protracted physiological activity and the psychophysical implications of the ceremonies' symbolic content.[127] The point of the ceremonies was not only to determine the precise location of the treasure, but also to "bind" it in place, since it was thought that treasures could either move of their own accord or be moved by spirits.[128] Furthermore, the magical ceremonies were also designed to protect the participants from the influence of or drive away any demons that might be guarding the treasure, either in addition to or instead of the spirit of a dead person, or the Devil, who was lord of both the underworld, where the treasure was buried, and the damned, and who therefore didn't want trapped souls to be set free.[129] In one particularly notable case the spirits began dispensing moral advice and prophesy, inspiring a quasi-religious cult following that caused considerable uproar in the early 1770s.[130]

This ambivalent moral orientation, the combination of avarice, which is perhaps base but is not directly or inherently injurious to others, with the facade of charitable concern for the poor soul trapped by the treasure, means that while treasure-hunting clearly involved a form of necromancy that shows that ordinary Württembergers were aware of and ready to use ceremonial magic in groups, it was not really sorcery, the use of ritual magic to injure or manipulate others.[131] Similarly, the related phenomenon of the "treasure-man" (*Geldmannlin*), a spirit that could be summoned or even bought (appropriately enough) and would procure for the controlling person as much money as he wanted, was reminiscent of the concept of a witch's familiar, a spirit that helped a witch do her *maleficium*, that played a major role in English witch beliefs but played only a limited role in Württemberg and elsewhere on the Continent.[132] However, the "treasure-man" himself, like the Christopher Prayer and unlike the familiar, did not harm others.[133] The readiness of many ordinary Württembergers to not only participate in but also to later candidly testify about these activities indicates that while they may have realized these spirits were probably something they really shouldn't mess with, they did not consider them to be particularly evil.

The Duchy's clerical and secular authorities, on the other hand, considered magical treasure-finding and the associated commerce with spirits to be sacrilegious and disobedient, and called them "devil conjuration" (*teuffels beschwehren*).[134] This association of treasure-finding with the Devil was in line with their broader association of magic with the Devil, an association that was not altogether foreign to the common people. We have seen that in order to spook horses Maria Gekin recited an incantation that explicitly referenced the Devil – "You are the Devil's ... You must the Devil's be," – and even if she created it herself, she was not the only Württemberger to think of appealing to the "evil enemy" in a spell. In one of the duchy's earliest trials, in 1541, a man was prosecuted in Urach for trying to invoke the Devil in a village churchyard.[135] In 1619, a "death's head" was found in a graveyard in Bietigheim "with many words written on it."[136] The skull was white, "as if it had been cleaned ... the letters" were "fresh and clear" and spelled out "Boach, Sarrith, Lucifer." In 1660 in Böblingen, "Wild Georg" Schaff told a smith's apprentice that to get a magic ring "that would help him hammer" better, he should "walk backwards through the smithy on Good Friday night between eleven and twelve o'clock in the Devil's name."[137] A few years later, Catharine Decker reported that Anna Schnabel's "grass spell" included the lines:

> Dass du verkrummest,
> Dass du verlahmest,
> Dass du verstiebest,
> Dass du verblindist,
> Dass dich der Teuffel gar hinwegfurhre,
> Ehe du zue mihr kommest.
>
> (That you become bent
> That you become lame
> That you disappear
> That you become blind
> That the Devil leads you away
> Before you come to me.)

These lines were intended to prevent the forest ranger from coming near them, and two other women gave similar accounts.[138] Finally, Margaretha Wagner, the girl who told the magistrates of Marbach that she had magically "pressed" people in 1740, also said she knew spells that would make a cow give extra milk and affect the weather that were carried out, she emphasized, not in the name of God, but "in the Devil's name."[139]

While these examples show that some people in Württemberg and elsewhere were ready to call on the Devil's aid in their magic, it is difficult to tell from them how significant his role was in the malefic aspect of witchcraft. Some of the spells recounted above were not harmful at all, like the blacksmith's, while others could have been harmful but do not seem, in these cases, to have been used maliciously: Maria Gekin seems to have used her spell to spook horses more to show off than to cause injury; Margaretha

Wagner does not seem to have tried to use her weather spells to affect anyone's harvest; and Anna Schnabel's "grass spell" seems to have been motivated by a desire to debilitate the forest rangers in order to hinder their surveillance rather than a malicious desire to harm them. In the case of more serious *maleficium*, the problem is that torture was used so liberally that most of the suspects' testimony is useless for determining what they actually did. However, some glimpses are offered by several of the other trials in the duchy.

The first took place in Rosenfeld in 1603, and involved Margretha, Michael Stainer's wife.[140] While all that remains of this trial is her tortured testimony, what makes this testimony unusual is that the magistrates investigated the 27 malefic acts she confessed to and noted the results of their inquiries in the margins of the transcript. They also followed the more routine practice of reviewing her confessions with her after the torture session and noting which she confirmed and which she retracted. She claimed to have killed and lamed a number of horses and cows and a goose, specifying that she hit many with a stick or a stone; poisoned a servant girl; and killed a number of children by hitting, kissing, or blowing on them.[141] In most cases, she said she inflicted the injuries "in the Devil's name," and in one she specifically said she told the boy "I kiss you in the Devil's name." In many of these instances, she described the specific motives that led her to perpetrate these acts: a man "refused to carry her wood" in his wagon; a woman dishonored her by asserting that she had "had borne a bastard child;" an employer had "beat her badly." Outside of the torture chamber, Margretha retracted six of her stories, but confirmed the others, and when the magistrates investigated the accounts she left standing, most of the people interviewed verified the quarrels and the injuries, with a few confirming some but not all the details, and only one denying any knowledge of what she said. This combination of partial retraction and partial confirmation, substantial corroboration but sporadic disagreement, detailed discussions of motives, and simple, for the most part directly physical violence set in the context of what we know about the intensity of conflict that was possible in early modern villages, makes it seem likely that Margretha did in fact do many of the things she said she did. Whether she specifically invoked the Devil as she did them, or whether this detail was added by her or the magistrates during her interrogation is less clear, but the fact that the lethal power of poisons, touch, and breath were supposed in early modern popular culture to come from the malevolent intent invested in them rather than simply from their physical force or properties, plus the evidence in other cases of incantations that specifically invoked the Devil, makes it quite possible that she did exploit the symbolic power of his name to intensify her malign impact.

Evidence from other parts of Europe also supports the possibility that Margretha was conscious of the Devil's hand in her actions as she attacked the children and animals, for trials elsewhere revealed that he was on occasion called upon in both relatively benign and deadly serious magical rituals. In nearby Augsburg, a woman who claimed to be a white magician told a client "to burn brandy in the name of the devil ... to win back stolen goods."[142] In Holstein, "the Devil came into play" in some sorcery cases, and the same held true in southern Italy.[143] In Spain, when a desired person proved resistant to regular love magic, "evil forces" like "St. Marta ... 'the wicked,' and ... Satan, Barabbas, the same Devil – were invoked directly or indirectly."[144] In England, a witch suspect confessed in 1662 that she stole milk from a cow by plaiting "rope the wrong way in the Devil's name."[145] In Scotland, a sorcerer named Reid performed image magic and buried enchanted objects in doorways. He had "learned his craft directly from the Devil," who "seems to have played a large part not only in Reid's instruction in magic but in its practical applications," and this was "a not uncommon feature of Scottish operative magic."[146] In Hungary, several cases of diabolic sorcery were recorded, while in Renaissance Florence several sorcery trials involved books with rituals for invoking the Devil to cause injury and death, and in one case a hired sorcerer clearly tried to kill someone using several magic rituals that he carried out while saying "in the name of Lucifer, of Satan, and Beelzebub."[147]

Two other sampled cases from Württemberg offer further evidence of the Devil's role in some instances of *maleficium*. The first was the very early case in which Magdelena Horn confessed to having injured several animals and killed a boy by hitting him. She said not only that she "had done so many bad things to animals and people, that she could not describe them all" at the Devil's instigation, but also implied that he had played a role in making her actions effective.[148] Since she said she hit the child, the Devil's role in his death would have been the same as in Margaretha Stainer's assaults, a magical intensifier that carried as much if not more weight than her hand. How she injured the animals is not so clear, however; it may have similarly combined physical and spiritual assault, but a portion of the testimony from Maria Braittingen, the young woman who said she slept with the Devil "in the form of her boyfriend," suggests that when she said the Devil did her evil she meant something rather different. Maria testified that when her employer "smacked her hard" for poor performance on her job, "from then on she became his enemy." She "appealed to her presumptive lover, the Evil Spirit, to kill the master's cow, which then happened."[149]

What is striking about Maria's account is the matter-of-fact relationship between her, the Devil, and the death of the cow. There is no suggestion that she undertook rituals or even cursed in the normal sense of the word; it is more like a woman heatedly insisting to her lover that he take her side in some interpersonal conflict. On a practical level, it is quite possible that she conveyed her hostility to the animal in the course of her daily routines as a servant in the household through the channels discussed in Chapter 1. On an experiential level, though (and regardless of her actual role in the animal's death in this case), there is something more than the direct line between the feeling of anger, the expression of anger, the perception of threat, and the onset of illness outlined there. Instead, she experienced the Devil as an intermediary in a way that comes close to the witch ideology's notion that a person self-consciously given to the Devil not only acted in the Devil's interest, but also gained thereby the power to inflict injury. Maria did not say she had made a formal pact with the Devil, but she did say she flew at night to witch dances and had sex with him, so this would seem to be a case of malefic witchcraft directly connected to the experience of diabolism. The connection, however, does not seem to have been a simple adoption of learned notions by a commoner, but instead an original fusion of personal emotion and popular ideas about *maleficium* and malign spiritual agency, with little of the demonology preached by the elite.

These examples from Württemberg were not the only ones in which malefic practices were undeniably linked to diabolism. In Scandinavia, the creation of a "milk hare," essentially a spirit familiar to steal milk for a witch, was sometimes "accompanied by the witch selling herself to the Devil and a satanic pact" that might involve sacrilegious use of a communion wafer and the recitation of a charm such as:

> I give you blood,
> the Devil gives you vitality,
> You'll run on earth for me,
> I'll burn in Hell for you.[150]

In England, the "Lancashire witches," two secluded families that openly practiced magic, constitute "probably the most challenging witch episode for the researcher to understand fully" because "all these prisoners testified freely against each other, in addition to admitting to all the allegations," which included causing 16 deaths, the killing of livestock, and damage to property, and one woman "confessed to having made a pact with the Devil" and leading her son, daughter, two grandchildren, and a neighboring woman into witchcraft.[151] In Hungary, a person could become a malevolent clan shaman, a zdhač, either by being born with a caul or "by learning and concluding a pact with the Devil."[152] In one of the sorcery cases in Renaissance Florence, the suspect was confined so that "without any physical pressure or torment, he might have the opportunity to repent," but instead "he spent his time commending himself to Lucifer, Satan, and Beelzebub, 'proclaiming himself to be in their spirit and body."[153]

While the witch demonology emphasized the relationship between diabolism and popular *maleficium*, before the early modern period, learned ceremonial magic was more commonly associated with the Devil because the difference between conjuration and adoration was not always clear-cut. Pagans commonly offered to give a particular god particular reverence in return for its help, and necromancers sometimes carried this practice over into their relationship with the demons they conjured.[154] As the culture became Christianized and the Devil came to be seen as the overlord of evil in the world, sorcery came to be seen as supplication of Satan, its power "gained, not by skill, but by compact, a sealed document delivered over to the Devil."[155] Whether or not any professional magicians actually practiced in this way in late antiquity is unclear, but there is evidence that some people did create broad pacts with the Devil in exchange for supernatural powers, and by the early modern period there is no question that some people did this.[156] The Faust legend has been traced to an actual person in the early sixteenth century, a student born in the village of Knittlingen, which became part of the Duchy of Württemberg in 1634, and who attended Heidleberg University, which lay about 50 miles down the Neckar from the Duchy's capital.[157] Nor was Faust alone, for there are documented examples of "other adventurous students who signed pacts with the devil" as well.[158] In some cases, like the trial of Urbaine Granier, purported pacts were almost certainly forgeries, but in others they appear to have been genuine.[159] A few such documents have survived; in one case a man's pact explicitly stipulated that he would enjoy the Devil's gifts for a period of nine years, after which the Devil would get him body and soul.[160]

Attempts to establish a compact with the Devil were not confined to the educated elite, for by the early modern period the idea that one could make a deal with the Devil to attain some temporal end was part of the common culture.[161] A criminal in Montaillou in the early fourteenth century observed that "sometimes the Devil has more power than God, and I have no choice but to help myself, either with the aid of God or with that of the Devil."[162] His is supposed to have been "an isolated case" at the time, but over the next three centuries awareness of the Devil and his power spread, until, as we have seen, Apolonia Walther expressed her conviction that, "her prince is the most powerful in the world, and therefore she must follow him."[163] Soldiers were known to make pacts with the Devil for protection in battle, and a man in Sweden admitted to having had a pact with the Devil after he had already been condemned for sodomy.[164] Contrary to the witch ideology, men appear to have been readier to conclude a formalistic relationship with the Devil than women, but women, like Maria Baittingen, also turned to him in an attempt to tap his powers.[165] One woman in Naples, for example, claimed not only to have had a relationship with the Devil, but also to have "counseled the Devil's help to others."[166] Another woman offered to have sex with a young man if he would make a pact with the Devil, while yet another said that she did homage to him, praying "I worship you, oh lord and Devil, attend my soul."[167] This last admission is rather similar to Maria

Gekin's testimony, for not only did Maria recite the invocation of the Devil that she used to spook horses, but also another incantation that dedicated herself to him:

> Dem Teuffel will ich seye,
> Dem Teuffel will ich bleiben,
> Dem Teuffel will ich verbunden seye,
> Dem Teuffel will nimmer aus seinen handen,
> Der Teuffel hat mich gemacht,
> Der Teuffel hat mich erlöst,
> Der Teuffel hat mich geheiliget,
> In seinen hande will ich bleiben
> Dem Teuffel will ich imer und ewig seye.
>
> (To the Devil I want to be,
> To the Devil I want to stay,
> To the Devil I want to be bound,
> To the Devil want never from his hand,
> The Devil has made me,
> The Devil has saved me,
> The Devil has sanctified me,
> In his hands I want to stay
> To the Devil I want always and eternally to be.)[168]

In addition, she recited a similar prayer she called "the Devil's woman's saying," which included lines like "We should go together in the Devil's service" and "With him eat drink celebrate / and [for] them testify praise and thank."[169] Maria was not the only person in Württemberg to recite such prayers to the Devil, for about 70 years, or two generations, earlier, in 1668, a young boy from a village near Bebenhausen had recited a similar hymn to the Devil that he claimed was sung at a witch dance during an investigation of his claims of having flown to a witch dance.[170]

In Württemberg, as in most of the rest of Europe, Christianity was the official religion, so any commerce with the Devil constituted apostasy.[171] The most extreme expression of this logic was the demonological argument that all magic required the intercession of demons, and therefore constituted an implicit pact with the Devil. In practice, of course, most Württembergers, and even Württemberg's legal system, treated beneficent magic as at most a moral lapse rather than an act of heresy, which was in line with most other parts of Europe.[172] Popular healers routinely protested that they did not use magic, confining themselves to natural methods or, at most, advised their clients to pray.[173] Most cunning folk who used magic, like most learned magicians, saw that their activities as helpful and therefore morally justifiable even if the authorities disagreed, and even people who used malefic magic often justified it as "a holy art ... a deeper, if not higher, morality, in the case of learned necromancers, or as righteous retaliation for wrongs inflicted on them, in the case of village witches.[174] Even some people who made pacts with the Devil appear to have thought that they remained Christian, and others assumed that it was relatively easy to renounce such an agreement later on, as folklore commonly assured them.[175]

Nevertheless, theologians were not the only ones who recognized the conflict between magical practices and the expectations of the Christian religion. Not only did pacts with the Devil generally include a provision that the person renounce Christianity, but also participation in some extra-Christian cult activities could also involve renunciation of the dominant religion. The "antipathy of fairies toward Christianity" in Ireland was "frequently mentioned," and "Cornish miners refused to make the sign of the cross when down in a mine, for fear of offending the fairies in their own subterranean territory by making a gesture that invoked their enemy."[176] In 1457, Nicholas of Cusa interviewed two women who "told him they were in the service of Domina Abundia, and went with her to revels" and "had vowed themselves to 'Richella' in return for good fortune and had promised to abstain from all Christian observances."[177] In Italy a woman who followed a "Madonna di Finemundo" said she went to mass "for fear of being excommunicated," but "when the high point of the mass was reached I didn't look at the Host or Chalice ... but hid, turning my face the other way, because I knew I was given to the Devil and damned."[178] Somewhat similarly, a woman in upper Swabia reported that "she believed that she must have blasphemed God" because "she had a 'lover who came from Hell, [and] he wanted that she deny God.'"[179] Among the sampled witch suspects in Württemberg, a number confessed, under torture, to having renounced God and pledged allegiance to the Devil, but these confessions appear to have been made to stop the torment, with, at most, an admixture of retroactive recognition that habitual recourse to *maleficium* was tantamount to having allied with the Devil and thereby turned against God and the Christian religion. However, we have seen that some suspects did confess freely, and they recognized the conflict between membership in the Christian church and their relationship with the Devil. Apolonia Walther said without coercion that "her Hannß, the Devil, had threatened to beat her if she told the preacher everything, and if she prayed with" him, and went on, as we have seen, that "her prince is the most powerful in the world, and therefore she must follow him."[180] We have also see that when Hanß Jacob Langen took his third trip "on a pitchfork ... a barber named Hannß ... drew several drops of blood, [and] he had to renounce the Holy Trinity, and sign with his blood in a book, whereupon" his friends "promised him they would teach him how to make lice and fleas." Ordinary Württembergers, like common people elsewhere, understood the incompatibility of Devilish behavior and the requirements of Christianity. Some of the duchy's people held themselves strictly to the dictates of Christian morality, most strove to keep their lapses limited enough that they could hope for forgiveness and salvation in the end, some came to the realization that they had strayed to the Devil's path, and a few consciously crossed over to his side. For some people illicit magic was an occasional transgression, for others, perhaps, a bad habit they alternately fell into and tried to break, but for a few, at least, it became a defining feature of their lives.[181]

Not only did the ideas of the pact with the Devil and the renunciation of Christianity have roots in the practice of sorcery, but also the notion that witches worked in groups was related to sorcery and other magical practices as well. We have seen that treasure hunters worked in groups, and while their practices were not malefic, hostile weather magic was also a collective activity.[182] One of the sorcery cases from Florence discussed earlier involved "a substantial group ... which engaged, actively or vicariously, in the practice of the black arts," while another involved "a colony of sorcerers" who, an inquisitor reported based on the book they used, "adore and invoke Satan and Beelzebub and ... worship idols."[183] Four centuries later, in 1741, a woman named Maria Salinaro claimed to have 21 disciples, at least one of whom she told to seek the Devil's help, and four of whom she led in beating a Capuchin exorcist "who they were afraid was aware of" one woman's "use of sorcery to cause a man's death."[184] In the Balkans groups of healers "practiced a kind of possession cult" that practiced "collective ecstasy" to heal illnesses caused by fairies, while in Sicily "women who belonged to the organization of the 'living' fairies maintained contact with them through trance and in dreams."[185] The members of these last two groups did not think of themselves as dealing with the Devil, but they, and similar groups in Hungary, were taken to be witches. Similarly, in Paris in the late seventeenth and early eighteenth centuries magical practitioners of various sorts "often ... acted together," forming loose networks that the police called "'cabals' or ... sects" they found "extremely difficult to 'penetrate.'"[186] In general these practitioners were more or less benign fortune-tellers and treasure-seekers, but in some cases they offered manipulative love magic and poisons (called "inheritance powders" due to their use by aristocrats in a hurry to get their hands on their family fortune), and there was evidence of some practicing of black masses.[187] In Sweden, there were several cases in which "two or three people drew up a joint agreement" with the Devil for nonmalefic purposes, while in southern Germany "vagrant juvenile bands" engaged in "threats ... violence ... sorcery and witchcraft ... believing in the effectiveness of magical formulas and rituals."[188] Among the sampled witch trials in Württemberg there was no evidence that the suspects engaged in collective *maleficium*, but, as we have seen, there were several examples of small groups who undertook nonmalefic forms of magic like Anna Schnabel's "grass prayer" and three brothers who attempted to fix shooting contests magically, and the numerous cases in which several or even many people engaged in magical treasure-seeking.[189]

Do these individual and collective incantations of prayers to and pacts with the Devil indicate that there really was an underground diabolical counter-religion in Württemberg, and Italy, and potentially across Europe, between the 1560s and the 1740s, and presumably before and after? Although the use of torture contaminates most of the evidence from the period of the witch trials, making it impossible to tell for sure, it does not seem very likely at all. The incidents cited are too isolated and too idiosyncratic, like the examples of prayers and hymns from Württemberg that were clearly derived from local culture and individual imaginations rather than any cohesive set of beliefs or organized ritual behaviors. Other investigations of purported witch gatherings have similarly come up empty, and historians understandably have concluded that the whole idea was nothing but an illusion generated by some combination of institutional self interest on the part of church and state; the sociocultural processes that enable large groups of people to generate, accept, and act upon collective myths; and psychopathology on the part of the people, some of whom feared the Devil's conspiracy, and others of whom, an insignificant minority, who imagined that they were part of it.

However, the evidence from Württemberg and elsewhere reviewed here indicates that belief in the Devil's conspiracy had stronger roots in reality than this interpretation acknowledges. First of all, it is clear that the idea that one could deliberately solicit the Devil's help to gain magical powers was in wide circulation by the turn of the seventeenth century. Secondly, there is no question that some people acted upon this idea either on a limited basis to help with specific acts of *maleficium* or to conclude a more general relationship in order to obtain a more lasting power. We saw in Chapter 3 that the Devil could be understood to be the source of inspiration for bad actions, either in retrospect or at the time they were committed, but here we can see that some people went beyond this and actively solicited the aid of the Devil in their illicit activities. Thirdly, there is no doubt that sometimes people who practiced such magic worked in groups, teaching or swapping techniques, collaborating in their performance, and sharing, or at least being prepared to share in, their fruits. While the Devil does not seem to have traveled around Europe physically, with his tail tucked into his pants, organizing and leading an underground sect of worshippers, the idea of the Devil did, and thereby lent a degree of cohesion to the disparate practices and beliefs of angry and alienated people in various corners of Christendom.

From one perspective, the Devil can be thought of as a kind of collective id, the sum total of all the negative forces in human life. Like the id, the Devil is not an independent conscious entity, but instead is a functional subset of a larger whole. Nevertheless, the fact that the disparate elements making them up are functionally related means that they often seem to act in a coordinated or mutually supportive way that makes it reasonable to speak of them as having a cohesive will and autonomous volition. Within a person, the primitive drives and destructive complexes that make up the id act in an often mutually reinforcing way so that psychoanalysts speak of the id motivating actions as if it were an independent conscious entity. Similarly, the primitive drives and destructive complexes shared among people, along with forces of nature inimical to peoples' welfare, often act in a mutually reinforcing way so that Christians think of the Devil as an independent conscious entity motivating peoples' actions. And, as we have seen, believing this can lead to visualizing, hearing, and interacting with the Devil as an independent conscious entity, endowing him with a high degree of experiential reality.

From another perspective, the Devil can be thought of as a meme, a cultural artifact that both organizes an individual's thoughts and behaviors and, since it propagates from brain to brain, organizes collective beliefs and actions as well.[190] Like a gene, from which the word was derived, a meme is not an independent conscious entity, but instead is an autonomous replicator subject to the forces of natural selection.[191] Memes that find purchase in new minds and mobilize their hosts to defend and disseminate them flourish, while those that cannot establish themselves in new brains or do not use them to steer behavior in a way that protects and spreads them die out. From this point of view, the Devil was an organizing principle for both the people who feared him and the people who followed him. For those who feared him, he worked in tandem with God, part of the stick God used when his carrots didn't sufficiently motivate the faithful, and also the leader of the enemy whose menace helped bind believers together. For the smaller number who followed or flirted with the Devil, though, he did compete directly with God, stimulating and facilitating thoughts and actions at odds with the reigning orthodoxy. For this reason, there was a tension in the Christian attitude toward the Devil, for while the Devil played a role in God's order, God was a meme himself, and for people to actually renounce God and venerate the Devil threatened the God-meme's control over the resources it needed to survive and reproduce.[192] The monotheistic concept of God had an inherent antipathy toward all competing deities, and the complex of memes associated with it, the beliefs and institutions of the Judeo-Christian tradition, had long since developed mechanisms to combat them, for memes, like genes, evolve as well as replicate, and natural selection had shaped the complex of ideas and the institutions that embodied them that made up Christianity into a formidable cultural competitor.

While thinking of the Devil as a sort of collective id or a meme helps us see how he could be something less than an independent conscious agent but more than simply a passive cultural symbol or individual psychological malfunction, they illuminate his role as a source of motivation more than his role as a source of power. To understand that, we need to consider more closely his role within peoples' minds and his role in society. In particular, he could be a source of power in two ways. First, to invoke him in a particular instance through a magic ritual was to call on the maximum power available for use in illicit spiritual activity. In a Christian society this was the ultimate form of inversion, which would strengthen the sorcerer's psychological resolve by categorically defying social dictates while, if made publicly, bringing a powerful force against the psychological defenses of his target. Secondly, to go beyond a specific invocation by pledging oneself to the Devil was a different form of inversion, a way of reversing the social order so that a person who felt disadvantaged could feel empowered. While successful people were sometime suspected of having gotten that way with the Devil's aid, in general the people who turned to him seem to have been relatively low in the social hierarchy. People with low social status by definition enjoy less social power than higher-ranked people, but they also suffer from poorer physical health than higher-ranked people and from psychophysical debilities that make it difficult for them to function at an optimal level psychologically.[193] For a peasant woman to assert that "her prince is the most powerful in the world" reverses the established hierarchy, at least in her mind (which is where it counts), in order to gain the enhanced cognitive capabilities that come with higher social status, and from them more tangible manifestations that such status brings. Furthermore, the extent to which other people in the community accept that a person has a special relationship with the Devil, they are drawn into an alternative hierarchy in which their status is relatively lower, counteracting to some extent the beneficial effects that being high in the dominant hierarchy have. Both invocation and worship of the Devil are ways a person can alter her own and her neighbors' cognitive functioning in order to strengthen her while weakening them. Historians have recently come to acknowledge that a reputation as a witch could be used to gain influence in the community, but this line of analysis suggests that this affected not just neighbors' opinions and actions, but also the witch's self-conception, and through that the levels of her own sense of well-being, her ability to project confidence and interpersonal power, and, inversely, her neighbors' psychophysical ability to resist the influence of these.

An intriguing example of how the idea of the Devil could be adopted as a form of empowerment in the early modern period took place at the very edges of the European world, in the colonial society of Spanish America. Here, the Catholic conquistadores encountered innumerable gods and classified them as demons subservient to the Devil. After a generation or two the old gods had almost disappeared as the natives converted to Christianity, but then in remote areas a new challenge to the Catholic Church arose, worship of the Devil![194] The idea of the Devil itself came from Christianity, of course, and the idea of worshipping him was suggested by the Christian accusation that followers of the old religions had been in fact worshipping him, but the stimulus to turn to the Devil as an alternative to worshipping as a Christian came from the Native Americans themselves. One man insisted, for example, that "nobody had taught him to pray to the devil and ask for his help," instead he came up with the idea on his own when he heard that his ancestors had worshipped and gotten help from him.[195] In 1597 a book in a Native American language was found that encouraged the "reader to 'offer and commend' himself to the Lord Lucifer'" and to stop taking the sacrament and saying the rosary.[196] Some people who turned to him withdrew to the mountains or caves, where "they would invariably be asked to forsake God ... take off the rosary ... promise to stop going to mass, praying to God ... or observing any ... teachings of the Church." For those who wanted to tap the Devil's power to aid in their magic, "any acknowledgement of God, any reference to the mysteries of the faith or manifestation of Christian devotion was not only invalid but positively detrimental."[197] One man who found the Devil more attractive than God flagrantly avoided church, while another was seen trampling and spitting on Christian images belonging to a devout neighbor.[198] This recourse to the Devil usually came after the person had tried and failed to enlist the support of God, was sometime followed by a contrite return to the Church when the Devil didn't come through, and these practices never amounted to a widespread or serious challenge to the Church's hold on the population as a whole, but it does show how people could respond to the idea of the Devil and work through its implications in a way that fulfilled, at least in part, the Church's fears about his influence.[199]

It seems possible that a similar process was at work in the Swiss valleys in the fourteenth and fifteenth centuries when missionary Catholic monks came into conflict with a mixture of Waldensianism, folk magic, and sorcery that they understood to be a "new witchcraft" combining organized Devil worship and malefic magic. More loosely, it seems like a model for a process of alienation and reorientation that took place on an individual level in some disaffected people across the Christian world. Timing seems particularly important in this regard: while the Devil was known and invoked in the Middle Ages, his role in magical culture was not static. Instead, over the course of the early modern period, it appears that, just as awareness of his role in motivating anti-social acts grew, so, too, recourse to him became more frequent and more specific. He appears to have gone from being one of a number of malign spirits invoked (along with demons such as Beelzebub, Berich, and so on) to being the primary, and to many, the sole source of malign power, even as the nature of the relationship to him shifted from primarily one of occasional dealings to exercise specific powers to a broader allegiance exchanged for broader powers or generalized fortune. To some extent, of course, these changes reflected the diffusion of the witch ideology, but to ascribe them all to this seems to put too much emphasis on the influence of elite culture and not enough on the autonomous inventiveness of ordinary people. An ability to reason logically appears to be one of the innate cognitive abilities that humans are born with, and, while we have seen that people have a powerful ability to dissociate thoughts and feelings and hold simultaneously (or, in terms of conscious awareness, serially and alternatively) to contradictory propositions, this ability appears to vie with a strong impulse for psychological integrity, a compulsion to rationalize their thoughts and feelings into logical consistency.[200] It did not take a theologian to see how the Devil could be the instigator of evil intentions or how he could be called upon to facilitate malevolent magic, and the evolution of popular culture involved its own internal dynamics as well as the influence of developments in elite culture, which themselves would seem to have involved the influence of developments in popular culture along with their own internal dynamics.

None of this is to suggest that there was actually an underground organization of Devil-worshipping witches in early modern Europe or that the cruel and bloody campaign to eradicate them was necessary or justified. Instead, the point is that fear of it was not simply a paranoid fantasy, nor was the experience of participating in it simply an isolated pathological delusion. Instead both the fears and the experiences were rooted in a way of understanding the world, a system of meanings that not only involved symbols and beliefs, but also connected to a variety of experiences and practices, so that the complex found apparent confirmation in a variety of concrete circumstances. Furthermore, this complex of beliefs and practices was not itself static, but was undergoing profound developments over the course of the early modern period as travel, trade, printing, and the propaganda campaigns of the elite diffused and mixed knowledge of various magical and spirit traditions and connected them ever-more strongly to larger developments in religious and intellectual culture.

Witchcraft and shamanism

The witch demonology combined ideas about the practice of sorcery with fears about underground heretical movements, reports of dream experiences, and belief in the immanent presence of the Devil into a myth that both distorted and exaggerated the individual elements that made it up. So far as can be determined, no Luciferan conspiracy, no cult of Devil worshipping witches existed; the witchcraft constructed by the demonologists served as a metaphor for the process of alienation that drove some women into such intense conflict with their neighbors that they harmed them, either intentionally or inadvertently. Yet, while the content of the witch ideology combined real but disparate elements into a fictitious whole, the structure of the whole was based on something real as well: the process of shamanic initiation.[201] Shamans, men or women who specialize in entering altered states of consciousness to travel to the spirit world, have been found in numerous societies around the world, and the process by which they become shamans has striking parallels to the process by which people in early modern Europe were thought to become witches.

Shaman is a term that is used in many different ways. At its most restrictive, it refers to members of certain Siberian tribes who conduct performances in which they enter an altered state of consciousness in which they experience the flight of their soul to the spirit world so that they can gain information and influence the spirits on behalf of other members of their community, primarily to heal them.[202] At its broadest, it is used to refer to virtually anyone who alters their consciousness and conveys some sense of insight from the experience to other members of their society. In between, the most common use of the term refers to practitioners in a wide variety of hunting, pastoral, and agricultural societies scattered around the world who enter an altered state of consciousness in order to "fly" to the spirit world on behalf of their communities. Another, somewhat broader but also broadly used definition of shamanism includes anyone who enters an altered state of consciousness in order to contact spirits.[203] Under the first intermediate definition, in the nineteenth century shamans were found in Asia, North and South America, and Southern Africa, but not in the rest of Africa, which had mediums, specialists who entered altered states of consciousness in which spirits possessed them, or in the Mediterranean and European worlds, whose spiritual practices were dominated by priests and an admixture of mediums, saints, and mystics. Under the second, African spiritual specialists would also be included, along with mediums, saints, mystics and ritual magicians in the Mediterranean and European areas.[204]

We will start by contrasting the classic structuralization of shamanic initiation under the first intermediate definition with the process by which people purportedly became witches.[205] To begin with, candidates for shamanhood are generally dreamy or going through a crisis, and are usually chosen by a spirit, or else because they are related to an existing shaman. Similarly, people were thought to become witches because they were melancholic and/or depressed when the Devil came a-calling, like Johann Bebion's wife and Anna Eberlin, or because their mother or another female relative initiated them into it, as was said of of Agatha Stosser and as Margaretha Wagner claimed. A crucial step in classic initiation is the use of ritual, sometimes with and sometimes without the aid of intoxicating agents, to induce an altered state of consciousness in which the shaman experiences a journey, usually flight, to the spirit world to interact with different spirits; the next step in a witch's initiation was to fly to a witch dance at which she worshipped the Devil with other witches. Shamans gain from their spiritual encounters extraordinary knowledge and magical powers, which they then use for divination, healing, and, possibly, bewitching. Witches were thought to gain from their attendance at the Sabbaths the power and knowledge to commit *maleficium*. Shamans also sometimes gain the aid of helping spirits, and, as part of their practice, routinely return to the spirit world or send their helpers; witches were believed to have familiar spirits in some traditions (particularly in England, although to a lesser extent in Germany as well). Witches were also believed in some areas to travel in spirit to attack their victims, and they were generally thought to return periodically to Sabbaths. The correspondence is not exact, for shamanic initiation often, but not always, involves a ritual experience of death and rebirth, while a witch's initiation did not. However, the witch's renunciation of her Christian identity and assumption of a new, diabolical one could be seen as a symbolic equivalent, and overall the parallels seem strong enough to raise the question of what possible connection there might be.

Most witch suspects were not shamans, of course, but there is evidence that significant elements of shamanism did exist in Europe in the early modern period. On the periphery, the Sami people of northern Scandinavia practiced a full-blown shamanism closely related to that of Siberia; immediately adjacent to them, folk magicians in southeastern Finland performed shamanic healing ceremonies; and Norse literature contains accounts of trance-flight experiences.[206] Around 1500, the Swedish historian and geographer Olaus Magneus described a diviner who fell "to the ground, like a corpse, from which the soul is gone," lay still for a time, and then gave "information about the far away place just as if he had seen it himself."[207] In northeastern Europe, evidence of the shamanic practice of shape shifting has been found, while in southeastern Europe there was an extensive spirit (fairy) cult in which a goddess presided over an otherworld to which magicians initiated by spirits would travel to share in festivities and learn "about healing and the use of herbal grasses."[208] In Romania, female magicians would lie down, whimper, roll their eyes, and contort, lie still for hours, and then wake up and tell of the events they had witnessed, performances reminiscent of shamans'.[209] In Greece, "holy healers ... converse with the saints" who either lead them in trance into the spirit world or possess them.[210] In Slovenia sorcerers flew to fight against each other in trance or dream, as some Siberian shamans claimed to, and some Hungarian witches both fell into trances to make soul journeys and also were said to abduct victims and transport them similarly to their revelries.[211] Hungarian *taltos* flew in spirit to battle witches and the malevolent dead to protect their communities' crops, and also healed, identified thieves, and located lost objects and treasure.[212] Other Hungarian practitioners specialized in traveling to the land of the dead while in trance.[213] Similarly, some *benandanti* in the Fruili flew in spirit to fight for the fertility of the crops, while others walked with the spirits of the dead. In nearby Milan, four women claimed in the late 1300s that they had "ecstatic experiences with the 'good lady and her folk' and were therefore able to cure and to look into the future."[214] Farther south, in Sicily, the people who met with "the ladies from outside" did not do so simply to party, but also to gain the power to help heal people inflicted with diseases caused by the fairies.[215]

In the British Isles, popular magic included significant elements of non-Christian spirit beliefs that contained important elements of shamanism. "Seeing women" in Ireland and Scotland went into trance in order to contact the dead, tell fortunes, and observe remote scenes.[216] Irish legends contain references to people who travel to other worlds and battle in spirit, and Irish popular culture contained a strong admixture of beliefs about fairies, spirits thought to reside in pre-Christian burial mounds (the Irish word for fairy, "sí," means "mound").[217] These fairies and their cousins in England and Scotland were thought to be able to cause and cure diseases as well as impart hidden knowledge and perform other magical feats, and so they were contacted for aid against illness, and as witches' familiars to cause it, and for other beneficial and malevolent purpose.[218] In 1438, "a Somerset fortuneteller and healer ... was charged ... with communicating with fairies, and claiming that she 'sought their advice whenever she pleased," and in 1499 three members of another family were convicted of "heretical depravity" for consorting with what they called "gracious fairies" who performed various deeds on their behalf. In 1566, a cunning man from Dorset said he went into the hills "where there were 'great heaps of earth'" to learn from the fairies, "which of his clients was bewitched and where stolen objects could be found."[219] In the sixteenth century the "fairies" were often said to have bestowed magical powers on people, and in Scotland human witches were commonly thought to use "elf-shot" supplied by fairies to cause illness.[220] English witch beliefs were distinguished by the prominent role played by familiars, and "fairy beliefs ... underpinned the whole construct of the witches familiar."[221] British fairy beliefs were not the same thing as shamanism, of course – traveling in spirit in particular seems to have played relatively little role in them, – but they did involve the shamanistic features of communing with spirits and sending them out on ones' behalf. Interestingly, the lack of reference to the Sabbath in English trials is generally explained by the inability of magistrates to use torture to compel suspects to recite fantastical details, but trials did include plenty of fantastical details about familiars, so perhaps the difference in trial records is more connected to differences in the elements of shamanism in popular culture than the traditional legal explanation allows for.

Back on the continent, in France there is more evidence of the experience of soul flight. In the 1230s, William of Auvegne, the Bishop of Paris, "described the cult of the Lady Abundance, whose retinue of flying female spirits were known as the 'nighttime ladies'" who claimed to "bestow great good things on the households that they visit."[222] Some women claimed to belong to this cult, and to experience the flight it involved, like a woman who told Etienne de Bourbon, "Lord, you ought to thank me ... for when I was going with the good things, in the middle of the night, we entered your house" and she covered his sleeping body because if "Our Lady" had seen his nakedness, the ladies "would have beaten you to death." Three centuries later, Jean Bodin reported on "seven magicians who, in the presence of many people ... lost consciousness ... for three hours. Then they sat up and said what they had seen" in various remote locales.[223] In the south of France, in addition to "love magic, harmful magic, [and] the belief in spirits" the Cathars in the early fourteenth century told a "story of a soul leaving the body in the form of a snake," a variant of shamanic soul travel, while one Waldensian in southwestern France claimed to "see the dead not only in his dreams, but while he was awake," and he "served as a courier for the deceased," taking instructions from the living to the land of the dead. He said "his cousin had been able to walk with the dead" as well, "and sometimes she had gone with them for three or four days."[224]

This connection with between Waldensianism and soul travel, at least at the popular level, was not confined to France. In the fourteenth and fifteenth centuries "the priestly power of binding and resolving was central for the brethrens' abilities, at least in the eyes of their followers ... all over Europe," and an investigation in Austria in the 1310s revealed that "two of the brothers had to go to Paradise every year, to receive the power."[225] Similarly, "in northern Germany in the late fourteenth century ecstatic experiences were commonly thought to be a Waldensian affair" also involving "periodic trips to Paradise." However, Waldensians were far from the only Germans to have such experiences; in fact, "it is striking ... how far popular beliefs contained ideas about other world journeys independently of any allusions to witchcraft or Waldensianism."[226] Also from northern Germany, a "legend tells of a midwife who was fetched into the mountain by a 'white witch'" where "a little 'elves' salve' under her eyes ... made it possible for her to see the inhabitants of the lower world" once she "returned to the realm of mortals."[227] In the German-speaking Alps in the sixteenth century, men like Chonrad Stocklin and Hans Tscholi "were serving their communities as healers, diviners and messengers to the other world ... characteristic features of shamanism."[228] As late as 1600, Lucerne chancellor Renward Cysat reported "dozens of stories of well-known contemporaries, who were members of the good society."[229]

A few years later, an incident in Württemberg took place that provides evidence of and insight into one more example of shamanism that was current during the early modern era. Hans Haasen, a "very poor" 68-year-old "transient drinking at the barber Simen Stiekhels' house ... claimed to be an 'itinerant scholar' famous for many magical arts like treasure-finding, fortune-telling, and healing of people and animals."[230] Word of his claims reached the magistrates, who brought him in for questioning. He told them his father had died when he was still young, and his mother abandoned him when she remarried. "Suffering under great poverty, he then herded animals, which gradually reduced him in his youth to a pitiful man," particularly since he had been "injured by a horse" so badly that he could "still feel the effects." When he was around 30, though, a man named "Little George from Ladenberg" said that "if he followed him, he would teach him so that the rest of his life would be good." Hans agreed, so Little George "took him on a ram to a dark mountain called the Venusberg, where he saw many magnificent people, particularly a very large, well-built woman" who, "in front looked like a normal person, but behind looked all light and fiery." He said that he stayed there nine years, and, under questioning, added that he "left behind a rib from his right side ... that the Devil took from him, and gave him instructions that he could heal himself with burdock."[231] He added that "he had learned so much that with his healing art he was able to help people and animals with many conditions and illnesses," for which he accepted "no wage, but was content with what one gave him with a good will." In healing, "besides the herbs used, he ... always recited a special prayer" as well. Just the day before he was brought in he had "helped a citizen's child" who had heart problems and a deformity; he "laid the right hand on the chest, recited something, and instructed the child to be bathed in the Kressich spring, upon which it quickly improved." He claimed that there were only nine people like him in the world, including Little George, a man from Nuremberg and another from Passau.

Hans told the magistrates that actually "he could not boast of treasure-seeking and fortune-telling," but "let run" talk about it in order to "occasionally earn a piece of bread thereby, and to make the healing he had learned more noticed." He said that when learning his healing arts he had agreed that if he should die within the next 38 years "he would be and remain the Devil's," but if however he should live longer than the specified time he should be free." He vehemently denied having "ever wanted to injure or afflict people or animals," and he said his prayers came "from the Holy scriptures." The magistrates, and the officials in the High Council in Stuttgart, were particularly interested in the details of Hans' visit to the Venusberg, such as what he ate, and what language was spoken there, but when he was questioned further, after a week in custody, he denied "that he was in the Venusberg, and had dealings with the evil Spirit."[232] He blamed his earlier statements on the drink, pointed out that he was not missing a rib but instead had a mark where the horse had kicked him, and said that he had learned healing "from an old aunt, and a hangman's apprentice."

Hans may have made up the story as he claimed, but his denial is itself suspect under the circumstances. In the first place, he had obvious reasons to downplay his incautious remarks. Secondly, "itinerant scholars" who practiced ritual magic had been known at least since the high middle ages. They were described in the Middle High German poem "Vita Vagorum," and their "heyday" came at the end of the fifteenth century.[233] The "itinerant scholars were particularly associated with Swabia, even in the twentieth century, and they were mentioned in a number of other trials, but similar figures were known elsewhere, like the "garabonciás" in Hungary, "wandering sorcerers of uncertain adherence and ambiguous functions."[234] In the sixteenth century the "itinerant scholars" came to be depicted as "swindlers and tramps ... who sold amulets, knew how to work magic formulas, effect miraculous cures, find treasures, exorcize demons, make prophesies, recover stolen goods, and possessed old magic books."[235] By the seventeenth century they were just one element in the floating population of "wandering performers, fortune-tellers, exorcists, rat-catchers, quacks, and similar itinerant outsiders ... who not infrequently got caught up in the witch persecutions."[236] They claimed to comprise a larger group, were thought to have made a pact with the Devil, were known to use a "wonder salve" to experience flight, and were thought to practice black magic. They also maintained that "the Venusberg was ... the schoolplace where" they "learned magic."[237] Zuanue delle Piatte, a wandering witch-doctor in the Italian Alps, who was "well known in many villages ... claimed to visit regularly the Venusberg, where the Fairy Queen was living," while just a few years after Hans Haasen was investigated, in Calvinist Isenburg-Büdinger a man named Diell Breull said that he "visited Frau Holle in her mountain castle and was therefore able to foresee the future."[238] The conflation of Holda, Venus and the Fairy Queen was not unusual, and Holda, in particular, was known for "bathing and binding up the lame and maimed."[239]

It seems clear that Hans did not physically live in a mountain, dark or otherwise, for nine years, but a number of aspects of his story suggest that he had, in fact, been initiated into an offshoot of the shamanic tradition. First, candidates to become shamans are often moody or depressed, and Hans said he had been "reduced ... to a pitiful man" when Little George approached him.[240] Second, while magical flight is the most typical mode of transport to the spirit world, transformation into, or riding on, animals, as Hans rode on a goat, is also common.[241] Third, the Venusberg was particularly associated with a school of magic supposedly founded by Virgil on a mountain near Naples where a temple to Venus had been erected, by the early modern period the term was associated with the "itinerant scholars, and, as the connection to Holda suggests, was linked to Germanic traditions which also contain references to several mountains to which departed souls migrated and which could be visited by the living to gain magical knowledge.[242] "The idea of a Cosmic Mountain as the Center of the World," the "connection between earth and sky" which the "shaman climbs in dream during his initiatory illness and that he later visits on his ecstatic journeys" is widespread among shamanic cultures, and was probably the source of the classical belief.[243] Third, shamans acquire occult knowledge and power through instruction by benign spirits and struggle against hostile ones, and Hans met "many magnificent people" on the mountain, one of whom ("the Devil" in the magistrates' report) removed his rib before instructing him how to heal himself.[244] Fourth, Central Asian shamans often have "celestial wives" who "help ... either in instruction or in ... ecstatic experience," a role which Holda played in Germanic legend and the "large, well-built woman" seems to have played for Hans.[245] Fifth, shamans retain from their initiations healing and other magical powers which they use to help other people; so, too, did Hans. In fact, the only important aspect of shamanic initiation Hans' story omitted was the "drama of ritual death and resurrection," the initial experience of classic Siberian shamanism held by older authorities to be the defining feature of shamanism.[246] However, more recent investigations suggest that experience of death and resurrection in trance is not as common as was once thought; in many cultures training involves a less dramatic withdrawal from society for a period of time.[247] In any case, the parallels between what he did discuss and the general features of shamanism suggest that he was intimately familiar with a magical tradition rooted in the prehistoric past.

The general correspondence of Hans' story to regional lore about wandering magicians and to shamanism highlights some connections between the "itinerant scholars" to shamanism, but these do not settle whether he actually was an "itinerant scholar" initiated by Little George from Ladenberg and schooled on the Venusberg, as he boasted over beer, or just a humble herder who knew a little about healing from "an old aunt and a hangman's apprentice," as he protested when facing prosecution. However, while the documentary evidence cannot settle the question definitely, and his claim of having been in the mountain for nine years suggests that his story was not entirely factual, some details in his testimony suggest that he was speaking from real, if imagined, first-hand experience rather than just hearsay. For one thing, the fact that he did not identify the female figure by name, but instead described her, suggests that he was not simply reciting a legend. For another, his discussion of the removal of his bone is a singular detail, somewhat reminiscent of shamanic stories about dismemberment of animals that are then reconstituted from their bones that were current in the region, and also of the shamanic experience of being dismembered during initiation, and, finally, may be related to a Hungarian belief that witches removed bones in order to bewitch, but his seems to have been original and directly related to his actual condition.[248] Furthermore, and even more telling, the fact that the spirit who removed the bone instructed Hans on what herb to use to heal himself, and that this appears to have been his initial healing experience, are both typical of shamanic initiatory experiences.[249] Finally, in his initial interview he was asked "if one also ate and drank in this mountain, and what kind of language was used there?" He replied that "he had indeed seen bread there, but did not know if it was real bread or what was in it," and he said "the language sounded like "Haio, Kaio, which," the magistrates added, "means blasphemies." His response regarding the bread, not knowing "if it was real bread," suggests his experience was a real dream experience rather than a fictional real experience, and the sounds he reported sound like a chant, which is one of the things shamans typically learn during their sojourns in the spirit world, but which does not seem to have been contained in myths and legends current in the region.[250]

There are three ways that this healer in Altensteig could have been connected to the larger phenomenon of shamanism. The first is a regional tradition based on a continuous line of descent from some ancient forbearers, the transmission down through the centuries of beliefs and techniques, undoubtedly modified over time, but maintaining and conveying a core of knowledge and practices used by generation after generation. And, indeed, shamanism does seem to have been an important element of the religion of the original Germanic tribes that settled the area.[251] Tacitus reported that the religion of the Semnones, who lived in Brandenburg at the time he was with them but who migrated southwest and formed the Alemanni confederation during late Roman times, "seems to have been shamanistic – involving trance and possession – and devoted to goddesses as much as to gods."[252] Soon thereafter, Christianity was introduced, and its influence steadily grew until by the early modern period it dominated popular consciousness as well as official culture, but magical practices reminiscent of shamanism continued to be used widely, albeit with a heavily Christian symbolism. Many of these practices were ritualized memories, but some, like Hans' spiritual apprenticeship on the Venusberg, appear to have been vital experiences.

However, the very fact that he called his magic mountain the Venusberg indicates that his connection to shamanism was through more than just a local or regional tradition. Instead, it was also linked to the larger phenomenon of shamanism in a second way, for it manifested the diffusion not just of one, but of numerous spiritual traditions which not only spread but mixed and cross-fertilized to feed an enormous network of ever-evolving local traditions. Popular magic is a far more fluid and eclectic set of traditions than religions tend to be. To begin with, Christianity itself absorbed, developed, and transmitted numerous elements that were similar to magic involving appeals to God, Christ, the Virgin, and the saints for health, wisdom, and success. These elements infused local magic with symbols and rituals that not so much disguised pagan beliefs as manifested peoples' evolving consciousness and reflected their desire to both tap and avoid alienating the most potent spiritual forces they knew of. Further, as we have seen with sorcery, learned traditions, easily transported in the form of manuscripts and books, influenced and were in turn influenced by various local cultures.[253] Some of the learned traditions involving "sending out ... bad spirits with malicious intent," and weather magic, for example, appear to have been derived from shamanic traditions originally performed by unlettered practitioners, while we have seen numerous examples of local practitioners using books and incorporating elements of learned ritual magic in the practice of treasure-seeking.[254] Next, local cultures themselves undoubtedly came into growing contact as trade and human mobility increased in the later Middle Ages, so that practices from one area were carried by merchants and other travelers directly to others; it may have been this, more than the rise of learned necromancy or the activities of Waldensian brethren, that stimulated the development of novel magical practices that inspired inquisitors to speak of a "new witchcraft" in Switzerland, which, far from being an isolated backwater, lay athwart the single most important trade route within Europe, the main link between northern Italy, the Mediterranean, and the east to the Rhine Valley, the Low Countries, and the northern seas.[255] Finally, diffusion undoubtedly occurred imperceptibly via the age-old process of cultural osmosis by which ideas and techniques slowly seeped from one locality to the next, more quickly within cultural zones and more slowly across frontiers of language and ethnicity. As a result of all these processes, Hans, whose distant ancestors may have repaired to a sacred grove where the spirits would possess them, ended up on a mountain named for a classical Roman goddess, but whose chief spirit had the attributes of an ancient German deity and associations with contemporary Slavic and Celtic spirit queens, and who was quickly transformed under interrogation by Altensteig's Christian magistrates into the Christian Devil.[256]

The third way that Hans could have been linked to the larger phenomenon of shamanism is through a process of re-creation or re-discovery, a similar "experiential" process to the one that, as we saw in Chapter 1, generates the "Old Hag" phenomenon. Like the "Old Hag," shamanism is not an ordinary cultural tradition dependent on ongoing continuity, not "a set of beliefs that manifest themselves through a set of customs."[257] Instead, it is a "chameleon-like phenomenon" that has been "reinvented or rediscovered by diverse cultures" around the world and at different times. This understanding of shamanism, of course, depends on adopting a specific definition of the term, rejecting the narrow view of it as the specific practices of Central Asian shamans and also the intermediate views of it as the much more broadly distributed altering of consciousness to experience soul flight to the spirit world and the even broader definition of shamanism as the altering of consciousness to experience contact with spirits, whether by "traveling" to them, being possessed by them, or summoning them to appear and dispatching them on errands, and adopting the broadest definition of all, the deliberate altering of consciousness to access knowledge and manifest powers not accessible to normal waking consciousness.[258] The adoption of this definition is not necessary, but for our purposes here (and, perhaps, in the overall scheme of things) it is most useful. The narrowest definition may be preferred for a close study of North-Asian religion (although it is worth noting that Siberians do not actually have a cohesive concept of "shamanism" and it is just one element, "and rarely the dominant one" in their spiritual practices, so even this usage is an artificial European construct), and the intermediate views may be useful in discussing the global anthropology of magic and religion, but in the present context we will get less insight from applying exclusionary criteria that highlight the distinctiveness of what happened in Württemberg from other practices in other locales around the world than we will get from adopting a broad frame of reference that emphasizes what is common in shamanistic phenomena cross-culturally.[259] In this way we can see how shamanism can occur by "spontaneous generation": the altering of consciousness shamanism involves, and the experiences that occur during it, "reflect latent human potentials, a psychobiological capacity of the species, structures common to mankind."[260] These alterations of consciousness can occur spontaneously, and techniques for inducing them deliberately can therefore be discovered and developed independently. Anthropological studies have found that almost 90% of the worlds' cultures (3500 of 4000) have institutionalized means of inducing and utilizing ASC experiences, and the remainder have informal induction procedures.[261] Many of them undoubtedly diffused from one culture to the next, but this cannot account for all instances of it. Instead, "shamanism was apparently reinvented or rediscovered in diverse cultures and geographic regions" as "cultural adaptations to the biological potentials of altered states of consciousness ... and certain ecological conditions and social demands."[262]

The concept of altered states of consciousness implies the existence of a normal state of consciousness, and the definition of shamanism given here states explicitly that the altered states in question give access to information and powers not accessible to "normal waking consciousness." Therefore, a necessary departure point for our discussion is to specify normal waking consciousness, since it is being altered. Physiologically, it appears that there are three basic states of ordinary consciousness, or modes of consciousness, which are distinguished by differences in neurochemistry, neuroelectric activity, centers of activity in the brain, muscle tone, and phenonemological experience: waking, nREM sleep, and REM sleep.[263] REM sleep, as we saw in Chapter 3, is characterized by high levels of acetylcholine and low levels of the aminergic neurotransmitters; high frequency, low amplitude (beta) brain waves; greater limbic and less forebrain activity than in waking; control by the brainstem; loss of muscle tone, reflexes, and capacity to move (except, of course, the eyes and some facial muscles); and internally generated perceptions, illogical thought, and strong emotionality. On the other hand, nREM sleep is characterized by declining levels of aminergic neurotransmitters and rising levels of acetylcholine; a succession of lower frequency, higher amplitude brain waves (alpha, theta, and delta); a balance of limbic and forebrain activity similar to REM sleep; control by the basal forebrain; reduced muscle tone but retention of reflexes and the ability to move; and dull or absent perceptions and logical sequential thought. Waking consciousness, in contrast, is characterized by high levels of aminergic neurotransmitters; high frequency, low amplitude beta waves, like REM; relatively greater forebrain than limbic activity than during sleep; control by the hypothalamus; full muscle tone, reflexes, and ability to move; and externally oriented perception, logical and progressive thought, and relatively high levels of executive control over emotional impulses.

Waking consciousness, however, is not as uniform as this contrast to the two modes of sleep suggest. For one thing, during waking the nervous system goes through regular 90–120 minute fluctuations between a particularly alert and aroused state and a drowsier, more lethargic state, the "ultradian cycle," which is somewhat similar to, although less dramatic both physiologically and phenomenologically than, the 90–120 minute fluctuations between REM and nREM sleep. The particularly alert stage, the "ultradian high" is characterized by the dominance of the sympathetic (fight/flight or ergotropic) nervous system, peak levels of aminergic neurotransmitters, peak levels of beta wave activity, left-hemisphere dominance, and "external vigilance and verbal, logical, and analytical mental activity."[264] The drowsier stage, the "ultradian low" involves the dominance of the parasympathetic (rest/recover or trophotropic) nervous system, increased levels of acetylcholine relative to the aminergic neurotransmitters, right-hemisphere dominance, and "global decline" in "motor behavior ... including increases in response latency, reduced muscle tonicity, and ... bodily activity." Sensory perceptions include increased "after images and hallucinations," "cognitive behavior manifests regressions, dissociations, amnesia, confusion, autonomous ideation, a wandering of the mind, fantasy, and time lags in response," social and affective behaviors are characterized by greater relaxation and contentment, and "transpersonal ... blissful experiences" are more likely to occur. If the ergotropic state is pushed to extreme, the result is like a functional psychosis involving mania, audio hallucinations, and paranoia.[265] In contrast, if the trophotropic state is pushed to extreme, the result is like an organic psychosis involving euphoria and visual hallucinations.

The ergotropic-trophotropic balance is affected by external events as well as internal rhythms, of course, for the body and mind respond to external dangers by activating the ergotropic system, and then recovers by switching to the trophotropic. Similarly, but much more frequently, the brain switches between right and left hemisphere dominance, for while the two work in tandem, they specialize in different sets of cognitive abilities, and their relative contribution to ongoing activity will reflect the nature of that activity.[266] "We are biologically equipped to process information in two distinct and complementary modes" and these modes are associated with the two halves of the neo-cortex. The left hemisphere, which controls the right side of the body, functions in a primarily rational, chronological, and linguistic mode, while the right hemisphere specializes in intuitive, gestalt, holistic, and largely unarticulated cognition. When a person writes, for example, the left hemisphere shows patterns of electrical activity indicating that it is engaged while the right hemisphere shows an idling pattern, but if the person switches to arranging blocks, hemispheric activation reverses.

We are seldom conscious of these alterations in systemic and hemispheric dominance, however, because our consciousness is made up of a patchwork of sensations and inputs whose seams and gaps are "papered over" in the process of synthesis, just as we are not aware of the movements of our visual point of focus, the difference between updated, remembered, and hypothesized portions of our visual field, or of our "blind spot" where the optic nerve meets that back of the eyeball.[267] In fact, our waking consciousness involves constant unperceived shifts of attention between different perceptions by the five senses and inputs from a variety of internal cognitive systems as the serial processor of our conscious experience integrates the results of the massive parallel processing going on behind the scenes in our minds (it has been said that, examined closely, dreams are actually more coherent than our waking stream of consciousness, but because the stream is all we can be aware of, it is very difficult to perceive its shifts and jumps directly). We are actually most likely to notice this effect when we have become focused on a limited set of perceptions and actions, have ceased to attend to the full range of stimuli we normally pay attention to, and are suddenly confronted with a change that has taken place outside our awareness. This ability to focus on a limited set of stimuli by unconsciously filtering out irrelevant ones is called dissociation, and is one of the neurobiological universals responsible for the ubiquity of shamanism, for one form of dissociation is what we call trance, the state of consciousness that shamans are said to enter in order to shamanize. As we saw in Chapter 3, most products of dissociation are the opposite of trance, they are the spinning off into unconsciousness of perceptual processing and motor activity that previously required conscious attending (like driving a car or playing the piano, which require great concentration at first, but later can be done while thinking about other things, or even carrying on a conversation). However, it is possible for our stream of consciousness itself to become dissociated, disconnected from sensory inputs and internal impulses that normally would draw at least fleeting attention, which can happen to different degrees ranging from brief periods of distraction through prolonged periods of catatonia. It has been posited that our waking mode of consciousness is made up of a series of mini-trances, or altered states of consciousness, and while this formulation may seem excessive, it seems clear that normal waking consciousness does routinely include frequent lapses of general attentiveness as we focus on specific stimuli or tasks. Whenever we engage in a specific form of activity, like conversing, reading, writing, watching TV, or playing sports, we focus our attention by attending to the relevant stimuli and ignoring irrelevant ones, subtly (or in the case of a teenage boy playing a video game, not so subtly) altering our consciousness.[268] Furthermore, dissociations happen during waking consciousness due to diffusion rather than focusing of attention; during the cyclical periods of parasympathetic dominance we are particularly likely to experience short periods in which we cease to attend to external stimuli while we follow unfocused interior mentation, and we even experience brief intervals of "micro-REM" dreaming while awake.[269]

In most cases, we do not intend to enter these trance states, but merely do so in the course of doing whatever activity they are associated with, and we do not do so with the intent that we will thereby gain access to unconscious information or powers. However, the process of concentrating on a limited range of stimuli and ignoring the rest does seem to enable us to better generate, retrieve, and utilize unconscious knowledge and skills, and sometimes we do consciously cultivate trance states, altered states of consciousness, in order to access knowledge and manifest powers normally inaccessible to our waking consciousness. In modern Western culture, these alterations of consciousness range from the rituals athletes use to psych themselves up before a game through hypnosis employed by therapists to hallucinogens used by psychonauts to explore the outer reaches of consciousness. In more traditional cultures, they ranged from charms and prayers used to instill confidence in the face of unpredictable misfortune through incantations and drumming used to promote healing to hallucinogens used by shamans to contact the denizens of the spirit world.

The nature, and even more the underlying neurophysiology, of dissociation has bedeviled psychology for centuries. Some psychologists have argued that it does not really exist, that people purportedly under hypnosis, say, or claiming to suffer from multiple-personality disorder are merely role-playing to gain some calculated advantage or to fulfill some social expectation. Other psychologists think that it does constitute a discrete psychological state or set of states in which conscious awareness and conscious control are reduced, but have been unable to account for the phenomenon, why some people under hypnosis, for example, claim to be unaware of what they are doing or completely unable to control their actions while others report some awareness and sense of volition yet claim to have felt unable to act on these, and still others neither act nor report feeling different at all. Furthermore, clinical studies have shown that subjects' entrance into, behavior and reported experiences during, and exit from purported dissociative states are strongly influenced by social cues and reinforcements, and the situation was made murkier when early EEG studies of hypnosis revealed no distinguishing pattern of brain-wave activity.[270]

Research has established, though, that some people are more hypnotizable than others. Some people are completely resistant to hypnotic induction, some are moderately susceptible, and some are very affected by it. Furthermore, "highly hypnotizable" people not only enter hypnotic trance more readily, but also display a stronger detachment from external stimuli, experience a complete loss of volition, and visualize imaginary scenes more powerfully during the trance.[271] They also focus their attention better outside of the hypnotic state, and are more likely to enter dissociated states spontaneously, have vivid dreams in sleep, and report having had religious and paranormal experiences.[272]

Recent brain-imaging studies have shown that cerebral activity in hypnotizable people is markedly different under hypnosis than when they are consciously role-playing, indicating that while some people may role-play dissociated states for the reasons suggested above, some purported dissociations involve real, physiologically based alterations of consciousness.[273] "During the hypnotic state ... many hypnotic subjects have high electrical activity of the type that indicates a relaxed state in the left frontal region of the cerebral cortex, which controls planning and decision-making," and hypnotized subjects exposed to painful heat have "a distinctly different pattern of brain activity compared to when they were not hypnotized ... brain activity was reduced in areas of the pain network, including the primary sensory cortex, which is responsible for pain perception" and there was " increased activation in two other brain structures – the left anterior cingulate cortex and the basal ganglia" which "may be part of an inhibition pathway that blocks the pain signal from reaching the higher cortical structures responsible for pain perception."[274] Furthermore, there is evidence that hypnosis is connected to an increase in brain wave activity in the theta range, which generally is characterized by drowsy, unfocused thinking.[275] Hypnosis is clearly something more than simple role-playing; it does induce real changes in brain functioning, both in terms of inducing a specific state of relaxed, detached, and suggestible consciousness and in terms of a wide variety of alterations that can be induced via suggestions made while the person is in that state. However, it does so to different degrees in different people, with some people less able to enter the state and implement the suggestions than others.

Differences in hypnotizability reflect both genetic and environmental factors. Studies comparing identical and fraternal twins showed a "genetic basis" with an "overall heritability index ... between those usually reported for personality measures ... and ability measures." On the other hand, it has been shown that "childhood absorption" in imaginative creativity "or dissociation due to abuse" foster the "development of hypnotic capabilities."[276] Like many other talents, hypnotizability is a product of both nature and nurture, and is found throughout the human race, although not in every human being in equal measure. (In this light, it seems significant that many shamanic societies assume that anyone can become a shaman, but that proclivity tends to run in families, and, similarly, early modern witchcraft beliefs similarly held that anyone could be a witch, but that people related to witches were particularly likely to be as well.)

Everyone dissociates, but not everyone is capable of dissociating to the same degree, or necessarily even in the same ways. The readiness with which and degree to which any individual goes into trance states, particularly the more pronounced states in which behavior and experience are noticeably affected, and the experiences they will have in them reflect not just individual genetic and psychological factors, but also the degree to which society fosters or discourages the cultivation and expression of this ability, the terms in which it is understood, and the ways in which it is institutionalized or suppressed. "There are many degrees of trance" and also many types, with "general similarities" that "arise through common experience and human proclivities" and "differences" that "reflect particular societies' cultural styles and objects."[277] Each individual culture, from the innumerable indigenous tribes through the great agricultural civilizations to modern Western civilization, provides its own set of symbols to guide the trance experience, from the spirits of animals and ancestors through genies and goblins, angels and demons to the metaphysical musings of mystics and musicians.[278] Furthermore, not only do many specific features of trance experiences reflect specific cultural traditions, but also general forms of trance experience are also correlated with general levels of socioeconomic and cultural development.[279] The shamans of hunters and gatherers typically fly to meet the spirit counterparts of animals, and when they die they go off to enjoy the eternal hunt. Horticulturalists see villages not unlike their own, while desert nomads dream of a lush, green paradise.[280] With the rise of political integration beyond the local level and the development of social classes, mediumistic possession replaces soul flight as the dominant mode of deliberate trance experience, and the utilization of spiritual power to inflict injury on personal enemies becomes an important social concern. In the great agricultural civilizations, trance experiences came to be steered by elaborate institutional structures to conform to the strictures of canonical texts, and approved experiential traditions increasingly emphasized achieving a sense of dissolution of self and communion with the overarching spirit of the universe rather than harnessing particular spirits to accomplish mundane goals. In modern industrial society, trance experiences are actively discouraged by materialist philosophy's denial that there is a spiritual aspect of reality that they can facilitate contact with, and the medical community's tendency to regard them as pathological, although some psychologists and lay people treat them as purely psychological phenomena that can be used to enhance creativity or other forms of productivity or as a form of psychotherapy. In general, as social complexity increases, deliberate induction of trance states declines, becoming increasingly limited in terms of the range of people who practice it, the range of experiences encouraged or accepted, and the intensity of the experience.[281] However, this trend is somewhat counteracted by the fact that as social complexity increases, it is likely that practices from previous levels will continue to be utilized, at least unofficially. Hence, the great agricultural civilizations tended to have practitioners who dealt with the spirit world for mundane practical ends, within or outside official institutional structures, even when the official religion disapproved of such activities. Similarly, modern societies include people who induce trance states for spiritual purposes as part of traditional religious observances, as part of traditional magical practices, and as part of the "New Age" movement that, dissatisfied with materialism, seeks a synchronistic spirituality drawing on many older traditions.

While it is useful to define the word "shamanism" in a way that focuses our attention on the commonalities linking the wide variety of ways human beings deliberately manipulate their nervous systems to alter their consciousness to access normally unconscious knowledge and skills, it is also useful to have a vocabulary that enables us to distinguish between different degrees and kinds of such manipulations. Naturally, different cultures have their own vocabularies to describe the trances their members induce and experience, which both situates them in their specific cultural context and distinguishes them from similar but distinct traditions of other peoples. Thus, for example, the Waldensian brethrens' visits to paradise were related to the entire complex of Waldensian beliefs and were not the same experience as the "itinerant scholars'" sojourns on the Venusberg, and the *taltos'* combats in spirit played a specific role in Hungarian culture and therefore differed somewhat in both content and meaning from those of *benandanti*.[282] However, while the use of culturally specific terms is entirely appropriate in discussing specific cultures and regional groupings, it shifts focus away from the universal features that they involve, making it difficult to relate them to similar (and to contrast them with not so similar) experiences of other people, and to appraise what aspects represent unique cultural constructs, what aspects represent biological universals, and what aspects manifest common responses to similar experiences and features in the environment. Broader terms like soul flight, possession, and invocation are useful in conveying commonalities in the phenomenal aspects of trance experiences, but do not convey much about the degree or depth of dissociation they involve, while terms like ecstasy and catalepsy lack connection to any larger understanding of how the nervous system works.

Fortunately, the concept of shamanism can be further articulated using existing noun and adjective structures to provide a framework within which various trance states, traditions of trance experience, and the people who practice them can be situated, not only in relationship to each other, but also in relationship to the neurocognitive processes they involve. Specifically, "shaman" can be reserved for a person who engages in practices involving alterations of consciousness in order to perceive and interact with spirits in order to gain knowledge or power inaccessible in normal waking consciousness, and "shamanic" used to refer to such practices. In contrast, "shamanist" can be used for someone who engages in other deliberate manipulations of consciousness to access unconscious information and skills not ordinarily accessible in waking consciousness, practices that do involve deliberately manipulating consciousness, their own or someone else's, but do not generate the experience of perceiving spirits, and "shamanistic" can be used to refer to such manipulations. Since both variants of shamanism involve deliberate actions, they can be distinguished as "shamanic practices" or "shamanistic practices," with the difference being whether they involve perception of spirits.

These distinctions are not just semantic, nor are they rooted in differing cultural traditions. Instead, they are connected to the effects of another neurocognitive process, a particular, and particularly dramatic, form of dissociation referred to as "tuning the nervous system," which involves activating both the sympathetic (ergotropic) and parasympathetic (trophotropic) nervous systems simultaneously.[283] Normally, as we have seen, the systems work in a complementary way, with one dominant and the other quiescent. However, if the nervous system is subjected to either overstimulation, leading to an overload of the ergotropic system, or understimulation, leading to an overload of the trophotropic system, it responds by triggering the other system while the overloaded system remains active. The result is a hybrid state of consciousness characterized by some features of sleeping and some features of waking.[284] It is thus somewhat similar to REM sleep, one of the basic modes of consciousness, and because of this, and because of the fact that there seem to be several different specific states of consciousness that can result from it (soul flight, possession, visions), just as there are several different specific states of consciousness that can occur during REM (normal dreaming, OBEs, lucid dreams, vivid dreams), and waking consciousness (absorption, daydreaming, hypnotic trance), it has been proposed that the "tuned" nervous system be considered a fourth basic mode of consciousness.[285] It is uncertain whether it is really equivalent to the other three since it is not an automatically triggered phase of our normal daily cycle of alterations of consciousness, and it is beyond the scope of this study to settle such an issue, but since the main states of consciousness related to shamanic practices appear to share a distinct physiological basis, it seems reasonable to refer to them collectively as the "shamanic states of consciousness."

The shamanic states of consciousness (or SSCs) can be induced by a wide variety of stimuli, or drivers, and can occur spontaneously or as a result of deliberate induction.[286] Stimuli that are particularly likely to generate SSCs spontaneously, although most can be and sometimes are deliberately sought for the purpose, include personal stress, traumatic or disorienting events, sex, acts of violence, hunger and nutritional deficiencies, high altitudes, severe physical injury or illness, and near-death experiences.[287] Stimuli that tend to be generated deliberately include repetitive rhythmic activities like drumming, dancing, and chanting; music and singing; sensory deprivation, meditation, or deep hypnosis; direct electrical stimulation of the brain; and the ingestion of hallucinogenic substances.[288] The latter, which are used widely but not universally, include tobacco, cocaine, amphetamines, marijuana, alcohol, beetlenut, ayahusca, aminita muscara, and various members of the nightshade family. Most of these stimuli, like the various forms of psychological stress, bodily injury, rhythmic activities, and hallucinogens, have the effect of driving the sympathetic nervous system, although a few, like meditation and sensory depravation, drive the parasympathetic system. In addition to their general effects as ANS drivers, hallucinogenic drugs have specific and complex chemical effects as well, as we saw in Chapter 4, and they and many of the other driving mechanisms have symbolic meanings that contribute to the nature and content of the experiences they generate.[289] Furthermore, learned associations between symbols associated with drivers and the states of consciousness they generate make it possible for the symbols to act later as triggers, stimuli that enable at least some of the effects of the shamanic states of consciousness to be produced with significantly less of the strenuous physical or mental activity originally required to produce them.[290] Note that the activity or substance used to drive the nervous system itself can become such a symbol, triggering the effects more quickly or more strongly through the combination of its direct physical effects and the indirect effects of association.[291]

These various means of tuning the nervous system cause a set of common physiological effects, including changes to the balance of neurotransmitters in the brain, general changes to its bioelectric activity, specific changes in brain center activity, and general physiological changes as well. In terms of the mix of chemicals in the brain, there appears to be " a shift in the neuromodulatory balance ... from aminergic to cholinergic dominance."[292] In terms of bioelectric activity, "desynchronized fast wave activity of the frontal cortex" characteristic of "normal waking conditions" is replaced by "high-voltage, slow-wave electroencephalogram (EEG) activity," particularly in the theta range, "originating in ... the brain stem and hippocampal-sepal area."[293] In terms of brain centers, "certain brain structures are deprived of the normal supply of neural input," including "the orientation association area," which consists of "the left orientation area," which "creates the brain's spatial sense of self," and the right orientation area, which "creates the physical space in which that self can exist."[294] In terms of general physiology, "compounds indicating stress" in the blood serum rise slightly and then drop below normal levels, the brain synthesizes beta-endorphin, "the body's own analgesic," which persists long after the other effects of the trance have worn off, blood pressure drops "to low levels," the pulse races, and "a negative charge that the brain gives off during learning tasks" can rise as high as "1,500 to 2,000 microvolts," far beyond 100 microvolts level normally observed during learning.[295]

This list can hardly be regarded as the last word on the physiology of shamanic states of consciousness, but it does suggest some physiological explanations for some of the experiences commonly associated with these states. First of all, the shift from aminergic to cholinergic dominance is similar to the situation during REM sleep, and accounts for the strong intrusion of internally generated stimuli on consciousness, for aminergic neurotransmitters, particularly serotonin, are responsible for our focused attention during waking because they block internally generated stimuli.[296] Second, the change in bioelectric activity from desynchronized fast wave activity in the frontal cortex to high voltage, slow wave activity originating in the hippocampus and brainstem is also similar to the situation during sleep, and synchronizes "the different levels of the brain and the frontal lobes" to "integrate information from the lower levels of the brain into the processing capacity of the frontal cortex ... integrating nonverbal emotional and behavioral information into the frontal brain ... providing intuition, understanding ... and personal integration."[297] Third, the deactivation of the orientation association area creates a disembodied sensation that can be manifested either as an out-of-body experience, as the intrusion of some external presence into the body, or a feeling of oceanic oneness with the universe.[298] Fourth, the synthesis of beta-endorphin contributes to a sense of well-being that often concludes shamanic experiences. Fifth, the combination of accelerated heart rate and reduced blood pressure is an unusual condition "known otherwise only from life-threatening situations ... when a person is close to death from an infectious disease or bleeding," which may be why shamanic states of consciousness are thought to involve journeys to the land of the dead, contact with the spirits of the dead, or a form of death itself.[299] Finally, the heightened bioelectric activity associated with learning suggests why shamanic states of consciousness are not only associated with the revelation of unconscious information, but also with the generation of new insights and heightened creativity.

Looking at shamanic states of consciousness in terms of their underlying physiology is instructive, but is somewhat like trying to understand an elephant by examining each of the organ systems that make it up. In order to get an integrated understanding of these integrative experiences, it will be helpful to look at them from another point of view, from the point of view of the perception of spirits which, as mentioned, is what distinguishes shamanic from shamanistic practices. Belief in and perception of spirits is another cultural universal (even the American currency proclaims that "In God We Trust," while most European countries have significant institutional ties to Christian churches), and while cultural factors strongly influence the way they are contacted and apprehended, there are some common aspects to the experience.[300] First of all, the person is generally conscious of coming into contact with another world or aspect of reality, or at least that something is profoundly different about the world from the way it is usually.[301] This realization usually occurs at the time, but if not, then in retrospect. This is often conveyed by some transitional experience like flight, passing through a portal, being entered by some external agent, or the perception that some of the normal constraints on the world are not operating, so that, for example, animals can talk or objects can change size or even transform into living beings.[302] Secondly, the person experiences interaction with autonomous, animate, conscious beings or beings, spirits, that may seem either ethereal or physically real, but are understood to be of a different nature than the people and animals that are interacted with most of the time.[303] These autonomous entities may merely be sensed presences, but more often they are experienced as heard voices or seen physical bodies, although in the case of mediumship they are manifested through the medium's own body in a manner similar to involuntary possession. Thirdly, through contact with these spirits the person gains occult, or hidden, knowledge and enhanced abilities of two types. On the one hand, and more immediately, the person experiences access to information that is not accessible normally, either because it is about things that are secret or unacknowledged or because the information is about things remote in space or time, and also may be able to perform acts of unusual physical prowess, like exhibiting unusual strength or endurance, or intervene in the spirit world to create effects in the normal world, like retrieving a sick person's soul in order to heal them.[304] On the other hand, and more generally, the person gains broader insights into people and nature, like what makes people ill or unhappy and how to correct (or cause) these conditions, how people and animals interact with each other and with their physical environment and how these interactions can be facilitated or exploited, how the physical world itself works and can be better manipulated, and what motivates the spirits and how best to interact with them.[305] Overall, the insights and abilities thus gained generally involve an intuitive or descriptive understanding of and ability to act on people and things, rather than a highly rationalized, logically structured body of knowledge, although a general framework may be conveyed, and the long-term power that is gained is control over spirits, the ability to initiate and steer the actions of these extraordinary agents. Finally, the experience of interacting with spirits generally leaves the person with a feeling of both depletion and satisfaction; the encounter is often experienced to be strenuous, but usually ends with a positive sense of closure.

While spirits may be sensed as simple presences, in shamanic states of consciousness they usually manifest themselves in more tangible form. In mediumistic shamanic experiences they seem to occupy the shaman's body and sometimes they are experienced as heard voices, most commonly they are perceived visually as well, as bodily entities that exist within the normal world or within a separate spirit world. We have seen many of the physiological bases for these experiences in early modern peoples' encounters with the Devil and flight to the witches' Sabbaths: the way that cognitive modules or demons can develop into autonomous centers of consciousness that can compete for control of the body, manifest as auditory hallucinations, or appear in the visual representation of the world, either as details superimposed on perceived objects, as free-standing figures, or within an entirely imaginary environment. In most of the cases we have seen, however, these experiences occurred spontaneously, as with Maria Braittingen, Endris Miembler, Johann Bebion's wife, and Anna Eberlin, and in most of the cases in which they were deliberately induced they were utilized as a form of escapism, either a source of sexual gratification, as with Apolonia Walther, or idle amusement, as with Hanß Jacob Langen. However, the fact that Hanß Jacob's companions said that they would teach him simple magic suggests that his trips could have been part of some shamanic initiatory process, at least potentially, and Hans Haasen's sojourn on the Venusberg was clearly a shamanic use of the human ability to perceive a spiritual dimension to the world.

As these last few examples illustrate, shamanic practices involve more than just perceiving spirits, they involve perceiving them in order to gain insights and powers that are inaccessible under normal circumstances. In shamanic states of consciousness, the nervous system utilizes a "presentational" rather than reflectional mode of conceptualization because the dominance of the cholinergic system and high amplitude, low frequency bioelectric activity originating in the brainstem and the limbic system promotes diffuse, analogic, emotional cognition rather than focused, sustained, rational thought processes.[306] As a result, just as dreams, to which, as we have seen, shamanic visions are closely related, often reveal unconscious information and sometimes generate creative insights, shamanic practices manifest unconscious knowledge and facilitate innovative solutions to problems.[307] The difference is that shamanic practitioners retain more elements of waking consciousness than ordinary dreamers, so they may be able to steer their experiences more deliberately, and can better attend to and remember the results of their dream-like cognition, or, in the case of mediums, whose normal personality may well not be conscious during possession and who often suffer from amnesia afterwards, directly report it as it takes place. The important thing is that this mode of cognition is not simply an alternative way of presenting thoughts to consciousness, it is a different way of thinking them in the first place.[308] The rational and linguistic thought that dominates our waking consciousness is a form of symbolic processing: ideas or information are encoded in symbolic form and the symbols are manipulated according to the rules of grammar or logic. Shamanic visions, in contrast, involve an analogue process: scenes are imagined or encounters simulated and their implications are resolved as an unfolding of experience, just as dreams manifest the processing of information, the generation of associations and the resolution of inconsistencies during sleep. Shamanic visions, like dreams, are often symbolic in the sense that the characters and scenes represent something else, of course, and so the analogue processing may map only imperfectly onto the situation that it represents, just as the results of rational linguistic processing may map more or less well to the real world the symbols reference, but the point is that cognition in shamanic states of consciousness is a different form of cognition than the rational processing in waking consciousness, able to generate some kinds of knowledge better, and some kinds less well.

The difference between the two modes of cognition does not just involve the mechanics of thought, but also the content as well, for the low levels of aminergic neurotransmitters, the enhanced role of limbic structures, which govern the emotions, and, at least during initiatory experiences, the disorientation, means that the usual restraints on thought are reduced, so that entrainments that are normally kept uncoupled from consciousness can be manifested during shamanic experiences.[309] This may also be facilitated by the fact that it is presented to consciousness as coming from an external source. Furthermore, the sense of organic connection between what are sharply delineated as self and environment in waking consciousness by the deactivation of the orientation association area plus the "cross-modular integration" generated by "the psychophysiologically induced integrative brain states produced by shamanic ASC" resulting in "extension" of "the modules for social perceptions of 'others,' their intentionalities (mind reading), and animal behavior," the "theory of mind" that enables us to anticipate the behavior of other people and animals by understanding and simulating their conscious processing in our own consciousness ... are manifested ... in concepts of animism," and perception and experience of spirits "and the spirit world."[310] In other words, because of "the neurognostic structures and processes of the paleomammalian brain" that are entrained to consciousness during shamanic ASCs, practitioners experience and therefore understand the physical world to be governed by pervasive organic processes as well as mechanistic ones and filled with autonomous consciousnesses.[311]

Shamanic practice is not generally undertaken simply to gain increased insight into the world, however. Instead, it is generally seen as a means to gain enhanced power. Of course, knowledge is power, as the cliché goes, so enhanced access to information and heightened learning in themselves represent a form of power, or at least raw material that can be transformed into power in terms of physical skills and social manipulations. For example, cats in REM sleep can be seen, if their brains are altered so that movement is not suppressed, to be practicing, or probably more accurately, remembering, cataloging, and storing, hunting routines.[312] In a development of this dreamwork (which, as we have seen, is similar in principle to that of humans), aboriginal men in some South American tribes have been observed to take "advantage of the properties of" the hallucinogenic vine ayahusca by re-creating "in their visions the most minute, difficult movements and activities of the animals they stalked and hunted ... to learn ... in the conscious mind, the aspects of animal behavior which they knew almost at a subliminal level, so that in future hunts they could be at one with their prey to hasten their victory."[313] In more complex societies the emphasis in shamanic practice is on human affairs, and the experiences imagined in shamanic states of consciousness yield diagnoses of illnesses, prescriptions for their treatment, the identities of suspects when crimes have been committed, the location of missing objects and people, the cause and potential remedies of misfortune, contact with the spirits of deceased loved ones, and knowledge of the course of events in the future.[314]

In addition to these fruits of enhanced knowledge, shamanic states of consciousness also induce useful changes in perception, cognitive processing, physical abilities, and sense of self. The source of many of these effects is the intense arousal of the sympathetic nervous system, which causes "a surge through the ascending systems which release acetylcholine and glutamate," making "parallel processing ... spurt." This creates "the impression – not at all incorrect – that the brain's" inner "time has vastly accelerated."[315] We become "hypercognitive (so we can in vent ... strategies on the fly) and ... we form richly detailed memories (so we will never forget ... the survival strategy), and we have "the sense that *external* events" unfold "in slow motion and with great clarity." Perceptions of space are also altered, so that small objects appear large, and their details can be examined minutely. Perception of pain is suppressed by the release of endogenous opiads, primarily endorphin, which heightens endurance.[316] Heightened endurance contributes, along with the effects of epinephrine (adrenalin) also released in the flight/fight response, to acts of unusual physical prowess and power.[317] The mix of chemicals released into the system also boost self-confidence by heightening the feeling of well-being and power, and self-confidence promotes assertive and sustained action and creates interpersonal charisma.[318] The euphoria, or ecstasy, experienced during shamanic states of consciousness, however, is more than just an endorphin rush. Instead, it manifests as well the integration of different levels of cognition, the reconciliation of the thoughts generated by higher cortical processing and "deep limbic structures" in a way that not only makes the person feel good, but also creates "a sense of compelling experiential immediacy," giving an emotional validation to percepts and insights and the confidence and persuasiveness that flow from conviction.[319]

For many peoples, the sine qua non of shamanic states is evidence of supernatural powers, things like the ability to read minds, to know of distant events, to move objects without touching them, and to predict the future.[320] Many of these effects, of course, do not necessarily manifest supernatural or paranormal powers; as early modern demonologists put it, the Devil can work *mirables* as opposed to true miracles by tapping his vast knowledge of nature, and in particular his knowledge of hidden, or occult, natural processes.[321] For example, foretelling the future can be based on dispassionate waking analysis or integrative shamanic cognition, and appearing to read peoples' minds can come from prior knowledge, sensitivity to subliminal signals, or a knowledge of human nature. The association of these powers with shamanic states of consciousness is valid because they reflect the nervous system's heightened capacity to manifest them while in such states, but they do not require what we (or educated early moderns) would consider to be truly supernatural powers.[322] Whether such nonparanormal explanations, including fraud and self-delusion, can account for all the apparently extraordinary phenomena associated with shamanism is an open question, though, for as we have seen, there is a substantial body of evidence that a subset are caused by some process, or set of processes, that is not accounted for in the current scientific understanding of how the world works, yet there is vigorous opposition to this idea as well, and no scientific consensus on the question exists. Interestingly, though, "parapsychologists using controlled experiments ... find a relationship between hypnosis and extrasensory perception. Meta-analysis of 25 experiments from 10 different laboratories suggests that hypnosis and similar altered states of consciousness facilitate psychic performance."[323] These investigations thus support the "folkloric accounts from all regions and eras" ascribing supernatural powers to shamanic practitioners. Whatever the physical reality of paranormal processes, there does appear to be a correlation between shamanic states of consciousness and the ability to perform in experimental settings in ways that appear to manifest them.

If the reality of the paranormal phenomena connected with shamanic states of consciousness remains shrouded in uncertainty, the bases for their contribution to the activity most strongly associated with shamanism, healing, has become much clearer in the last decades. To begin with, like the authority of a modern doctor, the shaman's status as a trained healer itself promotes optimism in patients, especially when this is reinforced by a firm, confident "bedside manner," and that optimism, in turn, can promote healing. In addition, rituals, incantations, and herbal concoctions can exercise a similar placebo effect. However, herbal remedies may also contain chemically efficacious agents, and rituals and incantations can have restorative properties beyond the placebo effect. For one thing, shamanic healing rituals frequently draw members of the community into activities that culminate in "positive limbic discharges" that promote "decreased distancing and greater social cohesion," which reduces interpersonal tensions that can contribute to illness and promotes a supportive interpersonal environment that further contributes to healing.[324] Additionally, the rituals often induce in the patient a trance experience that provides a fertile environment for hypnosis-like suggestions to be implanted, and may also induce a parasympathetic-dominant state that resolves unconscious tensions and releases endogenous endorphins that reduce discomfort and relieve anxiety.[325] Much shamanic initiation, like the experience that Hans Haasen reported, centers on learning to diagnose and cure ailments with the help of spirits encountered in initiation and invoked during the rituals themselves.[326] Like Hans, candidate shamans often suffer from some malady that they cure themselves as part of their training, and their ability to cure themselves is the foundation for their ability to cure others.[327] To some extent, like Hans, they learn about herbal treatments, but the main thrust of their therapies is manipulation of the mind, first of all their own, and then their patient's.[328] This skill can not only promote relief of anxiety about disease and relief of symptoms, but can promote real, organic healing, through the various channels connecting mind and body outlined above.

So was Hans Haasen linked to the larger phenomenon of shamanism through a process of re-creation or re-discovery, as was posed as the third possible source of his practices after direct continuation of some archaic tradition or the diffusion of a tradition from elsewhere? In one sense he was, for everyone who goes into a shamanic state of consciousness embarks on an individual journey that, however much it is influenced by cultural expectations and traditions, is constructed in his or her own nervous system from innate biological capacities, a unique psychological history, and the contingent development of the unfolding experience as well as cultural forces, with far less reference to the external world than most human experiences. In another sense the answer would seem to be no, for his claim to be an "itinerant scholar," Little George from Ladenberg's role in initiating him, the identity of the mountain, and the nature of its chief inhabitant suggest that he was initiated into an ongoing tradition that had historical roots and geographic breadth. In the final analysis, though, it is possible that Little George, or some group he was part of, had substantially rediscovered the practices, drawing inspiration and images from regional lore and classical traditions, but independently developing the specific rituals and myths Hans learned, for there was no Hogwarts to train them in some standard curriculum or licensing agency to test their knowledge and skills. Anyone could call himself an itinerant scholar and claim healing powers derived from a stay on the Venusberg, and some who did were undoubtedly rank charlatans whose only altered state of consciousness came from a trip to the bottom of a beer stein, while most probably practiced a mix of longstanding local traditions, diverse elements diffused through word of mouth and written texts, and the products of their own unique experiences with peculiar pieces of bread or salves, ritual training or incidental deprivations, dreams and imagination.

Instead of looking on them as vestiges of some pristine archaic shamanism, though, or as inauthentic interlopers in folk culture, it seem more reasonable to recognize them as historically situated instantiations of this universal human capability. When a Siberian shaman appeared to go into a trance and narrated a soul journey, no one but he knew if he was really in ecstasy or just faking it, and even he might not have known how intense his experience was relative to that of other shamans, only a dozen of whom he might have observed in his lifetime. The relative poverty and mobility of early modern Europe's marginal population probably meant that it did have a larger proportion of conscious frauds than the more egalitarian, closed societies where classical shamanism flourished, but European healers had a relatively broad knowledge base to draw on, and an increasingly competitive market to practice in, while the isolation of small-scale societies meant that a slow degradation of local shamanic practices could take place unnoticed, so that what was once a vigorous ecstatic tradition could become a set of rote practices. Conversely, of course, an inspired shaman could appear in an isolated community who was able to deliver a far higher level of services than his pedestrian teacher or forbearers, and, similarly, a "highly hypnotizable" itinerant scholar or other shamanic practitioner in early modern Europe who entered shamanic states of consciousness to learn healing powers from the spirits could have delivered a level of services equal in efficaciousness to any Siberian or South American practitioner. The point is not to engage in some sort of intercontinental one-upsmanship, but to highlight the fact that shamanism is not an ordinary cultural tradition dependent on ongoing continuity, but rather is a "chameleon-like phenomenon" that changes over time, can be reconstituted based on a meme or two that trigger the necessary physical activity, or rediscovered from the effects of some spontaneous experience. Hans Haasen may well have learned a shamanism that combined ancient Swabian traditions (like his aunts' herbal remedies), elements of Europe's common magical culture (like the female healing spirit), and the unique practices of the group he fell in with.

The basis of shamanism is manipulation of the mind, the mind of the practitioner and the minds of others, in order to draw out knowledge and manifest powers that are not accessible in normal waking consciousness. Shamanic practices induce altered states of consciousness in which spirits are perceived and can be interacted with. Such dramatic alterations are called "tuning the nervous system," and involve specific changes to the biochemistry, bioelectric activity, and other processes in the brain that amount to a fourth mode of consciousness alongside the waking state, deep sleep, and REM sleep. Shamanistic practices induce less dramatic and much more variable changes in the way the brain functions, changes that can range from subtle reactions to aversive or attractive stimuli (like to the odor of human feces that were sometimes found hidden in peoples' houses) to mild dissociations that interrupt the normal flow of waking consciousness (like prayer during Sunday services) to pronounced hypnotic effects that open the brain to powerful symbolic penetration (like Maria Gekin's incantations). Across this range of alterations of consciousness, which can perhaps be thought of as "fine-tuning the nervous system," the effect can be to bolster or undercut the person's psychological power, depending on the nature of the ritual, any visceral effects of the materials it employs, and the meaning of its associated symbols. Shamanic and shamanistic practices are related not just because they both involve manipulating the nervous system to tap the unconscious, though, but because they have a hierarchical relationship as well. Specifically, someone who undergoes shamanic initiation and engages in shamanic practices gains increasing power to fine-tune as well as tune the nervous system, both his or her own and others'. For this reason, the demonologists' fantasies were not entirely unfounded; the most powerful practitioners of illicit spiritual contacts were, in fact, those who altered their consciousness – rode the pitchfork; flew to a sacred mountain – where they mixed with non-Christian spirits, and thereby gained the power to heal and to harm by manipulating people's nervous systems though contact with the spirits.

Conclusion

"The means to alleviate disorders ... also provide the knowledge to cause illness," so witchcraft and shamanism were linked in both early modern demonology and early modern popular culture.[329] And, as we have seen, there was a tradition of sorcery that enabled practitioners to assault their enemies spiritually, through rituals and symbols that mobilized the power of their own psyches and debilitated that of their opponents. Most of this sorcery was shamanistic, like Agnes Langjahr's placement of the eggs in Christian Cammer's bed, since it involved relatively limited manipulations of consciousness which may have called on or assumed the involvement of spirits but did not entail the alteration of consciousness to the point of actually perceiving them. Some forms, however, like necromancy and the ritual Margaretha Wagner described to prime herself to "press" other people while dreaming, were shamanic, since they involved the deliberate alteration of consciousness to perceive the spirit world. Sometimes both shamanistic and shamanic sorcery could involve the Devil, as Maria Gekin's incantations to spook horses and Maria Braittingen's appeal to the Devil to kill her master's cow did. Maria also claimed to have flown to witch dances, but she did not say that she learned magic there. In fact, she did not claim to know or practice magic at all. Similarly, Apolonia Walther claimed to have flown to witch dances, but when incarcerated she threatened to burn the village down, not something one needed to attend diabolic Sabbaths to learn how to do. The only suspect to connect magical flight and ritual sorcery was Hanß Jacob Langen, who said that after his third trip on the pitchfork his companions said that they would teach him how to make fleas, but this offer does not seem to have been made or suggest that the instruction would be given while he was tripping. There is credible evidence that most of the elements of the witchcraft that suspects were routinely tortured into confessing to really existed in early modern Württemberg, but there is not a single case in which all of them appear to have existed together as the demonologist imagined. It is possible that, given time, the various elements of sorcery, Satanism, and shamanism might have drawn together as the demonologists feared, given Europe's rapidly growing transportation and information infrastructures, but the demonologists seem to have anticipated this potentiality, and evidence of this convergence, like the Affair of the Poisons in the late seventeenth century, suggest that one of the prime movers in this process was, ironically, the demonology itself.

Even if there was a possibility that a diabolic shamanic cult along the lines the demonologists feared might have arisen, the malefic witchcraft that was at the heart of the popular fears was not only not shamanic, it was not even shamanistic. It did not involve the deliberate induction of altered states of consciousness at all because the unconscious powers it utilized to cause illness and other misfortunes were accessed unconsciously, as a spontaneous expression of the angry person's emotions. Some expressions of anger like curses and threats fell on the border since they can be made with the intention to induce injury as wells as to warn or to bluff, but on the whole the evidence presented here and in part I indicate that while the power of witchcraft and the power of shamanism are real, they were not really combined in the way posited in the early modern witchcraft demonology and the popular fears that it inspired. Both learned and popular beliefs were deeply rooted in reality, but the ideas grew in the hothouse environment of Europe's burgeoning communications system and bore fruit that existed only in its collective imagination.

However, if there was no underground movement of discontented women undergoing shamanic initiations into a Devilish cult in which they learned the secrets of sorcery, the example of Hans Haasen suggests that there were at least a few people who underwent shamanic initiations into beneficent traditions in which they learned the art of healing. Similarly, if only a limited number of discontented people supplemented the natural power of their anger with the artificial enhancement of shamanistic sorcery, a much larger number of Württembergers engaged in more benign shamanistic practices. Furthermore, because all forms of shamanism were thought to involve contact with spirits, and all contact with spirits outside of a few approved channels were thought to involve the Devil, most demonologists regarded these beneficent forms as at least as reprehensible as malefic ones, and called for their suppression along with malefic witchcraft. Therefore, we will next examine the evidence from Württemberg of the varieties and functions of beneficent shamanism, popular magic, before concluding this study by turning to the campaign by the Duchy's elite to suppress all witchcraft and magic from the sixteenth through the eighteenth century.

Part III The Realities of Beneficent Magic

Introduction

Late medieval Württembergers shared with their contemporaries throughout Europe – and, indeed, virtually with all premodern peoples – the belief not only in witchcraft and sorcery, but also in a wide variety of unseen spirits and supernatural forces capable of influencing human affairs for good or ill.[1] Learned men argued about their nature and the source and extent of their power, but none questioned their existence, and ordinary folk believed that the forests and hills, valleys and rivers were populated by a menagerie of mysterious beings: quasi-human giants and dwarfs, fantastic animals, and ethereal spirits that might be angelic, demonic, or neither.[2] They believed that the ghosts of the dead might remain on earth even as their bodies rotted away, or returned with the Wild Horde, and they thought that the malefic power of witches and sorcerers were just one of a variety of occult forces that could be tapped by human beings. Indeed, many sought to exploit these forces through practices that amalgamated Germanic folk traditions, Christian rituals and doctrines, and, to a lesser extent, esoteric traditions from classical paganism, either to protect themselves from malign powers that might threaten them or to advance their own interests. Such practices were considered superstitious by the religious authorities because they either attempted to tap non-Christian sources of power or attempted to tap Christian sources of power in unapproved ways, but the evidence suggests that the vast majority of people incorporated them to a greater or lesser extent into the routine conduct of their daily lives, and a great many made use on occasion of the informal network of specialized practitioners who offered a variety of magical services as well.[3]

Popular magical practices employed innumerable means to accomplish a variety of different ends, but at bottom they served one of two purposes: to gain information about the world or exert some influence on it. The latter involved a broad array of purposes and procedures ranging from simply wearing protective amulets to undertaking elaborate rituals intended to transmute base metals into precious ones, but the former comprised a smaller, more cohesive set of practices known collectively as divination. Divination could presumably be used as a form of sorcery, a way of gaining intelligence in order to better strike at an enemy, but it seems to have been used more frequently as a form of countermagic, to determine the identity of an occult attacker, or for more neutral purposes like identifying a future spouse, locating hidden objects or missing persons, or determining the prospects for a planned activity. Most sorcery, as we have seen, was manipulative in nature, intended to exert influence to promote one person's interests at the expense of another, but here, too, most manipulative magical activity appears to have been defensive or more neutral in nature, attempts to ward off malign influences or gain ends that did not involve injuring others.

In Part III we will look first at the various types of divination that were used in the duchy, in Chapter 6, and then at the diverse forms of beneficent manipulative magic, magic used to exert some benign influence in the world, in Chapter 7. In order to provide some idea of the relative importance of various sorts of popular magic in the duchy, both chapters will draw from a number of samples similar to the sample of witchcraft cases used as a framework for analysis in Parts I and II. Specifically, a stratified random sample was created including 40 percent of the cases of the major specific forms of beneficent magic identified in the archival index – *Segensprecherei* (literally "saying blessings," which will be referred to here simply as blessing), *Arznei* (illicit medical practices, or healing), *Schatzgraberei* (treasure-hunting), and *Geisterbeschwörung* (conjuring spirits) along with 20 percent of the cases called *Zauberei* (magic), *Magia*, and other less specific terms indicating miscellaneous magical practices.[4] The sample was stratified to reflect the relative proportion of cases in each category, so it includes nine of the 23 cases labeled as blessing, eight of the 20 healing cases, 13 of the 33 treasure-hunting cases, and seven of the 17 cases of conjuring spirits.[5] The reason that only 20 percent of the 48 general magic cases were included is that, as we have seen, half of the random sample of 21 of this type proved to be essentially late witch trials, with the less prejudicial label reflecting the government's changing understanding of witchcraft, and the other half were incidents similar to those labeled as specific forms of beneficent magic plus a few involving other apparently supernatural phenomena. Therefore, if half (24) of the 48 general magic cases can be assumed to have involved nonmalefic magic, ten would equal 40 percent of the relevant cases. Therefore, the first ten such cases among the sample of 21 were added to the beneficent magic sample.

The consolidated sample of 47 of 117 cases is statistically significant, but even more than with the witchcraft sample, there are many aspects of the phenomenon that were not recorded or were recorded unsystematically. Furthermore, the various contemporary participants in the cases often had different labels for what they were doing, so what the constable considered illicit healing, the villagers considered neighborly assistance, and there was a certain amount of overlap between the categories, since blessings were often made as part of healing rituals, and treasure-seeking, as we have seen, often involved conjuration of a spirit, so that the neat categorizations and quantification require oversimplification of the messy reality. Quantification has its value, but, once again, the intention here is not so much to engage in rigorous statistical analysis or to arrive at definitive quantitative answers, but instead to use the sample as a starting point for discussion of the range and relative importance of various practices and practitioners involved in beneficent popular magic.

6
Divination and Prophesy

In this chapter we shall look at the occult processes by which early modern Europeans, and in particular early modern Württembergers, attempted to access information that was normally hidden to them: the identity of people who had bewitched or stolen things from them, the location of people and objects that had gone missing, their prospects for marriage, and the outlook for the future more generally. For the most part this information was sought deliberately, through various magical techniques known as divination, but sometimes it came through spontaneous prophesy. We will start by looking at the various ways in which people engaged in deliberate divination that are contained in Württemberg's judicial archives, and conclude by examining the less frequent instances of spontaneous prophesy. The one gives insight into the mundane realities of popular magical activity; the other, a glimpse of the occasionally spectacular manifestations of and reactions to the revelation of extraordinary information to otherwise ordinary people.

The varieties of divinatory activity

Divination can be used to gain information about hidden or distant things in the present, like lost objects or missing persons, to predict the future, or, less commonly, to learn unknown things from the past. Divination is a universal human activity, practiced in hunting-and-gathering societies and simple agricultural societies as well as in complex agricultural and even modern industrial civilizations.[1] It appears to have originated in Paleolithic times and was used in tribal cultures and early civilizations, until Roman times in the West, to assist in communal as well as personal decision making.[2] Christianity frowned on the practice, though, as indicating a lack of faith in God's providence, implying a constraint on God's omnipotence, and, in at least some cases, appearing to involve demons, so public use of divination declined. Kings and other public personages, along with ordinary people, commonly prayed to God for certainty about the best course of action, and interpretations of natural omens and spontaneous prophesies were understood to be potentially legitimate sources of insight into God's intentions, although the latter in particular might prove to be diabolic deceptions. Furthermore, judicial ordeals, in which a suspect was put to a test in which the only connection between the outcome and a suspect's guilt was the assumption that God would not permit the innocent to be punished, can be considered a form of divination, as, too, could the practice of "swimming" a witch, deciding her guilt by seeing if she floated or sank in water.

By the early modern period these forms of judicial divination by ordeal were rarely accepted in court, but innumerable forms of divination were practiced in private life. The purposes for which it was employed could include virtually any problem that might be on a person's mind or decision they might have to make. The range of techniques by which divination might be conducted was vast. One formal classification scheme identified over one hundred, including scapulomancy (inspecting animals' shoulders), dactyliomancy (using a finger ring), oneiroscopy (interpretation of dreams), chiromancy (palm reading), and necromancy (contacting the spirits of the dead). Furthermore, there were a host of local and even personal techniques like forecasting the weather by interpreting ravens' cries, foretelling the future by the croaking of frogs, and predicting the price of grain by watching what happened to kernels placed on a hot hearth. However, most techniques fell into a few general categories. One included omens, dreams, and prophesies, which were not technically a form of divination when they were observed or interpreted spontaneously, but could be considered such when they were sought or interpreted deliberately, for divination is generally understood to involve ritual actions designed to reveal hidden information either through the generation of physical patterns or outcomes that are then interpreted or the inducement of subjective experiences (visual, auditory, or, less commonly, simple awareness) whose content is relevant to the issue at hand.[3] The sixteenth-century international financier Anton Fugger, for example, employed a diviner, a woman named Megerler, who gazed into a crystal ball to help him oversee his far-flung employees and manage his business affairs.[4] More commonly, divinatory powers were used to predict future marriage partners or determine the fidelity of current ones, locate lost relatives or report on distant ones' well-being, or locate lost or stolen objects and identify who took them. They were also used not infrequently to determine if misfortune was due to witchcraft, and, if so, to identify the witch.[5]

Early modern Württembergers practiced these sorts of divination, undoubtedly as readily as any of their contemporaries elsewhere in Europe, although it is difficult to make either relative or absolute quantitative judgments about the incidence of such activities since the great majority of instances almost certainly went unrecorded. Nevertheless, a number of incidents did

Table 6.1 Sampled uses of divination by trial type

	Magic	Bless	Heal	Treasure	Conjure	Total	%
Detect Witch	1	2	2	0	0	5	*19*
Identify Thief	0	2	0	0	1	3	*11*
Decide Guilt-other	0	1	0	0	0	1	*4*
Locate Person	0	0	0	0	0	0	*0*
Locate Object	0	1	0	0	0	1	*4*
Locate Treasure	2	1	0	10	3	16	*59*
Tell Fortune	1	0	0	0	0	1	*4*
TOTAL	4	7	2	10	4	28	

Source: Sampled beneficent magic cases (see the appendix).

come to the attention of the duchy's judicial authorities, and they provide some insight into both the nature and the number of at least some of the purposes and techniques of divination as popularly practiced (see Table 6.1).

Divination and guilt

In the overall sample of trials for beneficent magic, detection of witchcraft was the second most common divinatory practice, after treasure-hunting (see Table 6.1). In all of these sampled cases the identification of the witch was done by a magical specialist. Interestingly, these trials formed almost the same proportion of all sampled divination cases, 19 percent, that the sampled witchcraft cases in which specialist practitioners, cunning men or low-level medical practitioners like bathers, determined that witchcraft was involved: among those 27 witchcraft cases in the sample discussed in Parts I and II, five, about 19 percent, contain evidence that such specialist practitioners were involved in identifying the witchcraft.[6] This latter statistic suggests that in early modern Württemberg witchcraft diagnoses by specialized practitioners played a significant but not leading role in the generation of witchcraft suspicions. The former statistic indicates that they played a similarly significant but not leading role in the activities of cunning folk. This impression is reinforced when we consider that while, on the one hand, some investigations into this practice were subsumed in witch trials rather than investigated separately, suggesting that such diagnoses probably constituted a somewhat larger part of cunning folks' practices than the number in the sample of trials for beneficent magic indicates, on the other hand, witch identifications were particularly likely to draw official attention and be recorded in the criminal archives since they triggered or came out during an investigation into a capital offense. On balance, then, the evidence seems to suggest that though identifying witches was an important activity of cunning folk, it was just one of a number of divinatory services they offered.[7]

In addition to providing the raw numbers, some of the sampled cases offer insight into the process by which witchcraft was diagnosed in popular practice. In several of the sampled cases, unfortunately, the method by which witchcraft and the identity of the witch were determined is not specified, such as when the medical practitioner in Pfüllingen, whom Agatha Sacher's ex-boyfriend's bride consulted after she became "crazy" and suicidal at her own wedding, said that "her spirit had been taken," before giving her a drink that made her feel better.[8] Similarly, a cunning woman in Weÿldorf told a man who suspected that Agatha Stoßer had bewitched his cow to dig around the door, where he'd find a bone that he should get rid of to make the cow better, which he did, finding "such a bone ... from a rib."[9] How these healers arrived at these conclusions is not clear; perhaps they were simply reasoning from their knowledge of disease, in the first instance, and of popular sorcery, in the second, or they might have been among those specialists who seemed to simply "know" things.[10] In other cases, though, it is clear that the practitioners were using deliberate divinatory techniques. In one of the blessing trials, Othmar Kählin told the investigating magistrates in Lauffen, in 1594, that he identified "witches and evil women" through magic, and in the same year an investigation into the town bather in Cannstatt, Hans Brückner, revealed specific details about the illicit techniques he used.[11] It was not unusual for a bather to practice simple medicine as part of his services, and Brückner needed the money to pay for his expensive equipment and support his wife and two children, but he made the mistake of telling Fuchs Jäger's wife that "her illness came to her from evil women," whom he "could see" in a reflection in a glass plate. Specifically, he told her that she was made sick by "a goat cheese given to her to eat" by Margritha Ludwig, the widow of a town official, who, he said, lived on a lane populated by "downright malevolent people." Jäger's wife "became belligerent toward Margritha," but since Margritha and her neighbors were "honorable notables," the magistrates began to investigate the bather. They soon learned of another incident in which Brückner had also said that a sick boy "was afflicted by evil women," and offered to let his father see for himself who did it "in a mirror." Under interrogation, Brückner protested that Frau Jäger had told him she had become sick from eating cheese, said that he must have been drunk when he slighted the honorable people, and denied that he had a mirror.[12] However, the fact that two different witnesses testified that he had boasted of his ability to detect witches in a reflective surface suggests that this last statement was an evasion, for he had told Frau Jäger he saw the witch "in the window" and he did not tell the boy's father whose mirror he would use.

The divinatory technique Brückner used, called scrying, was a common version of the general approach of inducing a subjective experience, in this case a visual one, whose content was relevant to the issue at hand.[13] Variants of it utilized windows and mirrors, as in Brückner's case; crystal balls, as in

Anton Fugger's fortune-teller's case; and sword blades, water in a bucket, and even polished thumbnails.[14] All involved staring into the reflective surface until an image that supplied the desired information appeared. Any of them could be manipulated by an unscrupulous practitioner who could merely pretend to see an image to support a conclusion he or she had already reached consciously, but if undertaken earnestly, such scrying had the potential to reveal genuine insights. Since "the brain knows more than the mind reveals" and "much of what we know can't be stated," scrying can bring out unconscious knowledge by altering the practitioner's consciousness and prompting visual hallucinations.[15] Scrying promotes an altered state of consciousness that enhances access to unconscious knowledge because gazing steadily induces a focused concentration and dissociation similar to hypnosis, if it is relatively brief, or, if it is prolonged, the stronger tuning of the nervous system and simultaneous discharge of the ergotropic and trophotrophic nervous systems associated with shamanic trance. In either state, although to different degrees, "subconscious neural processing can dominate mental activity, producing ... unusual ... thoughts and images" and "an occasional ... flash of insight."[16] Gazing into a reflective surface promotes visual hallucinations in particular because it focuses attention on visual processing, and the ambiguous visual experience they create provides a favorable field onto which internally generated images can be projected, for even a clear mirror creates a disjunction between the reflection and the background imagery, and many of the types of surfaces used, like windows or water, introduced distortion to the reflected image itself. As we saw in Chapters 1 and 3, vision routinely integrates incoming sense data, recent visual memory, and internally generated imagery based on expectations and older memories, and we saw a number of examples of how the latter can be spontaneously superimposed on the former to create powerful visual experiences that manifest internally generated elements in apparently external perceptions. The technique of scrying appears to harness this process deliberately in a more controlled and directed way. Most if not all people are capable of attaining at least fleeting impressions in this manner, and roughly one in 20 persons by one estimation can generate not just a fleeting impression, but actually a sustained moving image.[17]

A case from Murrhardt, which took place 130 years later, in 1729, contains evidence of another form of divination, commonly used to identify thieves as well as witches, that was used widely throughout Europe.[18] The case began when a man complained that another man who had lost some money went to a "devil incanter" who said that the first man's daughter had taken it. The magistrates investigated and found that the cunning man was a potter named Hans Jacob Schiller who had been "divining for people where lost objects had gone," and who had taken them, for well over a decade, and he had also told a man named Christoph Ernst Dumme that a poltergeist in his house was caused by the son of a man involved in a lawsuit against him.

The technique he used was called "sieve driving" (*Sieb treiben*) locally, and "sieve and shears" in England. It involved balancing a sieve on the tip of a pair of shears, which was held point upward while the names of suspects were recited until the sieve began to rotate, which was taken to indicate that the guilty party had just been named.[19] The technique had been known since antiquity, was commonly used across Europe in general and in Southwestern Germany in particular, and was transmitted through oral channels as well as in writings by Agrippa and Mathers' version of the *Clavicula Salomonis*.[20] Since the Middle Ages the technique had been embedded in a ritual including a short blessing invoking "St. Petrus, St. Paulus, St. Kilian, in the name of God the Father, God the Son, and God the Holy Spirit" to introduce each name in turn, which served to mark off the activity from daily routine and helped focus the participants' attention.[21]

Naturally, like scrying, sieve driving could be manipulated consciously to validate a preselected conclusion, but when the ritual was conducted ingenuously it could also manifest unconscious knowledge. In contrast to the process of visual overlay in scrying, which induced a subjective experience whose content was relevant to the issue at hand, the sieve and shears method created an objective, physical outcome whose meaning was interpreted. While the source of the sieve's movement appears to us to have been random, it was more likely due to a process known as ideomotor action or the ideomotor effect, in which "quasi-independent modules in the brain ... initiate motor movements without necessarily engaging the 'executive module' that is responsible for our sense of self-awareness and volition."[22] As a consequence, "our muscles will behave unconsciously in accordance with an implanted expectation" while "we are not aware that we ourselves are the source of the resulting action" and, indeed, the actions generally "feel as though they are being propelled" by an external force. This effect was first investigated by the German Jesuit Fr. A. Kircher, who in his 1640 Latin folios reported that pendulums and divining rods only move when held in someone's hand, and not when held by a rigid support, and it was first ascribed to unconscious muscular movements by his protégé Gaspard Schott in *Magiae Universalis Naturae et Artis* (1658–9).[23] The French chemist Michel Chevreul rediscovered and investigated the effect in the early 1800s, and the psychologist and physiologist William Carpenter named and invoked it as an alternative to spiritualist and paranormal explanations of a number of related phenomena in the late 1800s. William James expanded on the concept to explain volitional as well as nonvolitional movement, since "whenever a movement ... immediately follows upon the idea of it ... all sorts of neuromuscular responses come between ... but we know absolutely nothing of them," so the only difference is whether the original impulse was generated by conscious or unconscious processing. Recent research goes even further than James and suggests that all decisions originate in unconscious processing and consciousness serves at most as a check that enables us to voluntarily suppress impulses that are on the verge of being executed (a capacity that's been dubbed "free won't").[24]

After James, psychologists' interest in ideomotor action declined, and today it is mainly mentioned by skeptics of the paranormal as an alternative to paranormal explanations of apparently anomalous physical phenomena involving contact with people. They tend to emphasize its potential to channel external suggestions and preconceived notions into apparently significant events, just as historians and anthropologists, to the extent that they pay any heed to the efficacy of rituals involving it, as well as to rituals involving scrying, tend to emphasize the rites' potential to manifest and validate preexisting awareness of socially defined roles or individual interests.[25] Of course, these rituals can do and do do all of these things, for the brain's unconscious processing is notoriously complex, integrating biological urges, cultural scripts, longstanding and self-reinforcing patterns of thought and behavior, and ongoing calculations of immediate interest, which is why the clergy regarded divination as one of the devil's snares.[26] However, in emphasizing the illusory and self-serving aspects of divinatory techniques like scrying and the sieve and shears, modern scholars are somewhat whiggishly advancing the point of view of one of the parties to the debate about magic in the early modern period, the religious and later scientific critics, while to fully understand these practices and practitioners, it is necessary to recognize what about them really worked, and why, as well. As we have seen in Chapter 1, people do perceive, evaluate, and react to stimuli unconsciously, and it is known that they can become aware that this has taken place through "gut feelings" and intuitions. These forms of cognition manifest as visceral sensations and "images ... verbal input ... [or] a general sense of knowing" since gut feelings are "the conscious experience of involuntary autonomic nervous system activation ... triggered by the limbic system," while intuitive insights are "transient, spontaneous altered states of consciousness consisting of particular sensory experience or thoughts, coupled with strong emotional reactions" that are generated by "the tuning in of emotion-based unconscious processing and the tuning out of logical operations."[27] However, these forms of understanding emerge spontaneously in consciousness strongly enough to form the basis for action or persuasion only sporadically, because they are often fleeting or obscure, because they are difficult to articulate and rationalize, and because there are often strong social and psychological pressures not to acknowledge or act on them.[28] Forms of divination like scrying and "sieve driving" are techniques designed to tap these visceral and intuitive sources of knowledge deliberately, to "access information channels of the limbic brain and lower brain centers, behavioral, nonverbal, and emotional communication processes ... [and] protomentation, paleomentation, and emotomentation" to help people "negotiate their lives, make decisions, cure ailments, and reknit [or acknowledge and adjust to tears in] social fabrics."[29]

Scrying and sieve driving are particularly useful in determining the source of ailments associated with witchcraft – that is, ailments caused or contributed to by stress resulting from interpersonal conflicts – for several reasons. First of all, awareness or acknowledgment of an interpersonal conflict may be suppressed because of sociocultural constraints or individual psychodynamics. Secondly, awareness of the specific interpersonal communication generating the stress may, as we saw in Chapter 1, be subliminal, and thus not available to consciousness to begin with. In either case, the process of divination can bring this awareness to consciousness either directly or indirectly. The process will be direct if the person involved conducts the divination, and indirect if a specialist undertakes the ritual. In the former case, the process is relatively straightforward. The ritual induces an altered state of consciousness, comparatively light in the case of sieve driving and deeper in the case of scrying, in which the person envisions the neighbor or associate whose word, gesture, or expression triggered the stress, and perhaps even the word, gesture, or expression itself, in the case of scrying; or in the case of sieve driving the person reacts unconsciously to the name of the person with tiny muscle movements generating a circular motion at the tip of the shears, and hence causing the movements of the sieve. As noted, both of these processes can be manipulated consciously, and can for various reasons lead the person to unconsciously see or name an innocent party, but these possibilities should not obscure the fact that done authentically, these processes can help bring to consciousness previously unacknowledged awareness of who and what triggered the psychophysical processes responsible for the person's misfortune.

If the process of divination is indirect, with a cunning person performing the actual divinatory act, as Hans Brückner did for Fuchs Jäger's wife, the mechanism by which unconscious information is found is more complex. Of course, it is possible for the cunning person to work entirely from his or her own personal knowledge of the client and the potential subjects (Hans seems to have known Margritha Ludwig and the other people on her street) but in many cases people consulted cunning folk who lived at some distance and would not have known the client or the likely suspects beforehand. This is undoubtedly why cunning folk often encouraged clients to actually name names themselves, either simply supervising the divinatory process or, perhaps more commonly, acting almost like a psychotherapist to draw out unconscious or unexpressed knowledge by asking questions and suggesting possibilities.[30] In this latter case, and even more when the cunning person actually performed the divination him- or herself, the process involved an intricate interplay between the client and the specialist. Having the specialist do the divination basically involved a trade-off. On the upside, as we have seen, different people have different capacities to enter trance and bring unconscious information to consciousness, and a cunning person was not only a specialist in this, but also, as a disinterested party, would be less susceptible to the social and psychological pressures to suppress or distort insights than the client.[31] On the downside, though, the cunning person obviously did not have the kind of direct knowledge of the people involved, their relationships, and the specific interactions that might have led to the malady in question. A cunning person's ability to do the divination therefore depended on his or her ability to "read" the client, to detect and register on an unconscious level body language, intonation, turns of phrase, unconscious activation of vocal cords during subvocalization, and other subliminal cues, as well as to assimilate this information with a general understanding of people, based on life experience and any overt information given during any preliminary discussion.[32] The actual process of divination could involve an ongoing process of both overt and subliminal interaction between diviner and client or the diviner could withdraw and conduct the actual divination in private, but in either case, the cunning person was sensing the unconscious knowledge of the client, on the one hand, and manifesting it in the form of the image seen or the movement of the sieve, on the other hand.[33] This process would be even more complex in cases where a third party was involved, as in a case from Angoulême, in 1596, when two young children were used to scry under the supervision of an adult diviner, which would have involved an intricate interaction between them, the magician, and the client before and quite probably during the ceremony, as the different parties negotiated, possibly consciously but presumably unconsciously, a consensual image of the act of witchcraft and the witch they described.[34]

There was another form of divination commonly used to identify witches in early modern Europe that involved performing rituals that were then connected to events that seem, from our point of view, to be entirely coincidental. For example, a Stuttgart apothecary advised a client's family to "fill a bucket of water in the name of Satan" and "put it under the bed" to compel the witch to appear, while in nearby Esslingen, an imperial city surrounded by Württemberg's territory, mixing the urine of a sick person with wax and a piece of cloth in a glass was supposed to cause the person responsible for the sickness to come within 12 hours. The people involved, of course, assumed that these rituals worked through supernatural means, that a causative connection was mediated either by some spiritual agency or some occult bonds of natural sympathy. Given that the rituals were well known, it is hard to see how the knowledge that a person had consulted a cunning man or woman would somehow prompt a suspect to show up (indeed, it would seem to ensure that anyone who knew would stay away for a few days); so, barring some sort of paranormal influence, the only mechanism linking the ritual and the "result" would seem to be pure chance.

Of course, some apparently random processes could be influenced consciously or unconsciously to provide a predetermined outcome, like writing the names of suspects on slips of paper, wrapping them in clay, and dropping them in water to see which unraveled first – it was apparently possible to wrap them in such a way that a particular one would unravel quicker than the others.[35] Furthermore, an event like the arrival of a particular person is not necessarily a random or coincidental occurrence; Agnes Langjahr was far from the only suspect whose frequent intrusions in a neighbor's household put members of the family under psychological stress, and a cunning person might choose this particular ritual in the expectation that such a person would likely be the next to come a-calling. In still other cases, there may have been wiggle-room in the process of interpretation: several people could show up in a 12-hour period, and then the client would have to choose among them, or (in the case of a related technique), the first person who showed up after the ritual was conducted could be excluded as out of consideration for some reason, and the next person, a more likely suspect, chosen. Nevertheless, it is important to recognize that rituals that existed depended on what we can only consider coincidence and were sustained by their integration with ideas about magical connections, the psychological satisfaction they gave by providing apparent solutions to pressing problems, a certain amount of unconscious bias in setting them up and a certain amount of conscious fraud, peoples' ability to see patterns and influences in random events, and dumb luck.

We have already seen that divination by sieve driving was used for purposes other than identifying witches, particularly the identification of thieves, which was probably the most common thing it was used for. The distinction was not always that clear, however, as in the case of stealing milk, for it was believed that witches could magically transfer milk from others' cows to their own; but there were also cases in which the loss of milk could also have resulted from surreptitious nocturnal milking. In one of the blessing cases, for example, a woman consulted a blind man named Jacob Geigler, who made his living by his "forbidden arts," because her cow was not giving milk, and he told her that a neighbor named "Bilfinger ... had taken her milk."[36] The blind man claimed to have arrived at this determination by examining the cow's urine, but the woman he accused was also seen sneaking around her neighbors' property late at night, which gave her the opportunity to simply steal the milk physically rather than through some arcane magic.

In the case we have already seen involving Jacob Schiller, the potter from Murrhardt who said that a poltergeist was caused by a boy whose father was in a dispute with Schiller's client, Schiller was accused of using "sieve driving" to identify who had taken missing items, and also to help several people determine if they had been cheated out of some of their inheritance.[37] Similarly, the cunning man Hans Köll, who helped Anna Eberlin when she started acting as if possessed after she had sex with a boarder, also got into trouble when he confirmed for a man named Hanns Dietscher that his daughter and her husband had taken 400 Reichtaler (a small fortune at the time) from him.[38] Relations within the family became "deadly hateful," and the daughter went to the magistrates demanding a "public retraction," but Köll insisted that his magic had "never yet failed him."

Table 6.1 suggests that divination was used to identify thieves somewhat less frequently than it was used to identify witches, but this may reflect the fact that the crime was less serious than witchcraft, and therefore cases involving it were less likely to come to the attention of the ducal government.[39] Divinatory rituals like this were well suited for the problem of identifying thieves as well as witches because, while the crime itself did not involve the subliminal actions and reactions that characterized *maleficium*, the aftermath did involve a certain amount of deception because most theft in villages and small towns at the time appears to have been by people who were part of either the same community as their victims or one nearby. Of course, some missing items were undoubtedly simply misplaced, but they tended to be valuables that people would pay special attention to, and there is no reason to doubt that many items that disappeared were in fact stolen. Some may have been taken by the vagrants who drifted across the countryside, especially during and after wars, and who would not hesitate to burglarize a house if the opportunity arose (they were particularly likely to strike on Sunday morning, which was a common excuse for not attending church), but by and large such raids were both infrequent and obvious (the presence of the vagrant in the neighborhood would likely be noticed, and the house would likely be ransacked). The kind of thefts people consulted cunning folk about were the mysterious disappearance of specific items, which were most likely taken by people with access to the house and knowledge of the members' possessions and routines. The thief would then have to live with the victim, and perhaps even rebuff inquiries and accusations, all of which required deception and lying.

Lying presents a complex social-psychological problem, for "there is ample evidence that people behave differently when they are lying than when they are telling the truth," and these "differences in behavior ... alert targets ... that a lie is being perpetrated upon them"; yet the evidence suggests that people are relatively bad at consciously recognizing that they are being lied to.[40] Perhaps because "lying is a fact of daily life," since "on average people tell at least one lie a day, and one lie in every five of their social interactions," accurately recognizing lies and calling people on them would simply be too disruptive socially.[41] While this assessment is only suggestive since it is based on modern research, there is good reason to think that that if anything, lying was more firmly engrained in early modern culture, and certainly Hanns Dietscher's accusation against his daughter and son-in-law created a firestorm in that family, while, similarly, the magistrates of Murrhardt noted that Jacob Schiller's activities "created great bitterness between the best of friends" and "set hearts bitterly against one another, so that all sorts of evil consequences follow from it."[42] People had recourse to divination because, if more mundane clues or proof that a particular person had stolen something from them were not available, it could confirm their awareness of or bring to consciousness their unconscious knowledge of who in their immediate social circle was displaying involuntary signs that they were lying. Historians have traditionally emphasized that people went to diviners because there were no police detectives with modern forensic techniques and technology available to them, which is true, but a somewhat anachronistic way of looking at things, sort of like saying that people invented writing because they hadn't figured out how to make televisions yet. Scrying and sieve driving to identify thieves were used because they could tap peoples' real awareness of other peoples' unconscious signals that they were hiding guilty secrets, a real awareness that was often difficult to bring to consciousness and even more difficult to articulate in order to justify social action. The alternative was not modern criminology; it was doing nothing. Divination was not an ineffectual substitute for effective action, it was an effective action that, while not entirely reliable, was neither random nor inherently unreliable. Among the sampled cases, for example, Jacob Schiller had been forced to admit on one occasion "that what he said at first was far off the mark," and on another that he had defended a man accused of assaulting another with a knife because he was drunk, but Jacob Geigler said Glaßer Bilfinger's wife was stealing milk before she was seen sneaking around her neighbor's property late at night, and while we cannot know the guilt or innocence of the accused in most cases, thefts do take place, and, outside the formal structure of law, a suspect's protestations of innocence are no more inherently credible than a theft victim's suspicions.

Historical analyses of divination to identify witches and thieves have generally proceeded from the implicit assumption that there was only one predetermined suspect, and the ritual was conducted merely to rubberstamp their vilification. This approach overlooks both the fact that it is quite possible for the most obvious suspect to be, in fact, guilty and the fact that there may well have been several people in a community who were potential suspects, for the aggrieved person may have been at odds with a number of people, so that the ritual was conducted not to validate suspicion of a single suspect, but instead to decide among a number of potential offenders. Furthermore, it is even possible that once in a while the aggrieved party was genuinely perplexed about who might have perpetrated the crime, and went into the ritual without any preconceived ideas about who might be guilty and ready to accept whatever answer the process revealed.

Locating hidden things

Another purpose of divination that was often closely linked to identifying thieves was locating missing persons and objects. None of the sampled cases involved locating a missing person, but a couple of others incidents in the duchy did involve related activities. One concerned Hans Köll again, who got into trouble a few months after his involvement in Anna Eberlin's case by claiming to know where a schoolmaster who had disappeared was, although when the schoolmaster's wife denounced him for magic he claimed that he had merely seen the missing man in Strasburg when he was there to sell a cow. The other related case took place in Stuttgart, in 1802, when the magistrates investigated 52-year-old Christina Dorothea Schulen for "bottle gazing" (*Bouteillen Gucken*), a form of scrying, which she used not to locate people, but rather to give people separated from their children or relatives information about them.[43] Only one of the sampled cases involved locating missing objects, the one in which Jacob Schiller made his divisive accusations, which followed from his efforts to determine "where things gone missing went."[44] Several other cases in the duchy also involved use of divination for this purpose, though. The investigation that uncovered Christina Dorothea Schulen's "bottle gazing" appears to have begun with an investigation into Johann Heinrich Haufler, a "devil incanter" who had made his reputation by finding a watch owned by a Jew in Aldingen.[45] More recently, Jakob Sauerzapf consulted him when he lost a kerchief with 150 Ehlen in it, and while the magistrates noted that this led Sauerzapf to denounce several innocent people, Sauerzapf said in fact that "he really recovered his kerchief" and the money.

To the extent that locating a lost valuable involved identifying who had it, locating lost objects could operate by the processes used to identify malefactors, as Haufler seems to have done in Sauerzapf's case. Furthermore, there was always the possibility of fraud, as Hans Köll claimed he had attempted.[46] Locating an object that was lost rather than stolen might also be facilitated by divinatory techniques that draw out unconscious knowledge, though, since people often forget the last place they saw something, or may have some idea of or be capable of calculating an unlikely place where it might be. Scrying to determine distant peoples' well-being, however, can only involve a fraud like Köll's; a more or less well-intended pandering to peoples' hopes and fears; a guess, perhaps based on some knowledge of the distant person's condition and situation, or some paranormal channel of communication.[47] Christina Dorothea appears to have genuinely believed in her ability to bottle gaze, making fraud and conscious manipulation or calculation unlikely, so she either disingenuously recited "news" to people, which involved some combination of informed guesswork and unrecognized negotiation with her audience, or else she was genuinely clairvoyant. In the past two decades there has been intensive research into "remote viewing," including an extensive series of investigations by the US military and several publications in refereed psychology and engineering journals, and a number of scientists have advanced theoretical explanations based on quantum physics, but the experiments, their statistical analysis, and the theories advanced to explain them have been subject to questions and criticisms, so at this point there is no scientific consensus about whether clairvoyance or remote viewing actually occur or are even theoretically possible.[48] Since the scientific status quo is that these phenomena do not occur and, once again, 200-year-old judicial records can hardly decide the issue, we must assume that what Christina Dorothea actually saw reflected in her bottle can only have been visualizations manifesting her subconscious processing of her own prior knowledge and information she received, consciously and unconsciously, from her audience, without any direct input from the ostensible remote sources.

As Table 6.1 shows, treasure-finding was by far the most common purpose for which divination was practiced among the sampled trials for beneficent magic.[49] The fact, as we saw in Chapter 5, that it tended to involve groups of people rather than just a practitioner and a client may mean that it was particularly likely to come to the attention of the authorities, but, on the other hand, the fact that it did not generally create an aggrieved party who had an incentive to call in the authorities, as identifying witches and thieves did, would have worked in the opposite direction, so it seems safe to conclude that treasure-seeking was a leading reason why people conducted divination, but probably not as dominant overall as within the sample of trials.

As we also saw in Chapter 5, *Schatzgraberei* referred to attempts to recover caches of valuables that had been buried or secreted in old buildings over the centuries. The practice usually but not invariably involved the use of magic to locate the treasure and also to deal with any supernatural forces that might, according to contemporary theory, cause it to move or disappear or afflict the people trying to recover it. Divination played a pronounced role in the practice, because of the need to determine where a treasure was among all the potential locations, and was definitely conducted in ten of the 13 sampled treasure-seeking cases.[50] Of the three remaining cases, one stemmed from baseless allegations against a family that became suspect because they entertained visitors until after midnight, the second involved a fraud in which the swindler disappeared with 75 Reichstaler 'seed money' when he went outside, saying he was going to mark the place to dig, and the third does not have enough detail about the treasure-finders' activities to tell whether they used divination to decide exactly where to dig when they went to an old church a "Catholic maid" had said contained buried treasure.[51] Furthermore, in four of the five cases of "conjuring spirits" in which treasure was sought, there is evidence that divination was used; while in the fifth, it is uncertain.[52]

The divinatory methods employed in treasure-finding included the use of devices whose movements were thought to indicate the location of treasure, reflective surfaces in which the location could be discerned, and a variety of rituals intended to establish contact with a ghost or spirit and get it to reveal where the treasure was hidden. The devices included a pendulum, divining rods, and knitting needles, and were mentioned in three of the sampled treasure-finding cases: the one that took place in Brackenheim, in 1683; the one that took place in Dornstetten, in 1721; and lastly, the one that took place in Herrenberg, in 1751.[53] How the pendulum was used is not described in the documents, but in general pendulums work rather like the sieve and shears, except that they are somewhat more articulate since they can swing back and forth as well as rotate. They are most commonly used to answer "yes" or "no" questions, although they can also indicate things like "maybe," "yes, but," and "no, but" to prompt further questions along the same lines, or convey direction and magnitude.[54] In the case at hand, the one in 1751, a man named Johannes Kohler used a pendulum to determine that yes, there was a treasure hidden in a garden wall as Christoph Keller, the owner of the property, suspected, and also to find out roughly where it was. Georg Jacob Hofen then used knitting needles that were "twisted together" to zero in on the supposed location by taking the contrivance "in both hands," and carrying the needles near the wall while "attention was paid to their movement, which indicated that the treasure had been located."[55]

Dowsing rods, which were used in the 1683 case as well as in the 1721 one, are forked sticks used in the same way as Hofen used the knitting needles, with one hand holding each arm of the "Y" and the stem sticking out in front, and they undoubtedly served as a model for the needle contrivance, for there is evidence that their use goes back to prehistory, and that they were employed by the Egyptians, the Hebrews, the Chinese, the Scythians, and the Romans.[56] The prehistoric and Biblical evidence suggests that they were used to find water, but the Scythians and Romans definitely used them for other divinatory purposes, and the earliest description of them being used to detect hidden substances comes from the sixteenth century, when Georgius Agricola described "German miners using a forked twig to find underground mineral veins" with apparent success in his *De Re Metallica* (the first confirmed modern instance dowsing for water, the most common use today, was in the mid-seventeenth century).[57] The miners insisted that the minerals rather than the operator caused the rod to move, although they also said that not everyone could use one successfully. Martin Luther condemned the practice for relying on illicit spiritual intervention, while natural magicians defended it as based on natural, if occult, forces like sympathy and antipathy. The first scientific explorations of dowsing were Kircher's investigation of pendulums and rods around 1640 and a report by Robert Boyle to the Royal Society about 20 years later. Theological debates about dowsing continued into the early eighteenth century, but scientific study languished until late in the century, gradually picked up over the course of the nineteenth and early twentieth centuries, and became quite vigorous in the last few decades.

The issues at hand are: first, can dowsers actually detect water or other hidden substances, or are they just guessing; second, if they can, do they do so by unconsciously processing normal sensory cues or is some other process at work; and, third, if there is some other process at work, what is it? The scientific studies include both laboratory experiments and field tests, and show that while "testing for dowsing in artificial environments showed no evidence for a dowsing effect ... testing for dowsing in natural environments showed that geological anomalies can be detected by the use of dowsing."[58] In some cases this ability clearly reflects and in other cases may well reflect "unconscious reactions to clues found in the lay of the natural environment," but in some experimental studies "highly skeptical" researchers "took great pains to ensure a uniform testing surface," while in some field situations "geologists agreed there could be no surface indication of any underlying water," yet "dowsers found water ... where orthodox methods had failed." The fact that experiments have shown that people are sensitive to electromagnetic fields and there is "evidence of correlation between magnetic gradient changes" in the environment "and dowsing reactions" suggests that "dowsing is a neurophysiological response ... to electromagnetic field gradients ... or ... electromagnetic radiation from the earth or even ... a complex combination of geomagnetic fields, electromagnetic radiation and other factors," with "rods or pendulums" acting "as a mechanical amplifier of otherwise unnoticeable small tilts and movements of the hand."[59] While not all experimental data are consistent with the electromagnetic hypothesis, and alternatives involving paranormal powers or some unknown form of radiation have been advanced, unconscious processing of normal sensory cues plus human sensitivity to natural variations in the electromagnetic environment seems to be the most likely explanation for dowsers' apparent ability to detect subterranean features and objects.

While modern studies of dowsing have focused on its use to detect water, its potential to detect minerals is of most interest here, since it was these, in the form of coins, jewelry, and similar valuables, that the treasure-seekers were after. Only a few studies have been done to test dowsers' ability to detect objects like these, and the results have been mixed. On the one hand, one of the experiments that pointed most strongly to peoples' ability to detect variations in environmental electromagnetism involved detecting the influence of a buried iron rod or wire, but, on the other hand, a direct test of dowsers' ability to detect brass or gold hidden in one of ten sealed boxes yielded results equivalent to or less than chance.[60] Perhaps the fact that iron is a good conductor and brass and gold are not accounts for the difference, but in any event, while dowsing may well have helped early modern miners to detect geological veins of ore in mountains, the cases from Württemberg suggest that it was less helpful for people seeking small items made from precious metals in the walls and gardens of old buildings. In the case from 1751, Georg Jacob Hofen said initially that he had detected 650 Reichstaler (roughly $20,000) worth of gold and silver and later claimed that it was actually worth 2,000 Reichstaler (around $60,000), and that there was a very deep cache worth 9,000 ($250,000), but no treasure had actually been recovered when a town watchman intervened and cut short the group's activity.[61] Similarly, the treasure in the case from 1721 was initially said to be a "gold cross, cup, nuggets, and several rings" worth around 800 Reichstaler ($25,000), and later a "dowsing rod indicated" that the cache was worth 25,000 Reichstaler ($750,000), but, similarly, the magistrates "took away" the magical "instruments, so that nothing further" could be "undertaken, but rather everything melted away."[62] Finally, the case from 1683 involved a group of six men who had been treasure-hunting together for years and had not found anything in the old castle where they were caught, although they appear to have been a well-organized and relatively practical band and there was some indication that they had been more successful in the past, although how they might have achieved any earlier successes is unclear.[63]

In all three cases the dowsing rod was used in conjunction with "other magical ... incantational arts" that clearly involved interaction with spirits in the two eighteenth-century cases and at least an appeal to spiritual agency in the earlier one.[64] However, in two of the three cases it is less clear whether the participants thought the dowsing process itself involved spiritual agency, for only in the one from 1751 was it noted that the dowser, Georg Jacob Hofen, "mumbled something secret" as he used the needles, suggesting that he assumed that the process depended on the cooperation of some autonomous conscious agency.[65] Authorities at the time were explicitly divided on the question, with some regarding dowsing as an expression of natural, if occult, processes, while others regarded it as dependent on spiritual intervention, and therefore involving an implicit pact with the Devil.[66] In either case, though, it was generally assumed that the movement of the dowsing rod was caused by some external force, which is understandable since, as we have seen, "we are not aware that we ourselves are the source of" ideomotor actions, and may "feel as though they are being propelled" by an external force. The movements of diving rods are particularly dramatic, "sometimes violent enough to peel bark from a Y-stick, and to scratch hands painfully," while "novice dowsers who were former skeptics" have "claimed they were trying to stop the rods" rather than trying to make them move.[67]

Whether they were regarded as manifesting some occult natural force or contact with some spiritual agency, dowsing and other divinatory techniques that express unconscious neural activity in ideomotor movements have a clear connection to the visual and aural experiences that were taken to be direct perception of independent spiritual entities, for in all cases what was taken to be externally generated phenomena appears to actually have been the product of internal processing. Dowsing does seem, in some cases at least, to manifest the direct effects of an external force on the internal workings of the nervous system, but equally or more important, particularly in searching for treasure in old buildings and farmyards, would be the evocation of hunches about the most likely hiding places at a particular site. Divinatory practices routinely included invocations that facilitated subtle or dramatic alterations of consciousness conducive to such manifestation of nonconscious neural processing, but their effect was not limited to the physiological impact of rhythmic and repetitive activity. The practitioners' assumption that they constituted communication with an autonomous consciousness was in fact true, since the content did, through symbolic penetration, influence the content of the nonconscious processing and its subsequent manifestation in perception or ideomotor activity.

Aside from questions about the ability of dowsing to locate small quantities of precious metals, given the number of potential locations, using the technique alone would be rather like using a stud-detector to look for a needle in a haystack: it would help a bit, but not much. Therefore, dowsing was in all cases used in conjunction with other means of determining the general location in which to search. The treasure-hunt in 1721 focused on a barnyard because, according to the farmer, a ghost had been making mischief with his animals for years, and he wanted to capitalize on the process of exorcizing the troublesome spirit. The group in the case in 1683, in contrast, seems to have focused their searches on logically probable locations of manageable proportions, while the treasure-hunters in 1751, as we have seen, used a pendulum to narrow the search to a specific portion of the garden wall where the treasure was thought to be hidden, and then used the knitting needles to pinpoint the exact location to excavate. In addition to these ideomotor-based instruments, a mirror for scrying was used in conjunction with a dowsing rod in one case, and mirrors were mentioned in two of the sampled cases, while a water glass was used, presumably for the same purpose, in another.[68]

Furthermore, in all three of the sampled cases involving scrying the process was explicitly linked to a spirit. This was not unusual, for while Hans Brückner, in the case discussed earlier, does not seem to have asserted that his scrying involved spiritual assistance, it was common for people to assert that their ability to see an image in a reflective surface involved contact with a spirit, and crystal balls, like that used by Anton Fugger's cunning woman, Megerler, were commonly thought to get their power from spirits that had been trapped in them.[69] In the case involving a glass, which took place in Urach in 1789, the woman who used it, Maria Agnes Scholl, was said to have used it to communicate with the spirits.[70] The first of the cases involving the use of a mirror took place in Ludwigsburg, just outside of Stuttgart, in 1739, and centered on an attempt to gain treasure via the St. Christopher's Prayer. Maria Juditha Knötzlerin, the 32-year-old daughter of a schoolmaster from Vaihingen, said that a Capuchin monk had shown her a book made by the Jesuits that showed how to summon a "treasure-man" who would then "make a mirror that she could see everything in."[71] In another case involving a mirror, which took place in Herrenberg in 1762, Hanns Jerg

Stadi, a usually honorable judge in the village of Effringen, with significant property, but who needed money because his house was falling apart, became convinced that there was a treasure worth 1,200 Reichstaler ($35,000) buried in his basement. He said that he could see it in a mirror that a local cunning man, "blind Jacob" Geigler (whom we met earlier identifying who was stealing milk from a cow by examining its urine), had instructed him to enchant by burying it at night in a graveyard near a dead man's head, an interesting twist on the folkloric connection between the spirits of the dead and hidden treasure.[72] Friends he pressed to look in the mirror said they couldn't see any money, but he insisted that it was there, and he enlisted several people to help him dig under his house. The constable in Wildberg got wind of the activity and put a stop to it before any treasure was found, but he had already dug in his basement pretty extensively, so there seems to be little question that, as a neighbor's wife had commented when Stadi began talking of the treasure a year before, it was just "a pitiful old wives tale"; Stadi's "visions" revealed nothing more than the intensity of his financial hopes and fears. As the opponents of magic have argued from antiquity to today, tapping the unconscious is a risky business, for there are many forces shaping what finally bubbles up, hopes and fears, and angers and desires, as well as sudden flashes of clarity and insight, so what seem at the moment to be our most potent perceptions can turn out to be our greatest follies.

While these instances involved the use of various devices in attempts to gain information about the location of treasures from occult sources, for the most part, treasure-hunting involved unmediated communication with spirits. That communication could be established in two ways – through deliberate ritual invocation and through spontaneous contact – and could involve several kinds of spiritual agents: ghosts, St. Christopher, the Christian trinity, demons, and the Devil. Rituals were also often used after a spirit had appeared spontaneously, to get it to divulge the location of a treasure and perhaps set the terms on which the treasure could be secured, and more than one of the different kinds of spiritual agents were often involved in a single incident.

Only two cases involved demonic spirits. One was the case mentioned in Chapter 5, in which a treasure-finder had a powder he snorted or smoked to contact his "evil spirit."[73] The other was the one involving the spirit plaguing the barnyard in 1721, for when Georg and Chrisoph Bernhard traveled from Dornstetten to Strasburg to engage the services of a cunning man to exorcize the spirit and hopefully get it to divulge the whereabouts of some treasure, he invited them to attend a ceremony held in a hut in the woods near Reichenbach.[74] After hanging a cross and lighting several candles, the cunning man made a circle around them and began reading incantations that "called on the evil Spirit." Soon both brothers "noticed something strange near the hut … as if something like a wind was blowing through the bushes," and then "during the last repetition of the incantation something hard trod before them, and upon completion [of the incantation, they] perceived [something] like a dog baying, whereupon the good spirit came." The "good spirit" was not identified, but it seemed to be the spirit of the dead person that had been haunting the barnyard, for the cunning man asked if it could be "set free," and it said yes, if "25 Reichstaler [$750] were given in penance, to a cloister or chapel." As we saw in Chapter 5, ghosts were thought to be bound to treasures as a punishment for the sin of avarice, and they could be liberated if the cache was recovered and at least a portion was used in some selfless way. The cunning man apparently used the "evil Spirit" to establish contact with the ghost in the barnyard, presumably because a haunting ghost was thought to be the spirit of a dead person who was being punished, and therefore under the control of the Devil, but from that point on, the search took the more usual form of redemption of the damned soul through the charitable use of a portion of the cursed treasure, with the remainder (the lion's share) given over to the treasure-hunters as a sort of payment for their troubles.[75] The invocation in this case was not technically to locate the treasure, since the ghost's presence in the barnyard established its general location and a dowsing rod was used to determine it's specific place, but instead the invocation established the terms upon which the treasure could be secured, and it confirmed the value of the cache established by the dowsing rod as well.

The cunning man's actual solicitation of the "evil Spirit" in this case was unusual, for all the other attempts to locate treasure through invocation of spirits involved appeals to St. Christopher and the Trinity or direct contact with the ghost itself, although treasure-hunters were generally aware that their activity skirted dangerously close to the Devil's territory. Standing inside a circle during necromantic rituals, for example, was supposed to protect the participants from contamination by the malign spirits they were calling, and so, to some extent, were the inclusion of Christian symbols like crucifixes and holy water (they might also be included to help drive away the spirit guarding the treasure, should it prove to be hostile).[76] An extreme example is provided by a case from Böblingen, in 1769, when three young treasure-hunters went to "Eÿsinger Hof" in the afternoon of John the Evangelist's day singing "God permit me to stay under your protection," festooned with "a belt of papers around their bodies covered with incantations like 'Thus has God loved the world,' and 'Get away from me, Satan,'" and carrying bread wrapped in paper with inscriptions calling on the "blood of Jesus Christ" to block the power "of the evil Enemy."[77]

The young men from Böblingen were calling on the power of the Christian deity to protect their souls from Satan, but in most cases the Trinity was invoked as part of the St. Christopher's Prayer, for the more positive purpose of locating and securing the treasure. The rituals were not, however, intended to establish direct contact with God or Christ, but instead, with the help of

St. Christopher, to enable the treasure-hunter to learn the location from a lesser spirit. In general, the spirit was the ghost of a sinner doing time on earth for its avarice, but it was possible in theory for a treasure to be guarded by another sort of spirit.[78] In one case from Besigheim, in 1747, "a number of citizens of Wahlheim" were investigated for conducting "the so-called great Christopher's Prayer" without a mention of a ghost, and, similarly, in 1795, two men tried the St. Christopher's Prayer during Christmas time, inspired by "a pamphlet they found" and kept well-hidden. It is possible that these groups hoped to use the ritual to summon the spirit of a dead person, but since the dead were thought to want to be noticed so that the treasure would be found and they would be released, someone using magic to locate a treasure "cold," independent of a spontaneous ghostly manifestation, could end up dealing with a demon determined to defend the treasure instead. This is why the cunning man working with the knitting needles insisted, the group needed holy water, various herbs, and "an iron spike that the head of a criminal had been stuck on": if the spirit of the treasure was hostile, he "needed the power" to dominate it.[79]

Whether the spirit to be contacted once God's permission had been gained was a demon or a ghost, we saw in Chapter 5 that the complex and protracted verbalizations and ritual acts and the variety of exotic items and substances that such treasure-hunting rituals involved served to both induce in the participants a state of mind in which nonconscious perceptions and cogitations could be brought to consciousness and suggest the content of the resultant experience in much the same way as a hypnotist suggests the content of an hypnotic experience. While a good many of the treasure-hunting incidents clearly involved calculated manipulation for fraudulent purposes, many others were equally clearly conducted by people who sincerely believed that they were conjuring spirits and that they could indeed learn the location of treasure from them. For example, during an investigation of an extensive series of treasure-hunting activities in Böblingen in the 1730s, one man reported that the ritual involved a prayer of "approximately ... three-quarters of an hour" and then an hour of silent prayer.[80] The ostensible results of this activity could be a physical outcome like knocks on the door or "something like a wind at the window," which were interpreted to indicate "where the money would come," but it could also be a subjective experience. One man said, "he had not seen the spirit, [for] it did not let itself be seen, but he once felt it in his room; it was as if a cloud enveloped him, and wanted to pull the bed sheet down, whereupon he called for help." A servant girl said that she "often heard and sensed but never saw" it – except once, when it appeared "in a white and gray gown."

The man's experience, with the sense that a cloud had enveloped him and something was pushing his bed sheet down, sounds like it could have been an instance of sleep paralysis similar to those linked to "pressing" in witchcraft cases, but this time interpreted as the treasure spirit. Even if this is true, however, it is quite possible that the physiological sensations he experienced did not happen by chance, but instead occurred, or were intensified, as some witch-related experiences appear to have been, by his expectation that a spirit was at large. And the girl's experiences, too, seem likely to have been prompted by the buzz in the household created by the magical activity.

While the experiences of people who were involved in rituals designed to invoke spirits were clearly influenced by their expectations, the source of the original encounters that preceded the ritual procedures, and in some cases supplied the desired information without them, are less clear. According to both Protestant and Catholic doctrine, there was no place for ghosts on earth. Souls went to heaven or hell or, in Catholicism temporarily to purgatory, but there was not supposed to be any contact between any of these and the land of the living.[81] Nevertheless, belief that some peoples' spirits remain on or close to earth and that the living can encounter them is "close to an anthropological constant," and they had been a ubiquitous feature of European popular culture since antiquity.[82] The legends of the Wild Horde and the Wild Hunt involved ghostlike creatures, and female *benandanti*, the *armariés* in Montaillou, and other seers across Europe specialized in contacting the souls of the dead.[83] There is no question that the frequency, content, and significance of ghost encounters vary from society to society and from period to period in connection with changing cultural concepts and social structures, but there is not only a common core to the belief but also a range of common experiences including the visual perception of apparitions, aural perceptions of various sorts, and the physical movement of objects associated with poltergeist activity.[84]

Various cases from Württemberg contain examples of all of these phenomena. In 1698, Georg Mutschler, a farmer near Alpirsbach, complained that both during the day and at night he and his wife had been bothered by a ghost in stocking feet that bounced from floor to ceiling in their house and made a metallic jingling sound like many coins dropping. He asked what it wanted, and it replied that it was there to help him, but wouldn't say how. The constable of Alpirsbach informed the High Council that "it can be concluded [that] money was buried in the house," and the councilors gave permission to search, so long as it was done "without any superstition or use of forbidden [magical] means."[85] Thirteen years later, a man named Salz, in the village of Abershausen, near Göppingen, claimed that he was plagued by a ghost so much that he spent more and more time in the preacher's house, until a treasure-hunter came, summoned the ghost, which came dressed like a monk, and got it to divulge where a treasure was.[86] Again, the council said to go ahead and dig where the spirit had indicated, but not to use any (more) forbidden magic in the process. In 1702, in contrast, the government punished a number of people near Heidenheim for using "a devil incanter" to locate a treasure when they were plagued by a ghost that "knocked" when the lights were out, wandered around at night, sometimes appearing like a light and sometimes appearing as a white figure with white hair, and once grabbing a woman "like a cold hand on the throat" so that the next day, "Easter Monday, her neck was very swollen."[87]

While these three cases involved unidentified spirits, in other cases the ghost was someone close to the people involved. In 1799, Ludwig Schnedler, a cobbler in Ludwigsburg, hired Johann Josef Michael Muhlmaÿer, a schoolmaster from Feldkirch, to exorcize a ghost that had been bothering him on the strength of a recommendation from the smith Bernhard's widow.[88] She had told him that when her husband's ghost kept coming back and appearing to her and "the preacher and the Capuchins" weren't able to help, she called in Muhlmaÿer, who located and recovered, using an ax, 300 Reichstaler Bernhard had hidden along with a note to his son. He had also told the widow that she only had four weeks to live, which apparently was equally on the mark.

Thirty-five years earlier, another case involving the ghost of a spouse took place in Göppingen when Jacob Schu, an unmarried 23-year-old servant, convinced "his master Johannes Fredrich, as a 79 year old and gullible man, that he had to give him 1040 Ducats on the pretext that he would redeem Fredrich's dead wife, who supposedly was going around the house as a ghost."[89] When the constable got wind of this he arrested Schu, but Schu stuck to his story, insisting that the woman's ghost had appeared to him at night and told him that she had done evil things with her parents and siblings and so she was now damned. He said that he had tried to find an exorcist, but when he couldn't decided to help her himself. The High Council wasn't buying it though, saying that he and a servant girl "had bad intentions" and decreeing that further investigation was to be conducted for four weeks at the Ludwigsburg penitentiary "to try to bring him to confess" that he had "no other intention than to swindle some money out of the old Fredrich."[90] In Ludwigsburg "he was ... given ten lashes, and since he then hardened in his wickedness approximately seven or eight more, [then] five or six [more], then again ten, and finally five more."[91] Since "he stuck to his story," which the councilors said "merited absolutely no belief, they instructed that he be incarcerated for four more weeks, and that the questioning be "much sharper."[92]

A final case of treasure-hunting through spontaneous contact with ghosts involved a group of spirits who were also said to have committed sexual offenses during their lives and a rather unusual treasure-hunter. Sigfried Sattler was a 36-year-old citizen of Tübingen who lived to the west of the town in Sindlingen, a village on the edge of the Black Forest. In 1772 he declared that "from youth on he had seen" and communicated with "ghosts in many forms."[93] His contact with them fell off in adulthood, he said, until about two or three years earlier, when it picked up again so much "that he had no peace from them many days and nights." He said he "was plagued" by them "until he spoke to them, and promised to redeem them." They told him "he should diligently pray for them for hours day and night, not engage in any incantations or adjurations, but rather appeal for their redemption ... in the Christian and Evangelical way. They advised him" to use "many psalms, prayers, and songs" and said that his praying helped "to bring their liberation from Hell's torment and pain nearer and nearer." The ghosts said that they were nuns and priests who had been in a monastery a few miles away in Bondorf, but "they did not conduct themselves in a monastic way, but rather led a sexually sinful life, and even went so far astray that they killed the babies which were born of their unmarried and sinful relations." They also said that they had buried a cache of valuables in Breitenberg, about 12 miles away, that he could have once they were released. Stattler requested permission to look for that treasure, insisting that he only prayed to God and "that this is all possible, even though it seems impossible to people and they can't and don't want to grasp or understand it." Attached to the main report, a Major General and Chevalier of the Military Order of St. Charles wrote in support that while "a basis for his account cannot be found in writing or history, at the same time things happen in the world whose basis one cannot always explain and yet ... cannot completely deny." The ducal consistory, however, found his story "incautious and untheological," an attempt at "fraud," and "a fantastical adventure." It noted that "similar ghost stories have begun to be common recently," and insisted that the government should "make an end of the thing for good," and especially that Sattler should not be permitted to present his case to the Prince himself. The councilors concurred, imprisoning him while "a precise investigation against him" was made and ultimately sentencing him to a two florin fine and four weeks in Ludwigsburg for his "fraudulence."

The authorities' harsh response to Stattler's request was inspired by more than theological rigidity or rationalist doubts, for during the previous several years they had had to contend with a situation in which an encounter with ghosts inspired not simply a hope to locate treasure, but a quasi-religious enthusiasm that challenged both the religious and civil establishment's moral authority. It began in 1770, when a 33-year-old servant named Anna Maria Freyin who worked for a butcher, Georg Buck, in Weilheim an der Teck claimed to have encountered two spirits, who came to her in her master's house.[94] Atypically, she claimed that they had already been in heaven, and while they said they needed to be liberated and eventually promised to reveal the location of a treasure, they also "quoted passages from the Bible, prayed, sang religious songs, and urged people to live morally impeccable lives according to Christian ethics." Buck and others could see them as well and "were awakened and transformed."[95] Soon informal visits developed into regular meetings, and continued even after Freyin was exiled. The growing circle of followers "came to regard the spirits' utterances as divine revelation ... claimed that the ghosts were capable of working miracles ... [and] that they received far better instruction in

Scripture from the spirits than from their minister." They said the spirits' songs were "of unearthly beauty" and "proof of" their "divine nature," and called Freyin a "redeemer of souls," a "right holy warrior, spiritual mother," and "worker of miracles." They celebrated Freyin's initial meeting with the spirits on Epiphany, which in German is the *"Fest der Erscheinung"* or "Celebration of the Appearance," and Buck adopted a six-year-old boy who did not attend church, communicated readily with the spirits, and knelt in veneration of them. The ghost worshippers said they "alone had bright, open eyes, whereas the other people were blind, perverse, and pitiable," that "the matter about the ghosts was something divine and those who were not chosen could not comprehend it," and called the town preacher the "preacher of lies" and the town scribe the "writer of lies."

Government opposition to the movement not surprisingly increased steadily during 1771, and in 1772, at the very time Stattler was petitioning to seek the treasure the ghosts he had contacted. Buck and another leader of the ghost-worshippers, Gallus Dürrner, were incarcerated in the hope that they could be forced to confess to being frauds. They refused, but in September 1773 Freyin was arrested. "Under massive pressure," including the threat of a beating, she said that she had hidden in Buck's house since she was exiled and had faked the ghosts' appearance with two white dresses, but then she escaped and disappeared for good. Buck accepted a conditional release in early 1774 that stipulated he say nothing more about the ghosts, while Dürrner, who insisted that "the things are godly" even after being flogged, was given a medical exam and judged "mentally sound" although a "fanatic," and was eventually pardoned by the Duke.[96] By this time, the leaderless and disillusioned sect had dissolved.

While the spirits in the ghost-worshipper case did promise a treasure, and Buck even borrowed from his followers against it, the spirits did not mention it until well after they first appeared, and, as the constable investigating the group observed, it was "not their main motivation," even if they "would thankfully accept it" if one was found.[97] In a few other cases, ghosts appeared with no connection to a hidden treasure. In one instance, in 1747, Christina Dietsch, a woman from Schwandorf, near Nagold, claimed that the ghost of Thomas Walzen Müller's widow had come to her to "beg her pardon" because the widow had stolen a bag with a camisole, some bread, and three spoons from her before the widow died, a claim which the widow's heirs disputed since they naturally did not want to make restitution.[98] Similarly, in a case from 1598, a young man from Rommelshausen, near Cannstatt, named Hans Schlenzer said that when he was coming home from courting, he saw the image of a man in a garden.[99] He said that it looked like a man named Conrad who had died a few years before. Conrad had had a good reputation, but the apparition told Schlenzer that this was wrong, that he had been involved in several adulterous affairs, and asked him to put money and some objects on his grave. These allegations naturally caused a stink in the village, and Schlenzer allowed that he should have kept his mouth shut. The constable noted that he was "quick to believe" and "that this only" came "from drunkenness." Church officials who questioned him found that he was reluctant to speak and varied somewhat in his description of his experience; he spent several days in jail and had to pay the cost of his confinement.

In considering the reality of these treasure-hunting activities and encounters with ghosts which were so closely connected in early modern Württemberg, the first thing that must be acknowledged is the extent to which they involved conscious fraud. A classic example of this came from Backnang, in 1776, when Christopher Wurt, a miller's helper from Brenzfeld, sought out an experienced treasure-hunter to help him locate a treasure.[100] He asked his friend David Silling from Murrhardt, who got him in touch with a shepherd, who in turn put him in contact with a "devil incanter," who asked for payment of five Reichstaler and arranged to conduct the procedure at eight o'clock at night. Wurt, Silling, and six other men met at the appointed hour, and the professional treasure-finder drew a circle on the ground with a dagger, in which the eight hopefuls had to stand silently while he spoke. Very soon a man in green appeared, "put down two cloths with money and a key on them and said, 'It is alright, you can have the treasure, but there are people among you who are not worthy." He went on to reveal intimate secrets about most of them, that "the mayor of Schöntal has committed adultery three or four times," that "the miller ... Jacob Hiller made a bastard with his servant girl," that "the mayor of Mittel Scheuthal has enough money and is not master in his house but his wife is," and that "Ludwig Kühler stole 400 Reichstaler and one horse and his deceased father bought him out of a beating." Nevertheless, the man continued, "the miller's helper is worthy, [so] he can have the treasure." However, to learn the location of the treasure, it would first be necessary "to send 75 Reichstaler to a friend of the man who buried the treasure ... in Bohemia" to get a paper with directions. Fortunately, the green man could fly, and he was willing to put up 25 of the 75 Reichstaler to boot, so Wurt and his friends contributed the remaining 50. The man in green took the money and came back shortly with the paper, saying that the treasure was 20,000 Reichstaler worth gold and silver. When the man in green left, the treasure-finder went out in the garden to draw a circle where to dig while the eager company waited inside. They waited, and waited, and waited some more, and when they finally ventured out they found that the magician had vanished. Adding insult to injury, he took with him the 5 Reichstaler that had been set aside for his fee and the dagger.

This case was particularly brazen, but there were others in which conscious fraud seems likely. We have seen how Jacob Schu got his bedridden master Johannes Fredrich to give him 1040 Reichstaler to redeem his dead wife's ghost, and while Schu maintained his innocence even when imprisoned and beaten, the fact that the money was found stuck up between some rafters makes it seem likely that the suspicions against him were justified. Similarly, the ex-soldier hired by the group from Dornstetten to exorcize the ghost in the barnyard refused to go directly back with them, but instead insisted that the brothers who came to get him attend a ceremony in his hut, where they heard strange rustling in the bushes, footsteps and something howl as the incantation ended; then said they needed to donate 25 Reichstaler, which he subsequently raised to 38, and then raised again, while actually donating, as far as could be determined, only 18 batzen (small change) to a charitable fund; and finally disappeared with the money when the magistrates intervened; all suggesting that the Dornstetters were victims of as deliberate a con as that worked by the treasure-finder and the man in green on Wurt and his friends.

However, there was some difference between the cases from Backnang and Dornstetten: while the con men in the former case worked in a very ham-handed way, dressing up in green and pretending to fly bodily to and from Bohemia, the ex-soldier worked in a more subtle way, playing on the fears and expectations of his clients. Did he have an accomplice in the woods, shaking the bushes and pinching a dog? It seems likely, but whether he did or didn't, his approach, taking the men out into the woods and letting them hear but not see things, played not only on their avarice and gullibility but also on the power of their imaginations. He may not have been a shaman in the sense of someone who altered his own consciousness to contact the spirit world, but by pretending to be through his ceremonies and, probably, his subterfuges, he did manage to manipulate his clients' psyches to tap their desires and weaknesses in a way that was, ironically, closer to what he purported to be than the swindlers in Backnang.

There were certainly more conscious frauds among the other professional treasure-finders; some ordinary people undoubtedly lied about encountering ghosts in order to support a request to look for treasure in what they had rationally decided was an auspicious location; and the government routinely accused people involved in treasure-hunting, particularly the specialists, of fraud. However, out of the 13 treasure-hunting and seven spirit conjuration trials sampled, the evidence for this is strong in only the three cases mentioned (15 percent), mixed or unclear in another five (25 percent), while it seems clear that all participants were sincerely hopeful in nine of the cases (45 percent) (the issue was not relevant in the last three because the investigation revealed no evidence that any treasure-hunting had actually taken place).[101] Thus, while conscious fraud played a significant role in magical treasure-hunting, it does not seem to have played a dominant role. Instead, it was an outgrowth of, one could even say a parasitical mutation of, a practice that was for the most part undertaken by people who genuinely thought that it was possible and some of whom really experienced encounters with spirits.

There were several different orientations among those who earnestly hunted treasure. First of all, while in theory searching for treasure did not inherently require the use of magical means or spirit contacts, in practice it almost always did. Even the government, which always stipulated that no magic be used, when it gave permission for a search, seems to have turned a blind eye to its use in some of the instances where it was directly involved.[102] Among the 14 relevant sampled cases (13 treasure-hunting and seven spirit conjuration, minus the three apparently based on fraud and the three which did not actually involve treasure-hunting) there is positive evidence that contact with spirits was sought in ten, and there is good reason to believe it was in at least two others.[103] One of these latter two involved the three young citizens of Döffingen, whose songs, inscriptions, and items appear to have been defensive rather than divinatory, but the fact that they felt them necessary suggests that they had engaged in some active magic that involved forbidden invocations of spirits.[104] In the other case the suspects were reported to have engaged in the St. Christopher's Prayer but denied it, and the allegation could not be proved.[105] In one of the remaining two cases, the one involving an old church that had been repeatedly ransacked, it is simply impossible to tell if any magical divination, spiritual or otherwise, was conducted at all, while in the last, the earliest case in the duchy, which took place in 1608, the fact that it was enthusiastically supported by Duke Friedrich, who was both the head of the provincial Lutheran church and interested in alchemy and mining, suggests that use of divining rods and pendulums may well have been permitted, but open invocation of spirits would not have been.[106]

This conclusion is bolstered by the fact that in a connected case four years later, the government expressed an interest in determining "who introduced the art of conjuring a ghost," suggesting that this element had been added since the original incident, which would mean that, in the terms of the present study, the activities involved were at most shamanistic, actions undertaken to manifest unconscious knowledge and power, but without the intention of contacting spirits.[107] Some of the other cases, as we have seen, also made use of techniques like dowsing and scrying that did not necessarily involve contact with spirits, but because of the close connection of treasure-hunting, St. Christopher, and ghosts, in practice the rest of these cases involved shamanic activity, the deliberate performance of activities that alter consciousness with the intent of contacting spirits. The main question in these cases is the extent to which the rituals altered the consciousness of those who performed them, whether they, in the terms used here, fully tuned or just fine-tuned their nervous systems, or, put another way, whether they drove themselves into an ecstatic trance or just achieved some degree of dissociation. In some cases it was simply noted that "the so-called great St. Christopher's Prayer" was "undertaken" or "the art of conjuring a spirit" was employed or simply that Catholic clerics were consulted to learn the necessary rituals, but not enough detail is given to know fully what these involved.[108] In other cases, it seems probable that any effects of the ritual activity were fairly superficial, like when the three young citizens of Döffingen festooned their bodies with defensive prayers and sang for God to protect them while they timorously disobeyed his will, or when the treasure-hunting group dowsed and muttered incantations while methodically exploring old buildings.[109] However, in some of the cases the evidence suggests that the ritual activity produced more dramatic effects. Most obvious is the one in which Maria Juditha Knötzlerin said one man gave her "a powder ... to smoke, so that his evil spirit would come."[110] In another case we have seen, Hanns Jerg Stadi gazed into a mirror he had buried near a dead man's head until he could actually see, at least in his mind's eye, the treasure he hoped was buried in his basement, and a number of people in other cases reported that after the prolonged and intense ceremonies and in the general air of excitement and expectation they actually heard and saw what they took to be ghostly manifestations.[111]

Of course, in considering the reality of this kind of magic, we must also consider what caused the participants to perceive these spiritual presences. They, of course, understood them to be exactly what they seemed, the perception of the souls of the condemned that were disembodied yet somehow existed in the external world. Anecdotal evidence of this abounds, and some of it has been collected systematically and with an eye to separating that which can be readily accounted for by known physical processes and that which is problematic from that point of view, but evidence obtained outside of strictly controlled laboratory settings has ceased to carry much weight in scientific discussions of paranormal phenomena.[112] A good deal of early psychical research was concerned with the question of survival after death and the ability of mediums to contact the souls of the dead, but control conditions were weak by modern standards, numerous cases of fraud were exposed, self-delusion seemed to be clear in others, and scientific investigations into the purported paranormal shifted to other phenomena. Some recent studies of psychics who claim to contact the dead have been conducted in laboratory settings, but significant problems with their methodology have also been pointed out.[113] Furthermore, even if it can be established that people can obtain information that no currently established channel of information transfer can account for from what they take to be the spirits of the dead, it is difficult to see how the existence of ghosts can be demonstrated over a combination of the construction of the internal representation of external reality in the sensorium and some combination of telepathy, clairvoyance, precognition, and retrocognition, all of which have stronger experimental support and more developed theoretical explanations than the continuation of individual consciousness after the associated neural activity has stopped. Since we have seen that fraud does not seem to account for most of the cases discussed here, some form of unconscious intrapsychic generation seems to be the most likely explanation for the aural and visual perceptions that were experienced as ghosts, with the incorporation of some information gained paranormally – if such a thing is possible. In discussing peoples' encounters with the Devil, in Chapter 3, we saw that internal cognitive processes routinely contribute to and in some circumstances can dominate waking perception, so that externally generated sights and sounds are modified or even replaced by internally generated "sense" data in the process of updating our internal representation of our immediate environment, our "sensorium," and the same process would seem to have been at work in these cases involving ghosts, with the difference that the percepts reflected the expectations that they were ghostly rather than diabolical.

Why did some people have ghost experiences while others thought they were dealing with the Devil? To some extent the difference undoubtedly reflects differences in personality, but there are other differences as well. Most encounters with the Devil were reported before the late seventeenth century, while most of the treasure-hunting and spirit conjuration cases came from the eighteenth century. The difference therefore would seem to reflect changes in the culture, though not so much in the sense that the same sort of person would have interpreted their experience as the Devil, in 1660, and a ghost, in 1760, but rather that one sort of person, or people with one set of problems, would have been likely to manifest them as an encounter with the Devil, in 1660, while another sort of person, or people with another set of problems, would have been likely to manifest them as an encounter with a ghost, in 1760. Both types of spiritual contacts were known and experienced in both periods, with distressed sinners meeting the Devil and hard-up optimists meeting ghosts, but the frequency changed, as we shall see in Chapter 8, as the socioeconomic circumstances and culture in southwestern Germany evolved.

A final aspect of treasure-hunting divination that must be considered in assessing magical treasure-hunting was its efficacy, how often treasure-hunters actually found the treasure they were hunting. The record, it must be said, was not very impressive. While a number of German states issued ordinances during the period asserting the government's claim to most if not all of "actual finds of treasure or coin-hordes," among the sampled treasure-hunting cases, none clearly resulted in a treasure being found, although we have seen that in the case involving the group of regular hunters in Brackenheim, in 1683, there was an intimation that they may have been more successful in the past, while during the big investigation in Böblingen, in the late 1730s, that was included in the generalized magic sample, it was said that some people did get money after using the St. Christopher's Prayer, and in a big investigation in Urach, in 1789, it was reported that some people had found money or things to sell, although in at least some of these instances the found objects appear to have actually been taken from other people.[114] Of the other cases recorded in the duchy's archives, three are known to have involved treasure actually being located. One, however, was related to a small accidental find in 1717 – in Plochingen, a village near Göppingen – which was judged not valuable enough to be followed up. A second "was the result of a carefully planned search near Grabenstetten in 1720," while the third, the only known success to result from a typical small-scale hunt by a local cunning man, was the one in which Johann Josef Michael Muhlmaÿer found the hidden 300 Reichstaler left by the smith Bernhard for his son.[115] Nor did treasure-hunters enjoy much more success elsewhere in the German south and west: "a small number of coin-hoards" are known to have been "accidentally" discovered in Hesse-Kassel during the eighteenth century, and an equal number, eight, were found "in the area around Lucerne between 1550 and 1681." One horde with "around 100 heathen silver coins from the Emperors Vespasian, Aurelius, Tragan, and others was found" in the Pfalz.[116]

Why people put such extravagant hopes and substantial effort into such a long shot, and why people during the eighteenth century did so in particular, will be considered in the last chapter, when we look at the evolving place of beneficent magic in society, but here we must consider briefly what this poor showing implies for the relationship of magical treasure-hunting techniques and physical reality. We have seen that dowsing involves the ideomotor manifestation of unconscious processing, but even if that processing involves physiological sensitivity to electromagnetic or other variations in the energetic environment along with subliminal sensitivity to sensory cues, modern studies suggest that it would not be particularly useful in finding small caches of precious metals. Appropriately, in the early modern cases it was used as an adjunct to ghost sightings and spiritual invocations, as a way of conducting the final search once they had determined that a general site was likely. The record of the overall lack of success of the hunts, however, argues against the contemporary theory that there really were ghosts tied to hidden caches that drew people to them in order to gain their release, or even that the invocatory rituals people engaged in somehow enabled them to utilize some more plausible form of paranormal perception. Significantly, the one run-of-the-mill case that was successful was the one that involved not some random ghost helping some random rescuer to find some random location, but instead involved members of a family and a cache hidden within their house. These are conditions that would seem to be particularly conducive to a spiritual contact, if such a thing is possible, and, failing that, they are also conditions that would have been particularly conducive to an accurate assessment on the part of the diviner that the woman was plagued by visions of her dead husband because she had some sense that he had hidden away some money, and of where the man would have hidden it away. The fact that ghosts and hidden valuables were so strongly associated in the culture made the first part of this assessment fairly mundane, but both the fact that the diviner was ready to take an ax to the suspected location and the fact that the suspected location was correct suggest that the second part of his assessment was based on some genuine insight. The other sampled cases, in contrast, seem to have been little more than shots in the dark.

Fortune-telling and prognostication

Ironically, fortune-telling, the kind of divination most modern people are familiar with, the attempt to foretell either the broad outlines or a specific aspect of a person's future, is conspicuous by its absence from the sampled cases from early modern Württemberg. The strongest suggestion of it came in 1623, when Hans Haasen "presented himself as an itinerant scholar, famous for many magical arts including treasure-finding, soothsaying (*Wahrsagerei*), and healing of people and animals,"[117] What exactly he meant by "*Wahrsagerei*" is not clear, however. He may have meant fortune-telling in our sense, but he may also have meant that he could identify witches and thieves and locate missing people and objects – a set of services, as we have seen, that was relatively common at the time, and that was usually prosecuted, when it was prosecuted, under the rubric of "*Segensprecherei*" since it involved, or was presumed to involve, illicit blessings or incantations. In any event, he later denied that he could actually perform soothsaying or treasure-finding, saying he just let people think he could "to occasionally earn a piece of bread that way." In a few other sampled cases cunning people were referred to as "soothsayers," but it was always in the context of an investigation into treasure-hunting, illicit healing, or one of the more focused forms of divination mentioned, and practicing fortune-telling in our sense was never raised even as supporting evidence against a sampled suspect. Similarly, of five cases labeled as "soothsaying" in the archival index, two were essentially treasure-finding cases and one was a typical case of illicit healing with blessings, so that only the remaining two actually involved foretelling the future. One involved the use of divination to foretell the future of the duchy as a whole, and only the last was a case of fortune-telling in the modern sense of foretelling individuals' futures. Evidence from elsewhere suggests that some ordinary Württembergers during the early modern period undoubtedly did try to determine the outlook for their future by interpreting naturally occurring omens and signs and simple private divinatory rituals as well, for specific evidence of such practices by specialists, semi-specialists, and ordinary people in the early modern period has been reported from many parts of Europe, but the criminal records suggest that fortune-telling in our sense of the term was neither an important part of cunning peoples' practices nor a notable semi-professional activity in its own right in the duchy.[118]

Significantly, the one case that did involve fortune-telling in the modern sense of predicting individuals' futures occurred at the very end of the early modern period, in 1802–3. This was the investigation by the city government in Stuttgart that uncovered Christina Dorothea Schulen's practice of "bottle gazing" to determine the welfare of peoples' distant relatives, but she was just one of eight women investigated for fortune-telling, and her variant on the traditional practice of scrying was not at all like what the others, or at least what six of the others, were doing (one woman's activities were not specified). The other six whose fortune-telling practices were recorded were engaged in "card laying" ("*Kartenschlagen*"), the first time, as far as is known, that this practice was discovered in the duchy.

Cards were first created in China some time after paper was invented in the second century, and were used primarily in a variety of games.[119] Paper, cards, and card games spread westward across Eurasia during the first millennium, reaching the Egypt around 1000, and Europe a few centuries later. Europeans began manufacturing paper in 1121, and appear to have begun gambling with playing cards in the mid-1300s, for the first mention of them was in 1367, when they were banned in Bern.[120] The earliest playing card decks were similar to the modern deck, with four suits containing ace through ten plus face cards, but a modified deck with an additional "suit" containing trump cards with allegorical figures, the tarot deck, was created in the early 1400s.[121] There is evidence that standard cards were used for divination in the late fifteenth century, and they were definitely used for this purpose in the sixteenth, although they were not "read" in the modern sense, but instead were used as an alternative to the more common practice of throwing dice to generate a reference to a corresponding written passage in a book. The *Merlini Cocai Sonnets* of 1527 contain the earliest known suggestion that the cards themselves were used for divination, and in this case the cards involved were the trump cards of the tarot deck.[122] There are several allusions to the use of individual tarot cards in coercive love magic in Venice, in the late sixteenth century (the Devil card was a handy image to incorporate into a malevolent ritual), but their divinatory use appears to have been mainly a form of party game in which peoples' characters, and possibly their general fates, were revealed through association with particular cards.[123] A hybrid deck of cards with the number cards of the standard suits and a series of individual, tarot-like cards instead of face cards was created specifically for divination in the late seventeenth century, in England, but the practice of card-reading appears to have been limited, and mainly confined to northern Italy, until the latter half of the eighteenth century.[124]

Two men were particularly responsible for the rapid spread of card divination at the end of the early modern period. One was Antoine Court de Gébelin, who in 1781 published the first occult interpretation of the tarot deck in his *Monde Primitif*.[125] He claimed that the tarot embodied an arcane system of knowledge that originated in ancient Egypt, and, while his historical theories were almost completely wrong, he systematically linked the symbolism of the cards to various strands of mystical philosophy, which gave them greater psychological resonance on a practical level while providing the theoretical framework that made them part of the cannon of learned magic during the nineteenth century. The other man responsible for the sudden spread of "cartomancy," a term he himself coined, was Jean-Baptiste Alliette, who wrote under the name Etteilla.[126] Alliette claimed that as a young man he studied traditional card divination in Northern Italy, and around 1767 he became a professional astrologer and alchemist and the first known professional card reader. He published a manual on card divination using the standard deck, in 1770, and in 1785 came out with a revised version that focused on the tarot cards and incorporated Gébelin's occult theories. In 1789 he published a new version of the cards, the first "made primarily for divination and to embody the views of the modern occultist."[127] More important, from our point of view, he also taught card-reading, claiming, in 1791, that he had instructed 500 students, of whom 150 practiced professionally. These numbers suggest a significant impact, even allowing for exaggeration.[128] And perhaps most important, one of his students, one of the two who he considered really good ("all the others are charlatans," he said), was "Hisler," a Prussian who had studied with him from 1769–70 and is thought to have prepared the German translation of the *Cours théoretique et pratique du livre de Thot*, which was published in Leipzig in 1793.

Etteilla was born in Paris in 1738, but during the late 1770s and early 1780s he lived in Strasburg, which lay just 70 miles west of Stuttgart and 30 miles from the duchy's western region in the Black Forest. The city was ethnically German, Württemberg's administration occasionally consulted the law faculty there, and, as we have seen, the ex-soldier treasure-finder recruited by the brothers seeking professional help in exorcising the spirit from the barnyard in Dornstetten in 1721 came from a village near the city. Strasburg was also a printing center; Etteilla, who appears to have supported himself mainly by selling prints, was a member of the guild that included printers and card-makers; and the city became an important center of tarot card production, supplying Etteilla with cards in the 1780s and producing several notable decks in the 1790s.[129] The judicial records from the Stuttgart investigation do not indicate what sort of deck or system the women used or how conscious they were of the historical pedigree or philosophical stature that had recently been bestowed upon the cards, but the timing of the investigation and the evidence it uncovered suggests that their activity was part of a broad popularization of card-based divination in Western Europe at the end of the eighteenth century, which Gébelin and Etteilla both manifested and strongly contributed to.[130] One woman, the wife of a grenadier corporal, named Christine, said that she had last read the cards 14 days before, but another one, Christiane Catarina Himmelreich, said she had stopped seven years before, when her husband died. Since she was 43 in 1802, she would have stopped in 1795, when she was 35, suggesting that she had been reading cards since the early 1790s or late 1780s at the earliest, around the same time that Etteilla's new divinatory deck was becoming available and the German version of his book appeared.

Whether these women used Etteilla's new deck, more traditional tarot cards, or even standard playing cards, there was good reason why they, along with innumerable other women, took up card reading so readily.[131] While scrying could produce a rich, specific image, we have seen that only a limited number of people could practice it successfully. Ideomotor systems like the sieve and shears and the pendulum could only produce limited answers to specific questions, and other divinatory systems like bean-casting, reading coffee-grounds, and dropping egg-whites or wax into water to discern the identity of a future mate fell somewhere between, allowing more room for interpretation than the ideomotor systems while requiring less dissociational skill than scrying. Nevertheless, in all of the traditional divinatory systems there was a strong trade-off between ease of use and scope for interpretation, a trade-off that card-reading avoided. The procedure of shuffling the cards and then laying out a set number in a predetermined pattern was easy to learn and conduct, and it was not hard to remember a pattern and the specific meaning associated with each space in it. The number cards of the regular suits, which were found in all decks, combined numerological and graphic symbolism which could be interpreted freely, or could be referenced against one of several sets of standard definitions (which themselves might have metaphorical as well as literal meanings), or the two approaches could be mixed eclectically.[132] Similarly, the face cards of the regular suits were in all the decks and included kings, queens, and some set of lesser figures who could symbolize specific people, personality types, social roles, or power relationships. The trump suit was found only in tarot decks, which made it particularly popular with readers because these cards offered a wide and deep set of symbols that enriched the spread tremendously, giving both strong guidance and wide flexibility. Each card represented some dramatic personality type or cosmological force, the Emperor or Justice or the Moon, while each image contained numerous elements that could be highlighted to support a particular line of interpretation. The tarot cards were to the sieve and shears what the railroad was to the donkey cart.[133]

The card reader did not, like the scryer, have to be able to be able to go into a trance-like state of dissociation in order to generate a rich image whole cloth in her imagination, or even have to work the client into a state of relaxed concentration so that unconscious movements could register. Instead, she just needed a facility for getting into a state of mind in which she could develop an insightful line of analysis leading to pertinent advice from the interplay between the possible meanings of the cards, their positions in the spread, and the conscious and unconscious feedback of the client. If the card-guessing experiments of J. B. Rhine and his followers are valid, and there are such things as clairvoyance and precognition, then these obviously played an important role in the creation and selection of the initial pattern as well as the fortune-teller's ruminations, but even if they are not, a skilled reader could still provide a client valuable insight and advice.[134] Naturally, there were some who cynically pandered to their clients, flattering them and predicting only what they wanted to hear, particularly itinerants who operated by fleecing by day and fleeing by night. However, those who were members of a community and wanted to maintain a steady clientele in this generally quite competitive marketplace, assuming that they weren't motivated by professional pride in honest service to begin with, would have found that strategy counterproductive, and their clients disillusioned and hostile. The magistrates of Stuttgart themselves noted, "in this matter no complaint ... has been presented."[135] Instead, the women had "been sought out" by people from "high and low classes and asked for advice."

Another case of fortune-telling divination that took place more than a century earlier, in 1675, involved a wine grower named Wolfgang Wagenhals from Schwieberdingen, near Gröningen. The investigation began unusually, with a missive from the central government to a district seat rather than vice versa. The ducal government wanted to know "if a man lives in [the village of] Schwieberdingen ... who prophesizes various things about future events, in particular the ruination and plundering of our capital," Stuttgart.[136] When the magistrates of Gröningen investigated, they learned that Wagenhals was a wine tender in "his ordinary profession" who also practiced "as a doctor," and "along with this, he utilizes astronomy and astrology."[137] He said that he had only been in school for 14 days in his life, and had learned this art partly because of his "clever ingenuity," partly because "his whole life" he had been "inclined" towards it, and partly because " for a time he was" a gardener "at the Jesuit cloister in Enzbruckhin," where he was able to copy from the books on the subject, which "often lay open." He insisted that "his religion was not affected" by his service with the Jesuits or his astronomical studies, and despite "repeated very sharp reminders" he "completely denied" that he had ever said, or even thought, what had been reported. He did allow, however, that "he could argue from the constellations and ... from the comet that had been seen eleven years before, that because it pointed to Sagittarius and Württemberg lay exactly under Sagittarius, the province would suffer from destructive military incursions." He admitted that he had told this to "several people who asked him, but without naming Stuttgart," and mentioned that "about four weeks before, in the ducal councilor Walter's house in Stuttgart, when asked" he had given his prognostication, whereupon "Walter asked if Stuttgart would be affected," and he replied "not Stuttgart" in particular, "but ... the entire province." Wagenhals stood firmly by this account, and once the magistrates were convinced that was all there was to it, they let him go.

Wagenhals clearly formed a bridge between learned and folk culture, and also between magic and religion in this case. He said that he got his healing skills in part from a natural ability and in part by learning from experience, which were both traditional sources, but he also practiced astrology. Astrology is an ancient system of prognostication that was begun by the Babylonians; developed by the Greeks, Romans, and Arabs; embraced by Renaissance intellectuals; and was incorporated into the educated early modern understanding of how the world works.[138] Johannes Kepler, who was an astrologer as well as an astronomer, was born in the duchy, and during the sixteenth century most educated people were familiar with astrology and many took it very seriously.[139]

Based on the presumed effects of the Sun, Moon, and planets and their changing locations relative to each other and the background of the fixed stars, astrology probably originated from and was clearly sustained by the obvious fact that recurring changes in the heavens determine some of the fundamental conditions on earth, like day and night, the tides, and the seasons. Furthermore, changing celestial relationships may influence terrestrial conditions more subtly; there is good evidence that moon's gravity has a tidal effect on the atmosphere and thereby on the weather, and there is evidence that the relative positions of the planets affect sunspot activity, which affects both weather and climate.[140] Most life-forms are influenced indirectly by regular changes in the heavens, in that both their evolved characteristics and their individual behaviors are affected by the cycles of illumination, temperature, and moisture these cause or contribute to, and many plants and animals have also been shown to be sensitive to the moon's effect on barometric pressure and the earth's geomagnetic field. It is possible that solar radiation also has an effect on living things via the impact of geomagnetic fluctuations on biochemical processes as well.

While the Babylonians did not know much about gravity or sunspots or how they or the moon might influence the weather, it is possible that they began their astronomical investigations because of a desire to predict these effects, given the importance of weather to their agricultural economy. However, this is only speculation, and even if the strongest extra-terrestrial influences for which electromagnetic and gravitational influences have been proposed turn out to be operative, there is still a huge leap from them to the kinds of influences on large-scale terrestrial events and intimate personal characteristics posited by the system of astrology inherited by and elaborated during the Renaissance. Most scientific studies have failed to support the hypothesis that personal characteristics or vicissitudes of fortune correlate with the positions of celestial bodies, the branches of astrology called "nativities" and, roughly, "elections" in early modern theory, and the few modern studies that offer some evidence involve modest statistical correlations that have little connection to astrological theory or practice.[141] Overall, the evidence suggests that peoples' frequent experience of self-recognition in and satisfaction with astrological characterizations reflects their own lack of self-knowledge (as measured by the general inability to recognize one's own standardized psychological profile), their tendency to notice and accept pertinent insights and to overlook or discount inapplicable statements, and astrologers' intuitive skill at analyzing them and fitting that analysis within the framework of astrological symbolism. So, while there may be some basis for the belief that celestial bodies have some terrestrial effects beyond the obvious ones caused by light and heat, what appears certain is that the system that Renaissance intellectuals inherited from antiquity and further elaborated was a complex conceptual structure constructed through a combination of deductions from astronomy and physics as they were understood at the time and symbolic associations that were assumed to have physical correlates or consequences. As with card reading, the main value of astrology seems to have come from providing a random data set, perhaps slightly skewed by some influence not currently recognized or accepted by the consensus of scientific opinion, and a rich set of symbols that the astrologer could weave together into an interpretation from which the client could glean insight and guidance. However, it should be noted that astrological charts are often generated and interpreted by the astrologer in isolation, without the involvement of the client that allows subliminal give-and-take between diviner and client in other forms of divination, even those involving interpreting physical results, as in card reading, or those involving other manifestations of the client's unconscious knowledge, as with the sieve and shears. Thus, despite the fact that astrological charts involve complex technical processing and usually result in an extended essay by the astrologer, whatever insights and guidance the client gleans from the process would seem ironically to be more dependent on his or her own unconscious emphasis and omission than most other forms of divination.

Renaissance astrological theory was based on Ptolemaic astronomy, in which the earth was thought to be the physical center of the universe; the sun, moon, and planets orbited around it at varying distances; and the fixed stars. It was also connected to Galenic medicine because the different planets were thought to transmit "different quantities of the four physiological qualities of heat and cold, dryness and moisture," which made it "necessary for the understanding of physiology and therefore of medicine."[142] Astrological theory "had some impact on formal medical education," and it was not uncommon for university-trained doctors to consider astrological factors in making diagnoses and prescribing treatments.[143] Furthermore, astrological conditions were also used "to explain epidemics and the advent of new and unusual afflictions" like syphilis. Some modern studies "have correlated solar storm activity to rates of heart attacks, lung disease, eclampsias, ... the activities of microbes ... flocculation ... the leucocyte (white blood cell) content of the blood ... individual reaction times, pain felt by amputees, and the number of suicides" as well as "epidemics of diphtheria, typhus, cholera, and smallpox," suggesting that the same fluctuations in solar radiation that are thought to affect the weather may also affect both individual and collective health, but few of these reported correlations have been studied in depth, and, like the proposed connections between planetary positions and personality characteristics, do not in any case relate directly to the actual theories and practices of astrologers, modern or early modern.[144] If Wagenhals made use of diagnostic astrology in his healing activities, his calculations would have been based on the learned theories of natal predilections and auspicious timing put in terms of planetary influences on the humors that he copied from the Jesuits' books, rather than the relative positions of the planets in relation to their possible influence on solar activity. The magistrates of Gröningen remarked critically that while he "has already often cured strong disturbances," he "sometimes also has been responsible for marked failures with his cures." Of course, this could be said of almost any medical practitioner, and it is important to recognize from our perspective that his diagnoses and treatments, with or without the aid of astrology, were just as likely to have been efficacious, or not, as those offered, with or without the aid of astrology, by a university-trained doctor at the time.

Of course, the government's interest in Wagenhals' astrological activities did not stem from his medical activities, but instead from his prediction that invading armies would cause "the ruination and plundering" of Stuttgart. This prediction was a form of "general prediction," in early modern terminology, which, "based on the future movements of the heavens ... related to the weather, the state of the crops, mortality and epidemics, politics and war" indicating " the fate of society as a whole."[145] It was the form of prognostication thought most reliable by Ptolemy, who developed the basic principles of Western astrology, along with the geocentric cosmology which framed it.[146] The government was particularly interested in it because the year before, 1674, in the opening campaign of Louis XIV's Dutch War, the first major military operation in the area since the end of the terrible Thirty Years' War almost a quarter century before, French armies under Turenne had devastated the Palatinate between the Main and the Neckar, just to the north of the duchy, destroying two towns and 20 villages.[147] Furthermore, the French had scored a notable victory during the winter, securing Alsace and knocking Brandenburg out of the war, and at the time of the incident, the 1675 campaign was about to get under way in the area from the eastern bank of the Rhine to the north of Strasburg, just 50 miles or so from Stuttgart. It is small wonder that Württembergers were anxiously discussing the possibility of an incursion, and the damage it might inflict, particularly since the French appeared to be repeating the scorched earth tactics used so destructively against Württemberg after the battle of Nordlingen.

In the event the summer campaign was waged in the Rhineland to the west and northwest of the duchy, and in 1676, when the French next ravaged a region, it was even farther to the northwest, between the Moselle and the Meuse. Württemberg suffered only from some foraging raids during these campaigns, but suffered substantial devastation a decade later, during the War of the League of Augsburg. In the first year of the war, 1688, the French did in fact capture Stuttgart, although they extracted 15,000 Florin (almost 25,000 Reichstaler) in tribute instead of plundering it.[148] Three years later, French raiders destroyed the town of Calw, Cloister Hirsau, and the surrounding villages.[149] In the next decade, during the War of Spanish Succession, Württemberg was specifically targeted and pillaged, with Stuttgart occupied for eight days, in 1707, and the duchy was transited several other times by armies. Wagenhals' prognostication had come true, albeit somewhat more tardily than he and Württembergs' leaders undoubtedly feared at the time. While the campaign of 1674 may well have inspired Wagenhals to undertake his astrological calculations to begin with, and certainly provided a hint of what might be in store for the duchy, he does seem to have used the relationship of comet and stars to accurately predict the troubles to come, despite the apparent invalidity of the system itself. Since there is no evidence that he consciously used astrology as a cover for some deliberate geopolitical analysis – Württemberg's location on the frontiers of Louis XIV's France and between it and its arch-enemy, the Habsburg empire to the east, could certainly have suggested that it would become a theatre of war – his success must have come either through dumb luck, or, under the circumstances more likely, an inspired reading of the heavens that articulated an intuitive understanding that Württemberg was, after enjoying a generation of peace, sooner or later going to suffer from the renewal of war.

Prophesy

Wagenhals' reference to the comet connected his prediction not only to the occult tradition of astrology, but to a long tradition of Lutheran apocalyptic prophesy. Prophesy – a prognostication, admonition, or warning that issued not from conscious rational calculation but from an experience of spontaneous or spiritual revelation – goes all the way back to ancient civilization, and has often sprung from the interpretation of natural phenomena as signs, or omens. Both prophesy and the interpretation of omens are recorded favorably in the Bible, and continued down through the Middle Ages as generally acceptable activities for Christians, so long as they didn't draw attention to themselves by challenging the spiritual authority of the church or the legitimacy of the secular order. Luther himself was steeped in the tradition of Biblical prophesy, and early Protestantism had a strongly apocalyptic character, assuming that the world was approaching its end in the climactic struggle between Good and Evil, specifically the reign of the Antichrist, an escalating series of natural and man-made disasters, and the return of the Savior, who would conduct the Last Judgment and inaugurate the Kingdom of God. Within this framework, Lutherans identified the Pope with the Antichrist, and saw portentous omens and calamities as signs from God calling on people to repent and reform in preparation for the Day of Judgment.

Astrological conjunctions had long been used to predict communal misfortunes, of course, and before the Reformation there was a series of prophesies predicting "profound troubles and suffering" and "great dangers for the ship of St. Peter and for the entire social order."[150] Shortly after the Reformation, a prediction that twenty planetary conjunctions, including sixteen with watery signs, would bring a universal deluge or some other great calamity in 1524 caused great consternation, and even though Luther ridiculed those who had not included a peasant uprising, the one prediction that some made that did come about, by the 1550s "astrologers and preachers" began "to develop a mutual accommodation."[151] A series of celestial conjunctions in the late 1500s were interpreted by astrologers and theologians alike as warning signs calling for repentance, and they were reinforced by singular portents like comets and the appearance of new stars which, while not strictly part of astrology, were connected in peoples' minds. By 1600 "the notion that there was a perfect concordance between true astrology and biblical prophesy was widespread."[152]

This trend reached an ironic climax with the comet of 1618; ironic because it was both an omen that was finally followed by a disaster of suitable scale and the beginning of a trend to connect such portents with specific terrestrial events that gradually decoupled apocalypticism from astrology, moving it away from an inspiration for repentance back to its traditional role of facilitating preparatory measures. By the 1630s orthodox Lutheran clergymen began to discourage apocalyptic prophesy; in Württemberg the leading churchman of the age, Johann Valentin Andreae, went from being an enthusiast in his youth to a skeptic as he aged. Celestial events like the comet of 1664 were still clearly capable of generating dire expectations, but these were no longer widely seen as evidence that the end was near. Wagenhals' limited prediction, which focused on the instrumental implications of the ominous event for Württemberg, came at the tail end of what had been a general tendency to ascribe portentous meaning to celestial events, and the same comet also generated considerable interest of a new, more dispassionate nature among scientists who were more focused on the mechanics of the comet's movement and their relationship to theories of planetary motion.[153]

Not all admonitory prophesy was connected to omens or astrology, of course. In addition, there was an ancient and ongoing tradition that involved contact with spirits. The tradition of spirit prophesy, however, shared with the tradition of cosmological admonition two basic elements: predictions of worldly woes and calls for moral improvement; the latter, either to avoid the former or to prepare for the judgment they presaged.

Strictly speaking, this sort of contact with spirits was not a form of popular magic, but instead a form of popular religion. However, it did share some features with popular magic, in particular the conviction that specific patterns of thought and behavior could influence physical processes through an extraordinary channel, and the experience of perceiving and interacting with autonomous intelligences. However, while the former could imply a magic-like mechanicism – if you act in a certain way, a certain result will come about – the general conception of repentance and reform differed strongly from magic, in that they were understood to be essentially supplicatory rather than coercive; most popular, like official, concepts of God generally accepted that His power and knowledge were far beyond the capacity of any human to control. On the other hand, while encounters with spirits who communicated admonitory prophesies differed from other spirit encounters in some ways, angels of the Lord bringing warnings and admonitions generally appeared and proclaimed whereas ghosts often rattled around until people figured out what they wanted, mirror-spirits communicated by projecting images and scenes, and the Devil tended more toward whispered seduction and conversation than proclamation, but Divine prophesies could also come in the form of discarnate voices and visions, some ghosts conversed or proclaimed, and the Devil might appear in the form of any of the others, so the differences in this case were more of degree than of kind.

We have already seen in the "ghost worshipper" case in Weilheim in 1770 that the ghosts were quite untypical, having been to heaven and back, rather than just being souls trapped on earth, and were preaching and singing to a congregation rather than, say, bouncing between floor and ceiling, or spooking the cows. They were so untypical, in fact, that they were closer to the general conception of angels, at least some of whom were thought to be the souls of the saved who had gone to heaven, and who were occasionally sent by God to convey messages to people; but in this case they were understood to be ghosts and connected to hidden-treasure, presumably because of the pervasiveness of that belief in Württemberg in the 1770s.[154] Furthermore, there were two other cases which centered on spiritual prophesy, one of which involved the appearance of a spirit that was explicitly identified as an angel, and the otherwhich involved perception of a star or light and contact with a man, St. John the Baptist, and God himself.

The incident that involved purported contact with an angel took place in 1648 when a vine tender named Hans Keil from the village of Gerlingen, near Leonberg, said that one morning while he was in his vineyard preparing to work by praying "for the Almighty to save the people from their distress ... a man dressed in white appeared and addressed him," saying, "Be comforted, your prayer has been heard by the Lord ... What I tell you, you must report to your prince ... God will punish the land and its people ... if they do not repent."[155] The angel pointed to the devastation "the Lord has visited" on "Württemberg ... Germany ... all Christianity," yet "no one pays any attention," and threatened "fire from heaven, the Turkish sword, and massive famine" if the people did not stop cursing, adultery, female vanity, extortionate taxation, usury, gaming on Sunday, priestly avarice, and hunting on Sunday. Since "the Lord does not want people to die in their sins but wants all men to be saved," the angel said, God was giving them six months to shape up, and to signify this, Keil said, he took Keil's knife and cut six vines, which began to bleed.

Keil hurried back to Gerlingen with the vines, recounted and then wrote down his story, and tried to arrange to deliver his message to the Duke. The central government put him off, telling the government of Leonberg not to let him travel the five miles to Stuttgart under any circumstances.[156] Three days later, Keil reported that the angel had come to him in the vineyard again, causing upwards of 200 vines to bleed and warning that if the government, who the angel called the "servants of Pharaoh," ignored this second sign he would return again bringing fire.[157] Meanwhile, news of Keil's story had begun to spread rapidly across southwestern Germany, at first via word of mouth, then via handwritten reports by Keil and others, and within a month via broadsides, chapbooks, and even folk songs. Keil's visions and the bleeding vines were seen by many as "a true wonder from God," and the angel's denunciations of common sins, especially the criticisms of excessive taxation, clerical worldliness, and governmental tyranny, found widespread support that eventually threatened to turn into an open tax revolt.[158]

While many members of the establishment were sympathetic to Keil's denunciation of common sins like cursing and vanity, which were staples of pious sermons at the time, they were less enthusiastic about his prophecy's challenge to their wealth, power, and privileged lifestyles. Their initial resistance to his claims led to an investigation, which turned into a full-blown prosecution, as evidence of fraud emerged. There were many reasons for suspicion: Keil was close to the village preacher, a pious, rigidly assertive old man who decried the sins of his congregation and preached penance. Keil himself was a voracious reader of religious materials, and had numerous broadsides and pamphlets in his house, including two hung on his bedroom door. Several mentioned bleeding grain, one spoke of a poor vine tender who encountered an angel when forced to work on Sunday, another called the war punishment for peoples' sins, and yet another reported on a baker's daughter who predicted terrible weather as punishment for peoples' sins while in a rapture. He not only read these materials to himself, but also pushed others to listen, and the previous winter he had irritated many local women by insisting on reading about the Faust legend to them during spinning bees. Furthermore, Keil was a relatively poor man burdened by debt, and the officials found in his Bible a letter he had written to the Duke pleading for a reduction in taxes, which he, in anticipation of the angel, blamed on the corruption inherent in tax-farming. Significant passages in the angel's message also seemed reminiscent of the pastor's sermons or the prophesies reported in the broadsides, and some people thought it strange that an angelic vision should produce such a detailed and extensive prophesy.[159]

The bleeding vines seemed particularly suspect. Beyond that fact that several of the broadsides in Keil's house reported about similar miracles, while many claimed to have seen the vines bleed, no one was willing to swear that they actually saw blood flowing out of the plants. Some people from nearby Waiblingen claimed that they had discovered additional bleeding vines after they prayed, but they seemed to be making the claim in jest. Keil himself admitted that some people thought he had dipped the vines in blood, and the most damning evidence came from the preacher of the neighboring village of Höfingen, who became suspicious when he examined the vines after Keil reported his second vision and "found a grassy plot just outside the vineyard that was full of blood" where "there was also a quill" which he thought "was used to paint the vines."[160] The ducal officials, who had ordered a careful investigation of the second encounter with the angel, concurred.

Despite the evidence that Keil had faked the miracle, the rumors and the pamphlet literature stoked popular anger about the officials' failure to respond positively to Keil's revelations. The constable of Leonberg and mayor of Gerlingen reported that Keil was actively encouraging the simmering discontent and that they feared it might well boil over, so about six weeks after his visions the government arrested Keil and took him to the fortress of Hohenneuffen where he was stretched on the ground for two days and kept on bread and water. On the second day he was found passed out with his prayer book on his chest, and he said that he had had a third vision in which a form dressed in white with a red cross on its breast appeared, repeated the basic points of the first vision, told him to give the warning and instructions directly to the Duke, and touched him "whereupon Keil fell over" and "lay there" he did "not know how long."[161]

After about three weeks of imprisonment in isolation on bread and water, and bleeding profusely from his nose, he wrote a confession, and after two more days stretched on the ground and then being subjected to mock torture he escaped but was soon recaptured and wrote another. He admitted that he had "sinned terribly" by cutting the vines and putting the blood on them himself, although he insisted "regarding the vision, that is certainly as I have ... reported.[162] He explained that when the angel first instructed him he "did not know" if "anyone would believe it from him," and when he fell and cut himself while hurrying back to his village he got the idea, since "the good spirit" had left him and "the bad spirit" had come, to collect the blood in his hat, cut the vines, and create the appearance of a miracle to bolster the angel's message. The second time, he said, he had made his nose bleed into his hat, added some spit, and "smeared it on the vines" with a quill, which he accidentally left in the clearing near where some blood had spilled. He insisted that he had acted alone, and said he would "willingly take" punishment for his transgressions.

The government, however, was not satisfied with either his claim to have acted alone or his insistence that his visions were real, and he continued to be confined, threatened, abused, and interrogated. Several weeks later he wrote another confession in which he stated, "I, Hans Keil, subjectly acknowledge my misdeeds in so far as the vision is concerned," and abjectly pleaded over and over that he would "gladly give up" his "entire property" if only his "Gracious Highness" would "again look favorably on" him and spare his life so he could "return to" his "wife and children."[163] He later described how the story of the vine tender whom an angel appeared to when he had to work on Sunday "gave me the start" of the story, while "I got from the [Acts of the] Apostles how an angel came to Cornelius the Centurion."[164] He further stated that his concern about adultery was inspired by two married men in his village who had other families with women elsewhere, that his complaint about hunting on Sunday was based on a sermon his pastor had preached after the villagers had been forced to help with such a hunt recently, and that his other points were based on his own observations, experience, and reading.[165] At one point under torture he broke down totally and confessed that the village preacher was in cahoots with him, but the preacher denied it in confrontation and the government did not punish him. Keil, however, was fined, whipped, and banished across the Rhine as a "false prophet" for his "self-made bloody cuts" and "falsely reported visions."[166]

At first glance, it seems pretty clear what happened in this case: frustrated by the impiety and greed exhibited by the majority of people of all classes around him despite the exhortations of the clergy and the numerous signs and admonitions reported from all over Germany, one day in early February, 1648, Hans Keil decided to "shock" people into behaving better so he "invented his vision," constructing it "from the bits and pieces he had at hand," and in an attempt to make his message all the more powerful, drawing on the same sources, he faked a miracle by smearing some of the vines with his own blood.[167] This is what the leaders of Württemberg concluded, this is what Keil confessed, and this is what makes the most sense to an educated modern Westerner. However, while it seems pretty clear that Keil's did fake the miracle of the bloody vines, it is not so clear that he made up his vision.[168] In the first place, while he confessed to using his own blood to coat the vines readily, even when he admitted that he insisted the visions were real. Secondly, he mentioned that the idea of using the blood came to him when he fell down while rushing back to his village after the vision, and since he must have traveled the path between his home and his vineyard innumerable times, his preoccupied haste suggests that he was genuinely excited about something. Thirdly, he only changed that story after an additional month of isolation, malnourishment, physical abuse, and threats of torture and execution; if he had confessed to a pact with the Devil and multiple counts of *maleficium* under these circumstances, we would take the circumstances to be good reason to discount the admission. Fourthly, the possibility of a genuine vision experience seems far greater than the possibility of a genuine physical miracle like bleeding vines, since if one discounts the possibility of miraculous or paranormal phenomena, the latter is impossible but the former, which can be explained by entirely natural, if not entirely normal, psychological and physiological processes, is perfectly possible (and even if one admits the possibility of miraculous or paranormal phenomena on religious or scientific grounds, in this particular case the evidence seems to argue against it). Finally, the motivation of the authorities to discredit Keil's entire story must be considered: they were faced not just with a call for moral reform, but a critique of the socioeconomic and political order that had sparked a growing restiveness that threatened to break out into open rebellion. While most of the attention was naturally focused on the bleeding vines, with Keil's supporters seeing them as evidence of a miracle and his detractors seeing them as evidence of fraud, the crucial issue to the government was actually the content of his prophesy and its impact on public opinion. Showing that Keil had committed fraud with the vines was less important for its own sake than as a way of undercutting his message, and it is not surprising that the government did not stop with that, but instead continued to pressure him to renounce the entire story, and then added injury to insult by torturing him after he did so. The "Princely Resolution" ordering torture said it was because of his "variations and confirmed great imprudence," in other words, not simply to reconfirm his complete confession, but also to punish him for his effrontery.[169]

If Hans Keil did not simply make up a fake story about the visions, then there are several possible things that could have happened to him in the vineyard in Gerlingen and the fortress of Hohenneuffen in February and March, 1648. One is that an angel of the Lord really did come down from heaven and appear to him, but even if we accept this as possible, the fake miracle makes it seem unlikely in this case. Another is that he did "see" a figure dressed in white who spoke to him in the same way that Endris Miembler and Maria Braittingen "saw" and "spoke with" the Devil.[170] This seems particularly likely in the case of the third vision, the one he had at Hohenneuffen in March before he passed out, because, first, his psychological and physical condition was particularly conducive to such an effect; second, his jailer reported that he exhibited signs of a genuine physiological disorder; and, third, it is hard to see what purpose he could have rationally calculated such a claim would serve at this point. Of course, even before the first incident his unsent letter to the Duke concerning his taxes, his fascination with broadsides about portents and warnings, which he said he read because "he could mirror himself in them and prevent himself from sinning," his compulsion to read about Faust to groups of women despite their objections, and the fact that in a threatening story he recounted to the mayor of Gerlingen about an avaricious official, he claimed that justice was done when the Devil skinned the man alive, all suggest that he was psychologically stressed by his financial problems and internal tensions between his ingrained obedience and anger toward those in power and between his strong piety and strong urges to sin, so it is possible that the first and second visions also involved genuine hallucinations as well. Late Medieval Spanish "lay seers" reported similar fully realized apparitions that walked, talked, and occasionally even touched them, and such experiences generally did not occur when the person was in a trance, but rather when they were "awake and in ... free control and judgment."[171]

On the other hand, Keil did describe the figure in white in a rather stiff way, and it is hard to see how he could have committed to memory and recited the long, detailed, and carefully formatted revelation, which suggests the possibility that the "angel" was more like a sudden series of generalized realizations and an overpowering compulsion to act that seemed to come from outside of him, that he really understood these to be divine inspiration rather than just some good ideas or well-founded conclusions, but to which he added the physical description of an apparition and claimed that the wording was recited to him because that was how he understood these things were supposed to happen, and, as he admitted about the vines, he was afraid that without the proper trappings people wouldn't take them seriously.[172] Finally, and perhaps most likely, is something between these last two possibilities: in the vineyards he visualized what seemed to be a spirit as his understanding crystallized and he felt the imperative to act, which he "heard" as the instructions of the angel (at least some people who say that they "hear voices" report that the experience is actually less like hearing word-for-word and more like just "knowing" what is meant), and he conventionalized the description and fleshed out the outline in order to convey what he had experienced to others (and, perhaps, in the process of remembering it, to himself), while the vision in the fortress was a more fully realized hypnogogic-like hallucination perceived as he passed out.

Interestingly, that Keil's experience lay somewhere between fraud and a miracle is more or less what the Church Consistory concluded when it considered his story soon after it was first reported.[173] The theologians noted that the bleeding vines could have been caused by a satanic illusion, but judged it more likely that he "had made the vines bloody himself ... either deliberately or unconsciously." Similarly, they found many reasons to doubt that an angel of God had actually given him a message, and thought it more likely that he "had taken up sermons or police ordinances into his imagination." They shared his concerns about corruption and impiety, but felt he was too strict in his criticisms and unrealistic in his call for precipitous action. Indeed, led by the reformer Andreae, they were already engaged in a long-term effort to promote moral improvement through the establishment of *Kirchekonvents*, morals tribunals that "probed into the most detailed aspects of the lives of individuals and the community," and Keil's prophesy may have actually served the church leadership's purposes by demonstrating the need for orderly reform.[174] For the civil administration, in contrast, Keil's claims and their resonance in society posed an immediate problem, and the High Council had less interest in a subtle understanding of the sources, nature, and value of Keil's experience than in a blanket discrediting of his dangerous challenge to the sociopolitical order.

While there was considerable controversy about whether Hans Keil actually had any visions at all, there was no question about the reality of the experiences in the other case of spiritual prophesy, although there was plenty of disagreement about their legitimacy and meaning. Anna Bechtold, the wife of a vine tender and citizen in the village of Niederhofen, near Brackenheim, first got into trouble with the church synod in 1656 when she insisted that a man had come to her in a vision and told her not to believe in the clergy, but instead to believe in him.[175] At the time, the synod concluded that Anna suffered from "severe melancholy," recommended that she "immediately undertake a 'corporal cure,'" and instructed the district church supervisor to work closely with her. Four years later, though, she was involved in another incident stemming from her visions that had far more serious consequences. It began shortly before Christmas, in 1660, when a church visitation learned that the widow Barbara Appten, the Bechtolds' live-in servant, refused to let her own 17-year-old daughter attend mass.[176] When the village officials investigated, Barbara said that she and her daughter didn't attend mass because Anna didn't. When they asked her why Anna didn't, she said Anna wouldn't go "until it is shown to her that she should go." Asked where Anna's visions came from, Barbara replied "God." She later told them that Anna "knows all things, even if she can't write or read," that before sermons "she says ... what the pastor will preach," that she "knows more than all men," and that not only Barbara and her daughter, but also Anna's husband and children and sister and brother-in-law all followed her.

When the magistrates questioned Anna herself, she said that "she would see a bright star and after the star [hear] a voice when a misfortune was imminent." She had "first seen [this] 16 years before in Heilbronn and since then often." Indeed, "only yesterday she had seen the star and the sun or clarity or the bright light itself," and "had had the Christ child ... on Christmas night in her arms." She said she "was baptized in the fashion of John the Baptist (who had been with her just a week before)," that she herself was "the prophet King David," and that she was also Christ and "has the voice therefrom." When asked if she would baptize a child if she had another, she replied that "she would not throw it in the water." She explained that she "wanted to be able to lead more" followers since "she is the way to truth and life" and "is charged with saving her sheep because she was not sent to judge but to save." When the magistrates asked her if she ever "went to the Devil's mass at night," she replied that "the preacher is the Devil." Furthermore, while the magistrates were first interviewing Barbara, Anna had burst into the room, said to them she "should throw all your papers out of the window, beat the preacher with her fists," told a councilor "I should throw something in your face," and threatened "Herr Andreas Holden, 'You I want to skin alive.'" She then led Barbara out, yelling as she left, "Your can all kiss my ass!" Later, when the magistrates asked Barbara why Anna "spoke so badly to the preacher and others," she explained that Anna "had to do it" since "it came not from her, but ... from God."

For their part, the village leaders called Anna's "visions, apparitions, and soothsaying ... vain and empty."[177] They reported her to the constable of Brackenheim, who in turn brought the case to the attention of the High Council. The constable took both Anna and Barbara into custody in mid-January, and a few days later, after consulting the Church Consistory, the High Council ordered them to be incarcerated in Hohenneuffen, the same fortress where Hans Keil had been cured of his spiritual pretenses just a dozen years before. By the time her husband was able to arrange to visit her in mid-March, pleading that she suffered from "imbecility and melancholy" and was needed by her "young and boisterous" children, she told him "she wanted to stop heeding all the voices, stars, apparitions, and other things that had driven her, but rather ... to ask God for forgiveness for her sins, pray faithfully, and take the holy communion ... with a joyful and devout heart."[178] She also agreed to let her husband take her to a doctor. By the end of the month the officials in Hohenneuffen could report that she had "gone to holy communion and renounced her longstanding deceit."[179] Accepting that Anna had "completely renounced" her beliefs, the High Council ordered that she be sent back to Niederhofen, although the councilors did stipulate that the village officials should keep an eye on her.

Like Wolfgang Wagenhals' and Hans Keil's prophesies, Anna Bechtold's claims had not only general antecedents in the long series of major prophets in the Judeo-Christian tradition, but also more specific forbearers in Germany in the recent past. Specifically, in the first decades of the seventeenth century, a series of popular prophets emerged alongside the learned mystics and astrologers who had dominated the prophetic movement earlier.[180] In 1606, for example, a baker from Ulm named Noah Alb "received a revelation that he was the Noah whom Luther had called for in his exegesis of Daniel 12," which excited "considerable uproar" and was considered "genuine by some of the local clergy," although in the end Alb was executed "as a threat to the peace of the city." Similarly, "a few years later one Philipp Ziegler of Nuremberg was inspired ... to declare himself a spiritual monarch ... promising a spiritual return of Christ as well as the advent of a new David," and from 1604 through the 1630s "Esaias Stiefel and his nephew Ezechiel Meth" taught that only "the living Word" was valid, rejecting "the written Word of Scripture along with all the sacraments."

However, while these and similar popular prophets provided both a model for inspired visionaries like Anna Bechtold and a stimulus for established theologians to begin to define an orthodoxy, the very profusion of divergent and conflicting prophesies and the repeated nonappearance of the predicted disasters (with the notable exception of the Thirty Years' War) and failure of the world to end on schedule gradually discredited inspired prophesy in the Lutheran mainstream. "By 1630, apocalyptic expectation was already becoming a characteristic of separatist groups, a mode of dissent," and, indeed, the church consistory connected Anna's little group to Anabaptism, while in other ways it seems to have been a precursor to the radical Pietism that emerged over the next several decades.[181]

Despite the similar claims made by others before her, Anna's visions and voices were never questioned in the way that Hans Keil's were. In part that may be because the presence of all the printed materials in Keil's house suggested that interpretation in a way that would not have been as obvious in the case of the illiterate woman. In part it may also have been the difference in the nature and scope of the threat they posed: Anna and her small group of followers challenged the secular and clerical leadership in the village, but had wider ramifications only by implication, while Keil inspired a regional disturbance that called for a more comprehensive repressive response. In addition, it may have also reflected gender stereotypes, the expectation that a woman would be subject to melancholic visions and irrational fits whereas a man would be less likely to be vulnerable to these (although the church consistory did say that Hans was "melancholy" and might have acted unconsciously when he bloodied the vines). Finally, the differing evaluations may have actually reflected the specifics of the cases at hand: Hans Keil's prophesy may have manifested some sort of unconscious realization and compulsion to act, but it was strongly grounded in the news and analysis he had been reading; was reported with suspiciously conventionalized, extensive, and elaborate details; took place when he was alone; and was supported by a faked miracle. Anna Bechtold's visions and voices, in contrast, had no immediate intellectualized inspiration as far as could be determined; were described in part with idiosyncratic and indistinct details, as if she was groping to find the words to describe a singular experience ("the star and the sun or clarity or the bright light itself"), and in part with unusual elements like claiming to have held the Christ child in her arms; and had publicly witnessed extraordinary validation (her ability to predict the preacher's sermon, which may have resulted from an insightful reading of him and how he might respond to local events, but which does not seem to have been the kind of conscious fraud that Hans Keil perpetrated with the vines).[182] Anna's visions were believed, in other words, because they were more believable.

Of course, just because the officials accepted that Anna had really had her visions did not make the officials any readier to accept them. They knew how much turmoil, conflict, and error had come from the unrestrained enthusiasm of prophets and other religious fanatics over the previous century, and she had shown how directly individual inspiration led to insubordination. Since her revelations were not diabolical in nature, though they challenged the established religion, and she did not seem to be a conscious fraud, the only thing left was to classify her as melancholy.

Conclusion

We have seen in this chapter how some people in early modern Württemberg, like some people all over premodern Europe, tapped sources of knowledge beyond their conscious minds, in order to identify people who wished them ill and people who had stolen from them, to locate missing persons, lost objects, and hidden treasures, and to predict the future and obtain guidance for individuals and the community as a whole. In some cases this information came spontaneously; in most, the people sought it deliberately. In a few instances, any validity of the knowledge these people might have gained could only have come by chance or from some process of information transfer that is on the fringe of or beyond modern scientific understanding, but for the most part the insights and revelations, guidance and instructions can be explained most efficiently as the results of unconscious cognitive processes that could rise to consciousness spontaneously, but access to which could also be cultivated through ritual and fostered by belief.

Just as the source of the knowledge revealed by divination and prophesy need not be mysterious to us, peoples' motivation for using them need not perplex us either. From one point of view, they did not have the computers and telephones, forensic and meteorological sciences, branch libraries and research centers that are available to support our systematic rational and scientific analysis, so they had to rely more heavily on received knowledge and intuition than we do. From another, more relevant, point of view, they were not making the best of a deficit, but instead were simply making use of the tools and techniques they had available, which were better than the real alternative, which was generally nothing. Cunning men, for example, did not use sieve and shears as a poor substitute for lie detectors, but instead as a good alternative to sheer guesswork, foredoomed searches for unlikely physical evidence, rational deductions based on all-but-nonexistent hard data, or simply doing nothing. Victims' unconscious reactions were hardly infallible, but they were more likely to be accurate than their haphazard guesses, casual prejudices, long-standing assumptions, ill-founded inferences, overt animosities, or consensual conclusions. Similarly, people did not visualize angels from God as a poor substitute for political science or ghosts as a poor substitute for an understanding of geology, but instead because spirits – autonomous intelligences with dream-like form and voices – are a natural way for the brain to manifest the results of intuitive insights generated by largely if not wholly unconscious thought processes.

Spontaneous forms of prophesy and shamanistic and shamanic divinatory techniques, in other words, were not the pathetic substitutes for effective action "enlightened" moderns often assume them to be, but instead were subtle and highly evolved means of accessing information normally inaccessible to our waking consciousness.

Finally, it is worth noting that these incidents, in particular the two instances of prophesy at the end and the "ghost worshipper" case, reveal how heavy a hand the early modern state could have when confronted with ecstatic experiences. Hans Keil was summarily imprisoned, put in solitary confinement on bread and water, stretched on the ground for days at a time, and tortured until he was ready to confess anything, and then whipped, fined, and banished from his lifelong home and community. Anna Bechtold was whisked off to the same fortress as Keil, where it took only two months to reduce her to abject submission. Anna Maria Freyin, the servant woman who first encountered the two spirits from heaven, was exiled, hounded, jailed, and put "under massive pressure," including the threat of being beaten (tortured), to compel her to confess that she had faked the spirit appearances, while Georg Buck, her master and the leader of the cult, was jailed indefinitely until he agreed to say no more, and his comrade Dürrner, who insisted "the things are godly," was similarly imprisoned and flogged in an attempt to get him to recant. In all three cases the government's repressive measures succeeded: the leaderless "ghost cult" dissipated, the agitation sparked by Hans Keil's prophesies petered out, and Anna Bechtold returned to Niederhofen ready to "pray faithfully and take holy communion ... with a joyful and devout heart." These cases were particularly notable because they directly challenged the established order, but we shall see in Chapter 8 that they were very much in keeping with the government's larger and more ambitious attempt to forcibly suppress all shamanistic and shamanic activity beyond the very limited range permitted by the established church: beneficent magic as well as diabolic sorcery, and even ecstatic forms of religious experience.

7
Beneficent Manipulative Magic

In the last chapter we looked at divination, the acquisition of information about the world through magical processes. In this chapter we will examine the forms of popular magic used to accomplish the other purpose of magical activity, to exert influence on the world. These are a much wider and more diverse set of activities than divination, and many of them came to light only occasionally, if at all, in the criminal trials that formed the basis of information for this study. In particular, the most common forms of popular magic were passive and defensive – heeding omens, avoiding activities at times and places thought to be dangerous, wearing amulets, making gestures, speaking words – that were not only seldom mentioned in court, but were also such an integral part of life that they generally went unremarked even in confession and church conventicles.[1] Furthermore, beyond their sheer ubiquity, in the early modern period many magical practices went unremarked because most of those that can be traced back to pagan times had been Christianized, while numerous Christian rituals and beliefs had been incorporated into popular culture in a way that made them virtually indistinguishable from magic.[2] Therefore, rather than binary opposites, popular magic and popular religion were poles on a continuum that ranged from some unchanged pagan forms through a much larger number of Christianized versions of pagan rituals to rituals of Christian origin that were employed like magic to Christian rituals employed in theologically acceptable ways. For example, the ringing of bells to ward off spirits was a pre-Christian practice which might be conducted by itself, without any religious reference, but when the ringing of church bells was said to interfere with the activities of witches there was a clear implication that their power was connected to religion.[3] Similarly, prayers could be employed as an illicit form of protective magic, as when the three young citizens of Döffingen festooned themselves with papers covered with prayers while looking for treasure, but prayer was routinely employed as an entirely approved way of supplicating God for help in warding off spiritual threats.[4]

Table 7.1 indicates that even without counting protective rituals, magic intended to project power was more common than magic intended to simply gain information, accounting for about two-thirds of all the magical practices recorded in the sampled cases. Furthermore, it shows clearly that among the manipulative uses of magic, healing was by far the most

Table 7.1 Purposes of sampled beneficent magic by trial type

Purpose type	Incant	Heal	Magic	Treasure	Conjure	Total	%
Divination	7	2	4	10	4	27	*35*
Treasure	1	0	2	10	3	16	*21*
Identify Witch	2	2	1	0	0	5	*6*
Other	4	0	1	0	1	6	*8*
Manipulation	13	14	13	5	6	51	*65*
Heal	7	11	6	2	0	26	*33*
People	6	8	4	1	0	19	*24*
Animals	1	3	2	1	0	7	*8*
Counter	3	2	0	0	1	6	*8*
Witchcraft	1	2	0	0	0	3	*4*
Theft	2	0	0	0	1	3	*4*
Love	*	*	*	*	*	*	*
Enhance	2	0	6	1	2	11	*14*
Strength	0	0	2	0	0	2	*3*
Wealth	0	0	0	1	1	2	*3*
Fortune	0	0	1	0	1	2	*3*
Job Skills	1	0	1	0	0	2	*3*
Marksmanship	1	0	1	0	0	2	*3*
Stealth	0	0	1	0	0	1	*1*
Love	*	*	*	*	*	*	*
Health	*	*	*	*	*	*	*
Milk Production	*	*	*	*	*	*	*
Exorcise	0	1	1	1	2	5	*6*
Place†	0	1	1	1	2	5	*6*
Person	*	*	*	*	*	*	*
Miscellaneous	0	0	0	1	1	2	*3*
Copper to gold	0	0	0	1	0	1	*1*
Summon stranger	0	0	0	0	1	1	*1*
Invulnerability	*	*	*	*	*	*	*
Anomalous events	1	0	0	0	0	1	*1*
Harassing vision	1	0	0	0	0	1	*1*
Cloth destroyed	*	*	*	*	*	*	*
House bombarded	*	*	*	*	*	*	*
Ball lightning	*	*	*	*	*	*	*
TOTAL	20	16	17	15	10	78	

* No sampled cases, but one or two instances among nonsampled cases.
† Includes only cases in which contact with spirit was not initiated to locate treasure. Note also that four of the eight cases labeled "Gespenst" and "Sortilegii" in the archival index but not included here also involved attempts to deal with ghosts that had spontaneously appeared.

important, accounting for half the manipulative cases, or almost a third of all beneficent magical practices, and was almost as numerous as all types of divination combined.[5] Furthermore, the other kinds of manipulative magic comprised a polyglot miscellany including various enhancements to normal human capacities like strength and marksmanship; a limited number of magical countermeasures against natural and supernatural aggression by others; exorcism of bothersome spirits; a few cases involving claims of truly supernatural powers; and a couple of occurrences that were anomalous even within the magical worldview of early modern Europe. Therefore, this chapter will begin by examining the forms and bases of magical healing rituals, will then turn to other deliberate attempts to harness supernatural power to produce magical effects, and will conclude by briefly examining the reports of truly anomalous, apparently magical phenomena.

Magical healing

All living beings are vulnerable to ill-health, in that they can be injured from outside or within by accidents, systemic malfunction, predation, or other forms of combat, and all but the simplest microbes go through a natural process of degeneration and death. Furthermore, most animals are subject to some degree to breakdowns caused by their own information-processing systems: even cockroaches can die from extreme harassment by a dominant insect; when caught by a predator many prey animals go into shock and stop struggling well before they actually die; and social mammals, as we have seen, are affected by threatening expressions and gestures as well as changes in their relative standing in their group. Human beings share with the rest of the living order a vulnerability to physiological injuries and disease, are affected to a much higher degree than most if not all other animals by disruptions of social relations, and are unusually if not uniquely vulnerable to disorders generated by the internal workings of their own cognition.

All organisms have restorative mechanisms to mend physical damage and destroy internal invaders, and some animals have rudimentary behaviors that supplement their autonomic damage-control systems through deliberate individual or, in the case of some advanced mammals, social action. Humans, of course, have by far the most developed supplemental systems for countering disease and restoring health, manifesting their capacities for utilizing tools, steering their behavior by long chains of complex associations and inferences, and encoding, transmitting, and developing these practices in a set of symbols shared with other members of their culture. Since before civilization, they have used a combination of substances and actions to help comfort and heal themselves and each other. Some of the substances have palliative or restorative chemical or physical properties, like medicines and plasters, and some of the actions contribute directly to the healing process, like staunching blood and setting bones.

Many of the substances and most of the actions, however, do not work directly to relieve or cure the damage, but instead work indirectly, through their visceral or symbolic effects on the nervous system to stimulate the body's own defensive, analgesic, and therapeutic mechanisms. In other words, they deliberately alter the patient's consciousness in order to mobilize unconscious processes not accessible in our normal waking state of mind. In some societies these interventions have been shamanistic in nature, but in most cases they have been shamanic, in the sense that diseases were thought to be caused by spirits, and so the healing process was conceived as involving contact with spirits.

The varieties of healing practices

The full repertoire of healing techniques developed during the stone age appears to have included ingesting plants and minerals, burning and inhaling them, applying them topically, wearing them or crafted objects, including both bandages and amulets, on the body or placing them near the sick person, touching or manipulating the injury or the sick person, engaging in ritual actions, both bodily movements and vocalizations, and mobilizing social support by resolving conflicts and organizing community participation.[6] Some of these techniques involved clear physical intervention in the manifest causes of distress, but most worked on problems and through processes that were occult, or hidden. Nevertheless, while the materials used differ from place to place and the rituals, symbols, and explanations vary in their details, "there is a cross-cultural similarity" in healing techniques, and, with the exception of modern allopathic medicine, they integrate material and spiritual therapies, generally with an emphasis on the latter.[7] "By the time humans began writing," in early civilizations, "all known medical systems were intertwined with religion," and this connection between body and spirit was maintained in classical Greece and Rome, informing the Galenic system that was the basis of the learned medicine practiced by specialized doctors through the Middle Ages, incorporated into Christian tradition, and transmitted from generation to generation in popular practice.[8] Healing practices show a remarkable mixture of continuity and discontinuity, with practitioners spontaneously modifying received rituals and spells or creating new ones to fit the specific circumstances they were confronted with, yet remaining within a basic conceptual framework and set of forms that lasted "not just over generations but over centuries."[9] As a result, popular healing, like popular magic in general, was not a consistent, coherent system, but instead an amalgamation of "many different systems of thought," mixing pagan and Christian, Germanic and Classical, and learned and popular notions.[10] With wide local variations a similar set of basic assumptions and procedures was employed across Europe by folk healers and ordinary people alike; typically, the folk practices in Württemberg were deeply rooted yet ever-changing, uniquely local yet part of a broad common

European tradition that was itself but a local instantiation of a world-wide tradition going back millennia.[11]

Instances of popular healing were included in four of the ten sampled cases of generalized magic, seven of the nine cases labeled "blessing," one of the thirteen "treasure-hunting" cases (as an additional charge against two of the leaders), and, naturally, all eight of the "healing" cases.[12] Nineteen of these cases involved healing of people, six of which involved healing of animals as well, and one case involved healing of animals only.[13] Between them, they included all of the major therapeutic techniques generally used in folk healing: vocalizations, medicines, other objects and symbols, and actions of various sorts, in some cases, performed at particular times and places or according to other special instructions. Of these different practices, vocalization, in the form of blessings, was easily the most common, being used in most (15 of 20, or 75 percent) of the cases.[14] In contrast, medicines, special objects, and special actions were only used in some cases (nine, eight, and ten, respectively, or about half for each).[15] Special instructions involving a specific number of repetitions of the healing activities were included in six cases, but drawn symbols and special times were only used in a few instances each, and none of the sampled cases involved a special place (although one nonsampled case did).[16] In order to gain a deeper understanding of what these healing techniques involved and what their effects were, we will first look at each type of practice in turn, then examine how they were employed together, and finally assess the ways in which they influenced people's health and well-being, by looking at the specific types of ailments they were used for and assessing their potential therapeutic effects.

The various invocations ranged from obscure mumblings through Christianized incantations to prayers and even religious songs. In some cases the incantation was said "so that no one could understand" it, while in others, it was only noted that the healer used "good words."[17] In one instance the healer was only heard "calling the horse" he was curing "by the name of its color," and saying "the swelling, stiffness, or growth will wane like the moon wanes," but most frequently it was explicitly noted that the invocation was similar to a prayer, done "in the name of God the Father, the Son, and the Holy Spirit."[18] In a few cases the healer told the patient to pray, either in place of or in addition to more magical incantations, and in one case the people involved were said to have used "biblical words and songs."[19] In most instances the magistrates did not record the content of the incantations, but along with the several healers who insisted that they spoke "in the name of" the Trinity, one maintained that he prayed to "St. John the Evangelist" along with his "truly good words."[20] The magistrates of Sindelfingen did note in 1596 that a woman claimed to be able to staunch bleeding by commanding it to, "Stand still in the name of the Father, Son, and Holy Ghost, Amen," while over the next few years the magistrates of a nearby town, Cannstatt, recorded two incantations used by a popular healer and cow herder named Jacob Schäffer.[21] The first was intended to be used by a man to heal his son, and went:

> God greet you beloved moonshine,
> What I stroke, that is mine,
> I stroke my blood, and my flesh,
> In the name of the Father, Son and
> Holy Spirit.[22]

The second he used for a woman with a bad cold:

> Here I go over the sea,
> I spew therein all my woe,
> In the name of the Father, Son, and
> Holy Spirit.[23]

All of the utterances in these cases, except the one used to cure horses, were "blessings" not only in the sense that they were labeled at the time with the German equivalent, "*Segen*," but also in the sense that modern folklorists distinguish "blessings" from "charms": they invoked the Christian deity rather than a non-Christian spirit or the Devil or, like the horse charm, implicitly relied on the intrinsic power of the words themselves.[24] In the cases where healers mumbled, it is possible, of course, that they were doing so to cover up the fact that they were *not* pronouncing a blessing in this sense; Hans Haasen, who said he had learned from a heterodox spirit on the Venusberg, may have mumbled when he healed for this reason, and the magistrates of Sindelfingen implied as much when they said they were "afraid" that Gertrudt Raitsen "has intentionally hidden many words" when she told them what she said to stop bleeding.[25] Significantly, Gertrudt's *Segen* also took the form of a command or adjuration, which is the closest standard type of charm or blessing to a magic conjuration ("*beschwörung*"), in which the practitioner exerts control over the spirit rather than calling on it for help.[26] At the other end of the spectrum from conjuration was prayer, or abject supplication of God, which was the only licit way to approach Him, although even here there was a distinction between approved forms within sanctioned rituals and suspect supplicatory blessings included in lay healing activities. Jacob Schäffer's blessings fell somewhere between these two poles. The second of the two quoted above was an example of the standard narrative form, in which an imaginary experience was described in the expectation that it would have analogous effects on the patient. This form was closely related to a final standard form of blessing, the comparative, in which the analogy is made explicit in the form of "as this, then that." The words used to cure horses are an example of this form, although since they made no appeal to God they constituted a charm rather than a blessing.

The narrative form of blessing bears a formal relationship to the classical shamanic healing technique of soul flight in which the shaman describes his or her journey to the spirit world to the patient and assembled audience, although the course of the shamanic journey is spontaneous and protracted, while the blessing is conventional and relatively short. Similarly, the command form also has a formal relationship to shamanic practice since the spirit flight generally climaxes in a confrontation in which the shaman commands the spirit responsible for the person's disease to leave their body or let their spirit return with him or her to the land of the living, although here the difference is that the shaman's command is the culmination of the extensive narrative development, whereas the healer's command comprises a relatively brief utterance that may or may not be embedded in other sorts of ritual. The comparative form of blessing, as we have seen, shares with the narrative-command structure the basic idea that an analogy between one thing and another, between an imagined experience and an existing physical condition, can be created, and by manipulating the former, changes can be caused in the latter; while a supplication shares with a command the basic structure of a human confronting a spirit, but with the difference that, recognizing the spirit's superior power, the human beseeches it to grant favor instead of attempting to compel it to act.

The formal parallels between the narrative and command forms of blessing and shamanic healing and their structural relationships to the comparative and supplicatory forms are suggestive of a more concrete, historical relationship, a gradual development from the one to the other, but they are no more than suggestive. Additional support for such a relationship, though, comes from cross-cultural anthropological studies which show a consistent connection between classic shamans and nomadic societies, shamanic healers and simple agricultural societies, and healers and more complex agricultural societies, with spiritual leadership invested in priests in the second and mediums taking over ecstatic spirit communication in the third socioeconomic configuration.[27] However, while these correlations suggest a line of historical development, even more concrete evidence comes from the specific development of European charms between the early and the late Middle Ages. The earliest recorded charms date from tenth century Trier, Strasburg, Bavaria, and Franconia, but it is clear that such high medieval charms were already "very archaic" when recorded.[28] Indeed, at least one nineteenth-century Swabian blessing has been shown to have a close parallel in Sanskrit poetry, suggesting ancient roots indeed.[29] The earliest recorded charms show evidence of alliteration and assonance, but their poetry was lost when they were Christianized and committed to paper, with Christ and the saints replacing pagan gods, and paternosters replacing magic formulas, and the written form reducing the importance of rhyme as an aid to memory.[30] Furthermore, the earliest German charms were lengthy narratives in which mythical figures – at first gods, and later Christ and saints – experience a series of events creating a problem of the type the charm is for, which the heroes solve in the narrative. The charm then proceeds to the command section, in which "the actual charm formula ... with its magical words" (or, later, supplication) is spoken, connecting the desired result to the resolution achieved in the narrative section.[31] The earliest charms were also "originally sung by priests, physicians, and magicians as an incantation," but their use gradually broadened, and, in parallel, their dramatic narrative component declined as "they became short, vivid, and simple in making their point."[32] They also gradually homogenized as they circulated from region to region during the second half of the Middle Ages, so that, if the evidence from England is indicative, distinctive local and regional traditions were gradually subsumed in a European wide stock of motifs.[33]

To sum up this line of development, in the early Middle Ages Germanic charms consisted of lengthy poetic narratives that set up an analogy to the problem to be solved and illustrated a solution, which was referenced in a briefer concluding portion when a magical formula was pronounced that was to cause the desired outcome to happen in reality. These charms, which were already quite ancient, were recited by specialists, and transmitted orally. Around 1000, the pagan spirits in these charms were replaced by Christian figures and their magic formulas were replaced by Christian benedictions, which destroyed their poetry, but around the same time they began to be recorded in writing, which, to the extent that poetry served to help preserve them in oral transmission, counterbalanced this loss. Over the next centuries, their use broadened while their narrative element declined. What this progression shows is that there does seem to have been a transition from a shaman healer stage associated with the simple agricultural society of early medieval Europe, in which the shaman healer recited a protracted journey in an imaginal world parallel to the realm of ordinary experience in which actions performed in the one could lead to changes in the other, to a healer stage associated with the more complex agricultural society of high and late medieval Europe, in which the healer recited a short, formulaic incantation whose focus was on manipulation of symbolic relationships rather than engagement of the patient in an imaged experience following a dramatic narrative arc. What this progression suggests is that this transition was part of a longer development along the lines suggested by the cross-cultural correlations in which at least some Germanic charms started as shamanic performances in which the shamans spontaneously described their experiences and combats in ecstatic trances that, by the time they were first recorded, had long since become conventionalized narratives and formulaic spells which, at most, inspired and guided shaman healers' ecstatic experiences, and, at least, provided a string of rhythmic vocalizations and a series of imagined scenes that, when recited by a skillful practitioner, created an emotional engagement, hypnotic dissociation, and viscerally cathartic release in the patient, similar to those produced by a shaman in an actual trance.[34] This latter projection back into the early Middle Ages and before cannot be proved, of course, and the different charm forms may have additional roots as well: the supplicatory in ancient forms of political entreaty and the long tradition of Christian prayer, the comparative in more abstract processes of association, and the command in infantile wish-fulfillment.[35] There was undoubtedly considerable innovation and cross-fertilization as well, but the later transition from narrative poetical to simpler formulaic forms rests on firmer evidence, and overall this evidence suggests that not only is the sharp divide that has been noted between northern Asia's shamanic and Europe's cunning folk/healer traditions a product of an historic, or, more properly, prehistoric, process of development, but also it is a specific manifestation of a more general process of human sociocultural evolution.[36]

Blessings did not just contain narratives and spells or benedictions, but they also contained recipes and instructions for the preparation of herbal concoctions and the performance of ritual activities.[37] Furthermore, there was extensive knowledge and use of medicines beyond the information about them contained in blessings. Local herbs were used most commonly, but roots were also employed, and some healers even recommended medicines prepared by apothecaries. This last form created a particular danger of being charged with illicit healing, but actually any administration of internal remedies infringed on the prerogatives of official, university trained doctors.[38] Of the 20 sampled cases that involved healing of different sorts, nine, or almost half included medicinal concoctions, and, since some cases involved more than one, a total of 21 different types were mentioned. In the "itinerant scholar" Hans Haasen's case, he said that he "used herbs" along with blessings, but did not specify how he administered them. In all the other cases, though, at least some indication was given.[39] Five cases involved herbal drinks or other "internal medication," while in one other incense was burned.[40] Several of the healers involved insisted that they used only "wholesome herbs that are found in the woods" which "God created and planted in the earth."[41] One, however, a widow named Barbara Maurer from Bietigheim, also obtained some of hers from an apothecary "so the poor people can get them," she explained, despite "their great cost, for I take no cut."[42] Jacob Schäffer, the healer from Cannstatt whose blessings we saw earlier, sometimes used alcohol as a medicine: in one instance he mixed herbs with wine; in some others he prescribed distilled spirits.[43] In three cases external plasters or salves were used in addition to internal medicines, and two instances involved externally applied preparations only. These ranged from "a noxious salve ... from a powder consisting of four kinds of wood" made by Georg Preisen in 1666 for a boy who later died to an ointment made of "the white of an egg, bark, and sap" that Jacob Schäffer used to treat a woman with cut on her right thigh.[44]

A healer identified as just "Bästlin" was found, in 1605, to possess several containers "with salve" and "a black powder," he admitted he gave a young man he was curing "a drink of several herbs," and he also gave him an amulet comprised of "a little sack with a root in it."[45] Roots, as we have seen, were used in medicinal concoctions, but here Bästlin was employing them in a different way, as magical objects whose potency came not from their direct physical effects, but rather from the occult power they were supposed to possess. Similarly, Hans Köll from Owen, the healer who tried to help Anna Eberlin when she saw the man she had just had sex with as the Devil, in 1660, hung, without telling her what it was, "a bundle" containing "bread and salt, many twigs and roots, and hazelwood ... on a cord" down her back between her shoulder blades.[46] Similar amulets were used all over Europe to "drive away diseases, avert infection, or protect one from ... supernatural or evil force," and amulets were just one type of object used for their magical powers to help in healing.[47]

In another of the sampled cases a healer named Christoph Wieland, in 1770, also used "amulets ... to help people regain their health," but his amulets contained scraps of paper with magic words written on them, and he also gave similar scraps of paper to people to eat to help them get well.[48] Pieces of paper were, in fact, the most common type of object used in the sampled cases, being mentioned in four of the eight cases involving objects; amulets were mentioned in the two discussed above, and the rest of the objects were only mentioned once each. The pieces of paper generally had short blessings, charms, or occult symbols written on them, in which case they are sometimes referred to as talismans.[49] The forest ranger named Walzen who was accused of using "biblical sayings and songs" to help heal his child in 1742, had two such talismans, one with a blessing in German and the other with a series of symbols like "ר'] ר" and "O λ ό."[50] Christoph Wieland gave one woman a talisman with the famous "SATOR" square on it, a palindrome of great antiquity that was thought to possess potent magical power, although the source of that power was in dispute since many held its hidden meanings to be Christian, while others, including, in this case, the magistrates of Backnang, thought that it contained diabolical incantations.[51]

One incident which may have represented a more common practice than its sole appearance among the sampled trials suggests was the use of a "healing stone," in this case a "red and gold crystal stone" used by Hans Röcklin "when a horse" suffered from "swelling, stiffness, or children [suffered from] a tumor."[52] Röcklin, who said he got the stone from his father, was investigated, as we have seen, because of the charm he recited while using the stone. The reason the use of this sort of object may have remained relatively unrecorded in the judicial archives is that the stone itself constituted neither an illicit form of religion nor an illicit practice of internal medicine, so that when Hans protested that he "does not use the name of God" in his ritual, but "promises, if it's not right, he can forego it," he may well have meant the charm only, and not the use of the stone itself.

The other objects used in the sampled healing cases constituted a miscellany utilized by a handful of the healers, and were mainly associated with curing ailments related to witchcraft. The one instance that didn't involve witchcraft was Jacob Schäffer's use of rose petals sprinkled on a mad woman's head as part of a healing ceremony.[53] An incident that did involve an object to be used to cure an ailment thought to be caused by witchcraft took place in 1769.[54] It started when a young woman named Barbara Calmbach claimed that an older woman named Agnes Luzin, a servant to her aunt, insisted that she give her "a fingernail with my scent" in order to cure her of a persistent ache, although, Barbara claimed, Agnes actually used it to perpetrate further witchcraft on her. The other use of an object to cure witchcraft occurred about fifteen years earlier, when a man named Jacob Kurzen used "a pair of soles" from shoes to cure a cow belonging to Agnes Böhmler, which wouldn't give milk.[55] In this case, the incident came to the magistrates' attention because suspicion focused on Agnes' neighbor, Agnes Jausen, and since by this time the authorities were very resistant to witch accusations, she lodged a complaint with them. Other cures used in cases that did not form part of the sample included the use of urine and a tooth in a home remedy for a fever, and home-made holy water used by one healer for in his cures.[56]

One type of object, books, served double duty in healing practices. Books are, of course, repositories of information and instruction, but they can also be seen as potent objects in themselves when their information and instructions concern magical powers. Books were mentioned in five of the 20 healing cases. In three, the books appear to have functioned purely as sources of information: Barbara Maurer, who denied using any blessings and said she used only "wholesome herbs" and some things she got from the apothecary, had learned healing from her uncle, and appeared to have inherited his herbals as well; a "professed doctor" named Peter Jergle from Neccar-Gröningen, who was prosecuted in 1751 and had, it was learned, once refused to perform a cure because he said he had to go home and look it up in a book; and Christoph Wieland, the healer who had the SATOR talisman, also had an almanac, a "planet book," and "Carichter's Healing and Herb book" at home.[57]

In two cases, however, the books were integrated into the healing rituals. Hans Brückner, the bather from Cannstatt who used a mirror to identify witches in 1589, read from a book during the healing ritual he performed afterwards; and Jacob Geigler, who was one of Hanns Jerg Stadi's technical advisors when his mirror showed him a treasure in his basement in 1762, had been in trouble the year before for supplying Hanns Jerg Kugel with a book containing blessings, and instructing him to carry it under his arm while performing healing rituals.[58]

While books were clearly useful sources of information for some healers, and had a prestige that endowed them with a certain mystical potency, overall they seem to have played only a modest role in popular healing. They were mentioned in five of 20 cases, but that means that in most cases, 75 percent, they were not. In Jacob Schäffer's case it was explicitly mentioned that he could neither read nor write, yet he was "known far and wide" for his healing powers, consulted by people who traveled from Horb and Rottenberg, which lay 40 miles to the southwest and 60 miles to the northeast, respectively, of his home in Zuffenhaus, a village near Cannstatt.[59]

Special actions of various sorts were the second most numerous healing technique after vocalizations in the form of charms and blessings. Of course, it should be noted that vocalization is in itself a form of action, as are the preparation and administration of medicines, the application of ointments and salves, the creation and bestowing of amulets and talismans, and even the simple fact of consulting a healer in the first place. However, in addition to these actions inherent in the other healing activities, healers and/or patients engaged in a number of actions that were performed to promote healing in-and-of themselves. Such special actions were mentioned in ten, or half, of the sampled cases involving healing.[60]

Most of them were actions taken by the healer, and most of these actions involved direct physical therapy to the patient's body. In two cases that were not part of the sample, the therapy actually involved more or less surgical procedures. In one, while the magistrates of Schondorf tried Johannes Knödler for magical treasure-hunting in 1712, they also investigated a cure he had performed that involved bleeding someone (their concern was that he had also performed "something superstitious," and not that he bled the person). In the other, the magistrates of Heidenheim punished a blacksmith for treating dog bites with a method called "St. Hubert's key" in which he apparently put a burning-hot key on the wound (again, the magistrates were not concerned with the physical procedure, but with the fact that it was a superstitious "Catholic" ceremony, for St. Hubert was particularly associated with rabies, dog bites, and, by association, teething).[61] None of the sampled trials involved any such invasive procedures, however. Among them, the most common action was touching. The healer Hans Röcklin used his special "red and gold" stone to cure swelling, stiffness, and tumors in horses and children by stroking them three times with it, and in three other cases the healers touched the patients directly with their hands.[62] Hans Haasen said that he put his hand on the chest of a boy he was treating for heart pains, while Bästlin stroked the head and shoulders of a crazy young man he was trying to help and Peter Jergle passed his hands three times over the places where his patient hurt.[63] Jergle also blew three times on the aching foot of one patient, and Jacob Schäffer was accused of "blowing, sucking, placing his hand" against the injured place, "and similar practices."[64] Hans Brückner bathed the boy he was trying to cure in water with herbs in it, and Schäffer also, as we have seen, put rose petals on the head of a woman who "lay out of her senses."[65]

In this last form of contact any direct physical effects the woman may have felt were clearly less significant than the symbolic meaning of the flowers, and healers engaged in other activities that did not involve any physical contact with their patients at all. We have seen that Hans Brückner read from a book and Jacob Geigler told Hans Jerg Kugel to carry a book that he gave him while healing animals. Hans Brückner also went around the room before he started healing and made signs of the cross on each door and wall to, he explained, keep out evil, while Bästlin went around the room he was in and made sure that all the doors and windows were closed up tight before he began.[66] Jacob Schäffer sat with the woman who lay out of her senses for two hours and urged her to pray with her husband.[67] Similarly, while healers often advised their patients to undertake certain activities on their own, in only two cases did these involve direct physical therapies: Hans Haasen told the parents of the boy he treated to take him "to the Kressich springs to bathe," and Christoph Wieland, as we have seen, gave a child three pieces of paper with writing on them "to eat." In the other instances, healers told their patients to undertake activities that were more ceremonial in nature. For example, Jacob Schäffer told a woman that she was to get up before the sun to say the blessing he had given her, and Sara Sauter said that she could stop babies from losing weight "if one brings her" the "child unannounced on Sunday before sunrise."[68] Prior to the ceremony with the rose petals, Jacob Schäffer also gave the woman's husband a "good handful of Benedict root" and told him to bury it on St. Benedict's day early in the morning "while the dew still lay on the ground."[69] Somewhat similarly, in 1589 Conrad Stier from Insfeld near Lauffen gave Hannß Binder, whose boy was sick, "Scheelkrautt" to plant and pray to, or, the magistrates reported, he at least believed that doing this would cure him. Hans Köll also instructed Anna Eberlin to gather a number of herbs and prepare them when trying to help cure her of her diabolic obsession.[70] Both Schäffer and Brückner involved the families of sick children in their healing rituals, with Schäffer leading one family in collective prayer, and Brückner, in contrast, enjoining the audience to remain absolutely still and silent.[71] In the one case involving a person's attempt to heal herself on her own, 70-year-old Catharina Meÿer was seen sneaking into a graveyard at nine o'clock on Pentecost evening as it was getting dark, where she buried a tooth and then urinated on it in the hopes that this, plus three appeals to the Father, Son, and Holy Spirit, would cure a fever and restore her health.[72]

Meÿer's carrying out of her ritual in specific place was unusual, for none of the sampled healing cases involved a special location, and even in this instance what she really was looking for was a cross to carry it out under rather than a graveyard specifically. Her need to carry it out at a particular time, however, was not as uncommon, for four of the sampled cases also included the stipulation when an action was to be performed. As we have seen, both Sara Sauter and Jacob Schäffer stipulated that certain actions take place early in the morning, with Sauter specifying Sunday morning and Schäffer saying that the Benedict root was to be buried in the morning of St. Benedict's day. Hans Röcklin's use of his curing stone involved a similar coordination of timing: he said it was to be "done on three days in a row after the [full] moon," which coordinated with the charm's command that the pain or swelling "should wane as the moon wanes."[73] Jakob Franck, otherwise known as "Schafer J," from Emmau, near Sulz, was prosecuted in 1597 for "curing through magic," "soothsaying," and "invoking blessings," and he told one woman to say a blessing for her sick child on three Fridays in a row.[74] Similarly, Peter Jergle conducted his healing rituals at night between Thursday and Friday. Apparently, Friday was "a propitious day for healing" in several regions of Europe, including Württemberg, for it was the most popular day specified in the sampled cases (although it should be noted the day of the week was only specified in a couple of the sampled cases overall).[75]

The instruction to repeat a procedure three times, however, was more common. In fact, actions frequently had to be repeated a certain number of times, and three repetitions was by far the most frequent. Repetitions like this were specified in seven of the sampled healing cases, and only one involved a number other than three. In 1596, Barbara Breüninger was investigated for treating goiter and rings around the eye with a blessing which she would recite and tell the patient to repeat on each of the next nine days.[76] The other six cases, in contrast, all involved three repetitions: Frank's three Fridays; Röcklin's three strokes with his stone for three days "after the moon;" Wieland's three pieces of paper for the boy to swallow. Similarly, Bästlin's stroked the young man's head and shoulders three times, and followed it up with three "Our Fathers," and Peter Jergle similarly gave his patient three strokes with his hand and three puffs of breath when he blew, which were done on three successive Thursday-to-Friday nights. In some cases the stipulation that an action be repeated three times may have been more-or-less a practical matter, much like modern instructions to take a medication in the morning, at noon, and before bed, which seems to have been the case when Schäffer instructed his patient to smear the salve made from egg, bark, and sap on, three times a day. Specific numbers, however, were held to have magical significance in Württemberg's as in many other folk cultures, and three was generally the most common positive number in healing and antiwitch spells.[77] The number had obvious associations with Christianity, but belief in its power goes back beyond Christianity to pagan times.[78] In most cases, it seems most likely that three in particular was specified because of its magical significance.

Numbers used to specify repetitions of a blessing had more than symbolic importance, however, for they transformed a simple prayer into an incantation, a series of words whose purpose was not just to express an idea, but to generate a spiritual power.[79] This observation is important because it reminds us that the elements we have been looking at did not exist in isolation, but instead contributed to a ritual process whose full impact was created by the cumulative effect of its parts working together.[80] In order to fully understand the way that healing worked, it will therefore be useful to look at a few of the healing sessions as complete experiences before considering the ailments for which they were employed and the ways that they could have contributed to their cure. There were a few instances in which herbs were given or blessings were said without embellishment, but most healing practices involved combinations of activities that ranged in complexity from the combination of a few modest words and props to elaborate "ceremonies" involving multiple objects, elaborate rituals, and protracted incantation or praying. In some parts of Europe empirics appear to have been strongly differentiated from magical healers, but in Württemberg the primary distinction was between licit and illicit practitioners, with the licit forming a functionally differentiated and strongly hierarchical structure, and the illicit forming an "amorphous assemblage" in which not only was little distinction made between natural and supernatural aspects of diseases and cures, but also cures that combined both were considered superior to those which relied on just one or the other.[81] Among the sampled cases, only one healer, Barbara Weylandt, claimed that she only used herbs and medicines and not blessings, while there was only one case in which only praying is mentioned. Furthermore, even in these two cases there is some uncertainty, for in the first there were conflicting statements, and in the second records are very scanty.[82]

Sara Sauter's use of the blessing to keep infants from losing weight is a good example of a very simple combination: she relied mainly on the invocation, but reinforced it with the special instruction that the parent had to bring the child unannounced in the predawn darkness on a Sunday. Hans Röcklin's use of his stone to cure horses and children illustrates a more complex combination of object, actions, and words: his distinctive red and gold crystalline stone was a venerable artifact that had been passed down to him from his father, and on three successive days during the waning moon he would use it to stroke the affected part of the patient three times while he spoke, using a pet name for a horse and recited the blessing which made an analogy between the waning of the moon and the desired lessening of the swelling or stiffness. Peter Jergle's treatment of Jacob Albrecht's wife's pains in her leg was only a bit more involved: he insisted that she state her first name for him to use, and then on three successive Thursday-to-Friday nights he had her stand naked while he passed his hands three times over the places that hurt, while mumbling something; blew three times over her foot; and told her as he left that "she should pray faithfully" so that "with the help of God he would be able to help her."[83]

Other healing practices were more protracted and complex, like Jacob Schäffer's attempt to cure the mentally disturbed woman by sprinkling rose petals on her head, staying with her for two hours, and persistently pressing to lead her in prayer with her husband.[84] Some were still more elaborate and imposing, like Hans Brückner's treatment of the woman and boy who he said were "afflicted by evil women."[85] He began by scrying to determine the source of the ailment, and offered to let the boy's father see for himself in a mirror, as we saw in the last chapter. Then he gave the boy an herbal bath, and, in front of him and his family, read from a book, and, after warning everyone to keep perfectly still, went around the room making the sign of the cross on each wall and door. As he left, he warned the family not to tell anyone what he had done. He used a similar procedure with the woman he cured, except that he gave her an herbal drink instead of bath, mumbled while sitting next to her bed, as well as read from his book, which he forbade people to look in. Similarly, to treat the young man who had been "crazy in the head for some time" and was kept in chains, Bästlin made sure all the doors and windows were closed, hung a cloth with a root around the patient's neck, mumbled some words "that could not be understood," prayed "in the name of God the Father, Son, and Holy Spirit ... stroked" him "three times on his head and arms and said at the same time three 'Our Fathers,'" and finally gave him "a drink made of several herbs."[86]

If the treatments these cases involved were multimodal, the ailments they were used for were similarly complex. They ranged from what appear to have been purely psychological disturbances, like the craziness of the young man Bästlin treated and the woman Jacob Schäffer ministered to, to problems that seem to be purely physical, like bleeding, which Gertrudt Raitsen had a blessing for, and jaundice, for which Barbara Weylandt had an herbal cure. However, as we have seen, psychological factors can cause or contribute to physical disorders, while mental disturbances can have physical roots, so even these apparently clear-cut cases may have involved both, and most of the ailments fell somewhere in between. The stomach aches and headaches that Schäffer treated, and the aching limbs Peter Jergle cured could have been anything from manifestations of hypochondria through psychosomatic problems and symptoms of minor infections to signs of a major disease. Since the healing practices these cases involved generally utilized multiple forms of treatment and the nature of the problems they addressed was so unclear, it is difficult to assess how, and how much, the cures worked by simply looking at specific examples of maladies and the way they were treated. Instead, we will look at the general mechanisms by which the sorts of healing activities we have seen conducted in early modern Württemberg worked, and then examine some examples from cases in which the documentation is best in light of those general observations.

The efficacy of magical healing

The sorts of healing activities we have seen conducted in early modern Württemberg were specific incidences of a much broader phenomenon generally called popular medicine or folk healing. This rubric is used to distinguish these practices from the official or learned medicine of literate, formally schooled, professional doctors, and groups together diverse traditions of people ranging from small-scale tribal societies to the rural peasantries of great civilizations, and even includes to some degree practices of the modern urban underclasses, particularly in the Third World. The distinction is problematic both for what it divides and what it unites, since, on the one hand, until modern times the differences between learned and popular medical traditions were limited in both theory and practice, and, on the other hand, there is enormous variety in the traditions of popular medicine or folk healing around the world. However, since the categorization is a product of the very period we are studying, the distinction between official and unofficial medicine was made and was becoming more marked at the time (process we shall examine in more detail in the last chapter of this book). Furthermore, despite the wide variety of popular practices around the world, there are a few basic commonalities that make it useful to draw upon folkloric and anthropological studies as well as modern medical investigations of related phenomena in order to understand the particular cases we are examining here.[87]

The starting point for any accounting of how folk healing works has to be the fact that, as we have seen, it includes a considerable amount of herbal lore and other knowledge of chemical and physical treatments.[88] While the actual physical potency of any particular one of these may be uncertain, there is no question of that such interventions have the potential to aid healing through direct physiological effects similar to those of modern medicine.[89] However, as we have also seen, the popular medicine in early modern Württemberg, like folk healing generally, contained a strong admixture of magic, the use of incantations, objects, and activities whose effects cannot be accounted for by some direct physiological effect.[90] And yet, there is no question that they do have physiological effects.[91] To some extent, of course, the efficacy of magical therapies, like the presumed efficacy of some physical agents, is illusory, a reflection of the body's power to heal itself and peoples' natural tendency to assume that actions taken are responsible for subsequent outcomes.[92] However, as with physical therapies, there is no question that symbolic and ritual activities can help the body heal beyond its unaided capacity. How they are able to do so is generally explained in the cultures that actually practice them in terms that modern science does not accept, in terms of occult forces and processes, which are often assumed to have autonomous consciousness. More specifically, it is commonly believed in these cultures that many diseases are caused by spirits, and the purpose of healing is to drive out the spirit or neutralize the spell that sent it.[93]

Nevertheless, recent medical research as well as the work of anthropologists and folklorists have shown that to a considerable degree their workings can be understood in modern medical terms, which is useful not only because of the general insights into universal aspects of human health and disease it provides, but also because it enables us to go beyond understanding what early modern Württembergers, and Europeans more generally, thought was going on when they used blessings and amulets when they were sick, to understanding what was going on a physiological level when they did so, to go beyond relating their healing practices to the cultural context in which they existed to relating them to the external and embodied physical realities to which they referred.

Of course, the materialist-rationalist tradition has always recognized that spiritual and other occult healing traditions have some degree of efficacy, and has explained it by reference to "auto-suggestion" or, more recently, the "placebo effect."[94] How, exactly, autosuggestion and the placebo effect actually work have never been entirely clear, but they clearly assume that the operative mechanism is essentially psychological, that by some process or other the patient's belief in the efficacy of the therapy stimulates the body's restorative mechanisms and thereby enhances healing.[95] This model has several significant implications: first, that the process is entirely intrapsychic (as opposed to involving some sort of external force like conscious spirits or nonconscious energy from the healer or the environment), and second, that its power comes from an active, more or less conscious subscription to a learned set of ideas about how the world and the body work (as opposed to an autonomic response to some physiological triggering mechanism). Since this model constitutes the current scientific consensus, we will begin by looking at the ways in which the healing practices contained in the sampled cases did involve the kinds of psychological manipulations posited by the positivist tradition.

To begin with the influence of conscious beliefs, the words "placebo" and "placebo effect" have come to be used for almost any psychological influence on health and disease, but technically "placebo" refer to a substance that appears to be a medicine but lacks a chemically active ingredient, or a procedure that is understood to be efficacious but does not have an activity that has a specific effect on the condition in question.[96] The "placebo effect" is the phenomenon that when given a placebo in the belief that it is an active medicine or procedure, patients recover better than if they are not treated at all. Furthermore, when given placebos in place of active medicines, patients often suffer the same side effects that the actual medicine causes.[97] However, a placebo does not have to be based on an active medicine to have an effect; what is critical is the patient's belief that the substance or therapy is efficacious.[98] Placebos have been shown to reduce not only "pain, nausea, [and] anxiety," but also swelling, involuntary muscle tension, "and even cancer cells," because "it is not just" patients' "attitude that changes; their biochemistry" also undergoes "a transformation."[99]

Further, another underappreciated characteristic of placebos that is nonetheless critical in understanding their role in folk healing is that there are different degrees of placebo effect. A placebo marked with a name brand, for example, will have a stronger effect than a placebo of the generic version of the same drug.[100] This effect reflects the fact that, paradoxically, even real medicines have a placebo effect, so that a pill containing a chemically active ingredient with a name brand will be more effective than a pill with the same amount branded as generic.[101] This last phenomenon makes sense of the common practice of mixing medicines and magic, for even chemically efficacious remedies will be more potent if presented as part of an impressive package of therapies.[102] Similarly, the variable degrees of placebo effect help explain why people sought out healers rather than just relying on home remedies, and why some healers were consulted more often than others. The more effectively they inspired belief in their patients that they would get better, the more readily their patients would, in fact, get better; and the more their patients did, in fact, get better, the more effectively they could inspire belief in them and others.[103]

The sampled cases contain numerous examples of healing activities that involved the exploitation of peoples' conscious beliefs about what could cure them, the placebo effect. To begin with, the very fact of seeking help could have a placebo effect; if the patient believed that using a home remedy or consulting a healer would help, they were already ahead of the game.[104] This may seem trivial to us, but for people whose real alternative was to lay despondently on a straw mat in the semi-darkness of a drafty hut, taking action was in itself a significant step.[105] Next, the words used in discussing the remedy could heighten the patient's belief, and hence the therapeutic effect, and any words incorporated in the remedy itself as a blessing or charm would contribute even more, like Jacob Schäffer's recitation of the line "I spew therein [to the sea] all my woes" to help cure a woman's cold. Similarly, symbols known for their beneficial potency like the crosses Hans Brückner traced on the doors and windows, objects with reputed power like Hans Röcklin's stone, and the talismans used by Christoph Wieland would have a had similar potential to trigger the placebo effect. Actions like touching and stroking the place on the body where an ailment was located, as Peter Jergle did to treat Jacob Albrecht's wife's pains in her leg, were thought to have therapeutic value, and hence, whatever other potential they might have had, this belief in itself endowed them with some. Finally, some healers used conscious tricks to enhance their patients' belief in their powers.[106] That would seem to have been the implication of the magistrates' charge that Jacob Schäffer engaged in "sucking" at the source of pain, and other instances of simulated "extractions" have been reported from elsewhere in Europe.[107] The role of sham in shamanism was noted by some of the earliest Europeans to observe the activities of Siberian healers, and they have been observed in numerous cultures around the world. Itinerant charlatans in early modern Europe, of course, cynically exploited these tricks to fleece credulous customers, and some cunning folk used them to impress people in order to build their businesses, but whatever use was made of them for fraud, as placebos they could have genuine therapeutic effect (and, ironically, even when they were consciously being used for fraud!), which would help explain why shamans who used practices involving sleigh-of-hand could nonetheless believe that they could genuinely promote healing.[108]

Another interesting feature of the placebo effect is that the patient's belief in the efficacy of a placebo is not the only factor influencing its effect; the doctor's belief about it also plays a role, which is why it is necessary to do double-blind drug tests in which neither the patient nor the medical staff with which he or she has contact knows whether the medicine or a placebo is being administered.[109] The problem is not so much that doctors and nurses might consciously cheat by telling the patient or inadvertently say something, but that they can convey their expectations in ways that are unconscious to them and to the patient, through the kind of subliminal communication that we saw as an important aspect of witchcraft in Chapter 1. Thus, optimistic doctors with a "therapeutic" approach can enhance the effects of both placebos and actual medicines, while skeptical doctors with an "experimental" attitude about a drug can not only suppress the placebo effect, they can also suppress the effects of the active medication![110] This aspect of curing highlights the fact that even in considering placebos, in which the patient's conscious belief plays a therapeutic role, we must keep in mind that influencing the conscious mind is actually a means of influencing the unconscious processing going on "behind the scenes," so to speak, for a tremendous amount of unconscious processing is needed to transform an idea, which is nothing but a configuration of neurons in the cerebral cortex, into bodily activities in the blood vessels in a swollen foot or the infected tissues in the lungs. The power of the doctor's unconscious expression of his or her conscious beliefs to affect patients' bodily functions without their conscious awareness also indicates that the placebo effect, the ability to manipulate patients' cognitive processing by influencing their conscious beliefs, is just one way of getting at those unconscious processes, and the evidence from the sampled cases in Württemberg and elsewhere shows that these sorts of mechanism were also exploited by traditional healing methods.

The other psychological explanation traditionally offered for the effectiveness of traditional healing is "auto-suggestion." As originally developed by Emile Coué in the early nineteenth century, it also involved consciousness, for he thought of it as a form of mental programming in which the person deliberately molds his or her unconscious by conscious imaging and repetitive thoughts, in effect performing a sort of "self-hypnosis."[111] Like the placebo effect, it has come to be used rather indiscriminately, as a general description of conscious thought impressing itself on the unconscious, but the two are not the same, for while, as we have seen, some personality types are more responsive to hypnosis (and self-hypnosis) than others, there seems to be "no correlation" of the placebo effect "with personality type."[112] Furthermore, the term "placebo" contains no indication of mechanism by which belief is translated into healing, whereas the term "auto-suggestion" points to a connection between conscious thought and unconscious processing, and hints at the existence of the entirely unconscious processes that lie beyond.

While Coué is best known today for his mantra "Every day in every way I am getting better and better," and his broader emphasis on positive thoughts and expression, he actually stressed the primacy of imagery over will in the activation of the unconscious.[113] Indeed, recent research suggests that "imagery seems to be the only conscious modality that can trigger autonomic response," perhaps because the right cerebral hemisphere both works with images rather than language and specializes in dealing with internal processes.[114] There is "a vast network of neural connections between the right hemisphere and the limbic system" so that "the verbal functions of the left hemisphere are one step removed from the autonomic processes"; verbal thoughts and perceptions "have to undergo translation by the right hemisphere ... before they can be understood by the involuntary, or autonomic, nervous system."[115]

Whether they arise as linguistic suggestions or as spontaneous visualizations, the influence of imagery on autonomic functioning can be quite powerful. Actors in an experiment told to visualize a scene not only felt the corresponding emotions, but also showed "changes in some hormones" in their blood "and indications of subtle changes in the immune system."[116] Visualization has been shown to "elicit changes in blood glucose, gastrointestinal activity, and blister formation," slow the heart rate, decrease blood pressure, increase salvation, and stimulate or inhibit the immune system.[117] Thus, when classic shamans report on imaginal flights to the spirit world to defeat the demon responsible for a disease or to recover the patient's spirit, they are not just motivating the sick in some vague inspirational way, but instead are inducing a series of images that trigger specific physiological changes with "direct therapeutic effect."[118]

As we have seen though, among the Germans the classic shamanic performances appear to have ossified into standardized narrative charms by the turn of the first millennium, and these gradually evolved into the much briefer commands, analogies, and supplications that were current in the early modern period. Among the sampled cases there are elements of imagery, like Jacob Schäffer's blessing describing spewing one's woe into the sea, Gertrude Reitsen's command to blood to "stand still," and Hans Brückner's visual theatrics of tracing crosses on the walls and doors, but these are very subdued compared not only to the extended narrations of classic shamans, but also to the visually impressive props like masks and altars and activities like acting out scenes and ecstatic swooning that are also utilized in some peoples' healing ceremonies. Instead, as is perhaps typical of people who have passed from the shamanic healer to the simple healer stage, early modern Württembergers' healing activities centered on another mechanism, that of vocalization.

Vocalization plays a secondary role in shamanic healing, transmitting the shaman's visualizations to the patient and audience, who then translate the words back into images. As with the blessings mentioned above, this role as a prompt to imagery remained in a much reduced form.[119] However, vocalization has its own ways of directly affecting unconscious processes in the nervous system, for vocalization (as opposed to subvocalization, the cognitive analogue to visualization) had prelinguistic origins that link it directly to the limbic system, the area of the brain responsible for emotions that is in turn linked to the autonomic nervous system. "Sound waves can actually modify the activity of nerve cells" in the temporal lobe, and "during primate vocalizations, heightened neuroelectric activity occurs in both the temporal lobe and the amygdale."[120] What is important in this process is not the conceptual content conveyed by the sounds (although these could, of course, trigger the placebo effect and Couéan autosuggestion), but their emotional tenor and rhythmic structure, for the amygdale is a limbic center that plays a prominent role in emotional memory, and rhythmic, sing-song sounds "are represented bilaterally in the anterior regions" of the brain, contributing to "synchronizing brain activity between the left and right hemispheres," a "psychophysical integration which manifests itself as emotional catharsis." We have seen in Chapter 5 how incantation could act as a psychophysical driving mechanism in sorcery, and here we can see one way in which, employed for benign purposes, they could have therapeutic rather than injurious effects.[121]

When performed by a group, rhythmic vocalization, like other rhythmic group activities, promotes not only individual psychophysical integration, but also group solidarity and cohesion, which play a critical role in health and disease.[122] Interpersonal conflicts, as we saw in Chapter 1, can contribute to ill-health in a variety of ways, and social isolation or loneliness has been shown to depress the immune system and contribute to heart disease, hypertension, and even cancer.[123] Social support, in contrast, helps maintain good health and promotes recovery. "Social attachments are important to normal human development and psychobiological function," so "a strong community can exert a very practical effect on physical well-being."[124] Social support contributes to reduced levels of stress and bolsters the immune system as well as promoting healthier habits and life-choices, reducing the incidence of and contributing to faster recovery from illnesses ranging from strep to heart disease to cancer.[125]

Promotion of social support is an important part of folk medicine generally, as it was in early modern Europe, although it did not play as prominent a role as the communal dancing and other rituals utilized by many tribal peoples. Villagers in Württemberg rang the church bells when members of the community became sick, and sickbeds were often placed at the center of the room so that friends and relatives could gather around the patient.[126] Among the sampled trials, we have seen that Hans Brückner's and Bästlin's healing ceremonies were performed in front of the patients' families; Hans Haasen involved the parents of the boy whose heart problems he treated in the healing process, telling them to bathe him; and Jacob Schäffer tried to get the woman he treated with rose petals to pray with her husband. The marshalling of social support and resolution of social conflicts was a standard technique of shamans and healers around the world, and while healers in early modern Europe, who had to keep an eye out for the clerical and secular authorities, made less prominent use of it than the shamans and shaman healers in many smaller scale societies, they still utilized it to some degree.[127]

How social support promotes health is not entirely understood. The traditional assumption has been that it works indirectly, cheering the patient up by inducing members of the community with whom he or she might have debilitating conflicts to let go of them and demonstrate their more fundamental amity, while reinforcing the feelings of love and companionship from the rest of the community. Indeed, lonely people have been found to have higher levels of cortisol, the hormone responsible for stress, in their blood, with correspondingly lower levels of the killer cells that attack viruses and tumors.[128] Recent research, however, suggests that in addition to this undeniably important channel there is another connection between people that exerts a more direct physiological effect. One of the important effects of collective rhythmic rituals is to synchronize autonomic functioning through parallel activity, but autonomic functioning has been found to be coordinated by a far more straightforward mechanism as well.[129] It has long been known that when a person thinks about performing an action, some of the associated motor neurons actually begin firing, and it has recently been discovered that the same effect happens when a person observes someone else performing an action: about 20 percent of the neurons in the appropriate regions of the brain, termed "mirror neurons," fire to recreate at a low level a brain activity corresponding to the others person's observed action.[130] Furthermore, not only motor neurons fire in response to the activity of others, but also neurons in other regions of the brain, the neocortex and the limbic system, indicating that intent and emotion are also being mirrored in the brain of the observer.[131] Finally, and most importantly from our point of view, this process of mimicry and synchronization takes place when facial expressions are seen, vocalizations are heard, and other forms of emotional expression are perceived, so that the act of perceiving an emotion results in its recreation in the nervous system of the observer.[132] "A certain part of the brain is activated when we feel sad," for example, "but the same area lights up, albeit to a lesser extent, when we see someone else in distress."[133] Thus understanding feelings and intents, sympathy and empathy, do not simply involve labeling them and positioning these labels within some constellation of symbols, but actually reproducing them neurologically and experiencing them viscerally. (President Clinton really did "feel your pain"!) Healing rituals that involve communal participation thus surround the patient with expressions of affection and hope and thereby do not simply inspire feelings of optimism and being valued, but actually induce such feelings directly, by stimulating the parts of the brains that correspond to the expressions and their motivations of the others (the same mechanism probably contributes to the efficacy of spontaneous *maleficium* and ritual sorcery, although the malign potential of this effect has to date been little studied).[134] Similarly, the power of a healer's performance, the "charisma" that plays a vital role in his or her ability to heal, comes not simply by performing symbolically meaningful acts to inspire the patient, but by exuding optimism and confidence that trigger corresponding patterns of neural activity in the patient.[135] Genuineness and expressiveness are therefore critical traits in healers because communication on this level cannot be faked; there are aspects of subliminal communication, as we have seen, that are not accessible to the conscious mind, and a simulated emotion will not exert the same persuasive power on the patient's unconscious processing as a real one.[136]

While loud, rhythmic vocalization serves as a driving mechanism and promotes social cohesion, quieter vocalization and subvocalization can have other beneficial effects on health. For one thing, "a quiet prayer ... can activate the body's quiescent function that has been shown to enhance immune system function, lower heart rates and blood pressure, restrict the release of harmful stress hormones ... and generate feelings of calmness and well-being."[137] Another is that which was originally proposed by Coué: recitation of a prayer or incantation can exert an hypnotic effect, promoting dissociation and facilitating the effects of suggestion. Prayer, blessings, and charms, like hypnosis, can induce relaxation of the body and focused attention through repetitive stimuli and explicit suggestion, creating "an altered state of consciousness ... which improves the physical and mental well-being of the individual."[138] Some of the healing effect of hypnosis is undoubtedly caused by the relaxation it involves, for hypnosis in humans seems to be related to "animal hypnosis" in which startled animals enter "catalepsies, or pretended death" to avoid predators, a response that is the opposite of the "flight/fight" mobilization that we have seen plays such a prominent role in psychophysical maladies.[139] However, the suggestibility people display under hypnosis makes it possible for a hypnotic trance to be used to facilitate healing in other ways. In particular, hypnotic dissociation appears to disentrain the conscious facility responsible for our "free won't," the neurological circuitry that enables us to voluntarily suppress impulses that are on the verge of being executed.[140] Since this normal waking consciousness is closely connected to the brain centers responsible for reality orientation (both go offline during sleep), hypnosis appears therefore to facilitate healing suggestions by avoiding realistic but unhelpful doubts about the prospects of recovery.[141] Furthermore, hypnosis would appear to also circumvent other, nonconscious entrainments that inhibit action for pathological reasons, perhaps because they are normally entrained with our (not completely) "free won't" as part of the assessment criteria that influence its decisions. Finally, as we saw in Chapter 5, there is evidence that hypnotic trance directly promotes learning, for physiological studies of subjects in mild trance states showed a "signal, representing a negative charge, that the brain gives off during learning" that normally amount to "at most 100 microvolts" reached much higher levels, "rising in several instances to 1,500 to 2,000 microvolts."[142] Of course, this activity may just be a manifestation of the reduction of normal inhibitions, but the upshot seems to be that people in hypnotic trance states are not just psychologically but also physiologically more open to new ideas and information, which can be utilized to promote healing.

While in some cases the patients themselves recited the healing blessings and prayers, as when Peter Jergle told Jacob Albrecht's wife to pray to help heal her sore leg and Jacob Schäffer told the woman with the cold to say the blessing about going over the sea, in others it was the healer (or, in the case of children, a parent) who voiced the incantation instead of the person who was actually sick, as when Gertrude Raitsen used her blessings against bleeding and burns and when Jacob Schäffer prayed for Hannß Schuten's son.[143] Of course, in some cases, like the latter, the healer actually led others in prayer, but even when the patient said nothing such a ritual could induce a therapeutic trance, for "dissociation" can be "imposed on individuals in some way by the actions of other persons through verbal or nonverbal suggestion."[144] In classic hypnosis, of course, the hypnotist induces the trance in the subject without entering a trance state him or herself, and the recitation of a blessing by a healer could work in this way, by getting the patient to follow along silently if not through direct suggestion, but in shamanic healing the healer him or herself enters a trance state in order to induce one in the patient.[145] To some extent, of course, the shaman's trance simply facilitates the performance of rituals that induce trance, but it seems that the healer's trance state itself acts as a sort of "emotional contagion," inducing in the patient a similar altered state of consciousness.[146] The specific mechanism could be the action of mirror neurons or some other form of subliminal communication, but whatever the means, it seems that healers' facial expression, vocalizations, and gestures combined with any other sounds, smells, and activities would act as "a form of hypnotherapy" that affected the patient and any other audience, and if there was an audience, then a similar process of nonverbal communication from audience to patient would second and amplify the interpersonal influence of the healer.

At its most extreme, shamanic healing appears to go beyond induction of hypnotic trance and implantation of suggestion – fine-tuning the patient's nervous system, in the terms discussed in Chapter 5 – to a full-blown "tuning" of the nervous system similar to that responsible for the induction of shamanic ecstasy: the driving of the ergotropic nervous system into overload to generate the simultaneous discharge of the trophotropic system, synchronization of the cerebral hemispheres with each other and the limbic system, and collapse into a pronounced trophotropic state.[147] This process "facilitates rapid cognitive reassignment of affect to object," and ends in the autonomic state designed for regeneration and restoration of bodily resources.[148] While this approach seems to be quite common in shamanic tribal cultures, none of the healing rituals described in the documents from early modern Württemberg suggests the kind of prolonged and intense ritual activity these involve. Some, of course, may have been more intense than the participants – who were, after all, suspects in a criminal investigation because of these rituals – conveyed to the investigating magistrates, but it is important to realize that healing rituals do not have to be frenzied in order to be effective. In fact, relatively restrained rituals and subtle alterations of consciousness can achieve notable results.[149] Highly hypnotizable people "do not require special suggestions to respond hypnotically," although "their response is facilitated by hypnotic inductions," and hypnotizablility, while genetically based, can be enhanced through socialization and learning.[150] In a society in which magic and religious beliefs and practices both promoted the alteration of consciousness through activities and beliefs related to hypnotic inductions, the kind of rhythmic activities we have seen in the cases from Württemberg, like Peter Jergle's repeated stroking of Jacob Albrecht's wife's sore leg; Walzen, the forest ranger's "biblical sayings and songs" used against sickness; and Jacob Schäffer's two hour prayer session with his disturbed patient, would have fine-tuned the sick people's nervous systems enough to promote relaxation and open them to hypnotic suggestion contained in the rituals and incantations.[151]

These various manipulations of sick people's conscious beliefs and unconscious processing in the kinds of healing activities we have seen in early modern Württemberg work through a number of underlying physiological mechanisms. Some, like the direct effects of vocalization, have been mentioned in the course of describing the manipulations, but since various forms of manipulation can affect the same underlying mechanisms, it will be helpful to discuss the underlying mechanisms systematically, one by one.

First of all, since, as we saw in Chapter 1, psychological problems and interpersonal conflicts cause or contribute to many ailments, sometimes with the force and intent that are perceived as witchcraft, but more often as lower grade, routine manifestations of the psychological stresses of human life and communal living. Sometimes these problems manifest as somatoform disorders, symbolic somatizations of psychological distress, but more often they manifest as psychophysical maladies, "real" physical disorders that result either directly from the effects of chronic stress, like headaches from tensed muscles and hypertension from constricted blood vessels, or indirectly, due to the stress response's suppression of the immune system and the body's consequent vulnerability to a wide variety of disease agents. In all these cases, healing rituals that promote intrapsychic and interpersonal integration thereby reduce or remove an important contributor to disease by helping resolve the psychological and interpersonal tensions that either generate it or make the body vulnerable to it. While this form of intervention may seem inconsequential in comparison to modern medicines and surgical procedures, it was the primary means of promoting health before the twentieth century, and is increasingly recognized by even modern doctors as a potent contributor to health and a tool against disease.

While reducing or resolving the psychological and interpersonal tensions that cause or contribute to disease can promote healing, there are other, more directly physiological mechanisms by which traditional healing helps sick people feel better. The first of these is by stimulating the release of endorphins and enkephalins, the body's natural opiates.[152] We have seen that pain is a complex construct created by the brain, with cultural expectations and psychosocial dynamics playing an important role in the perception of its intensity and tolerance of its effects, but these endogenous chemicals also play a role, helping to block the sensation of pain, "exerting analgesic effects" that can be "more powerful than those of narcotic drugs, and ... produce a sense of calm and well-being."[153] Placebos can trigger the release of endorphins, as can "cultural symbols that have been cross-conditioned with physiological, emotional, and cognitive responses"; prolonged rhythmic rituals; exhaustive exercise; anaerobic activities; and sleep deprivation.[154] Chanting and other vocalizations appear to have a particularly close connection with these pain-reducing chemicals, for the basal ganglia structures, which "play a major role in language" by integrating the cognitive and emotional components, "are a rich source of enkephalin."[155] Conversely, "the cortical areas" particularly "involved in affiliative interactions, social bonds, multimodal sensory information processing, selective attention, and top-down physiological regulation are also areas with the highest density of opioid receptors." Endorphin release can thus be triggered by a variety of mechanisms involved in ritual healing, and results in a real reduction of pain and real sensations of well-being and connectedness. These not only provide the direct benefits that help the patient feel better, but also indirectly aid in healing by reducing anxiety and stress and thus facilitating rest and recuperation.

While there is no question that the pain-reducing effects of endorphin release can have beneficial effects in healing, it should also be noted that reduced pain can lead to excessive activity detrimental to healing; in fact, endorphin is actually secreted as part of the "fight/flight" response so that people in extreme danger can ignore severe injuries that would normally cause debilitating pain. Furthermore, excessive amounts of endorphin in the bloodstream are at least one way that the stress reaction suppresses the immune function, so the beneficial effects of artificially inducing endorphin release can come at a price. However, another mechanism that is tapped by a variety of healing techniques that we have seen is specifically designed to counter the effects of the stress response, to aid in rest and restoration of the body and boost the immune system. This method involves deliberately activating the parasympathetic nervous system, the quiescent system that is the counterpart to the sympathetic nervous system responsible for the "fight/flight" response and the stress reaction. In contrast to the excitation produced by the sympathetic system, during the "relaxation response ... metabolism slows down, blood pressure drops, breathing slows, heart rate lowers, and ... brain waves are less active."[156] As we have seen, periods dominated by the relaxation response naturally alternate with more active periods on an approximately ninety minute cycle, and after an emergency activation of the "fight/flight" response the relaxation response kicks in when the crisis is over.[157] We have seen that a parasympathetic dominant state is the end-condition when the nervous system is "tuned" through simultaneous discharge of both halves of the autonomic nervous system, and it can also be fostered less dramatically through soothing activities like subdued rhythmic activity, incantations and prayer, meditation, and hypnosis.[158]

As noted above, calming healing rituals like Peter Jergle's repeated stroking of Jacob Albrecht's wife's sore leg, Walzen the forest ranger's "biblical sayings and songs" used against sickness, and Jacob Schäffer's two hour prayer session with his disturbed patient had the potential not only to promote the relaxation response, "with all its physiological benefits," but also open them to hypnotic suggestion contained in the symbols utilized in the ritual activities and the words of the blessings and prayers. Furthermore, these hypnotic processes are just one way of exploiting the third general healing mechanism, symbolic penetration. As we have seen in Chapter 5, when considering the effects of the eggs Agnes Langjahr put in the woman's bed in the Crammer's house, symbolic penetration in general is "the effects exercised by the neural system mediating a symbolic percept (or the entire perceptual field) upon other neural, endocrine, and physiological systems," giving symbols the "potential to evoke any neural network that becomes entrained to the network mediating the percept" which "may include lower autonomic and endocrine structures mediating arousal and metabolic functions; core brain and limbic structures mediating sentiment, emotion, or feeling; and cortical structures mediating conceptual organization, imaginal organization, logico-mathematical functions, cross-modal sensory transfer, and other functions."[159] This means, first of all, that symbolic penetration can be used to modify neural structures responsible for psychogenic disorders by "entraining deep levels of neurocognitive organization, evoking repressed structures and psychodynamic complexes and re-elevating them into consciousness," which can lead to beneficial "changes in ... behavior, personality, self-understanding, and autonomic balance."[160] Furthermore, symbolic penetration can promote health and combat disease by directly entraining organs in the immune system.[161] The immune system plays a vital role in combating viral and bacterial infections and the development of cancers, and while it was traditionally thought to be a relatively self contained unit, connected with the nervous and endocrine systems only through generalized trigger and modulatory mechanisms, recent research in psychoneuroimmunology has shown that "hormones and neurotransmitters can influence ... the immune system, and ... products of the immune system can influence the brain," so that there is "a constant flow of information ... back and forth between the brain and the immune system."[162] To some extent "the immune system is ... under the direct control of the CNS," or central nervous system, informing the brain when an infection has been detected and receiving messages from the brain via neurotransmitter receptors on immune cells which enable "the brain" to directly and specifically "manipulate the immune system."[163] Ritual healing techniques appear to exploit this connection by creating entrainments between "the neural system mediating a symbolic percept" and the lymphoid organs and tissues of the immune system that are distributed around the body in order to artificially stimulate the body's defenses against infectious agents and internal malignancies.[164]

In addition to these neural entrainments connecting symbolic percepts to the immune system, "the frontal lobes" also "regulate internal physiologic control systems such as the autonomic nervous system and limbic sites ... that are known to ... impact health status" as well.[165] The autonomic nervous system consists of the sympathetic and parasympathetic nervous systems, and we have seen the effects they can have on health and disease. The limbic system is the primary seat of the emotions, and can exert a pronounced effect on immune functioning not only by triggering the sympathetic and parasympathetic systems, but also through the direct effects of the chemicals associated with specific emotions. Different emotional states correlate with the release of different neuropeptides, and the "the receptors for those chemicals are found in almost every cell in the body."[166] Since viruses enter cells through their peptide receptors, peptide levels correlated with emotional states affect how vulnerable they are to infection.[167] Furthermore, "the chemicals that mediate emotion" affect cellular activity in the immune system, and emotional reactions quickly lead to changes in it.[168] Since symbols can be, and often are, entrained with emotions, symbols can be used to cause changes in emotion to artificially induce changes in cellular defenses and immune functioning.[169]

Symbolic penetration occurs constantly during normal waking consciousness, but the ritual activities involved in folk healing facilitate the process.

The state of relaxed dissociation promoted by incantation and prayer, gentle rhythmic movements, and hypnotic induction reduce defensive interference against symbols that threaten to disrupt the existing configuration of neural networks. The profound neural upheaval experienced during autonomic tuning and the subsequent collapse into parasympathetic dominance, in contrast, "can lead to erasure of previously conditioned responses ... and can produce an ultraparadoxical phase in which the conditioned behavior and responses are reversed."[170] Rituals are not necessary for symbolic penetration to take place, for it is a ubiquitous feature of human cognition, but they promote the kind of powerful, focused entrainments and re-entrainments needed to inhibit detrimental and promote beneficial processes deep in the autonomic, endocrine, and immune systems. In other words, healing ritual "does not merely refer to or talk about but *does something* in the world."[171]

Among the sampled trials, as we have noted, the single most common ritual action was touch. Hans Haasen touched the boy with heart trouble he was treating on the chest. Bästlin stroked the head and shoulders of the demented young man he was treating, while Peter Jergle stroked the leg of the woman he was treating where it hurt. "The skin is the earliest sensory organ to develop," and, with "a total of 900,000 sensory receptors ... is a giant communication system that ... brings messages from the external environment to the attention of [the body and mind]."[172] Touch has been found to be "one of" the "most powerful components" of healthy "social support," and for "people who enjoy regular, satisfying touch," it has been found that "their hearts are stronger, their blood pressure is lower, their stress levels are decreased, and their overall tension is reduced."[173] A recent survey of research on healing touch therapies concluded that touch can contribute to "reducing stress, anxiety, and pain; accelerated healing; some improvement in biochemical and physiological markers; and a greater sense of well-being."[174]

The beneficial effects of touch clearly owe much to the physiological mechanisms already discussed, for touch can have important symbolic meanings, rhythmic stroking can stimulate the relaxation response, and endorphins are released as part of social bonding as well as pain suppression.[175] However, the effects of touch are thought by many to go beyond these ordinary processes to involve some sort of extraordinary power.[176] During the early modern period, the monarch's "royal touch" in England was thought to cure scrofula and other diseases, and touch was used commonly by healers across Europe.[177] This effect was commonly attributed to a power the healer had that derived from his or her social position or a special endowment from some mystical source, and which was transferred from the healer to the patient. In most cases the healers and their clients asserted that the source of such power was God, but theologians and the more devout said it was the Devil. Some people held that it came from non-Christian spirits, like Hans Haasen's "very large, well-built woman" who "in front looked like a normal person, but behind looked all light and fiery," who he said played such an important part in his shamanic initiation on the Venusberg.[178]

Popular traditions of religious and spiritual healing by simple touch and more elaborate ceremonies involving the "laying on" of hands continued through the following centuries, but they came to be regarded by the medical establishment as either fraudulent, misunderstood instances of coincidental recovery, or psychological cures of complaints caused by psychological problems. The Frenchman Franz Anton Messmer caused a sensation in the eighteenth century when he developed a new healing technique based on what he called "animal magnetism," a vital force that he asserted emanates from within the body, is affected by regular magnetism, and can influence other people's magnetism, and his cures became quite popular at the top of society, but a blue-ribbon panel appointed by the French government, in 1784, concluded "that the 'magnetic fluid' was a myth" and any curative influence his methods exerted was purely psychological.[179] The dissociation Messmer's techniques created led to the development of hypnosis and thereby contributed to the development of modern depth psychology, and his physiological theories and curative methods influenced spiritualism and Christian Science, but the idea that the body produces some occult energy that can be transferred remained beyond the pale, scientifically and medically, until the second half of the twentieth century, when laboratory studies produced evidence that healers could accelerate healing of wounds and delay the onset of disease in mice, increase the reactivity of enzymes associated with the growth of tissue, increase hemoglobin levels in human blood, and produce other effects of the same nature, all without the healers actually touching the substance or organism but by merely passing their hands near them.[180] Based on this evidence, anthropological reports on "primitive" healing techniques, ancient medical texts, experiences with traditional healing methods, and theories about human "bioenergy," a variety of healing practices were renewed or developed, most notably a modern version of "laying on" hands called "Therapeutic Touch" that spread rapidly in the nursing profession.[181]

By the mid-1990s the method had "been taught to over 30,000 health care professionals at more than 80 colleges and universities in the U.S., and in more than 70 countries throughout the world."[182] However, the practice of Therapeutic Touch and related healing methods have come under increasing criticism because of their connections to mysticism (by fundamentalist Christians as well as scientifically oriented skeptics), the fact that the existence of the "bioenergy" that forms the theoretical base of the practice has not been established scientifically, the methodological problems with many of the early experiments that inspired them and are still often cited to support them, and the mixed results of attempts to replicate and expand upon them.[183] Additional support for touch therapies, on the other hand, has come not only from the experiments that do provide evidence of clinical benefits attributable to them, but also from parapsychological experiments in which changes in the activity of sensorially isolated targets' autonomic nervous systems, as measured by blood volume in the fingers, galvanic skin response, blood pressure, EEG, or EKG, appear to be correlated with isolated senders' randomly prompted attempts to cause them.[184] However, the parapsychological experiments challenge Therapeutic Touch and similar healing methods from another direction, as do much disputed experiments involving intercessionary prayer from afar, for in both cases the purported physiological influence is exerted not by the close proximity of a healer's hands, but from another room or even from another state.[185] Even some advocates of Therapeutic Touch emphasize the importance of healing intent and the possibility that rather than representing any local transfer of some sort of "bioenergy," any healing power conveyed by touch or near-touch beyond the mechanisms discussed previously are simply a focused manifestation of more general psychokinetic influences.[186] On the other hand, the possibility has also been raised that any benefits beyond the placebo effect attributable to touch and near-touch therapies can be explained by the effects of heat and the very weak electromagnetic field generated by electrochemical activity in the nervous system, which would vindicate the practice of Therapeutic Touch without requiring any paranormal form of influence.[187]

On balance, then, while early modern healing practices, not just touch, but also prayer and other rituals performed by healers and others, may have had some beneficial effect through some form of direct energy transfer, the kind of influence that would on the surface seem to be most closely associated with "magical" healing, even if the possibility of such transfers comes to be accepted by the scientific community, given that the healing rituals contained in the records from early modern Württemberg involved actions carried out in the presence of the patients and with their knowledge of the activities' purpose, this would seem to have been a limited influence in comparison to the effects of the internal physiological mechanisms discussed earlier. With or without any sort of power to transfer thoughts or energy from healer to patient, the power of early modern folk healing in Württemberg and elsewhere beyond the efficacy of herbal remedies they involved substantially if not wholly stemmed from the power of incantations, ritual actions, and symbolic objects to resolve psychological and interpersonal tensions, stimulate endorphin release, induce the relaxation response, and establish neural entrainments and stimulate the release of neuropeptides that reduced people's pain and promoted their recovery.

Some of these influences, like the placebo effect, depended on people's learned expectations, but others, like the hypnotic effect of incantation, acted more viscerally. Similarly, many of the maladies they could cure were psychological or psychosomatic, but many were purely or primarily organic; just as interpersonal conflicts could manifest somatically as psychological conversion reactions or stress-related organic problems, beneficent psychological manipulations could promote organic healing as well as cure hysterical symptoms. Gertrudt Raitsen's blessings to staunch bleeding and to heal burns were as realistic therapies as Jacob Schäffer's prayers and rose petals to bring Bernhardt Saÿer's wife to her senses; both Peter Jergle's touch therapy for Jacob Albrecht's wife's leg pains and Hans Röcklin's use of a stone to reduce the swelling of a child's tumor were equally likely to bring relief or even a cure. None could equal the power of modern surgery and antidepressants, antibiotics or radiation therapy, of course, but they were not competing with them. If their promise did not equal that of modern medicine, it certainly rivaled the alternative medical care available at the time, and it constituted a markedly superior way of handling illness to letting nature take its course.[188]

Magical countermeasures

Just as causing illness was by far the most common misfortune attributed to witchcraft and sorcery, healing was the most common form of beneficent magic, forming a third of all the sampled activities, and half of those involving manipulative magic (see Table 7.1). The other half of the cases involving manipulative magic were divided among a number of types: magical countermeasures used against those who had trespassed against a person through magic or theft, magical techniques for enhancing various attributes and abilities, exorcism of spirits (not including attempts to establish contacts with spirits to gain treasure, which was mainly a form of divination), and a few miscellaneous practices.

While magical enhancement was the second most numerous category after healing, there was a form of countermagic that had a strong relationship to healing which makes it appropriate to discuss this category first. The countermagic in question is magic used against witchcraft, and it is related to healing because, as was just noted, the most common form of harm ascribed to witchcraft was illness, and so the most common response was some sort of healing activity. Of the 31 informal responses to witchcraft recorded in all the sampled witchcraft and magic cases together, 15 involved healing; 12 involved divination (and of these, five also involved healing, so that the divination was used essentially as a diagnostic tool), three involved asking the witch to remove the spell, one involved removing a hidden object thought to be responsible for the spell, and two involved undertaking magical action against the witch.[189]

To some extent these figures surely distort the frequency with which the different types of measures against witchcraft were used. Some, most notably preventive measures like avoiding or appeasing a suspected witch, wearing protective amulets, deploying protective devices or signs around the house, and incanting protective blessings have been reported from other early modern sources and found by folklorists in twentieth-century Swabia, but they were not likely not to draw the attention of the authorities.[190] Similarly, people probably downplayed or avoided reporting magical countermeasures that they took on their own, since these could lead to a countercharge or prosecution for practicing illicit magic. Conversely, consultation with a healer was more difficult to cover up than a purely private action, and it involved an activity that was would have been expected when a health problem was involved, so the authorities were on the lookout for the use of magical remedies. Once an investigation got under way, however, both healer and clients had reason to downplay any magical elements. Overall, it seems likely that the records reflect the frequency of consulting healers more accurately than the exact nature of the cures they recommended.

Even so, while passive protective magic and aggressive countermagic undoubtedly played more significant roles than the trial records show, consideration of the evidence in both the witch trials and the trials for beneficent magic suggest that among the active responses available to a harm caused by suspected witchcraft, simply curing the ailment ascribed to witchcraft was the most common.[191] To begin by considering the situation from the point of view of the witch trials, of the 27 sampled witchcraft cases, 13 involved a doctor or healer of some sort, although one of the "healers" was actually a wise woman who recommended that the spell be defused by digging up a bone she said was causing it.[192] In some of these cases home remedies had been tried before the help of a specialist was sought, but in two other cases home remedies alone were used; so 14 cases of the 27 involved medical activity. However, nine of the 13 cases that did *not* involve some medical intervention were concerned with situations in which there was no party thought to have been injured by witchcraft, and therefore medical action would not have made sense: the incident that started when a rumor swept Wildbad in 1663, most of the cases that started with a confession of diabolism, and two cases in which the accusation of witchcraft was made by officials against a person originally arrested for theft. Therefore, it seems that there was some sort of medical response in the great majority of the cases in which witchcraft was seen as the cause of some type of injury (14 of 18, or 78 percent).[193] Of the four cases in which there was an injury but no medical response was mentioned, one involved the wise woman mentioned above, two started with a malady that quickly got better (the girl who collapsed when berated and hit by Katharina Masten recovered later that day, and the couple who got sick from Catharina Freyberger's goat cheese also improved on their own).[194] The last was the defamation suit by Hans Rueff against Margaretha Stuertzen, who claimed he had caused her to become ill by grabbing her some months before, but while there were seven witnesses who testified that she was indeed ill, whether and how she had tried to cure her ailment was not discussed.[195]

Among the cases that did involve medical care, in two a doctor was only called in by the authorities to offer an expert opinion on the nature of the complaint once the investigation was well under way, when Anna Maria Schelling's family said that she had been poisoned by an apple Barbara Gessler gave her, and when young Hanß Ferner said the Devil had cut his leg after they returned from the witch dance.[196] In some other cases, officially sanctioned practitioners were consulted by the afflicted party and treated the ailment as a physical disease, like when Johanna Fehlen got sick from the drink with the powder in it that Barbara Schmied gave her at a party, and she went to a barber who gave her a drink and "also opened a vein" to bleed her.[197] Similarly, when the preacher of Geradstetten's sister-in-law got sick after eating a piece of bread Maria Laichlin gave her, and the preacher took the young woman to the doctor in Schondorf, he treated the malady by bleeding her, even though he said that its cause was "preternatural."[198]

In a number of cases the character of the healer is less clear and the nature of the remedy difficult to determine. For example, when Agatha Sacher's rival became distraught at her wedding to Agatha's ex-boyfriend, she was taken to a "doctor" ("*artzt*") who said that her "spirit ('*muoth*') had been taken" and gave her a drink to make her better.[199] Since the "doctor" was in the town of Villingen when she went to him, but was not identified in any more specific way and since then he had moved to a small village, it seems more likely that he was a completely unofficial healer than a bather or apothecary who was practicing beyond his official competence. On the other hand, he was not identified by any other profession, either those identified with occult knowledge, like knacker or executioner, or a more regular trade, and he does not seem to have been a peasant, all of which suggests that he was an at least semi-professional healer. The fact that he diagnosed the woman's problem as having had her "spirit" ... taken," and went on to indicate that he dealt with the problem frequently suggests that he was a practitioner with some focus on spiritual or magical problems.

However, in describing the Ziegler's bride's problem, the healer used the word "*muoth*" (modern "*mut*") that means "spirit" more along the lines of "courage," "mood," and "state of mind" than some ethereal dimension of personhood.[200] This terminology stands in sharp contrast to the way another healer, Margretha Rencklern, who lived 25 or 30 miles away in Sindelfingen, near Stuttgart, talked about her practices around the same time, saying that she "knew how to drive witches out" as if they actually entered the sick person.[201] Margretha's use of the word "Unhold" for the "bad people" causing children's ailments connects her conceptualization to the old belief that some women's souls flew at night with Holda and that others' flew out to devour children, while simultaneously anticipating the modern idea that disease is caused by noxious invaders. The healer from Villingen, in contrast, seems to be simultaneously closer to the shamanic concept of disease as a loss of spirit and the modern idea that symptoms like

Ziegler's wife's are psychological rather than spiritual. This impression is reinforced by the fact that he does not appear to have used any blessings or ceremonies to treat her, but instead just administered a medicine.

However, before we conclude that the Villingen healer was simply a naturopath giving Ziegler's wife an herbal sedative to calm her down so she could recover her *"muoth,"* we must remember that, first, details of the session may have been kept secret for the reasons given above, and, second, herbs were generally thought to have magical as well as medicinal potency.[202] Indeed, many herbs thought to have curative properties affect the nervous system as well as or even instead of having a more direct physiological effect. Some recipes even included the same powerful psychoactive plants that were thought to be used in witch salves, in which case the psychophysical effects would not simply be a sort of "fine-tuning," but actually a full-blown tuning effect, causing the patient to experience the simultaneous discharge of the sympathetic and parasympathetic systems and collapse into parasympathetic dominance, which induces ecstasy but also has "inherent therapeutic effects," including "facilitating self-regulation of physiological processes, reducing tension" and "eliminating psychosomatic effects."[203] In most cases, of course, the herbs were more mild, but could have beneficial effects either as part of a larger ritual, like Hans Brückner's, or simply by relaxing or stimulating the patient. It seems significant that the healer who treated Ziegler's bride said that her spirit "had been taken," implying that he thought someone or something took it, and he said that this sort of problem was common, which suggests that even if he confined himself to using herbal remedies, he was using them at least as much for their spiritual potency as for any natural effects on the body. Early moderns did not sharply distinguish between physical, mental, and spiritual phenomena the way we do, but instead tended to see them as highly interconnected.

In any event, of the 14 cases involving medical practices, four involved practitioners who were clearly identified as officially sanctioned medical men employing authorized practices. Six, in contrast, were clearly identified as popular healers who appear to have offered supernatural or spiritual therapies: an executioner in Stuttgart who prescribed a lavender water rub and "fumigating powder that she must smoke" for Barbara Dannenritter when her arm hurt terribly after Anna Maria Rothin grabbed it; the knacker consulted by the girl who Margaretha Ada hit; a knacker consulted by Anna Schollen, Magdelena Kochen's well-to-do neighbor who had refused to buy mandrake from her, when her cow got sick; the "little woman" (*weiblin*, a wise woman) who told Agatha Stoßer's neighbor to dig for a bone when his cow got sick; and two cunning men: Hans Köll, who treated Anna Eberlin after she thought she had had sex with the Devil by hanging an amulet with herbs in it on her back, as well as giving her an herbal drink, and another one consulted by Christian Cammer when the three eggs were found in his wife's bed.[204] Of the four uncertain cases, one was a "medical man" (*medico*) in the town of Backnang who was consulted when Jakob Endris got sick from his stepgrandmother's lye-laced soup and who recommended a medicine from an apothecary, so he was probably a sanctioned healer, and in this case anyway offered only a natural remedy, while the other three might have been simple healers.[205] If these three are added to the five who were clearly cunning folk, that means that such practitioners were consulted in eight, just under one-third, of the 27 cases in all, or about half of the 18 cases involving medical issues, while the remainder of these "medical" cases included the four handled by licit practitioners, the one involving the Backnang "medico," and four in which there were medical issues but there's no evidence that any medical personnel were consulted.[206] As in the case of divination, seeking the aid of cunning folk and village healers to counteract maladies ascribed to witchcraft was a significant option in dealing with them, but it was far from standard practice.[207]

The reason for this variability undoubtedly reflects the varied circumstances surrounding witchcraft accusations and the diverse circumstances of the people involved. Some accusations, as we have seen, arose in circumstances that did not call for medical intervention, not just the unfounded rumor in Wildbad, but also most of the confessions of diabolism, and when the prosecution grew out of an investigation of some other crime.[208] In other cases, a physical malady was involved, but the circumstances were so manifest that no cunning person was needed to divine the identity of the witch, and the affliction was transitory. This was the case when Katharina Masten berated and knocked down the servant girl Catharina Baitinger; the girl soon recovered, and there was no mystery who was to blame.[209] In some cases, the simple availability of different medical practitioners may have played a role, while in still others economic resources and social status may have influenced the choice of healer; Johannes Brand, for example, being the preacher of Geradstetten, not surprisingly took his sister-in-law to the town doctor in Schondorf when she got sick after eating the bread Maria Laichlin gave her.[210] Finally, people undoubtedly selected consciously from the available options in the local medical marketplace that they could afford, choosing a doctor who specialized in physical remedies when the problem seemed clearly to be poison, and a cunning person when the cause was obscure or the symptoms suggested a magical affliction.

Looking at the situation from the point of view of beneficent magic rather than witchcraft reinforces the impression from the situation with divination that countering witchcraft was a significant but far from dominant aspect of beneficent magic. Among the sampled trials, three of the nine trials for blessing, three of the eight trials for illicit healing, and one of the nine trials for generalized magic were involved with this activity (23 percent).[211] Of course, the one magic trial, that of Hans Brückner, shows in significant detail the types of procedures that might be used by cunning folk to help those afflicted by witchcraft. As we have seen, he used a window or a mirror to scry for the identity of the witch, and then treated his patients with elaborate magical ceremonies that included protective magical rituals, drawing crosses on the walls and doors; incantations; and herbal potions and baths. However, in most of the other cases the cunning person focused on healing, like Conrad Stier, who offered general medical help as well as magical healing "for those who are afflicted by witches and such," and Othmar Kählin, who was rebuked by the magistrates for identifying witches through means he admitted were magical, but who insisted that he only used natural cures "and good words" as treatment. Similarly, Jakob Franck, "Schafer J" from Emmau, identified witches as part of his cunning practice, but, according to his clients, "then cures and heals people with proper means, like any other doctor."[212] Jacob Schäffer, who was the subject of a series of investigations from 1594 to 1619 and, as we have seen, treated a wide variety of ailments including boils, open wounds, swelling and pain in the limbs, stomach aches, headaches, and "craziness," was only accused of diagnosing witchcraft once, in 1616, and in that instance he said that he couldn't help with it, although he ended up giving the girl's father the recipe for an herbal drink that he said would offer some relief.[213] It is possible, even likely perhaps, that the treatments offered by some of these cunning men, Othmar Kählin and "Schafer J" in particular, judging by their reputations and demeanors, involved more pronounced occult elements, like defensive rituals similar to those conducted by Brückner and possibly even spells to force the witch to lift the curse or deflect it back onto her, than the investigations uncovered, but on balance the evidence suggests that prophylactic and healing measures played a much more prominent role against witchcraft than active countermeasures.

Nevertheless, there were several forms of informal countermeasures that were definitely used at times. One was to neutralize the spell, as when the *"weiblin"* consulted by Agatha Stosser's neighbor told him to dig up a bone. Another was to get the witch herself to remove the spell, as several of the people involved in the sampled witch trials attempted to do.[214] One instance involved the wife of the man who consulted the *"weiblin"*: by the time he returned from the consultation his wife had pleaded with Agatha to remove the spell, who, she said, agreed to. (Agatha denied the whole thing in cross-examination.) Another involved Anna Maria Rothin, who was accused of laming several people by hitting them or smearing something on them, but who then helped Michel Gännßlen recover, he testified, and a third concerned Agatha Langjahr, who when asked to lift a spell denied that she was responsible but said "God help you," which sufficed to cure the victim's pain. At times it was alleged that this could develop into a kind of racket in which cunning folk themselves would cause ailments for which they would then offer a cure, for a price.[215]

The most dramatic response to suspected witchcraft, of course, was a counterattack. While, as noted before, the extent to which people undertook occult countermeasures on their own, or even did so with the help of cunning folk, is difficult to determine, in some cases the magistrates' investigations did bring such activities to light.[216] In the one instance contained in the sample of magic trials, one of the trials for using blessings, which took place in Herrenburg in 1761, Glaßer Bilfinger's wife complained that blind Jacob Geigler, the man who, as we have seen, would advise Hans Jerg Stadi in his futile search for treasure in his basement, in 1762, and who was also accused of selling Hans Jerg Kugel a book on magic, not only accused her of taking the milk from Barbara Steinler's cow based on examining its urine, but also worked magic against her and hit her as well.[217] What magic he used isn't clear, but he also seems to have inspired Steinler to shun her, for Bilfinger said that when she "came to the weekly market and wished" Steinler "good morning three times, she did not thank her, but rather only said ... 'go on your way, I don't want to have anything to do with you.'"[218] It is possible that this rudeness was simply a brief show of anger, but breaking off social contacts, along with spreading rumors, in the hopes of isolating a suspected witch, has been noted elsewhere, and may have complemented the magic and battery Geigler was using against her.[219]

More detail about the kind of countermagic that might be employed against a suspected witch came out in one of the sampled witch trials. In 1676 George Raster, a butcher in Alpirsbach, found that his cow went dry after someone "broke in and took the milk" from it.[220] Following the advice of a soldier, he burned a mixture of herbs including Vervain, thyme, Solomon's seal, and salt, and let blood from the animal, which was supposed to cause the person responsible "to be covered with pustules." Shortly thereafter, "these pustules were seen ... on the left side, toward the front on the body" of the midwife Christina Mück. "[S]he used ivy ... and mangelwurzel" as a treatment, according to her stepdaughter-in-law and stepgranddaughter. Christina's stepson, who accused her of "acting cheeky and cursing his father" while he was alive, said that three years before when a calf was sick he had put asafoetida on charcoal to fumigate the stall, and "his stepmother ... scurried up and down, in and out of his house while this fumigation was going on." In the latter case, it seems that he only deduced in retrospect that the treatment of the stall caused her discomfort, but in the first case the intent from the beginning was clearly to afflict her, the presumed cause of the cow's malady. The ultimate objective of the counterattack, besides the pure satisfaction of taking revenge, was presumably to pressure the witch into removing the spell.[221]

In addition to these examples from the sampled cases, two other instances of countermagic against witchcraft were found in the duchy's archives. In one instance, from Urach, in 1740, Georg Weÿwadels, a citizen and vintner in the village of Eningen, tried several ways to deal with what he perceived to be evil people "squeezing and pressing on his chest."[222] This was presumably happening at night, and appears to have been a case of the "Old Hag" syndrome. Georg sought the advice of Peter Jäcklen, a 33-year-old barber who had a book on magic (that he said he could no longer locate, when the magistrates asked about it, and that he had gotten from an old "field barber" who had, in the meantime, died). One of the measures Jäcklen recommended appears to have been passively defensive, putting a talisman on his chest. Another was a more active defense, placing nails in the rooms of his house, while the third was still more aggressive: he was to put urine in a trough for three days, then pour it on "a glowing tile and throw it with a snap on the so-called nose of the tile, with the intention of smashing the nose of the presumed attacker, and compel her to come and thereby reveal herself."

The other case of countermagic related to witchcraft took place in Herrenburg in 1773. It involved Conrad Blencklen, a 42-year-old mason who had for ten years been meeting a ghost in a stall, a "white shadow" of a man, that assisted him in divination and other magic. In particular, he helped a woman whose milk was being stolen, a not uncommon form of witchcraft, as we have seen. The countermagic he used was a blessing that went, "Agatha, I don't know [who] has assailed you, the Devil or a follower, but may the Lord Jesus Christ, who now on Palm Sunday has ridden to Jerusalem, help defend you. Abraham, Isaac and Jacob and Maria, [lead] you to sincere repentance, so that this evil devil's work must melt away from you," followed by the three holy names repeated three times. For this he received 2 Reichstaler because the milk reappeared that very night.

Exactly how the milk was returned is not clear, but this outcome makes it seem more likely that the milk was being stolen physically rather than magically, although the people involved seem to have assumed it was a magical process. Similarly, it is not entirely clear whether Jacob Geigler and Margaretha Steinler thought that Glaßer Bilfinger's wife was stealing Steinler's milk magically, since she had been seen sneaking around the Steinlers' at midnight. While there is no question that early modern Württembergers believed that witches could cause cows to dry up and could even steal milk from them magically, there is also no question that very similar countermeasures were used against physical theft.[223] Among the sampled cases, for example, Christoph Wieland, the cunning man from Backnang who cured people by giving them pieces of paper with blessings on them to wear or eat, also "stood in particular credit with the people, that he can recover stolen and lost things through his superstitious art."[224] Unlike Blencklen, though, Wieland used curses rather than blessings and combined them with rituals, although the intent was the same: to project influence on the guilty party and make them return the stolen goods. In one instance he put three pieces of fat with salt on a pan over a fire and said "as this fat cooks and sputters, so should it in this his bowels cook, he who took what was stolen, until he brings it back." In another, when the considerable sum of 60 Reichstaler was at stake, he incanted "I lay for you, thief, bread, salt, and lard ... because of your sins and presumption, lay it on your lung and liver and heart, so that a great pain will come and strike you such a blow as if it was bitter death."[225] In another case, from Waiblingen/Winnenden, in 1747, in which 100 Reichstaler was stolen from Hans Jerg Nachtriben, Jerg Ulmer from the village of Retterstein recommended a ritual in which Nachtriben was to beg for 3 Pfennig from three different households, give them to Ulmer, and he would lay them under a millstone which would cause the thief to return the money.[226] In a final case when clothes were stolen from a wagon in Blaubeuern in 1696, the wagoner said that he was going to go to "the soothsayer Veltin in Richenbach," but then the clothes were returned.

It is significant that in this last case the threat of consulting a cunning man sufficed to bring the return of the stolen goods, for the threat of counteraction or even just exposure meant that recourse to a cunning person could work by spurring the guilty party to remove a spell or return purloined items.[227] Similarly, Blencklen's blessing calling for the milk thief to repent his or her evil ways also seems to have had the desired effect. Furthermore, while Christina Mück's agitation and the outbreak of "pustules" on her body during the two fumigation procedures may have been coincidental, it is quite possible that they were sparked by the threat of the countermagic being undertaken if she had, indeed, surreptitiously harmed the animals of Raster or her estranged stepson and his family out of anger with them, or even just wished ill on them. In those circumstances, for her to feel fear and anxiety because of the procedures would have been natural, and there is no reason to question that they might manifest as the agitation she displayed in the earlier instance. Similarly, as we saw in Chapter 1, feelings of guilt and fear of countermagic could clearly cause someone who had committed theft or sorcery to generate the experiences of pain Christoph Wieland's rituals and curses were designed to inflict.

For ritual actions to cause a skin condition may seem like more of a stretch, but the same psychophysical mechanisms that underlay *maleficium* could just as easily have worked the other way in circumstance like this. To begin with, direct suggestion can cause physical changes in the skin. We have seen that "severe marks, real burns or weals, appeared on the skin" of a sailor reliving a traumatic shipwreck under hypnosis, even though it had been "perfectly intact" before the session, and "disappeared again when the hypnotic trance was over."[228] Among the sampled trials for generalized magic, a similar effect may have been triggered when the dissolute young man named Viet Grossman stalked and eventually grabbed a young woman named Anna Beyler, for shortly thereafter her hands began to hurt and swell, and two days later her face had swelled up and "one could see the grip of his hands on her chin and neck."[229]

Such direct somatization is not the only way that emotional stress can affect the skin, though, and some of the conditions that can be caused or exacerbated by stress involve the kind of pustules the countermagical ritual was intended to inflict.[230] Acne, for example, is notoriously sensitive to emotional stress, and it is particularly likely to afflict older women as well as adolescents, because of the changes in hormonal balance they are going through.[231] Similarly, the most common form of psoriasis, plaque psoriasis, appears as raised, rough red skin with whitish scales, which could look like pustules from a distance, and there is also a form called pustular psoriasis that causes actual white pustules to appear.[232] The exact cause of psoriasis is not known, but it seems to result from a malfunction of the immune system that causes skin cells to mature too quickly. There is a genetic disposition to the disease, but "research indicates that a 'trigger' is needed," and stress is one potential trigger. The condition is chronic and usually starts early in life, but "people often experience flares and remissions," and "after age 40, a peak onset period occurs between 50 and 60 years of age."

Christina Mück was 50 at the time of the investigation, and it is possible that the stress Weÿwadels' countermagical ritual put her under triggered either the onset or a flare-up of the disease in her, but the point is not to try and diagnose Christina Mück, or to judge her, across 325 years, but instead to illustrate how countermagic, like spontaneous *maleficium*, deliberate sorcery, and healing rituals, had the potential to really work, and really work not just in the sense of causing psychological disturbances or symbolic somaticizations, but in the sense of causing psychophysical reactions leading to fully physiological dysfunctions. The main difference between this form of magical assault and the others, in this regard, is that in this case it would be important that the target know that he or she was being targeted, not so that the harm could be inflicted – for we have seen that this can occur through subliminal channels, even without the person believing in magic or knowing that they are under attack – but because the goal of the exercise is not simply to inflict harm, but to get the person to lift the curse or return the stolen goods. Of course, even without getting a suspected witch to take back a spell, an ill person would gain the psychophysical benefits of fighting back, and it is possible that a thief with a guilty conscience might return stolen goods if struck with an inexplicable malady, but overall countermagic would seem to have depended more than the other forms of magical manipulations of health on the target's belief in the power of the rituals and knowledge that they were being performed. Like divination to identify witches and thieves, it was most effective when the very possibility that it might be used deterred an angry or covetous person from casting a spell or stealing something valuable, and when that failed it's primary purpose was to get an explicit renunciation of a curse or the recovery of the stolen property.

Magical enhancements

While magical counteraction may have been more carefully hidden than most forms of beneficent popular magic because of the direct harm it was designed to cause the target, which made it very similar to the *maleficium* it was supposed to counter, the form of manipulative magic that was second most common after healing among the sampled prosecutions was what might be called magical enhancement, the use of magic to heighten or gain some ability or characteristic that occurs naturally or can be cultivated. It, too, was undoubtedly very underreported, but for the opposite reason from magical countermeasures: magical enhancements usually did not involve a victim, or at least not a victim who was directly affected by the magic. Two of the cases involved the use of magic to enhance marksmanship, two involved the use of magic to enhance job skills, two involved unusual strength ascribed to magic, one involved unusual stealthiness ascribed to magic, and the last involved the use of magic to enhance a person's ability to endure the pressures and setbacks of a bitter political conflict.

Some of the rituals, of course, not only assumed but also required that truly supernatural processes be at work. For example, we have seen that in 1660 "Wild Georg" Schaff told a smith's apprentice in Aitlingen that he could get a magic ring that "would help him smith," by "entering the smithy backwards between eleven and twelve o'clock on *Charfreytag* while chanting the Devil's name, whereupon he would find one in the [blacksmith's] leather apron."[233] For this to actually work, a ring would have had to materialize out of thin air, which is more than even most parapsychologists would claim could really occur. In the event, it was a moot question since both the young man and "Wild Georg" claimed that they had never actually tried the ritual.

On the other hand, one of the cases concerned with marksmanship shows particularly well how magic really could be used to enhance performance. It took place in Münsignen, a town on the Alb southwest of Urach, and began when Young Jerg Gestenmaier, a carpenter, accused his three brothers – Johannes, Ludwig, and Christopher – of cheating in shooting contests by using magic to help them shoot more accurately. Jerg said that the three went home between rounds and refused to say why. He went on to say they used a ritual that involved burying a Bavarian coin, visiting it periodically, and after three weeks, digging it up, filing it, and mixing the particles into their gunpowder. "Through this means," he said, "no one could shoot better than them."[234] An older man, Hanns Hermann, admitted to the magistrates that he had taught the youths this magic, but the brothers denied it vehemently. Some of their neighbors began to say that Young Jerg should not press matters so hard against his own kin, and, indeed, two days later Johannes was seen attacking Young Jerg with a knife. The ducal government ordered the magistrates to "earnestly warn" the youths against these forbidden practices and "watch their activities and behavior well," and sentenced Hanns Hermann to "two days and nights in jail."[235]

The ritual Hermann taught the youths involved two distinct activities: first, burying and visiting the coin, and second, filing off shavings and mixing them into the gunpowder. The specific activity of mixing the shavings into the gunpowder cannot have been very old, for firearms had been in general use for less than two centuries, and it is hard to see how it could have contributed physically to the accuracy of the gun, but the ritual as a whole was connected to a far older tradition of using magical rituals to enhance one's aim. This form of magic probably dates back to the preparatory practices of prehistoric hunters, and it is found in most folk and many learned traditions. Superhuman aim was a common power of the heroes in Germanic sagas, and the *Malleus Maleficarum* contains evidence that magical marksmanship was a highly developed art in late medieval Swabia.[236] Its authors called archer wizardry one of the "three ways in which men ... may be ... addicted to witchcraft."[237] It reported that by offering "homage of body and soul to the devil," archer wizards gained the ability to "shoot an arrow with such precision as to shoot a penny from a person's head without hurting his head, and they can continue to do this indefinitely." Additionally, it claimed that by shooting a crucifix and bending "their whole will on killing" a man, "the arrow ... will be carried and stuck into him by the devil" no matter where he might hide. A related belief was reported in Augsburg, in 1579, which held that the ashes of a suicidal man's colon mixed into gunpowder would bring a sure shot, while elsewhere criminals' bones were thought to bring luck in shooting.[238] Why sinners' remains were thought to be helpful is not known, but in twentieth-century Swabia, bats' eyes were sometimes put in the barrel of guns so that the bullet would find the target like a bat finds insects in the dark.[239]

In this last example the mechanism thought to be at work is clearly sympathetic magic, the idea that an attribute of the bats' eyes can be magically transferred to the behavior of the bullet. In the previous two, the accuracy was thought to be caused by some power in the dead people's remains, which perhaps is linked to the mechanism posited in the *Malleus Maleficarum*, diabolic intervention. In the Gestenmaiers' case, the use of silver from a coin could have to do with some assumptions about the magical potency of silver, or it could be linked to the idea of sacrifice or payment in exchange for the extraordinary power, but the symbolic importance of it being a Bavarian coin is not clear (since Bavaria was a large principality that lay about 50 miles to the east, perhaps they were just unusual enough to be special while common enough to be reasonably obtainable). From our point of view, however, the substances themselves do not seem to have had any intrinsic properties that would make them contribute to the accuracy of a shot; what did give them that ability was the meaning the marksmen attached to them and, even more important, the process or ritual by which they obtained or prepared them.

The meaning that the marksmen attached to the substances and preparatory processes could influence their aim, because expert military marksmen studied to determine the source of their skill said they "believed that shooting was 20% physical and 80% mental."[240] The substances employed by the marksmen acted like amulets or talismans that helped avoid the jitters caused by anxiety and bolstered confidence to create a kind of self-fulfilling prophesy. However, in this case the power of symbolism would seem to be less important than the process of preparation. In the Gestenmaiers' and archer wizards' cases there were clear ritual preparations involved. In the cases of the powder made from a suicide's colon or possession of a criminal's bones no ritual was specified, but the process of obtaining a suicide's colon and making a powder with it or purloining a criminal's bones from a decaying corpse rotting on a pillory or digging up a skeleton buried under six feet of earth, or even just buying them from some illicit middleman such as a shady executioner or itinerant sorcerer would have been a fairly involved and nerve-wracking process. Also, there may well have been some unspecified rituals involved in preparing and using them, since in general "in folk-magical conceptions ... a magic ritual" was needed "to bestow its power" to a magic object.[241] Athletes and stage performers often use elaborate ritualistic activities to prepare themselves for action, and simple magic rituals like the one used by the Gestenmaier brothers would appear to have been a formalized version of this. By enhancing "concentration on the task at hand ... faith in ... future triumph and the psychological presentment of victory," these "forms of genuine magical observance ... actually influence reality."[242] Rituals foster "alert attention to detail" by "requiring behavior explicitly contrary to routine patterns" which "heightens awareness by interrupting the trophotrophic response that prevail in habitual acts."[243] It seems particularly significant in this regard that the Gestenmaier brothers went home between each shot to perform the ritual, because this suggests that the physical process of going through the ritual at the time, and not just awareness of the symbolic meanings of the ritual and materials, which could have been prepared beforehand, played a critical role in the enhancement of their performance.

Just how much ritual preparation can influence marksmanship is illustrated by the practice of archery in Zen Buddhism. In it, the initiate is taught to enter a detached state of consciousness in which it becomes possible to hit the bull's eye repeatedly without consciously aiming, or even necessarily looking at the target at all. The German philosopher Eugen Herrigel studied under a Zen master, and recounted how the initiate learned to wait with bow drawn to "the point of highest tension until the shot falls ... before he even thinks of it."[244] After years of practice, Herrigel found that he could enter a state of mind "in which nothing definite is thought, planned, striven for, desired, or expected," and therefore could shoot with uncanny accuracy time after time. While this ritual clearly differs from medieval archer wizardry and the magic practiced by the Gestenmaier brothers, and none seems likely to enable archers to shoot around corners or into closed rooms, as the *Malleus* suggests, they would seem to be related by the ability of ritual activity to free the mind from the self-consciousness and anxiety that inhibit performance and thereby enable it to enter the state of relaxed dissociation, the "flow state," associated with peak performance.[245]

In another case suspicion started from unusual performance rather than from evidence that a ritual had been performed. It took place in the village of Altdorf near Bebenhausen in the summer of 1705, when a weaver named Conrad Hahn complained that his tools were being damaged and materials destroyed by a poltergeist.[246] During the subsequent investigation it came out that some time before, he had produced an extraordinary amount of cloth in a single day, "which raised the suspicion that he had engaged in some "prayer against God the Almighty" and joined "the Devil's empire" in order to increase his output, with the unnatural damage he suffered being, presumably, the punishment for his sinful folly. The example of Georg Schaff's ring ritual shows that the idea of invoking the Devil to enhance work skills had been current in the region for at least half a century (and folklorists would find the same notion still current in the twentieth century), but while the government was convinced he had "used a forbidden means," the magistrates could not find any evidence of it, and so the ducal chancellery merely instructed that he be "told privately that from the testimony of several masters" they knew that "36 'els' [of cloth] cannot be made in one day naturally" and that frequent prayers should be performed in his house."[247]

Two other cases from the late seventeenth century also hinged on the inference that enhanced performance must have been created by magic rather than from direct evidence of magical practices. One took place near Altensteig in 1683 when the distraught preacher of Zwerenberg complained that a young man named Jakob Staibers had threatened to invoke the Devil against him, paraded past his house carrying a pitchfork, and had tried to burn down his house.[248] The magistrates learned that Jakob, a small man, had exhibited such "unnatural strength" by carrying a live steer on one occasion, several men on another, and a huge stone mortar on yet another that they suggested he must have used some "forbidden medicine." They also reported that Jakob was a "restless man who runs around at night and cannot be still," habitually carried a pitchfork, fought a lot, and had been overheard when drunk to say, "I am the Devil's" and that "if they [the preacher and supervisor] get in my way again, I'll complain to my Lord." Jakob said that he meant the government, not the Devil; that he carried a pitchfork because there were soldiers in the area; and vehemently denied that he had tried to burn down the preacher's house, although he pointed out that "the house is actually not the preachers," presumably because he was given housing by the parish, suggesting that he did have some resentment about the preacher's perk. The High Council was more concerned about his unruliness than any suggestion of magic or diabolism though, and after ten days in jail, he was let off to care for his sick wife.

The other case, from Illsfelden, near Neuffen, in 1662, concerned a more mysterious combination of strength, dexterity, and stealthiness. Christoph Martin, a cooper and new resident, complained that "a magical thief" had sneaked into his house several times, sometimes while Martin, his wife, and others were in the house, and even when the doors were locked and the windows nailed shut.[249] While in the house he had ransacked rooms, left some things tied in bundles and stole others, and left a series of warnings. "Even if you lock your door, I'll get in like I did before," read one, and the later ones were more ominous. In one he wrote "Kieffer, if you had given me three pieces the first day, I would not have come into your house again, for I have vowed to get three pieces from a woman," and his last one warned "Kieffer, God protect your wife." Eventually 20 people tried to catch the mysterious intruder, chasing after him but he "sprang over the preacher and others" and got away. Kieffer claimed that he had no idea who the man was or what he wanted, and it is not known whether he was ever caught or bought off. In any case, while there was no evidence that he practiced magic or did anything that could not be plausibly explained naturally, it was assumed that the unusual dexterity, strength, and stealthiness he demonstrated in the course of his escapades came from magic.

While no incantations or objects thought to confer strength or dexterity were recorded among the sampled or known trials, but just allegations that they must have been used, we have seen in Chapter 5 that an incantation for invisibility was current in the area, the "grass blessing" Anna Schnabel got in trouble for just one year later in Cannstatt, about 15 miles away. Similarly, in the last case of personal enhancements, the one involving a person's ability endure the pressures and setbacks of a bitter political conflict, the actual blessings were recorded by the person involved and preserved in his own handwriting in the judicial archive. The incident took place in 1709, near Kirchheim, and involved Leonard Weißinger, a 50-year-old judge in the village of Weilheim, who owned a "moderate amount of property."[250] He had already been in trouble once for practicing magic, when he was 25 and influenced by a comrade in the army. "One thought then that the memory of such forbidden acts had been lost to Weißinger," noted the magistrates, for he became a respectable citizen and rose to serve as *Bürgermeister* for a number of years. He became "rather imperious" late in his tenure, however, and "the common suspicion" held that he had "managed the ... office for the public not so well as for himself." He conflicted with the other *Bürgermeister*, Hans Kurtz, particularly. Their enmity apparently survived Weißinger's retirement from office in 1704, for in 1709 his old opponent brought forth a piece of paper he claimed to have found five years earlier. On it were "three blessings ... written in Weißinger's own hand." The first went

> Slander and complaint,
> cares and anger,
> all that restrain and compel be yielding,
> depart from me as the moon withdraws from the sun.

The second read

> Bullets hold fire and flame
> as when Christ on the holy cross came,
> his innocent blood forgotten,
> so should he stand their shot.

The third went

> There flow two streams,
> the one is named the Daradra,
> the other the wedge doesn't bite,
> it is not God's will.

Weißinger noted that "all are to be repeated three times in the name of God the Father, and the Son, and the Holy Spirit," but while this might have technically sufficed to make them Christian blessings rather than pagan charms, both the wording and the instruction to repeat them three times make it clear that they were basically magical incantations. The second, in fact, could well be a modification of a magical formula Weißinger had used to for protection in battle 20 years before; the first combines command and analogy; and the third, what appears to involve a segue from an initial analogy that was not completed into a second that was. However, unlike most blessings, which were intended to achieve some manifest effect, these were intended to bring emotional resilience and consolation very much like prayer. The first has intimations of manipulating some external forces, pushing out the impositions that "restrain and compel," but overall seems more focused on helping the person ignore the "slander and complaints" and let go of the "cares and anger." The second and third focus exclusively on helping the incanter endure external pressures stoically or accept failures as God's will. While all blessings competed with prayer in that they sought to magically compel what prayers were supposed to be used to piously request, for the most part they were used for the kind of purposes they were originally designed for, and for which Christian prayer's appropriateness was always a bit questionable: to transform desire into reality. Here, however, the blessings intrude on prayer's home ground, emotional consolation and acceptance of God's will. The blessings which Weißinger used to bolster himself amidst his bitter conflict with his fellow *Bürgermeister* Hans Kurtz remind us – like the "ghost cult" that formed around Anna Maria Freyin, Hans Haasen's quest for a better life by learning from the spirits on the *Venusberg*, and Apolonia Walther's dedication to "her prince," the Devil – how strongly magic can come to overlap religion.

Supernatural powers and anomalous events

In addition to his incantations, Leonard Weißinger's case also contains evidence of a different kind of magic – a magic intended to exert what we would consider a truly paranormal influence on the world. This distinction was not meaningful in popular usage at the time, but it does correspond to some degree to the contemporary theological distinction between *mirables*, tricks on the senses played by the Devil and true supernatural miracles worked by God, directly or through the saints, and it seems worth noting that, such magic played a limited role in beneficent manipulative magic, just as it played only minor role in actual cases of *maleficium* and "magical" healing, only a limited role in sorcery and most forms of divination, and a major role only in treasure-hunting, as we have seen. In Leonard Weißinger's case, the kind of supernatural effect in question was the invincibility spell that he was said to have used while he was a soldier, and upon which he seems to have based his blessing to stoically stand up to the fire of his political opponents. Spells to confer physical invincibility in battle were quite common during the Thirty Years' War and appear to have continued to be practiced during the French wars later in the century, when Weißinger served. The best known was the "Passauer Kunst," named after its reputed place of origin, the city of Passau near the border between Bavaria and Bohemia, about 100 miles east of Stuttgart.[251] This particular spell involved a talisman that was supposed to protect the wearer from bullets and blades, in some versions at least, through a compact with the Devil. Similar spells were known elsewhere in Europe, and were developed later by various Third World people opposing gun-armed Europeans with traditional weapons. While incantations and amulets to enhance prowess in combat go back to ancient and probably Paleolithic times, protective magic seems to have been particularly popular in early engagements involving guns because of the "occult" (hidden) connection between a soldier's action of firing and the almost instantaneous infliction of injury some distance away by an agent that was invisible to the naked eye. There are, however, no known instances in which these spells achieved significant success.

A second form of paranormal beneficent manipulative magic was mentioned by one of the suspects in one of the treasure-hunting cases, Maria Knötzlerin, the 32-year-old woman from Vaihingen, who said in 1739 that she had got two books with the St. Christopher's Prayer from a priest.[252] The priest also showed her a book with which she could conjure "strangers" to appear – and she claimed that when she tried, three unfamiliar men did show up unexpectedly – a spell that would seem to have been a variant of the divinatory spells discussed in Chapter 6, which were supposed to cause the guilty party to come to the house of a person afflicted by witchcraft. A third paranormal form of magic mentioned in the sampled cases was a claim, or really an accusation, by another treasure-hunter, one of the group that was duped by the man in green who "flew" to Bohemia and his partner who disappeared with the group's seed money in Backnang in 1766. One of the secondary participants, David Silling from Murrhardt, said that the main instigator of the scheme, Christoph Wurt, had claimed that three years before, he and "Schafer Jerg," the cunning man who got them in touch with the treasure-hunter, had changed 30 Reichstaler worth of copper into gold.

Attempting to transmute base metals into precious metals was a venerable magico-scientific activity, alchemy, a branch of the learned tradition of magic on par in terms of intellectual respectability with astrology.[253] Just as works in astrological observations contributed to some degree to the development of astronomy, alchemical experiments contributed to the development of chemistry. Similarly, just as astrology may have some basis in reality, since, as we saw in Chapter 6, sunspots do affect the earth's magnetosphere and may affect the weather and other physical processes, some elements change spontaneously, through radioactive decay, while others can be changed artificially through nuclear reactions. However, there is no credible evidence of such a transmutation having been achieved through alchemy or other magical rituals.

There was, as we saw in Chapter 6, a manipulative aspect to treasure-hunting itself, for it was thought that treasures could move on their own accord or be moved by spirits, and so magic was needed not only to determine their location, but also to fix them in place. In practice, while people undoubtedly performed the rituals designed to fix as well as find the treasures, the main practical effect of this belief would seem to be to help explain away the frequent failure of the hunters to uncover the treasures they hunted. An alternative manipulative magic associated with treasure-hunting was the attempt to get a spirit to bring the treasure to the hunter rather than vice versa. Not surprisingly, this was not the favored approach, but Maria Knötzlerin did say that the books the priest gave her showed "that one can conjure the great Christoph so that he has to bring as much money as you want."[254] Somewhat more common was the *"Geldt-mannlen"* ("treasure-man"), familiar spirits that were supposed to procure money for their owners, and which, as we have seen, were bought and sold during the eighteenth century. Maria Knötzlerin also claimed that the priest's books showed how to conjure up one, although this one did not get money itself, but instead would "create a mirror, wherein she could see everything," including, presumably, the location of treasure. Treasure-men were mentioned in two of the other sampled treasure-hunting cases but did not play a significant role in them. Three other cases centered on people's attempts to procure treasure-men: one in 1694, one in 1748, and one in 1792.[255] Significantly, the earliest of the three started when a man tried to buy a familiar spirit that he hoped would bring good health, and only broadened to include one to get money, when another man got involved, suggesting that it was something of a transitional case between the more traditional focus of magic on health-related issues and the eighteenth-century fad of treasure-hunting. The one in 1748 involved a group of men who tried to conjure up a treasure-man on their own, and the last involved a commercial transaction for one. Like St. Christopher in Maria Knötzlerin's conception, a treasure-man was supposed to procure as much money for the possessor as he wanted, but how this was to be delivered seems somewhat unclear.[256]

Maria's, as we have seen, was only supposed to help locate treasure, presumably so it could be dug up as in regular treasure-hunting, but in the other cases it's not so clear if the treasure-man was just expected to point the way to a treasure, was expected to do the heavy lifting as well, or even, as appears to have been the case in a couple of the "treasure-hunting" conjurations, was thought to deliver via natural means, by guaranteeing particular success in ordinary remunerative activities.[257]

We have seen that one of the main roots of the treasure-hunting activity was the belief that the ghosts who haunted places might be connected to some hidden treasure, and by the mid-eighteenth century virtually every reported ghost or spirit appearance was assumed to be connected to this, either by eager commoners hoping to score a windfall or by government officials on the lookout for illicit magic and fraud. Not all ghosts and spirits were assumed to be linked to treasure, however, especially during the seventeenth century, and sometimes magic was used not to summon or bind them, but instead to get them to go away. In these cases, magic was being used not as a supernatural manipulation in order to influence physical reality, but instead as a supernatural manipulation of another aspect of the supernatural, basically to cause a presumed supernatural entity to cease entering people's perceptions. The earliest known incident was mentioned during the investigation of "Schafer J" Franck by the magistrates of Sulz in 1597 for his illicit blessings, healing, and counterwitchcraft.[258] A man from Neckarshausen, a village near Esslingen, about 30 miles distant from Sulz, said that he had asked Franck to drive a ghost from his house, although he claimed to have backed out when he learned that the cunning man was going to use magic, and there was no mention of treasure. The next such incident was in 1672 in Bottwar, when the residents of a nursing home, "old women, children, and maids were seized by terrible fear" because some had seen a ghost.[259] The curator of the home, Philipp Jacob Ruethandten, was put in contact with an exorcist by an ex-Catholic, Matthew Lipp, the 73-year-old, illiterate steward of a dairy farm. The exorcist was also an ex-Catholic from Bavaria, named Frantz Beurlin, who had been living in the duchy as a Lutheran for a long time, and he conducted a ceremony that involved reading a book while sitting at a table. Again, there was no mention of treasure, for the object of the exercise was simply to get rid of the troublesome spirit. The third incident, which took place 24 years later in Blaubeuern, also involved a magical specialist, Paul Zürn, who was offered 5 Reichstaler to try to drive a ghost from the house of a man in Ulm, with the promise of 10 more if he succeeded.[260] Zürn, a 51-year-old cobbler who said he had been doing this for 25 years, used a mix of folk and Catholic elements in his exorcism. He started by laying a talisman with the blessing "God greet you beloved sun, God greet you beloved moonshine, God greet you son holy spirit, I ask you holy trinity, protect this house from all woes, in the name of God the Father, Son, and Holy Spirit" along with a root under a stone or stoop on three Fridays in succession, and then conducted "the Catholic mass by it, with the placement" of two burning candles where the ghost had appeared. The ceremony was said to have worked, although it's not clear if Zürn simply said so or if the man who hired him really ceased to perceive the specter. Zürn insisted that he drove out the Devil with God's help, justified performing a Catholic mass since "the Emperor himself receives it every day," and said that the spirits he exorcized were bad people who were condemned to wander long on earth, again without any reference to treasure.

In the course of the next case, which took place in 1702, however, what started as a desire to stop the annoying banging sounds ended up becoming a treasure-hunt. Barbara Wenzel Morus, the hospital master's wife, in Izelberg, a village near Heidenheim, began being bothered by banging noises when the lights were out, and she saw an apparition that sometimes looked like a light, and sometimes like a white figure with white hair, that wandered around every night.[261] At one point she felt its touch "like a cold hand on the nape" of her neck, and the next day her "neck was completely swollen." She first tried praying, but when that didn't help, she enlisted the help of Jacob Schweizer in trying to drive it out. Eventually, it was decided that the ghost would not leave until a treasure was dug up. From then on, most appearances of a ghost or spirit led to a treasure-hunt by the commoners involved, the suspicion that the commoners involved were engaged in a treasure-hunt on the part of the government, or some other connection to cash. We have seen, for example, the case in 1721 in which a ghost had been plaguing a farmer's animals, which ended up with the ex-soldier from a village near Strasburg being brought in to help locate a treasure. In the case from 1773 in which Conrad Blencklen's blessing to help a woman whose milk was being stolen resulted in it being returned, it was said that he had been meeting a spirit, a "white shadow" of a man that Blencklen said demanded money for its services, in a stall for the last ten years, which led to him being punished for "blessing, treasure-hunting, and similar superstitious and sinful activities."[262] A structurally related case was the one that took place in the following year in which young Jacob Schu persuaded his 79-year-old master that he had met his deceased wife's ghost, which had said that she would remain trapped on earth unless the old man paid out 1040 Reichstaler to compensate for her sins with her parents and siblings. This also reversed the usual presumed flow of money, but seems related to swindlers' common practice of asking for "advance" or "seed money" as well as the belief that ghosts were bad people condemned to wander long on earth. Even the spontaneous medium Sigried Sattler, who said that "since youth" he had "seen appearances of spirits in many forms" which badgered him "to faithfully pray for them for hours day and night" in order to "release them" got in trouble because he asked permission to hunt for a treasure he said some of them had told him of. This preoccupation with the cash potential of ghost sightings was an historical anomaly, however, for both before and after the eighteenth century the dead were more likely to be thought of as a source of occult knowledge, lost souls who needed help from the living making atonement for some sin that did not involve money, or, most commonly, menacing intruders who sometimes appeared and left on their own, but who sometimes required the magico-religious services of a spiritual specialist to conduct rituals to put an end to their invasive activity.

While cultural conceptions about ghosts and spirits clearly shaped early modern Württembergers' understanding of their perceptions of what they took to be supernatural phenomena, in a few cases they were confronted with events that seemed anomalous even within the extremely broad and variegated framework of their combined folk and elite culture. One of the sampled magic cases and two other incidents recorded in the judicial archive particularly challenged their understanding of the way the world works, just as trying to understand what really happened during them challenges ours. We will look at each in turn, considering how the participants and the government attempted to understand them as well as what they reported took place, and then consider the various possible explanations that might make sense of them in our terms.

One of the incidents took place in Böblingen, a small town just outside of Stuttgart, in 1724. It began shortly after a 78-year-old widow, Jacobina Hutelerin, died and was buried in the communal graveyard. Soon people began seeing strange, fiery lights at night by her grave, and then in her house, in both the room where she died as well as the room where her child had died.[263] Numerous witnesses testified that they saw a "terrifying, first fiery, then dark figure, now like a burning ball, another time like a line going straight up, and another like a bright straw basket that was first in one place and then moved quickly here and there." It was seen "almost every night by all sorts of people in the houses next to the graveyard and even on the graveyard wall," and watching it became so popular "the worldly government found that it had to forbid the activity with threats of punishment." But while some people seem to have enjoyed the show, others were disturbed by it, taking it to be "a trick of the evil enemy" showing that "the person who had been buried in the communal graveyard did not belong there" and foreboding "miserable misfortunes" like fire or destructive storms for the "negligent community."

The only problem with this interpretation was that Hutelerin had led a blameless life. She "went to church faithfully, carried herself quietly, and was buried honorably." After she died and the fiery display started, however, the magistrates reported that "suddenly she had had a treasure-man, because she left behind ... 6000 R. in all; suddenly she was a witch and had a pact with Satan; suddenly she had several times taken and misused earth from the graveyard when the grave digger was digging a grave; suddenly she never agreed to be a godparent when she was asked in order to avoid renouncing Satan; finally it was said, she did not call for a clergyman as she died," because "the evil enemy carried her away." As a consequence, "if not the whole, then the majority of the citizenry" wanted her to be removed from the town cemetery and "transported to a neighboring forest."[264]

The magistrates feared for their lives if a fire or hailstorm should seem to confirm the dire warnings, particularly since a Capuchin monk from nearby Weil der Stadt was stoking people's fears. While they hesitated to recommend that the popular outcry be satisfied by removing Hutelerin from the cemetery, they did suggest to the High Council that her coffin be dug up and opened "to see if anything suspicious was put with her in the casket." However, their investigation had revealed that no-one would come forth and swear to any of the allegations against the woman, and furthermore, while there were many witnesses to the remarkable display, the "figure" it involved was actually a "light as high and thick as an average man that threw fiery sparks out, and other times a dark shape on which one however could not see head nor arms or other human features." In addition, once a guard was posted at the graveyard the ghostly fireworks stopped, so the High Council told the magistrates to hang tough and have the minister preach a sermon against "the unnecessary fear and superstition of the people," pointing out how the government's "firm stand against Satan" defeated "this transparent diabolical illusion."

While both the elite and the people tried to assimilate the fiery show into their conceptual frameworks, neither succeeded very well. The popular notion that such a phenomenon must mean that the recently buried woman was a sinner unworthy of burial in the communal graveyard may have made logical sense of the situation, but it ran afoul of the fact that no one had any evidence, even by the standards of the time, that it was true. The official version that the entire episode was a "transparent diabolical illusion" would seem to have carried the day, except that the one thing that the magistrates' extensive and rigorous inquiry established was that numerous people had, in fact, witnessed the various fiery spectacles, and they agreed substantially about the details of what they saw. The Devil may have been trying to sucker the superstitious people into dishonoring an honorable woman, but his bait seems to have been not an illusion but something that was really there.

It is possible, of course, that the reports were some sort of mass hallucination. However, there is no evidence that the observations followed from any sort of suggestion, for the rumors about Hutelerin appear to have arisen after the displays began rather than vice versa, and they took place not in a single emotional incident, but on a number of different occasions. Furthermore, there are thousands of reports from many different parts of the world going back to antiquity of displays similar to those observed in Böblingen. Skeptical scientists, like the ducal government in Württemberg, long maintained that these observations were illusory, explaining them as some combination of optical illusion and hallucination, but the scientific consensus today is that they reflect a real physical phenomenon called ball lightning.[265] In general, ball lightning appears as a luminous sphere that floats above the ground moving along an erratic path at varying speeds for about a minute and then disappears, but "two of the most characteristic features of ball lightning are the unpredictability of its behavior and the variability of its properties."[266] It often appears during thunderstorms, but can appear in other conditions. It often comes from a lightning strike, but can also come from "a lightning channel in the sky," "fall from a cloud base," appear out of a solid object on the ground, or seemingly come from nowhere. It typically forms a ball from six inches to two feet in width, but can be much larger and it can take other shapes. It generally lasts less than a minute, but can last for several minutes. It usually appears bluish white, but can have other colors. It sometimes creates a hissing sound or an acrid smell, and it sometimes emits a white or bluish mist or sparks. It often enters and moves about in buildings, sometimes through open doors or windows, sometimes through small openings or screens, and sometimes by passing through closed windows or walls. When passing through things, it sometimes causes damage and sometimes does not. Similarly, ball lightning does not put off discernable heat, and yet it can inflict severe burns when it touches people.

The existence of ball lightning may be generally accepted in the scientific community now, but scientists still have little idea what it is. "One of the main problems in understanding ball lightning is that its properties, taken together, seem to be inconsistent with the laws of physics."[267] Another is that "we need to be able to achieve, in the laboratory, conditions that will" create ball lightning in order to systematically study it, but "we do not know how to do this." A wide variety of theories have been put forward to account for the phenomenon, "but none of these theories seem to have gained general acceptance because they fail to explain all the observed characteristics of the phenomenon."[268] Despite the lack of experimental evidence and theoretical explanation, the existence of ball lightning is generally accepted because "most physicists given a description of the natural phenomenon readily suggest an explanation, usually in terms of a plasma" and "only on more complete consideration of the problem" do " the difficulties become evident."[269] Furthermore, despite the lack of experimental evidence or theoretical explanation, ball lightning is now routinely invoked to explain other, even more anomalous luminous phenomena ranging from angels to UFOs, and even the inexplicable movement of heavy objects otherwise ascribed to poltergeists.[270]

While this promiscuous use of the phenomenon may or may not be justified in general, in the case of Böblingen it does seems to be appropriate. The fact that the glowing objects were mainly spherical, bluish-white, moved about erratically and apparently in a horizontal plane, were associated at times with a glowing vertical streak of similar light, emitted sparks, and entered and moved about Hutelerin's house suggests that ball lightning is most likely what the people of Böblingen saw in 1724. However, it should be acknowledged that in reaching this conclusion we are making a leap of faith, an extrapolation based on our generalized confidence in the correspondence of rationalist materialism's symbolic matrix to physcial reality, despite our lack of experimental evidence or a theoretical explanation of this specific phenomenon, or even complete agreement among experts in the field that it actually exists. Furthermore, there are some ways that the observations recorded in the archives don't fit ball lightning or that ball lightning can't explain, specifically the dark form that was observed, the repeated appearances night after night, and, most significantly, the fact that the glowing globules not only appeared at the graveyard, but also entered the woman's house and went to the very rooms where she died and where her child had died.[271] Of course, we can hypothesize that the dark form could have been some sort of an afterimage produced by staring at the bright light and the repeated appearances on succeeding nights were a meteorological anomaly, and, scientifically speaking, we have to regard the choice of rooms as either a misperception or false memory on the part of the witnesses or, if the testimony was accurate, simply a coincidence. However, these explanations, like the explanations of ball lightning itself at this point, are just speculation. In its way, the eerie display of nocturnal lights in Böblingen in 1724 challenges our scientific explanatory system as much as it did the magical and religious explanatory systems of the people at the time.

The second of the three anomalous cases took place over 100 years earlier, in the village of Stauffen, near Göppingen, in 1614. In late July, Hannß Vogel, the mayor, who was married and had five children, complained to the district magistrates that "three weeks" earlier his "family noticed" that "all was not right in" their house.[272] "Specifically, cherry pits began to fall on it," and "no one could figure out how this could happen or where they came from." This mysterious bombardment continued for three days and then subsided, but then resumed with the cherry pits "replaced by other, larger stones ... which weighed 1, 2, 6, 7, up to 14 pounds each." They "continued the fourth day ... and almost every day" thereafter, although the projectiles had changed to hazelnuts. Furthermore, Vogel's daughter's "new dress in a locked trunk, and also the calendar on the wall were torn," and the day before the report was written, Vogel unexpectedly "smelled smoke strongly," but when he and his "family thoroughly searched every nook and cranny of the house" they "could find nothing." By this time he not surprisingly "feared that this mysterious thing threatened" him and his family's "lives and property," and so turned to the government for help, even though he had to admit that neither he nor anyone else had "any idea or suspicion" who might be responsible.

The High Council told the magistrates of Göppingen to find out "what the mayor of Stauffen, his wife, and entire household's conduct has been until now, if they faithfully go to church to hear sermons on God's word and also take the Holy Sacraments." They also instructed them to "find out about the neighbors, if they are not suspected of witchcraft or other things," and told them to move the family "into another house, and carefully watch if the audacious activity can be seen to continue around the empty house." The magistrates followed these instructions, and found that witnesses confirmed that the barrages had taken place, that Vogel and his family had a good reputation, and that no one in the area was suspected of witchcraft.[273] Two women also testified that they had "heard a pitiful cry of misery and wail of sorrow, like a young child or sick person" coming from the area of the mayor's house, although they were not sure if it came from inside or out, and a man testified "that he knew that a fiery specter had been seen there twenty years before." Further investigation by the magistrates revealed that the mayor had four daughters, the youngest of whom was seven, and a young son; no one in the house had been sick recently; they had not heard the cries the women reported, although they had heard the yowling of cats.[274] "In the meantime," though, "no further tumult, knocks, throwing, or such" had "been detected" at the house. Presumably the barrages had ceased, for this was the last report.

At the time, several explanations for the mysterious barrages were proposed, at least by implication. Vogel's insistence that he had no "idea or suspicion" of who might be responsible indicates that he thought in terms of some malicious person. Similarly, the High Council's inquiry about his and his family's reputation and witchcraft suspicions suggests that they also thought so, although their question about the Vogels implies that they were considering the possibility that the complaint might be unreliable or that someone within the household might be responsible for the problem, as well as the possibility that it was a malicious neighbor. Vogel's initial complaint does not make it clear if he thought the projectiles were being thrown by someone hiding in the bushes or magically, but the High Council's question about witchcraft indicates that they were open to the possibility of magic. The neighbor who mentioned the "fiery specter" from 20 years before was suggesting another source of magical power, a ghost or spirit, but nobody seems to have picked up on that. Similarly, the magistrates ruled out witchcraft, found no evidence of a surreptitious vandal, and established the Vogels' reliability, so the incident ended as ambiguously as it began.

From our point of view, there are four possible explanations for this incident. The first is that it was all a lie made up by Vogel and his family for some unknown reason. The second is that it was some sort of collective delusion or series of mass hallucinations. The third is that it was a malicious prank played by someone with a secret grudge against the man or someone in his family, and the fourth possibility is that it was a genuine poltergeist phenomenon, assuming such things can happen. The magistrates' investigation makes the first possibility seem very unlikely, for not only did the Vogels have a good reputation, but there was no motive for a fraud, and other witnesses said they had heard the stones hitting the house and seen them on the ground. This last bit of evidence also rules out the second possibility; something clearly was really going on physcially. Poltergeist incidents have been reported since antiquity and studied by scientists, and incidents in which stones are said to have flown against the outsides of houses are not unknown.[275] In fact, one of the earliest known cases, a story about an incident in 355 AD. "recounted by Jacob Grimm in his *Deutsche Mythology* ... reported how a house was bombarded by stones while blows erupted from its walls." Items also are supposed to have been removed from locked containers, and objects are frequently reported destroyed or damaged. However, the reality of such poltergeist phenomena is strongly disputed within the scientific community, and the various phenomena reported in this case could well have been caused by a vandal, so we must conclude, despite the lack of evidence, that what most likely plagued the Vogel family in Stauffen in 1614 was a stealthy secret enemy (somewhat like the one who broke into Christoph Martin's house in Illsfelden in 1662), who repeatedly hid near the house – at first with a basket of cherry pits, then a collection of stones, and finally a bunch of hazelnuts – and chucked them onto the roof, later broke into the house and ripped up one girl's dress and a calendar on the wall, and finally brought a smoldering stick or something into the house to create a smoky smell and snuck it out before anyone could find it. Once the family had been driven out of the house, the vandal stopped. Whether the Vogels ever returned to the house is not known.

The incident in Stauffen was just one of a number of cases reported to the ducal High Council that we would call poltergeist incidents, whatever the source of the disturbances they involved. To begin with, one of the ghost appearances connected with treasure-hunting had poltergeist-like features: the case in Alpirsbach in 1698 involving the apparition that bounced around Georg Mutschler's house "making a loud noise" (*"starkhen Poldern"*) that sounded like many coins dropping.[276] Another of the cases was the investigation already mentioned of the weaver Conrad Hahn in 1705 for suspected use of magic to enhance his productivity. The magistrates' inquiry started when Hahn sought help because his tools and materials were being mysteriously destroyed and his house ransacked, a perplexing streak of vandalism which climaxed, after repeated but futile efforts to secure them, as his family was moving its things "for safe keeping from the house to the church." As the family's belongings were being carried, suddenly, "in the open," in front of "the preacher and his son-in-law ... three bolts" of cloth that had been "put in the arms of a boy" were "seized and destroyed" by something imperceptible.[277] Although they tried strenuously, the magistrates could not find a way to explain either the destruction of tools and household items or the dramatic scene with the cloth, and in the end had to content themselves with warning Hahn that they knew his extraordinary production must have been achieved unnaturally, intimating that his woes were therefore an unnatural retribution for his sin. Hahn, however, denied having engaged in any magic to enhance his productivity, and by implication that his troubles stemmed from any blowback from a diabolic pact, leaving the explanation for the incident contested. The third case involving a poltergeist occurred in 1729 when Christoph Ernst Dumme testified that he consulted the potter and cunning man Hans Jacob Schiller from Murrhardt about a "rambunctious spirit" ("*Polter Geist*," the origin of modern German as well as English term) in his house, and Schiller said it was caused by the witchcraft of a boy whose father was involved in a lawsuit against him. No witch trials seems to have resulted from this allegation, however, and in general these cases suggest that while poltergeist experiences were known to early modern Württembergs, they proved as difficult to integrate into their collective understanding of the world as they are for ours.

This impression is reinforced by consideration of one of the sampled cases of generalized magic, which combined poltergeist phenomena and a hostile apparition. It took place in the district of Balingen in 1744, and centered on Agnes Beck, a 35-year-old woman from the village of Walstettin who had suffered from an arthritic malady since birth.[278] She had always managed to be lively and spry, however, until after her second child was born. When she became pregnant for the third time her condition worsened considerably. She had to remain in bed, for her hands and feet became completely paralyzed. When she was in what she calculated to be her tenth month of pregnancy, she came to the attention of the magistrates because she complained that she suffered from a most unusual affliction.

Agnes said that for more than a year, but particularly since her pregnancy had immobilized her, she had been plagued by a ghost that hit her and scratched her so hard that it drew blood.[279] For most of the time she had not seen anything, just felt the blows and scrapes, but more recently she had seen the figure of a woman who carried out the assaults. One day, she impulsively struck at a cat, and that night the apparition berated her as it attacked, crying, "Barren one! ... You could not get me with your lame bones."[280] Agnes also reported that "splinters, fragments of glass, trash, scrap metal, and needles" came out of her uterus, and her sister-in-law confirmed seeing these objects lying beneath her on the floor. Agnes said that she had consulted a healer, who had not been able to help, and a doctor who refused to believe her. The magistrates called her problems the "illusions of a corrupt fantasy" caused by the pain of her overdue pregnancy, while the High Council commented, "one does not know what to believe of what she says."[281] They instructed the magistrates to bring her to Balingen, separate her from anyone who might help her with a fraud, have the town doctor and the preacher try to help her, and have the surgeon keep her under observation.

The town fathers dutifully brought Agnes from her village and set her up in the surgeon's house.[282] The first night she was there, she slept alone in the living room while the family retired to their bedrooms. Between 11 o' clock and midnight, she suddenly began screaming in terror, and when the surgeon ran out of his bedroom he saw that her face was covered with blood, but "her hands and her fingers were not in the least stained with blood." When she calmed down, Agnes told the surgeon that the apparition had attacked her again, while snarling, " You bad woman! What do you think you are doing here?"

The next night, the surgeon's son, who was himself a surgeon, remained in Agnes' room with the light on, and nothing happened. The following night, however, all was quiet until about midnight, when suddenly three milk pitchers on the far side of the stove from Agnes "did not fall," the young man reported, "but rather were hurled forcefully against the oven so that they broke into many pieces, and at the same time the oven bench was thrown with great force to the floor." The witness said he was awake when it happened, and he jumped up and saw Agnes still in bed under the covers. Nothing more happened in that room, but the surgeon's son-in-law who was sleeping in another room "reported that just after the great tumult ... a noise ... went by his room" that sounded "like a flock of pigeons brushed their wings on his wall and flew out through the back window."

Almost immediately after that night the magistrates noted that "the woman had a strong impatience to go home" to her family. The doctor treated her with incense so she would "remain further from the fascination" while the town preacher gave her spiritual counseling, but they soon concluded that their efforts had had such "good effect" that she could go, although it was "recommended that her pastor exercise further close spiritual oversight" over her.

As with the incident in Stauffen, there were several competing interpretations of Agnes' travails at the time. She herself clearly thought that she was being attacked by a ghost or spirit, a disembodied being who somehow was able to inflict injuries and talk to her while both visible and invisible. We don't know what the healer's diagnosis or treatment was, but the doctor she consulted thought she was simply making her story up. The High Councilors also indicated they thought this was possible, at least in part, while the magistrates called her initial complaints "illusions" and "fantasy" caused by her condition. It seems notable that not only was there no talk of witchcraft, as there was in 1614, but also there was not even any talk of the Devil, as there had been in 1705. Nevertheless, in the end the members of the local elite and the ducal councilors seem to have come to a consensus that her problem was both medical and spiritual, although exactly how the two were combined, and how these problems of hers related to the various moving objects and the sound that was heard in the hall was left unresolved.

From our point of view, there are three possible explanations for Agnes Beck's story: fraud, delusion, or some paranormal phenomenon, a poltergeist. The first, fraud, seems very unlikely based on the documents. Claims of visions, convulsions, and the passing of strange objects from various orifices had long been made, and the possibility of fraud was recognized long before there was scientific concern because of the church's desire to screen out false miracles.[283] A number of cases in Württemberg occurred around the time in which children made such claims, and it was established that they had been "encouraged by ... godless" parents hoping to "make a business" on their "pretended visions."[284] One of these incidents took place just a few years earlier, in Marbach, about 40 miles to the north, in 1739. One more followed in the same town six years after the incident involving Agnes, in 1750, while a third similar case took place in Onstmettingen in 1752. It is certainly possible that, inspired by talk of the first incident, Agnes made up her stories about the apparition, which, after all, only she could see, inflicted her cuts and bruises on herself, and surreptitiously put the objects that appeared beneath her there. However, the government was clearly alert to the possibility of fraud, made provision to block it, and concluded that it was not the answer in this case. Neither Agnes nor her family appears to have tried to profit from the situation or had any other motive to commit fraud; she would have had to have performed some feats of sleight of hand that she was by all accounts incapable of; and she would have had to persuade people to participate in the fraud who had no reason to do so, who had, in fact, been selected for their disinterestedness and reliability.

If fraud seems unlikely, delusion, the conclusion of the provincial elite, seems more probable. As we have seen, apparitions can be generated within the visual cortex by mixing percepts and internally generated imagery, while "ugly looking welts, red scratches, or actual teeth marks ... can be produced ... by the use of hypnotic suggestion." In one modern poltergeist case centered on a young girl, "the raising of these bite and welt marks were even filmed ... A close up shot shows horrid looking welts raising on her body."[285] Agnes was clearly a person in deep distress, and the apparition's bitter words suggest that she was tremendously frustrated by her disability; her lively mind rebelled at being encased in a paralyzed body. It is possible that this psychological pressure drove her to commit conscious fraud for some reason, but it seems more likely that she really did perceive the hallucinations and inflict the injuries through the kind of psychophysical processes we have examined earlier.

The physical movement of objects recorded in the documents, however, and the sounds in the hall heard by the surgeon's son-in-law pose a challenge to this theory. The young man's hearing, of course, could have been affected by fears and expectations generated by the spooky events that had already happened, and it is possible that Agnes collected the items that collected between her legs while in a dissociated state, a sort of waking sleepwalking, since the only witness, her sister-in-law, admitted that she had not actually seen the items come out of Agnes, and things coming out of the womb from a woman disabled by an overdue pregnancy seems like a pretty clear form of symbolic acting out. The smashing of the three pitchers against the oven and the slamming of the bench to the floor, however, cannot be accounted for so easily. There seem to be four possibilities: first, collusion between Agnes and the surgeon's son; second, the young man's account is inaccurate either because he misperceived a natural fall of the pitchers and bench as they happened or he misremembered what had happened after the fact; third, some sort of focused geological or other environmental disturbance that dislodged the pitchers and upset the bench without disturbing anything else in the house or being noticed by anyone; and fourth, some sort of paranormal psychokinesis.

The first of these possibilities, fraud, has already been discussed, and, while it cannot be ruled out categorically, in this case seems unlikely. The second, some sort of misperception or mistaken memory on the part of the surgeon's son, is also possible, but since there is no evidence for it, it seems reasonable to consider it only if the other possibilities are ruled out or deemed less likely. The third, some sort of subtle environmental disturbance, is theoretically possible, but while some attempts have been made to correlate apparent paranormal phenomena with geomagnetic forces, no specific physical mechanism for the movement of large objects has been set forth that has garnered even the level of support of the theories of ball lightning, and most accounts involve a role for human actors in the events as well as environmental forces.[286] The fourth possibility is unlikely on a priori grounds, but, given the weakness of the other three possibilities, would seem to warrant closer consideration.

To begin with, poltergeist phenomena can be understood in two ways. One is a phenomenological one: a set of events and experiences that are understood to be caused by poltergeists regardless of their actual physical origin. About 375 events that can be seen as poltergeists had been recorded since antiquity at various places around the world before systematic study began in the 1960s, and a number have been reported and studied since then.[287] They have been found to conform to "a rather standard pattern." The most common features are that "objects" are seen to "move about or break by themselves." They often seem to have been "flung across rooms or ... moved along weird trajectories." Other features include apparent teleportation, in which "objects ... turn up in unusual places," apparitions, and "bite marks, lacerations, and wounds." The perceived disturbances generally center on one person, and appear to "follow ... if they move to a new residence." The central figure is often an adolescent, but "sometimes it is a mentally disturbed child or adult." The phenomena generally last only a few weeks or months, "and once a poltergeist" incident ceases, "it rarely recurs."

By this standard, the events surrounding Agnes Beck constitute a poltergeist incident, and, as we have seen, mostly involve phenomena which, while dramatic, can be understood as normal, if uncommon, physical and physiological processes. However, within the phenomenological descriptions of poltergeist phenomena are events like the flinging of the pitchers and overturning of the bench that, if they really happen, can only be explained paranormally, which is the other, more specific meaning of the word. There is no way to systematically examine the events of 1744, of course, but in trying to determine what actually happened in that historical incident, it would seem to be worth noting what recent scientific studies have found. First of all, there is no question that frauds have been perpetrated, in which mysterious noises and movements of objects were faked, sometimes via elaborate, carefully prepared means. Secondly, most of the other reported poltergeist events have occurred in circumstances where systematic study has not been possible, and all that is known is what the witnesses claim. However, thirdly, several incidents have been the subject of extensive systematic study. One, which occurred in 1967 in Miami, a poltergeist was reported to be "creating havoc in a local warehouse, breaking numerous beer mugs, ash trays, vases, and other crockery."[288] Over the next 24 days "police, reporters, and TV and radio men" investigated and "witnessed numerous activities no one could explain." A local magician "was called upon to duplicate the crashing and falling of objects, but he could not." Eventually several physicists were "brought in ... to analyze the movements of the objects." They concluded that the "torques and twists ... are not explainable according to the laws of physical motion, as understood today." The second incident took place in Rosenheim, Germany in 1968, was even more thoroughly studied by a professor at the University of Freiburg, and the movements of objects were filmed. It involved inexplicable noises and movements of objects, but perhaps the most significant feature in terms of the systematic study was "frequent calls ... to the local time number." These so disturbed the German post office and telephone company that the telephone system was completely overhauled, and then sealed off." Eventually, "the postal authorities tore up the offices and the road outside, trying unsuccessfully to find out how the telephones could ring when no one was dialing a number." Two physicists from the Max Planck Institute undertook an elaborate and intensive investigation. They "carefully eliminated or controlled all the conceivable physical causes" and concluded that "the phenomena are not explicable by the available means of theoretical physics." However, they noted that, "the anomalous deflections only occur when a certain employee ... is in the immediate vicinity ... a case unforeseen in physics."

While these accounts may seem compelling, the possibility of the phenomena they describe has not been confirmed to the scientific community's satisfaction in controlled laboratory experiments. There have been a number of studies of purportedly gifted individuals in laboratory settings who, it is claimed, were able to cause objects to move without physical contact or known remote influences like magnets; repeated and refined experiments involving rolling dice using increasingly automated mechanisms and procedures to remove the effects of human movements, the weight differentials caused by the different number of holes on each side, and conscious or unconscious misrecording of the results; repeated and refined experiments in which attempts were made to influence the generation of random numbers by computers; and a variety of other experiments to test for some sort of psycho-physical influence.[289] Some of these experiments have generated impressive statistical results; some have not. Many have been criticized for methodological flaws, and replicability, while sometimes achieved, has not been reliable.[290] Meta-analyses have been conducted showing overall positive results, but the statistical procedures have been disputed, and the validity of using statistical analysis of trials against chance expectations at all has been called into question.[291] There is a community of scientists who accept the reality of these phenomena and now work to understand the factors that generate and influence them better, but there is a community of skeptics who hotly dispute the very existence of any paranormal effects, and most scientists, who have no direct involvement in the debate, pay little attention to it, perhaps believing that there might be something there, but at the same time believing that it has not been conclusively established. The current deadlock leaves the status quo in place, which means that phenomena like those reported in Miami, in 1967, and Rosenheim, in 1968, cannot have happened, and since, once again, we can hardly provide a decisive voice in this matter based on a single 250-year-old incident, best scientific explanation for the "hurled pitchers" and "thrown bench" is that the three pitchers must have all been carelessly left in a precarious position and due to some vibration in the floor or gradually slipping fell against the oven, and as they broke the shards pushed over the bench, all of which the young man, in his excited state, misperceived as the objects being "hurled" and "thrown."

Conclusion

If recent scientific works leave us with an uncertain understanding of the sort of phenomena like the fiery display in Böblingen and Agnes Beck's poltergeist experience that early modern Württembergers, too, found difficult to explain in terms of their understandings of the world, we have seen in this chapter that it does provide significant insight into the much larger body of activities that made up beneficent manipulative magic. In particular, we have seen that the great bulk of beneficent magic was employed for healing, and involved a wide array of activities that mobilized a variety of bodily mechanisms that do, in fact, promote health and well-being. Some of these worked through conscious beliefs and symbolic meanings, but others, as we have seen with sorcery and witchcraft, worked through unconscious, autonomic processes that had direct physiological effects unmediated by personal belief or cultural meaning. Similarly, magical rituals could be performed to effectively counter occult aggression and enhance performance in other aspects of life. As with sorcery and shamanism, a crucial aspect of beneficent magic is that to a very considerable degree it works by manipulating – tuning or fine-tuning – the human nervous system, dramatically or subtly altering consciousness in order to access knowledge and powers not accessible in normal waking consciousness. The point is not simply to recognize that there were more valid features of early modern popular magic than is generally currently acknowledged, but to understand that beneficent popular magic, sorcery, and witchcraft were all part of a system of activities, experiences, and beliefs that not only made sense in terms of their relationship to each other, but also made sense in terms of their relationship to physical reality: the physical reality of the external world, the physical reality of the human nervous system, and the physical realities of the interactions between the two.

Part IV Repression and Reality

Introduction

We have seen in the first three parts of this book that witchcraft and popular magic in the early modern period were significantly more strongly connected to reality than most historical and other scholarly accounts currently portray. The question this raises, of course, is why this should be so. The answer, of course is a huge topic that stretches far beyond the bounds of the current study geographically, chronologically, and conceptually, having to do with the whole series of cultural, socioeconomic, and even political changes that have taken place over the last few centuries to produce the modern understanding of nature, humankind, and the relationship between the two. However, since the changes that led to this situation began in many ways during the period under consideration, and to a significant extent were because of developments in learned culture that reflected as well as informed the experiences of local elites like those in Württemberg, examining the changing place of magic in the duchy's society and culture should shed some light on this process. In examining the realities of early modern *maleficium*, diabolism, and beneficent magic we have already seen a number of specific changes that were part of the larger development of the early modern understanding of the world: the shifting framework of moral judgments from the local community to the wider world; evolving mechanisms of psychological control; changing concepts about the boundaries of the self; competing explanations for unusual perceptions, abnormal abilities, and anomalous events; and a growing awareness of the credulous misconceptions, deliberate misrepresentations, and outright fabrications in the theory and practice of much magical activity. To conclude this study, in Part IV we will look systematically at the changing place of magic in Württemberg in particular and Europe in general by examining the interaction between the provincial government and the ordinary people during the course of the trials that took place as part of the elite's systematic attempt to suppress popular magic from the beginnings of the witch persecutions in the sixteenth century through the triumph of the Enlightenment in the eighteenth.

8
Magic and Society

In this chapter we will examine the ways in which the systematic campaign of repression that the trials for witchcraft and beneficent magic alike were part of affected the place of magic in early modern society and culture. We will start by looking more directly than heretofore at the social position of practitioners of beneficent magic, then consider the range of repressive mechanisms that were in place in early modern society, and conclude by examining the changing pace of prosecutions for various magical activities in relationship to the intertwined evolution of elite and popular culture. The upshot of this process, as we shall see, was that while the duchy's elite did not succeed in eliminating all unauthorized magical practices, as it had hoped, its systematic campaign of repression, along with other changes in society and culture, did alter reality to the point that the elite's concept of reality could be altered in turn, consolidating the gains (and losses) of the early modern period by putting in place crucial cultural constraints on perception and cognition that are central to our enlightened modern sensibility.

Practitioners of beneficent magic

We have seen that people throughout early modern society employed a variety of forms of shamanistic activity to gain insight into their situations, protect themselves from occult threats, and mobilize their own spiritual resources. At one extreme, the devout prayed to God, and in Catholic territories his agents, to guide them, defend them, and advance their interests. At the other extreme, a segment of the population knew "hardly the least of God's Word," but deployed a full arsenal of "blessings and other forbidden arts" to achieve their ends.[1] In between, the great majority of people casually employed an eclectic blend of magic and religion in their daily routines, while utilizing the services of spiritual specialists in moments of particular need. The religious specialists, of course, were the clergy, while the magical specialists were a variety of popular practitioners. In Württemberg, some of these were actually Catholic clergymen from neighboring territories, and gypsies and other itinerants were occasionally consulted, but the great majority were local practitioners, known by a variety of titles like *"Segensprechern"* (blessers), *"Wahrsagern"* (soothsayers), *"Teufelsbannern"* (exorcists), *"Teufelsbeschworern"* (demon incanters), *"Teufelsmänner"* (Devil's men), *"Zauberern"* (magicians), *"zauberische Leute"* (magical people), and even plain *"Weiblin"* (little woman).[2] Many historians have come to refer to these magical practitioners collectively as "cunning folk," but others have argued to restrict this designation to the subset who offered a range of magical services, as opposed to charmers, fortune-tellers, and other specialized practitioners who offered just one.[3]

In previous chapters, we have used the term "cunning folk" casually, in its broader sense of anyone who practiced magic for others, but here we will begin by focusing on a different distinction, a distinction between practitioners of healing and other beneficent magic for themselves and their immediate circle of household and family, who will be referred to as private practitioners, and those who served a broader clientele, public practitioners. The line between them was not always hard and fast, of course, for someone who acted mainly as a private practitioner might minister to a person they were less close to in certain circumstances, particularly since neighborliness seems to have included the provision of soups and home remedies when a member of the local community fell ill, *gratis* and sometimes even unsolicited, but there does seem to have been a discernable distinction between people who generally confined their activities to their close circle and offered them casually and others who offered them more deliberately and more widely.

The cases discussed in the previous two chapters suggest that the public practitioners played an important role in the practice and transmission of popular magical traditions, and that they were frequently the objects of the judicial prosecutions of beneficent magic. There is also evidence that the witch persecutions affected at least some of them strongly, and, indeed, the effects of the witch persecutions on them constitute one important strand of evidence that these, and the broader prosecution of magic that the witch trials were part of, had a more significant impact on European society and culture than historians have generally recognized.

Among the sampled cases of blessing and illicit healing (which together involved most health-care-oriented magic) the majority of suspects, 16 of 23, or two-thirds, were public practitioners, and they were involved in 14 of the 17 cases, or over 80 percent.[4] In contrast, in the 20 sampled treasure-hunting and incantation trials (most of which, as we have seen, basically involved treasure-hunting), public practitioners made up only about 12 percent of the 109 suspects and were involved in only half of the 20 incidents.[5] The difference may have been that ordinary Württembergers were readier to undertake treasure magic than healing magic, but may also have been that treasure-hunting tended to be a group effort which involved going to the location where the treasure was thought to be hidden, and was therefore difficult even for casual practitioners to keep secret, while magical healing rituals could be conducted by one or two people in the privacy of their home.

Among the ten sampled general magic trials that did not involve witchcraft, one was the extensive treasure-hunting scandal in Böblingen that involved at least 20 participants, two of whom were known to have been specialized consultants.[6] Another four of these cases stemmed from the activities of healers who practiced publicly, while five involved individuals (or in one case a small group) investigated for using magic to enhance their own abilities.[7] Overall, these cases support the impression of the more specific samples discussed earlier: while ordinary Württembergers may have practiced magic on their own, there was a network of public practitioners available to supplement their amateur efforts with greater skills and esoteric knowledge that they patronized when the potential rewards seemed great or the need particularly compelling.[8] These practitioners dominated the healing cases and the cases involving divination to detect lost objects and identify thieves, and they often acted as consultants brought in by the leaders of the much larger groups of ordinary Württembergers involved in treasure-hunting. They reinforced the place of magic in popular culture by their general example, by showing specific techniques to clients in the course of rendering their services, and by teaching their techniques to protégés.

In Part III we looked at the magical practices that were employed by both public and private practitioners in early modern Württemberg; here we will take a closer look at the practitioners themselves. Our focus will be on the public practitioners, although we will take a brief look toward the end of this section at the relatively small number of private practitioners who were caught up in the judicial process. The public practitioners offered a wide range of services: healing of people and animals through a combination of incantations, medicines, ritual actions, and magically potent objects; divination to identify witches and thieves and to locate lost objects and treasures; counter spells against witches and thieves; and exorcism and invocation of spirits, most commonly as part of treasure-hunting, but occasionally for other purposes. The proportion that each of these practices made up of the services they rendered was generally similar to the rates at which the activities were recorded in the sampled trials overall, except that treasure-hunting was somewhat less common, and healing correspondingly more. Healing made up almost 45 percent of all the services offered by public practitioners in all the sampled trials for beneficent magic (22 of 51), identifying thieves and witchcraft and locating things made up about 20 percent (10), and helping with treasure-hunting just under 30 percent (15).[9] As we have seen, public practitioners may have been underrepresented in treasure-hunting cases because ordinary people were particularly ready to undertake this on their own, without the help of a specialist, but it may also be that ordinary people were particularly likely to get caught in this activity since it involved a group, whereas most other forms of magic could be conducted secretly when done privately, and these other forms were therefore most likely to come to the authorities' attention when a specialist became involved. In any case, the important point here is that public practitioners were involved in a wide range of magical activities, both practicing them themselves and acting as examples and as sources of knowledge for ordinary folk.[10]

There were two basic types of public practice, although many actual practitioners' activities fell somewhere between the two poles. At one end were single-service practitioners, who specialized in one specific type of magical activity. Hans Röcklin, for example, used his "crystal stone" and slight variants of a single charm to cure tumors in children and swelling and stiffness in horses, and most of the practitioners involved in treasure-hunting appear to have worked that kind of magic alone.[11] Similarly, two of the three women tried in Sindelfingen in 1596 for blessings seem to have had an equally limited repertoire: Gertrudt Raitsen used blessings to heal burns and staunch bleeding, and Sara Sauter had one to help babies gain weight. The third, however, Barbara Breüninger, who was being investigated for curing goiter and rings around the eyes with blessings, "uttered many bad words" when she was questioned and said that even "if a gaggle of preachers" were to interrogate her, "she would still not tell everything that she used," implying that her healing practices were considerably more diverse than the officials were aware, and thus fell closer to the other end of the spectrum, practitioners who offered an array of services instead of just one.[12] Clearer examples of such practitioners included Wieland, who used divination to identify thieves and locate lost objects in addition to using amulets and talismans to heal various ailments; Georg Hofen – who served as the expert in the treasure-hunt led by Christoph Keller, dowsing with two knitting needles to pinpoint the treasure's location and size, specifying the items needed in the ceremony to contact the spirit guarding the treasure, and then leading the invocation itself – and also gave Keller's wife "internal medicine" and performed other "forbidden cures" as well; and Zimmerman Scholderer, who advised Hanns Jerg Stadi in his hunt for the treasure he saw in his mirror, and admitted that he had practiced magical healing since he was a child.[13] One particularly good example of the well-rounded generalized practitioner who formed the other extreme from Röcklin, Raitsen, and Sauter, a "cunning man" in the narrower sense of the term, was Hans Köll, the cow herder from Owen, near Kirchheim, who treated Anna Eberlin, in 1660, after she thought she had had sex with the Devil. Owen had her gather and prepare herbal medicines and put an amulet around her neck. Around the same time he was investigated for divining who stole a man's money and also for claiming to have located a missing person, and he said that he had treated other women plagued by the Devil in the past. Another good example of this sort of robust generalist was "Schafer J," who used both herbal medicines and blessings to cure people and animals of natural ailments and to counteract *maleficium*, identified the witches responsible for the latter, and offered his services to exorcize a bothersome spirit from a house.[14] Overall, 18 of the 35 public practitioners in the sampled cases of beneficent magic, just over 50 percent, were generalists, while 17, just under 50 percent, appear to have been single-service providers.[15] Public magical practitioners thus seem to have been rather evenly divided between those offering a single service and those offering a variety.

The 17 specialists tended to offer one of the two services: healing of natural ailments (6) or treasure-hunting (10).[16] Only one, Hanns Jacob Kurzen – an extremely poor old man from Steinach, prosecuted in 1752 – specialized in identifying and treating supernatural injury caused by witches, specifically harm to animals, and none identified thieves, located missing people or objects, or performed invocations or exorcisms unrelated to treasure-finding.[17] In contrast, while 15 of the 18 generalists helped with healing and five assisted with treasure-hunting, about a third (6) identified witches and treated the ailments ascribed to witchcraft, three identified thieves, and several located objects and exorcized bothersome spirits from houses.[18]

Just as the services provided by the two types of practitioners overlapped considerably but differed in some significant ways, the ways in which the two types learned their techniques also showed important commonalities and differences. Unfortunately, while the magistrates often tried to determine where a suspect had learned his or her art, this information is only known for 16 of the 35 public practitioners. Of the seven single-service providers for whom this is known, two learned from their fathers, one from an "old aunt" (which might mean a relative or might mean an elderly neighbor), one from a man she knew in a neighboring village, and one from a treasure-hunter with whom he worked, while only one learned from an "itinerant" (*Landfahrer*) and one appears to have learned from a book.[19] In contrast, among the eight generalists for whom this information is known, only two learned from a relative or neighbor, the healer Barbara Weylandt, who said she learned from her uncle (who she said had learned from a barber), and Barbara Breüninger. One appears to have been self-taught from books, while three said that they had learned from "itinerant scholars" – Hans Haasen, who said he had become one himself after his stay on the Venusberg; "Schafer J"; and Paul Zürn, who exorcized spirits from houses. "Schafer J" said he had also learned from someone who had been burned as a witch in Nagold.[20] Jacob Schäffer said he learned from an Anabaptist and Conrad Stier said he learned from shepherds and an executioner. While the numbers are small, there does seem to be a definite tendency for specialists to have learned from a family member or neighbor, while the generalized practitioners seem to have learned more commonly from itinerants or other more distant, marginal figures. This difference, like the difference in emphasis in services offered, does not suggest a polarized occupational structure, but instead a gradation from practitioners who were ordinary members of their community with a simple sideline to more distinct practitioners who had stronger ties to the marginal members of the community and the itinerants who circulated around the region. Like Apolonia Walther, the witch suspect who called the Devil "her prince" and associated with magical practitioners in the Reutlingen area, and Hanß Jacob Langen, the young ne'r-do-well who fell in with a charlatan and traveled "on the pitchfork" at various brewers' houses, these cases suggest that there was in the region a loose network of magical practitioners, some of whom led a peripatetic existence and some of whom were part of the settled community, who shared techniques and, to some extent, materials, sometimes practiced together, and who passed on their knowledge and skills to younger people, who carried on the traditions.

Information about the socioeconomic circumstances of the various specialized practitioners reinforces this impression of substantial similarities, with important differences indicative of a subtle gradation between relatively well-integrated members of the community and more marginal characters overlapping with the itinerant population. Overall, the practitioners came from what might be called the lower middle class and lower class of provincial society. The information that was recorded about them most consistently was about where they lived. It is given for all but four of the 35, and can be inferred for two from their occupations (shepherd and forester).[21] Only one, Hans Haasen, seems to have been itinerant; the rest had a fixed residence.[22] Both generalists and specialists included people from both towns and villages, but only three of the 18 generalists were from towns, while seven of the 17 single-service providers were townspeople, suggesting that generalist practitioners were more commonly found in the countryside, while, perhaps not surprisingly, practitioners in towns were more likely to specialize.[23]

Occupational information was recorded for 20 of the 35 suspects, which shows that they included a few minor officials (an almshouse administrator, a scribe, a former village headman, and a priest); a number of tradesmen (a cobbler, a potter, a smith, two masons, a bather, and a weaver); a charcoal maker; several herders (two shepherds and a cow herder); a forest ranger and a hunter; one day laborer; one former farmer who had lost his farm; a man with no real job; and the "itinerant scholar" Hans Haasen.[24] Miscellaneous observations about the general financial status of suspects was recorded for 13 of the 35, ten of whom, it was noted, were doing poorly, while two were doing well, and one had a servant.[25] Interestingly, all four of the officials were single-service providers (and all were involved in treasure-hunting), and only two of the single-service providers were noted to be poor, although most of the others had somewhat marginal positions like forest ranger, hunter, shepherd, and laborer. In contrast, all the tradesmen but the smith were generalized practitioners, and eight of the ten people who were noted to be financially distressed were generalists.

It has been noted elsewhere in Europe that magical practices were frequently a supplementary and sometimes a primary source of income for poor, marginal people, and that seems to have been the case in Württemberg as well.[26] Pricing structures were not recorded in many of the sampled trials, but while Barbara Weylandt protested that she often charged nothing or just the cost of medicines procured from an apothecary, two, Jacob Schafer and Peter Jergle, had standard fees of 3 Reichstaler and 2 Reichstaler respectively if they succeeded, with Jergle saying that anything more was up to the patient. Significantly, Schafer's price was in 1600 Reichstaler, while Jergle's was in 1750 Reichstaler, which were worth about 50 percent less, so Schafer's fee was actually three times higher than Jergle's.[27] This may explain not only why Jergle mentioned being open to additional payment, but also why Schafer was the only healer about whom it was said that he made enough to "buy real estate every year". Financially successful practitioners have been noted from England as well, but most practitioners in Württemberg, like those in most other places, appear to have either been people of modest means who offered their services for little profit, like Weylandt, or who lived in strained circumstances and enjoyed at most a modest profit from small cash payments and contributions in kind.[28]

Since all of the tradesmen lived in villages, where they had a less central position than urban artisans did in their towns, this data again suggests that while most specialized practitioners of magic were on the lower side of the social hierarchy, generalists tended to be somewhat more marginal than single-service providers, an impression reinforced by the information the magistrates recorded about ten of the practitioners' reputations in their communities. Two, one generalist and one specialist, were well regarded, but the other eight were regarded poorly by their communities.[29] The magistrates of Heidenheim reported that Georg Preisen, for example, was "a crooked man," those of Murrhardt said Hans Jacob Schiller was considered "right evil," and "Schafer J" was called at various times a "sorcerer," a "witch," and a "warlock" [Hexenman], while Jacob Schafer's neighbors reported that he consorted with sorcerers and was thought to be one himself. Of course, patients, who benefited from the practitioners' powers while generally living at some remove from them, often testified enthusiastically on their behalf, particularly in the case of Jacob Schafer, but the point here is that these men, including him, apparently, were clearly alienated from their immediate communities, and all of those who were so negatively regarded were general practitioners.[30]

Similarly, nine of the ten public practitioners for whom we have information indicative of their age were generalists, and all but two were clearly old (as was the one specialist whose age was recorded). The two whose ages are not clear were said to have been practicing for 15 and 17 years, respectively, which suggests that they were well into middle age at least.[31] Of those whose actual age was set down, one was 50, one was 51, two were over 60 (including the single-service provider), one was 62, and one 68.[32] Finally, the healer Barbara Weylandt was a widow, and Christoph Wieland had a grown child.[33] While lack of information is admittedly shaky ground for historical conclusions, we saw in Chapter 2 while considering the age of witch suspects that magistrates appear to have recorded ages when they were either notably young or notably old, but not when they were middle aged adults, so the evidence here suggests that generalized practitioners tended to be older than single-service providers. Why this should have been so is not clear: it may be that people who started with a single service gradually broadened their repertoire, it may be that older people picked up magical practices as they ceased to work in other ways (as was clearly the case with Wieland, who had lost his farm), and it may simply have reflected the fact that many single-service providers were involved in treasure-hunting, which was a form of magic particularly attractive to young and middle-aged men.

A final social characteristic of the public practitioners, gender, does not correlate at all with the division between single- and full-service providers, mainly because there were too few women in both areas combined, four in all, for any meaningful generalizations to be made.[34] Instead, what seems notable about the gender of public magical practitioners is, first of all, that there were so few women among them, and, second, that all four of the female practitioners were investigated early in the period, 1596 and 1608, while none at all were included in the later trials.

The proportion of female practitioners in the sampled cases, 11 percent of the 35 suspected practitioners, is significantly lower than the 20 percent of 23 magical practitioners found in a study of church visitation records for the districts of Tübingen and Tuttlingen between 1581 and 1621, but this is mainly because there were no treasure-hunters in this later study.[35] Treasure-hunting was an overwhelmingly male activity, as we have noted, and almost all cases took place more than a century later. All four female practitioners in the sampled trials under consideration here were involved in blessing and illicit healing, and they made up 22 percent of all suspects in those categories, which matches the figures from the visitation records almost exactly. It is also roughly consistent with the situation in other parts of southwestern Germany and many, although far from all, other parts of early modern Europe.[36]

Why women should have made up such a modest and declining proportion of the accused practitioners of beneficent magic seems perplexing, since women were particularly responsible for tending the sick in the domestic division of labor, they were commonly thought to be more inclined toward magic then as now, and many of the physiological characteristics that made them particularly good at affecting peoples' health negatively, as we saw in

Chapter 2, like their involvement in gardening and food preparation, their greater ability to recognize emotional signals between people, and their greater ability to express themselves verbally, would seem to have also equipped them to promote health through both the herbal remedies and psychological manipulations we examined in Chapter 7. There are two possible explanations for the lack of women among the accused practitioners: either women actually did engage in magical healing activities less than men, or they were equally or even more active but came to the attention of the authorities less often. Consideration of various kinds of evidence suggests that the reason for the low number of women practitioners in the early trials is the second explanation: women traditionally used magical healing in ways that were less likely to come to the attention of the authorities. The reason for their declining numbers over time, in contrast, would seem to be a combination of the two: women's traditional tendency to practice in a low-key way was strongly reinforced as they came to avoid activities like magic that ran the risk of drawing attention to themselves, and thereby exposing them to denunciation for witchcraft either because of the extent of their clientele or because of the nature of their activities.

As far as women's modest representation among suspects in early trials is concerned, it is possible that a greater public practice of magical healing by women had declined in the period before the late sixteenth century, either because of the moral suasion of the Reformation or the coercive power of the witch persecutions. However, the studies of the impact of the Reformation indicate that it's impact on popular culture during the sixteenth century was limited, and does not seem likely to have caused the kind of far-reaching alteration that would have been necessary here.[37] Similarly, the witch trials were only getting under way at the turn of the century, and therefore do not seem likely to have had such a marked impact in the time available. Instead, it seems more probable that the lower number of women practitioners around 1600 denounced to both church visitors and the magistrates reflected the genders' different social roles and the public visibility these created.[38] Specifically, it seems that male healers were more likely to establish public practices that paralleled men's public practice of other trades, while women's practices were more likely to grow out of their informal engagement with family and neighbors. This should not be taken as a hard-and-fast division, for there were women like Barbara Weylandt whose diverse practice seems to have been comparable to those of prominent male healers like Jacob Schäffer and Jakob Franck, and, conversely, there were men like Hans Röcklin, who appears to have practiced with his healing stone casually, as a minor sideline to his primary occupation as a smith. However, the other three women, who were investigated together in Sindelfingen in 1596 – Gertrudt Raitsen, Barbara Breüninger, and Sara Sauter – seem to have been more typical of female practitioners. Raitsen and Sauter appear to have been women who simply knew a few blessings that they had learned as children and seemed to have success with, and they were ready to help others with them when the need arose. Breüninger hinted that she knew considerably more than the one blessing for which she was being investigated, but the magistrates were not able to get any more information about her activities. In contrast, their peers were able to uncover copious information about Weylandt and a number of male healers around the same time, which suggests that whatever Breüninger did, it did not have the same level of public visibility that the men's practices did.

When a woman named Margretha Rencklern was investigated in Böblingen in 1609 for "forbidden herbal healing" and blessing, along with three of her clients, Rencklern told the magistrates that she had learned her arts from her mother, who used them more than she did and taught her even though she didn't really want to know about them.[39] She may have said she was less eager to practice than her mother because, the magistrates noted, "due to her ... magical healing" she was "strongly suspected by many of witchcraft." Magical healing was not witchcraft, of course. Both the *Carolina* and Württemberg's laws prescribed lesser punishments for magic involving neither harm nor a pact with the Devil, both the magistrates and the general public appear to have generally understood the difference between beneficent magic and *maleficium*, and the witch trials seldom focused on women simply because they practiced some form of healing.[40] However, evidence of such activity counted against a woman if she became a suspect for other reasons. Cures that went wrong or even just seemed unpleasant might become evidence against them, as in the cases of Anna Schnabel and Barbara Gessler, and female healers were particularly vulnerable when suspicions broadened into a panic.[41]

The possibility that the witch persecutions had a significant impact on the extent and nature of women's healing activities is supported by two of the nine sampled trials for beneficent magic (excluding treasure-finding) that involved private practitioners.[42] However, before we see how they did so, it is worth noting that these cases also support the general impression that the magical practices involved a range of people from solid citizens to marginal vagrants, but with the more heavily involved practitioners toward the lower edges of society. In three of the cases there was either no information about the suspect (the purported magical thief who bothered Christoph Martin and his wife), no evidence that the suspect had actually practiced magic (Jakob Staibers, who exhibited unusual strength), or no suspect (Agnes Beck's poltergeist experience), but the other six cases involved 11 suspects about whom there is some record. Only three lived in villages: one was the judge who used blessings to help himself get through his political travails and the other two were the smiths who knew the magic to gain enhanced skills by walking into the smithy backwards at midnight while invoking the name of the Devil. The judge was clearly a leading citizen of the small community, but he was said to have only "middling property" and he was "rather imperious, and therefore ... not in particularly good standing" with many of his neighbors.[43] One of the smiths was 26 years old and still an apprentice, while the other, Georg Schaff, was older, and a legal resident rather than a citizen of the village, but his nickname "Wild Georg," suggests that he was not exactly a pillar of the community.[44] All of these three men appear to have been established members of their villages, but none, even the judge, was entirely respectable.

Similarly, while the rest of the suspects resided in towns, they were mostly rather marginal. The three brothers who used magic to enhance their marksmanship were described as "dirt poor fellows" who had learned the magic from a neighbor who said he had learned it 20 years before, around 1650, from "a conjurer" he had given a ride in his wagon. Another suspect, a 42-year-old "acknowledged mocker of the communal leadership and everyone else," got in trouble when he admitted that he had a magic book in his house, which the magistrates found while searching for stolen goods; he was said to live in "great poverty." Yet another case involved the forester and his wife, who were investigated for using biblical sayings and religious songs they learned from their widowed servant in an attempt to heal their child, while the last case involved another servant, 56-year-old Agnes Luzin, who was accused of bewitching a young cousin of her employer, 24-year-old Barbara Calmbach, under the guise of healing her.

These last two cases, both of which took place in the eighteenth century and were the ones involving women suggest how women's role in healing and magic had changed since the sixteenth century, apparently as a result of the witch trials. In both, elderly women acted as the givers of healing advice, and in the case of the forester, may have actually led the sessions, but in both cases they were acting within the limited circle of household and family, and even then Luzin ended up being accused of witchcraft for what appears to have been a casual bit of advice in a chance meeting at church.[45] However, instead of further considering the evidence that the witch persecutions had succeeded in discouraging women from practicing magical healing in general, and practicing beyond their immediate domestic sphere in particular, as an isolated issue, we will consider it in the larger context of the rise and decline of the witch hunts and the even broader campaign against magic overall that took place in Württemberg, just as it did in Europe more generally, during the early modern period. Before we try to assess the impact of these though, we will first look at the various mechanisms of repression that were brought to bear against magical practices during this campaign in order to be in a better position to assess the impact of the cases recorded in the ducal archives.

The mechanisms of repression

There were four primary mechanisms of repression used against magic: the judicial system, the church, the bonds of local community, and the workings of individuals' psychophysiologies. In Württemberg the first two were both arms of the same institution, the state, which was ruled by the duke and run by a bureaucracy of professional civil servants and clergy. This structure had some direct contact with individual Württembergers, but they mainly felt its influence through its connections with the structures of local government, which formed not only the lowest rung of ducal government, but also the administrative embodiment of the local community. In addition to this formal governance structure, communities had a variety of informal means by which they constrained and compelled individuals, who had to, finally, regulate their own behavior by modulating their instinctive and individual-emotional responses with a combination of rational calculation and enculturated norms and values. For some time historians depicted the repression of magic, along with other disruptive or disreputable aspects of popular culture, as a top-down process, with the organs of state imposing a new, alien set of values on the communities and their individual inhabitants below them, but more recently they have come to recognize that the process was far more interactive than this.[46] Not only did different groups within local communities react differently to these initiatives, but some also took the lead in applying and even in formulating them, while the extent to which and the ways in which individuals internalized them, paid lip service to them, or rejected them are difficult to establish and subject to ongoing debate.

The impetus to repress magic, for example, did not simply come from government officials concerned about the spread of a diabolic conspiracy. The witch demonology was, of course, concocted by late medieval and early modern theologians and jurists, with important elements derived from the written tradition of secular and religious opposition to magic stretching back to antiquity and disseminated primarily through written tracts accessible only to the elite; but, as we have seen, other important elements derived from their experiences in the field, their encounters with actual practitioners and practices, and prosecutions were generally initiated by individuals with specific complaints about their neighbors. In the case of malefic magic, in particular, the great majority of the people appear to have been ready not only to cooperate with the judicial process, but also to initiate it when they felt that an accusation had merit.

The judicial system

At the top of the state and church hierarchies stood the duke, of course, but there was also a provincial diet whose powers were enshrined in the "Tübingen Contract" of 1514, the duchy's *"magna carta"* that gave its leading citizens (who were nonnoble, since most of the region's nobles were independent of the duchy) a voice in government throughout the early modern period. However, significant as the diet was from a constitutional point of view, aside from supporting, and at times even prompting laws governing morals, it played little role in administration or justice. The duke held supreme executive and judicial authority, which he exercised, advised by a "privy council" that was made up of an ad hoc group of high officials until it was formalized in 1628, through four main departments of state: the Chancellery, or secretariat; the Treasury; the *Oberrat*, or "High Council"; and the Church Council. The Church Council not only oversaw religious affairs, both administrative and doctrinal, but also the educational system, while the High Council, which was so named because it originally met in a room on an upper floor of the chancellery building in the fifteenth century ("*Oberrat*" literally means "upper council"), was responsible for judicial affairs.[47] It was the court of first instance for cases beyond the jurisdiction of lower courts; it helped formulate judicial policies, heard appeals from district courts, and oversaw the conduct of criminal cases by district officials via written reports and instructions. Its membership evolved over the sixteenth century from a majority of nobles assisted by a few legally trained burghers to a majority of legally trained professional administrators drawn from the duchy's leading families.

Württemberg was divided into 45 to 58 administrative districts – the number varied over time – which were the basis for ducal control of the countryside. Each included a market town that served as the district seat and the surrounding villages, although they ranged in size from a few that encompassed a number of other towns and dozens of villages to a few that included only a handful of nearby communities.[48] The chief administrative officer in each district was the constable (*Vogt* or, later, *Amtmann*), a ducal official who was responsible for, among other things, enforcing the Duchy's laws (in theory, there were supposed to be two constables, a chief constable [*Obervogt*], who was usually a noble, and an assistant constable [*Untervogt*], who was a burgher; but in practice the higher office became increasingly honorific and was often left unfilled, and most of the work was done by the "assistant").[49] The constable was assisted in his judicial duties by the district seat's town scribe, and he worked in conjunction with the town court, which was the court of first instance for civil cases in the town and felony cases in the district, and was the court of appeals for civil matters originating in the village courts. Town government also included a town council, a mayor, and other officials. All of the town officials, including the judges as well as scribe, were selected by and from the local urban elite, the *Ehrbarkeit*, and constables, while appointed by and responsible to the duke, were often from a prominent municipal family.[50] The town court originally passed judgment in cases tried before it by the constable, but since town judges were seldom trained jurists, the High Council asserted increasing control over the proceedings: demanding reports, issuing instructions, insisting with increasing frequency on written consultations with the law faculty at the University of Tübingen, and, in 1644, reserving the right to oversee judgments in witch trials.[51] The district court usually operated in the town that served as the district seat, but constables visited each village at least once every year or two to examine their accounts, hear appeals from their courts, and "after oral reading of the ordinances" to the assembled citizenry, ask each man in turn "to report conscientiously everything improper" he knew of (called the *Vogtgericht*).[52]

Village governments formed the bottom rung of the ducal administration, and were structured much like the town governments, with a mayor, other executive officials, a communal council, and judges who made up a court that heard civil complaints and handled misdemeanors.[53] Village mayors were originally appointed by the duke, but by the late sixteenth century were elected for life by the council from among its members, which also supplied and appointed the other village officials. Village officials played no formal role in criminal prosecutions of witchcraft and magic, beyond alerting the constable when evidence of a crime was uncovered, but they held regular assemblies of the citizenry at which local affairs were discussed; they could initiate informal inquiries; they assisted the constable in his formal investigations; and they could impose fines and even confinement for misdemeanors. Furthermore, villages, like the towns, had extensive power over their inhabitants' work, whether that was plying a trade or farming; their living arrangements, including the ability to migrate and settle; their marriages; their leisure activities; the sale and purchase of land; and their inheritance. These powers gave them formal means to punish people who failed to conform to informal community standards.[54]

Criminal laws originated from the ducal government within a series of broad provincial ordinances, in more specific police ordinances, and in numerous individual mandates and edicts.[55] The First provincial ordinance appeared in 1495 and others followed over the next century and a half, while the First Police Ordinance appeared in 1549. The provincial ordinances had not only provisions to promoted commerce and general welfare, but also sanctions against a wide variety of moral transgressions and breaches of the peace. In 1552 the Fifth Provincial Ordinance first proscribed the public practice of magic, calling on magistrates to first identify and warn "soothsayers and other Devil incanters," and then punish any who did not desist from practicing, with banishment for a second offense and death for a third.[56] Fifteen years later, the Sixth Provincial Ordinance followed the imperial government's model law code, the *Constitution Criminalis Carolina*, in prescribing death for harmful magic, but imposed the same penalty on a "Pact with the Devil" even if "no one [is] done harm." This statutory framework remained in place throughout the rest of the early modern period, down to 1806.

The standard form of execution for witchcraft in Württemberg, as in many other jurisdictions, was burning. There were several other forms available that were used for other offenses, including quartering (cutting the body into four pieces, imposed for treason), drowning (imposed for poisoning or theft by a woman), breaking on the wheel (used for male poisoners, and involving tying the convict spread-eagled to a wheel, breaking his limbs, and leaving him to die of exposure), live burial (for infanticide, but abandoned in the sixteenth century as it seemed cruel; awkward to carry out, since convicts tended to writhe around a lot; and insufficiently visible to a crowd of spectators), decapitation (for murder), and hanging (armed robbery).[57] Some of these could be intensified by having the convict dragged to the place of execution by horses or tearing the flesh with hot pincers. All of these sentences were carried out publicly, and the body (or part of it) was generally put on display near town gates.[58] The reason for the performative aspect was, from the authorities' point of view, to enhance their deterrent effect, and, from the populace's point of view, to demonstrate that justice had been done. The reason for the different forms of execution with different degrees of suffering involved was in part to reflect both official and popular estimations of the heinousness of the crimes – poisoning was worse than murder because it involved a secret betrayal of trust, and infanticide was worse than poisoning because it took a wholly innocent life as well as betraying trust – and in part to reflect specific aspects of the crime: arson, for example, was punished with burning as an obvious form of justice. Witches were burned partly because it was an extremely painful way to die, and both *maleficium* and diabolism involved a betrayal communal bonds, and partly because witchcraft involved a spiritual power that was thought to remain potent unless the witch's body was thoroughly destroyed (for this reason, even when the sentence was reduced to beheading as an act of mercy, the convicted witch's body was still burned afterwards).

In addition to the ultimate punishment of death, there were a variety of lesser penalties imposed for crimes related to witchcraft and magic in early modern Württemberg.[59] Banishment was originally tantamount to a death sentence, for in the early Middle Ages being expelled from the community put the person at the mercy of their enemies and predators both human and animal, and in the early modern period it still meant not only the disruption of social bonds, but also the loss of communal status and rights, property, and livelihood that could lead to destitution, misery, and even an early death.[60] Incarceration ranged from a few days in the local jail to years in the penitentiary (once one had been built in 1719), and, while conditions varied, jail time meant long days, weeks, or months on end spent in dank confinement, often in shackles and/or in the company of hardened criminals, while consignment to the penitentiary meant months or years of confinement, often combined with hard labor and disciplinary floggings.[61] Fines were obviously less severe than execution, banishment, or incarceration, but could make what might have seemed like an inconsequential transgression unpleasantly costly. Probation meant release from custody with the stipulation that community leaders keep a close eye on the person's conduct, with the threat of renewed prosecution if there was evidence of further misdeeds.

Prosecution always held the danger that it would end with punishment, but prosecution itself could be a punishing experience regardless of the verdict. The most obvious way this was so was when a trial involved torture, which was employed routinely in witchcraft cases (as in other capital cases) until the second half of the seventeenth century, and occasionally thereafter. Officially, torture in Württemberg had to be justified according to strict standards, at first to the High Council and increasingly to the Tübingen faculty of law in addition, before each session; it was limited in terms of the form and duration; proceeded through a series of grades of severity in sessions, which had to be separated by a day at least, and much longer as recurring consultations became routine; was supervised directly by the judges as well as the constable and town scribe; and had to be followed up with an interview outside of the torture chamber a day later during which the suspect had to confirm any confessions made during the session. Forms and duration proceeded from exposure to the torture chamber without any actual torture to torture by thumbscrews or leg presses for 15 minutes, strapado (elevation by the wrists tied behind the back) for a half hour, and strapado with 50 or 100 pound leg weights for three-quarters of an hour.[62] The presiding officer could extend the time limits for a recalcitrant suspect to one hour but no longer, but what actually could happen in the torture chamber depended on the individual integrity and group dynamics of the magistrates. Even a limited session with thumbscrews, strapado, or strapado with weights was an agonizing experience, to say the least, and in other jurisdictions in Europe, controls either did not exist or were less earnestly enforced, and there are plenty of examples of suspects subjected to unrestrained torment until they either broke down and confessed or expired. Even in Württemberg, we have seen that torture was imposed punitively by the highest authorities in the state in the case of the prophet Hans Keil.[63] Torture following this model was a mainstay of the witch persecutions, because it played a vital role in creating confessions of stereotypical diabolism, which not only sealed the individual suspect's fate, but also appeared to validate the witch stereotype. However, even as judicial torture fell into abeyance in the eighteenth century, we have seen the ironic spectacle of "enlightened" administrators having suspects whipped repeatedly (and, apparently, without any of the safeguards built into the process during the witch trials) to get them to deny their claimed encounters with spirits.

If a suspect avoided torture, there were other ways in which being the subject of a criminal investigation was a punitive experience. Incarceration during an investigation and trial could last anywhere from a few days to, in a few cases, years, and among the sampled witch cases the average stay of incarcerated suspects was almost three months.[64] While it was routine to incarcerate suspects in capital cases since the motivation to flee was strong, a few prisoners appear to have been left to languish in a deliberate attempt to coerce a confession or punish them without a conviction, for the gaols in which suspects wiled away the hours waiting to hear what fate had in store were similar to if not the same as those in which people were incarcerated as punishment: dark, cold, uncomfortable, unhealthy to the point that elderly suspects sometimes died while awaiting judgment, and quite possibly containing other, menacing suspects. Similarly, to be arrested and taken from one's home by armed men, thrown into jail, and grilled intensively and repeatedly by a battery of hostile magistrates was a humiliating, intimidating, and demoralizing experience. Furthermore, the humiliation was heightened by both the knowledge that somebody had denounced you and others might well testify against you and the knowledge that some stain at least would almost certainly remain on your honor for the rest of your life – that even if you were exonerated, personal enemies and malicious gossips in the community could use it against you at will; that should any further official problems arise, you would have to start out with one strike against you; and that the dishonor would extend beyond you to some degree to your family, both in the present and into the next generation. Certainly there were early moderners who did not care about their reputations and prospects in the community, and others who were so self-possessed that they could maintain their pride and self-confidence in the face of arrest, incarceration, interrogation, and even torture, but for most people in this honor-bound culture, a public scandal was a matter of profound emotional as well as practical consequence, a prospect that they would take considerable pains to avoid. To some extent the horrific violence of the mass burnings has desensitized us to the potential impact of less drastic forms of prosecution and punishment. Compared to torture and burning, prosecutions that "only" involved arrest and incarceration, interrogations, and prolonged uncertainty, and punishments that "only" involved expulsion from home and community, loss of freedom, or endurance of miserable conditions for months or even years on end seem less serious and to have had less significant deterrent effect. However, in fact, the great majority of people want to avoid trouble if they can and will practice behavioral self-censorship based on a cost-benefit analysis of transgressions, weighing the need they satisfy or the advantage they confer against the likelihood of being punished and the severity of the penalty.

Sometimes in cases of witch suspicions, the suspect actually initiated proceedings in order to clear her name, for not contesting an informal accusation could be construed to be an implicit admission of guilt, but most of the time witch trials began when one commoner lodged a complaint against another, for justice in Württemberg was based on the Germanic tradition of the accusatory principle, "the necessity for a formal accusation in capital crimes."[65] However, in some cases the magistrates became involved because they heard rumors and investigated, thereby drawing an accusation out rather than passively waiting for it to be brought to them, and in less serious crimes like magic without a pact or harm they had even more latitude to take the initiative. Furthermore, commoners were required to attend both constables' annual visitations and regular communal gatherings and report any illegal activities, and far from being reticent, people used them as an opportunity to lodge so many complaints that one official lamented, "experience teaches that people bring up all sorts of complaints which cannot be substantiated ... thereby increasing time and expenses."[66]

The church

In addition to these direct inputs into the criminal justice system, magistrates might also become aware of illicit magical activities through the church, which in Württemberg was an arm of the state, and whose officials not only cooperated in law enforcement, but also relied on the secular administration to enforce its own authority. The church had both formal and informal ways of eliciting information about the behavior of its parishioners and a number of nonviolent ways of punishing wayward parishioners on its own. Furthermore, the church had a variety of means by which it could exhort and admonish the people to behave better, making sure that they knew what they should and should not do, threatening them with eternal in addition to temporal punishments, and appealing to their innate virtue and desire to do right. These intangible forms of persuasion may seem weak in comparison to the physical means of coercion available to the civil authorities, but people are more easily and completely ruled by internalized norms and values than by external threats and punishments.[67] In the long run, this sort of internal repression promoted by the church probably played a greater role in the decline of magic than the repressive power of the government.

Württemberg became Lutheran in 1534, and under the leadership of Johann Brenz, its state church became a model for Protestant Germany in a series of acts that culminated in the Great Church Ordinance of 1559. At the top stood the duke, of course, with the Church Council (*Kirchenrat*) one of the four main departments of state. The Church Council consisted of four "political" councilors, who managed the church's financial and other secular administrative affairs, and three theologians, referred to as the Consistory, who were responsible for doctrinal and personnel issues. The local agents on the "political" side were church stewards, who paid the salaries of church personnel, maintained church buildings and schools, and distributed funds for alms houses and poor relief. The Consistory worked through a more complex hierarchy. It examined and appointed clergymen and teachers itself (subject to a rarely used veto by the congregations over new pastors) and determined "what needed to be done to satisfy any pastoral needs or correct any clerical abuses that could not be dealt with locally."[68] In addition, twice a year it met with the "general superintendents," traditionally the "evangelical 'prelates' ... in charge of the" duchy's "four secularized monasteries," in what was called the Synod, to review reports on local congregations, recommend "new legislation or other measures" that this review might indicate were needed, and excommunicate incorrigible sinners. The reports the Synod reviewed consisted mainly of the biannual reports of the 28 "superintendents," the next lower level in the hierarchy to the general superintendents, which reported on the superintendents' biannual visitations to the individual parishes in their districts, during which they investigated "the life and doctrine of the pastors, schoolteachers, local officials, and residents, and ... how carefully the duke's various ecclesiastical ordinances were being observed." In addition to submitting these standard full reports, the superintendents informed the consistory directly of any matters requiring immediate attention.

Beneath the superintendents, the local pastors ministered directly to the people by administering the sacraments, preaching God's word, and monitoring and correcting their actions and words. Both of the latter two were explicitly aimed at producing general changes in popular practices, as well as specific changes in individual behavior, as part of a comprehensive effort to create a more Christian commonwealth that was conducted by church officials in concert with the secular administration.[69] Preaching involved a combination of exhortation to goodness, including obedience to authority, and warnings of the penalties for sin, including recourse to magic with or without invocation of the Devil, which would fall not only on individual sinners but on the entire community. Parishioners were expected to come to services regularly, weekly at the least, and more frequently was desirable.[70] Monitoring and correcting actions and words involved a number of mechanisms. First of all, the pastor lived in the community, and so could see for himself some of what was going on, and was informally privy to rumors and some local gossip as well. Secondly, as we saw in Chapter 3, confession was obligatory before communion, and could bring to light not only individual but also collective transgressions. Thirdly, starting in 1644, village consistories consisting of the pastor and a select group of male parishioners were put into place to hear about and punish moral offenses, and they were assisted by "secret censors," or wardens, who spied on their neighbors and received a percentage of any fines levied as a result of their reports.[71] Similarly, ordinary villagers "who initiated a successful prosecution of a neighbor for immorality" could claim a monetary prize, and, lastly, the superintendents' regular visitations included interviews with ordinary people and some of the 300 standard questions concerned activities in the community, as well as the conduct of the officials.

Once church officials learned of a transgression, they could impose a range of sanctions that intertwined with those imposed by the state. The mildest sanction was private admonishment by the pastor. The local consistory could issue public citations, which were "a universally feared form of public humiliation."[72] It could also impose fines and brief jail sentences. Repeated and more serious offenses were reported to the secular authorities, for moral transgressions like magic were also against the secular law, and would be prosecuted accordingly. Witchcraft, both malefic and diabolic, was, of course, a capital offense, and if a suspect was found guilty the punishment removed her from the community through banishment if not execution, while if she was not, she was usually released into a form of probation with supervision by both the pastor and the village officials and the threat of renewed secular prosecution. Beneficent magic, like other lesser offenses, was subject to fines or imprisonment, after which the offender would return to the community. Repeated offenses could result in repeated trials and escalating secular punishments, but the church had another form of sanction in these cases: a series of admonishments by the local pastor, the district superintendent, and the ducal Synod; and if these failed, excommunication.[73]

The church's admonishments and symbolic sanctions were far less powerful external forms of repression than the punishments that the secular arm could impose, but the church had far more potent means of instilling internal forms of repression than the state. To begin with, sermons served to both educate and indoctrinate, informing parishioners of the do's and, more importantly from the point of view of magic, the don'ts of Christian morality, and of the rewards to be gained by conforming to them and the penalties in this world and the next for transgressing against them. By the late sixteenth century pastors were generally the best educated people in villages and among the most educated in towns, having passed through a stringent educational process starting with elite "Latin" schools for the university bound, continuing in special cloister schools for prospective clergy, and culminating in a course of study in a special section of the university, the "*Stift*," and generally an additional year or two of theology.[74] Their sermons (and conduct and conversation in general) reflected both the knowledge and values they inculcated during their education and specific instructions they received from the church hierarchy, as when the Sixth Provincial Ordinance of 1667 made both harmful magic and a pact with the Devil capital offenses and instructed preachers to inform "the people ... of what magic really involves."[75] With literacy limited among the ordinary people, sermons formed an important source of ideas and information, and so, for example, the "official duty of the preacher ... to hold witch sermons ... was the strongest impulse behind a rapid popularization of" the witch demonology.

Sermons not only conveyed important ideas to the people, but, at least when delivered well, also generated strong emotions in them, instilling fear and inspiring devotion, which exert a stronger influence on behavior than ideas alone. Similarly, confession, which we saw in Chapter 3, increased in prominence in the sixteenth century, also had the potential to intensify people's awareness of their shortcomings, forcing them to experience the humiliation of publicly acknowledging their sinful thoughts and actions, the guilt of hiding them and then taking communion dishonestly, or the public dishonor of avoiding confession and communion altogether.[76] Whatever the parishioner's course of action, in one way or another, the exercise forced the person to make a conscious decision that highlighted the disjunction between the prescriptions of Christian morality and their own thoughts and actions.

The church's last major direct means of enculturation was the catechism, as we saw in Chapter 3 in connection with the diffusion of the diabolic witch stereotype. As with the Devil, magic does not figure prominently in it, but Luther's small catechism, which was used for basic instruction, mentions it in regard to the second commandment, which says to "not misuse the name of the Lord," and explains that this means to "not curse, swear, use satanic arts, lie, or deceive by his name," while his large catechism, used to expand believers' understanding of the Christian message, says in regard to the first commandment, to "have no other Gods," that "sorcerers and magicians ... make a covenant with the devil, in order that he may give them plenty of money or help them in their love-affairs, preserve their cattle, restore to them lost possessions, etc. For all these place their heart and trust elsewhere than in the true God."[77] Both these passages are directed not only, or even primarily, against malevolent magic, but also against beneficent forms, as misuse of God's name in blessings or as constituting an implicit if not explicit compact with the devil, even if the ends are not malign.

The catechism was originally created to help people prepare for communion, but it quickly became a staple of religious instruction generally, and knowledge of it became a prerequisite for confirmation, which was instituted in 1722.[78] It was taught in special classes several times a week, which at least some children attended, and by the late seventeenth century there were instructional sessions for older people on Sundays after church services. However, the primary means of dissemination was in schools, where the catechism formed the main element of the curriculum at the elementary level, for moral instruction was at least as important an objective in the educational system as teaching reading and writing.[79] This orientation was most clearly indicated by the facts that the school system was overseen by the Church Council; teaching was not an independent profession but the first stage of service for prospective pastors after finishing their studies; and one of the duties of pastors was to visit schools weekly to check on the students' progress in learning the catechism. Children were expected first to memorize "the Ten Commandments, the Creed, the Lord's Prayer, etc. ... word for word," then study the short explanations of each element in the Small Catechism, and finally move on to the lengthy exposition of the Large Catechism.[80]

The school system was divided into a higher track, which led from the urban Latin schools through high schools to the university, to educate not only prospective clergymen, but also lawyers, government officials, and doctors, and a lower track, which introduced the mass of people to the rudiments of book-based knowledge in "German" schools. The system of public education was first established in the Great Church Ordinance in

1559 for both boys and girls, and attendance became compulsory for children in 1649.[81] Attendance tended to be spotty until the end of the eighteenth century, but seems to have become more regular over time, and exerted correspondingly increasing influence on the mass of people in the duchy. The number of schools in Württemberg grew from 50, mostly Latin schools, in 1534, to over 400, a majority German ones, by 1600, and they were staffed by men whose "own education had ensured their theological orthodoxy, and this they passed on to their ... pupils."[82] Württemberg was particularly advanced in the development of this system of public education, but its initiatives were paralleled by similar developments throughout Europe during the early modern period, and there is no question that all but the most marginal of the poor were significantly more educated in 1800 than in 1500, particularly in the rudiments of official morality.[83]

A final area of influence connected to the church in Württemberg, at least formally, was medicine, for public health in the duchy was overseen by the Church Council and paid for from church funds, although the court physicians functioned as expert advisors on medical questions and conducted triennial visitations.[84] Medical regulations impacted magical beliefs and practices strongly, since healing was the single most common reason people consulted magical practitioners and was undoubtedly among the most important uses of magical practices privately as well. Starting in the sixteenth century, the ducal government steadily increased its regulation of medical practices in a campaign that put into place a system of official medicine to replace the customary system that existed at the end of the Middle Ages. The customary system included the whole range of medical practitioners available – university-trained doctors, apothecaries, barber-surgeons, midwives, bathers, and local and itinerant healers – who offered a range of services that commonly overlapped with each other.[85] In contrast, the official system included only doctors, apothecaries, barber-surgeons, bathers, and midwives and, furthermore, insisted that each type of practitioner offer only the services that constituted his or her specialty. Theoretically, each district was to have a doctor in its service, who would also function as the town doctor in the district seat, and who was selected and paid by the local church administration and was responsible for both providing charity services for the poor and overseeing the work of the other practitioners. Only the doctor was supposed to diagnose illnesses and prescribe internal remedies, which the apothecary would prepare and supply, while barber-surgeons performed operations, bathers ran therapeutic mineral springs, and midwives delivered babies. All were expected to limit their practices to their specialties and employ natural methods only – midwives were explicitly prohibited from incanting blessings to help with childbirth in 1720 – but even healers employing only natural remedies were prohibited from practicing if they were not trained and recognized members of one of these official groups.[86]

Württemberg's first medical regulation, the First Apothecary Ordinance, appeared in 1486, and the First Police Ordinance of 1549 contained the first law governing midwives, requiring them to be familiar with a printed handbook on midwifery, but the official system really began to be put into place in the Great Church Ordinance of 1559, which subordinated medicine to the church, began to incorporate barber-surgeons, who had their own guild, into the system, and prohibited illicit medical practices, both healing by unofficial practitioners and healing activities by official practitioners beyond their field of competence.[87] The Seventh Provincial Ordinance of 1621 created the first comprehensive overview of the duties of each profession. The policing aspect of this activity became more explicit three years later when the government offered a reward to apothecaries who reported people who were dispensing medicines illicitly, and in 1643 it issued an ordinance that specifically targeted blessers, and also prescribed punishments for people who used the services of illicit practitioners as well as for the practitioners themselves.[88] In 1658 midwives were ordered to report unmarried mothers in a *Generalreskrept*, and there were all of eight acts against illicit practitioners in the late seventeenth century.[89] More followed in the early eighteenth century, at which time "the fight against charlatanism was pursued particularly strongly."[90] Among the measures were instructions for apothecary visitations that specifically targeted "self-made bunglers, blessing incanters, and similar people" and a measure that barred executioners and knackers, whose status as healers owed more to their association with death than any practical knowledge deriving from their trades, from practicing. The high points of the effort to consolidate the system of official medicine was the passage of comprehensive Medical Ordinances in 1720 and 1755, which, although they did not free medicine from the oversight of the church, contributed to a general decline in illicit practices to the point that by the late eighteenth century "the court physicians Gesner and Reuss even spoke ... of rooting out the evil once and for all."[91]

While Gesner and Reuss may have been somewhat overoptimistic, at least in the short run, it is important to remember that the "evil" they were referring to was not just illicit healers but also illicit practices by licit healers, and in the endeavor to stamp out both, the ducal administration was aided immeasurably by the zeal displayed by official practitioners in defending their turf from both unsanctioned practitioners and poaching by sanctioned specialists in other areas. For example, doctors were quick to complain about apothecaries who diagnosed illnesses and recommended remedies instead of just filling prescriptions, while apothecaries were equally ready to denounce bathers who kept a stock of medicines for the visitors at mineral baths. In fact, early modern Württemberg, like the rest of early modern Europe, was a corporatist society made up of numerous communities bound by tradition, interest, and statutory identities that were determined to defend their territory from outsiders and regulate their own internal affairs, and the ducal bureaucracy's success in its efforts to repress various aspects of traditional popular culture generally reflected the extent to which one or more of these groups supported the reforms, which in turn reflected the extent to which they perceived them to be furthering their interests and ambitions.[92] In addition, these groups had their own autonomous agendas that involved repression of various practices by their own members as well as competing groups, and they possessed a variety of formal and informal means of rewarding conformity and penalizing nonconformity.

Local communities

The most numerous of these communities, of course, were the peasant villages, which also held the greatest proportion of the population. The remaining percent lived in towns, most of which were barely larger than overgrown villages. In both, there were two main classes of inhabitants, citizens and permanent residents, with the citizens enjoying greater security and rights, but both defined legally and subject to considerable regulation by the community.[93] Villages functioned as collectives toward the outside, but internally were divided along a number of lines beyond those between citizens and permanent residents: different kinship and clientage networks; tenant farmers vs cotters and boarders; long-term residents vs temporary residents, like servants; long-established families vs recent immigrants; agriculturalists vs artisans (although many households involved some of each, some were more dependent on one than the other); agriculturalists vs herders; cow herders vs shepherds; male heads of households vs dependents; and often a few well-to-do rural "patricians" and their families vs everyone else.[94] Towns had similar divides, although the balance between tradespeople and agriculturalists was skewed in the opposite direction not only numerically, but also in terms of economic and social prominence, for while farmers dominated in the villages, and artisans tended to be marginal protoindustrial workers, tradesmen dominated the towns, and agricultural workers were more likely to be marginal workers such as vine tenders.

In addition, the district seats had a more pronounced local notability, the *Ehrbarkeit*, which was made up of the constable, the scribe, the preacher, the schoolmaster, the town councilors, and the judges, along with all of their families. They formed a distinct and self-conscious community that held itself and was held at some distance from the common citizens. They also had ties to the provincial elite that staffed the government offices in Stuttgart, which, along with their families, formed the pinnacle of provincial society. These two groups, the local honorability and the provincial elite, formed two overlapping but distinct communities, each with its own collective interests and internal divisions. Traditionally historians have tended to depict them as a monolithic social and cultural block that pressed relentlessly on those below, but they were actually as much divided as the peasantry, along similar or analogous lines of family, clientage, professional affiliation, wealth, geographic ties and mobility, and intellectual exposure, and we shall see that their interrelationship and internal dynamics played an important role in the forms and extent of the repression of magic.

Some of the local means of repression have already been mentioned because they formed the lowest tier of church and state: village or town courts and assemblies, church courts after 1644, the intrusive activities of mayors and other communal officials in the course of their normal duties, the formalized neighborly snooping by the "secret Censors" or wardens and ordinary people seeking the monetary rewards offered for denouncing immorality, and the supervisory responsibilities of doctors, apothecaries, and midwives. At least as significantly, though, each of Württemberg's villages and small towns "operated as a self-contained ... informal jural unit" that "incubated successive generations whose members had to learn to live in each other's shadow."[95] Members of these communities were acutely aware of matters of honor – worthiness measured by public standards and the esteem of others (as opposed to virtue, or worthiness, measured by private conformity to an inner sense of right) – because the communities were held together by a combination of reciprocity and fear: a finely honed sense of balance of responsibilities and rewards from cooperation and a knowledge that failure to maintain an esteemed status would lead to the loss of position within the community and the critical resources that it conferred.[96] Since "villagers shared in ... accomplishments ... and also in ... dishonor" and "the more severe a transgression, the wider the circle of associates whose honor was compromised," they felt an intense sense of communal destiny, the sense that underlay the frequently expressed fear that tolerance of an individual sinner would lead to divine retribution on the entire community.[97] As a consequence, "some of the most zealous agents of social discipline were located in the village," and "no mercy was shown to those who wandered from the path straight and narrow."[98]

While the fear of divine retribution may have expressed an acceptance of sin as defined by the cultural elite, it is telling that the dominant discourse was couched in the terms of honor, which referenced the more immediate context of interpersonal and communal relations. Furthermore, examining the specific aspects of life that these local communities asserted their right to control reveals that they had an even more practical basis: control of behaviors and actions whose implications impacted material resources. To begin with, each village and town had "a plethora of community officials": in 1717 the small district seat of Wildberg, with 300 households and 1,328 inhabitants, had 95 separate community offices including three mayors, nine judges, five church wardens, four building and road inspectors, two school inspectors, two field inspectors, three horse inspectors, four corvée officers, four bread inspectors, three fire inspectors, three brick inspectors, one church administrator, and four gatekeepers, while the village of Gültingen, with all of 860 inhabitants in 1752, had 51 officials including the mayor, 12 judges, six church court members, two horse and cattle inspectors, two wine valuers, four fire inspectors, three inventory makers, two church administrators, one sexton, one hay inspector, and four tax settlers.[99] Some of the matters these officials oversaw concerned public safety, like fire inspections, and many were purely economic issues like taxation, use of common land, participation in the obligatory communal labor services, sale and mortgaging of property, methods and timing of cultivation, and the conduct of craft, protoindustrial and commercial activity.[100] Theoretically, regulation of these fiscal and business matters was governed by purely economic considerations, both those of the communal officials involved and those of villagers who might dispute or seek to manipulate them. However, in a small-scale, face-to-face community, it would be naïve to think that either group was immune to trading favors or settling scores, factional maneuvering, ostracism of deviants, status conflicts, or interpersonal animosities.[101] Furthermore, economic considerations led communities to assert control over a much wider range of more personal aspects of life that gave even wider scope for noneconomic coercion and retribution. Particularly strong was the desire to minimize the obligation to provide poor relief, for families had only limited legal obligations to support indigent kin, while communities were "responsible for citizens until death," which "created incentives for communities to demarcate membership clearly and prevent members from taking risky decisions."[102] Consequently, from the early eighteenth century communities compelled young people to get permission to marry from the communal leaders even if their parents consented, and sometimes "forbade marriages outright on grounds of poverty or inability to support a family." Communities also closely controlled geographic mobility, refusing to allow temporary immigrants unless they could demonstrate citizenship in a home community (which would be responsible for them if they became destitute), forbidding citizens to give temporary shelter even to family members who were noncitizens without a written guarantee that they would not become a financial burden, and regulating the residence and work of unmarried women.[103] Within families, communities directed both inheritance practices, "to protect themselves against possible future burdens," and residential arrangements, commanding estranged spouses "to move back together to reduce living costs, married offspring to move out of the parental house or build a separate parlor to prevent conflict, [and] unmarried daughters to move back home to obviate separate house rents." Finally, similar fears of potential burdens led communities to punish parents and children both when the latter failed to attend school, "neglected their apprenticeships, habitually went fishing, or ran away from their masters." Adults, too, could feel the weight of this communal interference in living habits which were thought to threaten their own or the community's viability. Idleness, profligacy, slothful housekeeping, holding "evening gatherings (especially of unmarried people), tobacco-smoking, drinking, and gaming were reported by neighbors and punished by the authorities, often explicitly to reduce welfare risks," but also to deter "disorderly discourse concerning" social "superiors." In some cases these transgressions were formally punished in communal or church courts, but other formal means of control like permits for marriages and residential arrangements, allocation of labor duties, or resolution of tax and property disputes could be withheld ostensibly on the basis of some technicality, but in fact because of the official's, and often some significant portion of the community's, opinion of the applicant. Appeals were possible in many matters, of course, but they took time and were uncertain in a system dominated by behind-the-scenes manipulation by small groups of men, and in some matters, like application for citizenship, nothing more than "a poor 'Praedikat' (reputation) constituted legal grounds for rejection," so that "a sexual misdemeanor, a father who had been in prison, personal prodigality, or general dislike" could bar entry.[104] Furthermore, there were numerous informal means by which a community could punish one of its members: direct insults, gossip, temporary shunning, long-term ostracism, charivaries, threats, and physical violence, whether individual belligerence or collective vigilante action. Once a person was dishonored, the stigma would adhere to him or her personally and to those associated with him or her for the foreseeable future, and would not only prejudice their future dealings with the authorities, but also would informally undermine their position within the community.

Conversely, there were numerous positive inducements that rewarded conformity to community standards including favorable judgments, ready access to assistance like loans and labor, support in lawsuits and judicial investigations, and cover from intrusive agents of church and state. These sorts of positive inducements, like the exhortations of the preachers, could persuade people to repress things in themselves, to *not* engage in sex despite temptation and opportunity, *not* consort with disreputable people despite the pleasure of their company, and *not* engage in behaviors that ran the risk of arrest despite the possible gains they might bring. In fact, this sort of self-censorship is both necessary for and is in itself a stronger means of control than external sanctions, particularly if it develops from internal calculation of interest into, or is inculcated as to begin with, "subconscious ... moral acceptance" that "produces feelings of remorse or shame" when transgressed.[105] Membership in an early modern village was a two-edged sword: it was central to a person's psychological as well as legal identity, bestowing material benefits and psychological support, but at the price of submission to pervasive communal supervision and conformity to exacting communal standards which affected each member's "estimation of his own worth, his *claim* to pride," by affecting the community's "acknowledgement of that claim ... his *right* to pride."[106]

Of course, village communities were far from the monolithic social units they are sometimes imagined to have been. Communal opinion was a contested, shifting discourse, not a fixed verdict, and the micropolitics of family and faction could color the interpretation and ameliorate the effects of dishonorable conduct. Furthermore, at the lowest levels of society concern about reputation was often overshadowed by both the expediencies necessary for survival and a fatalistic acceptance of inherent disreputableness, so that the "deterrent value from the extraordinary significance attached to honor ... was always more effective against substantial villagers than against the poor."[107] Nevertheless, even the poor "possessed honor," and while interpretations of specific incidents were subject to negotiation, the standards against which villagers were judged remained relatively stable from the sixteenth through the eighteenth century.[108] Furthermore, although rationale and emphasis may have varied somewhat, to a considerable degree both the mechanisms of control and the standards of morality found in the village were paralleled in the other communities that made up the duchy: the populations of the small towns, the local notability, and the provincial elite in Stuttgart.

The small towns of Württemberg were almost indistinguishable from the larger villages. To begin with, the populations were not that different, since the latter could have a thousand inhabitants while many of the former had only two or three times that number.[109] However, in other parts of Europe there was nevertheless a sharp divide between towns and villages of similar population sizes, so the situation in the duchy must have had more to do with the fact that the villages, as we have seen, exercised as significant a degree of self-government as the towns, and had similar institutional structures.[110] If anything, however, the towns exercised even greater control over their peoples' lives, perhaps because more people were crowded into a confined space, than the villages. Everybody's business was literally everybody's business, and so citizens "would not buy their sausages from an adulterer, a liar, a blasphemer, a cheat, if only for fear of what their neighbors would say if they did; and if a neighborhood butcher was one of those things they would know it and his business would fail."[111] As in the villages, there were formal mechanisms of repression like civil, criminal, and church courts and "secret censors," and urban guilds additionally "were custodians of morality ... along with their economic and political functions," enforcing standards of conduct on their members "often to the point of amazing prurience."[112] Furthermore, as in the villages, formal controls could be "used ... to exclude persons held undesirable for other reasons," and, finally, informal controls could be implemented with devastating effect as well: the undesirable's "business could drop off; he could be slandered and ignored; his children could be ridiculed and bullied by their fellows."[113] Small towns "maintained a steady pressure on all members" via "the subjugation of everybody ... to everybody." It was impossible to maintain "multiple standards and compartmentalized lives"; citizens of small towns had to be "integrated personalities, caught like ... flies in a three-dimensional web of community."[114]

Most small towns, like villages, were dominated by a "group of influential insiders," but even though the town leaders were addressed as "Mister" ("*Herr*") and could wear a sword, and their wives and daughters could wear jewelry, all of which were signs of membership in the upper rather than lower orders, theirs "was a regime not of oligarchs but of communarchs, a regime of uncles" whose lives were tightly integrated with those of their communities.[115] The upper strata in the district seats, however, formed a more distinct class, a patriciate or notability known as the *Ehrbarkeit* through most of the early modern period, and the *Honoratioren*, toward the end of the eighteenth century (and will be referred to as "honorability" here). A person's profession, or the profession of a woman's husband or father, was the key to membership in the upper orders, and a series of five "police ordinances" from 1549 to 1712 and various rank and funeral ordinances in the eighteenth century set out in increasing detail the occupations that belonged in an ever-changing system of stratifications.[116] The untitled portion of the population, the vast majority, generally included the peasantry and all other agricultural workers, including village leaders, servants, and workers and most artisans in the towns, who were all lumped into the first three of six to nine classes.[117] The lowest ranks of the titled portion of the population included town officials, large-scale merchants, and apothecaries (referred to here as "notables"). The higher ranks arrayed the ducal officials at the district and central levels and members of the court in a relatively large number of gradations involving increasingly few people. This inverse relationship may indicate that status and rank became objects of ever more intense concern the higher one rose in this society, since one had more to gain and more to lose, which made the honor that they both reflected and bestowed even more important to the inhabitants of these rarified heights than it was to the already highly status- and honor-conscious commoners below. Of course, it may also just indicate that people were most conscious of fine gradations of rank among those closest to them, which in the case of the authors of official ordinances were the leaders of the duchy, but a pig-herder's wife might well have been able to make an equally finely graded but inversely proportioned hierarchy lumping everyone at court together and showing the exact order of the notables in the nearest town and the even finer distinctions between groups within her village.

In any case, the divisions that are relevant for our purposes here are the divides between (1) the lowest level of notables, basically the leaders of the secondary towns, (2) the honorability, the leaders of the district seats, (3) the bureaucrats in the duchy's central government, and (4) members of the court.[118] The distinction between groups (1) and (2) was that except for their right to wear a sword and fine clothes and to be addressed as "Herr," the local notables were quite similar to the village leaders in cultural terms: they were virtually indistinguishable from the other members of their communities except for their somewhat greater wealth and local power.[119] The honorability in the district seats, however, not only played a much greater political role in the duchy, dominating the lesser towns and villages in their districts and participating in provincial affairs via their control of district representation in the diet, but also were distinguished culturally because for all but some of the judges, who were leading artisans in local guilds, the occupations that gave entrée to this level of society were professions that involved reading and writing.[120] The path into these professions started with attendance at a Latin school, which were explicitly created to produce "good citizens for the use of the church and state."[121] By the late sixteenth century, all members of the clergy, who "belonged without exception to the honorability," came up through these schools, but the clergy quickly developed into a relatively closed caste, and because their education was subsidized, competition for entry into the program was fierce. There were places in the cloister schools for only about 10 percent of the students enrolled in the Latin schools, and many of those who did not make the cut simply returned to their towns, and in some cases villages, to work at some form of manual labor for which their education was irrelevant. However, they were particularly likely to become members of the local notability and, even if they didn't, their literacy meant that "there was in Württemberg rather early a relatively broad layer ... with at least a certain amount of advanced education." For those who could afford it, though, education in a Latin school offered other paths into the honorability if a clerical position was unobtainable or not desired: through the university to a degree in law or medicine, a position as a scribe (which often had to be purchased), or training as an apothecary or merchant. The "honorability was [thus] an educated strata," steeped in a curriculum that emphasized strict Lutheran orthodoxy, veneration of the classics, and a strict adherence to the established order.[122]

If the honorability at the district level were distinguished by their education, the bureaucrats in the central government were even more highly educated, and most had also traveled to other parts of Germany and Europe.[123] The central bureaucracy included both nobles, who often came from independent knighthoods and small principalities near Württemberg, and commoners, who were mainly drawn from the district honorability.[124] The nobles staffed some positions alone, particularly those that required practical experience more than an advanced education.[125] Some served with honorables in specialized bureaus like the High Council, despite having no legal training, but by the seventeenth century even nobles in this body had to pass an exam and write a sample brief, and gradually "for ... even the aristocrats, the study of law" became "an essential preliminary to appointment" to high bureaucratic office.[126] This had always been the case for the commoners, for they were referred to as "learned councilors," and were brought in specifically to provide legal expertise they had gained through their studies at the university, most often the University of Tübingen, which most of them capped by earning a doctorate in law. However, in addition to studying at this local institution, the majority spent several years at universities in other parts of Germany, other Protestant countries in Northern Europe, and even Catholic France and Italy. The guidelines for hiring councilors in the sixteenth century stipulated that they be "men of open character, shrewdness, and bearing," and the advanced study and cosmopolitan experiences their education involved, their exposure to the problems of provincial government at the highest levels, and their contacts beyond the duchy meant that, while they were confirmed Lutherans and considered themselves to be custodians of the duchy's laws and traditions, they had a broader, more cosmopolitan outlook than the district-bound members of the honorability.

Furthermore, their advanced education and administrative experience gave these officials habits of thought and methods of problem solving that set them apart from the provincial population, and even to some extent from the more provincial honorables. At the university, "the official ... learned to sort things out in the ways taught there: into the forms of books, lectures, and outlines ... he studied system and consequence from men whose task it was to create them; he learned ordered argument, cause and effect: intellectual patterns" far removed from the visceral, emotionally charged processing of immediate experience.[127] In the conduct of high administration, sequestered in quiet chambers reading reports from the districts and writing analyses for their colleagues and summaries for their superiors, conferring on technical matters in routine interactions with their peers and offering learned judgments in conferences with other officials, the central administrators were developing a novel way of perceiving, conceptualizing, and influencing the world, a way that involved gaining information solely through written descriptions, conceiving it in relationship to an intricate system of written prohibitions and imperatives, and exerting influence by issuing of written instructions. While they of course lived their daily lives, like the rest of society, in face-to-face encounters in emotionally charged situations, both in their work relationships with other high officials and their off-duty hours, their professional activities put them in a different mental world than the great mass of people they governed and connected them to a peer-group that extended far beyond the duchy's borders. Increasingly, the central bureaucrat's:

> skill lay in dealing with people and pursuits at a distance ... people and pursuits he did not fully know, and which therefore he categorized. He was constantly obliged to sort out his situation and his duties in ways that accorded with general instructions, and which could be reported briefly and systematically to his superiors. His occupation was to reconcile the particularities of his sphere of authority with the laws and general aims of his employers and of his caste, with the making of order; what could not be ordered had to be ignored.[128]

These bureaucrats, in short, both administered the repression of behaviors and practices that had been deemed illicit, and repressed in themselves ideas and information that could not be processed bureaucratically.

The professional bureaucrats in Stuttgart were not the only component of the ducal government that became increasingly separated from Württemberg's provincial society and culture during the course of the early modern period, while at the same time contributing to the repression of magical practices, beliefs, perceptions, and cognition. The court was always somewhat removed from regular society, of course, separated by rank and purpose and tied in with the regional and national nobility, but through the middle of the seventeenth century it remained strongly rooted in provincial society and culture.[129] Beginning in the late seventeenth century, though, the ducal court rapidly distanced itself from these, emphasizing in their place ties to the international aristocracy and the culture emanating from France. In 1677, Duke William Ludwig died just three years after his father Eberhard III, the last of the traditional "provincial fathers," and his brother Friedrich Karl became regent for William Ludwig' son Eberhard Ludwig. Friedrich Karl's education had been "shifted away from the humanistic-theological concerns of traditional Württemberg education to focus on the practical arts of governing," and he had traveled widely and "mingled with ... European noblemen."[130] He consciously separated himself from ... his father's retainers" and "introduced ... operatic performances, ballets, and balls" in place of "the long drinking bouts ... hunting and feasting ... around which ... Eberhardine festivities had centered." His chief privy councilor "presided over the [duchy's] first ... salon" where, "to the horror of the estates, the assembled notables and literati were expected to converse in French and to show a knowledge of and a concern for the fashions current at Versailles." When Eberhard Ludwig came of age, he quickly showed that he "not only shared his uncle's perception ... completely, but took it to new heights."[131] He had taken "meticulous note of the resplendent Catholic centers at Versailles and the Hofburg ... internalized these standards and sought whenever possible to surpass them."[132] He justified his extravagant court [and] ... flagrant marital infidelities ... by making references to Versailles."[133] The high point of the court's fascination with French culture came under Carl Eugen, who "from 1748 on ... employed a full-time consultant at Paris whose sole responsibility was to supply the duke with all new French publications, court circulars, and manuals of ... style."[134] Since the dukes set up cabinet governments staffed by courtiers in order to administer the duchy without the interference of the recalcitrant provincial bureaucrats for a significant period of the century, this Francophile orientation opened up a significant conduit for the French Enlightenment to influence the duchy's internal administration and elite culture.[135] Further, the courtiers of Württemberg, like the aristocrats of France, came to see themselves as a distinct, superior form of humanity, distinguished by their familiarity with the latest developments of Enlightened culture and by their self-control, which meant not only the control over one's own bodily functions and emotional displays demanded by refined courtly manners, but also the imperviousness to emotional displays and bonds of human sympathy required to demonstrate and defend the superior position of members of the ruling bloodlines.

While the honorability, central bureaucracy, and court nobility all had cultural features that set them apart from the popular culture of the mass of peasants and townspeople who inhabited the duchy, all three were still committed to repressing aspects of that culture, particularly magic, through legal prosecution as well as religious and educational indoctrination, and all three had motivations for and mechanisms of both formal and informal repression within their own memberships. To a considerable extent, these were the same as or analogous to those at work in the lower classes. The upper classes, too, were subject to legal penalties and church sanctions for illegal and immoral activities; their professional and business opportunities reflected their informal standing among their peers; and their marital and other social prospects were strongly affected by their reputations. Their dress, weddings, and funerals were also regulated, even if they were permitted to be fancier than those of the lower classes. Both district and central officials had to swear to uphold Lutheran orthodoxy in order to take office, and no one with an "unsavory reputation" could sit in the diet.[136] This rule was used by the "cultivated, class-conscious patriciate" from the leading cities who made up the executive committee to "screen out ... undesirables" from the smaller towns. In the late seventeenth and eighteenth centuries this inner circle, who were "embarrassed" by "the coarse manners of the delegates from the smaller market towns," gradually separated "themselves from the rank and file of the estates," seizing effective political control while asserting their social superiority. Simultaneously, they drew closer to the high officials in the central bureaucracy through ties of marriage and recruitment, and these "close ... ties to the Ehrbarkeit brought many of its values."[137]

Even the cosmopolitan court could not escape traditional values entirely. When Eberhard Ludwig made it clear that he intended to marry his mistress despite the fact that his wife was still alive, the provincial elite, which was both scandalized by the affair and furious about the Duke's high-handed rule, expensive tastes, and foreign values, made common cause with his estranged wife, who heightened their resistance by claiming that he planned to convert to Catholicism to get the marriage annulled and planned to take control of taxation from the estates.[138] With the support of the privy council and the estates she appealed to her father, the Margrave of Baden-Durlach, for help, and faced with a looming national scandal and the possibility of imperial intervention, Eberhard Ludwig backed down and sent his mistress away. He eventually brought her back married to a minor nobleman who agreed not to consummate the marriage in return for high office, but in the meantime he had already begun to ice out the high bureaucrats from policymaking by ceasing to attend meetings of the privy council and setting up an alternative cabinet of courtiers with whom he made decisions and issued orders that the bureaucrats simply put into effect. The point here is not only that the affair illustrates well the interplay of formal sanctions, informal manipulation of formal institutions, and informal sanctions at the highest levels of ducal society, but also that the basic scenario could have played out with different characters, different costumes, and only somewhat different issues at the local level: the combination of moral outrage and political interest, the use of rumor and maneuvering of factions, the appeal to a distant statutory authority and the threat of scandal, and, finally, the negation of formal powers through *fait acompli* all had their parallels at every level of society. Furthermore, while the court may have defied the moral values of the surrounding society, it enforced its own values fiercely, employing ridicule and accolades, gossip and rumor, social ostracism and access to privilege, power, and office to enforce an exacting conformity to the prevailing standards of courtly behavior and belief. It has been said that "beyond the walls of the ducal residence cultural conformity was a salient characteristic of Württemberg society," but with the one caveat that the culture within those walls was somewhat different from that outside, the statement was just as true within them as well.[139] For that matter, the same could be said of village, small town, and court societies most everywhere else in Europe at the time, almost certainly in theory and most often in practice too.

Individual psychophysiology

While it is important to understand the many and varied social mechanisms that were available to repress magical beliefs and practices in early modern Württemberg, in the end all of them depended for their efficacy on their ability to affect individual peoples' mental processing, to induce them to act differently, think differently, and ultimately to experience the world differently. Therefore, before we consider that actual record of repression in the duchy, we need to investigate the ways in which repressive social mechanisms could be translated into repressive psychological mechanisms. In considering this, four major issues need to be examined: first, the modes of transmission, the means by which society communicated the need to repress ideas and intentions to individuals; second, the modes of assimilation, the ways in which individuals cognized the social insistence that ideas and intentions be repressed; third, the integrability of the repressive imperative, the compatibility of the call to repress with existing knowledge and belief; and, fourth, the "direction" of repression, whether it involved rejecting ideas or suppressing intentions that people were already conscious of or precluding them from coming into consciousness in the first place.

There are two basic modes of transmission by which societies communicate their knowledge and beliefs to their members: explicit and implicit.[140] The explicit mode involves conscious instruction, either a formal educational effort or informal instructions given in the course of other activities.

The implicit mode works through example and inference in which a person participates in group activities, imitates others' actions, deduces values from actions and incidental utterances, and extrapolates more general principles which are then applied in other circumstances. In general, implicit transmission employing imitation and inference is the more important, if only because it is more pervasive: on the one hand, the amount that people must learn in order to function in any society is far too great to be codified and communicated explicitly, while on the other hand values and beliefs are embodied in every action and utterance of every member of society, so this is not necessary. In the case of repression, however, explicit transmission would seem to play a relatively greater role than in the process of socialization overall since it is less clear what someone has not done than what they have done, and, in any case, explicit transmission clearly played a prominent role in the repression of magic because the need for it was largely defined by the conscious deliberations of a small, highly educated elite and communicated through treatises and tracts, laws and instructions, sermons and summonses. This is not to underplay the extent to which implicit forms of communication would have played a role as the elite's desire to eliminate magic from the culture was assimilated into local communities, but just to highlight the importance of explicit instruction in the case of imperatives arising not from long-established local traditions but instead from recent innovations at the highest levels of society.

Once transmitted, there are two modes through which the need for repression are cognized: conscious and nonconscious. There is currently some debate as to whether consciousness is an active agent in decision making or merely a retrospective awareness of decisions already made, but in either case it does seem clear that it is closely connected to a special form of focused, top-level processing in which perceptual and cognitive outputs converge and the final determination is made about what actions are to be taken.[141] One of the main functions of this special processing is to facilitate learning; again, there is some debate whether any learning can take place without this processing, but there is no question that it plays a crucial role in handling critical and novel situations and in learning involved tasks, complex ideas, and substantial bodies of information.[142] This conscious processing has an obvious connection to explicit means of cultural transmission, and it clearly plays at least some role in imitation and inference as well. It also plays an important role in repression prompted by social rules, not only because they are often transmitted explicitly, but also because previously existing or newly generated ideas and intentions must be evaluated in light of the newly learned prohibition in order to weigh the costs of transgressing it against the benefits of maintaining or manifesting them. If the calculation is to implement the prohibition, then the idea is classified as wrong (in either the factual-linguistic or moral-emotional sense) or the intention to act is suppressed through activation of the frontal cortex's inhibitatory neural network. The neurological process by which ideas are evaluated and linked to qualitative judgments is not well understood, but there is evidence from neuroimaging that ideas that are consistent with beliefs are processed in different brain regions than ideas that contradict them. Conscious suppression causes ideas to be recalled less frequently, and there is reason to believe that "the left frontal lobe" of the neocortex "may play a significant role in ... the rejection, inhibition, and forgetting of information that is consciously recognized as undesirable."[143] In any case, the existence of an inhibitory system controlled at least in part by the highest processing regions of the neocortex has been well established by neuroimaging, and it has been show to influence motor functioning, the experience of pain, perceptual processing, and even executive functions like reality testing and critical evaluation.[144]

While conscious attention plays a critical role in much if not all learning, as skills, including cognitive processing like making evaluations and implementing inhibitory reactions, are mastered, their performance becomes "internalized" or "automotized" through the process of dissociation.[145] Dissociation, in which neural networks capable of performing "effortlessly, concurrently, and without awareness" are put in place, is "a fundamental aspect of cognitive processing" in general, and neural imaging studies have shown that this process changes some of the brain areas activated during the cogitation involved in performing the same task.[146] "Repeated attempts to forget ... may develop into a practiced coping strategy that no longer has to be put into effect deliberately," while not only can complex judgments of consciously perceived stimuli be made outside of awareness, but also they "can be performed even on subliminal stimuli."[147] In this way, externally imposed prohibitions of beliefs and behaviors go from being consciously weighed decisions about costs and benefits to "ingrained and habitual" internal repression of ideas and intentions.

Both the ease with which this process of internalization takes place and the degree to which the "ingrained and habitual" self-censorship will come to feel "natural" reflect the third issue involved in the implementation of sociocultural repression through psychological repression, the integrability of the repressive imperative. As we have seen, neural imaging studies have shown that ideas that are consistent with existing beliefs are processed differently than those that conflict with them, and they have also shown that "syllogistic reasoning is impaired when the outcome ... is in conflict ... with belief."[148] Cognitive studies support these observations, for "having a belief changes the way evidence is collected and evaluated," and, in particular, people tend "to evaluate incoming evidence in support of current beliefs."[149] Repeated exposure to an assertion increases the likelihood in itself that it will be believed, and "pre-existing notions of the world and human nature can determine and constrain interpretations and explanations."[150] It is well known that individual beliefs exist as part of a "web of belief," that, to switch from a cognitive to a semiotic idiom, symbols exist as part of a system of symbols, and these complexes act as "mental scaffolding" for "appraising, explaining, and integrating new observations."[151] Hence, the "acquisition of beliefs must be understood in the context of ... other aspects of cognition, experience, and behavior.[152] If a new idea does not fit well into the pre-existing "web," the process of internalization will be inhibited and once accomplished will be experienced as oppressive and exert a relatively weak hold, while if it does integrate easily, it "becomes so ingrained and habitual that ... it comes to feel 'natural,'" and the person will "seldom feel the weight of it upon" him or her.[153]

The last aspect of the psychological dimension of repression that needs to be considered is the "direction" of repression, to what extent it involved rejecting information or suppressing intentions that people were already conscious of and to what extent it involved preventing them from coming to awareness in the first place.[154] This issue is particularly important for understanding the repression of magic because while the traditional modern educated understanding could treat it as simply the expulsion of wrong ideas from the conscious belief system so that they could not be used to misinterpret perceptions of the external world and internal sensations, and more recent postmodern interpretations treated it as simply the replacement of one more-or-less arbitrary set of signs with another, we have seen that magical beliefs had considerable more reference to reality than heretofore recognized, so it is also necessary to account not only for how their invalid elements came to be recognized and rejected and for how the evolving constellation of signs that made up modern educated culture changed in ways incompatible with magical significations, but also how these real inputs came to be routinely excluded from consciousness, so that the traditional modern educated psyche came to be unable to recognize the influence of interpersonal relations on health or the utility of ritual systems that manifest information and abilities inaccessible to normal consciousness.

To begin with, it must be recognized that physiologically there appears to be a certain amount of overlap between conscious and non-conscious processing, a "gray area" between fully conscious activity and fully automated, dissociated activity.[155] Specifically, four separate conditions affect the degree of conscious involvement in actions: intentionality, voluntariness (control over activation), autonomy of execution, and awareness. It is possible, for example, to have the intention to do something and set it in motion, but not to have conscious awareness of the process of carrying it out or control over its execution. Similarly, it is possible not to consciously intend that something happen but to initiate and control the activity that carries it out consciously, while remaining unaware of the consequences even as they unfold. Furthermore, which parts are conscious and which are unconscious are not absolutely determined, for distraction, sedation, and strong external command can redirect consciousness, diverting or focusing it to increase or decrease the number of aspects to which it will attend.[156]

Another thing that must be recognized is that not all information in the brain that cannot be brought to consciousness is being repressed; some, like early memories, may not be retrievable because it was coded in a way that can no longer be accessed, like files on a computer disk written by an obsolete operating system, or because the neurons responsible have been overgrown by newer ones that physically prevent direct connections.[157] Similarly, because the human brain includes two autonomous and complementary cognitive and memory systems, a rational-linguistic system primarily located in the left cerebral cortex and particularly tied in to the external network of linguistic culture, and associational-imagic system primarily located in the right and particularly tied in with the internal limbic (emotional) and autonomic nervous systems, it is also possible for the right hand not only to not know what the left hand is doing, but to be incapable of understanding why it is doing it as well.[158] While the division between the two systems has been exaggerated in many popular accounts over the past few decades, for they are significantly interconnected and mutually supportive, both clinical and experimental experience has shown that information can exist in one half that is inaccessible to the other when the primary connection between them is severed.[159] In these cases, the person can continue to function because of interconnections at lower levels of the nervous system, but with noticeable disjunctions in higher cognitive functioning.[160] In particular, the left hemisphere will confabulate explanations to account for knowledge generated by the right, invent spurious reasons for actions initiated by it, and may even conceptualize the left half of the body as being controlled by some alien being.[161]

Of course, these exaggerated phenomena have been noted in extreme cases in which the connection between the two hemispheres has been completely severed, but more selective disconnects can be created in a normal brain because the frontal lobes on either side can actively inhibit the transfer of information between them, or because the information is in a form that is not directly comprehensible to the other system and it lacks mediating structures to represent it in a form that it can apprehend.[162] This situation can presumably exist on both sides, but it is most significant in terms of understanding magical beliefs, and their repression, when it involves the left hemisphere blocking, neglecting, or distorting information from the right, because magical beliefs and experiences are strongly associated with increased neural activity in the right hemisphere and decreased activity in the left. Belief in the paranormal has even been characterized in the neurocognitive literature as constituting an "over-reliance on right hemisphere processes," but to turn this around, disbelief in magic could equally be characterized as an overreliance on left hemisphere processes, one which is only achieved through a concerted and active repression of perceptions apprehended and cognitions generated by the right.[163]

To return to the question of directionality, it seems likely that the repression of magic involves both expulsion and exclusion. On the one hand, at the risk of oversimplification, magical beliefs can be seen to be rational-verbal representations of associational-imagic processes and their products. Explicit renunciation of these beliefs serves the purpose of excluding them from the conscious network of linguistic representations of the world and precludes their employment in the conscious formulation of deliberate actions, an exclusion from consideration that can become automatic through internalization so that not only are magical beliefs not actively incorporated into rational-linguistic cogitations, but even the suggestion that they might be at work is processed via the alternative, resistant neural circuitry employed for unwanted evidence. Even more powerfully, the repression of these concepts inhibits their function as mediating structures through which right-brain processes can be represented to the left brain, depriving the brain as a whole of the ability to bring this significant body of understanding into rational-linguistic awareness.[164] Furthermore, it is possible for the left frontal lobe to block information "that is consciously recognized as undesirable" from being transferred from the right hemisphere at all, and, finally, for the right frontal lobe, which "appears to maintain bilateral inhibitory... control over information processing in both halves of the brain and limbic system... to prevent information that has been emotionally recognized" as forbidden "from spreading across the corpus callosum, thereby preventing the disruption of information processing in the left half of the brain" by the inadmissible evidence from the right.[165]

Thus, just as the repression of magic at the social level worked through a variety of mechanisms ranging from formal prosecution to informal ostracism, so too the repression of magic at the psychological level worked through a variety of mechanisms ranging from the expulsion from consciousness of pre-existing beliefs and any impulse to act on them through the destruction of mediating constructs facilitating the incorporation into consciousness of perceptions and insights associated with magic, whether reported by others or experienced first hand, to the reflexive inhibition of intersystemic transfers of disallowed inputs, insuring that subliminal perceptions and unconscious cogitations remain inaccessible to consciousness. The repression of magic thus involved a form of neurological fine-tuning in itself, a kind of reverse-shamanism that inhibited the accessing of knowledge and powers inaccessible to normal waking consciousness, initially because accessing such knowledge and powers outside the framework established by the church was seen as devilish, incompatible with the moral strictures of the Christian faith, and later because it was seen as foolish, incompatible with the cognitive processes connected to rationalist materialism. There is no question that this repression made it possible for a large number of invalid assumptions and conclusions and misleading ideas about how the world works to be cleared out and kept out of the way while the new, mechanistic model of reality was being constructed, but we have seen evidence that in the process valid and useful insights and procedures were also repressed. While it is important to understand how the large quantities of bathwater were thrown out of the culture during the Enlightenment, it is also important to understand how in the process a few babies came to be thrown out as well. This process, at the level of the interaction between the central government, the local elites, and the ordinary people in the duchy of Württemberg, will be the subject of the final section of this chapter.

Repression and the marginalization of magic

There were a variety of formal and informal means through which repression could work in early modern Europe, ranging from explicit legal sanctions against illicit activities formulated and enforced by the highest levels of government through informal ostracism from social groups for the expression of unacceptable opinions to the unconscious suppression of perceptions inconsistent with socially defined reality. Some of these worked in ways that most of the time were hidden even from the individuals involved. Many worked in ways that were apparent to the participants but left few historical traces that can be studied systematically. The judicial process, however, left a significant body of records that contain both quantitative and qualitative evidence about the repression of magic from the sixteenth through the eighteenth centuries. We have been using these sources to study the nature of magical practices and the characteristics of magical practitioners throughout this book, and in this final section we will use them to gain some insights into the process of repression and its effects on the place of magic in provincial culture and magical practitioners in provincial society. We will start by looking at a statistical overview of the pace of prosecutions, and then take a more qualitative look at the main periods of rise and decline they reveal. The evidence in these records is naturally biased toward formal judicial forms of repression, so in addition to providing statistics about the pace of prosecutions they are richest in information about the formal interactions between the central bureaucrats, district and local officials, and ordinary Württembergers, but they also contain incidental evidence about the attitudes, beliefs, and practices held by members of these different levels of society and the way they changed in response not only in general ways to larger currents in European culture, but also in specific ways to the dynamics of their ongoing interaction.

Figure 8.1 shows the overall pace of prosecution for magical crimes in Württemberg from the mid-sixteenth century to the beginning of the nineteenth century. The most striking trend is the twin peaks associated with the period of intense witchcraft persecution, rising from virtually nothing in the 1570s to over 50 per decade in the 1610s and 20s, falling to less than a third of that number in the 1640s, and then rising back to over 50 in the 1660s, before falling to half of that total in the '70s and '80s and then again to under ten in the 1690s. The only other notable feature is that instead of

Figure 8.1 Witchcraft and magic trials

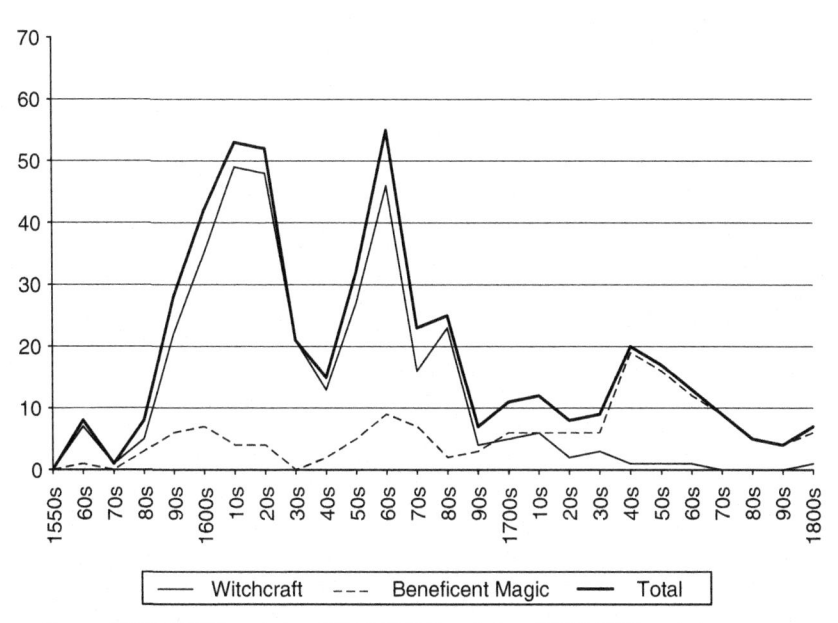

Source: WSAS A209 Repertorium; WSAS A213 Repertorium; WSAS 309 Repertorium; Index to witch and related cases in Tübingen Universtätsarchiv 84/1–70 by H. C. Erik Midelfort; Midelfort, *Witch Hunting in Southwest Germany*, Appendix.

gradually tailing off in the eighteenth century, the number of trials fluctuated around ten in each of the next four decades and then doubled to 20 in the 1740s before declining slowly back to below ten toward the end of the eighteenth century.

Before considering what questions this pattern raises, however, it is worth looking at the pace of prosecutions from another point of view, from the standpoint of trials per capita, because, as we saw in Chapter 2, the number of inhabitants in the duchy fluctuated widely over the course of the period, rising steeply to 450,000 people around 1630, falling to less than 25 percent of that total around 1640, rebounding to about 225,000 in the early 1650s, rising slowly over most of the next century to reach 450,000 again only around 1730, and then rising more steeply to 650,000 by 1789.[166]

Figure 8.2 shows the trials per 100,000 inhabitants, and suggests one important modification to the pattern conveyed by the simple total of trials per decade. Instead of two equal peaks during the witch persecutions with a dramatic drop between them, because the population was so much greater before the 1630s than in the 1660s, the earlier peak represented only about two-thirds the intensity of the 1660s, and the drop in the 1630s and '40s

380 Realities of Witchcraft and Popular Magic

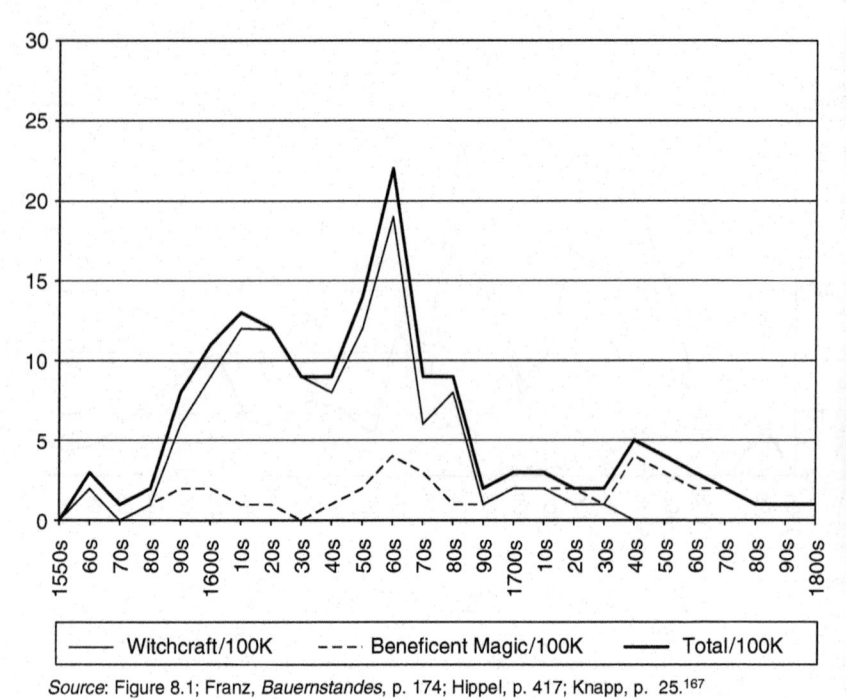

Figure 8.2 Witchcraft and magic trials per 100,000 inhabitants

Source: Figure 8.1; Franz, *Bauernstandes*, p. 174; Hippel, p. 417; Knapp, p. 25.[167]

represented a far smaller decline in intensity than the absolute drop in numbers would suggest. This modification simplifies the situation somewhat. The overall trend is the rising intensity of trials in the duchy from the 1560s to the 1660s and their decline thereafter, with one major interruption in each direction: the significant but temporary decline from the 1620s to '40s, and the sharp but temporary rise from the 1740s to the 1760s. Therefore, in this section we will look first at the reasons for the initial surge of trials from the mid-sixteenth century through the early seventeenth century. Second, we will look at the period of flux to determine why the rate of prosecutions fell off in the 1630s and '40s and then rose again so dramatically. Third, we will look at the reasons for the equally dramatic downturn in the rate of prosecutions from the late seventeenth century into the early eighteenth century. Fourth, we will consider the reasons for the spike in prosecutions in the 1740s, and finally, fifth, we will examine the reasons for the gradual decline over the second half of the century. Throughout, our primary concern will be to see how the changing pace of prosecutions relates to the larger campaign against magic, in terms of the motives and means being used and their effects.

The roots and rise of judicial repression

The drive to repress magic was deeply rooted in European culture, although exactly what was meant by magic and the reasons why it should be repressed changed over time.[168] Sorcery, of course, is antisocial by nature, since it involves the occult manipulation of natural forces and interpersonal bonds to cause harm, so ancient religions contained numerous countermeasures and governments have punished it "from the very earliest times."[169] The term "magic," however, is derived from the Persian *magu*, priest, which the Greeks began using around the time of the Persian Wars to disparage other Greeks who employed nontraditional beneficent magic or belonged to novel ecstatic cults.[170] The basis of this hostility was the concern that unconventional spiritual activity might disrupt the community's relationship to its traditional gods. Similarly, the ancient Hebrews were concerned that magical practices invoking gods or spirits other than Yahweh would anger him since he had explicitly forbidden them from venerating any other deity. However, just as Greek priests employed a variety of ritual practices that were very similar to those they opposed, early Hebrew priests produced magical effects to demonstrate the power of their god and allowed ordinary people to practice divination and other forms of beneficent magic as long as they ascribed their power to Yahweh. Gradually the Hebrew prohibitions came to be understood to forbid all ritual practices that went beyond supplication on the basis that they impiously presumed to coerce the almighty, though, and Christianity inherited Judaism's rejection of magic, explaining the apparently magical effects produced by biblical figures and Christian saints and the supernatural features of the sacraments as miracles manifesting God's power freely given, while considering all other magical effects to involve the agency of demons, evil spirits led by the Devil, who led practitioners to think they had magical power in order to tempt them to sin. Furthermore, late-Classical theologians combined the Judeo-Christian insistence on the omnipotence of god with a strain of pagan philosophy that held that all magic was produced through fraud, illusion, and natural processes to argue that while God might occasionally let demons exercise supernatural power if it suited his purpose, they mainly worked through illusion and occult natural processes, duping people into believing that they could produce miraculous results. Thus, by the end of antiquity, the concept of magic had evolved from the unsanctioned practice of heterodox rituals that threatened the community's relationship to its official gods to the idolatrous invocation of evil spirits based on a false understanding of the causes of magical effects.

This dual objection to magic, that it was both idolatrous and illusory, an affront to God and foolish to boot, opened up the possibility of repressing it on two levels, through public sanctions to suppress overt behaviors and practices offensive to God and through psychological processes to suppress private thoughts and feelings leading to misperceptions and miscalculations.

While both were pursued simultaneously over the centuries, the emphasis shifted depending on the power available to the authorities and the severity of the threat magic seemed to pose.[171] When Rome became Christian, it already had a long history of persecuting unsanctioned ritual activities as potentially damaging to both individuals' interests and Imperial authority, and "the early Christian emperors began their prosecutions where the pagans had ended theirs," suppressing competing religious movements and making most magical practices capital offenses.[172] "Under Valens, the terrorized citizens burned their books, fearing that they might be indicted for witchcraft."[173] However, while the Empire largely succeeded in eradicating formal pagan cults, it was less successful at rooting out popular practices, and even though the Germanic successor states maintained their own laws against sorcery and adopted Imperial laws against magic more generally they lacked the power to uproot popular magical practices. Instead, during the early Middle Ages the church pursued a policy that emphasized superimposing Christian content on traditional forms, like having clergymen bless fields and animals as pagan priests had done, and turning animal sacrifices into Christian feasts (a policy that was furthered by popular magic's readiness to substitute Christ, the saints, and the Virgin Mary for pagan deities in blessings and other ritual activities), combined with vigorous denials by theologians and priests of the power of (nonmiraculous) magic. Thus, St Boniface declared belief in witches and werewolves to be unchristian, and the *Canon Episcopi* condemned the belief of some women that they flew at night on the backs of animals with the goddess Diana as an illusion. Even though many magical practices flew in the face of a strict understanding of Christian theology, the early medieval church treated them relatively mildly – while the *Episcopi* called for banishment of sorcerers and malefic witches, it prescribed penance for those who said they flew with Diana, for example – and it turned a blind eye to innumerable popular magical practices that were either thinly Christianized or, like some of the blessings we have seen, simply noncommittal about the source of their power. Lacking the coercive power to suppress them physically, the church's most potent countermeasure was to undercut them psychologically.

During the High Middle Ages the church decisively rejected a call by natural magicians to accept their branch of magic, which was based on a revival of classical learning and the importation of Arabic scholarship beginning in the twelfth century, as an acceptable branch of philosophy concerned with understanding and manipulating the hidden forces of nature, the occult sympathies and antipathies that they claimed permeate the universe and knowledge of which they claimed could lead to wisdom and contribute to an understanding of God.[174] Instead, the church's leading thinkers reiterated that any invocation of spirits constituted idolatry, there are no good or neutral spirits, magical activities cannot lead to knowledge of god or the Holy Spirit, and miracles and magic are fundamentally different.

Consequently, while natural magic enjoyed general acceptance as a body of knowledge about hidden processes in nature until the Scientific Revolution, it never won general acceptance as a set of legitimate spiritual practices or as a source of wisdom or knowledge of God. Furthermore, as part of the scholastic movement in which the church rationalized its beliefs, theologians systematized ideas about the supernatural into the demonology that included beneficent practices along with *maleficium* and diabolism as part of the Devil's conspiracy against Christian community, a way of luring the unwary away from the true Christian path in the guise of doing good, an alternative form of temptation to the direct appeal of doing bad. This understanding of the relationship between magic and the Devil, the witch demonology, was formulated between the mid-fourteenth and late fifteenth century, and disseminated, with elaborations and increasing numbers of examples of actual cases, in the early sixteenth century. It constituted a call to switch the emphasis of the repressive impulse from denial to suppression, and fit with both the growing potential for effective coercion by the Renaissance state and the growing extent and coherence of the beliefs and practices both beneficent and malefic in the "common tradition" that had emerged, as we have seen, over the course of the High Middle Ages.

The impact of this growing concern in Württemberg appears to have been limited through the middle of the sixteenth century. The first known witch trial in the duchy took place in 1497, and only one of the 30 trials for magic of all types that took place over the next six decades is known to have ended with an execution.[175] Most of these trials were handled locally, with little involvement of the central government, and the first measure against magic at the ducal level was simply an instruction to the clergy to identify and admonish "fortune tellers and similar Devil incanters" in 1546.[176] The words of the instruction, its recipients, and the prescribed action to be taken all indicate that while it may have been influenced by the demonology's association of magical practitioners with the Devil, it was not concerned with an underground conspiracy of malefic witches, but instead with the improper activities of beneficent magicians. Similarly, the first statutory measure against magic in the Fifth Provincial Law Code of 1552 simply shifted responsibility for identifying and admonishing practitioners to the magistrates, although it added the threat of banishment for a second offense and execution for a third. Furthermore, while the explanation of the law called magicians "idolaters" who had "fallen from god," it mentioned neither the Devil nor malefic magic, complaining instead of the "unnecessary costs" to the clients of practices, "which should be held" it said, "to be shameless lies." This law indicates that the ducal government was still thinking in terms of the early medieval, "*Episcopi*," tradition that emphasized the illusory nature of magic, not the late medieval witch demonology.

Fifteen years later, however, the Sixth Provincial Ordinance of 1667 that crowned the reign of the reforming Duke Christoph included new statutes concerning "Magic, Devil Incantation, and Soothsaying" that signaled the government's absorption of the witch demonology.[177] Following the *Constitution Criminalis Carolina*, the imperial law code that Charles V had issued in 1532 to serve as a model for the member states of the Holy Roman Empire, the new law adopted its decree that harmful magic deserved death "almost word for word." However, while the *Carolina* simply left magic without harm to local custom, the Sixth Provincial Ordinance referred to a "pact with the Devil to the deteriment and injury of men, with which however no one [is] done harm," calling it an "abomination before God" that was "in no way to be allowed," but rather immediately prosecuted with torture, and that could in some circumstances justify the death penalty by itself.[178] Magic involving neither harm nor a pact, specifically "magical soothsaying, advising, and helping, especially with healing" was to be punished less severely, as we have seen, but at the same time preachers were instructed to "inform the people ... what magic really involves."

The specific process by which this dramatic change of policy came about is not known, but several trends and events suggest the changes that were taking place just after mid-century. The pace of prosecutions in southwestern Germany as a whole picked up in the 1550s and '60s, spurred on especially in the second decade by the proliferation of publications concerned with witchcraft, a number of hailstorms that were thought to be the work of witches, and the first mass trials in the region.[179] The question had particular urgency since a number of trials took place between 1562 and 1565 in and around Stuttgart. One of them was the sampled trial of Magdelena Horn, who confessed without coercion to having perpetrated several acts of *maleficium*; came to see them under questioning, at least, as having been instigated by the Devil; and added that she been to dances on the Feuerbacher meadow.[180] This and others were connected to a large-scale trial in Esslingen, a free city surrounded by Württemberg's territory that lay only few miles from Stuttgart, and there was during the same years a mass trial resulting in 63 executions about 25 miles to the southeast, in the independent county of Helfenstein's major town, Wiesensteig.[181] The increased activity in the region created a kind of informal peer pressure among the men who ran the governments in the area that was made explicit by a question posed by the neighboring Count Philipp of Hanau-Lichtenbeg to the ducal chancellery in 1563, "concerning the prosecution of women who are accused of witchcraft."[182] The chancellery had to inform the neighboring ruler that "until now no common opinion has been established," but four years later the ducal government had an answer. Not only harmful magic but even a mere pact with the Devil could be sufficient cause for the death penalty, and the connection of all forms of magic to the Devil's conspiracy was to be preached throughout the land.

The promulgation of the Sixth Provincial Ordinance in 1567 set the stage for an upswing in prosecutions for witchcraft and magic in the duchy, but it does not seem to have caused one. Only a handful of trials are known to have occurred in the 1570s and 80s, and almost all of them took place in 1589. Thereafter the pace of prosecutions increased rapidly, rising to 28 in the 1590s, 44 in the 1600s, and 54 in the 1610s and again in the 1620s.

There are three possible explanations for the lag between 1567 and 1589. The first is suggested by the fact that the lag corresponded roughly to the reign of Duke Ludwig (1568–93), who was "loved by his subjects for his good nature and mildness" and is most strongly remembered for his patronage of the arts and his opulent court.[183] The big rise in prosecutions began in the 1590s, when Ludwig was succeeded by Duke Friedrich I, a "hard and relentless man" who strove to strengthen princely power. However, the pace of prosecution began to pick up while Ludwig was still alive, in 1589, with eight trials in that year alone and another seven between 1590 and his death, in 1593. Furthermore, while four trials started in 1594, Friedrich's first year in office, they dropped off to one to three per year thereafter, with the number reaching that of 1589 only in 1603, after Friedrich had been ruler for a decade. While his energetic style of administration may have contributed to a more aggressive police effort in the countryside in general, it does not seem that he created or even systematically intensified the persecution of witches.

The second explanation of the 20-year lag is that it is more or less an illusion, that it reflects not a change in the pace of prosecutions but the imposition of stricter reporting requirements by the central government in 1597.[184] However, while there is no question that the reporting requirements were tightened under Duke Friedrich and it is reasonable to assume that some early trials did take place for which we have no records, there are several reasons to think that the overall trend corresponded to that suggested by the known trials. First of all, information about early cases comes from a variety of sources, not just the ducal archives, and the fact that there was only one trial reported for the whole duchy between 1564 and 1589 while dozens of cases were recorded in neighboring territories makes it seem unlikely that a vigorous persecution managed to go entirely unnoticed.[185] Second, the reports of prosecutions to the ducal government began to increase significantly before Duke Ferdinand tightened the requirements, suggesting that it reflects something more than that. Third, it is known from incidental evidence within the recorded trials that there were also trials from the later period whose records have disappeared, so any estimation of the trend taking unrecorded trials in the early period into account would also have to take a "dark figure" for the later period into consideration as well.[186] Fourth, and, last, since the conditions promoting witch persecutions worsened in the decades around 1600, it seems unlikely that the pace of prosecution would have actually fallen after 1590, so while it may have increased somewhat more steadily than Figures 8.1 and 8.2 show, it seems clear that what followed from the Landesordnung was a gradual rise over the course of decades to the peak rates, not some sudden storm of persecution imposed or even directly promoted by the central government.

The third explanation for the relatively low rate of prosecutions before 1590 and the swelling number through the first decades of the 1600s is that they manifested the gradual confluence of two processes that were under way at the local level in the duchy in the late sixteenth century: first, the dissemination and assimilation of concern about magic and the Devil among local officials, and, second, the intensification of interpersonal conflicts and their manifestation as suspicions and acts of *maleficium* among the common people brought on by the deteriorating socioeconomic situation, both of which grew slowly during the 1570s and '80s and then reached a "tipping point" around 1590.[187] On the one hand, from the mid-1560s to the late 1580s a wave of persecutions swept through the neighboring Catholic jurisdictions in the region, and a rash of pamphlets and treatises appeared describing them and the diabolic conspiracy behind them.[188] On the other hand, the duchy, as we saw in Chapter 2, could only support about 360,000 people (85 percent of the 450,000 who inhabited it around 1630), and it reached that point of saturation, crossing into overpopulation, sometime in the years around 1590. The upsurge in trials thus appears to have happened when the idea of a diabolic conspiracy seemed to be confirmed by numerous instances in nearby territories, while at the same time socioeconomic conditions that promoted both fears of *maleficium* and acts of *maleficium* reached an acute stage.

Both were necessary to create the upsurge of prosecutions around the turn of the seventeenth century, for the ducal government could exercise only loose control over local administration and hence depended on the initiative of constables, preachers, and communal officials to implement its policies and enforce its laws, and they, in turn, depended to a considerable extent on the active cooperation of ordinary people. For one thing, it was impossible for them to know first hand more than a fraction of what was going on in their jurisdictions and who was doing it, so they had to rely on a combination of formal investigative opportunities like the *Vogtgericht* and annual church visitations and informal channels of communication that fed them reports and rumors from the community. For another thing, Württemberg's legal system, enshrined in the Tübingen Contract, the duchy's basic constitutional document that has often been compared to the English *Magna Carta*, guaranteed a legal and systematic trial, and so the magistrates had to temper "the inquisitorial process" of Roman and Canon law "with the accusatory principle," the Germanic traditional that criminal investigations could only be undertaken upon an accusation by a private citizen.[189] While constables had gained the power to instigate an investigation in the name of the Duke early in the sixteenth century, the necessity for a formal accusation in capital cases was never lost.[190] Only one of the sampled cases took place solely at the initiative of the magistrates, although significantly this was one of the two earliest among them. In 1604 the magistrates of Freudenstadt arrested Barbara Tolmayer for theft, and then accused her of witchcraft because her husband had recently been burned for it in Balingen.[191] Similarly, only one of the sampled trials began purely because of a complaint by a preacher: in 1659 Johannes Brand, the pastor of Geradstetten, accused Maria Laichlin, the wife of the mayor, of poisoning his sister-in-law, and even in this case Brand was acting essentially as a private citizen bringing a complaint of *maleficium* directed against someone in his household.[192]

Officials did have one important means of generating accusations other than making them themselves, of course: the use of torture during ongoing trials to extract the names of other witches a suspect would presumably have seen at witch dances. While they were not supposed to suggest names, this undoubtedly happened, and even if they didn't, many tortured suspects offered up lists with anywhere from a handful to dozens of potential suspects. These could be investigated in turn for other *indicia* or cross-referenced against the names on other suspects' lists to see if they appeared on several, which could lead to a person being prosecuted purely on the basis of coerced denunciations.[193] This process was the mechanism responsible for mass panics in which dozens of suspects were arrested, tortured, and executed, and it also generated a good number of smaller trials spread across different jurisdictions or over several years.[194] While mass panics were most characteristic of small independent jurisdictions like territorial bishoprics and imperial cities where there was no central authority to insist on systematic legal procedures, a number of towns in the duchy did experience them, like Dornhan in 1608, where a constable investigating complaints brought at an annual *Vogtgericht* used torture to produce an ever-widening circle of accusations until, as the husband of one of the suspects complained, "it seems as if the constable's private obsession has taken over this place."[195] Smaller trials in the duchy also began because suspects were implicated in trials in neighboring jurisdictions, as happened in the village of Rhodt, near Reichenbach, in 1592, when a woman named by a number of suspects in the nearby bishopric of Speyer was arrested and tortured by the constable, who appears to have been driven by a combination of zeal and avarice, until she confessed and implicated three other women, whom he proceeded to arrest and torture illegally.[196] The High Council was able to intervene before the situation developed into a mass panic, but suspicions and hatreds engendered by this incident festered among the people and resurfaced in a new round of investigations, this time sparked by accusations made by a suspect who had escaped from jail, a few years later.

Officials' initiative appears to have played a particularly prominent role in the very early trials, but by and large even then they formulated charges in interaction with commoners, investigating rumors, drawing out suspicions, stimulating confessions, and, more than anything, adding the stereotyped diabolic elements of pact, flight, and Sabbath to the commoner's initial concerns about *maleficium*, and gradually officials came to play a less prominent role and commoners a more prominent role in initiating trials (see Table 8.1). We have seen how Magdelena Horn's confession and confirmation of harm to animals and a child in 1565 broadened into a confession of contact with the Devil and participation in a witch dance over the course of two days of counseling by the preacher in Cannstatt.[197] Similarly, it was the mayor of Dietersweiler who connected Agatha Sacher's deleterious effect on her rival at her wedding in 1611 to the allegation made against her in the previous year by old Benedict Benne, and the mayor of Ebersbach who commented in 1619 that Maria Braittingen "appeared to be no Christian, but given over to the loathsome Satan" when he had her in custody for theft, prompting her to offer that she had had sex with the Devil "in the form of her boyfriend."[198]

Maria's spontaneous response to the mayor's accusation in 1619, in contrast to the coaching that appears to have been involved in Magdelena Horn's confession of diabolism in 1562, suggests that by the early seventeenth century the diabolic aspects of witchcraft were becoming more firmly established in popular understanding and experience. So, too, does her description of her relationship with the Devil, although the facts that she initially called her dreamy flight a trip to a "night dance," called the first two festivities she attended "feasts," and confessed to attendance at witch dances, without elaboration and with inconsistency as to number, only after further conversations with the magistrates, all indicate that the process was still incomplete. Similarly, while Hans Jacob Langen's description in 1631 of his experiences "riding the pitchfork," included a renunciation of the Trinity signed in blood that would seem connected to the idea of a pact, the trips themselves resembled traditional descriptions of the raids by women who flew at night to neighbors' wine cellars rather than the stereotypical flight to the Sabbath.[199] Furthermore, Maria's description of how she got the Devil to kill her hostile employer's cow for her suggests that diabolism was also becoming explicitly linked with *maleficium* in popular understanding and practice. So, too, does Margaritha Steiner's description of the various forms of *maleficium* she confessed to practicing in 1603.[200] While her testimony was extracted by torture, we have seen that most of the injuries she claimed to have caused were confirmed by the victims, and there was no need for the magistrates to prompt her to add "in the Devil's name" to her *maleficium* since the confession of a pact and attendance at the Sabbath that they also tortured from her were the expected proofs of diabolism, so it seems likely that she did invoke the Devil as part of her spells, which means her case represents an intermediate point of development along the path from traditional forms of *maleficium*, like Magdelena Horn's 40 years before, that referenced the Devil retroactively, to the elaborate diabolic incantations recited by Maria Gekin more than a century later.[201]

Table 8.1 Sources of accusations over time

Date	Official	Mixed	Commoner
Before 1600		1	
1600–9	1		
1610–9		2	1
1620–9		1	5
1630–9			1
1650–9	1		1
1660–9		3	3
1670–9		1	2
1680–9			2
1700–9			1

Source: Sampled witchcraft cases (see the appendix).

The rising per capita trial rate and the trend in accusations suggested by Table 8.1 suggest that over the course of this period Württembergers became increasingly ready to both perceive and to perpetrate acts of *maleficium*. Certainly Magdelena Horn's confessions indicate that some people resorted to such things earlier on, but the sheer growth in the number of people and the declining standard of living after 1590 makes it reasonable to think that, between the increasing competition for resources and the readiness to resort to violence in many forms we saw in Chapter 2, such things became more common. Similarly, one of the striking things about Magdelena Horn's story is that none of her victims seems to have been anxious to connect her to their woes, even the woman whose child confirmed that she had hit him before he died, but such innocence does not seem to have persisted. We have seen how, in the milieu of the 1620s, Anna Gebhard's sexual horseplay with Konrad Streich at his wedding was construed to be an act of *maleficium* when it seemed to have caused him to become impotent, and how, similarly, a residue at the bottom of a wine glass could give rise to rumors that Barbara Schmied tried to poison Johanna Fehlen.[202] On the other hand, we have seen that during the same decade Katharina Masten did berate and beat the servant girl Catharina Baitinger when she prevented her from settling a debt with her master by taking goods without permission, and that the evidence does strongly suggest that Maria Schneider tried to poison her step-grandson, the rival to her own natural grandchildren.[203]

The prosecutions falter

On the other hand, the 1620s was the first decade since the 1570s in which the number of trials declined, albeit slightly, beginning a much steeper fall that would last through the 1640s (see Figure 8.1). The steep decline in the 1630s and 40s is actually easier to explain, for this is when the Thirty Years'

War ravaged the duchy, killing or driving out the majority of the inhabitants, throwing the government into chaos, and all criminal proceedings fell off.[204] In the 1620s, however, the war did not affect Württemberg directly, so the end of the rising tide of prosecutions must have been caused by something else, by some endogenous factor within the duchy.

The explanation would seem to lie in the beginnings of a change in attitude toward the prosecutions and the demonology that informed them, the beginnings of a "crisis of confidence" that influenced a wide range of people, although it was most influential in the highest social circles, the courtiers and central bureaucrats in Stuttgart. To begin with, mass panics, the chain reaction trials that swept up dozens of suspects, tended to proceed "logically and relentlessly" from the initial stereotyped poor, elderly suspects through a sampling of the ordinary womenfolk to the wives and daughters of leading citizens like the "teachers, innkeepers, wealthy merchants" and even the magistrates themselves, people who the men running the trials knew personally or by reputation.[205] This progression, which reflected the tendency of people under torture to think of stereotyped suspects first and then name people they either knew and didn't like or knew of but didn't know as they cast about for names to satisfy their tormentor (as well as, presumably, sometimes wanting to get back at the rich and powerful people who ran the very government that was responsible for their misery). The "magistrates as well as ... members of the populace" came to see "that one could not accurately tell who the witches were"; and "that if the law were given free rein, no one would be safe from its relentless grasp." It did not necessarily stop people from believing in witches, but it did make them question whether the danger they posed could justify the cruelty and injustice of the trials. To people who went through the experience, who lost friends or relatives, or even just heard the screams of agony from the basement of the town hall day after day, and smelled the stench of burning flesh, people who heard the pleas and denunciations of the condemned on the executioner's block or the pyre and heard the pitiful cries and bitter arguments of heartbroken relatives, the mass trials seemed surely to be pulling up the wheat to get at the tares.[206]

While these doubts from experience affected only people who lived in the towns and villages that were directly involved, and even in them there were many who believed in the guilt of the condemned and the danger they posed, the doubts were fed by and fed into a broader movement that questioned different aspects of the persecutions and the demonology that sustained them. In the first place, the *Episcopi* tradition that held magical experiences to be illusory had strong roots in southwestern Germany, was maintained throughout the sixteenth century, and became increasingly influential in the seventeenth.[207] Its earliest application to witchcraft in the region was probably by Ulrich Molitor, a theologian and official in Tyrol, who argued that witches' crimes were illusory, although he still advocated death for anyone who actually swore allegiance to the Devil.[208] The position was first expressed in Tübingen by the theologian Martin Plantsch in 1505, after one off the duchy's earliest known witch trials, and was given its definitive formulation in the 1520s and 30s by Johann Brenz, Württemberg's leading reformer and religious advisor to Duke Christoph.[209] In particular, Brenz argued that witches could not raise storms, but instead the Devil merely inspired them to undertake rituals before storms that would have happened anyway, and in general he argued that storms, famines, and other misfortunes should be regarded as God's warning rather than evidence of human malevolence, a moderate, "providential" interpretation that would ultimately become a basic tenet of the Pietist movement in the late seventeenth and eighteenth centuries.[210]

Proponents of this position could still agree with advocates of a harsh policy that some people really did try to inflict harm through magic and that a true pact with the Devil deserved death, but Johann Weyer started another tradition that opposed witch prosecutions more forcefully by arguing that women who thought they inflicted harm magically or had a relationship with the Devil were simply melancholic, and reports of flights to Sabbaths were caused by hallucinogenic drugs.[211] He said that any "old deluded woman" misguided enough to admit to or even practice witchcraft needed Christian instruction, not death; that even learned magicians, men who "used the Devil" and therefore deserved punishment should not be executed; and that only poisoners, who committed a physical crime, deserved to die. In southwestern Germany, Weyer's call for leniency was taken up as early as 1585 by the Heidelberg mathematician Hermann Witekind, who published under the pseudonym August Lerchheimer and argued that "foolish, stubborn, miserable women" who thought they were powerful magicians capable of smiting their enemies were just "poor" and "insane" and should be punished mildly.[212] Similarly, Johann Georg Gödelmann, a Swabian jurist who had a position on the faculty at Rostock, argued in 1591 that witches only imagined that they worked magic and therefore should be treated mildly, although, like Weyer and Witekind, he called for harsher punishments for male magicians.

In 1600, Thomas Birch, the pastor of Untertürkheim, a village near Stuttgart, combined Weyer's position with the *Episcopi* tradition in a play entitled *A Mirror of Witches*, and in 1604 the Tübingen jurist Heinrich Bocer revised his opinions to take medical and providential interpretations into account, although he continued to support harsh punishments.[213] A pamphlet from the region published in 1616 gave a sensational account of the crimes associated with witchcraft, but then called them all devilish delusions. A few years later the Tübingen theologian Theodore Thumm articulated a more consistent formulation of Weyer's perspective, arguing that melancholic fantasies should not be punished and that while *maleficium* and a pact merited death, a pact alone did not. In 1630 the famous

Tübingen jurist Johann Harprecht, who had already endorsed Weyer's medical interpretation in 1615, adopted Thumm's position that a pact alone did not deserve death. In 1631 the Jesuit priest and theologian at Paderborn university Friedrich von Spee published an impassioned and influential argument against witch trials that focused on the brutality of and injustices resulting from the use of torture, and in 1659 Christoph Besold of Tübingen revised his comprehensive 1629 thesaurus of terms in general use in the German Empire so that, while the first edition had no reference to the word "melancholy," the new one did.[214] While Johann Brenz had created an indigenous argument in the German southwest against the claim that witches had to be destroyed because they presented a physical danger, Weyer and Spee provided the arguments that were gradually adopted in the region undermining the position that witches deserved death for their apostasy by arguing that either the evidence was tainted because it was obtained through torture or, if not, that it was actually *prima facia* evidence that the suspect was mentally incompetent.

The growing criticisms of the theory and practice of witch hunting by learned authors in the early 1600s may have contributed to the leveling off of actual witch hunting in the 1620s, but their impact on formal policies was limited, for the view that a true pact alone merited execution prevailed among the Tübingen jurists into the eighteenth century, and the ducal government continued to use torture for decades.[215] However, the government's handling of witch cases in the decades following 1620 betrayed a growing sense of unease with them that reflected both the impact of the criticisms and its own experience with trials, and climaxed in a distinct shift of policy around the middle of the century. These long-term trends can be seen in the evolution of the trial procedures and the legal vocabulary used. During the first third of the century of intense prosecutions, from 1590 into the 1620s, the government was very open to accusations and dealt harshly with suspects, both before and after conviction. During the second third of the century, from the 1620s to around 1660, it continued to try suspects, torture confessions from them, and banish or execute those convicted, but it was less inclined to initiate proceedings and was more careful about procedures and judgments. (see Tables 8.2, 8.3, and 8.4) By the 1660s, the ducal government displayed little inclination to try witch suspects, and less to kill them.

The changes between the 1620s and the 1660s resulted mainly from a series of small steps to reduce abuses in trials. The High Council contributed to this by directing trials increasingly closely and with ever stricter conformity to legal forms.[216] We have already seen that the Council could exercise a moderating influence on the conduct of early trials, for magistrates had been required to report capital crimes and prosecute only with ducal approval since the 1530s, and in 1563, during the first spate of witch trials, the central government had prohibited magistrates from using the popular "quick trial" against witch suspects.[217] The reason for this moderation was not a disbelief in witchcraft, of course, but a professional concern that trials be conducted

Table 8.2 Torture in sampled cases

Dates	Used	Not used	Percent tortured
To 1620	4	1	80
1620–1660	5	6	45
After 1660	0	11	0

Source: Sampled witchcraft cases (see the appendix).

Table 8.3 Executions for witchcraft in Württemberg

Dates	# Suspects	# Executions	Percent Executed
1500–89	13	6	46
1590–1629	45	23	51
1620–49	15	8	53
1650–79	44	6	14
1680–1709	11	2	18

Source: Midelfort, Witch Hunting, pp. 201–30.
Note: Figures have been given only for those whose fate is known.

Table 8.4 Terminology used by Tübingen law faculty for witchcraft

Date	Teufels Ergebung	Hexenwerk/ Hexerei	Maleficium	Veneficium	Magia, Zauberei
1600s	3	6		2	2
1610s	6	20			2
1620s	4	5		7	1
1630s		5	1	4	
1640s	1		2	3	2
1650s			3	9	1
1660s	1		2	23	16
1670s				9	6

Source: Index to witchcraft and related cases in Tübingen Universitätsarchiv 84/1–70 compiled by H. C. Erik Midelfort.

properly and a practical concern about their costs. In 1621 in a General Decree stipulated that magistrates had to hold a hearing and report to the High Council within three days of arresting a suspect in any capital crime and then await instructions.[218] In 1625, six years before Spee published his book, a member of the Council warned that "in cases of magical crimes torture is a very dangerous and dubious thing," while in 1629 the central government issued a decree criticizing constables for being too ready to use their power to launch investigations. A decree in 1644 insisted that constables investigate contested testimony thoroughly and punish false accusations, and rebuked them for sometimes continuing trials after the suspect had been acquitted.

Another in 1663 insisted that legally educated lawyers be involved in all capital trials. The Council did not hesitate to assert itself by reprimanding magistrates for procedural mistakes in particular cases, ordering investigations into alleged misconduct, and on occasion sending outside officials to districts to take over proceedings. On a more mundane level, the necessity of preparing and submitting increasingly frequent and detailed reports, knowing that they would be reviewed carefully for irregularities, and simply waiting for instructions, forced magistrates to scrutinize their own actions and introduced delays that can only have had a restraining effect on their passions and conduct.

In addition to the moderating influence of the High Council, increasingly frequent consultations with the Tübingen law faculty also worked to restrain trials.[219] As early as 1554 the ducal government had required judges who did not have legal training to consult the jurists whenever they "felt uncertain," and in 1567 it required consultations in all cases of "magic without harm." During the early seventeenth century legal consultations became standard practice at crucial points in capital cases, particularly before the use of torture or the issuing of a verdict. By the 1660s, without having repudiated the existence of magical crimes or the use of tortured testimony, the Tübingen jurists were recommending against torture and for acquittal most of the time.[220] Furthermore, their careful legal scrutiny not only kept the specific case they were consulted about on course, but also created guidelines and precedents that guided the High Council in future trials. Their overall impact is suggested by the complaint of one frustrated magistrate, who said that "it is well known that the legal faculty of Tübingen is much too lenient in criminal matters, and especially in *delicti occultis.*"[221]

The way in which technical legal changes by the law faculty could diffuse into the governmental administration, and finally influence provincial culture as a whole, is suggested by the adoption of precise legal terms for the crimes associated with witchcraft. During the pre-war period, the law faculty generally labeled the cases with the German word *"hexerei"* (see Table 8.4). They gradually dropped that word and adopted the Latin terms *"veneficium"* during the 1620s and *"maleficium"* during the 1630s and 1640s. This change in vocabulary signified a significant shift in their conception of witchcraft. *"Hexerei"* carried with it all the theological connotations of a pact with the Devil and attendance at witch dances along with the popular association with malefic magic. *"Veneficium"* referred merely to the use of magic – spells and, in particular, potions – to cause injuries. *"Maleficium,"* which at its root meant "wrongdoing" but had long been used for bad magic, implied some relationship between moral character and behavior, but the law faculty did not use the term much, and abandoned it altogether in the 1660s, when they began making more use of *"magia,"* which, like *"veneficium,"* concerned a criminal act rather than a moral orientation.

A similar change occurred in the High Council's vocabulary a quarter century later. In the 1640s it still used *"Hexerei"* almost exclusively, and in the 1650s adopted the Latin *"veneficium"* without abandoning the German expression.[222] The two coexisted through the 1660s, but in the 1670s the Council dropped *"Hexerei"* altogether. Furthermore, it began to distinguish more clearly between bewitchings and poisonings, again following the lead of the Tübingen faculty.[223] From the 1660s to the 1670s the number of cases identified as witch trials plunged from 46 to 16, while the number of trials for poisoning rose from six to 17, more use of the charge than had been made during all the decades before 1660 (see Figure 8.3). Magistrates continued to use *"Hexerei"* somewhat longer, and commoners used it through the eighteenth century, although more and more often as an insult rather than as a serious allegation.[224]

While these gradual changes were taking place, in 1656 a trial at Neuenstadt sparked a crisis that marked a more pronounced turning point in ducal policy toward witchcraft. As the trial developed into Württemberg's first mass trial in decades, drawing in over 30 people, Duke

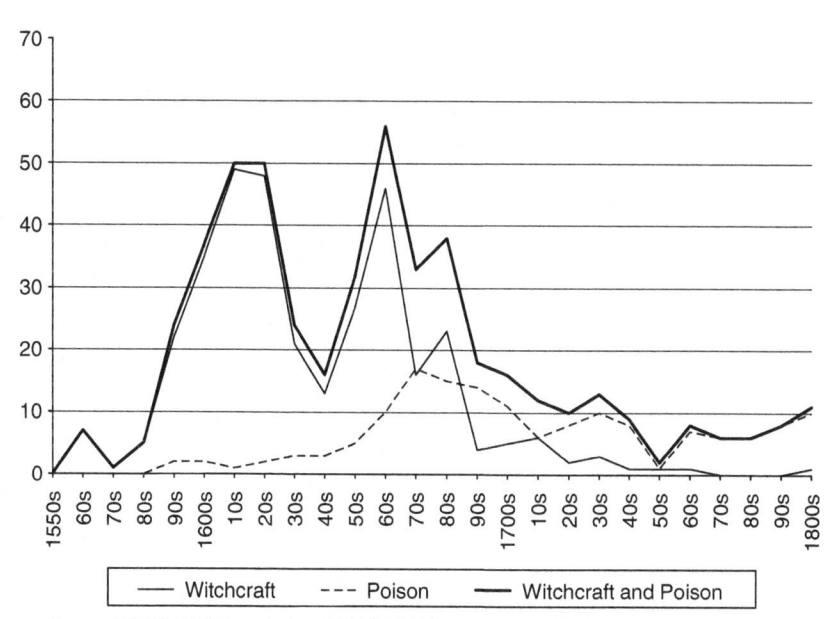

―― Witchcraft   --- Poison   ―― Witchcraft and Poison

Source: WSAS A209 Repertorium; WSAS A213 Repertorium; WSAS 309 Repertorium; WSAS A202 Repertorium; Index to witch and related cases in Tübingen Universtätsarchiv 84/1–70 by H. C. Eric Midelfort; Midelfort, *Witch Hunting in Southwest Germany*, Appendix.

Figure 8.3 Witchcraft and poison cases

Eberhard III got involved personally to bring it to an end.[225] He rebuked a number of officials for the "appalling errors" that had been committed, and demanded that the High Council draft a proposal for reform that would include the direct participation of a lawyer or legally trained jurist in every trial. He even suggested that that person might be a member of the Council itself, who would be dispatched to oversee a trial in person. In its response, the High Council proposed that trials proceed on the basis of the General Decree of 1621, with the strict stipulation that trials not proceed without its explicit permission. To the suggestion that they oversee the trials personally, the councilors responded, "there is a great difference between writing an opinion drawn from documents and personal interviews, confrontations, and attendance at torture."[226] Such a commission was "not commensurate with a councilor's class and honor," for these trials involved "things which plague even the hardest conscience, and have cost honorable people ... their health and well-being." Furthermore, "this work ... is very abstruse, because one can understand it in uncountable ways." The Duke decided to spare his councilors the distress of personal attendance at trials, but ordered that two of them become experts on the subject so they could serve as special advisors.[227] He also deputized a retired constable and sent him to end the trial at Neuenstadt forthwith, and he had a special instruction sent to the district magistrates throughout the duchy admonishing them to investigate witchcraft accusations and conduct trials more carefully.

As a consequence, during the following decade, the 1660s, less than half the trials that began were carried through to sentencing.[228] In the following decade the number of trials handled as simple poisonings shot up, while the number handled as witchcraft trials decreased commensurately. The High Council stopped calling for theological examinations, and allowed torture only very occasionally (see Tables 8.2 and 8.5). In their place, it began to emphasize specific evidence of specific acts and routinely solicited medical testimony about both the causes of maladies blamed on witchcraft and the state of mind of suspects who confessed.[229] Instead of executing or banishing convicted suspects, it usually imposed only fines, probation, or

Table 8.5 Theological examinations

Date	Used	Not Used
To 1620	3	1
1620–60	5	5
After 1660	1	11

Source: Sampled Witchcraft Cases (see the Appendix).
Note: The table does not include two trials in which the documents did not contain sufficient evidence, one from before 1620, and one from 1620–60.

confinement in a public shelter.[230] The duchy's last mass trial, a child-centered panic in Calw in 1684, ended when the central government dispatched a special commission and, eventually, troops to halt "this lamentable and mainly illusory witch business," quashing it with only the first two suspects having been executed.[231]

The first of these changes – the disengagement from denunciations, the abandonment of torture, and the discontinuance of the theological examination – indicate that the Duke and his councilors had become disillusioned with the demonological fears that underlay the trials. Not only did they realize that tortured people tell lies, but also they stopped caring whether suspects knew their catechism. They continued to believe in magic, but they no longer feared it. They continued to punish individual magicians and wrongdoers, and they even tortured them from time to time, but they no longer treated them as part of some vast underground conspiracy that threatened to overthrow Christian civilization.

The second change, the reliance on medical testimony about the causes of illnesses and the mental health of confessed witches, indicates the direction of the government's shift away from the witch ideology. Instead of seeking the guidance of theologians, the government turned to doctors. This shift complemented its increasing reliance on juridical rather than theological concepts: the government was transferring its intellectual and institutional allegiance from preachers to secular professionals.

The doctors' new role in the witch trials was but one sign of their rising prominence in Württemberg in the early modern period. Ever since its founding in 1477, the University of Tübingen's medical faculty had enjoyed wide authority over the practice of medicine in the duchy, and that authority evolved into real power as the number of doctors and the control exercised by the government bureaucracy increased.[232] The Great Church Ordinance promulgated by Duke Christoph in 1559 formally subordinated doctors to the church, but in 1621 they were explicitly placed at the top of the medical hierarchy, and their subordination became less consequential as their effective dominance of health care grew.[233] Only university trained doctors were allowed to practice internal medicine, and all other licit practitioners – surgeons, wound-dressers, barbers, and midwives – had to pass tests administered by them. Each town came to have an official doctor, whose duties included this supervision.[234]

The government turned from theologians to doctors in deciding witch cases because it lost faith in contemporary religious guidance in this aspect of social relations, and found a satisfying solution in the medicalization of the problem. The early seventeenth century had produced famous advances in medical theory, as in other sciences, and these created an optimism about what medical science could do.[235] More importantly, while lawyers, doctors, and preachers were all university educated, lawyers and doctors shared a common orientation to problem solving that emphasized instrumental relationships among natural phenomena. Just as traditional jurisprudence dealt with magic and morals, traditional medicine incorporated occult processes as one set of influences on health, but just as jurisprudence was coping with the difficulties magic and morals were causing by focusing on discrete, empirically verifiable crimes, medicine was being increasingly influenced by the idea that the body works like a machine through ordinary physical processes. Few late seventeenth-century doctors categorically denied the possibility of spiritual influences on health, just as few late seventeenth-century jurists denied the possibility of magical crimes, but doctors, like jurists, were predisposed by their training and their day to day responsibilities to think in terms of practical relations of cause and effect, and increasingly privileged natural explanations over supernatural ones.[236] As the two professions were moving down the same road in the same direction, they made congenial traveling companions.

The government's crisis of confidence in the witch ideology had two interrelated effects on elite culture in the duchy. First, it inspired a reinterpretation of the provincial intellectual tradition away from the demonology and toward the views of Spee and Weyer. Second, in so doing, it encouraged a new religious attitude whose challenge to orthodoxy became the dominant theme of religious life for more than a generation.

In 1669 the Tübingen jurist Erich Mauritius codified the new orientation by citing Weyer, Thumm, and Harprecht to argue that a "mere pact was not to be punished as severely as genuinely harmful magic."[237] He thus emphasized the physical problem over the spiritual, transforming witchcraft from a moral to a medical question. Some of his colleagues and successors held to the harsher position toward the pact into the eighteenth century, but a growing consensus among the jurists turned away from the ideology's conspiracy fears.

Far from resisting the new skeptical consensus, the religious establishment appears to have readily adapted to the new situation. The orthodox theologian at Tübingen, Johann Adam Osiander, advanced a similarly moderate view of the pact in chance reflections in a lengthy commentary on the Pentateuch published in 1674, and over the next decade he expanded them into a *Tractatus Tehologius de Magia* of 140 separate theses.[238] In them he championed Thumm as the guide to a Lutheran "middle way" between the ideological excess of the Catholics and Calvinists and the dangerous skepticism of the Weyerian tradition.

Two years before Osiander's longer work appeared, his colleague Georg Heinrch Haeberlin published a tract based on sermons he gave at Calw while serving in a ducal commission sent to help quell the duchy's last mass panic.[239] He recited the old Brenzian argument that the Devil only deceived women into thinking they raised storms, and urged his audience to turn its attention from the search for agents of the Devil to a contemplation of divine providence. He did not mention Weyer or Spee, but his words betray their influence. In one of his sermons he said that "one of the Devil's worst tricks was to get a town so excited that it uprooted the wheat with the tares," a clear echo of Spee's admonitions that it was "better to let the weeds grow with the grain."[240] Just as the provincial intellectual tradition accepted the demonology's insistence that witches be identified and destroyed at the turn of the century by focusing on their evil intentions while accepting the Brenzian denigration of their power, so, too, it proved flexible enough to forge a new consensus with the fresh intellectual current.

By reviving the providential emphasis of the *Episcopi* tradition, Württemberg's religious establishment contributed to the broader religious movement known as Pietism that ultimately challenged its orthodox doctrines and institutional position. Johann Spener, the father of German Pietism who brought the first stirring of the movement to Tübingen in 1662, wrote several works discussing the proper Christian attitude for a patient, the doctor, and the community.[241] He and other early Pietists opposed the orthodox emphasis on the Devil's role in causing disease by appealing to certain of Luther's writing that emphasized the role of guilt and sin. They insisted that God was the ultimate cause of all misfortune, and that to blame intermediate agents, including the Devil, was to lose sight of the positive meaning of disease and its relationship to the patient's moral state.[242] The early Pietists did not so much refute the witch demonology as ignore it. Without denying the possibility of diabolical agency in disease, they seldom considered it a significant cause.[243] It failed the test of usefulness by which they evaluated traditional theology. The early Pietists considered disease not as a manifestation of the Devil's malignant influence, but as an "allegory for the sins and miseries of men."[244]

Second surge and the decline of witchcraft

While the ducal elite's growing crisis of confidence in the theoretical underpinnings and practical implementation of the witch persecutions between the 1620s and the 1670s helps explain the leveling off of prosecutions in the first decades of this period and the dramatic decline in the last, it does not explain the dramatic upsurge in the 1650s and '60s to prewar levels, in absolute numbers, and all-time high, on a per capita basis. For that, we have to turn to the activities and beliefs of the commoners, for, as we have seen, they became the prime movers of witch-hunting during the period when the government began to disengage. However, one further administrative measure deserves mention, the introduction of church courts in the mid-1640s, for they increased the intrusive surveillance of the populace, creating not only another channel by which popular activities and concerns could be reported, but also contributing to the perception that society was rife with sinners whose nefarious activities needed to be curtailed. How great a role such reinforcement played, however, is uncertain, for by the 1650s three generations of Württembergers had already been subjected over the course of almost a century – 60 years of prosecutions and at least 30 years of propagandizing before that – to the idea that society was infested by malefic women who had committed their lives to the Devil's evil cause. Even as the government began to disengage from the persecutions, the ordinary people not only took up any slack in formulating accusations, but also showed a variety of signs of having internalized the beliefs and values of the witch demonology, melding the moral implications of the Devil's involvement to their traditional concerns about malefic magic.

We have already seen a number of signs of this internalization, and the trial records contain other evidence of it as well. One we have seen was the increasingly spontaneous reports of contact with the Devil, from Magdelena Horn's retroactive interpretations in the 1560s through Endriss Miembler and Maria Braittingen's ready admissions in the 1610s when accused of misconduct to Johann Bebion's wife and Anna Eberlin's elaborate reports of their experiences with him in the 1660s.[245] Another was eight-year old Hanß Ferner's dream in 1663 in which he unconsciously used the witch demonology to make sense of his own place in the world, which was just one of many cases stemming from children's dreams involving the Devil and the flight to the Sabbath during the late seventeenth century.[246] Still another sign of this assimilation was evidence that the psychological and even somatic manifestations of hostile interpersonal exchanges evolved in response to changes in the culture and the government's policy. In particular, it seems that what might be called "accusatory symptoms" became ever more common, at first because the government promoted witch fears, and later as a way to try and persuade it to take them seriously. For example, in 1631, when Margaretha Stuertzen complained that Hans Rueff had grabbed her and caused her to become lame, she said her symptoms were just pain and immobility.[247] In contrast, when Veit Grossman stalked and grabbed Anna Beyler in 1673 the result was that not only did her arms hurt and swell, but also her face swelled up so much she had trouble seeing and "one could see the grip of his hands on her chin and neck" (and even with that the *Oberrat* rejected her charge because he had never explicitly cursed or threatened her).[248] Similarly, whereas Margaretha Stuertzen's pain had come after Hans Rueff physically grabbed her, and rough handling precipitated disproportionate somatic symptoms in other early cases, like when Katharina Masten caused Catharina Baitinger to collapse by hitting her or Christoph Schweiklin said Agatha Stosser caused his son's arm to hurt by grabbing it, when Bueschelin Rogel simply borrowed a hoe from Johann Laisslin, who thought that she had already killed a pig of his in retaliation for his dishonesty in a business deal, in 1667, "the thumb of [his] right hand curled into a fist," became "completely rigid, so no one could move it," and then began to hurt fiercely, with the pain spreading to the rest of his body and "causing unbelievable agony."[249] The magistrates began investigating when a surgeon was unable to help him by letting blood and the girl who had helped him in his deception began feeling pain, but their report to the High Council in early March, and their follow-up letter in mid-April, got no response until mid-June, when the councilors told them they could question Bueschelin, but to arrest her only if "something truly culpable is found about her."[250]

An even stronger contrast is suggested by a case that took place in the village of Moessingen, near Tübingen, in 1720. One Saturday, Johann Jakob Wagner, the 17-year-old son of a cartwright, citizen, and village councilor was sitting outdoors with his master and workmates eating dinner when Christina Nethen, the 70-year-old wife of a citizen and smith passed by. Johann claimed that as she brushed by "she said to him, 'Taste good?' and, halting briefly, blew a light breath in is face and mouth," that made him feel something stick in his throat.[251] The men with him noticed nothing, but he claimed that he began to feel sick immediately. On Tuesday he collapsed at his job, vomited repeatedly, and "howled like a dog." He was carried home unconscious, and when he awoke he said that he had dreamed of being in heaven and God had told him Christina was a witch. He said that in the dream he had sex with her, which "created horrible progeny," and later he complained that all women reminded him of her. He remained sick for well over a month, recovering somewhat but relapsing periodically. At one point he cut off a lock of his hair, and, shouting that the "malevolent woman" should eat it, tried to throw it out of the window."[252] When the wind blew it back in his face, Johann fell into despondency, saying he would always be miserable and tried to kill himself with a knife. The doctor concluded that while his illness was "gout or some other disease ... the cause ... is not natural but rather supernatural."[253]

Christina and her relatives protested vehemently against the youth's charges in a series of letters to the government. "Whenever someone happens to contract an unusual disease," they wrote, "ignorant and simple peasants decide that some forbidden magical acts must be behind it." They cited the variations and contradictions in his story, pointing particularly to the time lag between the supposed bewitching and the onset of his illness, and said that his enthusiastic participation in a snowball fight the day after she passed him was "clear evidence that nothing ailed him." The High Council agreed, and she was not arrested.[254]

That Johann's ailment had a strong psychological dimension seems clear. He may well have had "gout or some other disease," but the doctor was probably right that the physical problem was not the only, or even the primary, cause of his distress. Instead, his main problem, like Konrad Streich's a century before, seems to have been that an encounter with an older woman unleashed some sexual fear or insecurity. However, the two incidents differed in several important respects that are suggestive of the changes that had taken place in the society and culture during the intervening period. In the earlier case, Streich's malady was simple and straightforward, a psychophysical reaction to the stress triggered by his insecurities and her jokes. In the later incident, Wagner's ailment was literally baroque, with a heavy overlay of symptoms drawn from the witch demonology. This difference suggests that the diffusion of the demonology and its incorporation into popular culture proceeded apace even as the government broke off the persecutions, and that it exerted more and more influence on the symptoms people experienced. Both the continued influence of the demonology and the official reaction against it may have fueled the accusers' increasingly dramatic psychosomatic reactions – the demonology by supplying the forms, the official indifference by creating the need to emphasize the interpersonal causes of distress.

Of course, the development of the symptoms of bewitchings, like the role of the Devil in people's experience, was not as linear as these examples suggest: some people suffered from complex symbolic afflictions or spontaneously experienced contact with the Devil early on, and some bewitchings manifested simply in later cases, but they do convey what seems to be an overall trend from mostly simple, relatively straightforward maladies precipitated by disturbed interpersonal relations to more complex, symbolically rich somaticizations, and from contact with the Devil as a retroactive interpretation of diverse moral lapses and spiritual experiences to an immediate conceptualization of immoral impulses and an actual set of apparent perceptions projected in the sensorium. They seem to be linked to tangible changes in governmental policy, socioeconomic conditions, and provincial culture, and suggest that despite important continuities in form and content, popular beliefs, practices, and behaviors were not some sort of static edifice erected in the Middle Ages that lasted until industrialization, but, like elite culture, they changed in response to developments in their sociocultural context and also to the their own internal and collective dynamics.

In addition to shedding light on the popular roots of the upsurge in prosecutions in the 1650s and 1660s, consideration of the dynamic nature of popular behaviors can help shed light on the second great change in the prosecutions for magical crimes after mid-century: why they fell off almost as steeply between 1670 and the 1690s as they had risen in the two decades before. Even if poison trials are added in because of their overlap with witchcraft, the decline is still dramatic, particularly if it is considered on a per capita basis (see Figures 8.4 and 8.5). While to some extent the apparent decline of witchcraft trials simply reflected their reclassification as poisonings, something more must have been going on since the combined total of both kinds of trials fell significantly from the 1660s to the '70s, and then, after increasing slightly in the '80s, fell significantly again in the '90s, and continued to dwindle into the middle of the eighteenth century (the brief fall-off of poison trials in the 1750s and rebound in the 1760s is probably due to records being lost since the handling of these cases was being changed at the time).[255] The decrease could reflect nothing more than an unwillingness on the part of the magistrates to investigate alleged poisonings, or it could reflect

Magic and Society 403

Figure 8.4 Witchcraft, magic, and poison trials

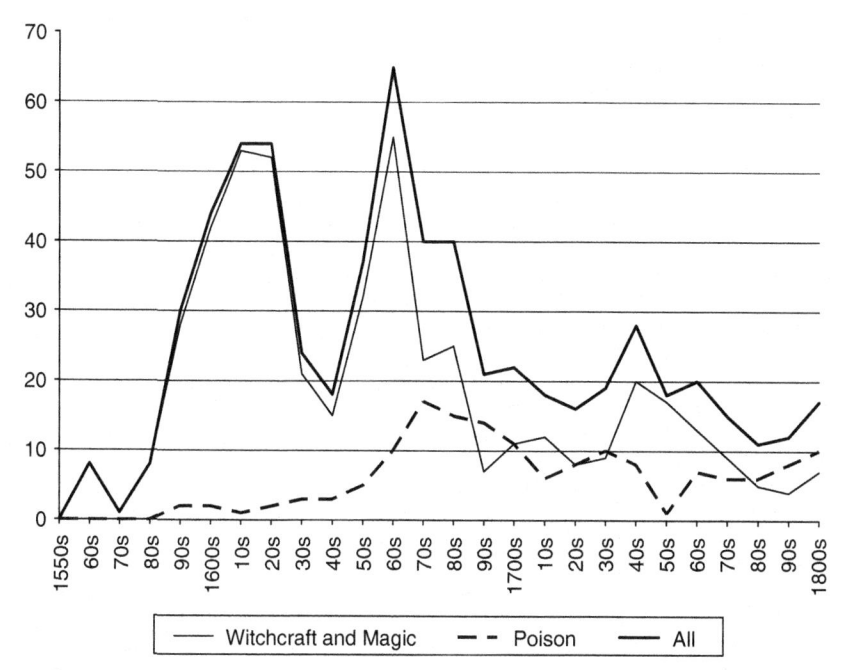

Source: Figures 8.1, 8.3, and W209 archival index.

a genuine decline in peoples' fear of being poisoned. The latter could simply reflect a decline in people's fears, or it could reflect a real decline in the danger of being poisoned.

To consider the first possibility, while magistrates seem to have begun holding back on their investigations into witchcraft allegations in response to the central government's admonishments, and probably the growing doubts about the demonology in elite culture in general, poisoning was considered even by Weyer to be a real and serious crime. Therefore, even magistrates inclined to dismiss stories of witch dances or vague malign influences could be expected to investigate an allegation of poisoning, and even if it were ultimately decided that the allegation was groundless, as a potential capital crime it would have left traces in the ducal archives.

So, if the decline in poisonings cannot be accounted for simply by official indifference, then it must represent a genuine decline in the number of cases in which people feared that they had been poisoned. This, of course, could just represent the decline of "fear itself" as people realized that that their fears of witchcraft had been overblown, but while this probably played a role in the decline, there is reason to believe that it also reflected a real

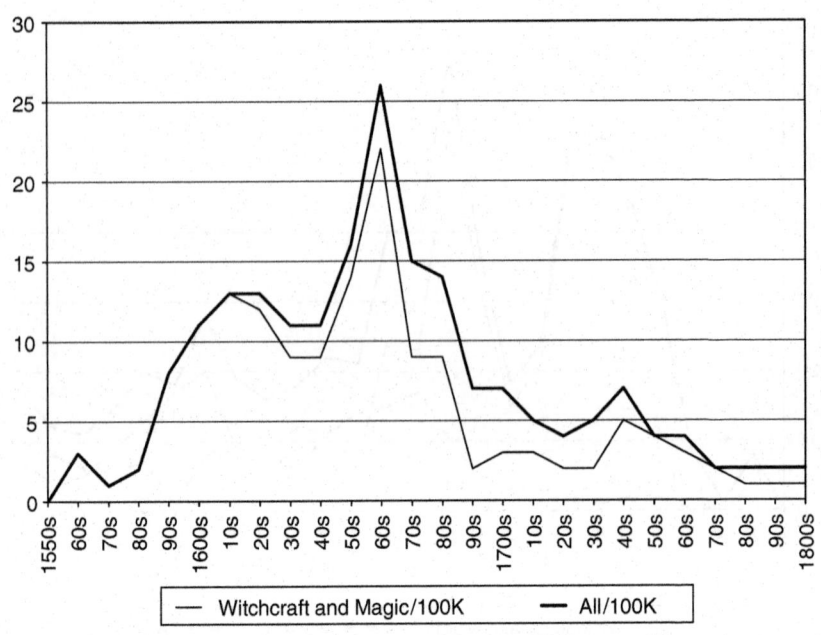

Source: Figure 8.4; Franz, *Bauernstandes*, p. 174; Hippel, p. 417; Knapp, p. 25.
Note: See endnote 167 for explanation of population figures.

Figure 8.5 Witchcraft, magic, and poison trials per 100,000 inhabitants

decline in the danger of being poisoned. To begin with, it must be recognized that there was, in fact, a danger of being poisoned in early modern times: we have seen that it is very likely that Maria Schneider did poison her stepgrandson Jakob Endriss in 1628; the doctor who examined Anna Maria Schilling in 1674 said that she had been poisoned, as she claimed, even if there was not enough evidence to sustain an accusation against the woman Schilling accused, Barbara Gessler; in several other cases there were at least some reasonable grounds to believe that suspects had given poison to people or animals.[256] Furthermore, there are several reasons to think that the danger of being poisoned did decline in the seventeenth century. To begin with, regular inspections of apothecaries by town doctors were first stipulated in the Second Apothecary Ordinance of 1626, and given the disruptions of the war shortly thereafter, could be expected to have begun to make a real impact only at mid-century. Secondly, apothecaries ran an increasing risk of punishment if they dispensed poisonous substances that were used in a crime; in 1653, when a shepherd named Michael Ellwein was tried and executed for poisoning his wife and children, the apothecary of Gröningen was fined 10 Reichstaler for selling him the poison. Third, the frequent prosecution of suspected poisoners, whether under the rubric of witchcraft or simple poisoning, probably had some deterrent effect, for while the threat of punishment does not do much to deter impulsive crimes of violence, poisoning is generally a deliberate, premeditated act. Before the 1660s, even being suspected of poisoning someone could lead quickly to torture and death, while after that date, even if a the suspicions were not substantiated, as with Barbara Gessler, the suspect would have to live with the possibility of punishment for some months and would end up on some sort of probation, whether a formal order to the magistrates and pastor to keep an eye on her, or just a public record of this incident and any prior suspicions that the investigation had brought to light. Furthermore, not only the suspect, but also everyone in the community, would have seen the potential for suspicions to become inquisitions. Whereas prosecutions for poisoning in any guise appear to have been infrequent before 1590, by the 1660s they were frequent indeed. While the deterrent effect of policing and punishment can undoubtedly be overestimated, it would be a mistake to conclude that they therefore have none. There is no question that some Württembergers continued to use poisons down to the present, but it seems reasonable to propose that the decline in poison cases in the late seventeenth century to some extent reflected the increase in the likelihood of being prosecuted for it during the previous hundred years.

Similarly, there is reason to think that the witch trials, and the more general moral supervision of which they were part, had a significant impact on the activities of healers and other beneficent magicians in the seventeenth century. We have seen that these practitioners were actually the original targets of ducal legislation, in the Provincial Ordinance of 1552, and while beneficent practices, those which involved neither *maleficium* nor a pact with the Devil, were treated more mildly, than witchcraft, punishment for repeated offenses could include banishment and even death. Furthermore, the distinction between beneficent practitioners and witches was not always clear. A good number, particularly male ones, presented themselves as the enemies of witches, capable of identifying them and countering their malign influence, but officials often referred to them as "Devil's men" and their activities as "Devil's work." During the period before 1660 they could come under suspicion of witchcraft themselves.[257] At one point the magistrates of Sulz, for example, asked the healer Jakob "Schafer J" Franck, "where he got such Devilish magical arts," and a pastor reported that he not only practiced magic, but also derided the "holy ministry," associated with an itinerant, and was considered to be a "witch."[258] While such suspicions rarely developed into an actual witch prosecution – both the male healers investigated during sampled witchcraft cases escaped prosecution because it was determined that they were not malevolent, – one of the earliest cases involved a man executed for magic and witchcraft, another practitioner was tortured during the course of his trial, and such practitioners were particularly likely to end up on multiple lists during mass trials.[259] Women who practiced healing or other beneficent magic were even more vulnerable to being suspected of witchcraft. In 1609, for example, when Margretha Rencklern from Sindelfingen was investigated for "magical healing," the magistrates noted that "due to her ... herbal medicine" she was "strongly suspected by many of witchcraft," and a reputation as a healer was indeed legal grounds for suspicion.[260] Eight of the 36 female suspects in the sampled witch trials were noted for healing activities, three of whom used magic rituals.[261] All three of the ones who used magic were punished: Maria Laichlin, accused of poisoning the preacher Johannes Brand's sister-in-law, was said to use blessings while midwiving, and she was incarcerated and placed on probation. Her friend Maria Rau, a reputed magical healer, was jailed and tortured three times before being released on probation. Anna Schnabel was jailed for her "grass spell" and other magic, including noxious remedies, fined, and put on probation.

As a more general consequence of this campaign of repression, both the specific, if moderate, penalties for beneficent practices and the less directed but more drastic danger of being accused of witchcraft, which were implemented by the combination of the state's police system and the church's supervisory system, all trials for beneficent magic appear to have fallen off during the late seventeenth century, at least in part because the practices they punished were suppressed: practiced less frequently and/or more furtively. As with poisoning, it is tempting to look at the higher levels of society for as causative agent, and ascribe the decline in magic trials to the gradual disengagement of the ducal administration from the drive to reform popular practices that undoubtedly did take place during this period, starting with Duke Eberhard III's refusal to support aggressive initiatives after the death of Johann Valentin Andreae, the religious advisor who created the system of church courts and secret spies, and continuing with his successors' preoccupation with French culture and life at court.[262] However, while this undoubtedly had some dampening effect, the officials handling these matters at the local and district level and in the central government were far more closely tied to the provincial estates, which continued to press for moral supervision and effective policing, and seem to have actively resented the frivolous and immoral lifestyle of the ducal court.[263] The French Wars also caused some disruptions in the decades around the turn of the eighteenth century, but these were local and temporary, nothing like the widespread devastation of the Thirty Years' War, when soldiers ravaged the countryside and the court fled to Strasbourg. There may have been a general reluctance to use the criminal courts to punish beneficent magicians as part of a general recoil away from the excesses of the witch persecutions, but since the punishments were mild and the offense was different in practical content and moral implications, there was no necessary connection between the prosecution of the witchcraft and the prosecution of beneficent magic. Furthermore, officials were not the only ones to have reason to initiate proceedings, for people who felt wronged by magical practices, either because they were denounced as witches or thieves or because the magic was thought to give an unfair advantage, as when the Gerstenmaier brothers used magic to win shooting contests in 1668, could bring charges, or just raise a ruckus, and some people have even been known to expose immoral activities because they feel bound by their conscience to do so. Yet these channels also generated few trials at the time. Magical activities remained both sinful and illegal, and when they did come to the attention of the ducal administration they were punished with fines and incarceration, and any magic books discovered were burned.[264]

Such punishments seem tame in comparison to the torture and executions of the witch trials, but there is other evidence that magic in general had become more marginalized during the century of witch prosecutions. Among the early trials, two, one in 1596 and the other in 1613, involved groups of three women who were prosecuted for saying blessings in healing, not as professional activity, but as a casual neighborly service.[265] Most were open about what they knew and where they learned it, indicated that such things were done by others, and said they never knew that it was forbidden. By the 1650s, however, saying blessings while serving as a midwife was one of the supporting charges against Maria Laichlin when the preacher Johannes Brand accused her of witchcraft when he thought she had poisoned his sister-in-law, and in 1709 the judge from Weilheim Leonard Weißinger was disgraced when his rival revealed that he had a talisman with three blessings.[266] While it was also revealed that he had used magic as a young man in the army, this was seen as a manifestation of the corrupting influence of that institution, the book he brought back with him had been confiscated and burned, and it was assumed that he had put such sinful and undignified folly behind him. Overall, the trajectory these examples suggest is that blessings went from unremarkable parts of daily life to furtive transgressions, if they were used at all. While suspects often claimed that they "never knew that it was not right" to use blessings and such around 1600, nobody could credibly make this claim a century later.[267] While many people continued to use trivial forms of beneficent magic to get luck or avoid malign influences, more involved magical practices seems to have become less common and more furtive.

While Leonard Weißinger's trial came at the beginning of an upsurge in prosecutions that would see more men tried for healing than ever before, the proportion of women in the same series of trials would sink to less than half than it had been previously. The prosecutions in which the gender of the suspects is known fall into three groups, 1580–1619, 1640–1689, and 1710–79. Ten men were tried in the first period, along with five women. In the second period, four women were tried and eight men, so the proportion of women to men, 1:2, was the same in each. In the third period, however, only five women were tried, as opposed to 21 men (plus one more between 1800 and 1809), or less than 1:4 women to men.[268] What this suggests is that while women had always been in the minority among public healers, their participation in this activity dwindled while that of men grew. Consideration of a few examples of women healers in the different periods reinforces this impression. In the earliest period, to be sure, the two groups of women mentioned above indicate that many women's involvement had always been relatively casual, but women like Barbara Weylandt, who we have seen was tried in 1608 for a thriving practice as an herbalist, and three clients were investigated along with Margretha Rencklern from Sindelfingen, who was held "by many in strong suspicion of witchcraft" because of "her ... herbal medicine" and blessings.[269] During the witch trial of Agatha Stosser in 1659, as we have seen, one of the men who suspected she had bewitched his cow consulted a "weiblin" who had a reputation for helping counter witchcraft, but Anna Schnabel, who similarly had a reputation as a powerful magical practitioner, was tried for witchcraft herself less than ten years later. During the eighteenth century, in contrast, the only sampled healing trial that focused on a woman for healing Barbara Saüberlichin who supplied amulets and led biblical songs to cure by warding off the Devil, but only for her immediate household, her employer, Forest Ranger Walzen and his wife, in order to cure their child.[270] In another case, a woman was involved in magical curing and thief detection, but was the sole female along with four men.[271] No cases from the eighteenth century are known that involved a public practitioner along the lines of Barbara Weylandt and Margretha Rencklern, and none of the cases suggests the kind of robust neighborly magical help that was shared by the groups of women in 1596 and 1613. It was said that at one point the witch persecutions drove every midwife from the city of Cologne, and if they did not have quite such a dramatic effect in Württemberg, it seems probable that they had a less spectacular but far longer lasting on effect on women's practice of beneficent magic there.[272]

We have already contrasted the reactions of Konrad Streich and Johann Jakob Wagner to the sexuality they perceived in their interactions with Anna Gebhard and Christina Nethen, respectively, noting how straightforward Streich's was in 1622 in comparison to Wagner's a century later. There is another contrast between the two stories, however: the difference between the actions of the two women. On the one hand, Gebhard was openly, boisterously sexual. On the other hand, Nethen's sexuality was literally in Wagner's dreams. It is possible, of course, that the breath she blew on him was a spontaneous kiss, or a conscious curse (remember Margaritha Steiner back in 1603 claimed to have bewitched several children by blowing on them), or simply the pant of an elderly woman carrying a heavy burden. Perhaps she neither spoke to him nor breathed on him at all; since she did nothing that anyone but Wagner claimed to have seen, we can never know.

In fact, just suggesting the possibility that she actually did anything more than pant with fatigue seems somewhat silly, although Freudian psychology suggests that there is often a highly sexual unconscious dimension to human relationships, and so it is certainly possible that Christina did actually send some emotionally charged signal to Johann. If she did, though, it was so subtle that even she may well have been unaware of it, and he only recognized its meaning in his dreams.

More importantly, even if she did, she was just one person and Anna Gebhard was just one person, and while two points make a line, two people's stories don't make a social trend. Nevertheless, it has been observed that in the sixteenth century women were thought to be the more sexually aggressive gender, while by the eighteenth century they were coming to be seen as uninterested in, or even resistant to, sex.[273] While cultural stereotypes are not necessarily social reality, they often relate to it, and they do suggest a trend. Furthermore, the witch demonology was famously concerned with the "defect in the formation of the first woman" that, according to the *Malleus Maleficarum*, made her "an imperfect animal," subject to "inordinate affections and passions" and slave to "insatiable" lusts.[274] This opinion was not the isolated pathology of that tome's author, but instead expressed a view common among late medieval and early modern men that women were "generally more easily moved by their feelings," were "morally degenerate," and altogether more vulnerable to the Devil.[275] The solution, as one author pointed out, was provided by the "example of the two holy women, Elisabeth and Maria" who "by chaste modesty remained clean and pure."

There were undoubtedly boisterously sexual older women in eighteenth century Württemberg, just as there were certainly chaste ones in the sixteenth century, but none of the former are known to have made it into the duchy's criminal records. Of course, an argument from a lack of evidence is a weak reed, but several of the sampled cases provide more positive evidence that women were going through some important psychological changes during the period of the witch trials. We have seen that in 1660 Anna Eberlin confessed to having fornicated with the Devil after having sex with a farmhand she had admired, and her ambivalence was manifested beforehand in the bird that urged her to "pray, pray" and the mouse that countered "don't pray," during the encounter by his resistance to his advances despite her attraction, and afterwards in the fact that she suddenly perceived his "great stink," saw that he had "goat's feet," and later fell into a dramatic despondency in which she threw up, her teeth chattered, her eyes rolled back in her head, and she "acted as if she was possessed."[276] And this does not seem to have been an isolated incident; Hans Köll, the healer who treated her, said that he had dealt with several similar cases recently, and three years later Johann Bebion's wife also said that she had sex with the Devil in a dreamy state every night.[277]

Johann Bebion's wife did not just connect her sexuality to the Devil, but she also ascribed her desire to "kill her husband and children in their sleep" to him, which suggests that she was internalizing another aspect of the witch demonology and the larger discussion of the "woman problem" in early modern Europe: the perceived greater aggressiveness of women than men, the Devil's manipulation of this, and the need for women to suppress it. According to the *Malleus Maleficarum*, women's weakness made them vulnerable not only to their "insatiable" lust, but also to their anger and desire for revenge, so that "there is no wrath above the wrath of a woman."[278] This opinion was echoed by the Lutheran preacher Kaspar Huberinus, who devoted an entire chapter of his "Mirror of Domestic Discipline" to the "evil woman," observing that women were "much more wicked then men," and "poison, shoot, [and] corrupt people," practice magic to make hail and storms, and, under torture, admit to being the Devil's tool.[279] "It is easy to believe" he concluded, "that such evil women eventually ... become nothing but witches (*Unholden*)." A suggestion of the lengths to which women were thought to go was conveyed by an early pamphleteer in the region, who described how 63 witches had killed many old people, often their own husbands.[280] The witch demonology tapped a widespread fear that some women, left to their own devices, would not shrink from violence and murder.

This pessimistic assessment of what women were like had much to do with the corresponding prescriptions about what women should be like. "Their proper functions were to be submissive wives, responsible mothers, and attentive, frugal housekeepers."[281] Men were therefore given physical control over their dependent womenfolk, including corporal punishment, and women's separate activities and recreations fell increasingly under male supervision. However, this coercive approach was complemented and ultimately superseded by the inculcation of the value system in women themselves. Male authors admonished women to internalize the Christian beliefs that would keep the Devil at bay. In a "warning to women" at the end of his early "moderate" discussion of witchcraft, Ulrich Molitor admonished them to remember, "your vow ... in holy Baptism, as often as the Devil visits you. Be resolute, don't let yourself be led astray through his evil encouragement, rather ... restrain yourselves ... and know that he has no power over you."[282]

Consideration of the sampled witch trials suggests that, just as Johann Bebion's wife's diabolical sexual experiences were part of the transition from one pattern of female sexuality to another, so, too, her "general acknowledgement that she is driven by the evil enemy" was part of a transition from one pattern of female aggressiveness to another. The early suspects from before 1660 included a number of women whose words and behavior were overtly violent. Katharina Masten assaulted a servant girl, hitting her and berating her until she collapsed in a heap.[283] Maria Schneider poisoned her stepgrandson. Magdelena Kochen hurled abuse at those who denied her favors, while Magdelena Horn harmed the animals of those who rebuked her. Agatha Sacher's threats contributed to her rival's sudden illness at her wedding, and Catharina Ada assaulted people, cursed them, and poisoned them, and her daughter Margaretha followed in her footsteps. Fewer of the later suspects manifested such overtly violent behavior: Agnes Langjahr and Barbara Gessler exhibited violent anger, but such women seem to have been a smaller proportion of the suspects and been less overt in their violence. The legal historian Paul Gehring reported a similar impression in his 1937 study of the Tübingen law faculty's relationship to the witch trials, noting that acquittals due to a lack of evidence of a bad reputation rose significantly over the course of the seventeenth century.[284]

More indirect evidence of the change in women's behavior is suggested by the rising concern for male violence during the late seventeenth century, precisely the time when official concern about female violence was waning. In Württemberg, "some time around the middle of the seventeenth century there was more concern about husbands behaving badly" than there had been before.[285] By the eighteenth century, the provincial church court "distanced itself from the notion that women were intrinsically evil, that they harbored hidden malice which could erupt at any time, and "on the whole ... judges were more inclined to see marital violence grow out of the impetuousness and willfulness of men then out of the anger of women."[286] Peasant women, in fact, came to be seen as "strong proponents of disciplined behavior."[287] Finally, in literature, it has been noted that "only in the last decades of the [seventeenth] century do we find increasing reference to women's 'softness.'"[288]

The witch persecutions arose in part because the men who ran society thought that women's sexuality and aggressiveness were an important problem and that they had to be punished or even killed if they let them get out of hand. Of course, the witch trials were not the only way that the need for better female behavior was communicated or enforced, but the evidence suggests that over the course of the seventeenth century women were gradually getting the message.

The witch trials themselves can be seen to have consisted of a series of checkpoints at which a suspect's, which 80 percent of the time meant a woman's, behavior was evaluated, and if it did not measure up, she was subjected to a new level of punishment. First of all, communal opinion judged her, and if she was suspected of causing injury through her ill-will, she was subject to increasing degrees of social isolation and informal retribution. Second, if some event brought this behavior and judgment to the attention of the authorities, she would be arrested and interrogated, put in a position of existential crisis as the quality and length of the remainder of her life was put in question. Third, if her demeanor under questioning, her behavior in the precipitating incident, or her reputation in her community were found sufficiently wanting, she would be arrested and incarcerated in a cold, uncomfortable cell, possibly in chains, accompanied by criminals of various types, and increasingly threatened by what the future probably had in store. This incarceration could go on for months, costing her family her upkeep and herself her health, and would be punctuated by further interrogations, examinations, and confrontations with accusers. If she failed these tests, she would then be hung by her wrists bound behind her back, wrenching her shoulders from their sockets, and then questioned. If she maintained her silence or retracted her confession she might be hung up again, for longer and with weights, and this could be repeated a third time. While the goal of this torment was ostensibly to get her to confess to creating a pact, participating in Sabbaths, and harming her neighbors, what was created was a fiction that rationalized the transgressions (if any) for which she had fallen under suspicion by connecting them and any asocial or antisocial impulses she might have felt to a mythical conspiracy led by the Devil. The torture chamber was the crucible in which a suspect's self-conception was fused and remolded, like an Old Bolshevik compelled to recognize his dissent from the party line as collusion with the counterrevolution in Soviet Russia. If the suspect held out, she would go free, possibly with her body broken and quite probably into a hostile community with few or no remaining means. If, on the other hand, she succumbed and confessed, she would die, beheaded if she was contrite and burned alive if she was not. Even someone who got out early in this game would have gone through a searing brush with pain and death, and everyone in the community would have seen the danger into which interpersonal aggression or excessive sexuality could place a woman. The fact that these trials went on for three generations, so that a woman born in 1570, her daughter, and her granddaughter would have all have lived their adult lives in the shadow of the pyre, and a greatgranddaughter in the fourth generation would have grown up amidst widespread popular concern, frequent rumors, and occasional accusations, and she herself might have been caught up for a brief spell as a youngster because of a fantasy or a dream. As Bob Scribner observed, "changing hearts and minds proved to be long, hard slog, spread over many generations."[289]

Scribner went on to challenge the "'behavior-modification' model, encapsulated by the notions of 'social discipline' and 'acculturation'" because "it is usually observed only at the level of injunction" with little indication of "how the process actually worked." Here, however, we have seen precisely that. And to continue, the fact that the persecutions took the form of both a steady stream of small trials and occasional mass panics would have heightened their effects. The small trials focused on a particular type of woman, and everyone knew who was particularly suspect. However, small trials could draw in quite innocent women, and panics engulfed them by the dozens. Yet what innocent woman could honestly deny ever having felt strong anger or desire? The trials combined a relentless specificity with sudden, blind outbursts that might force any woman to confront the asocial, amoral side of being human. This dual focus meant that one type of woman suffered endless harassment, threat, and persecution, while all other women were forced to confront the witch-related impulses within them that are inherent in the human condition.

The persecutions declined in the later part of the seventeenth century in part because of their very success in promoting the civilizing process. Men in 1580 could look around and see dangerous witches; a century later they could not. They stopped believing in witches in part because over the course of the century women had learned to try to avoid acting like witches. Some women still did, of course, a few chronically and many on occasion or to some degree, but a critical threshold, another "tipping point," had been crossed. The behavior modification program of the witch persecutions and the process of internalization of the values that informed them were not the only reasons for this, of course, for there were other currents promoting the changing behavior and attitudes of women and defusing the social strains that set up the interpersonal conflicts central to witchcraft fears and malefic effects, but the witch persecutions, protracted, brutal, and pervasive, would seem to have formed the cutting edge.

Interestingly, one of the other developments that fostered the emergence of the modern woman arose just as the period of witch persecutions came to an end. We have seen that in 1662 (that decade again!), Johann Spener introduced the Pietist movement to the duchy, and in 1684, the year after the duchy's last mass panic, the first Pietist conventicle, a small discussion group that met outside of church to discuss religion and pray, appeared in Göppingen, and other conventicles were soon formed in other towns.[290] The Pietists rejected orthodox Lutheranism as sterile dogmas and empty rituals, and cultivated instead an individual religiosity that stressed an emotive understanding of God's will; strict adherence to Christian morality; the importance of mystical, prophetic, and apocalyptic visions; the ultimate authority of the Bible; and the perfectibility of the world. Initially most members came from the urban elites, but the radical separatists tended to be lower on the social scale than the more moderate groups, and the movement gradually broadened so that by the mid-1700s there were "pietistic groups all over in the villages."[291] The leaders of church and state were ambivalent about the movement, appreciating its religious zeal but put off by its challenge to established religion, its exclusiveness, and its emphasis on inspired insight. Initially they resisted it, but gradually accommodated it, and eventually assimilated it.[292] On their side, most Pietists accepted necessity of the state church and hoped to live within it, reforming it from within so far as possible, but a radical faction known as separatists held themselves aloof from it.

There were a number of striking but enigmatic parallels between this radical Pietist movement and the supposed witch conspiracy. Women played a prominent role in both.[293] Both centered on ecstatic spiritual experiences induced by illicit ritual activity, and both stood self-consciously at odds with the established religion. Like their opponents, the preachers, both supposed witches and actual Pietists were connected to a significant degree by family relationships.[294] Most Pietists and some actual convicted witches were relatively well to do, and, finally, both confessed witches and radical separatists came to be seen by the authorities as having "the predisposition to hysteria that is a common evil that most women are afflicted with." The significance of these similarities is problematic because, as we have seen, the witch demonology patched together many disparate popular beliefs and practices, ascribing to them an intellectual coherence and organizational structure that did not exist, to create an illusory whole, whereas the separatist conventicles were quite real. However, their chronological relationship suggests that they were linked. So, too, does the advice given by Jacob Graeter in 1589 to women tempted to witchcraft to emulate Elisabeth and Maria and:

> fix their gaze on God, speak of His works ... praise his wonders, exhort each other with spiritual songs and psalms ... watch out for their neighbors, serve each other ... and always supplicate and pray.[295]

These words could have been written about the Pietists; they suggest that the movement at least in part manifested the internalization of the goals for women driving the persecutions, while at the same time manifesting the desire for ecstatic experience that had been fulfilled by some of the practices subsumed in the witch demonology and suppressed by the witch persecutions. However, since the women who participated in the separatist movement had significantly different personae and standing in the community than the typical witch suspect, their rebelliousness and abrasiveness notwithstanding, the two phenomena can hardly have had a straightforward connection (although one "completely hateful" woman named Magdelena Elrich was said to have fallen into a "deep sleep" amounting to a "cataleptic state," while hearing the scriptures read and "and after awakening, she had transformed ... to a dear sister in Christ").[296] For the most part, though, to the extent that the Pietist movement arose in response to changes in women's lives caused by the witch persecutions, it would seem to have helped women cope with the restrictions on female behavior the persecutions imposed, not so much on the women actually targeted by them, but on all the women who hoped to avoid being targeted by them, or who defined themselves in a more positive way by how different they were from the type of woman targeted by them. This in turn suggests that the most significant impact of the witch persecutions in terms of the history of women may not have been on the women they immolated, or even women in the rural and artisanal classes to which most of the victims belonged, but who stubbornly maintained many behaviors and attitudes reminiscent of, if somewhat more restrained than, their rural and small-town forbearers, but instead may have been their indirect influence on women in the upper bourgeois strata, the women who set the standards for comportment and self-definition in the milieu that formed the kernel from which modern urban industrial society and culture grew.

If the Pietist movement was a primary positive means by which changes in women's behavior and attitudes were promoted, improvements in the duchy's economic situation in the late seventeenth century were an important factor in defusing the social strains that set up the interpersonal conflicts central to witchcraft fears and malefic effects. Socioeconomic change was uneven and gradual, but on the whole the half-century following the government's crisis of confidence around 1660 did not suffer from the desperate conditions responsible for the growth of the persecutions a century before.[297] To begin with, the population remained significantly lower than it had been before the Thirty Years' War for most of this period, and as it began to approach prewar levels after the turn of the century a substantial out-migration relieved some of the pressure.[298] Agricultural depression and periodic wars disrupted the economy, but gradual improvements in agricultural productivity and manufacturing kept the situation in Württemberg's small towns and villages from being as bad as they had been earlier.[299] The court and nobility, of course, garnered the richest benefits from the improving economy, enjoying a glittering lifestyle that became increasingly disconnected from the lives not only of the masses, but from the provincial elite.[300] The honorability also prospered, however, even if they enjoyed it in a more restrained and traditional way, while the less well to do gained more reliable food supplies, a more varied diet, and access to more and cheaper manufactured goods. For the poor, the founding of a "poor commission" in 1665; the rise of private charitable foundations to help the poor, and especially poor widows, in the late seventeenth century; and the establishment of two "orphan houses" that functioned as reform schools, workhouses, penitentiaries, and asylums in the early eighteenth century alleviated some of the worst suffering.[301] Later, in the mid-eighteenth century the ducal government created a commission to distribute alms to immigrant poor who did not qualify for help from their localities, and in the 1750s it founded a voluntary widows and orphans chest. After mid-century local government began creating more "hospitals" whose primary role was to serve as old people's homes, while fire-fighting services and fire insurance were introduced in the 1740s and '50s.[302] Most of these improvements arrived too late to have played much of a role in the decline of witch accusations, but they did help prevent conditions from developing that would have fostered their return.

Enlightenment and repression

Had witch accusations surged as conditions deteriorated in the eighteenth century, it seems unlikely that the ducal government would have responded, for it adopted an increasingly reflexive rejection of witch suspicions as the seventeenth century gave way to the eighteenth. For one thing, the spate of child-centered witch trials late in the century accelerated its disillusionment, for it became increasingly clear that these involved individual dreams and fantasies, collective suggestion, and vengeful lies, and while in some cases the adults whom the children drew in may actually have practiced magic of one sort or another, it was more often clear that they had not.[303] Similarly, the officials began to treat the testimony of elderly women as equally unreliable. In 1704, for example, the magistrates of Herrenberg tried Agatha Weil, who "readily acknowledged, yes she was a witch ... led astray in her childhood by her mother," and who, we have seen, claimed to have "pressed" several people at night (who confirmed that they had noticed a presence) as well as a number of other acts of *maleficium* (most of which were also confirmed by the purported victims).[304] The High Council's response was to order the magistrates to go through the testimony again very carefully, and to investigate "if she is sane and mentally integrated, or if she isn't melancholy and leads a tedious life."[305] Agatha did acknowledge that she had misremembered some details, and "varied ... in the interrogation about the witch congregation," but the staff of the poor house where she lived said, "no one ... perceived her as melancholy."[306] The High Council ordered the magistrates to re-examine the witnesses and have a doctor or barber determine if the ailments were enchantments or natural, even though Agatha had claimed to have used natural means in most cases, and while the witnesses stuck to their stories, the barber dutifully diagnosed the ailments as natural.[307] The magistrates wrote a long report emphasizing the variations and contradictions in Agatha's statements, although they did not make much of the fact that the barber had contradicted himself at one point.[308] The officials similarly raised no objections when the doctors wrote a letter saying that Agatha was melancholic after all, but, of course, by Weyer's logic any woman who admitted to being a witch was by definition melancholic, so by the medical standards of the day there was really no question to begin with. The High Council did not dismiss the case out of hand at this point – the investigation lasted three months – but the tone of the councilors' instructions were always skeptical, emphasizing the mundane possibility over the sensational, and ready to overlook evidence of phenomena and contradictions in testimony that went against their expectations. Evidence that does not fit with our beliefs, as we have seen, is processed differently than evidence that does.

A similar process seems to have been at work 35 years later when the High Council oversaw the investigation of Margaretha Wagner, the girl who admitted using love magic, went on to describe various types of magic that she said she had learned from her grandmother, and said that she had gone to witch dances, and given herself to the Devil. The magistrates noted that "she must be in the power of Satan, even if one does not want to believe everything the girl says," indicating that, in 1740, these local officials still saw the Devil as an active agent in the world, but were aware that not everything believed about witches was true, and that the girl might have answered because of the pressure of her interrogation or because she was deceived by "an illusion of Satan."[309] However, when Margaretha was sent to the orphan house at Ludwigsburg for further examination by the preacher and town doctor, while she initially insisted that everything she had confessed was true, as the authorities went through the transcripts question by question she confirmed most of her answers, even complaining that they asked too much about some things, because she had told them everything she knew back at Marbach, but denied a few statements, citing as the reason a spanking that had been administered and the pain of having her hands bound at one point.[310] Then, in a later examination, she denied ever having practiced magic, although she still insisted her grandmother "held to the Devil," and said she had concocted her story from hearsay because she was afraid.[311]

When the High Council got this last report, it ordered the constable of Ludwigsburg to study the transcripts and interview the officials involved in the trial. His investigation showed that there were some irregularities in trial procedure and recording, but while the constable of Marbach had spoken sharply to Margaretha at times, and that the executioner had spanked her at one point, this was because she was denying things she had already said or that other witnesses had already established.[312] He determined that the constable of Marbach had started out "speaking nicely to the girl," that "the answers had not been suggested to" her, and she had already confessed to practicing magic before the executioner was called in. While Margaretha apparently did "wet herself from fear" at one point, "she was not spanked so hard it could be called a form of torture."

On balance it appears that while not all that the girl confessed to was true, neither was all of it false. Not only did Margaretha confess to and apologize for having sex with the boys and for using magic, but several of her friends also said that she was involved with simple sorcery, and other witnesses confirmed that she had threatened them with it.[313] All of this seems to have come out before there was any threat of corporal punishment, so it seems almost certain that she did use love magic and probable that she backed up her threats with curses or incantations, just as Maria Gekin did, around the same time, in Güglingen, about 15 miles away. Which, if any, of the other magic she talked about she actually practiced is not certain; although her first, partial retraction in the orphan house suggests that she may have done some. Certainly, some of the spells she recounted were common forms of popular magic, like getting extra milk from a cow or causing a storm, and some of her answers suggest that she had first-hand experience with hallucinogenic drugs, or at least knew someone who did, for rather than giving a stereotyped answer that she smeared a pitchfork with a salve and flew through the air to a witch dance, she said, to make it work best "you also smear the temples and the veins of the hands," and she described feeling "as if she sat in a wagon and her feet just scraped over the ground." Finally, while her stories about having had sex with the Devil, having been visited by him in jail, and having "renounced God given herself over to the Devil," seem particularly dubious, she did she stick to her claim that her grandmother "held to the Devil," at least in the sense of blaspheming, throughout.

The High Council reprimanded the constable of Marbach for using "illegal inquisitorial methods," made him pay the costs incurred by the constable of Ludwigsburg in investigating his conduct, and ordered Margaretha's release the next year, once she had gone through "instruction in Christianity" and confirmation.[314] While there definitely were irregularities in the way that the constable had handled the investigation, and Margaretha clearly had made up some of the things she confessed to, the changes in her story after she arrived in Ludwigsburg and the High Council's handling of the case suggest that by the 1740s, the same process that had helped to diffuse the witch demonology in the 1560s was now working in reverse.[315] Faced with an indefinite sentence in an inhospitable institution, Margaretha rapidly adapted her testimony to the skepticism of the doctor and preacher, and was soon using its stock features to undercut her own confession. She started by denying the one part of her story that was patently false, but, claiming that she now felt comfortable to tell the truth, went on to contradict not only her partial confirmations earlier in her stay at Ludwigsburg, but also her original testimony, including the parts that she had given apparently quite readily and before she was spanked, and the parts that witnesses had confirmed as well. Her step-by-step adoption of skeptical answers suggests that the enlightened authorities at the orphan house fell victim to the same process that had led witch hunters astray two centuries before. Just as elite beliefs then had found support when aligned with commoners' interests, so elite skepticism gained strength from the same process. Having tragically overblown the dangers of witchcraft for two centuries, the elite reacted by trying to dismiss it altogether.

Maria Gekin, who was investigated for her diabolic incantations and other claimed witchcraft at almost the same time, was sentenced to an indefinite stay in the Ludwigsburg penitentiary "because of her almost blasphemous words and prayers verified in the protocol," but when Barbara Calmbach said that she became ill after Agnes Luzin got her to give her a nail cutting in 1769, the central officials sharply noted that there were "no formal facts" and that "we would have wished that the entire inquiry had not happened.[316] The magistrates, they said, should have "applied more ardor and diligence to discover" Calmbach's "fraud and malice." They let Luzin go and sentenced Calmbach and her father to pay a fine for their use of magical countermeasures, and most of the other incidents involving witchcraft in the eighteenth century were actually recorded in the context of investigations into the healers who diagnosed it, with the officials totally disregarding the alleged *maleficium*. For example, in 1752, Jacob Kurzen was punished for his "magical practices and superstitious cures" that brought "godless calumny" on the woman he accused of harming animals, while in 1803 an itinerant man's claim that a farmer's animals' problems were caused by witchcraft, which he sold him a medication to counteract, was called by the government simply "fraud."[317]

This growing skepticism toward and final curt dismissal of witchcraft allegations was consistent with the way that the government's general handling of magic trials evolved over the course of the eighteenth century, as the skepticism about a diabolical conspiracy that triumphed among the elite during the crisis of confidence evolved into a reflexive dismissal of anything related to magic. This hardening disbelief in the duchy's leaders in turn both reflected and contributed to the detachment of magical beliefs from popular culture. The government's crisis of confidence in the witch demonology had led it to adopt an attitude of pious skepticism toward the related elements in social behavior and cultural concepts: while it disapproved of such activities as both impious and disobedient, it sought to minimize rather than emphasize their social importance. This orientation gradually weakened but on the whole prevailed among the ruling elite for about a century, from the climax of the crisis of confidence, in around 1660, to the triumph of enlightened disbelief, in the 1760s.

We have already discussed in the previous section one of the three phases that the prosecutions for magic went through during this century, the period of decline along with the decline of the witch trials between the 1660s and the 1680s/'90s. However, before we consider the last two we must note two crucial changes that occurred gradually throughout. The first was the steady growth of cosmopolitan French culture and its influence on the elite, with its enlightened disdain for the "brainless caprices of an ignorant villager ... the crackbrained head of a ridiculous shepherd."[318] As French and German presses poured out the early enlightenment denunciations of magic, the fashionable elite adopted their condescending view of witchcraft and magic as nothing but the "foolish superstitions" of "stupid and uncouth" peasants.[319]

Many enlightened discussions of magic were nothing but satirical polemics designed to disparage rather than dispute these beliefs, but these rested on more sober works which systematically rejected the concept of occult or supernatural causation, except perhaps for biblical miracles. The keystone of the edifice of the enlightened cosmology was Newton's success at explaining physical motion in terms of mechanistic principles of physical interaction.[320] The French Cartesians took this view to an extreme by insisting that all physical processes rely on direct physical contact, essentially separating the physical world from all spiritual or religious causation, although, as Newton acknowledged, his system was not entirely material since it had to treat gravity as a regular but perplexing force that acts across empty space. Meanwhile, enlightened thinkers in Germany focused on reconciling the new cosmology with the still-strong traditional religious understanding. Christian Thomasius was the most prominent German contributor to the intellectual assault on magical beliefs, and in 1721 he published a work in which he argued on theological grounds against belief in the Devil's power to perform supernatural miracles.[321] His desire to reconcile the "revealed insights of the Bible and the claims of reason" was shared by Christian Wolff, a student of Leibniz, who brought together "rationalistic developments in England and France" and a positive attitude toward the historic Christian faith," concluding that "piety consists in acting rationally, i.e., in harmony with the nature of things, while sin consists in acting contrary to that which seems right under the same set of assumptions." His philosophy "made it possible for theologians, pastors, and laity alike to regard themselves as being faithful to the Christian tradition, on the one hand, while on the other they could pride themselves on being utterly relevant to the new age that was dawning." George Billfinger, a student of Wolff, enthusiastically expounded this synthesis after his arrival at Tübingen in 1721, and his efforts met "with much success."[322] The extent to which the new approach sought to reconcile faith and reason is suggested by the writings of Johann Albrecht Bengel (1687-1752), who "became the very soul of Swabian Pietism, and the center of a school of like-minded men."[323] He studied mathematics, philosophy, and the classics as well as theology, and even his eschatology was "mathematically and chronologically presented."[324] It was in this atmosphere that the concept of superstition ("*Aberglaube*") shifted from designating outmoded and invalid spiritual beliefs to designating outmoded and invalid beliefs about physical reality, without any significant change in what was actually considered superstitious.[325]

These new intellectual currents affected the duchy's social elite far more strongly than its provincial masses, but the gradual changes in communication and education over the century helped diffuse the new perspective into popular culture.[326] In particular, the balance between secular and religious education changed as the government followed its new set of priorities. On a high level, the regent Friedrich Karl founded a high school for science and modern languages in Stuttgart in 1686. On a lower level, primary schooling appears to have increased, or at least held its own over the century, while religious instruction decayed significantly. The dukes found the church coffers to be a convenient alternative to the recalcitrant estates as a source of revenue, and the number of parishes – and hence pastors – remained constant as the duchy's population climbed.[327] Primary education, in contrast, more autonomous, and literacy's growing importance as a life skill for all but the most marginal inhabitants appears to have insured continued progress in basic education. At any rate, evidence in the trials for magic, particularly for treasure-hunting, attests to a growing influence of written matter on popular awareness. At first, its effect was to diffuse and consolidate magical beliefs, but eventually it became more important as a conduit for enlightened disbelief.

The enlightened rejection of all magic spread only slowly, for it did not triumph even in the government until the last third of the eighteenth century, and popular practices during the transitional century were less influenced by the advances in scientific knowledge than by the government's specific policies toward magic. These, as already mentioned, went through three distinct phases, the first of which, the decline in trials from the 1660s to the 1680/90s, we have already considered in relationship to the decline of the witch trials. The second phase lasted from about 1700 until the 1730s, when prosecutions rose some but then remained at moderate levels. We did not highlight this change in discussing the overall pace of prosecutions, since in absolute and per capita terms the magic, witchcraft, and poison trials considered together declined overall (see Figures 8.4 and 8.5), but viewing magic trials by themselves suggests that this period had more in common with the last phase, representing a rise from the lows of the 1680s that set the stage for the sudden surge and then marked, though more gradual, decline in prosecutions during the third phase, which lasted from the 1740s through the end of the century (Figure 8.6).

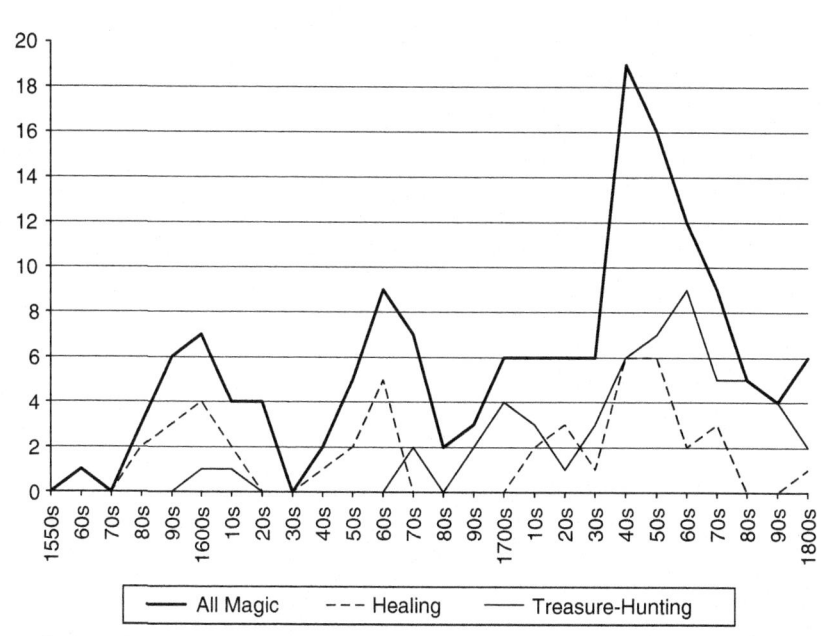

Source: WSAS, A209 Repertorium; WSAS, A213.
Note: Healing includes blessing as well as illicit medicine; Treasure-hunting includes spirit incantation as well as treasure-hunting. "All" includes "Healing," "Treasure-hunting," and miscellaneous cases.

Figure 8.6 All trials for magic, healing, and treasure-hunting

Four trends outside the prosecutions seem likely to have contributed to the gradual buildup of trials from 1690 to the 1730s, and then the sudden surge in the 1740s and the relatively numerous if declining prosecutions in the following decades. One was the gradual reconciliation of Pietists and orthodox Lutherans over the first decades of the century, and their statutory settlement in the 1730s, which steadily defused the religious tensions that dominated Württemberg's spiritual life.[328] The second was the fact that the reconciliation was part of a political development in which the estates were able to assert their leadership after the sudden death of Duke Karl Alexander (r. 1733–7), giving them the chance during the regency of his underage successor to shift the focus from his and his predecessor's absolutist, cosmopolitan policies to the traditional paternalistic concerns of the duchy's indigenous elite.[329] The third was the subsequent ascension of Duke Karl Eugen in 1744, who had acquired an enlightened, reformist worldview during a stay, in his youth, at Fredrick the Great's court.[330] The fourth was the crossing of a socioeconomic threshold that, like the one at the turn of the seventeenth century although less drastically, put the duchy's populace under increasing strain.

How significant the first development was is hard to say, although the repression of magic was certainly a goal on which the orthodox and the Pietists could readily agree. That the second may have played a role is suggested by the fact that all of the magic trials in the 1730s took place after 1737, suggesting that officials may have been too caught up on one side or another of Karl Alexander's attempt to impose military rule during the earlier part of the decade to deal with magical crimes, but once the estates were in control they may have actively promoted this goal.[331] This is supported by the probable effects of the third development, Karl Eugen's assumption of power, because while he came of age in 1744, "for the first decade of his reign he left his administration in the hands of his privy councilors," who continued "the policies of the regency."[332] In the 1750s, though, he "began to take matters into his own hands," and not only did rate of prosecution begin to decline again, but also this is when the government's attitude began to change from what we have called pious scepticism to what we might call dogmatic disbelief. The fourth trend, the crossing of a socioeconomic threshold, would clearly seem to relate to the rising tide of prosecutions, both because it is similar in nature to the developments that gave rise to the witch prosecutions and because it related to some specific developments within the popular practice of magic. We will look first at the threshold that was crossed and then look at some specific trends in popular practices that connected to the socioeconomic developments.

The duchy's population, as we have seen, took a century to reach the level of 1630 again and continued to expand despite periods of out-migration in the 1760s and the 1780s, standing at almost 150 percent of the pre-Thirty Years' War high, about 650,000 in 1789.[333] The fact that it could grow to this level at all is testimony to the impact of economic development during the preceding century. As the French wars came to an end in the 1710s and the military disruptions that had prolonged the post-Thirty Years' War depression ceased, the economy began to expand. However, there were continuing problems with "inflation, capital shortages ... retarded economic development," and the growing pressure of the burgeoning population.[334] While agriculture developed apace, the sheer number of people it had to support counterbalanced its growth, and manufacturing was hindered by the decline of some of the older centers of production even as new ones arose elsewhere.[335] Taxes and feudal dues burdened the peasantry, and wages in the putting-out industry were low. Bad harvest years recurred periodically, and increasing numbers of people became vulnerable to downswings in the business cycle.[336] A surplus of trained artisans in some areas after mid-century led to "bitter poverty ... among most of them," which posed "an almost insoluble problem."[337] Vagrants and bandits roaming the countryside became such a problem that the army had to be used against them, and every community contained a proportion of destitute paupers.[338] In some towns "the poor outnumbered all other classes," and overall about 10 percent of the people in each district were poor, according to a survey made in 1786.[339] The situation in the latter half of the eighteenth century was not as bad as on the eve of the Thirty Years' War, but poverty and insecurity remained grim realities amid the expansive civilization of the *ancient regime*.

How these economic developments, in particular the "inflation, capital shortages," taxes and feudal dues, low wages, and unemployment, connected to developments in popular magic are suggested by consideration of the trends of what we have seen were the two main types of magic in use at the time: healing and treasure-finding (see Figures 8.6 and 8.7).

The most obvious trend that that the graphs in Figures 8.6 and 8.7 convey is the growing importance of treasure-hunting. The increase in healing trials, as well as the miscellaneous others in the total, is clearly important as well, but they seem to have grown roughly in proportion to their earlier fluctuations, and on a per capita basis the peak decade for healing trials was the 1660s. Virtually all the treasure-hunting trials took place after the 1680s, though, and they were the single biggest contributor to the steady build-up of trials in the early 1700s and the sudden surge in the 1740s. The connection of treasure-hunting to things like "inflation, capital shortages," low wages and the other pressures of participating in a money economy seems clear, and it is the importance of the money economy (which made possible the tremendous growth beyond the subsistence level the duchy could support) that accounts, along with memories of the witch persecutions, for

424 Realities of Witchcraft and Popular Magic

Source: Figure 8.6; Franz, *Bauernstandes*, p. 174; Hippel, p. 417; Knapp, p. 25.
Note: See endnote 167 for explanation of population figures. "Healing" includes blessing as well as illicit medicine; "Treasure-hunting" includes spirit incantation as well as treasure-hunting. "All" includes healing, treasure-hunting, and miscellaneous cases.

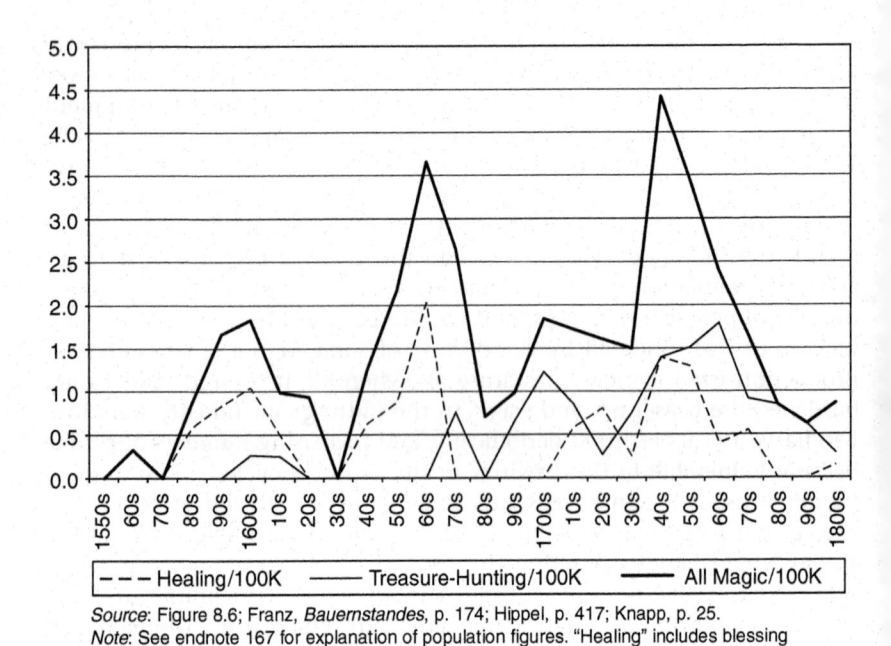

Figure 8.7 All trials for magic, healing, and treasure-hunting per 100,000 inhabitants

the failure of *maleficium*, the expression of displeasure and means of coercion through the threat of revenge on people's health (direct well-being and labor power) and capital resources (animals and, to a lesser extent, buildings [arson, which Apolonia Walther, for example, at least threatened to use]). Some people, like Christoph Wieland, who lost his farm in the 1760s, may have turned to healing as a source of income, but far more, like Hanns Jerg Stadi, the generally honorable judge whose house needed repairs, turned to treasure-hunting in the same decade, in this case the use of a magic mirror in his basement because he couldn't think how else to raise the money he needed.[340]

The importance of treasure-hunting also helps explain the fundamental changes in elite beliefs that took place at this time and also the steady decline of magic trials in the second half of the century. The fundamental change in elite beliefs was the transition from the pious skepticism that they had exhibited since their crisis of confidence in witchcraft to a dismissive, dogmatic disbelief. While individual beliefs of the elite's individual members about magic naturally varied, and continued to vary through the nineteenth century down to today, there is no question that in the late eighteenth century a fundamental rejection of magical cognition and perceptions, a disbelief in, and, indeed, reflexive repression of percepts, insights, experiences, ideas, and beliefs understood to be magical or supernatural, percepts, insights, experiences, ideals, and beliefs that at least partially, as we have seen, reflect the knowledge and powers inaccessible to normal consciousness that can be accessed through deliberate alterations of consciousness, took hold in the European elite's management of individual cognition and collective knowledge. The rise of treasure-hunting in the eighteenth century contributed to this because it was during the period from the 1730s to the 1770s, the peak decades for prosecutions of this activity, that officials began to use the word "fraud" routinely, and by the end of this period they focused on fraudulence or, as an alternative explanation, ignorance almost exclusively.[341] As we have seen, they had always held much magic to be fraud, although more in the sense of the Devil's misrepresentation of himself as the cause of a supernatural effect than in the modern sense of fraud as the deliberate misrepresentation of a natural effect as a supernatural one. Nevertheless, there had been since antiquity an awareness that some apparently magical effects were deliberately faked to fleece a mark (the duchy's first law against magic cited the "unnecessary costs" and "shameless lies" as well as the idolatry it involved).

As Table 8.6 shows, in the first few decades of the eighteenth century, the government's main emphasis was on the religious implications of magical offenses, especially since "superstition" ("*Aberglaube*") still had its traditional religious (and, connected to that, civil) connotations. During the transitional decades around mid-century, the government continued to exhibit concern about the religious and moral implications of magical activities, but began to refer frequently to them as fraudulent or foolish at the same time. Finally, after 1780 the government ceased

Table 8.6 Characterizations of magic in trial documents over time

Date	Sinful	Disobedient	Superstitious	Fraudulent	Foolish
1700s	3		1		
1710s			1		
1720s	1	1			
1730s	2		1	2	
1740s	3	1	4	1	3
1750s	4	1	2	2	
1760s	3		1	3	2
1770s	1	1	1	1	
1780s					1
1790s		1		2	
1800s				2	1

Source: Sampled magic cases (see the appendix) plus all unsampled trials read.[342]

using religious terms in discussing these cases, and instead focused on their presumed deceptiveness or irrationality, with some concern about the disobedience they involved. Just as the crisis of confidence in the witch demonology was signaled by the drift from *"hexerei"* to *"veneficium,"* the transition for pious skepticism to dogmatic disbelief was marked by the evolution in officials' discussion from terms connoting "impious and disobedient" to "fraudulent and foolish." By the time Karl Eugen established his most enduring legacy, the *Hohen Karlschule*, as a modern rival to the traditionalist University of Tübingen, in 1781, the government's transition to the enlightened understanding of magic was all but complete.[343]

In addition to this quantitative evidence of the elite's changing sensibility, and its interconnection with changes in the popular culture they were trying to remold, the documents contain qualitative evidence as well. In 1721, in reporting the treasure-hunting case that started with the farmer's desire to exorcize a ghost from his farmyard, for example, the magistrates of Dornstetten spoke of the participants "forbidden vexed means" for procuring money, which involved the "great misuse and desecration of God's name."[344] A generation later, in 1751, the magistrates of Herrenberg said that the "forbidden arts" of the treasure-finders who had been discovered by the watchman at work on Christmas were "highly sinful," but also referred to them as "their foolishness" and spoke of their "great simple-mindedness, false beliefs, frivolousness, [and] greed."[345] One generation after that, in 1789, the High Council sentenced Maria Scholl to a week in the penitentiary for her "fraud" in scrying with a glass for treasure during a large treasure-hunt, and said the groups' activities manifested their "gross ignorance."[346]

One of the most revealing documents contains the interrogation in Ludwigsburg 10 years later, in 1799, of a man named Heinrich Köhlern, who took part in complex, mass-like ceremonies and all-night prayer sessions to exorcize a ghost that plagued a family, appearing as the apparition of a woman and causing various poltergeist-like disturbances, and also to get it to reveal a treasure.[347] When asked by the magistrates in their 62nd question "if he believes that one can invoke spirits," he answered "he doesn't believe it because he has no proof of it," but when they then asked why he did it, he said that actually he did sort of believe, and later, in answer to question 175, said "he wanted to test whether the books" that described it were "good or not." When pressed once more whether he believed he insisted that he was conducting a test, but said that he had seen something and received signs, although he admitted it was not all that he had claimed. The magistrates asked "if he had had not" prayed too much which caused him to see things, but this he denied. The magistrates chastised him in question 206, saying "that one can't believe that he himself believed in this," and admonished him that "he should admit the truth, which is that he carried this exorcism out in order to be supported while he was in need." He then said that "at first he believed that it is possible, but later he saw that it is not," but in answer 208 he contradicted himself by insisting, "there are spirits, for many have been seen." At this point "all his earlier statements and contradictions could not make him admit that he did not believe." The magistrates were convinced that Köhlen must have been a conscious fraud from start to finish, but his testimony betrays a much more complex reality, an acknowledgment that some of the things that he was said to have experienced he had not, and uncertainty about what is really possible, but a conviction that there was in the end really something there, that the hours and hours of prayer and intricately conducted rituals did not simply create a trivial illusion, but instead a contact with something much deeper and more powerful than that.

The same progression can be seen in discussions of other forms of magic – indeed, one of the earliest harsh condemnations of "fraudulent" practices was made against Jacob Schiller for his thief detection using "blessings or magic arts," and healers were accused of "shameful supersition" – but the prominence of treasure-hunting in the eighteenth century would seem to help explain the decline of trials toward the end of the century in several ways.[348] First of all, the officials' growing conviction that magic involved nothing more than fraud and foolishness reflects, in part at least, the fact that a good deal of treasure-hunting *did* involve fraud and foolishness. A number of cases clearly involved cynical swindles by con-men of various stripes seeking to scam the credulous and the greedy, and commoners undoubtedly became more cautious as they, like the officials (although more reluctantly), came to this realization. Secondly, even when not fraudulent, almost all treasure-hunting activity was ineffective, for, while caches were occasionally found and we have seen that there are ways in which magical activities could theoretically facilitate locating hidden treasure, in practice this is a problem for which magic is particularly poorly suited, especially in comparison to divining the identity of a guilty party or projecting anger in a way that it induces illness, and as a result treasure-hunting was very rarely successful. While some commoners may have been hopeful to a fault, they were not as a group stupid, and many apparently came to realize that, sadly, treasure-finding was unlikely to work. Thirdly, as the officials came to believe all magical activities were essentially fraudulent or foolish, they found it harder to believe that the people who practiced them could be anything other than cynical swindlers or dupes, and became ever more determined to prove that this was the case, even to the point of using physical coercion (what would have been called torture in a witch trial) to get suspected con artists to confess. Thus, in 1764 the warden of the Ludwigsburg penitentiary had the young servant Jacob Schu "beaten with ten ... strokes, and when he remained firm in his badness approximately seven or eight more, further five or six, and again ten, and finally another five" in order to "bring him to acknowledge ... he had no other intention, then ... to steal money" from his elderly employer rather than use it to ransom his dead wife from punishment for incestuous sins he said her ghost had told him she had committed[349]. And if we are inclined to agree with the officials' conviction that the young man was, in fact, lying and was, in fact, perpetrating a fraud, we should remember Gallus Dürrner during the 1770 ghost cult incident in Weilheim, who was flogged in order to get him to stop insisting "the things are godly" and to confess that the cult was nothing but a treasure-hunting fraud, which he steadfastly, and apparently sincerely, refused to do.

Furthermore, by the mid-eighteenth century the government had a new means of punishment and coercion at its disposal: incarceration in the Ludwigsburg penitentiary. Before that, the duchy had few provisions for prolonged incarceration, and between the decline of torture and the completion of the facility came a half-century of relative laxity. Thereafter, however, sentences could be made much tougher without shedding blood. Several years in prison was a forbidding prospect, and sometimes the term was indefinite. Once warned, either personally or by example, a commoner had good reason to avoid further trouble, and once released, he had even better reason to avoid going back.

Even apart from the threat of flogging and/or prolonged incarceration, the repressive power of fines, short jail terms, and just the threat of prosecution should not be underestimated. As with the late witch trials, even probation could have a dampening effect on popular practices. Arrest carried social penalties quite apart from its legal results. Communities often stigmatized people convicted, or even suspected, of crimes, and we have seen that there were a variety of informal sanctions that such a stigma could trigger. This stigma could have life-long effects on the person's social standing, and that of his relatives and descendants as well, inhibiting upward mobility in particular. Thus, even mild repression intimidated established people, and the law affected the predominant mores of the marginal majority, making disreputable a set of activities that had previously been unremarkable.

Just as the witch trials may have influenced the ideals and actions of established women at least as much as the peasant's and artisan's wives who were their direct objects, so, too, the magic trials did not eradicate all magical practices, but had an important impact on the place of magic in society and culture all the same. As late as 1775, one magistrate commented that "it is indeed well known that magical healing is in full swing everywhere, and where not openly then secretly."[350] Nevertheless, these activities were endowed with a furtive, illicit character that hindered contact between magicians and local society and, most importantly, precluded the expansion of magical practices in step with the burgeoning population and the rapidly developing urban culture. At the end of the eighteenth century, Württemberg had three times the population of the 1660s, but only half the number of magic trials. Official indifference would seem to account for at most only part of this, for the men who ran the government tended to be responsible professionals alert to the need to protect the public from its own credulousness and the predation of swindlers. So, the marginal place of magic in the duchy's overall culture, and in its leading, urban, upper-middle-class sector in particular, would seem to be the cumulative effect of two centuries of repression from the witch persecutions in the seventeenth century through the enlightened repression of magic in the eighteenth century, which pushed magical practitioners to the margins of society, magical beliefs to the backwater of provincial culture, and magical experiences to the margins of perception.[351]

Conclusion

There are two final points to make about the repression of magic during the early modern period. First of all, it did not succeed in eradicating popular magical practices, as had been hoped.[352] Ordinary people have continued to believe in and employ a wide variety of magical activities down to today, and a range of public practitioners have continued to offer their services. In rural areas, traditional forms of magic continued to be practiced well into the twentieth century, and in urban areas innovative forms and uses of magic emerged and today command a major section of the bookstores in most malls. However, the second point is that the repression of magic was far from ineffective. In the 1400s, European society was full of people who employed magic routinely and fairly openly, despite the rather distant religious establishment's disapproval. In the 1800s only a subsection of Europe's society believed in magic, and an even smaller proportion practiced magic, and that only furtively. Economists emphasize that "informal (i.e., illegal) black markets" involve "high costs and risks" that affect "the options and behavior of many members of society, and thus the development of the entire economy."[353] The same can be said for the effects of repression on development of the entire culture. During the early modern period different forms of *maleficium* went from being a common weapon used in interpersonal conflicts, which were employed both consciously and unconsciously, overtly and surreptitiously, to being at most a furtive, barely acknowledged set of forbidden practices, and far more frequently nothing more than an alleged or imagined fear.[354] At the same time, beneficent magic went from being a central part of popular culture routinely employed to help with a range of problems to being a set of individual beliefs apologetically, defiantly, or only half-seriously practiced, while beneficent magicians went from being relatively open about, widely know for, and often well respected for the services they provided, to being secretive, marginal figures known and respected within the local community, perhaps, and occasionally able to develop a successful and visible practice, but always in danger of drawing too much attention. Finally, during this same period, magic went from being a vital part of Europe's intellectual heritage to being a discredited set of folk beliefs. There were certainly many reasons why magic lost its intellectual credibility – its vulnerability to fraudulent uses; the many specific ideas it incorporated that were wrongheaded; its very success at being integrated with classical science, Ptolomaic astronomy and Galenic medicine, whose displacement during the scientific revolution undercut its intellectual explanations; the subjective foundation of its approach to knowledge – but the fact that involvement with magic brought the suspicion of diabolism and the danger of prosecution must surely count among them.

As a final set of reflections, it is worth considering both why magic persisted and yet why it was so effectively suppressed. The answer to the second question has traditionally been that magic is fundamentally wrong, irrational and ineffective, and therefore suppressing it is nothing more than getting people to see the light. The corresponding answer to the first question has been that magic provides psychological satisfactions that seduce people into believing in it. We have seen, however, that much that was considered magic was valid and efficacious, not only the fact that specific magical beliefs and practices are true and work, like the conviction that one person's anger can cause another person's illness, or the use of ritual preparations to enhance skilled performance, but also the fact that magic as a whole, as a general body of knowledge and set of general practices, both references and enables manipulation of reality, since it is based on the deliberate manipulation of the nervous system and alteration of consciousness in ways that provide access to knowledge and powers that are not accessible in our normal waking state. Magic persists because it is real; whether or not this or that traditional idea is valid, whether or not any aspect of parapsychology ends up being vindicated, the cluster of beliefs at the core of magic – that people's psyches are intertwined at a visceral level, that thoughts can be read and projected through occult (hidden) channels, that patterned activity can enable us to understand and influence reality differently, and in some ways better, than normal deliberate actions – reference reality because the cluster of behaviors common to magical practices – deliberate, ritual actions that alter neural activity and the conscious experiences associated with it – provide access to reality, both enhancing knowledge of it and enhancing power over it.

The superficial answer to how magic could be effectively repressed during the European transition to modernity is that the specific magical beliefs of late Medieval Europe, like the specific magical beliefs of most people, contain a great deal of invalid information, because of the technical limits on traditional peoples' ability to test and refine their understanding of nature; because a considerable amount of magical knowledge is visceral and imagic, and therefore depends on metaphor and allegory to be expressed linguistically; and because magic, the manipulation of the mind, depends to some extent on creating illusions because of the possibility that in acting on them people will turn them into reality, the way that a sick person's belief she will get better may well help her get better. A deeper answer is that since magic works through deliberate behaviors to manipulate the mind, by prohibiting certain behaviors, magical practices, and imposing rigidities in the mind, disbelief, society and culture were able to distance the great majority of people from magic, making it dangerous, dishonorable, and ultimately futile to engage in these practices or express these beliefs, a process that became a self-reinforcing cycle since belief and interest in magic were further depressed if its effects could not be experienced firsthand.

However, this explanation, while it certainly contains some truth, distorts things in two ways. First of all, people naturally vary in their ability to achieve the dissociation necessary to experience magic, and even in traditional societies most people do not enter a magical state of mind easily, which is why they need extensive rituals, austerities, or drugs to help them, and also why they rely, as early modern Europeans did, on specialist practitioners. The difficulty people experience accessing magic is not just because of differences in dissociative ability, though; the fact of the matter is most people don't really want to access normally unconscious information, because it can be threatening to their self-image or force them to confront social facts that are disruptive. This latter reason is related to the second distortion in the foregoing answer to the question of why magic was so effectively repressed during the early modern period: the fact that there were powerful structural forces in the society and culture promoting the repression of magic, not simply the perversity or intolerance or insecurities of the ruling classes. In particular, magic is incompatible with some of the fundamental the needs of modern society: the need for people in densely populated settlements to act predictably, according to compartmentalized, explicitly stated bureaucratic rules and relationships; the premium in print culture for knowledge that is expressed, processed, and recorded in explicit, logical, linguistic terms; and the incentives in a capitalist economy for individuals to act as autonomous rational actors in the marketplace. Together, these developing structures fostered the redefinition of the self to emphasize an internally cohesive, independent, self-directed identity, an atomic individual that had no place for autonomous intelligences within or intrinsic connections with the world outside.[355]

Freud demolished the assumption of an internally integrated person, but not the ideal of it, for that is the goal of psychoanalysis, and he left in place the idea of the existentially independent psyche, the mind inside the brain that is fundamentally separated from the outside world. It is our need to protect the integrity and autonomy of our individual psyches, to suppress the autonomous intelligences within and the visceral interconnections with the world outside, both of which challenge our rational self-control, that have made it so difficult for educated moderns to understand the realities of witchcraft and magic for the past 200 years.

Conclusion

Taking the approach of trying to determine what was real about early modern witchcraft and magic has revealed a number of significant new insights. To begin with, *maleficium*, the aspect of witchcraft of most concern to early modern commoners, was real. Not every supposed harm inflicted by every supposed witch was real, of course, for some forms of *maleficium*, like weather magic, were, as far as we can tell, impossible, and since much *maleficium* was supposed to be perpetrated through occult, or hidden, channels, it was easy for fears, angers, jealousies, and rivalries to generate unfounded accusations. However, the great bulk of alleged *maleficium* concerned illness and other harm to people and animals, and not only did it involve a number of surreptitious physical activities whose potency has never been in question (although their significance has generally been minimized), but also it involved a combination of overt or subliminal communication of hostility and psychophysical vulnerability to stress that constituted a much more harmful form of interpersonal conflict than has been conventionally appreciated (see Chapter 1). Particularly noteworthy are the facts that, on the one hand, this interpersonal influence can be triggered by unconscious as well as conscious expressions of anger and by subtle as well as overt threat displays, and, on the other hand, it does not depend for its effect on some sort of symbolic somaticization, or even belief in its power, in order to work, although of course belief can intensify the effect and symbolic somaticizations do occur. Instead, it is an effect that can occur spontaneously, when one person's impulsive expression of anger triggers the stress response in another, although it can of course also be triggered consciously, with the explicit hope that an angry display will cause injury. In either case, and it is particularly potent when circumstances make it impossible for the recipient to respond or avoid the perpetrator, so that the stress becomes chronic.

This type of interpersonal interaction appears to be endemic to small-scale, face-to-face societies; if it is not a universal, it is certainly very widespread. In early modern Württemberg, as in much of early modern Europe, it was one among many forms of interpersonal combat utilized in the often-harsh environment of village and small town society. It was particularly likely to be employed by women, especially elderly women, because women had more limited options and tended to be better equipped to engage in *maleficium* owing to their social/domestic roles and their superior social, emotional, and linguistic skills (see Chapter 2). Furthermore, in the situation of acute competition for resources that was prevalent in Württemberg and neighboring parts of Europe during the "Iron Century," the use of *maleficium* and, more importantly, fears of *maleficium* intensified to the point of fueling witch hunts that drew in innumerable innocent victims who had never worked magic consciously or even unconsciously exerted a particularly malign effect on others.

The early modern discourse about witchcraft did not just concern *maleficium*, of course. Instead, it linked this traditional village witchcraft to diabolism, the idea that magical practitioners were bound together in an underground sect organized and led by the Devil and dedicated to the destruction of the Christian commonwealth. There is no good evidence that such a conspiracy existed, but the belief was constructed from numerous elements that did. To begin with the first stage of supposed recruitment into this conspiracy, the idea that the Devil approached depressed or angry people in order to seduce them into his service was both based on and fed into real experiences that people had as they assimilated a new, universalist moral orientation in which he served as the embodiment of evil, and a new set of expectations about internal regulation of feelings and actions (see Chapter 3). People under torture routinely made up stories about meeting the Devil to order, but other people confessed to such things because they really thought they had experienced them. In some cases this was just a way of talking about the theological or moral implications of the way that they lived, and in other cases it may have involved a retroactive reworking of memory to conform to a dawning realization about this, but in still others it appears to have been a direct experience in which the person worked through the process of realization in real-time, as a series of sensations, voices, visualizations, or even complex multisensory experiences that were projected into the parts of the brain that usually handle sensory input from the outside, the "sensorium," but were now in whole or in part filled with images generated in a different way, through the channels by which memories and expectations are added to immediate perceptions to create the image we understand to be external reality.

Similarly, the next step in the stereotyped recruitment process, flight to and participation in the Sabbath, was based on a range of actual experiences – vivid dreams, flying dreams, out-of-body experiences, and the effects of various hallucinogens – in which some people flew to Heuberg or raided neighboring beer cellars (see Chapter 4). As with encounters with the Devil, these were not merely folk beliefs or stories people told, but, in some cases anyway, actual lived experiences. In general, descriptions of these ceremonies are rather tame compared to the lurid sexuality and cannibalism of children described in the demonology, but some people did have sexual experiences in their dreams and others did "fly" to "devour" their neighbors' babies as they slept at night, so even here there was some basis in real experiences for the demonological fears. The incorporation of such reports into the generalized witch demonology suggests that there was a "ratchet effect" by which diverse elements that existed in isolation became standard components of the composite image.

After the Sabbath, witches were supposed by the demonology to return to normal life ready to perpetrate malefic crimes deliberately, which anthropologists call sorcery, as opposed to the spontaneous and unconscious infliction of harm they call witchcraft. Here again, not only were various forms of sorcery known and practiced widely in early modern Europe, but also they had the potential to inflict real harms (see the section "The realities of sorcery" in Chapter 5). The basic mechanisms of much sorcery were similar to the bases of spontaneous *maleficium*, but with one important addition: they included ritual activities whose performance artificially enhanced the practitioner's power to convey hostility and thus inflict harm. In some cases these were preparation of material substances, like poisons and sacks with noxious materials to secrete in their enemies' space, but most importantly from our point of view here were a variety of means by which practitioners could manipulate their own thoughts and feelings in order to project an effect similar to that caused by spontaneous emotions. Furthermore, there is much evidence that not just theologians, but ordinary people were aware of the relationship between such magic and the role of the Devil in the moral and spiritual universe, and they therefore sometimes invoked him or his agents in order to draw on his negative symbolic and spiritual power (see the section "Sorcery and satanism" in Chapter 5).

There is no good evidence, once again, that the witch demonology described an actual diabolic cult, an organized, underground sect led by the Devil and dedicated to subverting Christendom, but the demonology did involve more than just the scholastic conflation of diverse practices from around Europe. Instead, it was patterned as a whole after the structure of shamanic initiation, the psychological process by which magical practitioners in a wide variety of cultures enter the spirit world in order to learn how to heal, divine, and work other magic. Before summarizing this process and recapitulating its connection to European witchcraft and magic, though, what is meant here by shamanism must be clarified once more, for the term is currently surrounded by confusion and controversy. To begin with, shamanism does not exist as a cohesive set of beliefs and practices characteristic of any particular culture; whether it is understood to describe the spiritual healing practices engaged in by members of certain Siberian tribes, at one extreme; any alteration of consciousness used to convey inspired insights to others, at the other extreme; or one of several intermediate definitions that are used, it is an artificial construct created by Western intellectuals, an etic category rather than an emic one (see the section "Witchcraft and shamanism" in Chapter 5). The definition adopted for this study is an intermediate position that includes the range of practices designed to enable the practitioner to enter direct contact with spirits, whether through soul travel, invocation, or possession, and is based on cognitive rather than ethnographical considerations. In general, initiates display some predisposition to the calling, whether it is because they are going through a period of despondency or personal crisis or because they are constitutionally "highly hypnotizable," naturally endowed with an ability to dissociate. In any case, the crucial step is that the person is brought to experience a profound alteration of consciousness caused by driving the nervous system into the simultaneous discharge of the normally alternating sympathetic and parasympathetic systems and a subsequent collapse into parasympathetic dominance. During this process, called "tuning the nervous system," cognitive structures become fluid, synchronization of various parts of the nervous system occurs, body consciousness and reality-checking are distorted or suspended, physiological changes characteristic of both near-death and intense learning take place, and interactions with autonomous intelligences generally perceived – dream-like – as animate beings are experienced. Afterwards, the shaman uses the insights gained from the experience to work magic, most often healing and divinatory services for other members of his or her community.

While classic shamanic healing involves the shaman returning to the spirit world to defeat the spirits responsible for patients' illnesses or to rescue sick people's souls and engage in other activities in spirit that are thought to simultaneously affect the regular world, shamans often return to the spirit world to renew and expand their magical powers (as witches were thought to); and shamans sometimes induce profound "tuning" experiences in their clients as part of the healing process, shamanism as defined here also involves more limited alterations of consciousness, "fine-tuning" the shaman's own and others' nervous systems, so to speak. We have proposed to call these limited manipulations "shamanistic" practices to distinguish them from the more profound "shamanic" experiences of "tuning" that induce actual perception of and interaction with spirits and the spirit world (essentially entering a waking-dream state). The link between the two is the connection between alterations of consciousness – manipulations of the nervous system – whether overpowering or subtle, and the ability to access knowledge and powers that are normally inaccessible to the waking conscious mind. Shamanic experience is not necessary in order to utilize shamanistic practices, which can be learned by rote, improvised from examples, or developed from experience, but shamanic experience appears to foster the ability to do so. The witch demonology thus encapsulated the process by which people entered a state of mind conducive to shamanizing, either driving themselves into an initial spontaneous experience or opening themselves to tutelage by an established practitioner; tuning their nervous system in order to experience direct contact with spirits; and thereby gaining insight into the causes of human distress and ways to both induce and heal it. The demonologists understood the basic outline of what was going on as well as many details, but in their attempt to make sense of the variety of diverse, specific beliefs and practices people used to attain this neuropsychological experience in Christian terms they mistakenly took it for, and tortured people into confirming that it was, some sort of centrally organized, cohesive counterreligion that worshipped the Devil and was widely practiced by village witches and local healers.

There is evidence of ongoing shamanic practices in the activities of people across Europe in both elite and popular culture. First of all, learned necromancy was designed to "summon spirits" through extreme rituals involving extensive preparation and protracted and exacting ceremonies. (Here we're still in the section "Witchcraft and shamanism" of Chapter 5.) Secondly, popular practitioners like the *benandanti* in the Fruili, the "ladies from outside" in Sicily, the *taltos* in Hungary, the 'nighttime ladies' in medieval Paris, the Waldensian brethren, perhaps, the "itinerant scholars" like Hans Haasen, of course, and a variety of more idiosyncratic individuals and small groups reported magical flights and spirit encounters that were associated with spiritual powers. To some extent their practices may have been "vestiges" of some sort of pristine primitive shamanism, ongoing traditions passed down from generation to generation since antiquity, but it is important to keep in mind that, like the subliminal and psychophysiological processes underlying spontaneous witchcraft, shamanism as defined in this study is not a cultural tradition dependent on continuous transmission, but instead is a set of psychological experiences manifesting a physiological process that can happen spontaneously in situations of acute psychological or physical stress and, once (re)discovered, can be deliberately induced and taught to others. Whatever continuities late medieval and early modern shamanic practices in Europe may have had with the distant past, it seems likely that they owed at least as much to an ongoing process of collective cross-fertilization and individual improvisation.

Shamanic practitioners and practices clearly existed in late medieval and early modern Europe, and their experiences contributed the overall structure as well as some of the details to the witch demonology, but their role in European society and popular culture was far outweighed by shamanistic practices and practitioners. Shamanistic practices were extremely widespread; fused with religious symbols and rituals, they were utilized by most ordinary people for defense from spiritual dangers and to promote health and wellbeing, and the simple sorcery that was one form of *maleficium* used by some was another variant of such activity. Shamanistic rituals also formed the mainstay of the services offered by beneficent popular practitioners.

Most popular practitioners were beneficent, in that the services they offered were generally intended to help people (although helping one person might involve harming another, of course, like when conducting counter-magic against a suspected witch). Beneficent practices had two major functions: to divine unknown information, like the identity of a thief or the location of lost objects, and to improve people's situation in some way, like healing the sick or enhancing a skill. Some forms of divination relied on processes that would seem to us to be entirely random, but from the point of view of understanding the realities of magic it is important to recognize that other forms, like scrying and the "sieve and sheers" involved the creation of dissociative states in which unconscious knowledge could be manifested as visualizations or ideomotor activity, and even many apparently random processes have subtle biases or leave room for interpretation that can also bring out unconscious information (see Chapter 6). Similarly, some forms of manipulative magic aim to achieve what seem to be impossible effects, but the most common form, magical healing, is more efficacious, and efficacious in a wider range of ways, than historical accounts generally suggest (see Chapter 7). Specifically, it had the potential to mobilize and supplement the body's natural recovery mechanisms in a variety of ways, some of which depended on the hopes and beliefs of the patient, but others of which, like spontaneous *maleficium*, exerted direct physiological effects that did not depend on conscious mediation or cultural conditioning.

While the realities of the great majority of magical phenomena can be understood by reference to processes that seem well within current understanding of the ways the world works, at certain points such deliberations run up against reports of phenomena that our understanding of reality cannot accommodate. Furthermore, in many more places there is a significant disjunction between what we consider must have really been happening and what the participants thought was going on. In the latter case the reconciliation would seem to be to recognize that accounting for something in terms we can accept does not necessarily preclude the activity of processes that we don't accept. For example, we can account for someone perceiving and interacting with the Devil as the projection of images, sounds, and even smells into the sensorium and the animation of these by unconscious neural modules, but that does not necessarily mean that the source all of the information and intention in these percepts and intelligence is internal. We choose to believe that they are, while early moderns believed that some vital element in them came from outside, but the essential point is that whether the Devil miraculously appeared as a physical body, appeared as a spiritual or paranormal intrusion into the person's perceptual or cognitive processing, or was generated entirely by the internal workings of the person's nervous system, in the end all the person could know of him was a representation in the sensorium animated by an intelligence independent of the person's normal consciousness. Whether all the inputs into that intelligence came from the person's brain or some came from elsewhere is beyond our ability to judge historically; what we can know is that in dealing with the Devil, or invoking spirits, or traveling to the Venusberg, the person was accessing information not accessible in normal waking consciousness. In other words, whatever the source of input from beyond normal consciousness, at some point it must be translated into sensations registered in the sensorium in order for the person to have a conscious experience of it. In that sense, a vision is just as real as seeing an actual body, or, conversely, seeing an actual body is just as much an illusion as seeing a vision: in the end, all we can know, all we can experience, is what we assemble inside our brains.

Modern Westerners assume that the purpose of the sensorium is to model the outside world as accurately as possible, and all other input is a form of pollution, but that is actually false: the purpose of the sensorium is to help us survive to reproduce and rear children, if seeing an angel from God come to warn us from our evil, self-destructive ways helps us do that, it is just as valid a use of the sensorium as tracking prey or watching a play, and to ignore it or explain it away because it might not show up in a photograph would be the height of folly. Naturally, this process is not always reliable; sometimes the Devil appears as an angel from God and tries to trick us into doing wrong. But, then, perfectly rational thought can lead us astray just as easily, as the followers of a variety of modern "scientific" ideologies attest. If there is any resolution here, any moral, it is that we should not, and in fact cannot, choose between rationality and inspiration, for we are hard-wired for both. The question is not whether we will get input from both, just what we make of it and therefore choose to do with it.

This approach to the sensorium may help us reconcile the differing concepts of reality concerning voices and visions, but there is still the matter of reports of anomalous physical events: urns crashing to the ground for no apparent reason; cloth torn up before peoples' eyes by, apparently, no one; people flying through the night, even if in spirit, to "press" their enemies or touch their friends, who report having sensed the presence. Some of these may be reasonably explained as misperceptions or altered memories, but in the end there are reported experiences, in the historical and the experimental record, that strain these sensible answers. We have stressed repeatedly that it is impossible on the basis of 300-year-old documents to provide decisive evidence on this question, and these concluding remarks cannot magically produce some definitive answer. Instead, what it can do is point up the need, if we are serious about studying magic and witchcraft, for historical consideration of these issues. It is understandable, but at the same time lamentable, that in the past 50 years of modern social-scientific investigations of early modern witchcraft and magic not one has taken into account the body of serious scientific work on paranormal phenomena that has been done in the past century, along with the vigorous skeptical critique of it that has been ongoing. Without endorsing one side or the other of this debate, it is worth pointing out that historians have an important role to play in this discussion. They can explore how well different theories explain reported phenomena, they can assess the record of experiments and debates that determined our current understanding of what is possible and what is real, and they can place the changing consensus on what is real and what is possible in the larger context of social and cultural history and the history of mentalities.

We have taken some initial steps toward the first of these three tasks here in considering the reality of the various practices and experiences recorded in Württemberg's archives, and must leave the second to the history of science, but the third was the major focus of Chapter 8. Specifically, we saw there that the modern concept of reality was not formed in a vacuum, or through some peaceful process in which truth just naturally unfolded. Instead, the process was bitterly contested, involving a protracted, three century campaign of repression in which magical beliefs, practices, and practitioners were misrepresented and vilified, first as nefarious agents of the Devil and later as nothing but frauds and dupes. In the first phase, the full power of the state was brought to bear against suspected sorcery and evidence of contact with the Devil, and any involvement with magic was grounds for suspicion before and evidence during a trial that could lead to prolonged incarceration, agonizing torture, and a fiery death. Furthermore, even without charges of witchcraft, magical activities, however benign, could lead to arrest, incarceration, fines, and banishment from home and family, and this threat continued to hang over practitioners of magic long after the witch fires had died down. Furthermore, there were a variety of forms of repression beyond the force of the law, from the spiritual sanctions of the church through the moral strictures taught in schools and the myriad forms of supervision and punishment practiced by local communities to the individual psychophysiological processes by which the sociocultural mandate to suppress perceptions and block cogitations connected to magic ultimately took effect. As a consequence, popular beliefs were undermined, even if not obliterated; popular practices were suppressed, even if not eradicated; peoples' behavior was modified, even if not purified; and a new definition of self was put in place, a self that, at least in theory, was in rational control of its own actions and decisions, able to repress any irrational thoughts or illusory perceptions that might well up from within, and impervious to any direct contact with or irresistible influences from without.

Appendix

The lists below are provided to give an overview of the samples as well as the source documents for references in the notes. A discussion of the Witchcraft and General Magic samples is contained in the introduction to Part I of the book, and the Beneficent Magic samples are discussed in the introduction to Part III. All documents are located in the *Hauptstaatsarchiv* in Stuttgart. Note that "b." stands for *"Büschel,"* or file, which in A209 generally contains a single case, and in A213 generally contains several cases, which are distinguished by date.

Sampled Witchcraft Cases

Case ID	Archival ID
W1	A209, b. 719 (1565)
W2	A209, b. 1787
W3	A209, b. 2099
W4	A209, b. 1884 (1659)
W5	A209, b. 2096
W6	A209, b. 1924
W7	A209, b. 873
W8	A209, b. 2088
W9	A209, b. 1789
W10	A209, b. 449
W11	A209, b. 1856
W12	A209, b. 451
W13	A209, b. 1881
W14	A209, b. 1989
W15	A209, b. 852
W16	A209, b. 1223
W17	A209, b. 767
W18	A209, b. 1431
W19	A209, b. 1780
W20	A209, b. 851a
W21	A209, b. 546
W22	A209, b. 1486
W23	A209, b. 8
W24	A209, b. 434
W25	A209, b. 327
W26	A209, b. 782
W27	A209, b. 11

Note: Cases considered to be witchcraft in drawing this sample were those labeled as *"Hexerei"* or some variant "Pact with the Devil" in the archival index.

Sampled general magic cases

Case ID	Archival ID	Type
Zns	A209, b. 525	Beneficent
Z1	A209, b. 679	Witchcraft
Z2	A209, b. 1050	Witchcraft
Z3	A209, b. 1958	Witchcraft
Z4	A209, b. 773	Witchcraft
Z5	A209, b. 22	Beneficent
Z6	A209, b. 1436	Beneficent
Z7	A209, b. 466a	Beneficent
Z8	A209, b. 440	Witchcraft
Z9	A209, b. 552	Witchcraft
Z10	A209, b. 39	Beneficent
Z11	A209, b. 1587	Witchcraft
Z12	A209, b. 1388	Beneficent
Z13	A209, b. 757	Witchcraft
Z14	A209, b. 723	Beneficent
Z15	A209, b. 226	Beneficent
Z16	A209, b. 1258	Witchcraft
Z17	A209, b. 1634a	Beneficent
Z18	A209, b. 311a	Beneficent
Z19	A209, b. 1338	Beneficent
Z20	A209, b. 1092	Witchcraft

Note: General Magic cases were selected from those labeled "*Zauberei*" or other general terms for magic in the archival index. Cases designated "witchcraft" here were found to be essentially late witch trials where the government's changing terminology led the archival indexer to label them more vaguely as magic. Cases labeled "beneficent" were mainly instances of the more specific types listed below and miscellaneous others.

Beneficent magic sample

Sampled blessing cases

Case ID	Archival ID	Date of document
Ss1	A213, b. 8395	1770
Ss2	A213, b. 8406	1761
Ss3	A209, b. 1656	1729
Ss4	A209, b. 1855	
Ss5A	A209, b. 1424	1589
Ss5B	A209, b. 1424	1594
Ss7	A209, b. 307	
Ss8	A213, b. 8408	1751
Ss9	A209, b. 460a	

Sampled healing cases

Case ID	Archival ID	Date of document
Az+	A213, b. 8398	1751
Az1	A209, b. 1878	
Az2	A213, b. 8401	1769
Az3	A209, b. 1146	
Az4	A209, b. 654	
Az5	A209, b. 725	
Az6	A213, b. 8407	1752
Az7	A209, b. 368	

Sampled treasure-hunting cases

Case ID	Archival ID	Date of document
Sg1	A213, b. 8406	1762
Sg2	A213, b. 8406	1751
Sg3	A213, b. 8410	1795
Sg4	A209, b. 865	
Sg5	A213, b. 8399	1769
Sg6	A209, b. 1982	
Sg7	A213, b. 8419	1789
Sg8	A213, b. 8395	1766
Sg9	A209, b. 609	
Sg10	A213, b. 8395	1747
Sg11	A213, b. 8417	1770
Sg12	A213, b. 8397	1747
Sg13	A209, b. 1700a	

Sampled conjuring cases

Case ID	Archival ID	Date of document
Gb1	A213, b. 8396	1764
Gb2	A213, b. 8419	1789
Gb3	A213, b. 8411	1765
Gb4	A209, b. 433	
Gb5	A213, b. 8409	1739
Gb6	A209, b. 957	
Gb7	A213, b. 8397	1747

Note: "Blessing" cases are those labeled "*Segensprecherei*" in the archival indexes; "Healing" cases are those labeled "*Arznei*" or vaguer forms indicating illicit medical practices; "Treasure-hunting" cases were labeled "*Schatzgraberei;*" and "Conjuring," "*Teufelsbeschwörung*."

Notes

Part I The Reality of *Maleficium*

1. Bever, *Maleficium*, pp. 713–15; Levack, *Witch-Hunt*, pp. 4–7; Segelmann, pp. 2, 68–9; Baroja, p. 40; Maxwell-Stuart, *Witchcraft in Europe*, p. 10.
2. Maxwell-Stuart, *Witchcraft in Europe*, p. 10; Levack, *Witch-Hunt*, pp. 85–6; A209, b. 451, d. 2.
3. Midelfort, *Witch hunting*, p. 23. Note that I have substituted "magic" for "witchcraft" in this quote since, according to Ströhmer, "By '*zauberey*' the author [of the *Carolina*] understood ... traditional harmful magic, without the core elements of the witch demonology ... like the idea of nocturnal witches' flight, copulation with the Devil, or the witch Sabbath." n.p. (online). See also Schormann, p. 45.
4. Gehring, p. 169.
5. List from Thomas, pp. 436–7; note that Württemberg's theologians and jurists had a particular tradition of discounting the power of weather magic, although they were aware that some people tried to use it; see Raith, "Württemberg – Witch Persecutions," n.p. (online).
6. H. C. Erik Midelfort compiled this unpublished index to witchcraft and related cases in the University archive of Tübingen, 84/1–70, *Libri Sententiarum ... facultatis jur.*

1 The Varieties of *Maleficium*

1. MacFarlane, pp. 240–5; Clark, *Thinking*, pp. 3–10; Briggs, "Dangerous," p. 23.
2. Sebald, *Witch Children*, p. 89; MacFarlane, pp. 222–3; Briggs, "Dangerous," p. 23.
3. Briggs, *Neighbors*, p. 64.
4. Clark, *Thinking*, p. 4.
5. The sample is discussed in the introductory segment of this part, above.
6. Raith, "Hexenverfolgungen" n.p. (online) advances the theological explanation, but in "Oberrat," p. 114 reports that weather magic was routinely reported in tortured confessions, where the influence of ideas held by the educated elite would be expected to be strongest, and seldom mentioned in the complaints lodged by commoners, who could be expected to be least influenced by learned debates. For other areas, see Larner, pp. 60–1; Levack, *Witch-Hunt*, p. 220; Pócs, *Between*, p. 67; Briggs, *Neighbors*, p. 91; Thomas, p. 437.
7. MacFarlane, p. 153; Sharpe, *Bewitching*, pp. 66–7.
8. Thomas, p. 436; Briggs, *Neighbors*, p. 63; Pócs, *Between*, p. 59; for world, Mayer in Marwick, p. 47 and MacFarlane, p. 213. There were a further two reports of theft and witchcraft in the archival index.
9. A209, b. 1884 (1659), d. 2.
10. A209, b. 851a.
11. A209, b. 451.
12. A209, b. 8, Georg Raster; A209, b. 1884 (1659), Agnes Fritz. Note that where possible the specific document where an accusation is recorded is given; when not, then the name of the witness is given instead.

13. A209, b. 449, d. 2.
14. A209, b. 767, Margretha Ruchhinbrodt.
15. A209, b. 1787, d. 1.
16. A209, b. 1780, d. 9-7-60.
17. A209, b. 434.
18. Ray, pp. 347–8; Schultes, *Plants*, pp. 134–5; Schultes and Hoffmann, pp. 33–9.
19. Bever, "Drugs and Hallucingens," p. 298.
20. Sidkey, pp. 166–83; Matossian, pp. 70–80. Bever, "Drugs and Hallucinogens," p. 298.
21. Feulner, p. 6.
22. Walther, p. 89; Aker, p. 28; Beckmann and Beckmann, Chap. 4; Ortega, p. 67; Rogge, p. 158.
23. A209, b. 782, dd. 25-6-1674, 23-7-1674.
24. A209, b. 2096, d. 1.
25. Feulner, pp. 6, 12, 19.
26. A209, b. 719, dd. 3-5-1565 and 5-5-1655.
27. A209, b. 1223, dd. 1, 2, 5.
28. A209, b. 1856, d. 2; A209, b. 1856, d. 2.
29. A209, b. 11, d. 1.
30. A209, b. 1486, d. 11-6-1701.
31. A209, b. 1486, d. 6.
32. A209, b. 1258, dd. 1, 2, 7.
33. Duerr reports of a boy who said in 1571 that his mother "taught him how to paralyze people with a salve made from herbs (p. 137, n. 6), while Sebald reports of a woman near Bamberg who used a salve to poison the roots of trees (*Witch Children*, p. 191).
34. Bever, "Wuerttemberg," pp. 296–7; one sampled case contained an allegation that a suspect gave a neighbor just such a concoction: A209, b. 1989, Agnes Ostwald; see Chap. 4.
35. Rudgley, p. 94; Priesner, II, p. 35.
36. A209, b. 1881, Johann Koenbeckhen.
37. A209, b. 1486, Michel Gänsslen.
38. A209, b. 852.
39. Klaits, p. 15; Briggs, *Neighbors*, p. 64; Hansen, *Salem*, pp. xv, 10. Levi-Strauss, p. 168.
40. *Diagnostic and Statistical Manual* (*DSM-IV*), p. 445; Eisendrath, p. 982; Temoshek and Attkisson, pp. 158, 164; Krohn, p. 124.
41. Rief and Hiller, p. 529; Wolman, p. 183; Webb, "Pain," p. 199; Chapman and Wyckoff, p. 35.
42. Temoshek and Attkisson, pp. 164–7; *DSM-IV*, p. 455; Koller, "Psychogenic," p. 128; Chapman and Wykoff, p. 34.
43. A209, b. 1856, d. 1.
44. A209, b. 1881, d. 1.
45. A209, b. 1881, d. 1.
46. A209, b. 1486, d. 11-6-1701.
47. A209, b. 852, d. 1.
48. A209, b. 1431, Margaretha Stuertzen.
49. A209, b. 1884 (1659), d. 16-6-1659.
50. A209, b. 1856, d. 2.
51. A209, b. 1223, dd. 1, 2.
52. A209, b. 11, d. 1.

53. A209, b. 1787, d. 1.
54. *Oxford Companion*, p. 1170; Gatchel, pp. 10, 14; Nemiah, p. 217; Hafen et al., *Mind/Body*, pp. 7, 9, 13–16, 42, 46, 64–5; Adler, pp. 7–8; Gannon, "Psychophysiology," p. 6; Haynes, "Headache"; Natelson, pp. 412, 421–2; Bosch et al., p. 374; Walker and Sandman, p. 164; Heiman and Hatch.
55. G. Lewis, p. 94; Laungoni, p. 167.
56. Simon, "Somatic," p. 481; Gentilcore, "Fear" p. 190; Mullings, pp. 5–6; Gannon, "Psychophysiology," pp. 6, 11.
57. *DSM-IV*, 676–7; Gatchel, p. 15; Gannon, "Psychophysiology," p. 10; Gielen, p. xvii. Hafen et al., *Mind/Body*, pp. 49–50, 53; Pike, p. 447; Eck, p. 456.
58. Hafen et al., *Mind/Body*, p. 51.
59. A209, b. 873, d. 1.
60. Heiman and Hatch, p. 223; Simon et al., "Somatic," p. 481.
61. A209, b. 1856, dd. 16-7-28, 22-7-28.
62. Arieti and Meth, pp. 559–60; see also Webster, p. 486; Rush, p. 131; Hughes, p. 138; Cannon, pp. 169–81; Hafen et al., *Mind/Body*, p. 16.
63. Natelson, pp. 408, 422–3. Hafen et al., *Mind/Body*, p. 8. Note that Lex, "Voodoo," p. 821, discusses the possibility of an "acute trophotropic response," a "terminal lethargy due to the chronic activation of the parasympathetic nervous system. This seem possible in some cases, but the damage of chronic trophotropic activation does not seem to have explored as much as the opposite.
64. Hafen et al., *Mind/Body*, pp. 71–3; Adler, p. 9; Totman, pp. 91–2, 94, 96; LaVie, p. 138; Liang, p. 178; Gerritsen et al., p. 273; Cobb et al., "Psychosocial," p. 404; Gatchel, p. 17.
65. Thomas, pp. 511–12, 537, Levack, *Witch-Hunt*, p. 167.
66. A209, b. 1787, d. 3.
67. A209, b. 1856, Margretha Rettnier.
68. A209, b. 11, Andrea Leichten.
69. Bloom, p. 65.
70. A209, b. 1486, d. 5.
71. *DSM-IV*, pp. 676–7; Hafen et al., *Mind/Body*, pp. 6–7.
72. A209, b. 552.
73. Winkelman, *Shamanism*, p. 201.
74. Gerritsen et al., p. 273; Hafen et al., *Mind/Body*, p. 211; Adler, p. 8; Gannon, "Psychophysiology," pp. 19, 22; Totner, pp. 90–1, 129–31, 139.
75. A209, b. 1856, d. 3.
76. Susanna Catharina's symptoms included a racing heart, weakness in her limbs, hallucinations, vomiting, pain, uncontrollable movement at times, and paralysis at other times. These do not prove that she suffered from ergot poisoning, but they would be consistent with its direct effects combined with her distress. See A209, b. 1787, d. 1.
77. A209, b. 1223.
78. A209, b. 11, dd. 1, 3.
79. *Handworterbuch des deutschen aberglaube*, vol. III, p. 1874; Newell, p. 89; Roper, "Evil," p. 115; Wilson, *Magical Universe*, pp. 263–6, 269, 273.
80. Ahrendt-Schulte, "Weise," p. 107.
81. MacFarlane, pp. 110–11.
82. Jay, pp. 56–60.
83. A209, b. 852, Mayor of Dornstetten.
84. A209, b. 1856, Margretha Rettnier.

85. Wilson, *Magical Universe*, p. 431; Paracelsus quoted in Kiener, p. 217; Mazur links verbal aggression to dominance struggles, pp. 377, 392.
86. Neher, p. 35.
87. Argyle, p. 349; Maryanski et al., p. 184; Joseph, *Neuron*, p. 390.
88. Argyle, p. 127.
89. Argyle, pp. 19, 52, 115.
90. Masling, p. 263; Kihlstrom, p. 43; Bargh, p. 237.
91. Maryanski et al., p. 184; Joseph, *Neuropsychaitry*, p. 115; Alexander et al., p. 45; Neher, p. 30; Winkelman, *Shamanism*, p. 37; Donald, p. 268; Jay, p. 157.
92. Argyle, pp. 3, 129; Joseph, *Neuron*, pp. 126–7; Maryanski et al., p. 183; Kendon, pp. 110–11, 118; Winkelman, *Shamanism*, p. 46.
93. Maryanski et al., p. 183; Argyle, p. 128.
94. Argyle, pp. 125, 127, 129; p. 114; Laughlin and Throop, p. 334.
95. Argyle, pp. 211–2; Yrizarry, p. 131. Spooner, pp. 281–4, outlines four approaches to the evil eye. The first is merely descriptive. The second and third are similar: emphasizing social and cultural functions or social ecology causing the belief. These two have been integrated by Garrison and Arensberg, pp. 289–90, as well as by Roberts in "Belief" in Maloney. The fourth approach, a psychobiological one, has been most effectively presented by Meerloo, pp. 12, 15, 113–6, 120.
96. The belief played a role in an early case in Esslingen, an independent Imperial City surrounded by Württemberg, although in this case as part of an attempted fraud; see Lorenz, "Tübinger," p. 248, and was recorded by Swabian folklorists in the early twentieth century. Koestler, p. 209, claimed that Katharina Kepler, the astronomer's mother, was accused of using the evil eye to lame a girl during her trial, but it is unclear on what he based this account. More recently, Connor's, *Kepler's Witch* discusses the case without mentioning any incidents involving the evil eye, and the encounter Koestler apparently refers to seems to be one in which the woman was actually accused of hitting a girl on the arm and causing her hand to hurt and become lame (pp. 255–7). However, Sutter, p. 47, asserts that alleged battery never took place, calling it a "fantasy lie" by the girl, who was disturbed by seeing the old woman, whom her family was at odds with, at a distance, which would seem to make Koestler's account at least plausible. Evidence of the belief in other parts of Germany is Labouvie, "Hexenspuk" pp. 64–5 and other parts of Europe is in Levack, *Witch-Hunt*, p. 7; Martin, p. 196; Briggs, *Neighbors*, p. 113; Maclagan, p. 10; Gallucci, p. 14.
97. Argyle, pp. 33, 237, 245, 120, 233, 245; 230; Masson and McCarthy, p. 51.
98. Argyle, p. 245, Plate 10 and Figure 11.1.
99. Argyle, pp. 232, 245.
100. Hess, p. 110.
101. Mazur et al., pp. 377–89.
102. Yrizarry, p. 131; Laughlin and Throop, p. 334; Brown, *Universals*, p. 134.
103. Argyle, p. 216.
104. Argyle, p. 216; Rakover and Cahlin, p. 49; Blonder, p. 283; Smith and Bond, p. 58; Yrizarry, p. 133; Somby-Borgstrom, n.p. (online); Dimberg, p. 49; Laughlin, *Brain*, p. 56.
105. For various positions on these issues, see *The Psychology of Facial Expression*. However, it should be noted that the main point of the critique is to de-emphasize the emotional roots of facial expressions in favor of an emphasis on the role of context in their interpretation (see particularly Ginsburg, p. 349). However, in terms of the issues here, the potential for nonverbal communication to cause or

contribute to psychophysical maladies in the receiver, this would seem to be a secondary issue.
106. Peleg et al., pp. 15921–6; Galati, pp. 424–5.
107. Rakover and Cahlin, p. 117; Maryanski, p. 187.
108. Joseph, *Neuropsychiatry*, p. 191; Nelson and de Haan, pp. 184–9, 190, 198.
109. Laughlin and Throop, p. 335; Rakover and Cahlin, p. 120; Argyle, p. 362; Walsh, p. 72; Morris et al., p. 1680; Czyziewska, p. 107; Norretrandes, pp. 124, 157, 198, 208.
110. Laughlin and Throop, p. 335; Armstrong, p. 266.
111. Ginsburg, p. 380; Kirouac and Hess, pp. 182, 202.
112. Smith and Bond, p. 60; Yrizarry, p. 139.
113. Saville-Troike, p. 227; Smith and Bond, p. 63; Yrizarry, pp. 135–6; Smith and Bond, p. 62.
114. Armstrong, p. 268; Argyle, p. 136; Beatie, p. 180; Saarni, pp. 107–9.
115. Argyle, pp. 125, 218, 365; Yrizarry, p. 140; Brown, *Universals*, p. 134.
116. Donald, p. 190.
117. Brown, *Universals*, p. 131; Zagorin, p. 1; Maryanski et al., p. 191.
118. Yrizarry, p. 140; Argyle, p. 365; Maryanski, p. 188; Schiefenhövel, p. 64; Eckman, pp. 62, 66.
119. A209, b. 1884, d. 16-6-59.
120. Maryanski, pp. 190–1; Joseph, *Neuropsychiatry*, p. 116; Argyle, pp. 125–6, 130, 218, 114, 128.
121. One of the most recent expressions of this is Rowlands, "Old Women," pp. 55–7; Sebald recognizes that verbal "deception can normally be detected" but attributes this to "unconscious body movements" generated by "remorse about lying," thus focusing on psychodynamics rather than physiology (*Witch Children*, p. 220).
122. Argyle, pp. 286–91.
123. Hughes, p. 135; Argyle, pp. 34, 251.
124. Argyle, pp. 279–83, 126, 300.
125. Argyle, pp. 312–16.
126. A209, b. 1856, d. 22-7-26.
127. A209, b. 11, d. 1.
128. A209, b. 852, d. 8-8-11; according to Rösener, everyone in a community would attend weddings and was supposedly "entered fully into the spirit of the celebration;" so Agatha had not "crashed" the party in the modern sense, but her presence was noted as a contributing factor to Ziegler's bride's malady, suggesting that either her presence was unwelcome even though not culturally inappropriate, putting Ziegler's bride into a bind since she didn't want her there but couldn't bar her, or that Agatha failed to fully enter into the spirit of the celebration, at the very least.
129. Vogel, p. 23.
130. MacFarlane, p. 171.
131. Arieti and Meth, pp. 559–60; Rush, p. 131; Hughes, p. 138; Briggs, *Neighbors*, p. 64.
132. Laughlin and Throop, p. 346; Kihlstrom, p. 44; Argyle, p. 115.
133. A209, b. 767.
134. The incident is described in both the initial report of the visitation and in the record of the subsequent judicial inquiry; the two correspond fairly closely, with the inquiry giving more detail, but the word "something" (etwas) appears in the initial report.

Notes 449

135. Thomas, pp. 475, 578.
136. Reed, pp. 37–9, 46, 55–6; Slade and Bentall, pp. 8, 23.
137. Starker, p. 45; Slade and Bentall, pp. 58, 69, 72, 118; Pinker, p. 257; Bentall, p. 99 (70% of grieving people report hallucinations).
138. Reed, pp. 33, 59, 65, 192.
139. What is given here is a simplified overview of the process; Pinker, pp. 236–72, 295.
140. Starker, p. 44; Pinker, pp. 287–90; Johnson, p. 182; Slade and Bentall, pp. 107, 211, 126; Bentall, p. 100; Johnson, pp. 49–50, 169.
141. Bentall, p. 101.
142. Reed, p. 67; Johnson, p. 183; Slade and Bentall, pp. 206–7.
143. Slade and Bentall, pp. 78–81; Bentall, p. 97.
144. Slade and Bentall, p. 154; Reed, p. 48.
145. Slade and Bentall, p. 223; Reed, p. 60.
146. A209, b. 767, judicial inquiry.
147. Raith, "Tuttlingen," p. 126; A209, b. 1971, d. 16.
148. Reed, pp. 42, 190.
149. Bentall, p. 98; Slade and Bentall, pp. 85–6, 88–9.
150. Slade and Bentall, pp. 92, 221.
151. Slade and Bentall, pp. 85, 221.
152. Pócs reports of this same phenomenon, of *suspects* reporting "visiting" at night (as opposed to accusers experiencing "visitations"), *Between*, p. 114.
153. A209, b. 1258, d. 1, p. 24.
154. A209, b. 1587, d. Prefect's report, 10-10-1739; also Bachman, pp. 61–2. It should be noted that the girl said that her grandmother also did this, and later changed her story to say that she had only done it with her grandmother, and that she did not remember having done it, but only learned of it from her grandmother the next morning; d. Doctor and Preacher's Examination, 9-11 and 17-12-1739, p. 5. The circumstances and complexities of this case are discussed more fully in Chap. 8.
155. A209, b. 1587, Actum 26-9-1739, p. 53.
156. A209, b. 1258, d. 2.
157. Walther, p. 67; Oldridge, "General Introduction," p. 16; Briggs, "Dangerous," pp. 14–5; Roper, *Oedipus*, p. 209; Klaniczay "Hungary," p. 250; Oates, n.p. (online); Blecourt, "Bedding," n.p. (online); and Davies, "Nightmare," n.p. (online).
158. Cheyne, "Relations," pp. 313–17; Chayne, "Sleep," n.p. (online).
159. Hufford, *Terror*, p. 115; Parker and Blackmore, pp. 45–59, 58; also Cheyne (online).
160. Hufford, *Terror*, pp. 46, 113.
161. Hufford, *Terror*, p. 15.
162. Cheyne and Girard, "Spatial," p. 283.
163. *Basic Research in Parapsychology*, esp. Rao, "Introduction," pp. 3–37; also Parker and Brusewitz, pp. 33–51.
164. Irwin, *Introduction*, p. 319; Mishlove, pp. 339–42.
165. Humphrey, pp. 206–27; Alcock, "Null Hypothesis," pp. 29–50.
166. Ginzburg, *Night Battles*, pp. 6, 16, 19–20, 22.
167. Ways of harming animals were reportedly common knowledge, according to one study of Brandenburg-Ansbach: Dixon, p. 123.
168. Hutton, *Triumph*, p. 95 speculates that this may in part be caused by scent, although without trying to trace the precise mechanism.
169. A209, b. 2096, d. 1.
170. A209, b. 1856, d. 2.

450 Notes

171. Totman, p. 91.
172. Weiner, pp. 76, 364, 474.
173. Adler; Natelson, p. 425.
174. Ewing, p. 296.
175. Hemsworth et al., pp. 264–5, 272, 275–8, 274.
176. A209, b. 782, d. 25-6-74.
177. A209, b. 1884 (1659), d. 6a.
178. A209, b. 719, d. 5-5-1565.
179. Archer, pp. 252, 255–7; Spierenburg, "Crime," pp. 342–3, who also reports that arson was frequently used in personal disputes.

2 Maleficium and Society

1. Levack, Witch-Hunt, p. 192; Pócs, Between, p. 11.
2. Hippel, pp. 421–5; Sabean, "Landbesitz," p. 3; Ernst, 6000 Jahre, pp. 348–54; Sauer, "Not und Armut," pp. 131, 136; Ogilvie, p. 1.
3. Hippel, pp. 421–2; Weller and Weller, p. 197.
4. Hippel, pp. 424–5; Mayhew, p. 103.
5. Hippel, p. 418; Knapp, pp. 25, 86–7; Mayhew, pp. 104, 113.
6. Ernst, 6000 Jahre, pp. 133, 136; Mayhew, p. 133.
7. Hippel, pp. 418, 428–30; Ernst, 6000 Jahre, pp. 364, 368.
8. Vann, pp. 35–8.
9. Franz, Bauernstandes, p. 223 (note that values given in Florins have been converted into Reichstaler at a rate of 2 : 3 based loosely on table in Durant, The Age of Louis XIV, p. ix).
10. Hippel, p. 417; Mayhew, pp. 104, 131; Ernst, 6000 Jahre, p. 193; Berkner, p. 75; Rösener, p. 162.
11. Knapp, pp. 94, 100; Bever, "Wuerttemberg," p. 87.
12. Bever, "Wuerttemberg," pp. 97–9; Ernst, 6000 Jahre, pp. 205–7, 232–6; Knapp, pp. 6, 101–3; Wunder, "Bauerliche Oberschichten," pp. 143, 145–6; Franz, Bauernstandes, p. 224.
13. Sabean, "Self," p. 7; Scharfe, "Distances," p. 161.
14. Scharfe, "Distances," pp. 161, 165–8.
15. Wegert, p. 85.
16. Rösener, p. 163; Walz, "Schimpfende," p. 192.
17. Wegert emphasizes that while enmities could be bitter and specific conflicts intense, the countryside was not a state of chronic disorder: pp. 85–6. See also Krämer, p. 229.
18. Sabean, Power, p. 52.
19. Sabean, Power, p. 16; Walz, Hexenglaube, p. 521; Gaskill, "Kent," p. 286; Walz, "Schimpfende," p. 185.
20. Walz, "Schimpfende," p. 192; Sabean, Power, p. 136; Wegert, p. 151.
21. Wegert, pp. 34–5, 32.
22. Rösener, p. 161; Spierenburg, "Crime," p. 340.
23. Rösener, p. 161; Sabean, Power, p. 164.
24. Wegert, p. 127; Walz, "Schimpfende," p. 190.
25. Vann, pp. 39–40; Wintterlin, p. 55; Gehring, p. 191.
26. Sauer, "Not und Armut," p. 138; Ernst, Krankheit, p. 19; Jütte, "Social Construction," p. 27.
27. Sabean, Power, p. 110.

28. A209, b. 1881, d. 1.
29. Bever, "Wuerttemberg," pp. 205–6, 209, 213–17.
30. Bever, "Wuerttemberg," pp. 221–2.
31. A209, b. 1787.
32. A209, b. 1486.
33. Bever, "Wuerttemberg," pp. 222–3.
34. A209, b. 2099; A209, bb. 546, 1789.
35. A209, b. 2096.
36. A209, b. 1111.
37. *Malleus Maleficarum*, p. 45.
38. A209, b 449, A209, b. 852, A209, b. 873.
39. Bever, "Wuerttemberg," pp. 223–4.
40. Ibid., p. 224.
41. Ibid., pp. 209–11; Labouvie, "Perspektivenwechsel," pp. 55–6.
42. Bever, "Wuerttemberg," pp. 224–5.
43. Ibid., pp. 207–8.
44. Ibid., pp. 219–21.
45. Walz, "Schimpfende," p. 192. On the view his undercuts, see Matalene, p. 61; Gregory, p. 55; Finch, p. 38; Ingram, p. 67.
46. Walz, "Schimpfende," pp. 179, 182; Wegert, p. 86; Sabean, "Property," p. 138; Walz, *Hexenglaube*, p. 513. Note that in England and Scotland, scolds were generally women, Goodare, *The Scottish Witch-Hunt*, p. 299.
47. Walz, "Schimpfende," p. 213.
48. Bever, "Wuerttemberg," Appendix (especially cases 4, 11, 15, 17, 22, 24, 27); Walz, *Hexenglaube*, p. 516 acknowledges this himself.
49. A209, b. 1884.
50. A209, b. 852.
51. A209, b. 782.
52. A209, b. 1431.
53. A209, b. 552.
54. A209, b. 757.
55. Wegert, pp. 122, 124, 137; Walz, "Schimpfende," p. 189; *Gender Relations*, p. 7; Finch, pp. 27, 29; Schnabel-Schule, p. 195; Castan, pp. 476, 486–7; Ingram, p. 49.
56. Duley et al., p. 8; Björkqvist and Niemelä, p. 7; Segall, p. 244; Björkqvist, Österman, and Kaukiainen, p. 51; Pool, p. 54.
57. Rosser, pp. 71–2; Heyne, pp. 80–2; Segall, pp. 263–5; Björkqvist and Niemelä, p. 14; Keashly, pp. 185–6; Adams, p. 23; Lindfors, p. 231; Baron-Cohen, p. 35.
58. Björkqvist, Österman, and Kaukiainen, p. 55; Björkqvist and Niemelä, pp. 6–7; Parsons, p. 19; Blum, pp. 80–1; Rabbie, p. 223; Fraczek, p. 111; Björkqvist and Niemelä, pp. 8, 14; Björkqvist, Österman, and Kaukiainen, pp. 52, 61; Richardson and Green, pp. 173, 178; Moir and Jessel, p. 82.
59. Björkqvist and Niemelä, p. 14; Heyne, pp. 11–12; Hirsch, p. 152.
60. Feulner, p. 106; Rublack, *Women* pp. 227–9; Herx, p. 3. Other connections are the importance of conflicts in women's space in early modern Europe and cross-cultural tendency of women to conflict particularly bitterly with other women: Björkqvist and Niemelä, p. 12; Eichenbaum and Orbach, p. 137; especially in patrilocal societies like early modern Europe, Glazer, p. 170.
61. Wegert, pp. 122, 124, 137; for other areas, see Walz, "Schimpfende," p. 189; *Gender Relations*, p. 7; Finch, pp. 27, 29; *The Scottish Witch-Hunt*, p. 294. On the corresponding underrepresentation of women: Schnabel-Schule, p. 195; Castan,

pp. 476, 486–7; Ingram, p. 49. For caveats that women could be brutal, Schnabel-Schule, p. 196; Rublack, *Women*, p. 203; Walz, "Schimpfende," pp. 190–1 (but not as often as men). For modern studies of violent crime, Pool, p. 54; Barash, p. 86; Blum, p. 72 (who reports that chimps show even more sex differentiation in aggression (95 : 5 male : female vs. 80 : 20 for humans)).
62. The connection between indirect aggression and witchcraft is drawn specifically for Zapotec women in Fry, pp. 194–5. Kowalski, p. 216 notes use of aversive interpersonal behaviors to influence others' behavior.
63. Carli, p. 44; Rabbie, p. 223; Frevert, p. 37; Segall, p. 266. Walsh, p. 34, however, argues that metastudies "did not provide strong evidence for early gender-role socialization."
64. On modern women's social integration, *Women, Culture, and Society*, pp. 55–6; Chodorow, p. 57. On the connection to aggression, Rabbie, p. 225. On women's space: Behringer, "Witch Studies," p. 94 (citing Wunder und Labouvie); Briggs, "Victim," p. 447; Sharpe, "Northern," pp. 120, 187, 188, 192; Opitz, p. 262; Rublack, "Public Body," p. 62; Ahrendt-Schulte, "Alltag," p. 353; Purkiss, p. 414.
65. Van den Wijngaard, p. 47; Pool, pp. 109, 200; Lustig, p. 24; Rinisch pp. 37, 42; Eron, p. 96; Rosser, p. 73; Segall, pp. 251–2; Miller, "Hierarchies," p. 3; Pool, p. 216; Moir and Jessel, p. 75; Rosser, p. 65; Weingart, pp. 151–3; *Gender Relations*, p. 9; Garrett, p. 56 (on Durkheim); Clark, *Thinking*, pp. 6–7; Brauner, p. 21; Schnabel-Schule, p. 195; Rublack, "Gender," p. 1 states that "the theoretical question to all research on gender is whether sex differences is socially and culturally constructed, or to some extent rooted in a pre-discursive body."
66. Rinisch, pp. 41–2.
67. Jan-Erik and Öberg, p. 144; Ruble and Schneer, p. 165; Fraczek, p. 108; Glazer, p. 163; Rabbie, p. 223; Björkqvist and Niemelä, p. 14; Segall, p. 243; Parsons, pp. 18–19; Heyne, pp. 82–3, 89; Stoddart, p. 214; Richardson and Green, p. 176.
68. Harris, pp. 60–3, 69.
69. For example, Joseph, *Neuropsychiatry*, pp. 66–9.
70. Pool, p. 53.
71. Walsh, p. 87; Pool, p. 108; Moir and Jessel, p. 76; Blum, pp. 42, 43, 74; Newcombe and Ratcliff, p. 186; Lustig, p. 23; Barash, pp. 85, 175, 177.
72. Vines, p. 79; Segall, p. 268; Benton, p. 46; Wijngaard, p. 46.
73. Björkqvist and Niemelä, p. 6; Segall, p. 250.
74. Moir and Jessel, p. 79; Rosser, p. 74.
75. Walsh, p. 89; Segall, p. 250; Pool, p. 53; Baron-Cohen, pp. 1–6; Reid and Paludi, p. 204; Newcombe and Ratcliff, p. 194.
76. Reid and Paludi, p. 204; Lindfors, p. 230; Walsh, p. 90; Moir and Jessel, p. 19; Barash, pp. 189–90; Segall, p. 244; Brown, "Middle Aged Women,"p. 87; Pool, p. 107; Barash, p. 185; Newcombe and Ratcliff, p. 187; Kerrick and Hogan, p. 183; Lustig, p. 13.
77. Blum, p. 66. On face recognition, Pool, p. 204. Infant girls also seek out eye contact and mutual gazing more than boys; Brizendine, p. 15.
78. According to Blum, p. 67, these differences are not found to the same degree in females with a male fraternal twin (and who were hence exposed to higher levels of androgens in utero than other females); Walsh, p. 88; Moir and Jessel, p. 18. Stoddart, p. 135.
79. Blum, p. 37; Legato, p. 22.
80. Moir and Jessel, pp. 46, 48; Pool, pp. 111, 119.
81. Walsh, p. 89; Newcombe and Ratcliff, p. 189; Moir and Jessel, p. 48.

82. Blum, p. 78. Significantly, early modern women were commonly thought to exhibit both greater facility with as well as greater reliance on verbal power; see Brauner, *Fearless*, p. 19, Sabean, *Power*, pp. 137, 142; Popkin, "Marriage," pp. 336, 353; Ingram, pp. 49, 50; Raith, "bösen Weibern," p. 15 (citing Wunder).
83. Pool, pp. 55–6; Moir and Jessel, p. 46; Hiscock, p. 137.
84. Pool, p. 108.
85. Moir and Jessel, p. 49, quote Sandra Witlesan on women's "preferred cognitive strategy ... [of] playing to your mental strengths."
86. Herx, pp. 112–13; Weiler, p. 1; Ahrendt-Schulte, "Hexenprozesse," p. 213.
87. Popkin, p. 339; Rublack, *Women*, p. 202; Sabean, *Property*, p. 317; Ingram, p. 51; Wegert, pp. 137–8; Bender-Wittman, p. 27; Sharpe, "Northern," p. 194 citing Larner; Whitney, "International," p. 91.
88. Ahrendt-Schulte, "Hexenprozesse," p. 212; Hester, "Patriarchal Reconstruction," p. 298; Schnabel-Schule, p. 192.
89. Midelfort, *Witch Hunting*, pp. 201–29.
90. A209, b. 1780; A209, b. 449; A209, b. 873.
91. A209, b. 719 (1565); A209, b. 2096.
92. A209, b. 1856.
93. A209, b. 1486.
94. A209, b. 782.
95. A209, b. 11.
96. A209, b. 1884 (1659).
97. A209, b. 1881.
98. A209, b. 852.
99. A209, b. 1223; A209, b. 1431.
100. It is impossible to calculate precisely because the actual number of suspects involved in many of the trials, and particularly in the mass trials, was not recorded.
101. DeLisi, p. 6.
102. Levack, *Witch-Hunt*, pp. 142–3.
103. Demos, "Old Age," pp. 252, 251, quoting William Bridge. See also Rosen, p. 233.
104. Rosen, pp. 236–8.
105. Demos, "Old Age," p. 263; Fischer, *Old*, p. 72.
106. Bever, "Wuerttemberg," p. 241; Janzarik, pp. 391–2.
107. Pfeiffer, p. 653; Kuhlen, pp. 115, 124.
108. Geist, p. 34; Koller, pp. 49–50; Yarrow, p. 202.
109. Laslett, *World*, p. 101; Tilly and Scott, p. 28; Parker, *Seven*, pp. 477–8; Brizendine, pp. viii–xix, 140, 142, 149.
110. *The Curse*, pp. 179, 186–8; Parker, *Seven*, pp. 469, 480–8, 491; Notman, p. 1271; Posner, p. 183; Weideger, pp. 201, 203.
111. Ryan, "Summary," p. 3.
112. McCranie, p. 85; Weideger, pp. 196–7; Notman, p. 1270; Kuhlen, pp. 12–18; de Beauvoir, p. 27.
113. Niehoff, pp. 53, 149.
114. Hippel, p. 417; Franz, *Bauernstandes*, p. 174; Sauer, "Not und Armut," p. 137.
115. Hippel, p. 430.
116. Mitterauer, "Familienwirtschaft," p. 200.
117. Grees, p. 314.
118. Knapp, p. 27; Weller, *Sozialgeschichte*, p. 66.
119. Ernst, *6000 Jahre*, pp. 240–1.
120. Grees, p. 157.
121. Jaeger, pp. 193–5; Weller and Weller, pp. 193–5; Weller, *Sozialgeschichte*, p. 66.

122. Hippel, pp. 430–1, 434.
123. A209, b. 1881; A209, b. 1223.
124. This point of view is extensively developed in Kamen, *The Iron Century*.
125. Sauer, "Not und Armut," p. 138.
126. Hippel, pp. 425–6; Ernst, *6000 Jahre*, p. 383.
127. Franz, *Bauernstandes*, p. 177.
128. Franz, *Bauernstandes*, pp. 174–5; Hippel, pp. 437–8; Mayhew, p. 149.
129. Franz, *Bauernstandes*, p. 174. This figure undoubtedly reflects the temporary displacement of many people who came back as conditions improved, which would account for the rapid rise during the following decade.
130. See Chap. 8.

Part II The Realities of Diabolism

1. Nicholls, p. 234.
2. Labouvie, "Hexenspuk," pp. 77, 86–7; McGrath, p. 72; Gentilcore, "Folklore," p. 101; Oldridge, "Introduction," p. 7.
3. Midelfort, *Witch Hunting*, p. 30.
4. Rowland, "Fantastical," p. 161.

3 The Devil in the Duchy of Württemberg

1. Ginzburg, "Deciphering," p. 121; Borst, p. 109; Behringer, "Waldensians," pp. 156–7.
2. *Witchcraft Reader*, p. 22; Cohn, pp. xi–xii; Gurevich, p. 83.
3. Gurevich, p. 82; Fichtenau, p. 322; Kieckhefer, "Specific," in *New*, pp. 79–81; Kieckhefer, *Forbidden*, pp. 3, 10–12; Fichtenau, pp. 320–2.
4. Kieckhefer, *Middle Ages*, p. 157; Gurevich, p. 85; Stories that such promises might go so far as to constitute permanent pacts with the Devil go back to St. Basil: Roos, p. 43; Medway, pp. 58–60; Russell, *Lucifer*, p. 80.
5. *Witchcraft Reader*, p. 4; Zagorin, p. 269, "hints" that "in his youth" Agrippa "belonged to a quasi-religious secret brotherhood devoted to arcane knowledge and practices, and veiled allusions intimating his connection with some sort of clandestine society appear at a later period as well;" Dixon, pp. 121–2; Kieckhefer, *Forbidden*, p. 2.
6. Broedel, pp. 101–6, 134; see Gentilcore in *Witchcraft Reader*, p. 102; Verdon, pp. 54–6.
7. Brodel, pp. 104–5; Kieckhefer, "Children," pp. 95, 106–7; also, rites involving the drinking of human blood were known at least as late as the eleventh century in Germany: Gurevich, p. 92; Clark, *Thinking*, p. 443.
8. Henningsen, "Ladies," pp. 203–4, says she "explained to her followers that she ruled her *società* as Christ ruled in the world, and in order not to offend her it was forbidden to utter the name of Jesus during the meetings"; Kieckhefer in *Witchcraft Reader*, p. 32: her followers' souls belonged to her after death.
9. Henningsen, "Ladies," p. 204; McCall, p. 251; Gentilecore, "Witchcraft Narratives," p. 103.
10. *Witchcraft Reader*, p. 17.
11. Rice, pp. 8–9, 147; Eisenstein, I, pp. 3–5, and II, p. 703.
12. *Witchcraft Reader*, p. 12.

13. Roos asserts the rising number of "Devil books" in the late sixteenth century, discussed below, definitely resulted from the decline of religious tracts after 1550, p. 110.
14. *Schrochliche Zeitung*; Midelfort, *Witch Hunting*, pp. 38–40.
15. Widmann, pp. 2–5.
16. Clari, pp. 23–34, 127–9.
17. Bernhard, vol. 1, p. 77.
18. Tuczay, "Holda," p. 502. According to Tuczay, "Unholden" appears to have signified malevolent women from the beginning, in contrast to benovolent "Holden." Brauner, *Fearless*, p. 122, however, traces the term further back to a malevolent Nordic spirit that was used from the eleventh century on to describe both evil and good night-flying spirits that only became associated with sorcery in the fifteenth century.
19. Midelfort, *Witch Hunting*, p. 45.
20. Midelfort, *Witch Hunting*, pp. 36–7.
21. *Wahrafftige unnd Erschreckliche Thatten*; Alber and Bidenbach.
22. Gehring, pp. 167–9.
23. Lerchheimer.
24. For this insight into the pamphlet literature, I would like to thank Professor H. C. Erik Midelfort.
25. Examples of this influence are contained in two of the early sampled magic cases: Z14 (A209, b. 723) and Z18 (A209, b. 311a) and several of the cases involving blessings and illicit healing: Ss5B (A209, b. 1424, dd. 3, 7-1595). These are discussed in Chapters 6 and 7.
26. Siebel, p. 50. Württemberg's rulers frequently corresponded with neighboring nobles; see Dübber, pp. 72, 156–7. The Fugger newsletters, based on company correspondence, also reported, on occasion, witch trials; see *The Fugger Newsletter*, pp. 107–14.
27. Medway, p. 53; Cervantes, p. 17.
28. Carus, p. 283; Fichtenau, p. 318.
29. On popular notions: Oldridge, *Devil*, p. 3; Roos, p. 8; Gentilcore, pp. 251–3; Russell, *Lucifer*, p. 63; Russel, *Mephistopheles*, p. 44, n.34. On elite conceptions: Fichtenau, p. 308; Russell, *Lucifer*, pp. 203, 206.
30. Fichtenau, p. 312.
31. Carus, p. 287; Roos, pp. 8, 17–18; Russell, *Lucifer*, p. 68.
32. Stanford, p. 145; Verdon, p. 49. Cervantes, p. 19.
33. Carus, p. 342; Erikson, p. 243; Roos, p. 22.
34. Roos, pp. 31, 52.
35. Russell, *Mephistopheles*, p. 54; Zilka in *New*, p. 101; Roos, pp. 9, 56.
36. Carus, p. 347; Roos, pp. 22, 108.
37. Zilka in *New*, p. 101.
38. Roos, pp. 108–9.
39. *Witchcraft Reader*, p. 228.
40. Roos, p. 111; Clark, *Thinking*, p. 438.
41. Roos, p. 9; Zilka in *New*, p. 101; Clark, *Thinking*, pp. 438–9.
42. Clark, *Thinking*, p. 440.
43. Peters, "Destruction," p. 138.
44. Cervantes, p. 20; Clark, *Thinking*, p. 491; Russell, *Mephistopheles*, p. 45.
45. Clark, *Thinking*, p. 491.
46. Strauss, "Anticlericalism," p. 632; Tolley, p. 75.
47. Russell, *Mephistopheles*, p. 45.

Notes

48. Gurevich, pp. 100, 102; Sabean, "Self," p. 7.
49. Sabean, "Self," p. 7; Scharfe, "Distances," p. 161.
50. Roos, p. 8; *Witchcraft Reader*, p. 227; Oldridge, *Devil*, p. 3; Cervantes, pp. 2–3; Gentilcore, "Folklore," p. 105.
51. Roos, p. 110; Midelfort, "Devil," pp. 243, 245; Lynn et al., pp. 128, 130 gives modern examples of psychological conditions like Satanic Ritual Abuse and alien abduction increasing dramatically in the wake of publicity.
52. Aker, p. 8.
53. A209, b. 719 (1565), d. 5-5-1565.
54. A209, b. 719 (1565), d. 3-5-1565.
55. A209, b. 719 (1565), d. 5-5-1565.
56. Gentilcore, *Bishop*, pp. 250–2 notes that Italian trials reveal a similar combination of elite and folkloric elements.
57. Lynn, p. 127; Victor, p. 209.
58. Gentilcore, *Bishop*, p. 250.
59. Damasio, *Descartes*, pp. 220–2; McGrath, p. 137; Neher, pp. 20, 46–7, 55; Allport, p. 55.
60. Lynn et al., p. 133.
61. Lynn, p. 127, 132–3; Victor, p. 210.
62. A209, b. 327, d. 18-1-78.
63. A209, b. 327, d. 15-1-78; Aker, p. 19.
64. A209, b. 327, d. 21-1-78.
65. A209, b. 327, d. 28-1-78.
66. A209, b. 327, d. 6-2-78.
67. A209, b. 327, d. 3-2-78.
68. A209, b. 327, d. 14-3-78.
69. Koslofsky, pp. 101–2; Wegert, p. 105.
70. A209, b. 327, d. 4-4-78; Aker, pp. 21–2.
71. Sabean, *Power*, p. 36.
72. Jackson, p. 353 discusses how witchcraft confessions could be used by women to contextualize themselves, although she focuses on the context of women's cultural roles rather than moral values and behaviors.
73. Sabean, *Power*, pp. 50, 35.
74. Ibid., pp. 35, 92.
75. For example, Roper, *Oedipus*, p. 216; Forsyth, p. 12; Baumeister, p. 169; Ross, p. 59; and, less theoretically, Jackson, p. 358.
76. Verdon, pp. 48–53, discusses the extent to which people in Middle Ages also said their crimes were prompted by the Devil, which reminds us that the idea did not appear in the early modern period, but the extent to which the Devil was invoked was, he says, "slight," so these references may manifest an earlier phase of a process in European psychocultural development which reached its climax in the time and manner discussed here. Cervantes, p. 68 reports that after the Spanish conquest, half the visions Indians (who did not "see" the Christian Devil before the Spanish arrived) had were diabolical; what we are positing here is that a similar, although far more gradual, change in visionary experience occurred in late Medieval and early modern Europe. Another suggestive example is the wave of diabolic possession cases that occurred in the late sixteenth century in northern Germany. Possession cases tend to occur in waves or clusters, as one instance sparks others (Neher, p. 199; Slutovsky, "Divine," p. 256), Midelfort shows that there was a marked rise in reports in the second half of the sixteenth century and then an equally dramatic fall-off in the early seventeenth century (Midelfort,

"Devil," pp. 244–5). He considers the possibility that it could be an "optical illusion" caused by the increasing number of records and pamphlets, but notes that contemporaries commented on the increasing number of cases, ascribing them to the Devil's increased influence in the "old age of the world."
77. A209, b. 1789.
78. Sabean, *Power*, 208, 35, 48; see also Jackson, p. 361.
79. McGrath, p. 31; Argyle, p. 142; Hollan, p. 539; on nonconscious processing, see discussion in this chapter.
80. Inglis, pp. 15–16.
81. Hollan, p. 540; Libet, p. 97; Kihlstrom, p. 34; Czyziewska, pp. 9–10, 92; Bargh, pp. 239–40; Masling, p. 260; Velmans, "Introduction," p. 9; Towell, p. 77; Donald, p. 288.
82. Joseph, "Neuropsychiatry," p. 167; Donald, pp. 106–7.
83. Donald, pp. 197, 107.
84. Joseph, "Neuropsychiatry," pp. 161–2, 169–78.
85. La Cerra and Bingham, p. 155; Jackson, p. 359 discusses another example of this low-level influence on consciousness being interpreted as the influence of the Devil: postpartum psychosis.
86. Donald, p. 189.
87. Tomasello, p. 206.
88. A209, b. 546, d. 18.
89. Tuczay, "Incubus," pp. 546–8.
90. A209, b. 451, d. 2.
91. Similar cases are recounted by Jackson, p. 359 and Luther's belief in the Devil's seduction of young girls in the form of a handsome man is discussed in Carus, p. 343.
92. A209, b. 451, d. 10.
93. Erickson, p. 214.
94. Nicholls, p. 235; Carus, p. 284.
95. A209, b. 1989, d. 1.
96. A209, b. 1989, d. 2.
97. Norretranders, pp. 192–3; Neher, p. 18.
98. Donald, pp. 173–4; Allport, p. 197.
99. Hobson, *Chemistry*, p. 127; Wade and Swanston, p. 259; Norretranders, p. 186; Donald, p. 179.
100. Norretranders, p. 200.
101. Norretranders, p. 186, quoting Richard Gregory, *Eye and Brain*.
102. Shore, p. 4; Cole, p. 66.
103. Stephens, p. 2 reports on a similar experience, and Nicholls, p. 235 points out how important the rise of printing was in diffusing a concrete image of the Devil.
104. Segall, p. 86.
105. Slade and Bentall, p. 80; Cardeña, "Intro" p. 7.
106. Zilka, *Exorcizing*, p. 2.
107. A209, b. 546, d. 18, pp. 12–13.
108. Neher, p. 40; Austin, p. 389.
109. A209, b. 451, d. 2.
110. Roper, "Evil," p. 128; Cervantes, p. 116.
111. Furst, *Hallucinogens*, p. 83.
112. Johnson, p. 181.
113. Johnson, pp. 170, 173.
114. Jaynes, pp. 71–5, 85–7, 95; Norretranders, pp. 317–19.

458   Notes

115. Johnson, p. 57.
116. Clark, *Thinking*, p. 398 (speaking of possession, but his point is more broadly applicable).
117. Greenfield, pp. 111–14; Hollan, p. 538; Shermer, *How*, p. 37.
118. Tomasello, p. 203; La Cerra and Bingham, p. 186; Donald, p. 111.
119. Greenfield, p. 153; Donald, p. 177.
120. Donald, pp. 160–1, 177, 189, 212, 302–4.
121. Laughlin and Throop, p. 333; Donald, p. 258; Bloch, p. 11; Greenfield, p. 111; Wier, p. 42.
122. Norretranders, pp. 164–5; Bloch, p. 11; Towell, p. 77; Neher, p. 54; Wier, p. 29.
123. Wier, pp. 55–6; Neher, p. 80; Donald, pp. 230–2.
124. Hollan, p. 541; Klass, p. 114.
125. Hollan, pp. 539, 542.
126. Sökefeld, pp. 430, 418; Donald, p. 135; Hollan, pp. 539, 546.
127. Goodman, *Demons*, pp. 80–2.
128. Goodman, *Demons*, p. 5; Oesterreich, pp. 131–234.
129. A209, b. 1958, dd. 6-6-1720; 30-3-1720; 17-4-1720.
130. A210, II, b. 96, d. 1.
131. A210, II, b. 96, d. 4.
132. A210, II, b. 96, d. 7-8-1695.
133. A209, b. 375.
134. Slutovsky, "Divine," p. 260; Clark, *Thinking*, pp. 399, 392; Klass, p. 115.
135. Slutovsky, "Divine," pp. 257–8; Clark, *Thinking*, p. 394.
136. Midelfort, "Devil," p. 247; Slutovsky, "Divine," pp. 260–1; Cervantes, p. 101.
137. Hollan, p. 539; Neher, pp. 196–7; Haaken, pp. 248, 254; Slutovsky, "Divine," p. 261.
138. Slutovsky, "Divine," p. 261.
139. A209, b. 451, d. 3.
140. Slutovsky, "Divine," p. 261.
141. Cervantes, pp. 101–3, citing Freud.
142. Clark, *Thinking*, p. 393.
143. Clark, *Thinking*, p. 397.
144. Clark, *Thinking*, pp. 399–400.
145. Gianaro, n.p. (online).
146. Klass, p. 122.
147. Sebald, "Witch Children," treats possession as a form of role playing, saying, for example, it was "socially caused" by "group reinforcement" and an accepting audience.
148. Crapanzano, pp. 640–2; Klass, p. 115; Kenny, p. 270; Clark, *Thinking*, pp. 398, 401, 429.

4 Witch Dances and Witch Salves

1. The combined idea of flight and a Sabbath was only firmly incorporated into the demonology around the turn of the sixteenth century; see Clark, *Thinking*, p. 139; Maxwell-Stuart, *Witchcraft in Europe*, pp. 18–23.
2. Midelfort, "Heartland," p. 117; Broedel, p. 124.
3. *Malleus Maleficarum*, p. xxxix; Murray, *Witch Cult* and also her *God of the Witches*; Cohn, pp. 102–21.
4. Ginzburg, *Night Battles*.

5. Cohn, pp. 221–4.
6. Pócs, "Alternative," p. 133; Oldridge, "Introduction," p. 8; *Witchcraft Reader*, p. 110; Henningsen, "Ladies," p. 207; Behringer, *Shaman*, p. 65; Macdonald, "Devil in Fife," pp. 33; 43–4.
7. Fichtenau, p. 318.
8. Henningsen, "Ladies," pp. 206, 197; Goodman, *Ecstasy*, p. 47.
9. Ginzburg, "Deciphering," pp. 124, 126; Henningsen and Ankarloo, "Introduction," in Henningsen and Ankarloo, p. 6.
10. Gurevich, pp. 80, 91; Kieckhefer, "Children," pp. 101–2; 105; Behringer, *Shaman*, pp. 34, 60.
11. Gentilcore, "Folklore," pp. 100–1; Maxwell-Stuart, *Satan*, p. 215; Henningsen, "Ladies," p. 205.
12. *Witchcraft Reader*, pp. 110–11; Muchembled, "Satanic," pp. 139–40; Clark, *Thinking*, p. 134.; Rowland, "Fantastical," p. 166.
13. Muchembled, "Satanic," p. 148; Stewart and Strathern, p. 16.
14. Muchembled, "Satanic," pp. 149–50.
15. For example, Wilson, *Magical Universe*, pp. 129, 238.
16. Wunderlei, pp. 47–8.
17. Straus, "Anticlericalism," pp. 634–5; note that secular officials were also held in low repute as well: see Stuart, pp. 2–3.
18. Gurevich, p. 98; Kieckhefer, *Repression*, pp. 7, 111; Ginzburg, "Deciphering," pp. 126–7; Behringer, *Shaman*, p. 158; *Witchcraft Reader*, pp. 163–4.
19. Kieckhefer, *Middle Ages*, pp. 40, 190–1.
20. Lecouteaux, pp. 51, 58, 60, 79; Ginzburg, "Deciphering," p. 126; Behringer, *Shaman*, p. 43.
21. Behringer, *Shaman*, p. 130.
22. Russel, *Lucifer*, p. 83.
23. Graf, "Schwäbish-Gmund," p. 129; Midelfort, p. 202; Esslingen: Vöhringer-Rubröder, p. 153; the correspondence of these early witch trials and the trial of the Anabaptists was first pointed out to me by Anita Raith (personal interview in June, 2000).
24. Behringer, *Shaman*, pp. 59, 135–6; note that one participant was chosen "Queen of the Angel Land."
25. Bailey, *Dictionary*, p. 143.
26. Behringer, *Shaman*, p. 48.
27. Verdon, p. 59; Gurevich, p. 85 argues that there was a separate cult of Diana.
28. Gurevich, pp. 83–4; Zilka, "Hoodwink," p. 94.
29. Behringer, *Shaman*, pp. 97, 102, 57; Giger, pp. 136, 140–2; Monter, "Switzerland," p. 1100.
30. Giger, p. 146; Midelfort, *Witch Hunting*, p. xiv.
31. UATüb, v. 16, pp. 749–57; A209, b. 440.
32. Muchembled, "Satanic," pp. 149–50; Labouvie, "Hexenspuk, p. 84; Briggs, "Witchcraft and Popular," p. 347; Maxwell-Stuart, *Satan's*, p. 214.
33. A209, b. 2099, d. 2; A209, b. 1989, d. 24.
34. Weber, *Kinderhexen*, p. 40.
35. A209, b. 2088, d. 5-6-63.
36. A209, b. 2088, "Examination."
37. A209, b. 2088, d. 5-6-63.
38. A209, b. 2088, d. 6-6-63.
39. A209, b. 2088, d. 10-6-63.
40. A209, b. 2088, d. 12-6-63.

41. A209, b. 2088, d. 15-6-63.
42. A209, b. 2088, d. 5-6-63.
43. Midelfort, *Witch Hunting*, p. 194; Levack, *Witch-Hunt*, pp. 153–4; Briggs, *Neighbors*, pp. 247–8; Steward and Strathern, p. xi.
44. Verdon emphasizes that in the Middle Ages night was "the realm of fear ... the devil, of sin," and was associated with conspiracies and the subversion of public order, pp. 11, 24, 27. Schindler argues that "so many people were out and about" at night that it was less fearsome than is commonly supposed (*Rebellion*, p. 220), but Spör's story suggests that Verdon is closer to the truth.
45. Steward and Strathern note that gossip and rumor can grow out "attempts to guess at events that may not have occurred at all," p. 41.
46. Rosnow, pp. 14–15; Steward and Strathern, p. 39. On the differences, see also Steward and Strathern, p. 38; Neubauer, p. 3; Hafen, p. 3 (online).
47. Neubauer, p. 155; Allport and Postman, pp. 49–60.
48. Rosnow, p. 14; Allport and Postman, p. 161.
49. Schein, p. 151.
50. Allport and Postman, p. 33.
51. Rosnow, p. 17; Neubauer, p. 166; Allport and Postman, pp. 56, 60.
52. Neubauer, pp. 16–8.
53. Rosnow, p. 17.
54. Heath, p. 3; Anthony, p. 93; Allport and Postman, p. 36; Rosnow, p. 17.
55. Allport and Postman, pp. 38, 46.
56. Allport and Postman, pp. 51–3, 55, 197; Rosnow, p. 23; Neubauer, p. 162.
57. Allport and Postman, pp. 59–60.
58. Rosnow, pp. 12, 17–18; Shibitani, p. 163.
59. Shibitani, pp. 183, 167; Rosnow, p. 16; Steward and Strathern, pp. 43, 57.
60. Neubauer, pp. 169, 171; Rosnow, p. 13.
61. A209, b. 2088, d. "Examination."
62. Merry, p. 274.
63. Tebbutt, p. 13.
64. Wickham, n.p. (online); Luckman, p. x.
65. Hafen, "Gossip," n.p. (online); Tebbutt, p. 76; Bergman, p. 144; Wickham, n.p. (online).
66. Wickham, n.p. (online); Luckman, p. x.
67. Merry, p. 274.
68. Steward and Strathern, pp. 29, 37; Bergman, pp. 146–7; Wickham, n.p. (online).
69. Luckman, p. ix.
70. Schein, p. 140.
71. Schein, pp. 151–2; Merry, p. 296.
72. Tebbutt, p. 11; Kurland and Pelled, p. 5; Steward and Strathern, p. 29; Schofield, p. 34; Merry, p. 272.
73. Schein, p. 152.
74. Wickham, n.p. (online); Schein, pp. 141–3, 148; Levin and Arluke, p. 281.
75. Schein, p. 150.
76. Tebbutt, pp. 13–14; Coates, pp. 118–19.
77. Coates, p. 120.
78. Tebbutt, p. 183. She is speaking here of working-class neighborhoods in early twentieth century cities, but her point is at least as valid for early modern communities.
79. A209, b. 2099, d. 2; Weber, *Verführten*, p. 207.

80. A209, b. 2099, d. 1; Weber, *Verführten*, p. 207.
81. A209, b. 2099, d. 2, 4; Weber, *Verführten*, p. 208.
82. A209, b. 2099, dd. 3, 4, 5.
83. Walinski-Kiehl, p. 182; Sebald, *Witch Children*, pp. 38–41, 105.
84. Vasek, p. 288; Walinski-Kiehl, pp. 176, 181–2; Sebald, *Witch Children*, p. 164.
85. Weber, *Verführten*, p. 207.
86. Brown, *Universals*, p. 139.
87. Modern children are particularly likely to treat dream experiences as real, see Mack, pp. 31–2; Stevens, *Private*, p. 258.
88. Bulkeley, *Introduction*, pp. 13–24; Stevens, Private, pp. 35–45.
89. Bulkeley, *Introduction*, pp. 27–49; Stevens, Private, pp. 46–82.
90. Domhoff, pp. 135–47.
91. Mueller and Roberts, pp. 90–1; Bulkeley, *Introduction*, p. 74.
92. Flanagan, pp. 74–5, 87–9; Vedfelt, pp. 183–4.
93. Flanagan, p. 76; Joseph, *Neuropsychiatry*, p. 108.
94. Joseph, *Neuropsychiatry*, p. 108; Bulkeley, *Introduction*, p. 57; Domhoff, p. 148.
95. Flanagan, p. 92, n. 3.
96. Austin, pp. 381–3; Neher, p. 42.
97. Flanagan, p. 75; Bulkeley, *Introduction*, p. 55.
98. Domhoff, p. 15.
99. Hobson, "New", p. 322; Hartmann, pp. 199–201; Flanagan, p. 89.
100. Flanagan, pp. 13, 81, 83; Solms, pp. 200, 243, 246; Domhoff, pp. 12, 15.
101. Flanagan, pp. 89–90; McGrath, p. 216.
102. Joseph, *Neuropsychiatry*, pp. 61, 108; Sylwester, pp. 43–5; Restak, p. 248.
103. Domhoff, pp. 4, 12, 14; Hobson, "New," 324; Sylwester, p. 93; Rock, pp. 104, 110.
104. Bulkeley, *Introduction*, pp. 57–8; Hartmann, p. 197; Domhoff, pp. 142, 148.
105. Domhoff, pp. 4–5; note that small amounts of sensory information may be incorporated into dreams.
106. Bulkeley, *Introduction*, p. 58.
107. Flanagan, p. 86; Hartmann, p. 210; Bulkeley, *Introduction*, p. 54.
108. Flanagan, p. 86.
109. Stevens, *Private*, pp. 105–6; Rock, pp. 78, 188.
110. Stevens, *Private*, p. 94; Winkelman, *Shamanism*, p. 137.
111. Stevens, *Private*, p. 94; Winkelman, *Shamanism*, p. 137; Hartmann, pp. 203–4; Mueller and Roberts, p. 92; Bulkeley, *Introduction*, p. 55; Vedfelt, pp. 191–2.
112. Hartmann, p. 128; Stevens, *Private*, pp. 95–6; Rock, p. 188.
113. Greenfield, p. 151; Hobson, "New," p. 328; Vedfelt, p. 194; Domhoff, p. 163; Winkelman, *Shamanism*, p. 136.
114. Domhoff, pp. 12, 16, 136; Vedfelt, p. 194; Stevens, *Private*, p. 95.
115. Rock, pp. 105, 117; Vedfelt, p. 186; Stevens, *Private*, p. 95.
116. Vedfelt, pp. 187, 194; Hobson, "New," p. 326; Domhoff, pp. 16, 30, 32; Rock, pp. 104, 111, 188.
117. McGrath, p. 216; Rock, p. 188.
118. Rock, p. 188; Domhoff, p. 169; Solms, pp. 240–1.
119. Hobson, "New," p. 328; Domhoff, pp. 6, 158; Flanagan, pp. 100–1. Note that there is also some controversy about whether waking consciousness plays a critical role in mental functioning or is merely a spectator of unconscious mentation that has already taken place; see, for example, Norrentranders, p. xi and Donald, pp. 1–8.

120. Hobson, "New," pp. 322, 327; Domhoff, pp. 27, 34, 169; Rock, pp. 77, 119.
121. Domhoff, pp. 142, 169; Hobson, "New," p. 328; Hobson, *Chemistry*, p. 131.
122. Hobson, "New," p. 329.
123. Domhoff, p. 136.
124. Domhoff, pp. 27, 34; Hartmann, p. 234; Mueller and Roberts, p. 88.
125. Weber, *Verführte*, p. 209. Sebald, *Witch Children*, p. 204 makes a similar observation about the connection between childrens' stories and adult conversation.
126. Ginzburg, pp. 18, 6. Note that Ginzburg not only discusses the *benandanti's* experiences as taking place in "lethargy" or a trance state, but also as "dreams (p. 61); a "very deep sleep" they are "in bed" (p. 69); a "dream-like state" (p. 79) (the "prisoners of a myth" go out on "Embers days"), p. 82: "dream-states." Contemporary research supports the role that cultural constructs can play in dreaming, see Ullman, pp. 258, 266; Hobson, *Chemistry*, p. 131.
127. Stevens, *Private*, p. 90; Bulkeley, *Introduction*, p. 57, Flanagan, pp. 13, 20.
128. Labouvie, "Hexenspuk," pp. 77–83.
129. Hartmann, p. 216.
130. Flanagan, p. 146.
131. Sylwester, p. 148; Flanagan, p. 76.
132. A209, b. 451, d. 2; Roper, "Evil," p. 128; Cervantes, p. 116; Vedfelt, pp. 184–5; Domhoff, p. 19.
133. "Sleep disturbances are one of the most sensitive indicators of emotional distress in children;" Mack, pp. 21–3.
134. Weber, *Verführte*, p. 207.
135. It should be noted that in his third round of interrogation (A209, b. 2099, d. 4), Hanß said that the "black man" had taken him to a witch dance long before, after his grandmother said he would come to him. However, there are a number of reasons to doubt this story: (1) there was no independent evidence of a bad dream, as the watchman's testimony was in the case of the one that woke him up; (2) he was being pressed by the magistrates to identify who had led him into witchcraft, which presupposed that someone had, and they threatened to beat him if he didn't tell them; (3) he claimed the black man had taken him to Heuberg, the legendary witch mountain, rather than the local meadow, Strampfelbach, where he said the other dance took place; and (4) at first he said he couldn't recognize anyone there, but when pressed and threatened again, he said "all the same who were at the Strampfelbach dance," which, along with the close parallel between his grandmother's role in this story and that of the neighbor woman in his original story suggest that in this case he was just making up details to satisfy his inquisitors.
136. Weber, *Verführte*, p. 182; Walinski-Kiehl, p. 172; Weber, pp. 34–5.
137. Midelfort, *Witch Hunting*, pp. 133, 139–40; Briggs, *Neighbors*, p. 233; McGrath, p. 193, Sebald, *Witch Children*, pp. 36, 104; Walinski-Kiehl, p. 173; Midelfort, "Heartland," p. 117; Yeoman, p. 232; Roper, "Evil," p. 109.
138. Sebald, *Witch Children*, p. 37; Briggs, "Dangerous," p. 20.
139. Weber, *Verführte*, pp. 187–9.
140. Weber, *Verführte*, pp. 191, 198–9, 216, 220, 224 (*maleficium*), 191, 198 (contact with the Devil).
141. Weber, *Verführte*, pp. 214, 205, 210, 214, 220; Pócs, "Alternative," p. 130.
142. Weber, *Verführte*, pp. 203, 220–1.
143. Weber, *Verführte*, p. 223; Roper, "Evil," p. 115.
144. Weber, *Verführte*, pp. 182–3; McGrath, p. 195. There was a widespread belief that witchcraft ran in families, and some children did practice minor forms of sorcery,

so theoretically children could have been accused of witchcraft, but their possible involvement was not a prominent feature of traditional witchcraft beliefs.
145. Sebald, *Witch Children*, p. 177.
146. Walinski-Kiehl, p. 182.
147. Sebald, *Witch Children*, pp. 162, 203; Walinski-Kiehl, p. 180.
148. Walinski-Kiehl, p. 181; McGrath, pp. 55–7; Saarni, p. 119; Vasek, p. 285; Tomasello, p. 212.
149. Rock, p. 188; Domhoff, p. 21; Mueller and Roberts, p. 94, Hartmann, p. 214. Furthermore, children's dreams are often disturbing, and often involve "fears of witchcraft, ghosts, and malevolent spirits," Stevens, *Private*, p. 258.
150. Weber, *Verführte*, p. 215.
151. Weber, *Verführte*, p. 184; Weber, *Kinderhexen*, p. 37.
152. Weber, *Verführte*, p. 185.
153. Weber, *Verführte*, p. 184; Roper, "Evil," p. 118.
154. Weber, *Verführte*, pp. 185–6; Weber, *Verführte*, pp. 225–8; Walinski-Kiehl, pp. 183–4.
155. Weber, *Kinderhexen*, p. 40.
156. Weber, *Kinderhexen*, p. 37.
157. Yoeman, pp. 233, 237.
158. Briggs, *Neighbors*, p. 233; Sebald, *Witch Children*, p. 36.
159. Walinski-Kiehl, p. 175.
160. McGrath, p. 196; Yeoman, p. 232.
161. Sebald, *Witch Children*, p. 104, see Chap. 8.
162. Weber, *Verführte*, p. 183.
163. Harrington, p. 16.
164. Walinski-Kiehl, pp. 182–3.
165. On youth gangs: Sebald, *Witch Children*, pp. 41, 104, 191–5; Walinski-Kiehl, p. 184.
166. Walinski-Kiehl, p. 173; Weber, *Kinderhexen*, p. 35.
167. The impact of acculturation on dreams was highlighted by the anthrolopologist Roger Bastide, quoted in Ullman, p. 269; evidence of the impact of Nazi propaganda on Germans' dreams was collected by Charlotte Beradt, quoted in Ullman, p. 271.
168. See Chap. 3.
169. A209, b. 1924.
170. On the decline of witch beliefs and the role of the university in ending the witch persecutions, see Chap. 8. On the trials in Reutlingen, see Fritz, especially pp. 261–91.
171. Zarit and Zant, pp. 54–5; *DSM-IV*, p. 123; Stewart and Fairweather, pp. 592, 594.
172. *DSM-IV*, p. 126; Zarit, p. 54; Stewart and Fairweather, p. 604.
173. Zarit, pp. 54, 57; Stewart and Fairweather, pp. 597, 603, 610; *DSM-IV*, p. 123.
174. Zarit, pp. 54–5; *DSM-IV*, pp. 123, 126; Stewart and Fairweather, p. 604.
175. Stewart and Fairweather, pp. 592, 594, 599–600.
176. Hasher, et al., p. 288; Zarit, p. 60.
177. Stewart and Fairweather, p. 595. It is possible that Apolonia was showing the first signs of dementia, especially some memory loss (she said "Urbanle" was a butcher who had been executed recently in Reutlingen, but the last person named Urban known to have been executed there was a wheelwright put to death seven years before, in 1660; Fritz, pp. 247–9) and degraded executive (inhibitory) function. However, no other, stronger signs of memory loss, which is central to the diagnosis of dementia (*DSM-IV*, p. 134), were mentioned, and, as noted, some loss of memory and decreased executive function are more general characteristics of aging

(Zarit, p. 60). Similarly, it is possible that Apolonia was developing some form of schizophrenia, since hallucinations are characteristic of this type of disorder, but, as with dementia, the evidence is weaker than for delirium, and neither accounts any better for the central issue here, Apolonia's reported flights to witch dances. In any case, the point here is that to understand what was going on in this case, it is not sufficient to dismiss Apolonia as some crazy old lady, as the magistrates of Tübingen and the High Council did, and as traditional rationalists would, but instead it is necessary to place her reported experiences in their cultural context. I would like to thank Carlo Ginzburg, who first suggested to me to look beyond the medical issues in this case in a personal interview in 1986.

178. Ginzburg, *Night*, pp. 16, 23.
179. Henningsen in *Early Modern Witchcraft*, pp. 196–9; Pócs, *Between*, pp. 73, 96.
180. Maria was tortured during her earlier trial but denied any further thefts or contact with the Devil beyond what she had already admitted to (A209, b. 451, d. 16) and got off with only a punishment for stealing. The fact that she held to her original confessions while successfully refusing to go beyond them makes it seem unlikely that she made her confessions in 1622 either in fear of torture or out of some neurotic compulsion to confess or feeble-minded inability to resist interrogators' suggestions.
181. A209, b. 451, d. 7.
182. A209, b. 451, d. 6.
183. Ginzburg, *Night*, pp. 6–7, 16; Henningsen, "Ladies," p. 197; Pócs, *Between*, p. 73.
184. Henningsen, "Ladies," p. 197; Pócs, *Between*, pp. 76–7.
185. At least, as conveyed by Ginzburg in *Night*; see pp. 1, 3, 35, 67, for example.
186. Ginzburg, *Night*, p. 3; Pócs, *Between*, p. 77.
187. Henningsen, "Ladies," p. 200.
188. Pócs, *Between*, p. 73.
189. The *Canon Episcopi* established that at least some flights were imaginary, but there was still room to debate whether that meant all had to be; see Levack, *Witch-Hunt*, pp. 46–8; Maxwell-Stuart, *Europe*, pp. 18–21.
190. Broedel, pp. 104, 114.
191. Pócs, *Between*, pp. 73, 77.
192. Ginzburg, *Night*, pp. 19–20.
193. Henningsen, "Ladies," pp. 195, 204, 206.
194. Pócs, *Between*, p. 73.
195. See Alvarado, "Out-of-Body Experiences" for a review of psychological studies from the late nineteenth century through the 1980s, and Murray and Fox, for an overview of current theories.
196. Blanke, "Neural," p. 1414; Meyerson and Gelkopf, p. 90; Alvarado, "Out-of-Body Experiences," p. 183; Irwin, "Dissociation," p. 262. Alvarado insistst that the "experience must include the exteriorization of perceptual locus to be classified as an OBE," but does not establish by what criteria such exteriorization should be established, the person's subjective feeling or the physical possibility of the reported point of view.
197. Murray and Fox, n.p. (online).
198. Irwin, *Flight*, p. 135.
199. Neher, p. 191.
200. Irwin, "Dissociation," p. 162; Blanke, "Neural," p. 1414; Frist, p. 241; Meyerson and Gelkopf, p. 91. Parapsychologists have moved away from the physical question also because it is particularly difficult to test, since virtually every testable

phenomenon (knowledge that couldn't have been acquired any other way, otherwise inexplicable physical effects on the remote environment) can also be accounted for by other forms of paranormal phenomena (clairvoyance and psychokinesis) whose existence is also disputed but which are more readily testable.

201. Alvarado, "Out-Of-Body Experiences," pp. 197–9; Irwin, "Dissociation," p. 271. Schizophrenic hallucinations tend to be auditory rather than visual, have little consistency from patient to patient, and are not subject to the experient's control; Irwin, *Flight*, p. 245.
202. Irwin, *Flight*, pp. 246, 301, 248–9; Alvarado, "Out-Of-Body Experiences," pp. 193–4.
203. Irwin, *Flight*, pp. 110–11, 191–2.
204. Domhoff, p. 34.
205. Mishlove, p. 95; Irwin, *Flight*, pp. 250, 17, 19.
206. Murray and Fox, n.p. (online); Irwin, *Flight*, pp. 255, 208, 19, 134, 17; Meyerson and Gelkopf, p. 91.
207. Irwin, "Dissociation," p. 268; Cheyne and Girard, "Spatial," p. 297. Briggs, "Dangerous," p. 15 speculates that the belief in magical flight, and hence flight to the sabbath could be connected to sleep paralysis, but Cheyne's research suggests that the two are only coincidentally related.
208. Irwin, *Flight*, p. 253; Blanke, "Neural," p. 1414; Meyerson and Gelkopf, p. 90.
209. Irwin, *Flight*, p. 121; Meyerson and Gelkopf, p. 90; Alvarado, "Out-Of-Body Experiences," pp. 187, 196.
210. Alvarado, "Out-Of-Body Experiences," p. 188; Meyerson and Gelkopf, pp. 90, 92, 98; Domhoff, p. 34.
211. Irwin, *Flight*, pp. 250, 301; Irwin, "Dissociation," pp. 271, 263; Meyerson and Gelkopf, pp. 90, 99; Murray and Fox, n.p. (online); Alvarado, p. 196.
212. Irwin, *Flight*, pp. 154, 182.
213. Irwin, *Flight*, pp. 147, 149, 155; Irwin, "Dissociation," p. 272; Meyerson and Gelkopf, p. 90.
214. Blanke, "Neural," p. 1414.
215. Frist, pp. 239–40.
216. Sylwester, pp. 126, 160; Blanke, "Neural," p. 1415; Blanke et al., "Linking," p. 556.
217. Blanke et al., "Linking," p. 550.
218. Irwin, "Dissociation," pp. 261–4.
219. Blanke, "Neural," p. 1414.
220. This reinforces Brigg's observation that "dream-like experiences ... made a significant contribution to the confessions of the witches themselves, notably in their accounts of the sabbath," and Pócs' that "the sabbath is in essence a visionary experience." On the frequency and variability of reported OBEs, see Frist, p. 241; Meyerson and Gelkopf, p. 91.
221. Irwin, *Flight*, pp. 110, 155, 191.
222. Mishlove, p. 95; Ginzburg, *Night*, p. 16; Pócs, *Between*, p. 74.
223. It is suggestive that people who have OBEs are particularly likely to have lucid dreams as well; see Irwin, *Flight*, p. 20.
224. Duerr, pp. 3, 143, n. 14; Lecouteaux, pp. 83, 86, 88; Sidkey, p. 193, Ginzburg, *Ecstacies*, p. 307; Clark, *Thinking*, pp. 237–8; Broedel, pp. 108, 110, 112–3; Lerchheimer, p. 30; Saur, *Ein kurtze treuwe Warnung*.
225. Pócs, *Between*, p. 77; Gehring, p. 400; Klaits, p. 12.
226. Duerr, p. 143, n. 13.

227. Briggs, *Neighbors*, p. 56; Henningsen, *Advocate*, pp. 297–8, although because not all the pertinent records were preserved, he found it "an open question" whether there had been any hallucinogenic salves (p. 300).
228. On the *benandanti* and others, Ginzburg, *Night*, p. 17; Pócs, *Between*, p. 77; For some recent historians' skepticism, see Levack, *Witch-Hunt*, p. 49; Briggs, *Neighbors*, p. 56; Klaits, pp. 11–12; and Thurston, p. 174. For even more dubious positions, see Cohn, pp. 220, 222–3; Harte, n.p. (online). See also Duerr, p. 144, n. 16; Priesner, I, p. 23.
229. Quaife, p. 202; Priesner, I, p. 24, II, p. 36; Schöpf, p. 23.
230. Sebald, *Witch Children*, p. 190.
231. Schultes and Hoffmann, pp. 261–3; Schultes, p. 46.
232. Reyscher, vol. 13, p. 491.
233. Schultes and Hoffmann, p. 288; Karger-Decker, p. 97; Priesner, II, p. 36; Duerr, p. 137, n. 6; Richardson, *Encyclopedia*, p. 80; Melton, p. 227.
234. Schultes and Hoffmann, pp. 296–8; Priesner, II, pp. 36–8; Karger-Decker, p. 101; Richardson, *Encyclopedia*, p. 81; Rudgley, p. 99.
235. Priesner, II, p. 38.
236. Cohn, p. 220; Harte, n.p. (online); Duerr, pp. 9–10, 144, n. 16. Bever, "Drugs and Hallucinogens," pp. 296–8; Sidkey, pp. 190–4.
237. Duerr, p. 10.
238. Zilka in *New*, p. 95.
239. *Newe Zeitung aus Berneburgk*.
240. Sebald, *Witch Children*, p. 191. In addition, it is worth noting that "poor people" in Europe in the mid-twentieth century used "plants of the nightshade family as an opiate ... since wines and liqueurs are usually beyond their means" (Baroja, p. 254), while ethnographers in Hungary in the same period reported on people who used a "magic ointment to fly" (Duerr, p. 136, n. 4).
241. Duerr, pp. 2, 138, n. 7; Bever, "Drugs and Hallucinogens," pp. 296–8; Thomas, p. 524; Monter, "Toad," pp. 575, 594.
242. Reyscher, 13, p. 491.
243. A209, b. 449, dd. 1 and 2.
244. A209, b. 1123.
245. A209, b. 392, Lit. A.
246. A209, b. 434; A209, b. 1787, d. 1; A209, b. 449, d. 1.
247. UATüb, v. 16, pp. 749–57; A209, b. 1757.
248. Schultes and Hoffmann, pp. 35–7.
249. Sidkey, p. 169.
250. Schultes and Hoffmann, p. 35.
251. Schultes and Hofmann, pp. 35–6; Ginzburg, *Ecstasies* p. 304; its use during delivery was forbidden in Württemberg only in 1831, Nestlen, *Hebammen*, pp. 18–19.
252. Ginzburg, *Ecstasies* pp. 304–5; Schultes and Hoffmann, p. 36.
253. Alm, pp. 403, 405–9.
254. Sebald, *Witch Children*, p. 192.
255. A209, b. 1587, d. 4, pp. 6–11.
256. A209, b. 1587, d. 23-12-39; the identity of the place where she overheard the conversation is unclear, although it was most likely a tavern. See Bachmann, pp. 60–3 for a discussion of the irregularities in the handling of Margaretha's case, and further discussion of it in Chapters 5 and 8.
257. A209, b. 1587, d. 9-11-39.
258. A209, b. 1430, d. 1.

259. This sort of relationship was not unknown among itinerant charlatans; see Ramsey, *Medicine*, p. 158.
260. Note that some details are taken from A209, bsl. 1430, d. 2; the accounts given in d. 1, the magistrates' report, and d. 2, a transcript of statements made later by Hans Jacob, are somewhat inconsistent.
261. A209, b. 1430, d. 2.
262. A209, b. 1430, d. 3.
263. A209, b. 1430, d. 26-1-1631.
264. A209, b. 1430, d. 5.
265. A209, b. 1430, d. 7.
266. Quaife, p. 201.
267. Tek22, n.p. (online). The plant is referred to by its American name, jimsonweed, here, but it is the same plant, *Datura stramonium* (Schultes, p. 143).
268. Chembob, n.p. (online).
269. Briggs, *Neighbors*, p. 56; Clark, *Thinking*, pp. 237–8; Ginzburg, *Ecstasies*, p. 303.
270. Sidkey, p. 199.
271. Weil and Rosen, p. 133; Sidkey, pp. 193–4, 196.
272. Maverick, n.p. (online); Reformed, n.p. (online).
273. Irwin, *Flight*, p. 244; Sidkey, p. 196; Priesner, II, p. 39.
274. Reformed, n.p. (online).
275. Levitt and Criswell, p. 104.
276. *DSM-IV*, p. 129. See also Maverick, n.p. (online); The Watcher, n.p. (online); Crystallinesheen, n.p. (online).
277. Sidkey, pp. 194, 207–8. LSD use has also been noted to create a cumulative experience in which the experient's brain changes over repeated sessions, Austin, p. 421.
278. Weil and Rosen, p. 23.
279. Austin, p. 440; Beckmann and Beckmann, p. 60; Criswell and Levitt note that "no one agent duplicates the effects of ingestion of the mushroom *Amanita muscaria*, which contains at least four different alkaloids," p. 96.
280. Richardson, *Encyclopedia*, p. 77.
281. Ibid., p. 80; Priesner, II, pp. 35–8; Schultes and Hoffman, pp. 286–8, 298.
282. Schultes, p. 46; Priesner, II, p. 35; Levitt and Criswell, p. 104; Abel, p. 151.
283. Hobson, *Chemistry*, pp. 265–6; Priesner, II, p. 35; Levitt and Criswell, pp. 93, 104.
284. Levitt and Criswell, p. 116.
285. Sidkey, p. 199; Irwin, pp. 151–3.
286. Sidkey, pp. 199–200; Irwin, pp. 159, 242, 263, 289–90.
287. Fischer, p. 62; Abel, p. 151.
288. Austin, pp. 164, 486; Greenfield, p. 151; Gibbs, pp. 184–5; Hagan, p. 86; Levitt and Criswell, p. 109; Stewart and Fairweather, p. 604.
289. Gibbs, p. 184; Levitt and Criswell, p. 111, although they warn that it is difficult to tell if many of the effects are caused by specific mechanism or "a general disturbance of body chemistry, p. 105 (see below).
290. Domhoff, pp. 5, 6, 129, 151; Austin, pp. 312, 316–7; Greenfield, pp. 140, 151; Hobson, "New," p. 328.
291. Walsh, p. 75; Levitt and Criswell, p. 116; Hobson, *Chemistry*, p. 255; Beckman, p. 60.
292. Slade and Bentall, p. 154; Rios, p. 197; Pócs, *Between*, p. 75; Gentilcore, "Narratives", p. 101; Sidkey p. 205; Quaife, pp. 202–3; Cohn, pp. 223–4. Early modern demonologists argued that it was the incantations and intentions of the users and the action of the demons they invoked, not the power of the salves themselves, that were responsible for their effects; see Sidkey, pp. 200–2.

293. There is evidence, for example, that drunken behavior is culturally conditioned, Sabean, *Power*, p. 124.
294. Ray, p. 100; Santhouse, p. 2059; Levitt and Criswell, p. 105; de Rios, pp. 198–9. The "Marsh Chapel" experiment in particular demonstrated that subjects given psilocybin in a religious setting had qualitatively different experiences that controls given an active placebo; Austin, p. 437.
295. There has been some question in the historical literature about the possiblity of transdermal absorption of hallucinogenic chemicals, but the medical literature makes it clear that this is indeed possible if they are mixed with fats or oils; see Weil and Rosen, p. 133; Harner, "Role," p. 128; Richardson, *Encyclopedia*, p. 78; Rudgley, p. 94.
296. Sidkey, pp. 190, 199.
297. Duerr, p. 138, n. 7; Quaife, p. 203; "Apium graveolens" n.p. (online); "Celery seed," n. p. (online).
298. Rudgley, p. 95; Duerr, p. 138, n. 7.
299. Winkelman, "Altered," p. 397; Locke and Kelly, p. 6.
300. Austin, pp. 308–9; Irwin, *Flight*, p. 252.
301. Austin, p. 308; Meyerson and Gelkropf, p. 91.
302. Winkelman, "Altered," p. 397.
303. Austin, pp. 305, 450–1.
304. Austin, p. 324.
305. Differing ASCs: Austin, pp. 299, 306–7; Waking dream: Winkelman, *Shamanism*, p. 130; Winkelman, "Altered," p. 411.
306. Winkelman, "Altered," pp. 397–8.
307. Winkelman, *Shamanism*, pp. 118–23, 127–33.
308. Levitt and Criswell, p. 111.
309. Rudgley, p. 94; Priesner, II, p. 35; Schultes and Hofmann, p. 263; Beckman, p. 60; Winkelman, "Altered," p. 400.
310. Quaife discussed the possibility that users of hallucinogenic drugs were essentially drug addicts rather than members of a cult (p. 203), and Sidkey raised the possibility of that they formed a loose network (pp. 204–8), but neither offered any archival evidence to support these ideas. Also, "experients" is used here since cholinergic hallucinogens do not appear to be physically addictive.
311. A209, b. 1430, d. 2.
312. Hobson, *Chemistry*, pp. 248, 251; Wier, p. 27.
313. Goodman, *Ecstasy*, pp. 40–1; Winkelman, "Altered," p. 399; Samuel, p. 116; Austin, p. 313.
314. Perry, p. 448; Zarit and Zant, p. 57; Pollock, p. 321. The relationship to aging reflects the deterioration that commonly take place in elderly people's colinergic system: Gibbes, pp. 183, 185, 187; Milwain and Iversen, p. 62. The relationship to sex reflects the fact that estrogen plays an important role in the colinergic system, and declining levels of estrogen affect women particularly: Morley, p. 7; Gibbes, p. 193 notes that estrogen has been shown to mitigate the effects of scopolamine.
315. Wier, p. 78.
316. On "placebo" hallucinogens, see Locke and Kelly, p. 32; Priesner, II, p. 38. However, the "Marsh Chapel" experiment suggests that while experients using placebos may have felt effects, they may well have been different from and less powerful than those of people who used chemically effective drugs; see Austin, p. 437.
317. Austin, p. 432.

5 Sorcery, Satanism, and Shamanism

1. Winkelman, "Magico-Religious Practitioner Types," pp. 33–5, 40 presents indirect evidence that magico-religious practitioners evolved from shamans in hunting and gathering societies to priests and shamanic healers in simple agricultural societies to a combination of priests, healers, mediums, and sorcerer-witches in more complex societies, although he treats sorcerer-witches as persecuted shaman-healers rather than actually malevolent practitioners. Critics have pointed out that interpretations of shamanism as the primeval stage of magico-religious development rest on hopeful interpretations of scanty and ambiguous evidence (Hutton, *Shamans*, pp. 30–1, 43–4, and 112–27, for example), but this seems to be the only coherent theory of the prehistoric origins of religion and magic that accounts for the similarities of basic magico-religious beliefs currently in play.
2. Eliade, *Shamanism*, pp. 3–12, 33–4, 110–39; Vitebsky, *Shamanism*, pp. 8–25, 52–95; Hutton, *Shamans*, pp. 47–59, 69–75; Stutley, pp. 7–10, 37–8.
3. Hutton, *Shamans*, p. 78.
4. Hutton, *Shamans*, pp. 49, 56, 77; Métraux, pp. 97, 102; Winkelman, "Other," p. 334; Vitebsky, *Shamanism*, p. 50; Chaumeil, p. 272; Klaniczay, "Shamanistic," p. 136.
5. Chavers, p. 365.
6. Chavers, p. 365; Narby and Huxley, "Introduction," p. 7; Hutton, *Shamans*, pp. 77, 136; Rios, p. 278; Skafte, p. 236; Samuel, pp. 108–9; Siegel, p. 58.
7. Olsen, "Music," p. 214; Reichel-Dolmatoff, p. 219.
8. Lafitau, pp. 23–4; Chaumeil, p. 275; Brown, "Dark Side," pp. 251–6.
9. Thomsen, pp. 8, 139; Ogden, pp. 3, 71; Gager, pp. v, 15–17, 21, 26; Dickie, pp. 567, 577; Brown, "Sorcery," pp. 18, 22, 25, 26, 28, 34.
10. Gager, p. 27; Flint, pp. 40–1, 63; Kieckhefer, *Magic*, pp. 46–9.
11. Kieckhefer, *Magic*, pp. 56, 80–5, 187–8, 191; Kieckhefer, "Children," p. 92.
12. Kieckhefer, *Magic*, pp. 46–9.
13. Klaniczay, "Shamanic," p. 143; Fichtenau, p. 322; Gurevich, p. 89.
14. Kieckhefer, *Magic*, p. 82; Broedel, p. 139.
15. Kieckhefer, "Holy," p. 374; Peters, pp. 116, 120, 122–5; Kieckhefer, *Magic*, p. 96.
16. Brucker, pp. 23, 9–19.
17. On exploitativeness of love magic, see Ortega, pp. 62–3, 66, 83.
18. Kieckhefer, *Forbidden*, p. 10.
19. Kieckhefer, "Children," p. 106.
20. There is some evidence of shamans using magic "darts," (Chaumeil, p. 273; Somé, pp. 238–9), curses, (Skafte, p. 236) and thoughts (Rasmussen, p. 82), but it is not clear the extent to which these represent outgrowths of shamanic practices and the extent to which they are imports from other magical systems.
21. Muir, p. 218.
22. Merrifield, pp. 147, 155; Gager, p. 28.
23. Walsham, p. 43; other instances of image magic in early modern England are given in Hole, "Instances," pp. 82, 88–9.
24. Maxwell-Stuart, *Satan's*, p. 214.
25. Briggs, "Witchcraft and Popular," p. 347.
26. Monter, "Toad," pp. 577, 583.
27. Gentilcore, *Bishop*, pp. 222–3.
28. Ortega, p. 79.
29. Martin, p. 212.
30. Klaniczay, "Shamanistic," pp. 134, 136.

31. Professional sorcerers and sorceresses were found across Europe; see Klaniczay, "Witch-hunting"," p. 159; Maxwell-Stuart, *Satan*, p. 94; Ortega, p. 60; Hagen, "King," p. 261; Brucker, p. 12. On the other hand, Brucker, pp. 22–3, n. 39 notes that he found no references to sorcery in the many private correspondances he examined from the early Renaissance, even though he found evidence in judicial records of significant networks of practitioners and clients.
32. Broedel, p. 144; Roper, "Magic," p. 317.
33. Kieckhefer, "Holy," p. 380; Labouvie, "Hexenspuk," p. 85.
34. Sebald, *Witch Children*, p. 185; Walinski-Kiehl, p. 179.
35. Ahrendt-Schulte, "Weise," pp. 51–2. Roper, "Evil," p. 115 says that use of powders, which could be either poisonous or magical or both, was common in low sorcery.
36. Labouvie, "Hexenspuk," p. 85.
37. Sebald, *Witch Children*, p. 192; Midelfort, "Devil," p. 250. Note that according to Sebald, "Justice," pp. 244–5 and "Shaman," p. 310, a grimoire containing rituals for harmful magic, the *Sixth and Seventh Book of Moses*, was used by some members of the rural populace in Franconia in the mid- to late twentieth century.
38. Roper, "Magic," pp. 319–20, 322–3; Midelfort, "Heartland," p. 114.
39. Lederer, p. 39.
40. Sebald, *Witch Children*, p. 189; Oldridge, "Introduction," p. 17; Dixon, p. 123. Sebald, "Justice," pp. 245–6 reports that mid-to-late-twentieth-century rural Franconians who use magic are divided into two groups, one of which includes otherwise ordinary people who cast the occasional spell, and the other of which for whom the practice of sorcery has become a defining feature of their "lifestyle."
41. Weber, *Verführten*, p. 199.
42. Bachmann, pp. 68–9.
43. On curses as a form of sorcery, Cryer, p. 139.
44. A209, b. 1884, d. 24-7-45.
45. Bachmann, p. 41; based on A209, b. 1158.
46. See Chap. 4.
47. A209, b. 11, d. 3.
48. *HddA*, vol. III, p. 1874; Newall, p. 89; Roper, "Evil," p. 115.
49. A209, b. 11, d. 1, and see Chap. 1. Walther, p. 97 reports that in twentieth century Swabia the belief was current that something borrowed from the household could be used for witchcraft against a new mother.
50. A209, b. 11, d. 3.
51. Note that in other cases, like those of Barbara Gessler (Case 26: b. 782) and Anna Schnabel (Case 17, b. 767), suspects brought foodstuffs to a person in a sickbed which were acknowledged to have been brought as nourishment or as a cure, even when their noxious flavor or apparent ill effects were also cited as evidence of witchcraft.
52. Laughlin, *Brain*, p. 160.
53. Winkelman, *Shamanism*, p. 243.
54. Laughlin, *Brain*, p. 95.
55. Ibid., p. 189.
56. Ibid., p. 190.
57. Ibid., pp. 165, 190.
58. Laughlin, *Brain*, pp. 169, 212; Winkelman, *Shamanism*, p. 244.
59. Laughlin, *Brain*, p. 191.
60. Ibid., pp. 163, 167.

61. Ibid., pp. 92, 163, 172, 191.
62. A209, b. 1587, d. Constable's Report 10-10-1739, p. 7.
63. See Chap. 4.
64. Hobson, *Drugstore*, pp. 31–2.
65. Winkelman, *Shamanism*, p. 231; Newberg, *God*, p. 59.
66. Hobson, *Drugstore*, p. 31.
67. See Chap. 1.
68. A209, b. 767, initial report.
69. A209, b. 767, d. 3.
70. Warde, pp. 175–212; Ernst, *6000 Jahre*, pp. 260–3.
71. Warde, p. 175.
72. Warde, p. 183.
73. Warde, pp. 179, 188.
74. Meerloo, p. 15.
75. Lissner, p. 245.
76. Tart, p. 485. See also Kamiya p. 510; Kasamatsu, p. 501.
77. Winkelman, *Shaman*, pp. 72, 146.
78. Kieckhefer, *Forbidden*, p. 15.
79. A209, b. 1092, d. 10-7-1740, pp. 1–2v.
80. A209, b. 1092, d. 10-7-1740, pp. 7v, 9v.
81. Wier, p. 113.
82. Ekman, "Facial," pp. 62, 64–5; Ekman et al., "Autonomic," p. 1208; Somby-Borgstram, (online); Reichel-Dolmatoff, p. 221.
83. Olsen, "Music," p. 213; Winkelman, *Shamanism*, p. 254.
84. Mazur, "Gaze," pp. 50, 64, 72; Mazur, "Biosocial," p. 377.
85. Sebald, "Shaman," p. 320.
86. Donald, p. 157.
87. Somby-Borgstram, n.p. (online).
88. Gentilcore, *Bishop*, p. 211 suggests that the value of sorcery was purely the psychological comfort it gave the user.
89. See Chap. 1.
90. It seems worth noting that if parapsychological phenomena ever do gain scientific acceptance, in these cases, too, the primary object of the magic ritual will prove to be the manipulation of the practitioner's own nervous system, and only secondarily, through that, the manipulation of the physical world.
91. Labouvie, "Hexenspuk," p. 83.
92. Winkelman, *Shamanism*, p. 6; Langdon, p. 63; Sebald, "Shaman," p. 323.
93. Wier, p. 69.
94. A209, b. 1092, d. 10-7-1740, p. 3v.
95. A209, b. 1092, d. 11-6-1740.
96. Sebald, "Shaman," p. 315. Catharina Ada, whose mother was killed as a suspected witch, and Catharina's daughter Margaretha, who was accused of hitting a girl and causing her whole side to hurt, may have been a case of this sort of pattern; A209, b. 1856, d. 2.
97. UATüb, v. 16, pp. 749–57.
98. Hughes, p. 135; Kieckhefer, "Specific," pp. 80–1; Brucker, p. 13.
99. Rudgley, p. 93; see also Locke and Kelly, pp. 29–30. A209, b. 736, d. 4; d. 42, pp. 15, 18.
100. A209, b. 736, d. 42, pp. 6–7.
101. Levack, *Witch-Hunt*, p. 27.
102. Russel, *Mephistopheles*, pp. 89–91; Brucker, p. 11.

103. Thomas, p. 35.
104. Hole, "Instances," p. 86; Kieckhefer, *Magic*, p. 168.
105. Gentilcore, *Bishop*, p. 214; Martin, pp. 131, 162, 177–8.
106. Monter, "Toad," pp. 565, 590–2.
107. Olli, p. 109.
108. A209, b. 1431.
109. A209, b. 1784a.
110. A209, b. 1258, d. 2.
111. Kieckhefer, "Rationality," p. 833.
112. Kieckhefer, *Magic*, pp. 151–2.
113. Hermelink, p. 107; Sauer, *Herzog*, pp. 148–56.
114. Dillinger, "Ewige," pp. 242–50.
115. Dillinger, "Ewige," p. 221; Wilson, p. 60; for details about the divinatory techniques, also see Chap. 6.
116. Dillinger, "Ewige," p. 229; Martin, p. 88; Adam, p. 382.
117. For a case of such an accidental find, A209, b. 967.
118. Dillinger, "Ewige," pp. 231, 233–4; A209, b. 14; b. 865; b. 959; b. 967; b. 1176; A213, b. 8401/72; b. 8406/1762; b. 8409/99–03.
119. A209, b. 865.
120. *HddA*, II, pp. 73–4; Birlinger, "Schwaben," I, p. 398 and II, p. 424; Dillinger, "Ewige," pp. 235–6; A209, b. 525; b. 865; b. 1176; A213, 8397, d1; b. 8409/1739; 8410/1795, d. 11-3-95; b. 8419/1789.
121. A209, b. 433; b. 525, d. 4; b. 609, b. 865; A213, b. 8397/1747, d. 1; b. 8414/1750–1; 8409/1739.
122. A209, b. 433; b. 525, d. 5; b. 865; b. 1176; A213, b. 8395/1766; b. 8399/1769; b. 8409/1739; b. 8409/99–03. Dillinger, "Ewige," p. 238.
123. A209, b. 525, dd. 5, 24; A213, b. 8406/51; b. 8414/1750.
124. A213, b. 8406/1751; b. 8406/1762; b. 8409/1739.
125. A209, b. 865; A213, b. 8409/39.
126. Several instances were clear frauds, like A213, b. 8395/1766; b. 8401/1792.
127. In one late case, the magistrates asked a treasure-seeker point blank if he had not prayed so much it caused him to see illusions: A213, b. 8409. On the power of religious symbols to induce autonomic arousal, Winkelman, *Shamanism*, p. 259. Kieckhefer, "Holy," p. 377 conveys the physical demands of ritual magic. Mathiesen, "Thirteenth Century," pp. 156–7 explicitly suggests that the involved rituals of late medieval mages were a way of "tuning" the nervous system.
128. Dillinger, "Ewige," pp. 232–4.
129. Dillinger, "Ewige," pp. 234–5; A209, b. 1700a; A213, b. 8406/51.
130. This story is recounted in Dillinger, "American," and is also discussed in Dillinger and Feld, p. 175 and Dillinger, "Ewige," pp. 263–71, and is discussed in more detail in Chap. 6.
131. Virtually all cases involved several treasure-seekers working together, and some involved a half dozen or more (A209, b. 525; b. 865; b. 609; A213, b. 8406/1751; b. 8419/1789).
132. Thomas, pp. 445–6; Magdelena Horn said that she had two familiars in the second report on her, A209, B. 719, d. 5-5-1565; Martin, p. 207; Briggs, *Neighbors*, p. 30.
133. A213, b. 8401/1792; b. 8413/1748.
134. A209, b. 865; b. 1176; A213, b. 8395/1766. For a particularly vehement denunciation of the practice, see A209, b. 525, d. 24.

Notes   473

135. Schribner, "Urach," pp. 266–7.
136. A209, b. 371.
137. A209, b. 466a.
138. A209, b. 767, d. 3.
139. A209, b. 1587, Actum 2/26/1739, pp. 11r–14.
140. A209, b. 1753.
141. Blowing was a known way of casting a spell in Germany; see Labouvie, "Hexenspuk," p. 66.
142. Roper, "Magic,", p. 321.
143. Kramer, "Schaden," p. 227; Gentilcore, "Folklore," p. 101.
144. Ortega, pp. 66–7.
145. Wilson, p. 107.
146. Maxwell-Stuart, *Satan's*, p. 214. Note, though, that Maxwell-Stuart cautions that "the Devil" may be the court's interpretation of Reid's involvement with spirits, so this could be a case of nondiabolical necromancy, although the fact that the spirit in question "appeared to Reid on several occasions, sometimes in the shape of a man, sometimes in that of a horse" sounds more like instances elsewhere in which the spirit is explicitly identified as the Devil than it does of instances in which the magician was trying to contact fairies, or even deliberately conjuring demons.
147. Klaniczay, "Witch-hunting," p. 250; Brucker, pp. 14–5, 19.
148. A209, b. 719, d. 5-5-1565.
149. A209, b. 451, d. 7.
150. Nildin-Wall and Wall, p. 67.
151. Sebald, *Witch Children*, pp. 86–8.
152. Klaniczay, "Shamanistic," p. 136.
153. Brucker, p. 14.
154. Medway, p. 58; Gurevich, p. 85.
155. Brown, "Sorcery," p. 36.
156. Russel, *Lucifer*, pp. 80–1; Medway, p. 60; Russel, *Mephistopheles*, p. 58; Carus, p. 290.
157. Medway, p. 60; Russel, *Mephistopheles*, p. 58; Walther, p. 64; "Knittlingen," n.p. (online).
158. Midelfort, *Madness*, p. 77.
159. Rapley, pp. 152–3.
160. Medway, p. 64; Lederer, p. 52; Zilka, *Exorcizing*, p. 1.
161. Russel, *Lucifer*, pp. 82–3.
162. Ladurie, *Montaillou*, p. 342.
163. A209, b. 1924.
164. Medway, p. 332; Olli, p. 110.
165. Olli, p. 111.
166. Gentilcore, "Folklore," p. 104; Gentilcore, *Bishop*, p. 153.
167. Gentilcore, *Bishop*, p. 153.
168. A209, b. 1092, d. 11-6-1740, p. 13.
169. A209, b. 1092, d. 11-6-1740, p. 18.
170. Weber, pp. 220–1.
171. Brown, "Sorcery," p. 36 traces this back to late antiquity; Roos, p. 17 cites Paul and the Old Testament; Midelfort, *Witch Hunting*, p. 55.
172. See Chap. 8.
173. See Chaps 6 and 7.
174. Kieckhefer, "Holy," pp. 377–8; the best example from Württemberg is probably that of Frau Schölhornin, who as we have seen invoked God while cursing her

brother-in-law. Among the sampled cases, see particularly that of Magdelena Kochen, A209, b. 1881, and even the case of Margaretha Stainer, discussed above, who gave justifications for many of the acts of *maleficium* she confessed to.
175. Briggs, *Neighbors*, p. 26, though he emphasizes that most found they were in too deep to back out.
176. Thompson, "Hosting," p. 195.
177. Broedel, p. 109.
178. Gentilcore, "Folklore," p. 100.
179. Tschaikner, "Magie," p. 145.
180. See Chap. 4 for both these cases.
181. Many peoples hold that sorcery can exert a powerful draw on practitioners of magic and become addictive; see Harner, "Darts," p. 197; Payaguaje, p. 232; Somé, p. 239; Siegel, *Name*, p. 115; Sebald, "Shaman," p. 310.
182. Dillinger and Feld, p. 177; *Witch Reader*, p. 110; Ahrendt-Schulte, "Weise," p. 40; Olli, p. 105.
183. Brucker, pp. 17, 19.
184. Gentilcore, "Folklore,", pp. 101, 104.
185. Pócs, *Between*, pp. 155–7.
186. Krampl, p. 150.
187. Oliver, pp. 6, 9.
188. Sebald, *Witch Children*, p. 195.
189. For the magical marksmanship, see A209, B. 1634a.
190. The concept of memes as a cultural analogue to genes first suggested by Robert Dawkins in *The Selfish Gene* (1976), and has been used in an attempt to make a scientific theory of cultural evolution analogous to that of biological evolution by a number of writers, most notably David Dennett in *Consciousness Explained* (1991) and *Darwin's Dangerous Idea* (1995), Susan Blackmore in *The Meme Machine* (1999), and Robert Aunger in *The Electric Meme: A New Theory of How We Think* (2002). The attempt to make a rigorous science of "memetics" has been problematic, to say the least, but there seems to be general agreement that memetics provide a useful metaphor to help conceptualize the process of cultural development, which is how it is used here (see Edmonds, n.p. (online)).
191. Blute, n.p. (online).
192. Bloom, p. 192.
193. Bloom, pp. 197–8.
194. Cervantes, p. 54.
195. Ibid., p. 56.
196. Ibid., pp. 49–50.
197. Ibid., p. 81.
198. Ibid., pp. 82–3.
199. Ibid., pp. 78–9, 83, 86–8.
200. Joseph, *Neuropsychiatry*, pp. 413, 468–9, 561.
201. The connection between the shaman's soul journey and the witch's flight to the sabbath has been commented on particularly by Klaniczay, "Shamanistic," p. 146 and Pócs, *Between*, pp. 84, 126, 151, 157–8.
202. Definitions of shamanism are discussed in Hutton, *Shamans*, pp. vii, 124, 145; Samuel, pp. 106–7; Townsend, pp. 431, 433; Flaherty, p. 214; Price, p. 6; Hultkrantz, pp. 44–6; Kehoe, pp. 2–3.
203. Hoppál, "System," p. 129 points out that spirit possession and shamanic flight often coexist, so attempts to make a hard distinction between the two systems seems questionable. See also Stutley, pp. 3, 28–9; Winkelman and Peek, p. 11.

Notes 475

204. Ironically, Kehoe, who argues strongly for restricting use of the term "shamanism" to Northern Eurasia, in the process makes the strongest case for inclusion of European spiritual traditions along with others in the general category, just under one other label, pp. 59, 70.
205. On classic structure, see Eliade, *Shamanism*, pp. 13–14, 80, 86, 88–9, 266, 269; Winkelman, *Shamanism*, Chapter 2, esp. pp. 60–3; Winkelman, "Practitioner Types," pp. 29–33; Townsend, pp. 444–6. Cases mentioned: A209, b. 1789; A209, b. 1989; A209, b. 1884 (1659), Maria Meyer; A209, b. 852; A209, b. 1587.
206. Hutton, *Shamans*, pp. 137–40; Priesner, I, p. 23; Davidson, p. 37; Buchholz, pp. 240–2.
207. Tuczay, "Trance," p. 219.
208. Ginzburg, *Ecstasies*, p. 14; Pocs, *Between*, pp. 150–1.
209. Hutton, *Shamans*, p. 146, although he suggests that these practices could have been derived from Ottoman dervishes (rather improbably) or developed independently (more possibly, although on the relevance of this see below.)
210. Pócs, "Possession," p. 126.
211. Klaniczay, "Witch-hunts," p. 157; Pócs, *Between*, pp. 73–4.
212. Klaniczay, "Shamanistic," pp. 136–43; Pócs, *Between*, pp. 134–43; Hutton, *Shamans*, p. 145 points out that the Taltos did not cure through a public performance, "shamanism proper;" and also that the various abilities attributed to them are a composite, drawn from different figures at different times. Nonetheless, for our purposes here they do show a significant range of shamanic features existing in the early modern period only a few hundred miles away from Württemberg.
213. Pócs, *Between*, pp. 126–7.
214. Behringer, *Shaman*, pp. 54–5; Behringer, "How," p. 174.
215. Henningsen, "Ladies," p. 200.
216. Pócs, *Between*, p. 125.
217. Hutton, *Shamans*, pp. 134–5; Oldridge, "Introduction," p. 10; Thompson, pp. 194, 196.
218. Oldridge, "Introduction," p. 9.
219. Davies, *Cunning-Folk*, p. 70; Oldridge, "Introduction," p. 9.
220. Behringer, *Shaman*, p. 64; Hall, "Getting," p. 6.
221. *Witchcraft*, pp. 95, 105; Wilby, p. 1; Pócs, "Possession," p. 120.
222. Cacioloa, pp. 21, 24.
223. Lecouteaux, p. 88.
224. Behringer, "How," pp. 173–5; Ladurie, *Montaillou*, pp. 351–2.
225. Behringer, "How," pp. 175–6.
226. Behringer, "How," p. 179.
227. Duerr, p. 11.
228. Behringer, "How," p. 181.
229. Behringer, "How," p. 179.
230. A209, b. 22, d. 1.
231. Burdock is an herb used traditionally to heal wounds, among other things. See "Burdock," n.p. (online).
232. A209, b. 22, d. 2.
233. *HddA*, II, p. 1123.
234. A209, b. 1878; A209, b. 433; A209, b. 1338; Walther, p. 55; Klaniczay, "Shamanistic," pp. 140, 142–3.
235. *HddA*, II, p. 1123.
236. Biedermann, p. 166.
237. *HddA*, IV, pp. 143–4; Zilka, *Exorcizing*, pp. 14–15.

238. Behringer, "How," p. 178; Behringer, "Shaman," p. 56.
239. List, pp. 309–10.
240. Mediums also typically find their calling when in distress; Locke and Kelly, p. 34.
241. Ginzburg, *Ecstacies*, p. 165.
242. *HddA*, IV, p. 144; *HddA*, I, 1049.
243. Eliade, *Shamanism*, pp. 266, 269.
244. Ibid., pp. 86, 88–9.
245. Ibid., p. 80; McLaughlin, *Brain*, p. 273.
246. Eliade, *Shamanism*, p. 80.
247. Hutton, *Shamans*, p. 74; Winkelman, *Shamanism*, p. 81.
248. Ginzburg, *Ecstacies*, pp. 246–50; Klanciczay, "Shamanistic," p. 148.
249. Vitebsky, *Shamanism*, p. 156 discusses how the shaman cures himself of his initiatory illness to learn how to cure others. Pócs, *Between*, p. 153 points out that shamanic healers gain knowledge of herbs in dreams.
250. Stutley, pp. 16–18 mentions that learning secret language was not unusual.
251. Ernst, *6000 Jahre*, p. 418; Dankert, p. 219; Stutley, p. 35.
252. Jones and Pennick, p. 116.
253. Klaniczay, "Shamanistic," p. 143.
254. Pócs, *Between*, p. 124.
255. Kieckhefer emphasizes the contribution of learned necromancy in *Magic*, p. 191, while Behringer points to the activities of Waldensian brethren in "How," p. 182.
256. Jones and Pennick, p. 116.
257. Gennep, p. 51; Winkelman, *Shaman*, p. 77; Vitebsky, *Shamanism*, pp. 50, 154; Kehoe, p. 49.
258. Pócs, "Possession," p. 132 emphasizes the importance of distinguishing flight from possession phenomena in outlining the structures of European spirit-folklores. Note that flight and possession are often discussed in the anthropological literature, but the third gets less attention there. Invocation does seem to have played a more prominent role in the learned magical traditions of complex Eurasian agricultural civilizations than in simpler societies, but, as we have seen, the practice does seem to be related to both the spirit helpers shamans ally with and also with the mediumistic practice of calling spirits to oneself. Hutton, *Shamans*, pp. 88–90, points out that shamanic flight, mediumistic possession, and dispatch of spirit helpers are all used by Siberian shamans.
259. In general, having a word that enables us to discuss the commonalities of the phenomenon seems more important than having a precise label for an artificial subset of Siberian religious practice. In this regard, note that Hutton employs the first definition mostly, but in the end endorses the idea that "the traits which underpin Siberian shamanism occur naturally in individuals thorughout humanity; *Shamans*, pp. 147–9. Similarly, Kehoe argues against the use of the term "shamanism" outside the North Asian context, but recognizes that it is based on general human physiological potentials, and that whether to use "shamanism" to label the complex of behaviors that manifest it is essentially arbitrary, pp. 52, 55. Hutton, *Shamans*, p. viii, notes the Eurocentrism in referring to Siberian religions as shamanism.
260. Winkelman, *Shamanism*, pp. 117, 121; Taves, p. 357; Laughlin, *Brain*, pp. 273, 334; Atkinson, p. 308; Chavers, p. 363; Pócs, "Possession," p. 131; Winkelman, "Other," pp. 309–10; Winkelman, "Altered," p. 402; Kehoe, p. 4.
261. Locke and Kelly, p. 4; Winkelman, *Shamanism*, pp. 113, 117.
262. Winkelman, "Altered," pp. 402–3; Kehoe, p. 55; Hutton, *Shamans*, p. 127.
263. Flanagan, pp. 75–8; Hobson, *Drugstore*, p. 267; McClenon, *Healing*, p. 88.

264. Winkelman, *Shamanism*, pp. 143–4; Hobson, *Drugstore*, pp. 29, 207, 302–3; Klein and Armitage, p. 1326; McClenon, *Healing*, p. 88.
265. Hobson, *Drugstore*, pp. 302–3.
266. Ornstein and Galin, p. 23; Galin, p. 28.
267. Austin, p. 297; Jaynes, pp. 24–5.
268. For example, according to Wier, p. 75, "measured changes in alpha states ... occurs within 30 seconds" of beginning to watch TV.
269. Austin, p. 320.
270. Kasamatsu, p. 497.
271. Hobson, *Chemistry*, p. 251; Hobson, *Drugstore*, p. 317.
272. Hobson, *Chemistry*, pp. 251–2; McClenon, *Healing*, pp. 90, 92.
273. McClenon, p. 92.
274. "Hypnosis," p. n.a.; "Brain Imaging," p. n.a.
275. Winkelman, *Shamanism*, pp. 132–3; Wier, p. 46.
276. McClenon, *Healing*, pp. 24, 92–3; Winkelman, *Shamanism*, p. 130; Hobson, *Drugstore*, p. 317.
277. Stutley, p. 28; Kehoe, p. 52; Goodman, *Ecstasy*, p. 35; Laughlin, *Brain*, pp. 153, 274–5; Winkelman, *Shamanism*, p. 119; Locke and Kelly, p. 27; Neher, p. 19; Newberg, "God," p. 89; Hoppál, "System," p. 125; Hutton, *Shamans*, p. 72; Fuller, pp. 174–5.
278. Laughlin, *Brain*, p. 278.
279. Winkelman, *Shamanism*, p. 187.
280. Goodman, *Ecstasy*, pp. 42, 46; Winkelman, "Other," p. 336.
281. Winkelman, "Other," p. 337.
282. Ginzburg, *Ecstasies*, pp. 161–2.
283. Lex, "Voodoo," p. 820; Laughlin, *Brain*, pp. 147, 276, 323; Newberg, p. 39.
284. Winkelman, *Shamanism*, pp. 130, 133, 135.
285. Winkelman, *Shamanism*, pp. 113–14, 122–4; Winkelman, "Trance," p. 186; Andresen, p. 257; Goodman, "Neurophysiology," p. 377; Samuel, p. 108; Vitebsky, *Shamanism*, p. 146.
286. Winkelman, "Altered," p. 403; Winkelman, *Shamanism*, pp. 77, 128, 148–52; Laughlin, *Brain*, pp. 143, 317; Locke and Kelly, p. 37.
287. Persinger, pp. 31–2; Austin, p. 446; Locke and Kelly, pp. 21, 27, 30, 35; Austin, p. 445.
288. Hoppál and von Sadovszky, p. 16; Hutton, *Shamans*, p. 82; Grambo, p. 418; Tuczay, "Trance," p. 216; Hoppál, "System," p. 125; Locke and Kelly, pp. 30, 36; McClenon, *Healing*, p. 31; Hinde, p. 115; Newberg, *God*, pp. 79, 125; Goodman, "Neurophysiology," pp. 377–8; Olsen, "Music," p. 213; Laughlin, *Brain*, p. 205; Austin, p. 440. Kehoe, pp. 3, 58 suggests induction techniques are simply "learned cues" equivalent to a hypnotist's snapped fingers or dangeld object, but McClenon, *Healing*, pp. 24 and 31 in particular presents evidence that repetitive stimuli have a similar calming effect on animals connected to group cohesion and mating, while drumming "has been demonstrated to affect brain patterns inducing ASCs." Learned cues play an important role in shamanism, as we shall see below, but their role is secondary to the drivers discussed here.
289. Laughlin, *Brain*, pp. 312, 321–2.
290. Locke and Kelly, p. 37; Wier, p. 118; Laughlin, *Brain*, pp. 153, 316; Newberg, *God*, p. 97; Goodman, *Ecstasy*, p. 34; Andresen, p. 269; Taves, pp. 357–8; Hobson, *Drugstore*, p. 105.
291. Kalweit, p. 181.
292. Hobson, *Drugstore*, p. 251; Flanagan, p. 80.

293. Winkelman, *Shamanism*, p. 7; Goodman, "Neurophysiology", p. 378; Hobson, *Drugstore*, p. 217.
294. Newberg, *God*, pp. 4, 28, 87.
295. Goodman, "Neurophysiology," p. 378.
296. Winkelman, *Shamanism*, pp. 131, 221–2; Austin, p. 385; Hobson, *Drugstore*, p. 257.
297. Winkelman and Peek, p. 11; Winkelman, *Shamanism*, p. 187.
298. Newberg, *God*, pp. 6, 7, 116.
299. Goodman, *Ecstasy*, p. 39.
300. Klaneczay and Pócs, "Introduction," p. 1; Hutton, *Shamans*, p. 127; Winkelman, *Shamanism*, p. 75.
301. Goodman, *Ecstasy*, p. 44; Chavers, p. 363. Note that Klein et al., p. 388, state that Mixe shamans in southwest Mexico "reportedly do not differentiate between the dreaming and the waking state," and so question whether they would experience the distinction suggested here, and, in a larger sense, challenge the appropriateness of the concept of trance [ASC] because some indigenous cultures do not have a corresponding conceptual category. However, while it is possible that the Mixe shamans are not aware of entering a distinct state of consciousness when they move from waking to dreaming (and, as we have seen, laboratory studies have established that dreaming is a distinct state of consciousness in which the brain works differently to produce qualitatively different experiences than when awake), the authors do not prove that these shamans are not aware of some difference between the two states, and, even if true, this would seem to be an exceptional situation cross-culturally. Similarly, their wider assertion, citing Hamayon, that the word trance "'tells us nothing about what the shaman is actually doing' and, in any case, cannot be empirically verified," while literally true in the field, overlooks the laboratory research that supports the physiological distinctiveness of trance (hypnotic) states and has begun to provide information about what is happeneing during them, as discussed below.
302. Laughlin, *Brain*, p. 326.
303. Winkelman, *Shamanism*, p. 87; Laughlin, *Brain*, pp. 274–5.
304. Willis, "New Shamanism," p. 18; Locke and Kelly, pp. 43–4.
305. Goodman, *Ecstasy*, p. 47.
306. Winkelman, *Shamanism*, pp. 2, 39, 44; Tuczay, p. 223; Goodman, *Ecstasy*, p. 44, 46; Noll, p. 249; Hobson, *Drugstore*, p. 92; Laughlin, *Brain*, p. 277.
307. Wier, p. 107; Neher, p. 39; Grambo, p. 422; Hutton, *Shamans*, p. 90.
308. Winkelman, *Shamanism*, pp. 7, 38, 41, 90.
309. Fuller, p. 167; Austin, pp. 307, 433.
310. Winkelman, *Shamanism*, pp. 28, 29, 50, 51; Austin, p. 435.
311. Winkelman and Peek, p. 6.
312. See Chap. 4.
313. Rios, p. 196.
314. Winkelman and Peek, pp. 8–12; Métraux, p. 100; Hutton, *Shamans*, pp. 56, 97; Samuel, p. 111; Tuczay, "Trance," p. 216; Elkin, p. 106.
315. Austin, p. 450; Hobson, *Drugstore*, p. 273; Winkelman, *Shamanism*, p. 19.
316. Hobson, *Drugstore*, p. 273.
317. Stutley, p. 29; Hutton, *Shamans*, p. 97; Neher, p. 207.
318. Winkelman, "Altered," p. 402.
319. Laughlin, *Brain*, p. 321; Winkelman, *Shamanism*, pp. xii, xiii, 145; Austin, pp. 386, 411.
320. Hutton, *Shamans*, pp. 94, 96; McClenon, *Healing*, p. 70.

321. Clark, "Witchcraft and Magic," pp. 161–2.
322. Note that even extraordinary feats like firewalking, which is sometimes used by shamans to prove the genuineness of their trance, can be explained naturalisticly as a product of purely physical processes, probably involving the brain's ability to influence metabolic processes while in an altered state of consciousness; Labitau, p. 26; Burkan, n.p. (online).
323. McClenon, *Healing*, pp. 70, 92–3; Tuczay, "Trance," p. 228; Winkelman, "Other," p. 323.
324. Andresen, p. 261; Winkelman, *Shamanism*, pp. 197, 201–2.
325. McClenon, *Healing*, pp. 7–8, 47, 56; Winkelman, *Shamanism*, pp. 194–5, 198–9.
326. Winkelman, "Other," p. 322; Winkelman, *Shamanism*, p. 95.
327. Lex, "Voodoo," p. 821; Vitebsky, *Shamanism*, p. 157.
328. Laughlin, *Brain*, p. 213.
329. Lex, "Voodoo," p. 822.

Part III The Realities of Beneficent Magic

1. Peuckert, p. 119; Döbler, p. 12; Schöck, pp. 14–15; Mährle, p. 353; Wilson, pp. xvii–xviii.
2. Midelfort, "Devil," p. 242; von Dobeneck, pp. 72, 90, 97, 115; Walther, pp. 55, 69.
3. Clark, *Thinking*, pp. 283–4; Smallwood, p. 21; Dixon, p. 124; Clark, p. 247; Broedel, p. 151; Ramsey, p. 253; Hampp, p. 15; Holzmann, p. 37; Rowlands, "Witchcraft and Popular Religion," p. 115.
4. For the cases included in the samples, see the appendix.
5. Note that in addition five cases were labeled "*Wahsagerei*," which translates as "Soothsaying" or "Fortune-Telling": A209, b. 1675 and A213, bb. 8401(1772), 8406(1765), 8406(1773), and 8417(1802–3). However, none were included because their examination revealed that two were essentially treasure-finding cases, one was a typical case of charming, one was a case of political prophesy, and the last involved a number of card-reading fortune-tellers in Stuttgart in 1802–3. Since a proportionate random selection of one could hardly be representative of the group, and their contribution to the overall sample would be minor, it was decided to simply discuss them as appropriate on an individual basis.

6 Divination and Prophesy

1. Schiefenhövel, p. 62; Hutton, *Shamans*, p. 54; Tuczay, "Trance," p. 215.
2. Bever, "Divination," pp. 285–7.
3. Like most regions of Europe, Swabia had a rich local lore of omens, and dream interpretation was widespread; see Walther, pp. 69–72, 92–3; Thomas, pp. 128–46, 623–8; Wilson, pp. 375–90; Schiefenhövel, p. 62. On the distinction between "natural" and "technical" divination, Tuczay, "Trance," p. 215.
4. Tuczay, "Trance," p. 227.
5. Blécourt, "Witch Doctors," p. 298.
6. Witchcraft Cases W2, 4, 7, 11, 13, and 15 (see the appendix).
7. It should be noted that historians tend to regard witchcraft diagnoses and counter-magic as a more prominent part of the services provided by cunning folk, and also believed that these played a more prominent role in generating witchcraft suspicions, than is suggested here; see Clark, "Culture," p. 112 and also Davies, "Market-Place," p. 73; Gildrie, "Visions,", p. 288; and Blécourt, "Witch Doctors," p. 302.

8. A209, b. 852, d. 8-8-1611.
9. A209, b. 1884 (1659), d. 24-7-45.
10. Ramsey, *Medicine*, p. 269. One English cunning woman said she could identify witches because "the fairies told her," while others claimed to learn through the help of familiar spirits.
11. A209, b. 1424, d. 7-1595; A209, b. 723, d. 2.
12. A209, b. 723, d. 3.
13. Thomas, p. 186; Briggs, "Neighbors," p. 182; Walter, p. 67. Other ways of inducing such subjective experiences included the use of hallucinogenic drugs, including, in Europe, henbane (Duerr, p. 138, n. 6) and mandrake (Priesner, II, p. 37); see also Harner, "Darts," p. 199 and Rios, p. 203.
14. Bever, "Divination," pp. 285–7.
15. Hollan, p. 540; Norretranders, p. 300; Neher, p. 54.
16. Neher, p. 37; Winkelman, "Other," p. 323.
17. Tuczay, "Trance," pp. 225, 230, n. 12; Briggs, *Neighbors*, p. 182.
18. A209, b. 1656, d. 13-5-1729.
19. Thomas, p. 213.
20. Mährle, p. 252; Walther, p. 75; Martin, pp. 119–20.
21. A209, b. 1338, d. 3.
22. Benes, "Fortunetellers," pp. 130–1; Hyman, "Ideomotor," n.p. (online).
23. Barrett, "Reminiscences," n.p. (online); John, n.p. (online); Hatch, "Schott," n.p. (online).
24. Schwartz, *Mind*, p. 307.
25. Thomas, pp. 208, 216–7, 242–4; MacFarlane, pp. 110, 123; Blécourt, "Witch Doctors," p. 297; Waardt, p. 35; Dillinger, *Böse*, pp. 142, 144.
26. Briggs, *Neighbors*, p. 184.
27. Hobson, *Drugstore*, p. 92; Alexander et al., pp. 118–9.
28. Anderson et al., p. 401.
29. Winkelman and Peek, pp. 10, 7. Alexander et al., p. 118. Fichtenau, p. 320 discusses a form of divination to detect thieves that relied on the their unconscious processes. Specifically, suspects were subjected to extensive rituals and then required to eat dry bread and cheese; the guilty were presumed to be unable to swallow, and Fichtenau notes "We can well imagine how ... a guilty conscience would have constricted the throat of the thief" (although, like a modern lie detector, this method actually detects signs of nervousness – stress, the drying of the mouth – rather than direct indications of guilt).
30. MacFarlane, pp. 123–4; Briggs, *Neighbors*, p. 180.
31. McClenon, *Events*, p. 1.
32. Glucklich, p. 13; Neher, pp. 31–2, 34; Alexander et al., p. 120. Goodman, *Ecstasy*, p. 49, denies any role for "methods similar to a Rorschach test, or ... game theory for randomizing results," placing all emphasis on the "religious trance ... which the practitioner enters," but I think it is more reasonable to assume that diviners combine all these techniques, to different degrees in different cultures, traditions, and personal styles.
33. Note that this explanation assumes that no truly paranormal process was being tapped that gave the diviner direct access to the information, since, as we have seen, the existence of such processes is not accepted by a consensus of the scientific community.
34. Briggs, *Neighbors*, p. 182.
35. Thomas, p. 218.
36. A213, b. 8406, d. 6-2-1761.

37. A209, b. 1656, d. 1.
38. A209, b. 1338, d. 1.
39. Martin, p. 119; Thomas, pp. 253–4. Note also that in addition to the sampled cases, many other related cases were read for this study, and of them only one included divination for witchcraft (A209, b. 529), while four included divination for theft (A209, b. 1338; A213, b. 8406/1765; A213, b. 8406/1773; A213, b. 8422/1747.
40. Anderson et al., pp. 375, 382.
41. Anderson et al., pp. 377–8.
42. A209, b. 1656, d. 13-5-1729 and d. 1. See Zagorin on early modern lying.
43. A213, b. 8417, 1802-3, d. 17-11-02. Ladurie, *Montaillou*, p. 347 mentions contact with the dead being used for the same purpose.
44. A209, b. 1656, d. 1.
45. A213, b. 8417, dd. 31-8-03, 18-9-03, 27-9-03, 29-9-03.
46. Examples of using scrying to find lost objects are given in Monter, "Toads," p. 576 and Rowlands, "Popular Religion," p. 111.
47. Hutton, *Triumph*, p. 96.
48. Radin, *Entangled*, pp. 48–9, 95–6, 250–60, 292–3; Targ and Katra, pp. 36–78; Humphrey, pp. 128–37; Teresi, n.p. (online).
49. Note that treasure-finding was the most common form of learned magic in Italy; see Gentilcore, *Bishop*, p. 226 and Martin, p. 88.
50. Sg1, 2, 3, 4, 5, 6, 7, 9, 12, 13 (see the appendix).
51. Sg11, 8, 10 (see the appendix).
52. Gb1, 2, 5, 7; Gb6 (see the appendix).
53. Sg2, 4, 9 (see the appendix).
54. "The Pendulum," n.p. (online).
55. A213, b. 8406, d. 2-1-1751. Adam, p. 363, reports that diving rods were also used, in neighboring Baden anyway, to determine the value of the treasure by asking, "how much money is there?" and then counting the "strokes it then makes."
56. John, n.p. (online).
57. According to Eis, p. 146, there are relatively few incantations to be used with divining rods from the Middle Ages, but they were quite numerous in modern folklore, suggesting that use of the devices only became common during the early modern period.
58. John, n.p. (online).
59. Wolcock, n.p. (online); Miller, "Dowsing," n.p. (online); see also Hansen, "Dowsing".
60. This experiment was reported in Chadwick et al., DG and Jensen, L. (1971). "The Detection of Magnetic Fields Caused by Groundwater and the Correlation of such fields with Water Dowsing." Utah Water Research Laboratory Report PRWG 78-1, January 1971, US Geological Survey, Water Resources Division, which is summarized in John, n.p. (online) and Hansen, "Dowsing," pp. 349–50.
61. Sg2 (see the appendix). Note: conversion rate of 1751 Reichstaler was made to 1965 US dollars at 1R=$5, rounding off the 1:4 conversion ratio given in Durant, *Voltaire*, p. ix and then roughly converted from 1965 to 2005 dollars using the consumer price index value generated by the Economic History Services' "What is It's Relative Value?" utility at http://eh.net/hmit/compare/.
62. Sg4 (see the appendix).
63. Sg9. Note that they would not have been anxious to reveal any past successes since that might have created trouble for them either for their magical practices

64. Quote from A209, b. 609, d. 13-1-83.
65. A209, b. 8406/1751, d. 2-1-51.
66. Dillinger and Feld, p. 165, n. 28.
67. Wolcock, n.p. (online).
68. A209, 1811; Gb5; Sg7 (see the appendix).
69. Tuczay, "Trance," p. 277.
70. Sg7 (see the appendix).
71. A213, b. 8409/1739, d. 26-5-39.
72. A213, b. 8406/1762, d. 24-4-62.
73. Gb5 (see the appendix).
74. Sg4 (see the appendix).
75. Dillinger, "Ewige," pp. 234–5.
76. Circle: Gb5; holy water: Sg2. (See the appendix.)
77. Sg5 (see the appendix).
78. Dillinger and Feld, pp. 165–6.
79. Sg2 (see the appendix).
80. Zns (see the appendix).
81. Dillinger, "American," n.p. (online). Thomas notes that in the Middle Ages Catholicism accepted the possibility that God could send souls back to earth as part of their time in Purgatory, but Protestantism rejected the concept of Purgatory and insisted that ghost-like apparitions were demons sent by the Devil to test men's faith, so in the early modern period Catholicism became far more resistant to the idea of contact between the living and the dead as well. Neither faith denied that God had the power to return souls to earth, but both the faiths increasingly insisted that He did not do this in practice.
82. Lederer, p. 24; Wilson, pp. 301–4; Walther, pp. 54, 68.
83. Ginzburg, *Night*, pp. 37, 67; Pócs, *Between*, pp. 122, 125–6; Behringer, *Shaman*, pp. 22–34; Ladurie, *Montaillou*, p. 345.
84. Blécourt, "Witch Doctors," p. 200, gives an example of changing attitudes towards ghosts, in Holland.
85. A209, b. 14; Dillinger, "Ewige," p. 234.
86. A209, b. 959.
87. A209, b. 1176.
88. A213, b. 8409, d. 6-2-1799.
89. A213, b. 8396/1764, d. 5-6-64.
90. A213, b. 8396/1764, d. 9-6-1764.
91. A213, b. 8396/1764, d. 22-6-1764.
92. A213, b. 8396/1764, d. 3-7-1764.
93. A213, b. 8401, d. 15-7-1772.
94. This story is recounted in Dillinger, "American," and is also discussed in Dillinger and Feld, p. 175 and Dillinger, "Ewige," pp. 263–71. All quotes not otherwise identified are from the online version of "American," which is not divided into pages.
95. Dillinger, "Ewige," p. 265.
96. Dillinger, "Ewige," p. 271.
97. Dillinger, "Ewige," p. 266.
98. A209, b. 1669, d. 1.
99. A209, b. 727, d. 1.
100. A213, b. 8395/1766, d. 14-4-66.

Notes 483

101. Dillinger discusses several cases involving swindlers in the duchy in Dillinger and Feld, pp. 166-7, 169 and Dillinger, "Ewige," pp. 245-7. A case in which a regular person seems to have claimed to have encountered a ghost in order to support a request for permission to dig more where some items had already been found is in A209, b. 967, also discussed in Dillinger, "Ewige," p. 242. Strong evidence of fraud: 3 (Sg4, 8; Gb1); apparent genuineness: 9 (Sg1, 3, 5, 6, 9, 10, 12; Gb5, 7); uncertain: 5 (Sg2, 7, 13; Gb2, 6); not relevant: 3 (Sg11; Gb3, 4 – the first of these involved unsubstantiated allegations against people who were simply active at night, while the third involved a cunning man who simply exorcized ghosts, without seeking treasure). For case references, see the appendix.
102. Dillinger and Feld, p. 169; Dillinger, "Ewige," pp. 245-6.
103. Positive evidence: Sg1, 2, 7, 9, 12, 13 and Gb2, 5, 6, 7; possible: Sg3, 5 (see the appendix).
104. Sg5 (see the appendix).
105. Sg3 (see the appendix).
106. Sg10, 6 (see the appendix); Dillinger, "Ewige," p. 243.
107. Sg13 (see the appendix).
108. Sg3, 12, 13; Gb6, 7. Also Sg7, Gb2 (see the appendix).
109. Sg5 (see the appendix).
110. Gb5 (see the appendix).
111. Sg1, Zns. (See the appendix.)
112. Mishlove, pp. 194-5, 201-5, 207-19.
113. Schwartz, *Afterlife*; Hyman, "How Not," pp. 20-30, strongly critiques Schwartz's methodology; A relatively balanced overview of current scientific research is Roach.
114. Adam, p. 376; Sg9; Zns; Sg7 (see the appendix).
115. A209, b. 967, d. 1; Dillinger and Feld, p. 178; A. 213, b. 8409/1799, d. 6-2-99.
116. Adam, p. 375.
117. Z5 (see the appendix), A209, b. 22, d. 28-2-23.
118. Wilson, pp. 375-91, emphasizes the interpretation of omens and private rituals, but Thomas, pp. 237-44; Davies, *Cunning-Folk*, pp. 10, 73, 79, 87; Martin, pp. 113-24; Gentilcore, pp. 215, 219; Krampl, pp. 144, 149-50; and Benes, "Fortuneteller," p. 129 all demonstrate that various systems to divine peoples' fates were known and employed by specialists or semi-specialists in England, Venice, Southern Italy, Paris, and New England in the early modern period. On the other hand, this does not seem to have played an important part in the practice of folk magic elsewhere in Germany either; see Labouvie, "Wider." It may be that it tended to be an urban phenomenon.
119. Place, pp. 9-10.
120. Place, p. 14.
121. Decker, p. 27.
122. Place, pp. 14, 25.
123. Martin, pp. 162-3; Decker, p. 50.
124. Casanova claimed that a Russian peasant girl he bought and took as his mistress in 1765 read the cards daily and mentioned a 25-card spread she used to reconstruct "a debauch which had kept me out" the night before. This is cited as the first recorded example of cartomancy by both Decker (p. 74) and Ryan, *Bathhouse*, (p. 328), but both consider it "puzzling" that a Russian peasant girl would have used a relatively sophisticated system while the practice seems to have been completely novel to the urbane Casanova. The solution to this puzzle would seem to be that Casanova only wrote his memories in the 1790s, well after

484 Notes

card reading had been popularized in France (Caldwell, n.p. [online]; see also Emery, n.p. [online]).
125. Place, pp. 31–2, 41.
126. Place, pp. 52–4.
127. Place, p. 54.
128. Decker, p. 100.
129. Decker, p. 81; Simmons, n.p. (online).
130. Martin does not mention cards in her discussion of divinatory activity in Venice, pp. 113–24, nor does Thomas, pp. 237–44, in discussing England, nor Wilson in discussing Europe as a whole, pp. 386–91. Davies, *Cunning-Folk*, mentions them only in connection with a book published in 1784, p. 46. Evidence that card reading was a widespread semiprofessional occupation among women by the beginning of the nineteenth century is given in Decker, p. 117; Wigzell, pp. 32–3.
131. In the nineteenth century card reading appears to have become the most popular form of fortune-telling; Blécourt and Usborne, p. 388.
132. A sheet with divinatory meanings of 35 tarot cards and instructions on how to lay them from mid-eighteenth century Bologna has been found (Decker et al., pp. 48–50), and Etteilla's 1770 book contains a related but distinct set of instructions and interpretations for the 7-K plus ace in each of the suits of a standard deck (Decker et al., pp. 74–5). Furthermore, Etteilla's system for standard cards implicitly assigned general themes to the suits (clubs dealing with material goods and money, diamonds with relationships, and so on).
133. Mährle discusses the use of sieve and shears to divine adulterous relationships among neighbors and to identify the mistress of a priest, in Ellwangen, in 1528, pp. 352–3.
134. Note that if it exists, ESP would seem to have a limited impact on cartomancy. To begin with, successful card-guessing experiments typically result in some modest "hit" rate above chance, whereas fully psychic cartomancy would require accurate knowledge of all of the hidden cards. Furthermore, the procedure involves shuffling the deck and then drawing off some number of cards in a set order rather than picking out individual cards, which means that not only would the identities of many of the cards need to be known at once, but also the positioning of individual cards would have to be controlled through repeated shuffling. Consequently, a fully paranormal interpretation of cartomancy would require some far more comprehensive synchronicity than most ESP research claims to have demonstrated. Alternatively, it would seem that with or without the influence of ESP, the heart of this form of fortune-telling lies in the ability of the person doing the divination to interpret the symbology of the cards as laid in relationship to the circumstances of the person whose fortune is being told. On diviners' role as "social and psychological councilor," see Goodman, *Ecstasy*, p. 50.
135. A213, b. 8417, d. 24-11-02.
136. A209, b. 1018, d. 8-5-75.
137. A209, b. 1018, d. 16-5-75.
138. Thomas, p. 285.
139. Cohen, p. 59.
140. Watson, *Supernature*, pp. 24–34.
141. McGrew and McFall, n.p. (online); Mishlove, pp. 73–81; "Skeptico," n.p. (online); Thomas, p. 286.

142. Thomas, p. 285.
143. Wilson, pp. 312–13, 319; Siraisi, pp. 67–8.
144. Mishlove, pp. 78–80.
145. Thomas, p. 286; Wilson, p. 381.
146. Mishlove, p. 71.
147. Dupuy, pp. 564–5; Durant, *Louis XIV*, p. 692.
148. *Beschreibung ... Stuttgart*, p. 448; conversion based on Durant, *Louis XIV*, p. ix.
149. Dupuy, pp. 546–8, 617–27; "Söllingen," http://www.mallfamily.org/s%C3%B6llingen.htm.
150. Barnes, pp. 142–3.
151. Barnes, p. 145.
152. Barnes, p. 153.
153. McGuire and Tanny, pp. 349, 354–60.
154. Thomas, p. 590.
155. Sabean, *Power*, pp. 62–3; see also Theibault, pp. 456–8; Haag, "Frömmigkeit," pp. 127–41; and A209, b. 1462a.
156. Sabean, *Power*, p. 70.
157. Haag, "Frömmigkeit," p. 140.
158. Sabean, *Power*, p. 84; Haag, "Frömmigkeit," p. 136.
159. Sabean, *Power*, p. 77.
160. Sabean, *Power*, p. 74.
161. Sabean, *Power*, p. 86.
162. A209, b. 1462a, dd. 73, 77.
163. Sabean, *Power*, p. 87; A209, b. 1462, d. 73.
164. A209, b. 1462a, d. 107.
165. Sabean, *Power*, p. 90.
166. A209, b. 1462a, dd. 143, 146, 165; Sabean, *Power*, p. 88.
167. Sabean, *Power*, pp. 66, 90.
168. "Lay seers" who reported similar experiences were common in late medieval and Renaissance Spain; Christian, p. 7.
169. A209, b. 1462a, d. 127.
170. Spanish apparitions also appeared as fully realized figures who walked, talked, and even touched the seers; Christian, p. 8.
171. Christian, p. 186.
172. "Revelations that bypass the sense altogether" were recorded by others, and confirmatory by signs that anyone could see were common; Christian, p. 8.
173. Sabean, *Power*, pp. 70–3.
174. Schöck, "Ende," p. 382.
175. A209, b. 593, d. 5.
176. A209, b. 593, d. 22-12-60, Lit. A and Lit. B.
177. A209, b. 593, d. 22-12-60, Lit. C.
178. A209, b. 593, d. 13-3-61.
179. A209, b. 593, d. 22.
180. Barnes, pp. 230–1.
181. Barnes, p. 258; A209, b. 593, d. 6.
182. In late medieval Spain lay seers said they saw a lady clothed in light who was "brighter than the sun," who was understood to be the Virgin Mary, but Anna spoke only of a light rather than a figure when describing her luminous visions; see Christian, p. 6.

7 Beneficent Manipulative Magic

1. Wilson, p. xxvi; Gurevich, p. 89.
2. Walther, pp. 54, 62; Roper, "Magic," p. 315; Gentilcore, *Bishop*, p. 232; Cervantes, p. 58; Winkelman, "Other," p. 343.
3. Fichtenau, p. 321; Thomas, pp. 32, 49; Labouvie, "Hexenspuk," p. 86.
4. A213, b. 8399, d. 15-2-1769.
5. This was typical for Europe: Smallwood, p. 20; Roper, *English*, p. 189; Davies, "Healing," pp. 20–8; Sulzman, pp. 7, 50; Hampp, p. 31.
6. Fox, p. 255; Kiev, p. 455; Pattison, pp. 6, 10; Lambo, p. 956; Welborne, pp. 13–14, 17; Webster, p. 500.
7. Winkelman, *Shamanism*, p. 246; McClenon, *Healing*, p. 60; Schiefenhövel, p. 62; Pócs, "Possession," p. 129.
8. McClenon, *Healing*, pp. 23, 39, 41, 43; Stutley, p. 4; Pócs, "Possession," p. 105; Gay, pp. 34–5; Thomas, p. 181.
9. Ramsey, *Medicine* p. 238; Thomas, p. 184; Gurevich, p. 95; Labouvie, "Hexenspuk," p. 74; Smallwood, p. 12; Hutton, *Triumph*, p. 97; Garrett, p. 58.
10. Thomas, pp. 182, 185, 189, 222–31; Blécourt, "Witch Doctors," p. 299; Hutton, *Triumph*, pp. 93–4.
11. O'Connor and Hufford, p. 30; Clark, *Thinking*, p. 472; Clark, "Protestant," p. 205; Roos, p. 23; Walther, pp. 64, 72.
12. Z5, 7, 14, 19; Ss1, 2, 4, 5A, 5B, 7, 9; Sg2; all Az (see the appendix).
13. Both: Z5, 7; Sg2; Az1, 5, 6; people only: Z14, 18; Ss1, 4, 5A, 5B, 7, 9; Az+, Az2, 3, 4, 7; animals only: Ss2 (see the appendix).
14. Z5, 7, 14, 18; Ss4, 5A, 5B, 7, 9; Az+, Az1, 3, 4, 5, 6 (see the appendix). Note that Blécourt, "Cunning Women," p. 54, also found that words were the most commonly used form of therapy in the seventeenth century, and Hughes, p. 31, makes the same point.
15. Medicines: Z5, 7, 14, 18; Az1, 3, 5, 7; Sg2. Actions: Z5, 7, 14, 18; Ss1, 2, 5A; Az+, Az5. Objects: Z7, 14, 18; Ss1, 7; Az2, 5, 6 (see the appendix).
16. Special instructions: Z7, 18; Ss4; Az+, Az1, 5. Symbols: Z14; Ss7. Special times: Ss4; Az1. Special place: A209, b. 468a (see the appendix).
17. Z5, 14, also Z18 and Az+; Ss5B (see the appendix).
18. Z7 (see the appendix).
19. Ss5A; Az+; Az5; Ss7 (see the appendix).
20. Az1 (see the appendix).
21. Ss4 (see the appendix).
22. A209, b. 725, d. 10.
23. A209, b. 725, d. 17.
24. Sulzman, p. 4; Holzmann, pp. 28–9.
25. Z5, Ss4 (see the appendix). However, whispering may have simply been the preferred form of utterance, since some charms were whispered around 1000, when the need for secrecy was presumably not as urgent; see Sulzman, pp. 5, 70.
26. Holzmann, pp. 31, 55; Davies, "Healing," p. 20.
27. Winkelman, "Practitioner Types," p. 36; also note that in third configuration mediums appear to develop spontaneously rather than as an outgrowth of the shamanic/shamanic-healer traditions, and are sometimes absent, in which case witches are present. There is a fourth, more complex configuration of agricultural society in which all four types – healers, priests, mediums, and witches – are present.

28. Sulzman, pp. 26, 34, 37; Roper, *English*, p. 190; Smallwood, p. 14.
29. Sulzman, p. 33; Eis, p. 12.
30. Sulzman, pp. 10, 17, 20, 65, 73; Jütte, *Ärzte*, p. 154; Hampp, p. 112; Scribner, "Disenchantment," p. 481.
31. Sulzman, pp. 18–19, 55; Smallwood, p. 11. Ryan, "Eclecticism," p. 117 notes a similar structure in "the more complex" Russian charms.
32. Sulzman, pp. 5, 45–6; Smallwood, pp. 13–15, 21; Siraisi, p. 35.
33. Smallwood, pp. 15–16.
34. Sulzman, p. 65 notes that recitation of protracted rhymes can induce trance.
35. Hampp, pp. 110–1; Pócs, "Possession," p. 104; Ramsey, *Medicine*, p. 198; Scribner, "Disenchantment," p. 482; Ohrt, "Fluchtafel," p. 16; Hampp, p. 110.
36. Hutton, p. 137; Davies, *Cunning-Folk*, pp. 177–86.
37. Sulzman, p. 44.
38. Wessling, pp. 14, 67; Az7: A209, b. 368, d. 1.
39. Z14, 18, A+5; A+1, 3; Z5 (see the appendix).
40. Z14, Z18, A+5, A+7, Sg2 (see the appendix).
41. A209, b. 368, d. 1; Az5: A209, b. 725, d. 6.
42. A209, b. 368, dd. 1, 2.
43. A209, b. 725, d. 24.
44. A209, b. 1146, d. 6; A209, b. 725, d. 22.
45. A209, b. 311a, d. 26-5-1605.
46. A209, b. 1989, d. 1 (3/14/60).
47. Hughes, *Women Healers*, p. 33.
48. A213, b. 8395, d. 28-7-1770.
49. Kieckhefer, *Magic*, p. 77.
50. Ss7 (see the appendix).
51. A209, b. 8395/1770, d. 28-7-1770; Kieckhefer, *Magic*, pp. 77–8; Fishwick, pp. 30, 34; Labouvie, "Hexenspuk," p. 62.
52. Z7: A209, b. 466a. Owen Davies notes that this sort of healing activity was part of the tradition of charming that was carried on with less interference by the authorities than the activities of cunning folk; *Cunning-Folk*, pp. 83–4. There was one other known case involving an investigation of it in Württemberg: A209, b. 254.
53. A209, b. 725, d. 29, Extract 1.
54. Az2 (see the appendix).
55. Az6 (see the appendix).
56. A209, 468a; A213, b. 8399.
57. A209, b. 368, dd. 1, 3, 18-5-08; Az+; A213, b. 8395/70, d. 3-9-1770.
58. A209, b. 723, d. 2; A213, b. 8406, d. 6-2-1761.
59. A209, b. 725, d. 1.
60. Z5, 7, 14, 18; Ss1, 2, 4, 5A; Az+, Az5 (see the appendix).
61. Wilson, pp. 280, 327.
62. Z7 (see the appendix).
63. A209, b. 22, d. 1; Z18, d. 2; Az+ (see the appendix). Passing the hands over an injury was still practiced in Württemberg in the twentieth century; Walther, p. 78.
64. A209, b. 725, d. 5. Blowing was still practiced by folk healers in Württemberg in the twentieth century; Walther, p. 80.
65. A209, b. 723, d. 2.
66. A209, b. 723, d. 2; A209, b. 311a, d. 26-5-1605.
67. A209, b. 725, d. 29, Extract 1.

68. A209, b. 725 d. 17; Ss4: A209, b. 1855, p. 3.
69. A209, b. 725, d. 24.
70. A209, b. 1424(1589), d. 1; A209, b. 1338, d. 2.
71. A209, b. 725: d. 28; Z14: d. 2.
72. A209, b. 468a.
73. Z7 (see the appendix).
74. A209, b. 1878, d. 10.
75. Wilson, p. 455. Although Holzmann says that special times and days were common in medieval German incantations (pp. 47–51) this was not the case in early modern Scotland (Miller, "Devices," p. 102). Some days were thought to have magical significance in early twentith-century Württemberg (Walther, pp. 65, 75, 144–5), and, we have seen some were mentioned in early modern magic in the duchy, but overall, as in Scotland, they seem to have been of limited significance.
76. A209, b. 1855, p. 2.
77. Miller, "Devices," p. 101; Walther, pp. 65–7.
78. Sulzman, p. 22; Davies, "Healing," p. 29.
79. Jütte, Ärzte, p. 154.
80. Charms and blessings were often recorded without the ritual actions that accompanied them; see Roper, "Introduction," p. 6.
81. Ramsey, "Medicine," pp. 182, 236; Wessling, pp. 17, 63, 65–6; Lindmann, p. 166; Siraisi, p. 177; Walther, p. 74; Hughes, pp. 93–4; Hampp, p. 31; Jütte, Ärzte, pp. 149–50.
82. Az7; Ss9 (see the appendix). Weylandt denied using blessings in A209, b. 368, d. 2, but it is seems to have admitted using "gottes segen" in d. 1. Note that in Scotland, only 3 percent of charms relied on words alone, while 92 percent involved some physical action; Miller, "Devices," p. 98.
83. Az+ (see the appendix).
84. A209, b. 725, d. 29, Extract 1.
85. A209, b. 723, d. 2.
86. A209, b. 311a, d. 2.
87. Gentilcore, "Was there," pp. 151–2.
88. Walther, pp. 76–7, 81, 87.
89. Hughes, p. 35; Beck, p. 35.
90. Welborne, pp. 13–14, 17; Webster, p. 500; Hampp, p. 33; O'Connor and Hufford, p. 28.
91. McClenon, *Healing*, p. 62; Wortley, p. 159; Walther, p. 75; Hoppál, "System," p. 121.
92. Kehoe, p. 28; Thomas, p. 208; MacFarlane, pp. 128–9.
93. Labouvie, "Hexenspuk," p. 59; Hampp, p. 58; Pócs, "Possession," p. 104; Sulzman, p. 11.
94. Harpur, p. 186; Biedermann, p. 166; Hampp, p. 33; McClenon, *Healing*, p. 95; Csordas, *Sacred*, p. 3.
95. MacFarlane, p. 129.
96. Moerman and Jonas, pp. 471–2; Hafen, *Mind/Body*, p. 430.
97. Laderman and Roseman, p. 7; Hafen, *Mind/Body*, p. 434.
98. Hafen, *Mind/Body*, p. 431; Wortley, p. 160, for example, discusses healing relics as placebos.
99. Achterberg, p. 4; Wall, pp. 164–5; Hutton, *Shamans*, p. 53.
100. Moerman and Jonas, p. 472; Wall, p. 171.
101. Vyse, p. 136.

Notes 489

102. Davies, "Healing," p. 30.
103. Moerman and Jonas, p. 473; Laderman and Roseman, p. 7.
104. Moerman and Jonas, p. 473; Bloom, p. 112.
105. Wall, p. 168.
106. Hutton, *Triumph*, pp. 95–7.
107. Briggs, "Fancie," p. 262.
108. Davies, "Cunning-Folk in England and Wales," pp. 98–9; Taussig, p. 276. It is interesting to note that modern doctors often consciously prescribe placebos when there is nothing else to do, which is about 40 percent of the time, "according to one pharmacology textbook (Hafen, *Mind/Body*, p. 431).
109. Hafen, *Mind/Body*, pp. 434–6; Ray, p. 100; Schwartz, "NIH," p. 8.
110. Hafen, *Mind/Body*, p. 434.
111. Miladinovic, "Method," n.p. (online).
112. Wall, p. 169.
113. Miladinovic, *Emile Coue Web Site*, Main Page, and "Method."
114. Winkelman, *Shamanism*, p. 87.
115. Achterberg, pp. 122–3, 127.
116. Felten, p. 219.
117. Achterberg, pp. 114–5.
118. Achterberg, p. 6; Laderman and Roseman, p. 8.
119. Levi-Strauss, "Shamans," p. 110; Walther, p. 81.
120. Oubré, pp. 177, 179.
121. Oubré, pp. 170, 184; Winkelman, *Shamanism*, p. 193.
122. Newberg et al., pp. 80, 84; Marshall, p. 133; McClenon, *Healing*, p. 25; McNeill, *Together*, pp. 2, 8; Hafen, *Mind/Body*, p. 261.
123. Felten, p. 220; Hafen, *Mind/Body*, pp. 297–305; Frecska and Kulcsar, p. 70.
124. Frecska and Kulcsar, p. 70; Newberg et al., p. 131.
125. Kemeny, p. 198; Hafen, *Mind/Body*, p. 345.
126. Sabean, *Power*, p. 54.
127. Alver and Selberg, p. 22; Samuel, p. 117; Winkelman, *Shamanism*, p. 99.
128. Hafen, *Mind/Body*, p. 302.
129. Lex, "Voodoo," p. 821.
130. Achterberg, p. 114; "A Mirror," p. 87.
131. Iacoboin and Lenzi, p. 39; "A Mirror," p. 87.
132. Somby-Borgstram, n.p. (online).
133. Hawaleshka, p. 23.
134. "A Mirror," p. 87.
135. Laderman and Roseman, p. 6; Sebald, "Shaman," p. 313; Hutton, *Triumph*, p. 95; Devisch, p. 411.
136. Laderman and Roseman, p. 6.
137. Newberg, p. 131.
138. Bryan, pp. 28–9, 32; Newberg, p. 7.
139. McClenon, *Healing*, pp. 23–4, 28; Winkelman, "Other," pp. 322–3.
140. Schwartz, *Mind*, p. 307.
141. See Chap. 4.
142. Goodman, "Neurophysiology," p. 378.
143. Only three of the sampled cases involved the patient praying or incanting him or herself (Ss4; Az+, Az5), while in twelve the healer or a parent recited it (Z5, 7, 18; Ss4, 5A, 5B, 9; Az1, 3, 4, 5, 7);see the appendix. A209, b. 725, d. 28.
144. Klass, p. 120.
145. Klass, p. 123; Ilomäki, p. 47.

146. Wier, p. 120; Winkelman, *Shamanism*, p. 102.
147. Lex, "Voodoo," pp. 819–20; Winkelman, *Shamanism*, p. 114.
148. Laughlin et al., p. 147; Winkelman, *Shamanism*, pp. 191–5.
149. Rasmussen, p. 82.
150. McClenon, *Healing*, pp. 8, 47, 92; Newberg et al., p. 80; see, for example, Rasmussen, p. 82.
151. Az+, Ss7, Az5 (see the appendix).
152. Winkelman, *Shamanism*, p. 198; Lederman and Roseman, pp. 7–8.
153. Hafen, *Mind/Body*, p. 30.
154. Achterberg, p. 85; Kehoe, p. 28; Winkelman, *Shamanism*, p. 100.
155. Oubré, pp. 179–81.
156. Hafen, *Mind/Body*, p. 387; Winkelman, *Shamanism*, p. 195.
157. See Chap. 5.
158. McClenon, *Healing*, p. 28 (hypnosis and relaxation-related).
159. Laughlin et al., pp. 169, 212; Winkelman, *Shamanism*, p. 244.
160. Winkelman, *Shamanism*, p. 245.
161. Laughlin et al., pp. 169, 190.
162. Felten, pp. 215, 218, 219; *Understanding the Immune System*, p. 36; Harpur, p. 152; McClenon, *Healing*, p. 96.
163. Achterberg, pp. 9–10; Kemeny, p. 209; Felten, pp. 214, 220.
164. Winkelman, *Shamanism*, pp. 244–6; Laughlin et al., pp. 193–6.
165. McNamara, p. 250.
166. Pert, "Chemical," pp. 179–81, 184–6; Pert, *Molecules*, pp. 130, 145–8, 178.
167. Pert, "Chemical," pp. 185–6, 190.
168. Pert, "Chemical," pp. 185–6, Kemeny, p. 197.
169. Kemeny, pp. 195–9.
170. Winkelman, *Shamanism*, p. 195.
171. Laderman and Roseman, p. 3, emphasis in the original.
172. Hafen, *Mind/Body*, p. 285.
173. Hafen, *Mind/Body*, p. 286.
174. Wardell and Weymouth, p. 154.
175. Winkelman, *Shamanism*, p. 100.
176. O'Connor and Hufford, p. 22.
177. Thomas, pp. 192–200; Wilson, p. 344.
178. A209, b. 22, d. 1; see Chap. 5.
179. Mishlove, pp. 99–104.
180. Mishlove, pp. 322–5; Targ and Katra, pp. 109–11.
181. Targ and Katra, p. 239; Harpur, p. 136.
182. Targ and Katra, p. 240.
183. Mishlove, p. 324; Astin et al., p. 906.
184. Targ and Katra, pp. 208–9; Radin, "Event-Related," pp. 315–23; Standish, pp. 307–14; Richards et al., pp. 955–63.
185. Astin et al., pp. 905, 908–9.
186. Targ and Katra, p. 241.
187. Mishlove, p. 324.
188. Probst, p. 44.
189. Heal: W11, 13, 14, 15, 22, 23; Z4, 9, 14; Az5 (see the appendix). Request remove: W4, 13, 22. Remove object: W4. Counteraction: Ss2, Az6 (see the appendix). (Note that two other cases that were not sampled also involved countermagic: A213, 8406/1773; 8419a.)

190. Walther, p. 67; Clark, *Thinking*, p. 441; Rowlands, "Witchcraft and Popular Religion," p. 114; MacFarlane, pp. 103–4; Newall, *Egg*, pp. 90–2; Labouvie, "Hexenspuk," p. 70; Bever, "Countermagic," pp. 221–3.
191. Labouvie, "Hexenspuk," pp. 71–2 emphasizes the active responses.
192. W4 (see the appendix).
193. Doctor or healer consulted: W2, 3, 5, 7, 10, 11, 13, 14, 15, 22, 26, 27; Home remedies used: W23, 24; Diabolism; no injured party: W1 (acts of *maleficium* in past), 6, 8, 9, 12, 17, 20, 21, 25; theft: W12, 20 (see the appendix).
194. W16 and W19 (see the appendix).
195. W18 (see the appendix).
196. W26, also 3 and 22 (see the appendix).
197. A209, b. 449, d. 1; also d. 2.
198. W2 (see the appendix).
199. A209, b. 852, d. 8-8-11.
200. Answers.com, "Middle High German," http://www.answers.com/topic/middle-high-german; Answers.com, "Gemütlich," http://www.answers.com/topic/gem-tlich.
201. A209, b. 459a, d. 1.
202. Stannard, pp. 36–40.
203. Winkelman, *Shamanism*, pp. 193, 209–17.
204. Official: W2, 3, 10, 26; "popular": W22, 11, 13, 4, 14, 27 (see the appendix).
205. W5; others: 7, 15 (see the appendix).
206. Cases with health issues but no medical measures: W16, 18, 19, 24 (see the appendix).
207. Briggs, *Neighbors*, p. 185, noted that a similar proportion of witch trials in Lorraine (25 %) involved consultations with cunning folk. Many scholars emphasize the role of cunning folk in witchcraft suspicions and witchcraft suspicions in the activities of cunning folk: see Davies, "Market-Place," p. 73; Gildrie p. 288; Blécourt, "Witch Doctors," p. 302.
208. W8, also 17; W1, 6, 9, 12, 21, 25; W20 (see the appendix).
209. W16; also 19, 24 (see the appendix).
210. W2 (see the appendix).
211. Ss2, 5a, 5b; Az1, 5, 6; Z14 (see the appendix).
212. A209, b. 1878, d. 1.
213. A209, b. 725, esp. dd. 24, 28.
214. Blécourt, "Witch Doctors," p. 298 notes that this possibility was recognized all over Europe.
215. Klaniczay, "Witch-Hunting," p. 167.
216. Dillinger, *Böse*, p. 150.
217. A213, b. 8406, d. 6-2-61; A213, b. 8406, d. 24-4-62.
218. Ss2 (see the appendix).
219. Favret-Saada, "Unbewitching," pp. 46–9.
220. W23 (see the appendix).
221. Dillinger, *Böse*, p. 150.
222. A213, b. 8419/1740.
223. Labouvie, "Hexenspuk," p. 70.
224. A213, b. 8395/1770, d. 28-7-1770.
225. A213, b. 8395/1770, d. 3-9-1770.
226. A213, b. 8422/1747, d. 26-10-1747; A209, b. 433, d. 1.
227. Hutton, *Triumph*, pp. 96–7; Bönisch, p. 69.

228. Furst, p. 83.
229. A209, b. 552, d. 6-6-73.
230. Hafen, *Mind/Body*, p. 7.
231. "Menopause and Acne," n.p. (online).
232. "What is Psoriasis?" n.p. (online).
233. Z7 (see the appendix), A209, b. 466a, d. 24-1-60.
234. A209, b. 1634a, d. 21-8-68.
235. A209. 1634a, d. 21-8-68.
236. *HddA*, VII, pp. 1058–71.
237. *Malleus Maleficarum*, pp. 150–4.
238. Stuart, p. 161; Roper, "Magic," p. 319.
239. Walther, p. 91.
240. Alexander et al., p. 78; Fichtenau, p. 323.
241. Labouvie, "Hexenspuk," p. 70.
242. Lissner, p. 245. Vyse argues, pp. 81, 101, that "lucky behavior" before performances is superstitious and that "fluctuations in performance are a natural feature of any random enterprise" and that "hot" streaks are statistically "consistent with a simple random process" seems to overlook the importance of psychological factors in physical performance, particularly the fact that athletes perform at a heightened level of skill to which "lucky behavior" and "lucky" objects contribute, so that the mean around which their performance fluctuates is itself at an artificially induced high level, and periods of particular concentration and skillfulness are needed to maintain this against the periods when a high level of performance can't be sustained. He himself seems to acknowledge the basis for this when he notes that a "sense of control ... is associated with a more favorable response to ... setbacks" and "an optimistic attitude of self-deception is more effective" than realistic self-appraisal (pp. 131–2). See also Baumeister, pp. 177–8.
243. Lex, "Neurobiology," p. 140.
244. Herrigel, pp. 41, 54, 66.
245. Jaynes, pp. 25–7.
246. A209, b. 238, d. 27-6-1705.
247. A209, b. 238, d. 22-7-1705.
248. A209, b. 39, d. "Protocol".
249. A209, b. 1436.
250. A209, b. 1388, d. 8-10-1709.
251. "Passauer Schutzzauber," n.p. (online).
252. Gb5 (see the appendix).
253. Maxwell-Stuart, "Alchemy," pp. 27–9.
254. Gb5 (see the appendix).
255. A209, b. 1373; A213, b. 8413/1748, A213, b. 8401/1792.
256. Fischer, p. 276.
257. Sg7 (see the appendix); A209, b. 525, dd. 5, 24.
258. A209, b. 1878, d. 3.
259. A209, b. 536.
260. A209, b. 433, d. 26-5-96.
261. A209, b. 1176.
262. A213, b. 8406/1773, d. 15-4-73.
263. A209, b. 517, d. 1.
264. A209, b. 517, d. 6-3-1724.
265. Carroll, n.p. (online). "Ball Lightning Scientists," n.p. (online).
266. Turner, pp. 435–6; Wessel-Berg, pp. 439–40, 470–1, 474–6.

267. Turner, p. 435.
268. Wessel-Berg, p. 439.
269. Singer, pp. 7–8.
270. "Scientists Remain in the Dark," n.p. (online).
271. A209, b. 517.
272. A209, b. 909, d. 1.
273. A209, b. 909, d. 3.
274. A209, b. 909, d. 4.
275. Rogo, pp. 40–1.
276. A209, b. 14.
277. A209, b. 238, d. 27-6-1704.
278. Z15 (see the appendix).
279. A209, b. 226, d. 1.
280. A209, b. 226, dd. 1, 3.
281. A209, b. 226, d. 4.
282. A209, b. 226, d. 5.
283. See, for example Sharpe, *Bewitching*, pp. 44–5; Clark, *Thinking*, pp. 153–4, 177.
284. A209, bb. 1584 and 1589; Weber, *Verführte*, pp. 229–33.
285. Rogo, p. 78.
286. Persinger and Lafrenière, pp. 101–2, 201; Braud and Dennis, p. 1989; Roll, p. 84.
287. Rogo, pp. 38–41.
288. Moss, pp. 331–2; Roll, pp. 76–7.
289. Mishlove, pp. 232–40; Watson, *Supernature*, pp. 118–20; Rogo, pp. 20–31; Parker and Brusewitz, pp. 40–2; Braud, pp. 2–5; Durrani, n.p. (online); Pallikari, n.p. (online).
290. Jeffers, abstract; Etzold, pp. 367–9; Alcock, pp. 34–8.
291. Utts, p. 377; Radin, *Entangled*, pp. 146–58; Alcock, pp. 42–4.

8 Magic and Society

1. Rublack, "Luthertum," p. 102.
2. Examples of Catholic clergy: Sg4, Gb6 (see the appendix), A213, b. 8409/99; gypsies: Frick, pp. 408–24; Itinerant: Z5.
3. Davies, *Cunning-Folk*, pp. 83–4.
4. Ss1, 2, 3, 4, 5A, 5B, 9; Az+, Az1, 3, 4, 5, 6, 7 (see the appendix).
5. Sg1, 2, 4, 6, 8, 9, 13; Gb4, 5, 6 (see the appendix).
6. Zns (see the appendix).
7. Z5, 7, 14, 18; Z6, 7, 10, 12, 17 (see the appendix).
8. Similar specialized practitioners have also been found to have been very widespread in other parts of Germany and Europe: see Labouvie, "Hexenspuk," p. 77; Rowlands, "Witchcraft and Popular Religion," p. 115; Holzmann, p. 37; Hampp, p. 15; Broedel, p. 151; Ramsey, *Medicine*, pp. 238, 253; Garrett, "Witches and Cunning Folk," p. 56; Henningsen, *Advocate*, p. 303; Ortega, p. 58; Clark, *Thinking*, p. 457; Clark, "Protestant," p. 205; MacFarlane, pp. 115–21.
9. Public healing services offered in cases: Ss1, 2, 4, 5A, 5B, 9; Az+, Az1, 3, 4, 5, 6, 7; Sg2; Z5, 7, 14, 18. Identifying and locating services offered by public practitioners, in Ss2, 3, 5B; Az1, 6; Gb4. Treasure-finding, in Sg1, 2, 4, 6, 8, 9, 13; Gb5, 6. (See the appendix.)
10. The range of services they offered is comparable to those found in other regions of Europe, except that, as noted before, there was little evidence of the fortune-telling

regarding love and general fate until the very end of the period. See Blécourt, "Witch Doctors," p. 299; Davies, *Cunning-Folk*, pp. 73, 79, 87.
11. Z7; Sg6, 8, 9, 13; Gb5, 6 (see the appendix).
12. Ss4 (see the appendix).
13. Ss1; Sg2 (see the appendix).
14. Az1 (see the appendix).
15. General practitioners: Ss1, 2, 3, 5A, 5B; Az1, 3, 5, 7; Sg1, 2, 4; Gb4; Z5, 14, 18. Specialized: Ss4, Ss9; Az+, Az4, 6; Sg6, 8, 9, 13; Gb4, 5, 6 (see the appendix).
16. Healing: Ss4, 9; Az+, Az4; Z7. Treasure hunting: Sg6, 8, 9, 13; Gb5, 6; Zns) (see the appendix).
17. Az6 (see the appendix).
18. Healing: Ss1, 2, 4, 5A, 5B; Az1, 3, 5, 7; Sg1, 2; Z5, 14, 18. Treasure hunting: Sg1, 2, 4; Z5. Witchcraft: Ss2, 3, 5B; Az1, 5; Z14. Theft: Ss2, 3; Gb4. Locate and exorcize: Ss3, Az1, Gb4. (See Appendix.)
19. Father: Az+; Z7. "Aunt": Ss4. Man: Ss4. Other treasure hunter: Sg13. Itinerant: Ss9. Book: Gb5 (see the appendix).
20. Z5; Az1; Gb4. Father: Ss4. (See the appendix.)
21. Not given: Sg8. Occupations only: Sg9. (See the appendix.)
22. Z5 (see the appendix).
23. Generalists from towns: Ss4, Gb4, Z14. Single-service providers from towns: Ss4, Ss9; Gb5, 6; Zns. (See the appendix.) The results are similar to but not as one-sided as the urban/rural split reported by Rowlands, "Witchcraft and Popular Religion," p. 115.
24. Officials: Sg13; Zns; Sg6; Gb5. Tradesmen: Gb4; Ss3; Z7; Ss4; Az7; Z14; Az3. Charcoal-maker (Sg4). Herders: Az3; Sg9; Az5. Forest ranger, etc.: Sg9; Zns; Gb6; Ss1; Az6; Z5. (See the appendix.) These occupations are roughly comparable to those found elsewhere; see Holzmann, p. 37; Ramsey, *Medicine*, pp. 176, 216–17; MacFarlane, p. 167; Davies, *Cunning-Folk*, pp. 68–71, although herders seem to be less prominent than in some other areas; Garrett, "Witches and Cunning Folk," p. 60.
25. Poor: Ss1, 2, 5A; Az1, 6; Sg1, 6; Z5, 14. Well off: Az5, 7; Sg13. (See the appendix.)
26. Ramsey, *Medicine*, pp. 202, 218–19; Blécourt, "Cunning Women," p. 54.
27. Durant, "The Age of Reason Begins," p. ix, and "Rousseau and Revolution," p. ix.
28. Thomas, pp. 248–50; Davies, "Marketplace," pp. 71–2; Davies, "Cunning Folk in England and Wales," p. 95; Tangherlini, p. 295; Roper, "Magic,", p. 318.
29. Well regarded: Az+, 7. Bad reputations: Ss3, 4, 5A, Az1, 3, 5; Sg4, Gb4; Ss3; Az1. (See the appendix.)
30. It was not unusual in other areas for cunning folk to be similarly feared and disliked in their own communities; see Garrett, "Witches and Cunning folk," p. 59; Barstow, p. 117.
31. Ss3, Az1 (see the appendix).
32. Ss5A; Gb4; Az5, 6; Sg1; Z5 (see the appendix).
33. Az7, Ss1 (see the appendix).
34. Ss4 and Az7 (see the appendix); for the record, two of the suspects in these cases were generalists, and two were specialists.
35. Tolley, p. 67.
36. Southwestern Germany: Dillinger, *Böse*, p. 145. England: Davies, "Cunning Folk in England and Wales," p. 94; Holland and the Saarland: Blécourt, "Witch Doctors," p. 301. On the other hand, Gurevich, p. 83, argues that women healers were more common in medieval Europe, while Gentilcore, *Bishop*, p. 155

Notes 495

reports that they were more common in early modern Italy; Halpern and Foley, pp. 905–6 reports the same for the modern Balkans, and Blécourt, "Witch Doctors," p. 301, similarly for Cologne. Overall the anthropological record suggests that men take the role of public healers more often then women; see Winkelman, "Other," p. 333.

37. Strauss, *House*, p. 299; Estes, pp. 102–3; Tolley, pp. 64, 156 emphasizes that there were results, but doesn't provide evidence of anything this dramatic.
38. Blécourt, "Cunning Women," p. 44; Watson, "Hidden," p. 25.
39. A209, b. 459a, d. 1.
40. Gehring, p. 169.
41. W17 and 26 (see the appendix). Also, Mormando, "Bernardino," p. 134.
42. Ss2, 7; Az2; Z6, 7, 10, 12, 15, 17 (see the appendix).
43. Z12 (see the appendix).
44. Z7 (see the appendix).
45. A213, b. 8401/1769, Protocollem 10-1-69, p. 9.
46. Robischeaux, *Rural Society*, pp. 11–13; Warde, pp. 198–9.
47. Vann, pp. 62–3.
48. Vann, pp. 39–40; Scribner, "Police," pp. 106–7; Marcus, pp. 9–13; Wegert, p. 25; Wintterlin, p. 55; Gehring, p. 191.
49. Marcus, p. 10.
50. Vann, pp. 39–40, 99.
51. Gehring, p. 164.
52. Ogilvie, p. 58; Wegert, p. 25.
53. Wegert, pp. 24–5; Vann, p. 40; Scribner, "Police," p. 107; Ernst, *6000 Jahre*, pp. 205–7, 232–6; Knapp, p. 6.
54. Ogilvie, pp. 57, 72.
55. Scribner, "Police," pp. 107–10.
56. Gehring, pp. 167–9.
57. Wegert, pp. 97–110.
58. Wegert, pp. 97, 101.
59. Wegert, pp. 90–1; Bever, "Wuerttemberg," pp. 183–92.
60. Wegert, pp. 90–1; Spierenberg, "Body and State," p. 62.
61. Weller, p. 196; Spierenberg, "Body and State," pp. 72–6; Spierenberg, *Experience*, pp. 173–5; Nagel, p. 37.
62. Wegert, p. 95; Gehring, pp. 16–25.
63. See Chap. 6.
64. Bever, "Wuerttemberg," p. 153.
65. Gehring, pp. 170, 391.
66. Ogilvie, p. 58.
67. Wegert, p. 21.
68. *Godly Magistrates*, p. 21.
69. Wegert, pp. 22–4; Scharfe, "Distances," pp. 159, 161.
70. See Chap. 3.
71. Scharfe, "Distances," p. 159.
72. Wegert, p. 26; Hasselhorn, pp. 59, 61.
73. Estes, p. 96. It should be noted that excommunication was resented by the populace and little enforced by the secular arm, so it was seldom used.
74. Methuen, pp. 844–9.
75. Gehring, p. 169.
76. Also Scharfe, "Distances," p. 161.
77. Luther, "Small Catechism," p. 5; "Large Catechism – Part First," p. 1.

78. Scharfe, "Distances," p. 159.
79. Methuen, p. 849; Scharfe, Distances," pp. 159–60; also, see Chap. 3.
80. Luther, "Small Catechism," pp. 2–3.
81. Fulbrook, p. 69.
82. Methuen, p. 850.
83. Haag, *Predigt*, p. 340.
84. Wessling, p. 10.
85. Wessling, pp. 61–7; Nestlen, *Bekämpfung*, p. 4.
86. Nestlen, *Hebammen*, pp. 20–1.
87. Nestlen, *Bekämpfung*, pp. 3–7; Nestlen, *Hebammen*, p. 3.
88. Nestlen, *Bekämpfung*, pp. 7–8.
89. Nestlen, *Hebamme*, p. 8; Nestlen, *Bekämpfung*, p. 13.
90. Nestlen, *Bekämpfung*, p. 15.
91. Nestlen, *Bekämpfung*, p. 24.
92. Wegert, pp. 28, 35, 37, 88; Ogilvie, pp. 44, 83, 396–7.
93. Ogilvie, p. 45.
94. Wegert, p. 35.
95. Wegert, pp. 31, 87.
96. Wegert, pp. 32–4.
97. This concern was expressed in the disputes over the burial of both Dorothea Richer, A209, b. 327, d. 4-4-78 (see Chap. 3) and Jacobina Hutelerin, A209, b. 517, d. 6-3-1724 (see Chap. 7).
98. Wegert, pp. 34, 120.
99. Ogilvie, p. 59.
100. Ogilvie, pp. 66–70.
101. Ernst, *6000 Jahre*, p. 194.
102. Ogilvie, pp. 61–5.
103. Ogilvie, p. 53.
104. Ogilvie, p. 51.
105. Wegert, p. 89.
106. Wegert, p. 33; emphasis in original.
107. Wegert, p. 34.
108. Ogilvie, pp. 65, 72.
109. Fulbrook, p. 68.
110. Vann, p. 41.
111. Walker, p. 101.
112. Walker, pp. 57–8.
113. Walker, p. 103.
114. Walker, pp. 106, 134.
115. Walker, pp. 56–8; Vann, p. 42.
116. Gebhardt, pp. 111, 247.
117. Gebhardt, pp. 111–27.
118. Note that in common usage "*Ehrbarkeit*" was a slippery term, and depending on who was using it and when it was used could refer to everyone addressed as "Herr," or (increasingly over time) was restricted to the notables of the district seats and the members of the central government who came from their ranks; see Gebhardt, p. 246. However, for the sake of clarity here, the terms "notables" and "notablity" used for the inclusive sense, and "honorables" and "honorability" are used in the narrower sense.
119. Vann, p. 42.
120. Gebhardt, pp. 31, 87, 246–7.

121. Gebhardt, pp. 90–3.
122. Gebhardt, p. 102.
123. Vann, pp. 81–3.
124. Vann, pp. 63–4.
125. Marcus, pp. 13–17.
126. Vann, pp. 79–83.
127. Walker, p. 128.
128. Walker, p. 127.
129. Lehmann, pp. 25, 33, 51; Weller and Weller, p. 181; Fulbrook, p. 7.
130. Vann, pp. 135–7.
131. Vann, p. 161.
132. Vann, p. 173.
133. Vann, pp. 177, 193.
134. Vann, p. 259.
135. Vann, p. 268.
136. Vann, pp. 248, 250.
137. Vann, pp. 121, 128.
138. Vann, pp. 189–93.
139. Vann, p. 250.
140. Barrett, *Culture*, pp. 63–7.
141. Spence, "Action," p. 224; Sierra and Berrios, p. 279.
142. Donald, pp. 228–9; Zeman, p. 217.
143. Bell, p. 8; Spence, "Lying," p. 258; Joseph, *Neuropsychiatry*, p. 553.
144. Oakley, pp. 249, 251; Joseph, *Neuropsychiatry*, pp. 552–3; Sierra and Berrios, p. 267; Spence, "Action," p. 222.
145. Spence, "Action," p. 223; Joseph, *Neuropsychiatry*, p. 553.
146. Brown, "Dissociation," p. 139; Zeman, p. 219.
147. Brewin, pp. 176–7; Zeman, pp. 217, 219; Ferrai, p. 77.
148. Bell, p. 8.
149. Halligan, p. xv.
150. Halligan, pp. xiii, xvii.
151. Halligan, p. xiii.
152. Deeley, p. 51.
153. Barrett, *Culture*, p. 67.
154. Joseph, *Neuropsychiatry*, p. 571.
155. Ferrai, p. 79; Spence, "Action," p. 228.
156. Spence, "Action," p. 211; Spence, "Cognitive Executive," p. 222.
157. Joseph, *Neuropsychiatry*, pp. 523, 536, 538, 563.
158. Joseph, *Neuropsychiatry*, pp. 526–7, 564–5.
159. Joseph, *Neuropsychiatry*, pp. 528–9, 555.
160. Joseph, *Neuropsychiatry*, pp. 535–6.
161. Joseph, *Neuropsychiatry*, pp. 126–7, 528–9, 536, 538, 565.
162. Joseph, *Neuropsychiatry*, pp. 532–4, 553, 565.
163. Bell et al., pp. 9–10.
164. For example, the right hemisphere can recognize emotion in other peoples' faces and even tone of voice (both of which, as we saw in Chapter 1, were important ways of communicating the ill-will that could cause or contribute to illness) but does not have the ability to express these realizations verbally; Joseph, *Neuropsychiatry*, p. 527.
165. Joseph, *Neuropsychiatry*, p. 553.
166. Bever, "Wuerttemberg," pp. 373–4; Sauer, "Not und Armut," p. 137.

498   Notes

167. Note that approximate population figures for each decade were calculated using Franz's figure for 1630 and Hippel's growth rates for the period before the 30 Years' War, and Franz's figures for 1640 and 1652 plus Knapp's figure for 1789 and assumed growth rates of .007/year from 1653 to 1749 and .008 from 1749 and after.
168. Bever, "Magic and Religion," p. 692.
169. Segelmann, p. 2; Baroja, p. 40.
170. Bever, "Magic and Religion," pp. 692–3.
171. Bever, "Magic and Religion," pp. 694–5; Bever, "Wuerttemberg," pp. 32–9.
172. Segelmann, p. 69.
173. Segelmann, p. 70.
174. Bever, "Magic and Religion," p. 694; Bever, "Magic, Learned," pp. 700–2; Bever, "Wuerttemberg," pp. 39–40.
175. Raith, "Württemberg" in *Encyclopedia*, p. 1228; Raith, "Oberrat," p. 105; Midelfort, *Witch Hunting*, pp. 202–3; Willburger, pp. 135–7.
176. Gehring, pp. 167–8.
177. Gehring, p. 169.
178. Raith, "1592," pp. 91–2.
179. Midelfort, *Witch Hunting*, pp. 202–3; Willburger, pp. 136–8.
180. W1, and see Chap. 3.
181. Lorenz, p. 255.
182. Gehring, p. 165; Raith, "Oberrat," p. 103.
183. Stälin, p. 813; Weller and Weller, p. 171.
184. Raith, "Oberrat," p. 105.
185. Midelfort, *Witch Hunting*, pp. 202–9. Anita Raith reported to me in a discussion on February 27, 2007, that she knows of a small number of oaths to keep the peace resulting from local trials in the ducal archives that Midelfort does not list, but that they do not significantly change the overall trend.
186. Raith, "Oberrat," p. 109.
187. Gladwell, pp. 7, 9, 12–4.
188. Midelfort, *Witch Hunting*, pp. 66, 202–7, 262–70.
189. Weller and Weller, pp. 97–9; Gehring, pp. 390–1.
190. Note that it was reduced in the *Manudaktion* of 1621 if a *corpus delicti* and evidence of a crime was found, but since physical evidence was rarely found in witchcraft and magic cases, the impact of this on them was limited (Gehring, p. 172).
191. W20 (see the appendix).
192. W2 (see the appendix).
193. Midelfort, *Witch Hunting*, p. 85.
194. Raith, "1592," pp. 85–6 and personal communication.
195. A209, b. 844, d. 26.
196. Raith, "1592," discusses this trial in detail.
197. Labouvie, "Hexenspuk," pp. 77, 87, on Devil's lack of involvement in traditional witch fears and countermagic.
198. W15; W12 (see the appendix), and see Chap. 4.
199. A209, b. 1430, and see Chap. 4.
200. A209, b. 1753, and see Chap. 5.
201. A209, b. 1092, and see Chap. 5.
202. W10; W7 (see the appendix), and see Chap. 1.
203. W16; W5 (see the appendix), and see Chap. 1.
204. In a systematic sample of every other town contained in the archival index for the ducal High Council, the number of criminal prosecutions of all types rose from 39 in the 1610s to 70 in the 1620s, but then fell to 34 in the 1630s and 25

in the 1640s before rising again to 55 in the 1650s and 103 in the 1660s. Similarly, between 1623 and 1631 each of the three volumes of consultations by the Tübingen law faculty (volumes 5–7) covered an average of 3.2 years, while between 1648 and 1659 each of the three volumes (9–12) covered just 2.8 years. In contrast, only a single volume (8) was needed to include the consultations from the years in which Württemberg was directly affected by the war, 1632 to 1648, and still had room for some of the material from 1649 to 1653, for a total of 21 years in the single volume (Bever, "Wuerttemberg," Figures 2.4a and 2.4b).
205. Midelfort, *Witch Hunting*, pp. 162–3, 192, 195.
206. Kneubuehler, p. 176.
207. Midelfort, *Witch Hunting*, pp. 24, 34–56; Bever, "Crisis," pp. 145–8, 158–9.
208. Molitor, pp. 64–5.
209. Midelfort, *Witch Hunting*, pp. 34–41.
210. Zsindely, pp. 55–6, 74.
211. Baxter, pp. 68–70; Paulus, p. 87; Zilboorg, p. 149.
212. Lerchheimer, pp. 21–3, 41–6, 51–3; Midelfort, "Weyer," p. 250.
213. Midelfort, *Witch Hunting*, pp. 46–7, 50–2.
214. Weber-Unger, p. 91; Levack, "Decline," p. 8; Midelfort, *Witch Hunting*, p. 27; Kneubuehler, pp. 160, 164, 90; Midelfort, "Weyer," p. 253.
215. Midelfort, *Witch Hunting*, p. 54; Gehring, pp. 32–3.
216. Bever, "Crisis," pp. 149–51.
217. Gehring, pp. 164, 397; Bernhard, p. 20.
218. Schnabel-Schüle, pp. 91–5; Raith, "Oberrat," p. 117 .
219. Gehring, pp. 160–3, 378–81.
220. Levack, "Decline," p. 18.
221. Midelfort, *Witch Hunting*, p. 191.
222. This conclusion is based on a time-stratified, proportional sample of trials from the 1620s to the 1670s: A209, bb. 5, 9, 236, 380, 665, 685, 757, 782, 1001, 1123, 1125, 1289, 1291, 1342, 1467, 1469, 1611, 1721, 1757, 1759, 1779, 1857, 1881, 1883, 1884, 1916, 1929, and 1990.
223. Gehring, p. 390. Note that while the archival index was complied by an archivist in the nineteenth century and the documents themselves contain a mixture of terms, examination of a random sampling of thirteen "witchcraft" and "poison" trials from the 1660s and '70s (bb. 9, 236, 685, 782, 1342, 1469, 1611, 1721, 1757, 1759, 1857, 1929, 1990) suggests that the archivist's classifications convey a real shift in terminology and conception that took place.
224. On "witch" as an insult in eighteenth-century Württemberg, see Popkin, "Marriage," pp. 351, 353–4; Schöck, "Ende," p. 379.
225. Raith, "Oberrat," p. 119.
226. Gehring, p. 390.
227. Raith, "Oberrat," p. 120.
228. Raith, "Herzogtum," p. 204.
229. For example, among the witch trials contained in the Sampled Witch Trials (see the appendix), 6 of 11 cases (more than half) after 1660 involved medical testimony, medical investigations, or discussions of melancholy, whereas only 3 of the earlier 16 (less than a third) involved medical testimony. Furthermore, among the cases in the General Magic Sample (see the appendix), of the ten that proved to be late (post-1650) witch trials, five (again, half), included testimony from doctors or apothecaries or other medical involvement; see Bever, "Wuerttemberg," Chap. IX.
230. Bever, "Wuerttemberg," p. 192.

231. Raith, "Oberrat," p. 121.
232. Makowsky, pp. 1–2.
233. Makowsky, p. 41; Hermelink, p. 93; Wessling, p. 9.
234. Knapp, p. 24; Weller, pp. 62–3; Seidler, p. 312; Königer, p. 40.
235. Makowsky, p. 14; Seidler, pp. 305, 313.
236. An example is the reluctance of the medical practitioners to judge the cause of an ailment magical and their corresponding readiness to speculate on possible natural causes in the case contained in case Z9 (see the appendix).
237. Midelfort, *Witch Hunting*, p. 54; Gehring, p. 21.
238. Midelfort, *Witch Hunting*, p. 55.
239. Midelfort, *Witch Hunting*, p. 55.
240. Kneubuehler, p. 176.
241. Zsindely, pp. 15, 19.
242. Zsindely, pp. 55–6, 74; Ernst, *Krankheit*, pp. 81–4, 123.
243. Zsindely, pp. 45, 57–8, 61.
244. Zsindely, p. 53.
245. W1; W12, 21, 9, 14 (see the appendix); and see Chap. 3.
246. W3 (see the appendix); and see above Chap. 3.
247. W18 (see the appendix).
248. Z7 (see the appendix).
249. W16; W4 (see the appendix); and see Chap. 1; A209, b. 773, d. 3-3-67.
250. A209, b. 773, dd. 15-4-67, 17-6-67.
251. A209, b. 1958, dd. 6-6-1720 and 30-3-20.
252. A209, b. 1958, d. 17-4-1720.
253. A209, b. 1958, d. 31-3-1720.
254. A209, b. 1958, undated.
255. There are no poison cases in A209 after the 1740s, and they begin to appear in A202 in the 1760s, suggesting that the transition rather than an abrupt, temporary cessation of poisoning (and fear of poisoning) was the cause of the lacuna.
256. W5, W26; W24, W4 (see the appendix.) On the Apothecary Ordinance: Wessling, p. 13, n. 8. On the fine: A209, b. 757, d. 19.
257. A209, b. 311a; A209, b. 1424.
258. A209, b. 1878, dd. 3, 8.
259. Male healers: W14, 22 (see the appendix); Early case: A209, b. 720.
260. A209, b. 459a, d. 1; Gehring, p. 22.
261. W2 (two suspects – both used rituals – one jailed and probation; one jailed, torture three times and probation), W3, W11, W13, W14 (male), W17 (used rituals; jailed, fined, and probation), W22 (male), W23 (midwife), W26. (See the appendix.)
262. Fulbrook, p. 140, says that magistrates exhibited a notable reluctance to cooperate with the clergy to enforce morals regulations starting in "the 1690s or early 1700s," but this was when prosecutions for magic began to pick up.
263. Vann, pp. 136, 178, 191–2.
264. Sg9, Az3, Z17, Gb6 (see the appendix), A209, b. 536a.
265. Ss4, A209, b. 536a; A209, b. 576a.
266. W2, Z12 (see the appendix), A209, b. 536a.
267. A209, b. 1855. See also A209, b. 254.
268. Bever, "Wuerttemberg," Figure 10.3.
269. Az7 (see the appendix), A209, b. 459a.
270. Az2 (see the appendix).
271. A213, b. 8406/1752.

272. Hammes, p. 62.
273. Davis, *Society and Culture*, pp. 124–5; Bucher, p. 34; Fries, pp. 81–5.
274. *Malleus Maleficarum*, pp. 44–7.
275. Paulus, p. 79; Saur; Karant-Nunn, p. 41.
276. A209, b. 1989, d. 14-3-60; Po-Chia Hsia, p. 165, reports that "several women in Zurich committed suicide out of guilt," believing that they had had sex with the Devil, citing it as an example of evidence of the effectiveness of repressive policies on not just behavior but on emotions and self-definition.
277. W9 (see the appendix).
278. *Malleus Maleficarum*, p. 43.
279. Paulus, p. 91.
280. *Wahrafftige unnd Erschreckliche*.
281. Karant-Nunn, p. 41.
282. Molitor, p. 65.
283. W1, W 5, W11, W13, W15, W16 (see the appendix).
284. Gehring, p. 394.
285. Rublack *Women*, p. 4; Karant-Nunn pp. 26, 35–6; Wegert, p. 137; Lacour, p. 660.
286. Popkin, "Marriage," pp. 353–4.
287. Popkin, "Marriage," pp. 3, 13, n. 23.
288. Keeble, p. 71; Melton, p. 203; Rublack, *Women*, p. 15.
289. Scribner, "Desacralisation," p. 89.
290. Bever, "Crisis," pp. 159–60; Gestrich, p. 271; Lehmann, p. 34; Hermelink, pp. 156–82.
291. Lehmann, p. 34; Hermelink, pp. 156–82; Rochs, p. 114.
292. Fulbrook, pp. 100–1.
293. Hermelink, pp. 186–8; Fulbrook, pp. 130–7.
294. Ernst, *Krankheit*, p. 45; Gleixner, p. 327.
295. Graeter, n.p.
296. Stitziel, p. 351.
297. Bever, "Wuerttemberg," pp. 375ff; Bever, "Crisis," pp. 159–60.
298. Bever, "Wuerttemberg," p. 373.
299. Vann, pp. 97–8; Weller, pp. 88, 181, 197, 73.
300. Lehmann, p. 124; Stoeffler, p. 84.
301. Weller, pp. 81–2; Weller and Weller, pp. 64, 196; Wintterlin, p. 101.
302. Ernst, *6000 Jahre*, p. 245; Wintterlin, pp. 102, 107.
303. Bever, "Wuerttemberg," pp. 337–40; see also Weber, *Verführten*.
304. A209, b. 1258; Bever, "Wuerttemberg," p. 342; and see Chap. 1, above.
305. A209, b. 1258, d. 1.
306. A209, b. 1258, d. 4.
307. A209, b. 1258, dd. 5, 7.
308. A209, b. 1258, dd. 9-11-1704, 12, 13.
309. A209, b. 1587, d. Constable's initial report, 10-1739, pp. 14r, 18r.
310. A209, b. 1587, dd. 9–11 and 17-12-1739.
311. A209, b. 1587, d. 23-12-1739.
312. A209, b. 1587, d. 8-1-1740.
313. A209, b. 1587, d. Constable's initial report, 10-1739, pp. 6, 19r.
314. Bachman, pp. 62–3.
315. W1, and see Chap. 3.
316. Z20; Az2 (see the appendix).
317. Az6 (see the appendix); A213, b. 8417/1803.
318. Bergerac, p. 114.

319. Moser-Rath, p. 213; Daston and Park, pp. 350, 359; Midelfort, *Exorcism*, reviews these often bitter polemics.
320. Rabb, pp. 111–12.
321. Midelfort, *Witch Hunting*, p. 2; Kneubuhler, p. 224; Pott, *Aufklarung und Aberglaube*, pp. 4, 205; Reill, p. 6.
322. Kneubuhler, p. 224; Lehmann, p. 66.
323. Stoeffler, p. 94.
324. Lehmann, p. 123.
325. Dinzelbacher, pp. 1091–2. Daston and Park, pp. 337–8, note that the focus of the meaning shifted over time; the point here is that in practical terms a common set of activities was the core of what was being designated by it.
326. Behringer, "Communications," has recently championed the importance of the "communications revolution" in Germany during the eighteenth century, and a significant change in provincial culture would certainly be consistent with this. Midelfort, *Exorcism*, in fact, conveys well the growth and power of public discussions of these sorts of these very issues in southwestern Germany during the mid- to late eighteenth century, while Böning and Siegert give extensive evidence of the diffusion of Enlightenment thought to the lower classes.
327. Hasselhorn, p. 80.
328. Fulbrook, pp. 7, 101, 130, 137–46.
329. Vann, pp. 215, 243–55.
330. Vann, p. 259.
331. Fulbrook, p. 143.
332. Vann, p. 256.
333. Bever, "Wuerttemberg," pp. 373–4.
334. Weller, p. 75; Liebel-Weckowicz, p. 76; Sauer, "Not und Armut," pp. 137, 139.
335. Liebel-Weckowicz, p. 88; Weller and Weller, p. 199; Fulbrook, p. 69.
336. Nagel, pp. 13–25.
337. Liebel-Weckowicz, pp. 80, 76; Sauer, "Not und Armut," p. 137.
338. Sauer, "Not und Armut," pp. 142–4.
339. Liebel-Weckowicz, pp. 80–2.
340. Ss1; Sg1 (see the appendix).
341. Compare, for example, the government's rather mild response to the treasure-hunting case in Dornstetten in 1721 that grew out of the spirit in the cow stall, which it punished only by imposing fines and ordering a sermon against "the great misuse and injury to God's name" it had involved (Sg4), and its cautious investigation of the cunning man Jacob Schiller in 1729, letting him go at first despite considerable evidence against him and only authorizing a trial when he was caught a second time (Ss3), with its readiness to have Jacob Schu flogged repeatedly in 1764 in order to get him to admit he had "no other intention than to swindle some money out of" his aged employer (Gb3), or its harsh rebuke and heavy punishment of Barbara Calmbach in 1769 for her "fraud" in claiming Agnes Luzin had bewitched her (Az2).
342. The table is based on the sampled beneficent magic cases (see Appendix) from after 1700 plus A209 1176, 238, 1811, 1584, 1589; A213 8419a/40, 8420/47, 8422/47, 8413/48, 8409/49, 8414/50, 8408/51, 8406/65, 8405/66, 8401/72, 8406/73, 8401/92, 8409/99, 8417/1802, 8417/1803. The nonsampled cases include all magic cases from after 1700 that were read in addition to the sampled ones, and are included because they help show the general patterns better

(in the early and late parts of the century in particular). While they were not selected randomly, neither were they chose because of any specific connection to this issue, and since all were included, even those that went against the overall trends, the impression conveyed by the table seems valid.

343. Weller and Weller, p. 185.
344. Sg4 (see the appendix).
345. Sg2 (see the appendix).
346. Sg7 (see the appendix).
347. A213, b. 8409/99, d. 6-2-1799.
348. Ss3 (see the appendix), A213, b. 8405.
349. Gb1 (see the appendix), and see Chap. 6.
350. A213, b. 8399/1775.
351. Harley, p. 142.
352. The continuation of witchcraft and magic beyond the witch trials and Enlightenment has been the subject of considerable research recently. See Davies, *Witchcraft; Witchcraft Continued: Popular Magic in Modern Europe; Beyond the Witch Trials: Witchcraft and Magic in Enlightenment Europe*; Blécourt, "Continued Existence"; Blécourt, "Continuation". There is no question this is true, but there is also no question that magic's role in European culture, and even in popular culture, was considerably reduced between 1500 and 1800.
353. Ogilvie, p. 444.
354. For example, see Sebald, "Justice."
355. Sabean, *Power*, p. 35; Pott, *Aufklarung und Aberglaube*, p. 340; Daston and Park, p. 343. Haag, *Predigt*, p. 275.

Bibliography

Archival sources

Hauptstaatsarchiv Stuttgart

A202 Geheimer Rat, Akten: Repertorium.

A209, Oberrat, Kriminalakten: Repertorium; Büschel 2, 5, 8, 9, 11, 14, 17, 21, 22, 24, 39, 85, 144, 226, 230, 233, 235, 236, 238, 254, 263, 281, 307, 311a, 327, 330, 345, 347, 368, 371, 375, 380, 392, 404, 433, 434, 440, 449, 451, 454, 459a, 460a, 466a, 468a, 517, 525, 529, 536a, 546, 552, 576a, 593, 606a, 609, 654, 661, 665, 679, 685, 696, 719(1562), 719(1565), 719, 720, 723, 725, 727, 736, 742, 757, 767, 773, 782, 844, 851a, 852, 865, 873, 901, 909, 957, 959, 967, 985, 1001, 1018, 1050, 1091, 1092, 1111, 1123, 1125, 1146, 1176, 1190, 1215, 1223, 1258, 1289, 1291, 1338, 1342, 1373, 1382, 1388, 1424(1), 1424(2), 1430, 1431, 1436, 1462a, 1467, 1469, 1473a, 1486, 1492, 1508, 1575, 1584, 1587, 1589, 1611, 1616, 1634a, 1656, 1668, 1669, 1700a, 1721, 1742, 1753, 1757, 1759, 1779, 1780, 1784a, 1787, 1789, 1811, 1855, 1856, 1857, 1878, 1881, 1883, 1884(1654), 1916, 1924, 1929, 1957, 1958, 1971, 1982, 1990, 2059, 2073, 2088, 2096, 2098, 2099, 2104.

A210, Oberrat, Stadt und Amt Stuttgart: Repertorium; Büschel 96, 429, 463.

A213, Oberrat, Jüngere Ämterakten (Spezialakten): Büschel 8395(1747, 1766, 1770), 8397(1747), 8396(1764), 8398(1751), 8399(1769, 1775), 8401(1769, 1772, 1792), 8405(1766), 8406(1751, 1761, 1762, 1765, 1773), 8407(1752), 8408(1748, 1751), 8409(1739, 1749, 1799–1803), 8410(1795), 8411(1765), 8412(1756), 8413(1748), 8414(1750–1), 8417(1770, 1802–3, 1803), 8418(1748, 1803), 8419(1740, 1789), 8420(1747), 8422(1747).

A309, Kriminalakten der Ämter: Repertorium.

Note that in the Endnotes, "b." refers to a "Büschel" (file), while "d." refers to a specific document within a Büschel. For example, "A209, b.1587, d. 4" refers to document 4 in Büschel 1587 in the archival holdings A209. Multiple files are designated by "bb." and multiple documents within a file are designated by "dd."

Universitätsarchiv, Tübingen

84/1–70 *Libri Sententiarum ... facultatis jur*: Index of witchcraft and related cases compiled by H. C. Erik Midelfort; vols 6, 7, 11, 16.

Printed sources

Abel, Ernest. *Drugs and Behavior: A Primer in Neuropsychopharmacology*. New York: Wiley, 1974.

Achterberg, Jean. *Imagery in Healing: Shamanism and Modern Medicine*. Boston and London: New Science Library Shambhala, 1985.

Adam, Thomas. "'Viel tausend gulden lägten am selbigen Orth': Schatzgräberei und Geisterbschwörung in Südwestdeutschland vom 16. bis 19. Jahrhundert." *Historische Anthropologie: Kultur, Gesellschaft, Alltag*, vol. 9:3. Ed. Richard van Dülmen. Köln, Weimar, Wien: Böhlau Verlag, 2001, pp. 358–83.

Adams, David. "Biology Does Not Make Men More Aggressive than Women." In *Of Mice and Women*.
Adler, Helmut and Leonore Adler. "From Hippocrates to Psychoneuroimmunology: Medicine as Art and Science." In *Spirit vs. Scalpel*.
Ahnert, Thomas. *Religion and the Origins of the German Enlightenment*. Rochester: University of Rochester Press, 2006.
Ahrendt-Schulte, Ingrid. "Hexenprozesse." *Frauen in der Geschichte des Rechts: Von der Frühen Neuzeit bis zur Gegenwart*. Ed. Ute Gerhard. Munich: Verlag C. H. Beck, 1997.
Ahrendt-Schulte, Ingrid. "Hexenprozesse als Spiegel von Altagskonflikten." In *Hexenglaube und Hexenverfolgungen*.
Ahrendt-Schulte, Ingrid. *Weise Frauen – böse Weiber: Die Gescheichte der Hexen in der Neuzeit*. Freiburg-Basel-Wien: Herder, 1994.
Ahrendt-Schulte, Ingrid. *Zauberinnen in der Stadt Horn (1554–1603): magische Kultur und Hexenverfolgung in der Frühen Neuzeit*, Frankfurt, New York: Campus Verlag, 1997.
Aker, Gudrun. *Hexen und Zauberer in Besigheim*. Besignheimer Geschichtsblätter, vol. 20 (2000).
Alber, Mathew and Wilhelm Bidenbach. *Ein Suma etlicher Predigen vom Hagel und Unholden*. Tübingen, 1562.
Alcock, James. "Give the Null Hypothesis a Chance: Reasons to Remain Doubtful about the Existence of Psi." *Journal of Consciousness Studies*, vol. 10: 6–7 (2003), pp. 29–50.
Alexander, John et al. *The Warrior's Edge*. New York: William Morrow, 1990.
Allport, Gordon and Leo Postman. *The Psychology of Rumor*. New York: Russell and Russell, 1965.
Alltagsleben und Magie. Ed. Rita Voltmer and Günter Gehl. Weimar: Rita Dader Verlag, 2003.
Alm, Torbjrn. "The Witch Trials of Finmark, Norther Norway, during the Seventeenth Century: Evidence for Ergotism as a Contributing Factor." *Economic Botany*, vol. 57:3 (2003), pp. 403–16.
Altarriba, Jeanette. "The Influence of Culture on Cognitive Processes." In *Cognition and Culture*.
Alternate States of Consciousness. Ed. Norman Zinberg. New York: Free Press, 1977.
Altered States of Consciousness. Ed. Charles Tart. New York: Wiley, 1964.
Alvarado, Carlos. "Onset and Terminal Sensations in Out-of-Body Experiences." *The Journal of Psychology*, vol. 128:6 (1994), pp. 701–2.
Alvarado, Carlos. "Out-of-Body Experiences." In *Varieties of Anomalous Experience*.
Alver, Bente and Tourunn Selberg. "Folk Medicine as Part of a Larger Concept Complex." Reprinted in *New*, vol. 5.
The American Family in Social and Historical Perspective. Ed. Michael Gordon. New York: St. Martin's, 1973.
American Handbook of Psychiatry, vol. I. Ed. Silvano Arieti et al. New York: Basic Books, 1959.
Anderson, D. Eric et al. "Love's Best Habit: Deception in the Context of Relationships." In *The Social Context of Nonverbal Behavior*.
Andresen, Jensine. "Conclusion: Religion in the Flesh: Forging New Methodologies for the Study of Religion." In *Religion in Mind*.
Animal Social Psychology: A Reader in Experimental Studies. Ed. Robert Zajonc. New York: Wiley, 1969.
Ansha. *Wie sie wirkt Schwarze Magie und wie wir uns davon schützen*. Munich: W. Ludwig Verlag, 2001.

Anthony, Susan. "Anxiety and Rumor." *The Journal of Social Psychology*, vol. 89 (February 1973), pp. 91–8.
Anthropology of Religion: A Handbook of Method and Theory. Ed. S. Glazier. Westport, CT: Greenwood, 1997.
The Anthropology of the Body. Ed. John Blacking. London: Academic Press, 1977.
Anthropology of Violence and Conflict. Ed. Bettina Schmidt and Ingo Schröder. London: Routledge, Taylor & Francis, 1996.
Anticlericalism in Late Medieval and Early Modern Europe. Ed. Peter Dykema and Heiko Oberman. Leiden: E. J. Brill, 1993.
Anti-dementia Agents: Research and Prospects for Therapy. Ed. C. David Nicholson. London: Academic Press, 1994.
"*Apium graveolens dulce*. Celery" – (Mill.) Pers at "Plants for a Future," c. 1996–2003, last modified 2004, http://www.pfaf.org/database/plants.php?Apium+graveolens+dulce.
Apps, Laura and Andrew Gow. *Male Witches in Early Modern Europe*. Manchester, New York: Manchester University Press, 2003.
The Archaeology of Shamanism. Ed. Neil Price. London: Routledge, 2001.
Archer, John. *By a Flash and a Scare: Incendiarism, Animal Maiming, and Poaching in East Orua, 1815–1870*. Oxford: Clarendon Press, 1990.
Arden, John. *Consciousness, Dreams, and Self: A Transdisciplinary Approach*. Madison, CT: Psychosocial Press, 1996.
Argyle, Michael. *Bodily Communication*. New York: International Universities Press, 1975.
Arieti Silvano and Johannes Meth. "Rare, Unclassifiable, Collective, and Exotic Psychotic Syndromes." In *American Handbook of Psychiatry*, vol. 1.
Armstrong, Este. "'Making Symbols Meaningful': Human Emotions and the Limbic System." In *Biocultural Approaches*.
Astin, John et al. "The Efficacy of 'Distant Healing': A Systematic Review of Randomized Trials."*Annals of Internal Medicine*, vol. 132 (2000), pp. 903–10.
Atkinson, Jane. "Shamanisms Today." *The Annual Review of Anthropology*, vol. 21 (1992), pp. 307–30.
Atlas der deutschen Volkskunde, 2 vols. Ed. Matthias Zender. Marburg: Elwert, 1959–64.
Aus der Heimatsgeschichte: Jahresheft des Geschichts-und Altertumsverein Göppingen, vol. 4 (1965).
Aus der Zeit der Verzweiflung: zur Genese und Aktualität des Hexenbilder. Ed. Gabriele Becker, et al. Frankfurt am Main: Suhrkamp, 1977.
Austin, James. *Zen and the Brain: Toward and Understanding of Meditation and Consciousness*. Cambridge, MA: MIT Press, 1998.
Aversive Interpersonal Behaviors. Ed. Robin Kowalski. New York: Plenum Press, 1997.
Bachmann, Angelika. "Allerhand gottloses abgöttisches Werckhn: Glaube – Aberglaube – Zauberei. Magie in der dörflichen Gesellschaft Württembergs des 17. und 18. Jahrhunderts." In *Zauberer – Selbstmörder – Schatzsucher*.
Bader, Karl. *Das Mittelalterliche Dorf als Friedens-und Rechtsbereich*. Weimar: Hermann Boehlaus, 1957.
Bailey, Michael. *Battling Demons: Witchcraft, Heresy, and Reform in the Late Middle Ages*. University Park, PA: Pennsylvania State University Press, 2003.
Bailey, Michael. "The Disenchantment of Magic: Spells, Charms, and Superstition in Early European Witch Literature." *American Historical Review* (April 2006), pp. 383–404.
Bailey, Michael. *Historical Dictionary of Witchcraft*. Lanham, MD: Scarecrow, 2003.
"Ball Lightning Scientists Remain in the Dark." *New Scientist*, vol. 13:42 (December 20, 2001), n.p. (online).

Barash, David and Judith Lipton. *Making Sense of Sex: How Genes and Gender Affect Our Relationships*. Washington, DC: Island Press, 1997.
Barber, Paul. "The Real Vampire." In *Magic, Witchcraft, and Religion*.
Bargh, John A. "Does Subliminality Matter to Social Psychology? Awareness of the Stimulus versus Awareness of Its Influence." In *Perception without Awareness*.
Barnes, Robin. *Prophesy and Gnosis: Apocalypticism in the Wake of the Lutheran Reformation*, Stanford: Standford University Press, 1988.
Baroja, Julio. *The World of the Witches*. Trans. O. Glendinning. Chicago, IL: University of Chicago Press: 1964.
Baron-Cohen, Simon. *The Essential Difference*. New York: Basic Books, 2003.
Barrett, Richard. *Culture and Conduct*, 2nd Edition. Belmont, CA: Wadsworth, 1991.
Barrett, William. "Some Reminiscences of Fifty Years' Psychical Research," paper delivered to the Society for Psychical Research, June 17, 1924, posted by SurvivalAfter Death.org at http://www.survivalafterdeath.org/articles/barrett/years.htm.
Barstow, Anne. *Witchcraze*. San Francisco, CA: HarperCollins, 1995.
Basic Research in Parapsychology, 2nd Edition. Ed. K. Ramakrishna Rao. Jefferson, NC: McFarland, 2001.
Bath, Slicher van. *Agrarian History of Western Europe*. Trans. Olive Ordish. London: Edward Arnold, 1963.
Bauernschaft und Bauernstand 1500–1970. Ed. Günther Franz. Limburg an der Lahn: C. A. Starke, 1975.
Baumeister, Roy. "Lying to Yourself: The Enigma of Self-Deception." In *Lying and Deception*.
Bausinger, Hermann. "Aufklarung und Aberglaube." *Deutsche Vierteljahresschrift für Literaturwissenschaft und Geistesgeschichte*, vol. XXXVII:3 (1963), pp. 345–62.
Baxter, Christopher. "Johann Weyer's *De Praestigius Daemonium*: Unsystematische Psychopathology." In *The Damned Art*.
Beamtentum und Pfarrerstand. Ed. Günther Franz. Limburg/Lahn: C. A. Starke, 1972.
Beattie, Geoffrey. *Visible Thought: The New Psychology of Body Language*. London and New York: Routledge, 2004.
Beauvoir, Simone de. *Coming of Age*. Trans. Patrick O'Brian. New York: Putnam, 1972.
Becher, Gabriele. "Zum kulturellen Bild und zur realien Situation der Frau im Mittelalter und in der frühen Neuzeit." In *Aus der Zeit der Verzweiflung*.
Beck, Jane. "Traditional Folk Medicine in Vermont." In *Medicine and Healing*.
Beckmann, Dieter and Barbara Beckmann. *Alraun, Beifuß und andere Hexenkräuter: Alltagswissen vergangener Zeiten*. Frankfurt/New York: Campus Verlag, 1990.
Becoming Visible: Women in European History. Ed. Renate Bridenthal and Claudia Koonz. Boston, MA: Houghton Mifflin, 1977.
Behringer, Wolfgang. "Communications Revolutions: A Historiographical Concept." *German History*, vol. 24:7 (2006), pp. 333–74.
Behringer, Wolfgang. "How the Waldensians Became Witches: Heretics and Their Journey to the Other World." In *Communicating with the Spirits*.
Behringer, Wolfgang. *The Shaman of Oberstdorf*. Trans. Erik Midelfort. Charlottesville, VA: University Press of Virginia, 1998.
Behringer, Wolfgang. "Weather, Hunger, and Fear: Origins of the European Witch-Hunts in Climate, Society, and Mentality." Trans. David Lederer. *German History*, vol. 13:1 (1995), pp. 1–27.
Behringer, Wolfgang. *Witchcraft Persecutions in Bavaria*. Trans. J. C. Grayson and David Lederer. Cambridge: Cambridge University Press, 1997.
Behringer, Wolfgang. "Zur Geschichte der Hexenforschung." In *Hexen und Hexenforschung*.

Believed-in Imaginings: The Narrative Construction of Reality. Ed. Joseph de Rivera and Theodore Sarbin. Washington, DC: American Psychological Association (APA), 1998.
Bell, Vaughn, et al. "A Cognitive Neuroscience of Belief." In *Power of Belief.*
Bender-Wittman, Ursula. "Frauen und Hexen – feministische Perspektiven der Hexenforschung." In *Hexenverfolgung und Frauengeschichte.*
Benes, Peter. "Fortunetellers, Wise-Men, and Magical Healers in New England, 1644–1850." In *Wonders of the Invisible World.*
Benes, Peter. "Itinerant Physicians, Healers, and Surgeon-Dentists in New England and New York, 1720–1825." In *Medicine and Healing.*
Bentall, Richard. "Hallucinatory Experiences." In *Varieties of Anomalous Experiences.*
Benton, David. "Hormones and Human Aggression." In *Of Mice and Women.*
Benzing, Joseph. *Die Buchdrucker des 16 und 17 Jahrhunderts im Deutschen Sprachgebiet.* Wiesbaden: Otto Harrassowitz, 1963.
Bergerac, Cyrano de. "A Letter Against Witches (1654)." In *European Witchcraft.*
Bergmann, Jörg. *Discreet Indiscretions: The Social Organization of Gossip.* Trans. John Bednarz, Jr. New York: Aldiine de Gruyter, 1993.
Berke, Joseph. *The Tyranny of Malice.* New York: Summit Books, 1988.
Berkner, Lutz. "Inheritance, Land Tenure, and Peasant Family Structure: A German Regional Comparison." In *The American Family.*
Bernhard, Walter. *Die Zentralbehörden des Herzogstum Württemberg und ihre Beamten, 1520–1624,* vol. 1. Stuttgart: Kohlhammer, 1972.
Beschreibung der Stadtdirections-Bezirkes Stuttgart. Koniglichen Statistisch-Topographischen Bureau. Stuttgart: Eduard Hallberger, 1856.
Beschreibung des Obermts Sulz. Koniglichen Statistisch-Topographischen Bureau. Magstadt bei Stuttgart: Horst Bissinger, 1964, rpt. of 1863.
Bever, Edward. "Countermagic." In *Encyclopedia of Witchcraft.*
Bever, Edward. "The Crisis of Confidence in Witchcraft and the Crisis of Authority." In *Early Modern Europe.*
Bever, Edward. "Divination." In *Encyclopedia of Witchcraft.*
Bever, Edward. "Drugs and Hallucinogens." In *Encyclopedia of Witchcraft.*
Bever, Edward. "Magic and Religion." In *Encyclopedia of Witchcraft.*
Bever, Edward. "Magic, Learned." In *Encyclopedia of Witchcraft.*
Bever, Edward. "Maleficium." In *Encyclopedia of Witchcraft.*
Bever, Edward. "Old Age and Witchcraft in Early Modern Europe." In *Old Age in Preindustrial Society.*
Bever, Edward. "Witchcraft Fears and Psychosocial Factors in Disease." *Journal of Interdisciplinary History,* vol. 30:4 (2000), pp. 573–90.
Bever, Edward. "Witchcraft, Female Aggression, and Power in the Early Modern Community." *Journal of Social History,* vol. 35:4 (Summer 2002), pp. 955–88.
Bever, Edward. "Witchcraft in Early Modern Wuerttemberg." Ph.D. Dissertation, Princeton University, 1983.
Beyer, Christel. *"Hexen-Leut, so zu Würzburg gerechetet": Der Umgang mit Sprache und Wirklichkeit in Inquisitionsprozessen wegen Hexerei.* Frankfurt am Main: P. Lang, 1986.
Beyond the Witch Trials: Witchcraft and Magic in Enlightenment Europe. Ed. Owen Davies and Willem de Blécourt. Manchester: Manchester University Press, 2004.
Biedermann, Hans. "Schaden- und Abwehrzauber." In *Hexen und Zauberer.*
Biocultural Approaches to the Emotions. Ed. Alexander Hinton. Cambridge: Cambridge University Press, 1999.
Biological Treatment of Mental Illness. Ed. Max Rinkel. New York: Farrar, Straus and Giroux, 1966.

Bird-David, Nurit. "'Animism' Revisited: Personhood, Environment, and Relational Epistemology." *Current Anthropology*, vol. 40, Supplement (February 1999), pp. 67–92.
Birlinger, Anton. *Aus Schwaben*. 2 vols. Aalen: Scienta Verlag, 1969, rpt. of Wiesbaden, 1874.
Björkqvist, Kaj, Karin Österman, and Ari Kaukiainen. "The Development of Direct and Indirect Aggressive Strategies in Males and Females." In *Of Mice and Women*.
Björkqvistt, Kaj and Pirkko Niemelä. "New Trends in the Study of Female Aggression." In *Of Mice and Women*.
Blackwell, Jeannine. "Controlling the Demonic: Johann Salomo Semler and the Possession of Anna Elisabeth Lohmann (1759)." In *Impure Reason*.
Blanke, Olaf. "Out-of-Body Experiences and Their Neural Basis." *British Medical Journal*, vol. 329 (2004), pp. 1414–5.
Blanke, Olaf et al. "Linking Out-of-Body Experiences and Self Processing to Mental Own-Body Imagery at the Temporoparietal Junction." *Journal of Neuroscience*, vol. 25:3 (January 19, 2005), pp. 550–7.
Blauert, Andreas. "Frühe Hexenverfolgungen in der Schweiz, am Bodensee und am Oberrhein." In *Hexenglaube und Hexenverfolgungen*.
Blauert, Andreas. *Frühe Hexenverfolgungen: Zetzer, Zauberei, und Hexenprozesse des 15. Jahrhunders*. Hamburg: Junius, 1989.
Blauert, Andreas. "Schweizerische Hexenprozesse der frühen 15 Jahrhunderts." In *Hexenverfolgung: Beiträge*.
Blécourt, Willem de. "Bedding the Nightmare: Somatic Experience and Narrative Meaning in Dutch and Flemish Legend Texts." *Folklore* (August 2003), n.p. (online).
Blécourt, Willem de. "Cunning Women, From Healers to Fortune Tellers." In *Curing and Insuring*.
Blécourt, Willem de. "The Making of the Female Witch." *Gender & History*, vol. 12:2 (2000), pp. 287–309.
Blécourt, Willem de. "Mangels Beweisen: Über das Ende der Verfolgung von Zauberinnen in Niederländisch und Spanisch Geldern, 1590–1640." In *Das Ende der Hexenverfolgung*.
Blécourt, Willem de. "On the Continuation of Witchcraft." In *Witchcraft in Early Modern Europe*.
Blécourt, Willem de. "Preface: Situating 'Alternative Medicine' in the Modern Period." *Medical History*, vol. 43:3 (1999), pp. 283–5.
Blécourt, Willem de. "Witch Doctors, Soothsayers and Priests. On Cunning Folk in European Historiography and Tradition." *Social History*, vol. 19:3 (October 1994), pp. 285–303.
Blécourt, Willem de. "The Witch, Her Victim, the Unwitcher and the Researcher: The Continued Existence of Traditional Witchcraft." In *Witchcraft and Magic in Europe: The Twentieth Century*.
Blécourt, Willem de and Cornelie Usborne. "Women's Medicine, Women's Culture: Abortion and Fortune-Telling in Early Twentieth Century Germany and the Netherlands." *Medical History*, vol. 43 (1999), pp. 376–92.
Bloch, Maurice. *How We Think They Think: Anthropological Approaches to Cognition, Memory, and Literacy*. Westport, CT: Westview Press, 1998.
Blonder, Lee. "Brain and Emotional Relations in Culturally Diverse Populations." In *Biocultural Approaches*.
Bloom, Howard. *The Lucifer Principle*. New York: The Atlantic Monthly Press, 1995.
Blum, Deborah. *Sex on the Brain: The Biological Differences between Men and Women*. New York: Viking, 1997.

Blute, Marion. "Memetics and Evolutionary Social Science." *Journal of Memetics – Evolutionary Models of Information Transmission*, vol. 6 (2005).
Boas, Franz. "Seeking Contact with Spirits Is Not Necessarily Shamanism." In *Shamans through Time*.
Böning, Holger and Reinhart Siegert. *Volksaufklärung: Biobibliographisches Handbuch zur Popularisierung aufklärerischen Denkens im deutschen Sprachraum*, 2 vols. Holzboog: Frommann, 1990.
Bönisch, Monika. *Opium der Armen: Lottospiel und Volksmagie im frühen 19 Jahrhundert. Eine Fallstudie aus Württemberg*. Tübingen: Silberburg-Verlag, 1994.
Borst, Arno. "The Origin of the Witch-Craze in the Alps." Reprinted in *New*, vol. 2.
Bosch, Jos et al. "Psychological Stress as a Determinant of Protein Levels and Salivary-Induced Aggregation of *Streptococcus gordonii* Human Whole Saliva." *Psychosomatic Medicine*, vol. 58 (1996), pp. 374–82.
Bostridge, Ian. *Witchcraft and Its Transformations, c.1650–c.1750*. Oxford: Clarendon Press, 1997.
Bostridge, Ian. "Witchcraft Repealed." In *Witchcraft in Early Modern Europe*.
Bowyer, J. Barton. *Cheating: Deception in War and Magic, Games and Sports, Sex and Religion, Business and Con Games, Politics and Espionage, Art and Science*. New York: St. Martin's Press, 1982.
Boyd, Robert, and Peter Riderson. *Culture and the Evolutionary Process*. Chicago and London: University of Chicago Press, 1985.
Boyer, Pascal. *Religion Explained: The Evolutionary Origins of Religious Thought*. New York: Basic Books, 2001.
Boyer, Paul and Stephen Nissenbaum. *Salem Possessed*. Cambridge, MA: Harvard University Press, 1974.
"Brain Imaging Studies Investigate Pain Reduction by Hypnosis," *AScribe Health News Service* (March 14, 2005).
Braud, William G., and Dennis, Stephen P. "Geophysical Variables and Behavior; LVIII. Autonomic Activity, Hemolysis, and Biological Psychokinesis: Possible Relationships with Geomagnetic Field Activity." *Perceptual and Motor Skill*, vol. 68 (1989), p. 1243.
Braud, William G. "Can Our Intentions Interact Directly With The Physical World?" *European Journal of Parapsychology*, vol. 10 (1994), http://integral-inquiry.com/docs/649/intentions.pdf.
Brauner, Sigrid. *Fearless Wives and Frightened Shrews: The Construction of the Witch in Early Modern Germany*. Ed. Robert Brown. Amherst, MA: University of Massachusetts Press, 1995.
Brauner, Sigrid. "Martin Luther's Witchcraft: A True Reformer?" Reprinted in *New*, vol. 1.
Brewin, Chris. *Posttraumatic Stress Disorder*. New Haven, CT: Yale University Press, 2003.
"A Brief History of Comets I (until 1950)." European Organisation for Astronomical Research in the Southern Hemisphere. Last update, July 13, 2006. At http://www.eso.org/outreach/info-events/hale-bopp/comet-history-1.html.
Briggs, Robin. "'By the Strength of Fancie': Witchcraft and the Early Modern Imagination." *Folklore*, vol. 115:3 (December 2004), pp. 259–72.
Briggs, Robin. "Circling the Devil: Witch-Doctors and Magical Healers in Early Modern Lorraine." In *Languages of Witchcraft*.
Briggs, Robin. "Dangerous Spirits: Shapeshifting, Apparitions, and Fantasy in Lorraine Witchcraft Trials." In *Werewolves*.

Briggs, Robin. "Witchcraft and Popular Mentality in Lorraine, 1580–1630." In *Occult and Scientific Mentalities*.
Briggs, Robin. *Witches and Neighbors*. New York: Penguin, 1996.
Brizendine, Louann. *The Female Brain*. New York: Morgan Road, 2006.
Broedel, Hans Peter. *The Malleus Maleficarum and the Construction of Witchcraft: Theology and Popular Belief*. Manchester and New York: Manchester University Press, 2003.
Brown, Donald. *Human Universals*. Philadelphia: Temple University Press, 1991.
Brown, Judith. "Cross-Cultural Perspectives on Middle Aged Women." In *Cultural Constructions of 'Women'*.
Brown, Michael. "Dark Side of the Shaman." In *Shamans through Time*.
Brown, Michael. "Thinking about Magic." In *Anthropology of Religion*.
Brown, Peter. "Sorcery, Demons, and the Rise of Christianity from Late Antiquity into the Middle Ages." In *Witchcraft: Confessions and Accusations*.
Brown, Richard. "Dissociation and Conversion in Psychogenic Illness." In *Psychogenic Movement Disorders*.
Brucker, Gene. "Sorcery in Early Renaissance Florence." *Studies in the Renaissance*, vol. 10 (1963), pp. 7–24.
Bruyn, Lucy de. *Women and the Devil in Sixteenth Century German Literature*. Wiltshire: Compton, 1979.
Bryan, William. *Religious Aspects of Hypnosis*. Springfield, IL: Charles C. Thomas, 1962.
Bucher, Carl. *Die Frauenfrage im Mittelalter*. Tübingen: Laupp'schen Verlag, 1882.
Buchholz, Peter. "Shamanism in Medieval Scandanavian Literature." In *Communicating with the Spirits*.
Bulkeley, Kelley. *An Introduction to the Psychology of Dreaming*. Westport, CT: Praeger, 1997.
"Burdock (Arctium lappa)," *Medline Plus*, U.S. National Library of Medicine and NIH, 9/1/2005, http://www.nlm.nih.gov/medlineplus/druginfo/natural/patient-burdock.html.
Burghartz, Susanna. "Tales of Seduction, Tales of Violence: Argumentative Strategies before the Basel Marriage Court." *German History*, vol. 17 (1999), pp. 41–56.
Burkan, Tolly. "A Firewalking Theory That Can Benefit Everyone." Firewalking Institute of Research and Education, 2001, http://www.firewalking.com/theory.html.
Burke, Peter. *Popular Culture in Early Modern Europe*. New York: Harper, 1978.
Burstein, Sona. "Aspects of the Psychopathology of Old Age Revealed in Witchcraft Cases of the Sixteenth and Seventeenth Centuries." *British Medical Bulletin*, vol. 6: 1–2 (1949), pp. 63–9.
Buss, Hedwig. *Was die Alten Einst Erzählten ... Von Sympathiedoktoren, Hexen und Schräcksli: Geschichten aus dem mittleren Schwarzwald*, vol. 1. Waldkirchlichen Verlag, 1994.
Bütterlin, Rudolf. "Die Ärzte in Altwürttemberg: Ansehen und Selbstverständnis einer Berufsstands in Zeitalter der Barock." *Zeitschrift für Württembergische Landesgeschichte*, vol. 50 (1991), pp. 149–63.
Byloff, Fritz. *Hexenglaube und Hexenverfolgungen in den österreichischen Alpenländer*. Berlin: Walther de Gruyter, 1934.
Bynam, Caroline. "Why All the Fuss About the Body? A Medievalist's Perspective." *Critical Inquiry*, vol. 22 (Autumn 1995), pp. 1–33.
Cacioloa, Nancy. "Breath, Heart, Guts: The Body and Spirit in the Middle Ages." In *Communicating with the Spirits*.

Cannon, W. B. "Voodoo Death." *American Anthropologist*, new ser. 44 (1942), pp. 169–81.
Caldwell, Ross. http://www.tarotforum.net/showthread.php?t=63206.
Cardeña, Etzel et al. "Introduction: Anomalous Experiences in Perspective." In *Varieties of Anomalous Experiences*.
Carlen, Louis. *Das Recht der Hirten*. Innsbruck: Wagnerishche-Universität-Buchdruckerei, 1970.
Carli, Linda. "Biology Does Not Create Gender Differences in Personality." In *Women, Men, and Gender*.
Carroll, Robert. "Ball Lightning." *The Skeptic's Dictionary*. Last update 11/06/2005, http://www.skepdic.com/balllightning.html.
Carlton, Eric. *The Paranormal: Research and the Quest for Meaning*. Aldershot, UK: Ashgate, 2000.
Carus, Paul. *The History of the Devil and the Idea of Evil*. LaSalle, IL: Open Court Pub. Co., 1996, rpt. of 1900.
Cassidy, Frederick. "Chemical Approaches to the Enhancement of Cholinergic Function for the Treatment of Senile Dementia." In *Anti-dementia Agents*.
Castan, Nichole. "Criminals." Trans. Arthur Goldhammer. In *A History of Women in the West*.
"Celery seed / Apium graveolens / Marsh Parsley / Smallage / Wild Celery," 2001–6, at *Herbal Remedies*, http://www.herbalremedies.com/celeryseed-information.html.
Cervantes, Fernando. *The Devil in the New World*. New Haven and London: Yale University Press, 1994.
Chadwick, Paul et al. *Cognitive Therapy for Delusory Voices, and Paranoia*. Chichester, NY: Wiley, 1996.
Chapman, C. Richard and Margo Wyckoff. "The Problem of Pain: A Psychobiological Perspective." In *Psychosomatic Disorders*.
Charms and Charming in Europe. Ed. Jonathan Roper. Houndsmills, Basingstoke, Hampshire and New York: Palgrave Macmillan, 2004.
Charon, Veronique. "The Knowledge of Herbs." In *The Pagan Middle Ages*.
Chaumeil, Jean-Pierre. "Magic Darts as Viruses." In *Shamans through Time*.
Chavers, Ronald. "Trance, Social Transformation, and Ecstatis Practices." In *Shamanism: Past and Present*.
Chembob. "An Undisciplined Stunt: Belladonna." *Eorwid's Experience Vault*, http://www.erowid.org/experiences/exp.php?ID=22.
Cheyne, Alan et al. "Relations among Hypnagogic and Hypnopompic Experiences Related to Sleep Paralysis." *Journal of Sleep Research*, vol. 8:4 (1999), pp. 313–17.
Cheyne, Alan et al. "Sleep Paralysis and Associated Hypnagogic and Hypnopompic Experiences," http://watarts.uwaterloo.ca/~acheyne/S_P2.html.
Cheyne, J. A. and T. A. Girard. "Spatial Characteristics of Hallucinations Associated with Sleep Paralysis." *Cognitive Neuropsychiatry*, vol. 9:4 (2004), pp. 281–300.
Chmielewski-Hagius, Anita. "Wider alle Hexerei und Teufelswerk ... vom alltagsmagischen Umgang mit Hexen, Geistern und Dämonen." In *Hexenglaube und Hexenverfolgungen*.
Chodorow, Nancy. "Family Structure and Feminine Personality." *Women, Culture, and Society*.
Christian, William. *Apparitions in Late Medieval and Renaissance Spain*. Princeton, NJ: Princeton University Press, 1981.
Clari, Colin. *A History of European Printing*. London: Academic Press, 1976.

Clark, Stuart. "Inversion, Misrule, and the Meaning of Witchcraft." Reprinted in *Witchcraft Reader*.
Clark, Stuart. "Protestant Demonology: Sin, Supersitition and Society (c. 1520–c.1630)." Reprinted in *New*, vol. 1.
Clark, Stuart. *Thinking with Demons: The Idea of Witchcraft in Early Modern Europe*. Oxford: Oxford University Press, 1997.
Clark, Stuart. "Witchcraft and Magic in Early Modern Culture." In *Witchcraft and Magic in Europe: The Period of the Witch Trials*.
Clasen, Claus-Peter. *Anabaptism: A Social History, 1525–1618*. Ithaca, NY: Cornell University Press, 1972.
Coates, Jennifer. "Gossip Revisited: Language in All-Female Groups." In *Women in their Speech Communities*.
Cobb, Julie et al. "Psychosocial Stress and Susceptibility to Upper Respiratory Tract Illness in an Adult Population Sample." *Psychosomatic Medicine*, vol. 58 (1996), pp. 404–12.
Cognition and Culture: A Cross-Cultural Approach to Cognitive Psychology. Ed. Jeanette Atlarriba. Amsterdam: North Holland, 1993.
Cognitive and Behavioral Performance Factors in Atypical Aging. Ed. M. L. Howe et al. New York: Springer, 1990.
Cognition and Emotion. Ed. Eric Eich et al. Oxford: Oxford University Press, 2000.
Cohen, I. Bernard. *Revolution in Science*. Cambridge, MA: Belknap, 1985.
Cohn, Norman. *Europe's Inner Demons*. London: Sussex University Press, 1975.
Cole, Michael. *Cultural Psychology: A Once and Future Discipline*. Cambridge MA: Belknap, 1996.
Communicating with the Spirits. Ed. Gábor Klaniczay and Éva Pócs, with Eszter Csonka-Takács. Budapest: Central European University Press, 2005.
A Companion to Psychological Anthropology: Modernity and Psychocultural Change. Ed. Conerly Casey and Robert Edgerton. Malden, MA: Blackwell, 2005.
Conflict and Gender. Ed. Anita Taylor and Judi Miller. Cresskill, NJ: Hampton Press, 1994.
Conjuring Spirits: Texts and Traditions of Medieval Ritual Magic. Ed. Claire Fanger. University Park, PA: The Pennsylvania State University Press, 1998.
Connor, James A. *Kepler's Witch*. San Francisco: HarperSanFrancisco, 2004.
Conversion Hysteria: Towards a Cognitive Neuropsychological Account. Ed. Peter Halligan and Anthony David. Hove, UK: Psychology Press, 1999.
Cook, Harold. *The Decline of the Old Medical Regime in Stuart London*. Ithaca, NY: Cornell University Press, 1986.
Counterpoints: Cognition and Emotion. Ed. E. Eich et al. New York: Oxford University Press, 1998.
Crapanzano, Vincent. "The Etiquette of Consciousness." *Social Research*, vol. 63:3 (Fall 2001), pp. 627–49.
Criswell, Hugh and Robert Levitt. "Cholinergic Drugs." In *Psychopharmachology: Biological Approaches*.
Cross-Cultural Psychology: Research and Applications. Ed. John Berry et al. Cambridge: Cambridge University Press, 1992.
The Cross-Cultural Study of Women: A Comprehensive Guide. Ed. Margot Duley and Mary Edwards. New York: The Feminist Press, 1986.
Cross-Cultural Topics in Psychology, 2nd Edition. Ed. Leonore Adler and Uwe Gielen. Westport, CT: Praeger, 2001.

Crouzet, Denis. "A Woman and the Devil: Possession and Exorcism in Sixteenth Century France." Trans. Michael Wolfe. Reprinted in *New*, vol. 1.

Cryer, Frederick. "Magic in Ancient Syria-Palestine – and the Old Testament." In *Witchcraft and Magic in Europe: Biblical and Pagan Societies*.

Crystallinesheen. "A Tale of Nudity, Arrest, and Insanity ..." in *Eorwid's Experience Vault*, http://www.erowid.org/experiences/exp.php?ID=17700.

Csordas, Thomas. *Body/Meaning/Healing*. Houndsmill and New York: Palgrave Macmillan, 2002.

Csordas, Thomas. *The Sacred Self: A Cultural Phenomenology of Charismatic Healing*. Berkeley, CA: University of California Press, 1994.

Cultural Anthropology. Ed. David Hicks and Margaret Gwynne: New York: HarperCollins, 1994.

Cultural Constructions of "Women". Ed. Pauline Kolenda. Salem, WI: Sheffield, 1988.

Cultural Encounters: The Impact of the Inquisition in Spain and the New World. Ed. Mary Elizabeth Perry and Anne Cruz. Berkeley, CA: University of California Press, 1991.

Cunningham, Graham. *Religion and Magic: Approaches and Theories*. New York: New York University Press, 1999.

Curing and Insuring: Essays on Illness in Past Times. Ed. Hans Binneveld and Rudolf Delcker. Hilversum: Verloren, 1993.

Current Medical Diagnosis and Treatment. 1998. Ed. Lawrence Tierney et al. Stamford, CT: Appleton and Lange, 1998.

The Curse: A Cultural History of Menstruation. Ed. Janice Delaney et al. New York: E.P. Dutton, 1976.

Czyziewska, Maria. *Nonconscious Social Information Processing*. Wydawnictura Uniwersytetu Warszawskiega, 1989.

Daalen, Riencke Van. "The Emotion." In *Encyclopedia of European Social History*, vol. 4.

D'Andrade, Roy. *The Development of Cognitive Anthropology*. Cambridge: Cambridge University Press, 1995.

D'Aquili, Eugene. "Social Historians Entranced, or 'The Medium is the Message.'" In *Social History and Issues in Human Consciousness*.

Damasio, Antonio. *Descartes Error: Emotion, Reason, and the Human Brain*. New York: G.P. Putnam's Sons, 1994.

Damasio, Antonio. *Looking for Spinoza: Joy, Sorrow, and the Feeling Brain*. Orlando, FL: Harcourt, 2003.

The Damned Art. Ed. Sydney Anglo. London: Routledge & Kegan Paul, 1977.

Dankert, Werner. *Unehrliche Leute*. Bern: Francke, 1963.

The Dark Side of Interpersonal Communications. Ed. William Cupach and Brian Spitzberg. Hillsdale, NJ: Erlbaum, 1994.

Daston, Lorraine and Katharine Park. *Wonders and the Order of Nature, 1150–1750*. New York: Zone, 1998.

Davenport, John. *Aphrodisiacs and Anti-aphrodisiacs*. New York: Award Books, 1970.

Davidson, H.R. "Hostile Magic in the Icelandic Sagas." In *The Witch Figure*.

Davies, Owen. *Cunning-Folk: Popular Magic in English History*. London and New York: Hambledon and London, 2003.

Davies, Owen. "Cunning-Folk in England and Wales during the Eighteenth and Ninteenth Centuries." *Rural History*, vol. 8:1 (1997), pp. 91–107.

Davies, Owen. "Cunning-Folk in the Medical Market-Place during the Ninteenth Century." *Medical History*, vol. 43 (1999), pp. 55–73.

Davies, Owen. "French Charmers and Their Healing Charms." In *Charms and Charming*.
Davies, Owen. "Healing Charms in Use in England and Wales, 1700–1950." *Folklore*, vol. 107 (1996), pp. 19–32.
Davies, Owen. "The Nightmare Experience, Sleep Paralysis, and Witchcraft Accusations." *Folklore* (August 2003), n.p. (online).
Davies, Owen. *Witchcraft, Magic, and Culture, 1736–1951*. Manchester: Manchester University Press, 1999.
Davis, Natalie. *Fiction in the Archives: Pardon Tales and their Tellers in Sixteenth-Century France*. Stanford, CA: Stanford University Press, 1987.
Davis, Natalie. *Society and Culture in Early Modern Europe*. Stanford, CA: Stanford University Press, 1975.
Dawkins, Robert. *The Selfish Gene*. Oxford: Oxford University Press, 1976.
Dawson, George. *Healing: Pagan and Christian*. New York: AMS Press, 1977, rpt. of 1935.
Daxelmüller, Chrisoph. *Zauberpraktiken: Eine Ideengeschichte der Magie*. Zurich: Artemis & Winkler, 1993.
Deception: Perspectives on Human and Nonhhuman Deceit. Ed. Robert Michell and Nicholas Thompson. Albany: SUNY Press, 1986.
Decker-Hauff, Hans Martin. "Die Geistige Führungschicht Württembergs." In *Beamtentum und Pfarrerstand*.
Decker, Ronald et al. *A Wicked Pack of Cards: The Origins of the Occult Tarot*. New York: St. Martins, 1996.
Deeley, Quintin. "The Cognitive Anthropology of Belief." In *Power of Belief*.
Defining Females: The Nature of Women in Society. Ed. Shirley Ardener. New York: Wiley, 1978.
Delcambre, Etienne. "Witchcraft Trials in Lorraine: Psychology of the Judges." In *European Witchcraft*.
DeLisi, Matt. *Career Criminals in Society*. Thousand Oaks, CA: Sage, 2005.
Dementia and Normal Aging. Ed. Felicia Huppert et al. Cambridge and New York: Cambridge University Press, 1994.
Demos, John. *Entertaining Satan*. New York: Oxford University Press, 1982.
Demos, John. "Old Age in Early New England." In *Turning Points*.
Dennett, David. *Consciousness Explained*. New York: Penguin, 1991.
Dennett, David. *Darwin's Dangerous Idea*. London: Allan Lane, 1995.
Despret, Vinciane. *Our Emotional Makeup: Ethnopsychology and Selfhood*. Trans. Marjolijn de Jager. New York: Other Press, 2004.
The Devil, Heresy, and Witchcraft in the Middle Ages. Ed. Alberto Ferreiro. Leiden, Boston, Köln: Brill, 1998.
Devisch, René. "Witchcraft and Sorcery." In *A Companion to Psychological Anthropolgy*, pp. 389–416.
Devlin, Judith. *The Superstitious Mind: French Peasants and the Supernatural in the Ninteenth Century*. New Haven, CT: Yale University Press, 1987.
Diagnosis and Management of Dementia: A Manual for Memor Disorders Teams. Ed. Gorden Wilicolk et al. Oxford: Oxford University Press, 1999.
Diagnostic and Statistical Manual, 4th Edition. American Psychiatric Association. Washington, DC, 1994. Referred to as *DSM-IV*.
Diamond, Stephen. *Anger, Madness, and the Daimonic: The Psychological Genesis of Violence, Evil, and Creativity*. Albany: SUNY Press, 1996.

Dickie, Matthew. "Who Practiced Love-Magic in Classical Antiquity and in the Late Roman World?" *The Classical Quarterly*, New Series, vol. 50:2 (2000), pp. 563–83.
Differential Diagnosis and Treatment of Movement Disorders. Ed. Eduardo Tolosa et al. Boston: Elsevier 1998.
Dillinger, Johannes. "American Spiritualism and German Sectarianism: A Comparative Study of Societal Construction of Ghost Beliefs." *Bulletin of the German Historical Institute*, n.28 (Spring 2001), http://www.ghi-dc.org/bulletin 28S01/b23dillinger.html.
Dillinger, Johannes. *"Böse Leute." Hexenvervolgungen in Schwäbisch-Osterreich und Kurtrier im Vergleich*. Trier: Spee, 1999.
Dillinger, Johannes. "'Das Ewige Leben und fünfzehntausend Gulden": Schatzgraberei im Herzogtum Württemberg im 17. und 18. Jahrhundert." In *Zauberer – Selbstmörder – Schatzsucher*.
Dillinger, Johannes and Petra Feld. "Treasure-Hunting: A Magical Motif in Law, Folklore, and Mentality, Württemberg, 1606–1770." *German History*, vol. 20:2 (2002), pp. 161–84.
Dillinger, Johannes, Thomas Fritz, and Wolfgang Mährle. *Zum Feuer Verdammt: Die Hexenverfolgungen in der Grafschaft Hohenberg, der Reichstadt Reutlingen, und der Fürstpropstei Ellwangen*. Stuttgart: Franz Steiner Verlag, 1998.
Dimberg, Ulf. "Psychophysiological Reactions to Facial Expressions." In *Nonverbal Communication*.
Dinzelbacher, Peter. "Superstition." In *Encyclopedia of Witchcraft*.
Dissociation: Clinical and Theoretical Perspectives. Ed. Steven Lynn and Judith Rhue. New York and London: The Guilford Press, 1994.
Divination and Healing. Ed. Michael Winkelman and Philip Peek. Tuscon: University of Arizona Press, 2004.
Dixon, C. Scott. "Popular Beliefs and the Reformation in Brandenburg-Ansbach." In *Popular Religion in Germany*.
Dobeneck, Friedrich von. *Des Deutschen Mittelalters Volksglauben und Heroensagen*. Hildesheim: Georg Olms Verlag, 1974.
Döbler, Hansferdinand. *Hexenwahn: Die Geschichte einer Verfolgung*. Munich: Bertelsmann, 1977.
Domhoff, G. William. *The Scientific Study of Dreams: Neural Networks, Cognitive Development, and Content Analysis*. Washington, DC: American Psychological Association, 2003.
Donald, Merlin. *A Mind So Rare: The Evolution of Human Consciousness*. New York and London: W.W. Norton, 2001.
D'Ondrade, Roy. *The Development of Cognitive Anthropology*. Cambridge: Cambridge University Press, 1995.
Douglas, Mary. "The Pangolin Revisited: A New Approach to Animal Symbolism." In *Signifying Animals: Human Meaning in the Natural World*.
Dreams: A Reader on Religious, Cultural, and Psychological Dimensions of Dreaming. Ed. Kelly Bulkeley. New York: Palgrave Macmillan, 2001.
Drugs and the Brain: Papers on the Action, Use, and Abuse of Psychotropic Agents. Ed. Perry Black. Baltimore: Johns Hopkins Press, 1969.
Duerr, Hans Peter. *Dreamtime: Concerning the Boundary between Wildness and Civilization*. Trans. Felicitas Goodman. New York: Basil Blackwell, 1985.
Duley, Margot et al. "Biology Versus Culture." In *The Cross-Cultural Study of Women*.
Dülmen, Richard van. *Theatre of Horror: Crime and Punishment in Early Modern Germany*. Trans. Elisabeth Neu. Cambridge, UK: Polity Press, 1990.

Dupuy, Ernest and Trevor Dupuy. *The Encyclopedia of Military History*, New York: Harper & Row, 1970.
Durant, Will and Ariel. *The Age of Louis XIV*. New York: Simon and Schuster, 1963.
Durant, Will and Ariel. *The Age of Reason Begins*. New York: Simon and Schuster, 1961.
Durant, Will and Ariel. *The Age of Voltaire*. New York: Simon and Schuster, 1965.
Durant, Will and Ariel. *Rousseau and Revolution*. New York: Simon and Schuster, 1967.
Durrani, Matin. "Physicists Probe the Paranormal." PhysicsWorld.com. News and Analysis, May 1, 2000, http://physicsweb.org/articles/world/13/05/8.
Early Modern Europe: From Crisis to Stability. Ed. Philip Benedict and Myron Gutmann. Newark, DE: University of Delaware Press, 2005.
Early Modern European Witchcraft: Centers and Peripheries. Ed. Bengt Ankarloo and Gustav Henningsen. Oxford: Clarendon Press, 1990.
Eck, Marleen van. "The Effects of Perceived Stress, Traits, Mood States, and Stressful Daily Events on Salivary Cortisol." *Psychosomatic Medicine*, vol. 58 (1996), pp. 447–58.
Edmonds, Bruce. "The Revealed Poverty of the Gene-meme Analogy – Why Memetics per se has Failed to Produce Substantive Results." *Journal of Memetics*, vol. 9 (2005), http://jom-emit.cfpm.org/2005/vol9/edmonds_b.html).
Edwards, Allan. *Dementia*. New York and London: Plenum Press, 1993.
Edwards, Kathryn. "Introduction: Expanding the Analysis of Traditional Belief." In *Werewolves*.
Eichenbaum, Luise and Susie Orbach. *Between Women: Love, Envy, and Competition in Women's Friendships*. New York: Viking Penguin, 1988.
Eider, Herbert. "Elitenkultur Contra Volkskulture: Zur Kritik an Robert Muchembleds Deutung der Hexenverfolgung." In *Alltagsleben und Magie*.
Eis, Gerhard. *Altdeutsche Zaubersprüche*. Berlin: de Gruyter, 1964.
Eisendrath, Stuart. "Psychiatric Disorders," In *Current Medical Diagnosis*.
Eisenstein, Elizabeth. *The Printing Press as an Agent of Social Change*, 2 vols. Cambridge: Cambridge University Press, 1979.
Ekman, Paul et al. "Autonomic Nervous System Activity Distinguishes Among Emotions." *Science*, New Series, vol. 221 (September 16, 1983), pp. 1208–10.
Ekman, Paul. "Biological and Cultural Contributions to Body and Facial Movement." In *Anthropology of the Body*.
Ekman, Paul et al. "Facial Expressions of Emotions: An Old Controversy and New Findings." *Philosophical Transactions: Biological Sciences*, vol. 335, *Processing the Facial Image* (January 29, 1992), pp. 62–9.
Eliade, Mircea. "Observations on European Witchcraft." In *Occultism, Witchcraft and Cultural Fashions*. Chicago, IL: University of Chicago Press, 1976.
Eliade, Mircea. *Shamanism: Archaic Techniques of Ecstasy*. Trans. Willard Trask. Princeton, NJ: Princeton University Press, 1964.
Elkin, Adolphus. "Aboriginal Doctors are Outstanding People." In *Shamans through Time*.
Ellis, Bill. *Lucifer Ascending: The Occult in Folklore and Popular Culture*. University of Kentucky Press, 2004.
Elmer, Peter. "Towards a Politics of Witchcraft in Early Modern England." In *Languages of Witchcraft*.
Emery, Ted. "Casanova's Life: An Outline." At *Casanova Research Page*, Department of French and Italian, Dickinson College, last updated 7/30/2000, copyright 1998–2000, http://www.dickinson.edu/~emery/sketch.htm.
Emmerich, Wolfgang. *Germanistische Volkstumideologie*. Reutlingen: Braxmaier, 1968.

Encyclopedia of European Social History from 1350 to 2000, 4 vols. Ed. Peter Stearns. New York: Charles Scribner's Sons, 2000.
Encyclopedia of Witchcraft, 4 vols. Ed. Richard Golden. Santa Barbara, CA: ABC-Clio, 2006.
Das Ende der Hexenverfolgung. Ed. Sönke Lorenz and Dieter Bauer. Stuttgart: Franz Steiner, 1995.
Erickson, Carolly. *The Medieval Vision*. New York: Oxford, 1976.
Ernst, Gottlob. *6000 Jahre Bauerntum im Oberen Gau*. Korb i. Remstal: Gottlob Ernst, 1955/56/57.
Ernst, Katharina. *Krankheit und Heiligung: Die Medikale Kultur Württembergischer Pietisten im 18. Jahrhundert*. Stuttgart: Kohlhammer, 2003.
Eron, Leonard. "Gender Differences in Violence: Biology and/or Socialization?" In *Of Mice and Women*.
Eslea, Brian. *Witch-Hunting, Magic, and the New Philosophy*. Sussex: Harvester, 1980.
Estes, James. *Christian Magistrate and State Church: The Reforming Career of Johannes Brenz*. Toronto: University of Toronto Press, 1982.
Etzold, Eckhard. "Does Psi Exist and Can We Prove It? Belief and Disbelief in Psychokinesis Research." *The Parapsychological Association Convention, 2004: Proceedings of Presented Papers*, pp. 367–77.
European Witchcraft. Ed. E. William Monter. New York: Wiley, 1969.
Evans, Richard J. "Introduction: The 'Dangerous Classes' In Germany from the Middle Ages to the Twentieth Century." In *The German Underworld*.
The Evil Eye. Ed. Clarence Maloney. New York: Columbia University Press, 1976.
Ewing, L. S. "Fighting and Death from Stress in a Cockroach." In *Animal Social Psychology*.
Fabrega, Horacio. "Culture, Behavior, and the Nervous System." *Annual Review of Anthropology*, vol. 6 (1977), pp. 419–55.
Family and Inheritance: Rural Society in Western Europe, 1200–1800. Ed. Jack Goody et al. Cambridge: Cambridge University Press, 1976.
The Family Life Cycle in European Societies. Ed. Jean Cuisenier. The Hague: Mouton, 1977.
Farge, Arlette and Jacques Revel. *The Vanishing Children of Paris: Rumor and Politics Before the French Revolution*. Trans. Claudia Miéville. Cambridge: Harvard University Press, 1991.
Fausel, Heinrich. "Von altlutherischen Orthodoxie zum Frühpietismus in Württemberg." *Zeitschrift für Württembergischer Landesgeschichte*, vol. XXIV:2 (1965), pp. 309–28.
Favret-Saada, Jeanne. *Deadly Words: Witchcraft in the Bocage*. Trans. Catherine Cullen. Cambridge: Cambridge University Press, 1980.
Favret-Saada, Jeanne and Catherine Cullen. "Unbewitching as Therapy." *American Ethologist*, vol. 16:1 (February 1989), pp. 40–56.
Fear in Early Modern Society. Ed. William Naphy and Penny Roberts. Manchester: University of Manchester Press, 1997.
Feinberg, Benjamin. *The Devil's Book of Culture: History, Mushrooms, and Caves in Southern Mexico*. Austin: University of Texas Press, 2003.
Felten, David. "The Brain and the Immune System." In *Healing and the Mind*.
Ferrai, Robert, et al. "Volition and Psychosocial Factors in Illness Behavior." In *Power of Belief*.
Feulner, Walter. "Zum Giftmord und Seinem Nachweis." Dissertation, Medizinischen Fachbereichen der Reeien Universität Berlin, 1983.

Fichtenau, Heinrich. *Living in the Tenth Century: Mentalities and Social Orders*. Trans. Patrick Geary. Chicago, IL: University of Chicago Press, 1991.
Finch, Andrew. "Women and Violence in the Later Middle Ages: The Evidence of the Officiality of Cerisy." *Continuity and Change*, vol. 7 (1992), pp. 23–45.
Finks, Max. "Drugs, EEG, and Behavior." In *Drugs and the Brain*.
Fischer, Alan. "Chemical Stimulation of the Brain." In *Drugs and the Brain*.
Fischer, David Hackett. *Growing. Old Fischer Old in America*. New York: Oxford University Press, 1977.
Fischer, Hermann. *Schwabisches Wörterbuch*, vol. 3. Tübingen: H. Laupp'schen Buchhandlung, 1911.
Fishwick, Duncan. "An Early Christian Cryptogram?" In *CCHA (Canadian Catholic Historical Association) Report*, vol. 26 (1959), pp. 29–41.
Fiume, Giovanna. "The Old Vinegar Lady, or the Judicial Modernization of the Crime of Witchcraft." In *History of Crime*.
Flaherty, Gloria. "Sex and Shamanism in the Eighteenth Century." In *Sexual Underworlds*.
Flaherty, Gloria. *Shamanism and the Eighteenth Century*. Princeton, NJ: Princeton University Press, 1992.
Flanagan, Owen. *Dreaming Souls: Dreams and the Evolution of the Conscious Mind*. Oxford: Oxford University Press, 2000.
Flint, Valerie. *The Rise of Magic in Early Medieval Europe*. Princeton: Princeton University Press, 1991.
Folkbiology. Ed. Douglas Medin and Scott Atran. Cambridge: MIT Press, 1999.
Folktales of Germany. Ed. Kurt Ranke. Trans. Lotte Baumann. Chicago, IL: University of Chicago Press, 1966.
Forman, Robert. "Introduction: Mystical Consciousness, the Innate Capacity, and the Perennial Psychology." In *The Innate Capacity*.
Forsyth, Neil. *The Old Enemy: Satan and the Combat Myth*. Princeton, NJ: Princeton University Press, 1987.
Fox, J. Robin. "Witchcraft and Clanship in Cochiti Therapy." In *Magic, Witchcraft, and Curing*.
Fraczek, Adam. "Patterns of Aggressive-Hostile Behavior Orientation among Adolescent Boys and Girls." In *Of Mice and Women*.
Franklyn, Julian. *Death by Enchantment*. New York: Putnam's, 1971.
Franz, Günther. "Hexensalbe: Was Sie Schon Immer Über Herstellung und Gebrauch Wissen Wollten." In *Alltagsleben und Magie*.
Franz, Günther. *Geschichte des deutschen Bauernstandes*. Stuttgart: Eugen Ulmer, 1970.
Franz, Günther. *Beamtentum und Pfarrerstand*. Limburg/Lahn: Starke, 1972.
Franz, Günther. *Das Dreissigjährige Krieg und das deutsche Volk*. Stuttgart: Eugen Ulmer, 1970.
Frazier, Cynthia and Anthony Gloslock. "Aging and Old Age in Cross-Cultural Perspective." In *Cross-Cultural Topics in Psychology*.
Frecska, Ede and Zsuzsanna Kulcsar. "Social Bonding in the Modulation of the Physiology of Ritual Trance." *Ethos*, vol. 17:1 (March 1989), pp. 70–87.
Freedman, Joseph. Aging: Its History and Literature. New York: Human Sciences Press, 1979.
Frevert, Ute. "The Taming of the Noble Ruffian: Male Violence and Dueling in Early Modern and Modern Germany." In *Men and Violence*.
Frick, Thomas. *Zigeuner im Zeitalter des Absolutismus*. Centaurus: Pfaffenweiler, 1996.
Friedman, Howard. *The Self-Healing Personality*. New York: Henry Holt, 1991.

Friedrichs, Christopher. *Urban Society in an Age of War: Nördlingen, 1580–1770.* Princeton, NJ: Princeton University Press, 1979.
Fries, Maureen. "*Feminae Populi*: Popular Images of Women in Medieval Literature." *Journal of Popular Culture*, vol. 14:1 (Summer 1980), pp. 79–86.
Frist, Chris. "The Pathology of Experience." *Brain*, vol. 127, no. 2 (2004) pp. 239–42.
Fritz, Gerhard, "Des Herzogs ungetreue Diener. Vögte und Atleute in Altwürttemberg zwischen Legitimatät, Korruption und Untertanenprotest." *Zeitschrift für Württembergische Landesgeschichte*, vol. 63 (2004), pp. 119–68.
Fritz, Gerhard, "Fälscher und Betrüger im frühneuzeitlichen Württemberg: Das *Crimen falsi et stellionatus* al Indikator einer sich differenzierenden Gesellschaft." *Zeitschrift für Württembergische Landesgeschichte*, vol. 64 (2005), pp. 165–98.
Fritz, Thomas. "Hexenverfolgungen in der Reichstadt Reutlingen." In *Zum Feuer Verdammt.*
Frolkis, Vladimir. "Aging of the Autonomic Nervous System." In *Handbook of the Psychology of Aging.*
Fruth, Chris. "The Pathology of Experience." *Brain*, vol. 127 (2004), pp. 239–42.
Fry, Douglas. "Female Aggression among the Zapotec of Oaxaca, Mexico." In *Of Mice and Women.*
The Fugger Newsletters. Ed. Victor von Klarwill. Trans. Pauline de Chary. London: John Lane, 1924.
Fulbrook, Mary. *Piety and Politics.* Cambridge: Cambridge University Press, 1983.
Fuller, Robert. *Stairways to Heaven: Drugs in American Religious History.* Boulder, CO: Westview Press, 2000.
Funkenstein, H. Harris. "Cerebrovascular Disorders." In *Geriatric Neuropsychology.*
Furst, Peter. *Hallucinogens and Culture.* San Fransisco: Chandler and Sharp, 1976.
Furst, Peter. "'High States' in Culture-Historical Perspective." In *Alternate States of Consciousness.*
Gager, John. *Curse Tables and Binding Spells from the Ancient World.* Oxford: Oxford University Press, 1999.
Galati, Dario et al., "Spontaneous Facial Expression in Congenitally Blind and Sighted Children Aged 8–11." *Journal of Visual Impairment and Blindness*, vol. 97:7 (July 2003), pp. 418–29.
Galin, David. "The Two Modes of Consciousness and the Two Halves of the Brain." In *Symposium on Consciousness.*
Gallucci, Margaret, "Burned under the Tuscan Sun: A Newly Discovered Witchcraft Document in the Archivio di Stato, Florence," *Annals of Scholarship*, vol. 16: 1–3, pp. 11–23.
Gannon, Linda. "The Psychophysiology of Psychosomatic Disorders." In *Psychosomatic Disorders.*
Garrett, Clarke. "Witches and Cunning Folk in the Old Regime." In *The Wolf and the Lamb.*
Garrison, Vivian and Conrad Arensberg, "The Evil Eye: Envy or Risk of Seizure? Parnoia of Patronal Dependency?" In *The Evil Eye.*
Gaskill, Malcolm. "Witchcraft in Early Modern Kent: Stereotypes and the Background to Accusations." In *Witchcraft in Early Modern Europe.*
Gaskill, Malcolm. "Witches and Witnesses in Old and New England." In *Languages of Witchcraft.*
Gatchel, Robert. "Psychophysiological Disorders: Past and Present Perspectives." In *Psychophysiological Disorders.*
Gay, David. "On the Christianity of Incantations." In *Charms and Charming.*
Gebhardt, Werner. *Bürgertum in Stuttgart.* Neustadt and der Aisch: Degener, 1999.

Gehring, Paul. "Der Hexenprozess und die Tübinger Juristenfakultät." In *Zeitschrift für Württembergische Landesgeschichte*, vol. I (1937), pp. 157–188, 370–405.
Geist, Harold. *The Psychological Aspects of the Aging Process with Sociological Implications*. St. Louis: Warren Green, 1968.
Gender in Early Modern Germany History. Ed. Ulinke Rublack. Cambridge: Cambridge University Press, 2002.
Gender Relations in German History: Power, Agency, and Experience from the Sixteenth to the Twentieth Century. Ed. Lynn Abrams and Elizabeth Harvey. Durham: Duke University Press, 1997.
Gennep, Arnold Van. "Shamanism is a Dangerously Vague Word." In *Shamans through Time*.
Gentilcore, David. "The Fear of Disease and the Disease of Fear." in *Fear in Early Modern Society*.
Gentilcore, David. *From Bishop to Witch: The System of the Sacred in Early Modern Terra d'Otranto*. Manchester and New York: Manchester University Press, 1992.
Gentilcore, David. *Healers and Healing in Early Modern Italy*. Manchester: Manchester University Press, 1998.
Gentilcore, David. "Was there a 'Popular Medicine' in Early Modern Europe [1]." *Folklore*, vol. 115 (2004), pp. 151–66.
Gentilcore, David. "Witchcraft Narratives and Folklore Motifs in Southern Italy." In *Witchcraft Reader*.
Geriatric Neuropsychology. Ed. Marilyn Albert and Mark Moss. New York and London: The Guilford Press, 1988.
The German People and the Reformation. Ed. R. Po-Chia Hsia. Ithaca: Cornell University Press, 1988.
The German Underworld: Deviants and Outcasts in German History. Ed. Richard Evans. London and New York: Routledge, 1988.
Gerrig, Richard and Bradford Pillow. "A Developmental Perspective on the Construction of Disbelief." In *Believed-in Imaginings*.
Gerritsen, Welmoet et al. "Experiemental Social Fear: Immunological, Hormonal, and Autonomic Concomitants." *Psychosomatic Medicine*, vol. 58 (1996), pp. 274–86.
Geschlecht, Magie, und Hexenverfolgung. Ed. Ingrid Ahrendt-Schulte et al. Bielefeld: Verlag für Regionalgeschichte, 2002.
Gestrich, Andreas. "Pietism und Aberglaube." In *Das Ende der Hexenverfolgung*, pp. 269–86.
Geyer-Kordesch, Johanna. "Cultural Habits of Illness: The Enlightenment and the Pious in Eighteenth Century Germany." In *Patients and Practitioners*.
Geyer-Kordesch, Johanna. "Passions and the Ghost in the Machine: Or What Not to Ask about Science in Seventeenth- and Eighteenth-Century Germany." In *The Medical Revolution of the Seventeenth Century*.
Gianaro, Catherine. "Lahn's Analysis of Genes Indicates Human Brain Continues to Evolve." *The University of Chicago Chronicle*, vol. 25:1 (September 22, 2005), http://chronicle.uchicago.edu/050922/brainevolution.shtml.
Gibbes, Robert. "The Effects of Estrogen on Basal Forebrain Cholinergic Neurons and Cognition: Implications for Brain Aging and Dementia in Women." In *Hormones, Gender, and the Aging Brain*.
Gibson, Marion. "Understanding Witchcraft? Accusers' Stories in Print in Early Modern England." In *Languages of Witchcraft*.
Gielen, Uwe. "Forward," In *Spirit vs. Scalpel*.
Giger, Hubert. *Hexenwahn und Hexenprozesse in der Surselva*. Kommissionsverlag Desertina, 2001.

Gijswijt-Hofstra, Marijke. "Witchcraft after the Witch-Trials." In *Witchcraft and Magic in Europe: The Eighteenth and Nineteenth Centuries*.
Gildrie, Richard. "Visions of Evil: Popular Culture, Puritanism, and the Massachusetts Witchcarft Crisis of 1692." Reprinted in *New*, vol. 1.
Giles, Cynthia. *The Tarot*. New York: Paragon, 1992.
Ginsburg, G. P. "Faces: An Epilogue and Reconceptualization." In *The Psychology of Facial Expression*.
Ginzburg, Carlo. "Deciphering the Witches' Sabbat." In *Witchcraft Reader*.
Ginzburg, Carlo. *Ecstasies: Deciphering the Witches' Sabbath*. Trans. Raymond Rosenthal. New York: Pantheon Book, 1991.
Ginzburg, Carlo. *Night Battles: Witchcraft and Agrarian Cults in the Sixteenth and Seventeenth Centuries*. Trans. John and Anne Tedeschi. New York, Penguin, 1985.
Gladwell, Malcolm. *The Tipping Point*. Boston, MA: Little, Brown and Company, 2000.
Glazer, Ilsa. "Interfemale Aggression and Resource Scarcity in Cross-Cultural Perspective." In *Of Mice and Women*.
Gleixner, Ulrike. *Pietismus und Burgertum: Eine Historische Anthropologie der Frömmigkeit: Württemberg, 17-19 Jahrhundert*. Göttingen: Vandenhoeck & Ruprecht, 2005.
Glucklich, Ariel. *The End of Magic*. Oxford: Oxford University Press, 1997.
Godly Magistrates and Church Order. Ed. and Trans. James Estes. Toronto: Centre for Reformation and Renaissance Studies, 2001.
Good Gossip. Ed. Robert Goodman and Aaron Ben-Ze'ev. Lawrence, KS: University Press of Kansas, 1994.
Goodman, Felicitas. *Ecstasy, Ritual, and Alternate Reality*. Bloomington and Indianapolis: Indiana University Press, 1988.
Goodman, Felicitas. *How About Demons? Possession and Exorcism in the Modern World*. Bloomington, IN: Indiana University Press, 1988.
Goodman, Felicitas. "The Neurophysiology of Shamanic Ecstasy." In *Shamanism: Past and Present*.
Goody, Jack. "Inheritance, Property and Women: Some Comparative Considerations." In *Family and Inheritance*.
Gordon, Bruce. "God Killed Saul: Heinrich Bullinger and Jacob Ruef on the Power of the Devil." In *Werewolves*.
Graeter, Jacob. *Hexen oder Unholden Predigten*. Tübingen, 1589.
Graf, Fritz. *Magic in the Ancient World*. Trans. Franklin Philip. Cambridge, MA: Harvard University Press, 1997.
Graf, Klaus. "Hexenverfolgungen in Schwäbish-Gmund." In *Hexenverfolgungen*.
Grambo, Ronald. "Sleep as a Means of Ecstasy and Divination." *Acta Ethnographica Academiae Scientiarum Hungaricae*, vol. 22: 3–4 (1973), pp. 417–25.
Greenfield, Susan. *Journey to the Center of the Mind: Toward a Science of Consciousness*. New York: Freeman and Co., 1995.
Grees, Herman. *Ländliche Unterschichten und Ländliche Siedlung im Ostschwaben*. Tübingen: Geographischen Institutes der Universität Tübingen, 1975.
Gregory, Annabel. "Witchcraft, Politics, and 'Good Neighborhood' in Early Seventeenth Century Rye." *Past and Present*, vol. 133 (1991).
Grof, Ruth. *Critical Realism, Post-Positivism, and the Possibility of Knowledge*. London and New York: Routledge, 2004.
Grube, Water, *Der Stuttgarter Landtag*. Stuttgart: Ernst Klett, 1957.
Gurevich, Aron. *Medieval Popular Culture: Problems of Belief and Perception*. Trans. János M. Bak and Paul A. Hollingsworth. Cambridge: Cambridge University Press, 1988.

Gutman, David. "The Cross-Cultural Perspective: Notes Toward a Comparative Psychology of Aging." In *Handbook of the Psychology of Aging.*
Haag, Norbert. "Frömmigkeit und sozialer Protest: Hans Keil, der Prophet von Gerlingen." *Zeitschrift für Württembergische Landesgeschichte,* vol. 48 (1989), pp. 127–41.
Haag, Norbert. *Predigt und Gesellschaft: die lutherische Orthodoxie in Ulm, 1640–1740,* Mainz: P. von Zabern, 1992.
Haaken, Janice. "Women's Stories of Hidden Selves and Secret Knowledge: A Psychoanalytic Feminist Analysis." In *Believed-in Imaginings.*
Hafen, Susan. "Organizational Gossip: A Revolving Door of Regulation and Resistance." *Southern Communication Journal,* vol. 69:3 (Spring 2004), pp. 223–41.
Hafen, Brent et al. *Mind/Body Health: The Effects of Attitudes, Emotions, and Relationships.* Boston, MA: Allyn and Bacon, 1996.
Hagen, William. " Glaube und Skepsis einer magischen Schätzgrabers: Ein Fall aus den Prignitz und Mecklenburg aus den 1760er Jahren." In *Historie und Eigen-Sinn.* Weimar: Herman Böhlaus Nachfolger, 1997.
Hagan, J. J. "The Status of the Cholinergic Hypothesis of Dementia." In *Anti-dementia Agents.*
Hagen, Rune. "The King, the Cat, and the Chaplain: King Christian IV's Encounter with the Sami Shamans of Northern Norway and Northern Russia in 1599." In *Communicating with the Spirits.*
Hall, Alaric. "Getting Shot of Elves: Healing, Witchcraft and Fairies in the Scottish Witchcraft Trials." *Folklore,* vol. 116 (April 2005), pp. 1–8.
Halligan, Peter and Mansel Aylward. "Introduction: The Relevance of Belief for Understanding and Managing Illness Behavior."In *The Power of Belief.*
Hallucinogens and Shamanism. Ed. Michael Harner. London: Oxford University Press, 1981.
Halpern, Barbara and John Foley. "The Power of the Word: Healing Charms as an Oral Genre." *Journal of American Folklore,* vol. 92, n. 362, October–December 1978, pp. 903–24.
Hammes, Manfred. *Hexenwahn und Hexenprozesse.* Frankfort: Fischer, 1977.
Hampp, Irmgard. *Beschworung, Segen, Gebet: Untersuchungen zure Zauberspruch aus dem Bereich der Volksheilkunde.* Stuttgart: Silberberg Verlag, 1961.
Handbook of Aging and the Social Sciences. Ed. Robert Binstock and Ethel Shanas. New York: Van Nostrand Reinhold, 1976.
The Handbook of Culture and Psychology. Ed. David Matsumoto. Oxford: Oxford University Press, 2001.
Handbook of the Psychology of Aging. Ed. James Birren and Walter Schau. New York: Van Nostrand Reinhold, 1977.
Handworterbuch des deutschen aberglaube, 20 vols. Ed. Hanns Bachtold-Staubli (1927–42). Referred to as *HddA.*
Hansen, Chadwick. *Witchcraft at Salem.* New York: Braziller, 1969.
Hansen, George. "Dowsing: A Review of the Experimental Evidence." *Journal of the Society for Psychical Research,* vol. 51, no. 792 (October 1982) pp. 342–67.
Hansen, Joseph, *Zauberwshn, Inquisiton und Hexenprosess in Mittelalter.* Munich: R. Oldenbourg Verlag, 1900.
Harley, David. "Mental Illness, Magical Medicine and the Devil in Northern England, 1650–1700." In *The Medical Revolution,* pp. 114–44.
Harner, Michael. *The Jívaro.* London: Robert Hale, 1972.
Harner, Michael. "Magic Darts, Bewitching, Shamans, and Curing Shamans." In *Shamans through Time.*

Harner, Michael. "The Role of Hallucinogenic Plants in European Witchcraft." In *Hallucinogens and Shamanism*.
Harpur, Tom. *The Uncommon Touch: An Investigation of Spiritual Healing*. Toronto: McClelland and Stewart, 1994.
Harrington, Joel. "Bad Parents, the State, and the Early Modern Civilizing Process." *German History*, vol. 16:1 (1998), pp. 16–28.
Harris, Marvin. "The Evolution of Human Gender Hierarchies." In *Sex and Gender Hierarchies*.
Hasselhorn, Martin. *Der altwürttembergische Pfarrstand im 18. Jahrhundert*. Stuttgart: Kohlhammer, 1958.
Hatch, Robert. "Schott, Gaspar." *The Scientific Revolution*, Westfall Catalogue – Scientific Community, The Scientific Revolution Homepage, 2002, http://web.clas.ufl.edu/users/rhatch/pages/03-Sci-Rev/SCI-REV-Home/resource-ref-read/major-minor-ind/westfall-dsb/SAM-S.htm.
Harte, Jeremy. "Granny Takes a Trip: Drugs, Witches, and the Flight of the Sabbat." "Published at Beltane, 2001." Online at http://www.whitedragon.org.uk/articles/ointment.htm.
Hartmann, Ernst. *Dreams and Nightmares*. New York: Plenum, 1998.
Hasher, Lynn et al. "Inhibitory Control, Environmental Support, and Self-Initiated Processing in Aging." In *Perspectives on Human Memory*.
Hatch, Robert. "Schott, Gaspar." The Scientific Revolution/Westfall Catalogue – Scientific Community, The Scientific Revolution Homepage, 2002, http://web.clas.ufl.edu/users/rhatch/pages/03-Sci-Rev/SCI-REV-Home/resource-ref-read/major-minor-ind/westfall-dsb/SAM-S.htm.
Hawaleshka, Danylo. "Ready, Aim, Fire!" *Maclean's*, vol. 119:10 (March 6, 2006), p. 23.
Haynes, Stephen. "Muscle-Contraction Headache: A Psychophysiological Perspective of Etiology and Treatment." In *Psychosomatic Disorders*.
Healing and the Mind/Bill Moyers. Ed. Betty Sue Flowers. New York: Doubleday, 1993.
Healing Logics: Culture and Medicine in Modern Health Belief Systems. Ed. Erika Brady. Logan: Utah State University Press, 2001.
Health, Disease, and Healing in Medieval Culture. Ed. Sheila Campbell et al. New York: St. Martin's Press, 1991.
Heath, Chip et al. "Emotion Selection in Memes: The Case of Urban Legends." *Journal of Personality and Social Psychology*, vol. 81:6 (2001), pp. 1028–41, http://www.sscnet.ucla.edu/anthro/bec/papers/Heath_Emotional_Selection.pdf.
Heiman, Julia and John Hatch. "Conceptual and Therapeutic Contributions of Psychophysiology to Sexual Dysfunction." In *Psychosomatic Disorders*.
Heinze, Ruth-Inge. "Divination in Multireligious Southeast Asia." In *Divination and Healing*, pp. 167–79.
Hemsworth, D. H. et al. "Fear of Humans and its Consequences for the Domestic Pig." In *The Inevitable Bond*.
Hendry, Joy. *Other People's Worlds: An Introduction to Cultural and Social Anthropology*. New York: New York University Press, 1999.
Henningsen, Gustav. "Das Ende der Hexenprozesse und die Fortsetzung der populären Hexenverfolgung." In *Das Ende der Hexenverfolgung*.
Henningsen, Gustav. "'The Ladies from the Outside': An Archaic Pattern of the Witches Sabbath." In *European Witchcraft*.
Henningsen, Gustav. *The Witches' Advocate*. Reno: University of Nevada Press, 1980.
Henningsen, Gustav and Bengt Ankarloo. "Introduction." In *Early Modern European Witchcraft*.

Hermelink, Heinrich. *Geschichte der Evangelischen Kirche in Württemberg.* Stuttgart: Rainer Wunderlich, 1949.
Herrigel, Eugen. *Zen in the Art of Archery.* New York: Vintage, 1971.
Herx, Liselotte. *Der Giftmord, inbesondere der Giftmord durch Frauen.* Emsdetten: Heins & Lechte, 1937.
Hess, Eckhard. "The Role of Pupil Size in Communication." *Scientific American*, vol. 233:5 (November 1975), pp. 110–19.
Hester, Marianne. "Patriarchal Reconstruction and Witch Hunting." *In Witchcraft in Early Modern Europe.*
Hexe oder Hausfrau: Das Bild der Frau in der Geschichte Vorarlbergs. Ed. Alis Niederstätter und Wolfgang Scheffknecht. Sigmarungendorf: Regio Verlag, Glock and Lutz, 1991.
Hexen und Hexenverfolgung im deutschen Südwesten. Ed. Sönke Lorenz. Karlsruhe: Cantz, 1994.
Hexen und Zauberer: die grosse Verfolgung, ein europaïisches Phänomen in der Steiermark. Ed. Helfried Valentinitsch. Graz: Leykam, 1987.
Hexenverfolgung: Beiträge zur Forschung. Ed. Sönke Lorenz and Dieter Bauer. Würzburg: Königshausen and Neumann, 1995.
Hexenverfolgung und Frauengeschichte. Ed. Regina Pramann. Bielefeld: Verlag für Regionalgeschichte, 1993.
Hexenwahn: Magie und Imagination von 16–20 Jahrhundert. Ed. Richard van Dülman. Fischer Taschenbuch Verlag, 1993, rpt. of 1987.
Hexerei, Magie, und Volksmedizin. Ed. Bernd Schmelz. Bonn: Holos Verlag, 1997.
Heyne, Claudia. *Täterin: Offene und versteckte Aggression von Frauen.* Zurich: Kreuz, 1993.
A History of Women in the West, vol II, Renaissance and Enlightenment Paradoxes. Ed. Natalie Davis and Arlette Farge. Cambridge, MA: The Belknap Press of Harvard University Press, 1973.
Hilgard, Ernst, *Divided Consciousness: Multiple Controls in Human Thought and Action.* New York: Wiley, 1986.
Hinde, Robert. *Why Gods Persist: A Scientific Approach to Religion.* London and New York: Routledge, 1999.
Hippel, Wolfgang von. "Bevolkerung und Wirtschaft im Zeitalter des Dreissigjahrigen Krieges." *Zeitschrift der Historische Forschung*, vol. 5:4 (1978), pp. 413–48.
Hirsch, Miriam. *Of Women and Violence.* New York: Van Nostrand Reinhold, 1981.
Hiscock, Merrill et al. "Is There a Sex Difference in Human Laterality? IV. An Exhaustive Survey of Dual-Task Interference Studies From Six Neuropsychology Journals." *Journal of Clinical and Experimental Neuropsychology*, vol. 23 (2001), pp. 137–48.
History of Crime, Ed. Edward Muir and Guido Ruggiero, trans. Corrada Curry et al. Baltimore: Johns Hopkins University Press, 1997.
The History of Everyday Life: Reconstructing Historical Experiences and Ways of Life. Ed. Alf Lüdtke. Trans. William Templer. Princeton, NJ: Princeton University Press, 1995.
Hobson, J. Allan. *The Chemistry of Conscious States: How the Brain Changes Its Mind.* Boston, MA: Little, Brown and Company, 1994.
Hobson, J. Allan. *The Dream Drugstore: Chemically Altered States of Consciousness.* Cambridge, MA: MIT Press, 2001.
Hobson, J. Allan. *Dreaming as Delirium: How the Brain Goes Out of Its Mind.* Cambridge, MA: MIT Press, 1999.

Hobson, J. Allan. "The New Neuropsychology of Sleep: Implications for Psychoanalysis." In *Dreams: A Reader*.
Hodgkin, Katharine. "Reasoning with Unreason: Visions, Witchcraft, and Madness in Early Modern England." In *Languages of Witchcraft*.
Hole, Christina. *A Mirror of Witchcraft*. London: Chatto and Windus, 1957.
Hole, Christina. "Some Instances of Image-Magic in Great Britain." In *The Witch Figure*.
Hollan, Douglas. "Constructivist Models of Mind, Contemporary Psychoanalysis, and the Development of Cultural Theory." *American Anthropologist*, vol. 102:3 (2000), pp. 538–50.
Holmes, Ellen and Sowell Holmes. *Other Cultures, Elder Years*, 2nd ed. Thousand Oaks: Sage Publications, 1995.
Holzmann, Verena. *"Ich bescher dich wurm und wyrmin ..." Formen und Typen Altdeutscher Zaubersprüche und Segen*. Bern: Peter Lang, 2001.
Hoppál, Mihály. "Changing Image of the Eurasian Shaman." In *Studies on Shamanism*.
Hoppál, Mihály. "Shamanism: An Archaic and/or Recent System of Beliefs." In *Studies on Shamanism*.
Hoppál, Mihály and Otto von Sadovszky. "Introduction." In *Shamanism: Past and Present*.
Hormones, Gender, and the Aging Brain: The Endocrine Basis of Geriatric Psychiatry. Ed. Mary Morrison. Cambridge: Cambridge University Press, 2000.
Horsley, Richard. "Who Were the Witches? The Social Role of the Accused in the European Witch Trials." *Journal of Interdisciplinary History*, vol. IX:4 (Spring 1979), pp. 689–715.
Horsley, Ritta Jo and Richard Horsley. "On the Trail of the 'Witches': Wise Women, Midwives and the European Witch Hunts." In *Women in German Yearbook*, vol. 3, pp. 1–28.
Houdard, Sophie. "Mystics or Visionaries? Discernment of Spirtis in the First Part of the Seventeenth Century in France." In *Communicating with the Spirits*, pp. 71–83.
Hufford, David. "Beings Without Bodies: An Experience-Centered Theory of the Belief in Spirits." In *Out of the Ordinary*.
Hufford, David. *The Terror that Come in the Night: An Experience – Central Study of Supernatural Assault Traditions*. Philadelphia: University of Pennsylvania Press, 1982.
Hughes, Muriel. *Women Healers in Medieval Life and Literature*. Freeport, NY: Books for Libraries Press, 1968, rpt. of 1943.
Huisman, Frank. "Shaping the Medical Market: On the Construction of Quackery and Folk Medicine in Dutch Historiography." *Medical History*, vol. 43 (1999), pp. 359–75.
Hultkrantz, Åke. "The Place of Shamanism in the History of Religion." In *Shamanism: Past and Present*.
Human Behavior in Global Perspective: An Introduction to Cross-Cultural Psychology. Ed. Marshall Segall et al. New York: Pergamon Press, 1990.
Human by Nature: Between Biology and the Social Sciences. Ed. Peter Weingart et al. Mahwah, NY: Lawrence Erlbaum Associates, 1997.
Humphrey, Nicholas. *Leaps of Faith: Science, Miracles, and the Search for Supernatural Consolation*. New York: Copernicus, 1996.
Hutton, Ronald. *Shamans: Siberian Spirituality and the Western Imagination*. London: Hambleton and London, 2001.
Hutton, Ronald. *The Triumph of the Moon: A History of Modern Pagan Witchcraft*. Oxford: Oxford University Press, 1999.

Hyman, Ray. "How Not to Test Mediums: Critiquing the Afterlife Experiments." *Skeptical Inquirer* (January/February 2003), pp. 20–30.
Hyman, Ray. "The Mischief-Making of Ideomotor Action." *The Scientific Review of Alternative Medicine*, Fall–Winter 1999. Posted as "How People are Fooled by Ideomotor Action" at http://www.quackwatch.org/01QuackeryRelatedTopics/ideomotor.html.
"Hypnosis: Theory and Application Part II." *Harvard Mental Health Letter*, vol. 18:12 (June 2002).
The Hysterical Personality. Ed. Mardi Horowitz. New York: Aronson, 1977.
Iacoboni, Marco and GianLuigi Lenzi. "Mirror Neurons, the Insula, and Empathy." *Behavioral and Brain Sciences*, vol. 25:1 (February 2002), p. 39.
Ilomäki, Henni. "The Self as a Charm." In *Charms and Charming*.
Im Wilden Südwesten: Die Rauberbanden zwischen Neckar und Bodensee. Ed. Heiner Boehncke and Hans Sarkowicz. Frankfurt am Main: Eichorn, 1995.
Imagery and Cognition. Ed. Cesare Cornoldi and Mack McDaniel. New York and Berlin: Springer, 1991.
Impure Reason: Dialectic of Enlightenment in Germany. Ed. Daniel Wilson and Robert Holub. Detroit: Wayne State University Press, 1993.
The Inevitable Bond: Examining Scientist-Animal Interactions. Ed. Hank Davis and Dianne Balfour. Cambridge: Cambridge University Press, 1992.
Inglis, Brian. *Trance: A Natural History of Altered States of Mind*. London: Grafton Books, 1989.
Ingram, Martin. "'Scolding Women Cucked or Washed': A Crisis in Gender Relations in Early Modern England?" In *Women, Crime, and the Courts*.
The Innate Capacity: Mysticism, Psychology, and Philosophy. Ed. Robert Forman. New York: Oxford University Press, 1998.
Irwin, Harvey. "The Disembodied Self: An Empirical Study of Dissociation and the Out-of-Body Experience." *The Journal of Parapsychology*, vol. 64 (September 2000), pp. 261–77.
Irwin, H. J. *Flight of Mind: A Psychological Study of the Out-of-Body Experience*. Metuchen, NJ and London: The Scarecrow Press, 1985.
Irwin, H. J. *An Introduction to Parapsychology*, 3rd edition. Jefferson, NC: McFarland, 1999.
Itons-Peterson, Margaret and Mark McDaniel. Symmetries and Asymmetries Between Imagery and Perception." In *Imagery and Cognition*.
Jackson, Louise. "Witches, Wives, and Mothers: Witchcraft Persecutuion and Women's Confessions in Seventeenth Century England." In *Witchcraft Reader*.
Jacques-Lefèvre, Nicole. "Such an Impure, Cruel, and savage Beast ... Images of the Werewolf in Demonological Works." In *Werewolves*.
Jaeger, Herbert. *Reichsstadt und Schwabischen Kreis*. Göppingen: Kummerle, 1975.
Jan-Erik, Ruth and Peter Öberg. "Expressions of Aggression in the Life Stories of Aged Women." In *Of Mice and Women*.
Jänichen, Hans. *Beiträge sur Wirtschaftsgeschichte des schwäbisschen Dorfes*. Stuttgart: Kholhammer, 1970.
Janzarik, Werner. "Diagnostic Nosological Aspects of Mental Disorder in Old Age." In *Handbook of the Psychology of Aging*.
Jay, Timothy. *Why We Curse: A Neuro-psycho-social Theory of Speech*. Philadelphia/Amsterdam: John Benjamins Publishing Co., 2000.
Jaynes, Julian. *The Origins of Consciousness in the Breakdown of the Bicameral Mind*. Boston, MA: Houghton Mifflin, 1976.

Jeffers, Stanley. "Physics and Claims for Anomalous Effects Related to Consciousness." *Journal of Consciousness Studies*, vol. 10: 6–7 (June–July 2003).
Jens, Walter. *Eine deutsche Universitaet: 500 Jahre Tuebiner Gelehrtenrepublik*. Munich: Kindler, 1977.
Jerouschek, Günter. "Der Hexenprozeß als politisches Machtinstrument." In *Das Ende der Hexenverfolgung*.
John, Gareth. "A Scientific Investigation of Dowsing." Philadelpia Association for Critical Thinking, n.d. (latest reference 2000), http://www.phact.org/e/z/dowsepro.bak.
Johnson, Fred. *The Anatomy of Hallucinations*. Chicago, IL: Nelson-Hall, 1978.
Jones, Doug. "Evolutionary Psychology." *Annual Review of Anthropology*, vol. 28, 1999, pp. 553–75.
Jones, Prudence and Nigel Pennick. *A History of Pagan Europe*. New York: Barnes and Noble, 1995.
Joseph, R. *The Naked Neuron: Evolution and the Languages of the Body and the Brain*. New York: Plenum Press, 1993.
Joseph, Rhawn. *Neuropsychiatry, Neuropsychology, and Clinical Neuroscience*, 2nd Edition. Baltimore: Williams and Wilkins, 1996.
Joyce, Kelly. "From Numbers to Pictures: The Development of Magnetic Resonance Imaging and the Visual Turn in Medicine." *Science as Culture*, vol. 15:1 (March 2006), pp. 1–22.
Jütte, Robert. *Ärzte, Heiler, Patienten: Mediinesche Alltag in der Frühen Neuzeit*. Munich: Artemis and Winkler, 1991.
Jütte, Robert. "The Historiography of Nonconventional Medicine in Germany: A Concise Overview." *Medical History*, vol. 43 (1999), pp. 342–58.
Jütte, Robert. "The Social Construction of Illness in the Early Modern Period." In *The Social Construction of Illness*.
Kalweit, Holger. "Experiencing the Shaman's Symphony to Understand It." In *Shamans through Time*.
Kamen, Henry. *The Iron Century: Social Change in Europe 1550–1650*. New York: Praeger, 1972.
Kamiya, Joe. "Operant Control of the EEG Alpha Rhythm and some of Its Reported Effects on Consciousness." In *Altered States of Consciousness*.
Karant-Nunn, Susan. Review of Kathy Stuart, *Defiled Trades, Social Outcasts* in *Social History*, vol. 26:3 (October 2001), pp. 343–5.
Karger-Decker, Bernt. *Gifte, Hexensalben, Liebestränke*. Leipzig: Koehler and Amelang, 1967.
Kasamatsu, Akira and Tomio Hirai. "An Electroencephalographic Study on the Zen Meditation (Zazen)." In *Altered States of Consciousness*.
Kawerau, Waldemar. "Lob und Schimpf des Ehestandes in der Literatur des sechzehnten Jahrhunderts." *Preussische Jahrbücher*, vol. 69 (1892), pp. 760–81.
Keashly, Loraleigh. "Gender and Conflict: What Does Psychological Research Tell Us?" In *Conflict and Gender*.
Keeble, N. H. *The Cultural Identity of Seventeenth-Century Woman*. London: Routledge, 1994.
Kehoe, Alice. *Shamans and Religion: An Anthropological Exploration in Critical Thinking*. Prospect Heights, IL: Wavelength Press, 2000.
Kelly, Faye. *Prayer in Sixteenth Century England*. Gainesville: University of Florida Press, 1966.
Kemeny, Margaret. "Emotions and the Immune System." In *Healing and the Mind*.
Kemp, Simon. *Cognitive Psychology in the Middle Ages*. Westport: Greenwood Press 1996.

Kendon, Adam. "Gesture." *Annual Review of Anthropology*, vol. 26 (1997), pp. 109–28.
Kenny, Michael. "The Proof is in the Passion: Emotion as an Index of Veridical Memory." In *Believed-in Imaginings*.
Kerrick, Douglas and Robert Hogan. "Cognitive Psychology." In *The Sociobiological Imagination*.
Kertzer, Zauberer, Hexen: Die Angänge der europaischen Hexenverfolgungen. Ed. Andreas Blauert. Frankfurt am Main: Suhrkamp, 1990.
Kieckhefer, Richard. "Avenging the Blood of Children: Anxiety over Child Victims and the Origins of the European Witch Trials." In *Devil, Heresy, and Witchcraft*.
Kieckhefer, Richard. *European Witch Trials*. Berkeley: University of California Press, 1976.
Kieckhefer, Richard. *Forbidden Rites: A Necromancer's Manual of the Fifteenth Century*. University Park, PA: Pennsylvania State University Press, 1998.
Kieckhefer, Richard. "The Holy and the Unholy: Sainthood, Witchcraft, and Magic in Late Medieval Europe." Reprinted in *New*, vol. 1.
Kieckhefer, Richard. *Magic in the Middle Ages*. Cambridge: Cambridge University Press, 2000, rpt. of 1989.
Kieckhefer, Richard. *Repression of Heresy in Medieval Germany*. Philadelphia: University of Philadelphia Press, 1979.
Kieckhefer, Richard. "The Specific Rationality of Medieval Magic." Reprinted in *New*, vol. 1.
Kiener, Franz. *Das Wort ak Waffe: Zur Psychologie der verbalen Aggression*. Gottingen: Vanderhoek and Ruprecht, 1983.
Kiessling, Edith. *Zauberei in den geramisschen Volksrecht*. Jena: Gustav Fischer, 1941.
Kihlstrom, John F. "Perception without Awareness of what is Perceived, Learning without Awareness of what is Learned." In *The Science of Consciousness*.
Kihlstrom, J. F. et al. "The emotional unconscious." In *Counterpoints*.
King, Lester. *The Medical World of the Eighteenth Century*. Chicago, IL: University of Chicago Press, 1958.
King, Lester. *The Philosophy of Medicine in the Early Eighteenth Century*. Cambridge, MA: Harvard University Press, 1978.
Kirouac, Gilles and Ursula Hess. "Group Membership and the Decoding of Nonverbal Behavior." In *The Social Context of Nonverbal Behavior*.
Klaits, Joseph. *Servants of Satan: The Age of the Witch Hunts*. Bloomington: Indiana University Press, 1985.
Klaniczay, Gábor. "The Process of Trance, Heavenly and Diabolic Apparitions in Johannes Nider's Formicarius." Collegium Budapest, Institute for Advanced Study, Discussion Papers Series No. 65, June 2003, http://www.colbud.hu/main/PubArchive/DP/DP65-Klaniczay.pdf.
Klaniczay, Gábor. "Shamanistic Elements in Central European Witchcraft." In *The Uses of Supernatural Power*.
Klaniczay, Gábor. *The Uses of Supernatural Power*. Trans. Susan Singerman. Ed. Karen Margolis. Princeton, NJ: Princeton University Press, 1990.
Klaniczay, Gábor. "Witch-Hunting in Hungary: Social or Cultural Tensions?" In *The Uses of Supernatural Power*.
Klaniczay, Gábor and Éva Pócs. "Introduction." In *Communicating with the Spirits*.
Klass, Morton. *Mind Over Mind: The Anthropology and Psychology of Spirit Possession*. Lanham, MD, Boulder, New York, Oxford: Rowman and Littlefield, 2003.
Klein, Cecelia et al. "The Role of Shamanism in Mesoamerican Art: A Reassessment." *Current Anthropology*, vol. 43:3 (June 2002), pp. 383–401.

Klein, Raymond and Roseanne Armitage. "Rhythms in Human Performance: One and One-half Hour Oscillations in Cognitive Style." *Science*, New Series, vol. 204:4399 (June 22, 1979), pp. 1326–8.

Klinkhommer, Heide. *Schatzgräber, Weisheitssucher und Dämonenbeschwörer: Die motivische und themtische Rerception der Topos der Schätzsuche in der Kunst vom15. bis 18. Jahrhundert*. Berlin: Gebr. Mann, 1992.

Knapp, Theodore. *Neue Beitrage zur Rechts und Wirtschaftgeschichte des Württembergischen Bauernstandes*. Tübingen: Scientia, 1964, rpt. of 1919.

Kneubuehler, Hans-Peter. *Die Überwindung von Hexenwahn und Hexenprozesse*. Diessenhofen: Rügger, 1977.

"Knittlingen," International Civic Heraldry, Ralf Hartemink, 1996, http://www.ngw.nl/int/dld/k/knittlin.htm.

Koestler, Arthur. *The Watershed: A Biolgraphy of Johannes Kepler*. Garden City: Anchor, 1960.

Koller, Marvin, *Social Gerontology*. New York: Randon House, 1968.

Koller, William et al. "Psychogenic Movement Disorders." In *Differential Diagnosis and Treatment of Movement Disorders*.

Königer, Ernst. *Aus der Geschichte der Heilkunst*. Munich: Prestel, 1958.

Kontinuitet? Geschichtelichekeit und Dauer als volkskundliches Problem. Ed. Hermann, Bausinger und Wolfgang Brückner. Berlin: Erich Schmidt, 1969.

Koslofsky, Craig. *The Reformation of the Dead: Death and Ritual in Early Modern Germany, 1450–1700*. New York: St. Martin's Press, 2000.

Kowalski, Robin. "Aversive Interpersonal Behavior: An Overarching Framework." In *Aversive Interpersonal Behaviors*.

Krämer, Karl. "Schaden- und Gegenzauber in Alltagsleben des 16-18 Jahrhunderts Nach Archivalischer Quellen aus Holstein." *Hexenprozesse: Deutsche und Skandinavische Beitrage*. Ed. Christian Degen et al. Neumünster: Karl Wachholtz Verlag, 1983.

Krampl, Ulrike. "When Witches Became False: *Séducteurs* and *Crédules* Confront the Paris Police at the Beginning of the Eighteenth Century." In *Werewolves*.

Krankheit, Heilkunst, Heilung. Ed. Heinrich Schipperger. Freiburg i.B.: Alber, 1978.

Krohn, Alan. *Hysteria: The Elusive Neurosis*. Psychological Issues, Monograph vol. XII, 1978.

Kuhlen, Raymond. "Developmental Changes in Motivation During the Adult Years." In *Middle Age and Aging*.

Kuhn, Werner. *Die Studenten der Universitat Tübingen zwischen 1477 und 1534. Ihr studium und ihre spätere Lebensstellung*, 2 vols. Göppingen: A. Kümmerle, 1971.

Kurland, Nancy and Lisa Pelled. "Passing the Word: Toward a Model of Gossip and Power in the Workplace." *Academy and Management. The Academy of Management Review*, vol. 25:2 (April 2000), pp. 428–39.

La Cerra, Peggy and Roger Bingham. *The Origin of Minds: Evolution, Uniqueness, and the New Science of the Self*. New York: Harmony Books, 2002.

Labouvie, Eva. "Absage an den Teufel. Zum Ende dörflicher Hexeninquisition im Saarraum." In *Das Ende der Hexenverfolgung*.

Labouvie, Eva. "Hexenspuk und Hexenabwehr: Volksmagie und volkstümlicher Hexenglaube." In *Hexenwahn: Magie und Imagination*.

Labouvie, Eva. "Men in Witchcraft Trials: Towards a Social Anthropology of 'Male Understandings of Magic and Witchcraft." In *Gender in Early Modern German History*.

Labouvie, Eva. "Perspektivenwechsel. Magische Domänen von Frauen und Männern in Volksmagie und Hexerei us der Sicht der Geschlectergeschichte." In *Geschlecht, Magie, und Hexenverfolgung*.

Labouvie, Eva. *Verbotene Künste: Volksmagie und ländlicher Aberglaube in den Dorfgemeinden des Saarraumes (16–19. Jahrhundert)*. St. Ingbert: Röhrig Verlag, 1992.
Labouvie, Eva. "Wider Wahrsagerei, Segnerei und Zauberei." In *Verbrechen, Strafen, und soziale Kontrolle*.
Labouvie, Eva. *Zauberei und Hexenwerk: Ländlicher Hexenglaube in der Frühen Neuzeit*. Frankfurt am Main: Fischer Taschenbuch Verlag, 1991.
Lacour, Eva. "Faces of Violence Revisited: A Typology of Violence in Early Modern Germany." *Journal of Social History*, vol. 34:3 (Spring 2001), pp. 649–67.
Laderman, Carol and Marina Roseman. "Introduction." In *The Performance of Healing*.
Ladurie, Emmanuel. *Jasimin's Witch*. Trans. Brian Pearce. Gower House, UK: Scolar, 1987.
Ladurie, Emmanuel. *Montaillou: The Promised Land of Error*. Trans. Barbara Bray. New York: Vintage, 1979.
Lafitau, Joseph. "The Savages Esteem Their Jugglers." In *Shamans through Time*.
Lambo, T. Adeoye. "The Treatment and Management of African Psychiatric Patients." In *Biological Treatment of Mental Illness*.
Langdon, E. Jean. "Shamanism as the History of Anthropology." In *Shamanism: Past and Present*.
Languages of Witchcraft: Narrative, Ideology, and Meaning in Early Modern Culture. Ed. Stuart Clark. Houndsmill, UK: Macmillan, 2001.
Larner, Christina. *Enemies of God: The Witch-Hunt in Scotland*. Baltimore: Johns Hopkins, 1981.
Laslett, Peter. *Family Life & Illicit Love in Earlier Generations*. Cambridge: Cambridge University Press, 1977.
Laslett, Peter. "Societal Development and Aging." In *Handbook of Aging and the Social Sciences*.
Laslett, Peter. *The World We Have Lost*. London: Methuen, 1971.
Laungoni, Pittu. "The Influence of Culture on Stress." In *Cross-Cultural Topics in Psychology*.
Lazarus, Herbert and John Kostan. "Psychogenic Hyperventilation and Death Anxiety." *Psychosomatics*, vol. 10:1 (June 1969), pp. 14–22.
Laughlin, Charles & Jason Throop. "Emotion: A View from Biogentic Stucturalism." In *Biocultural Approaches*, pp. 324–363.
Laughlin, Charles et al. *Brain, Symbol, and Experience: Toward a Neurophenomonology of Human Consciousness*. New York: Columbia University Press, 1992.
La Vie, Mariano. "The Influence of Stress Intrusion on Immunoldepression in Generalized Anxiety Disorder Patients and Controls." *Psychosomatic Medicine*, vol. 58 (1996), pp. 138–42.
Lea, Henry Charles. *Materials Toward A History of Witchcraft*, 3 vols. Ed. Arthur Howland. Philadelphia: University of Pennsylvania Press, 1939.
Leavitt, John. "Meaning and Feeling in the Anthropology of Emotions." *American Ethnologist*, vol. 23:3 (August 1996), pp. 514–39.
Lecouteaux, Claude. *Witches, Werewolves, and Fairies: Shapeshifters and Astral Doubles in the Middle Ages*. Trans. Clare Frock. Rochester, VT: Inner Traditions, 2001.
Lederer, David. "Living with the Dead: Ghosts in Early Modern Bavaria." In *Werewolves*.
Legato, Marianne. *Gender-Specific Aspects of Human Biology for the Practicing Physician*. Armonk, NY: Futura, 1997.
LeGoff, Jacques. "The Learned and Popular Dimensions of Journeys in the Otherworld in the Middle Ages." In *Understanding Popular Culture*.

Lehmann, Hartmut. *Pietismus und weltliche Ordnung in Württemberg.* Stuttgart: Kohlhammer, 1969.
Lempens, Carl. *Geschichte der Hexen & Hexenprozesse.* St. Gallen, Switzerland: H. Fuhrmannsche, n.d.
Lerchheimer, August. *Christlich bedencken und erinnerung von zauberey.* Heidelburg, 1585.
Lewis G. "Some Studies of Social Courses of and Cultural Response to Disease." In *The Anthropology of Disease.*
Levack, Brian. "The Decline and End of Witchcraft Prosecutions." In *Witchcraft and Magic in Europe: The Eighteenth and Nineteenth Centuries.*
Levack, Brian. *The Witch-Hunt in Early Modern Europe*, 2nd Edition. London: Longman, 1995.
Levin, Jack and Arnold Arluke. "An Exploratory Analysis of Sex Differences in Gossip." *Sex Roles*, vol. 12: 3/4 (1985), pp. 281–6.
Levi-Strauss, Claude. "Shamans as Psychoanalysts." In *Shamans through Time.*
Levi-Strauss, Claude. "The Sorcerer and His Magic." *Structural Anthropology.* Trans. Claire Jacobson and Brooke Schoepf. New York: Basic Books, 1963.
Levitt, Robert and H. E. Criswell. "Cholinergic Drugs." In *Psychopharmacology.*
Lex, Barbara. "The Neurobiology of Ritual Trance." In *The Spectrum of Ritual.*
Lex, Barbara. "Voodoo Death: New Thoughts on an Old Explanation." *American Anthropologist*, New Series, vol. 76:4 (October 1974), pp. 818–23.
Liang, Sai-Woon et al. "Life Events, Frontal Electro-encepholographic Laterality, and Functional Immune Status after Acute Psychological Stressors in Adolescents." *Psychosomatic Medicine*, vol. 59:2 (1997), pp. 178–86.
Libet, Benjamin. "Neural Processes in the Production of Conscious Experience." In *The Science of Consciousness.*
Liebel-Weckowicz, Helen. "The Politics of Poverty and Reform: Modernization and Reform in 18th Century Württemberg." *The Consortium on Revolutionary Europe Proceedings*, vol. X (1981), pp. 76–85.
Lindfors, Bodil. "The Other Sex: How are Women Different? Gender, Dominance, and Intimate Relations in Social Interaction." In *Of Mice and Women.*
Lindmann, Mary. *Health and Healing in Eighteenth-Century Germany.* Baltimore: Johns Hopkins, 1996.
Lissner, Ivor. *Man, God, and Magic.* Trans. Maxwell Brownjohn. New York: Putnam, 1961, rpt. of 1958.
List, Edgar. "Holda and the Venusberg." *Journal of American Folklore*, vol. 73 (1960), pp. 307–11.
Lloyd, G. E. R. *Demystifying Mentalities.* Cambridge: Cambridge University Press, 1990.
Locke, Ralph and Edward Kelly. "A Preliminary Model for the Cross-Cultural Analysis of Altered States of Consciousness." In *Ethos*, vol. 13:1 (Spring 1985), pp. 3–55.
Lorenz, Sönke. "Die letzten Hexenprozesse in den Spruchakten der Juristenfakultäten." In *Das Ende der Hexenverfolgung.*
Lorenz, Sönke. "Die Rechtsauskunftstätigkeit der Tübinger Juristenfakultät in Hexenprozessen (ca. 1552–1602)." In *Hexenverfolgung: Beiträge.*
Lorey, Elmar. *Heinrich der Werwolf: Eine Geschichte aus der Zeit der Hexenprozesse mit Documente und Analysen.* Frankfurt am Main: Anabas, 1997.
Lottes, Gunther. "Popular Culture and the Early Modern State in Sixteenth Century Germany." In *Understanding Popular Culture.*
Luckman, Thomas. "Forward." In *Discreet Indiscretions.*

Lüdtke, Alf. "Introduction: What is the History of Everyday Life and Who are Its Practitioners?" In *History of Everyday Life*, pp. 3–40.
Lustig, Robert. "Sex Hormonal Modulation of Neural Development in Vitro: Implications for Brain Sex Differentiation." In *Males, Females, and Behavior*.
Luther, Martin. "Large Catechism – Part First: The Ten Commandments." Online at http://www.lcms.org/graphics/assets/media/LCMS/3_tencommandments.pdf#first.
Luther, Martin. "The Lutheran Confessions; The Small Catechism." Online at www.lcms.org/graphics/assets/media/LCMS/smallcatechism.pdf.
Lying and Deception in Everyday Life. Ed. Michael Lewis and Carolyn Saarni. New York and London: The Guilford Press, 1993.
Lynn, Steven et al. "Rendering the Implausible Plausible: Narrative Construction, Suggestion, and Memory. In *Believed-in Imaginings*.
Maclagan, R. C. *The Evil Eye in the Western Highlands*. London: David Nutt, 1902.
MacDonald, Michael. *Mystical Bedlam: Madness, Anxiety, and Healing in Seventeenth-century England*. Cambridge: Cambridge University Press, 1981.
MacDonald, Stuart. "In Search of the Devil in Fife Witchcraft Cases, 1560–1705." In *The Scottish Witch-Hunt*.
MacFarlane, A. D. J. *Witchcraft in Tudor and Stuart England*. New York: Harper, 1970.
Mack, John. *Nightmares and Human Conflict*. Boston: Little, Brown and Company, 1970.
Maggi, Armando. *Satan's Rhetoric: A Study of Renaissance Demonology*. Chicago: University of Chicago Press, 2001.
Magic, Faith, and Healing. Ed. Ari Kiev. London: Free Press of Glencoe Collier-Macmillan, 1964.
Magic and Modernity: Interfaces of Revelation and Concealment. Ed. Birgit Meyer and Peter Pels. Standford: Standford University Press, 2003.
Magic, Witchcraft, and Curing. Ed. John Middleton. Garden City, NY: The Natural History Press, 1969.
Magic, Witchcraft, and Religion: An Anthropological Study of the Supernatural. 3rd Edition. Ed. Arthur Lehmann and James Myers. Mountain View, CA; London; and Toronto: Mayfield Publishing, 1993.
Mährle, Wolfgang. "'O wehe der amen seelen.' Hexenverfolgungen in der Fürstpropstei Ellwangen" (1588–1694). In *Zum Feuer Verdammt*.
Mair, Lucy. *Witchcraft*. New York: McGraw-Hill, 1970.
Makowsky, Ludwig. *Funf Jahrhunderte Chirurgie in Tübingen*. Stuttgart: Ferdinand Ende, 1949.
Males, Females, and Behavior: Toward a Biological Understanding. Ed. Lee Ellis and Linda Ebertz. Westport, CT: Praeger, 1998.
Malingering and Illness Deception. Ed. Peter Halligan et al. New York: Oxford University Press, 2003.
Malinowski, Bronislaw. *Magic, Science, and Religion*. New York: Doubleday, 1954.
Malleus Maleficarum, by Heinrich Kramer and James Springer. Trans. Montague Summers. New York: Dover, 1971.
Mandrou, Robert. "Magistrates and Witches in 17th Century France." Trans. Robert Wagoner. In *European Witchcraft*.
Marcus, Kenneth. *The Politics of Power: Elites of an Early Modern State in Germany*. Mainz: von Zabern, 2000.
Marquardt, Ernst. *Geschichte Wuerttembergs*. Stuttgart: Mezlersche, 1961.
Maryanski, Alexandra M. et al. "The Social and Biological Foundation of Human Communication." In *Human By Nature*.

Martin, Ruth. *Witchcraft and the Inquisition in Venice, 1550–1650*. Oxford: Blackwell, 1989.
Marzell, Henrich. *Zauberpflanzen, Hexentraenke*. Stuttgart: Francl'sche Verlagslandlund, 1963.
Mascie-Taylor, G. C. N. *The Anthropology of Disease*. Oxford: Oxford University Press, 1993.
Masling, Joseph. "What does it all Mean?" In *Perception without Awareness*.
Masson, Jeffrey and Susan McCarthy. *When Elephants Weep: The Emotional Life of Animals*. Rockland, MA: Wheeler, 1995.
Masters, William and Virginia Johnson. "Human Sexual Responses: The Aging Female and the Aging Male." In *Middle Age and Aging*.
Matalene, Carolyn. "Women as Witches." In *New*, vol. 4.
Matossian, Mary K. *Poisons of the Past: Molds, Epidemics, and History*. New Haven: Yale University Press, 1989.
Matsumoto, David. "Cultural and Emotion." In *Handbook of Culture and Psychology*.
Maverick, "A Delirious Experience." *Eorwid's Experience Vault*, http://www.erowid.org/experiences/exp.php?ID=3286.
Mayhew, Alan. *Rural Settlement and Farming in Germany*. London: Batsford, 1973.
Mazur, Allan et al. "Physiological Aspects of Communication Via Mutual Gaze." *The American Journal of Sociology*, vol. 86:1 (July 1980), pp. 50–74.
Mazur, Allan. "Biosocial Models of Status in Face-to-Face Primate Groups." *Social Forces*, vol. 64:2 (December 1985), pp. 377–402.
Mathiesen, Robert. "A Thirteenth-Century Ritual to Attain the Beatific Vision from the *Sworn Book* of Honorius of Thebes." In *Conjuring Spirits*.
Maxwell-Stuart, P. G. *Satan's Conspiracy: Magic and Witchcraft in Sixteenth Century Scotland*. East Linton, Scotland: Tuckwell Press, 2001.
Maxwell-Stuart, P. G. "Alchemy." In *Encyclopedia of Witchcraft*.
Maxwell-Stuart, P. G. *Witchcraft in Europe and the New World, 1400–1800*. Houndsmills, UK: Palgrave Macmillan, 2001.
Mazzoni, Christina. *Saint Hysteria: Neurosis, Mysticism, and Gender in European Culture*. Ithaca, NY: Cornell University Press, 1996.
Mazzoni, Giuliana and Elizabeth Loftus. "Dreaming, Believing, and Remembering." In *Believed-in Imaginings*.
McCall, Andrew. *The Medieval Underworld*. New York: Barnes and Noble, 1993, rpt. of 1979.
McCranie, E. James. "Psychodynamics of the Menopause." In *The Menopausal Syndrome*.
McClenon, James. *Wonderous Events: Foundations of Religious Belief*. Philadelphia: University of Pennsylvania Press, 1997.
McClenon, James. *Wonderous Healing: Shamanism, Human Evolution, and the Origin of Religion*. Dekalb, IL: Northern Illinois University press, 2002.
McGrath, Malcolm. *Demons of the Modern World*. Amherst, NY: Prometheus Books, 2002.
McGrew, John H. and Richard M. McFall. "A Scientific Inquiry Into the Validity of Astrology." *Journal of Scientific Exploration*, vol. 4:7 (1990), pp. 75–83.
McGuire, J. E. and Martin Tanny. "Newton's Astronomical Apprenticeship; Notes of 1665/5." *Isis*, vol. 76:3 (September 1985), pp. 349–65.
McLeod, Hugh. *Secularization in Western Europe, 1848–1914*. New York: St. Martin's Press, 2000.
McNamara, Patrick. "Religion and the Frontal Lobes." In *Religion in Mind*.

McNeill, William. *Keeping Together in Time*. Cambridge, MA: Harvard University Press, 1995.
The Medical Revolution of the Seventeenth Century. Ed. Roger French and Andrew Wear. Cambridge: Cambridge University Press, 1989.
Medicine and Healing. Ed. Peter Benes. The Dublin Seminar for New England Folklife, Annual Proceedings. Boston: Boston University, 1990.
Medick, Hans. "'Missionaries in the Rowboat?' Ethnological Ways of Knowing as a Challenge to Social History." In *History of Everyday Life*.
Medway, Gareth. *Lure of the Sinister: The Unnatural History of Satanism*. New York and London: New York University Press, 2001.
Meerloo, Joost A. M. *Intuition and the Evil Eye*. Wassendar: Servire, 1971.
Mejer, Ludwig. *Die Periode der Hexenprozesse*. Hannover: Schmorl & von Seefeld, 1882.
Melton, James. *The Rise of the Public in Enlightenment Europe*. Cambridge: Cambridge University Press, 2001.
Men and Violence: Gender, Honor, and Rituals in Modern Europe and America. Ed. Pieter Spierenburg. Columbus, OH: Ohio State University Press, 1998.
The Menopausal Syndrome. Greenblatt, Robert et al. New York: Medcom Press, 1974.
Menopause and Aging. Ed. Kenneth Ryan and Don Gibson. Department of Health, Education, and Welfare Publication (NIH) 73-319, 1971.
"Menopause and Acne." Quick Acne Remedy, 2004–2005. Acne Treatment & Medication, http://www.quickacneremedy.com/acne-treatment/menopause-and-acne.html.
Merrifield, Ralph. *The Archaeology of Ritual and Magic*. New York: New Amsterdam, 1987.
Merry, Sally. "Rethinking Gossip and Scandal." In *Toward a General Theory of Social Control*.
Métraux, Alfred. "Climbing the Twisted Ladder to Initiation." In *Shamans through Time*.
Métraux, Alfred. "Using Invisible Substances for Good and Evil." In *Shamans through Time*.
Methuen, Charlotte. "Securing the Reformation through Education: The Duke's Scholarship System of Sixteenth-Century Württemberg." *Sixteenth Century Journal*, vol. XXV:4 (1994), pp. 841–51.
Meyerson, Joseph and Marc Gelkopf. "Therapeutic Utilization of Spontaneous Out-of-Body Experiences in Hypnotherapy." *American Journal of Psychiatry*, vol. 58:1 (2004), pp. 90–102.
Michelet, Jules. *Santanism and Witchcraft*. Trans. A. Allinson. New York: Citadel, 1969.
Middle Age and Aging. Ed. Bernice Neugarten. Chicago: University of Chicago Press, 1968.
Midelfort, H. C. Erik. "Das Ende der Hexenprozesse in den Randgebieten: Licht von draußen." In *Das Ende der Hexenverfolgung*.
Midelfort, H. C. Erik. "The Devil and the German People." In *Witchcraft Reader*.
Midelfort, H. C. Erik. *Exorcism and Enlightenment: Johann Joseph Gassner and the Demons of Eighteenth-Century Germany*. New Haven: Yale University Press, 2005.
Midelfort, H. C. Erik. "Heartland of the Witchcraze." In *Witchcraft Reader*.
Midelfort, H. C. Erik. *A History of Madness in Sixteenth Century Germany*. Standford: Standford University Press, 1999.
Midelfort, H. C. Erik. "Johann Weyer and the Transformation of the Insanity Defense." In *The German People*.
Midelfort, H. C. Erik. "Were there Really Witches?" In *Transition and Revolution*.

Midelfort, H. C. Erik. *Witch Hunting in Southwest Germany*. Palo Alto, CA: Stanford University Press, 1972.

Migliore, Sarn. *Mal'uocchi: Ambiguity, Evil Eye, and the Language of Distress*. Toronto: University of Toronto Press, 1997.

Mikolajczyk, Renata. "*Non Sunt Nisi Phantasiae et Imaginationes*: A Medieval Attempt at Explaining Demons." In *Communicating with the Spirits*.

Miladinovic, Milan. *Emile Coue Web Site*, Main Page. Created 12/6/98, last modified 5/17/06, http://www.emilecoue.com/.

Miladinovic, Milan. "Method of Emile Coue." At *Emile Coue Web Site*. Created 12/6/98, last modified 5/17/06, http://www.emilecoue.com/method.html.

Miller, Ann. "Dowsing: A Review." The Scientific and Medical Network, http://www.scimednet.org/Articles/SPSmiller.htm.

Miller, Barbara. "The Anthropology of Sex and Gender Hierarchies." In *Sex and Gender Hierarchies*.

Miller, Joyce. "Devices and Directions: Folk Healing Aspects of Witchcraft Practice in Seventeenth Century Scotland." In *The Scottish Witch-Hunt*.

Milwain, Elizabeth and Susan Iversen. "Cognitive Change in Old Age." In *Psychiatry in the Elderly*.

"A Mirror to the World." *The Economist*, vol. 375:8426 (May 14, 2005), p. 87.

Mishlove, Jeffrey. *The Roots of Consciousness*, revised edition. New York: Marlowe, 1993.

Mishra, R. C. "Cognition across Cultures." In *Handbook of Culture and Psychology*.

Mit den Waffen der Justiz: Zur Krimminalgeschichte des späten Mittelalters und der Frühen Neuzeit. Ed. Andreas Blauert und Gerd Schwerhoff. Frankfurt am Main: Fischer Taschenbuch Verlag, 1993.

Mitterauer, Michael. "Familienwirtschaft und Altenversorgung." In *Vom Patriarchat zur Partnerschaft*.

Mitterauer, Michael and Reinhard Siedler. *Vom Patriarchat zur Partnerschaft: Zum Strukturwandel der Familie*. Munich: C. H. Beck, 1977.

Modell, John. "A Note on Scholarly Caution in a Period of Revisionism and Interdisciplinarity." In *Social History and Issues in Human Consciousness*.

Moerman, Daniel and Wayne Jonas. "Deconstructing the Placebo Effect and Finding Meaning in Respose." *Annals of Internal Medicine*, vol. 136 (2002), pp. 471–76.

Moir Anne and David Jessel. *Brain Sex: The Real Difference between Men and Women*. New York: Carol Publishing Group, 1991.

Molitor, Ulrich. *Von Hexen und Unholden*. Trans. Conrad Lautenbach. 1575, trans. and rpt. of 1489.

Monter, William. "Switzerland." In *Encyclopedia of Witchcraft*.

Monter, William. "Toads and Eucharists: The Male Witches of Normandy, 1564–1660." *French Historical Studies*, vol. 20:4 (Autumn 1997), pp. 563–95.

Monter, William. *Ritual, Myth and Magic in Early Modern Europe*. Athens, OH: Ohio University Press, 1983.

Monter, William. *Witchcraft in France and Switzerland*. Ithaca, NY: Cornell University Press, 1976.

Morley, John. "Summary Chapter. The Endocrine Basis of Geriatric Psychiatry: An Integrative Approach." In *Hormones, Gender, and the Aging Brain*.

Mormando, Franco. "Bernardino of Sienna, Popular Preacher and Witch-Hunter: A 1426 Witch Trial in Rome." Reprinted in *New*, vol. 1.

Morris, J. S. et al. "A Subcortical Pathway to the Right Amydala Mediating 'Unseen' Fear." *Proceedings of the National Academy of Science*, vol. 96 (February 1999), pp. 1680–5.

Moser-Rath, Elfriede. "Geistliche Bauernregeln: Ein Beitrage zum Volksglauben der Barochzeit." *Zeitschrift für Volkskunde*, vol. 55 (1959), pp. 201–26.
Moss, Thelma. *The Probability of the Impossible*. New York: New American Library/Plume, 1974.
Muchembled, Robert. "Lay Judges and the Acculturation of the Masses (France and the Southern Low Countries, Sixteenth to Eighteenth Centuries)." Trans. John Burke. In *Religion and Society in Early Modern Europe*.
Muchembled, Robert. "Satanic Myths and Cultural Reality." In *Early Modern European Witchcraft*.
Muchembled, Robert. "The Witches of the Cambresis." In *Religion and the People*.
Mueller, Antje and Ron Roberts. "Dreams." In *Parapsychology: The Science of Unusual Experience*.
Muller, Ernst. *Kleine Geschichte Württenberg*. Stuttgart: Kohlhammer, 1949.
Muir, Edward. *Ritual in Early Modern Europe*. Cambridge: Cambridge University Press, 1997.
Mullings, Leith. *Therapy, Ideology, and Social Change: Mental Healing in Urban Ghana*. Berkeley: University of California Press, 1984.
Murray, Craig and Jezz Fox. "Dissociational Body Experience: Differences between Respondants with and without Prior Out-of-Body Experiences." *British Journal of Psychology*, vol. 96:4 (November 2005), pp. 441–57.
Murray, Margaret. *The Witch Cult in Western Europe*. Oxford: Clarendon, 1962, rpt. of 1921.
Nagel, Adelbert. *Armut in Barock: Die Bettler und Vaganten Oberschwabens*. Weingarten: Drumlin, 1986.
Narby, Jeremy and Francis Huxley. "Introduction." In *Shamans through Time*.
Narby, Jeremy and Francis Huxley. "The Understanding Deepens." In *Shamans through Time*.
Narr, Dieter. *Studien zur Spätaufklärung im deutschen Südwesten*. Stuttgart: Kohlhammer, 1979.
Natelson, Benjamin. "Cardiac Arrythmias and Sudden Death." In *Psychosomatic Disorders*.
Nash, June. "Devils, Witches, and Sudden Death." In *Magic, Witchcraft, and Religion*.
Neher, Andrew. *The Psychology of Transcendance*. New York: Dover, 1990.
Nelson, Charles and Michelle de Haan. "A Neurobehavioral Approach to the Recognition of Facial Expressions in Infancy." In *Psychology of Facial Expression*.
Nemiah, John. "Alexithymia: Present, Past – and Future?" *Psychosomatic Medicine*, vol. 58 (1996), pp. 217–18.
Nestlen, Dr. *Die Bekämpfung der Medikastrierens in Herzogtum Württemberg*. Stuttgart: Stuttgart: K. Hofbuchdruckerei zu Gutenberg Carl Grüninger (Klett and Hartmann), 1905.
Nestlen, Dr. *Die Entwicklung der Hebammen-wesens und der praktischen Geburtshilfe im Herzogtum Württemberg*. Stuttgart: K. Hofbuchdruckerei zu Gutenberg Carl Grüninger (Klett and Hartmann), 1906.
Neubauer, Hans-Joachim. *The Rumour: A Cultural History*. Trans. Christian Braun. London/New York: Free Association Books, 1999.
Neuhaus, John. *Toward a Biocritical Sociology*. New York: Peter Lang, 1996.
New Perspectives on Witchcraft, Magic, and Demonology, 6 vols. Ed. Brian Levack. New York: Routledge, 2001.
Newall, Venetia. *An Egg at Easter*. Bloomington, IN: Indiana University Press, 1971.

Newberg, Andrew, et al. *Why God Won't Go Away: Brain Science and the Biology of Belief.* New York: Ballantine, 2001.
Newcombe, Freda and Graham Ratcliff. "The Female Brain: A Neuropsychological Viewpoint." In *Defining Females.*
Newe Zeitung aus Berneburgk / Schrecklich und abschewlich zu horen und zu lesen / Von dreyen Alten Teuffels Bulerin / Hexin oder Zauberinnen / ... (n.p.: "eine Liebhaber der Warheit," 1580).
Newman, Paul. *A History of Terror.* Stroud: Sutton Publishing, 2000.
Nicholls, David. "The Devil in Renaissance France." In *Witchcraft Reader.*
Niehoff, Debra. *The Biology of Violence.* New York: The Free Press, 1999.
Nildin-Wall, Bodil and Jan Wall. "The Witch as Hare or the Witch's Hare: Popular Legends and Beliefs in Nordic Tradition." In *Folklore,* vol. 104:3 (1993), pp. 67–76.
No Matter, Never Mind. Ed. Kunio Yasue et al. Amsterdam/Philadelphia: John Benjamins, 2002.
Noll, Richard. "Shamans, 'Spirits,' and Mental Imagry." In *Shamans through Time.*
Nonverbal Communication: Where Nature Meets Culture. Ed. Ullica Segerstråle and Peter Molnár. Mahwah, NJ: Lawrence Erlbawm Associates, 1997.
Norretranders, Ted. *The User Illusion.* Trans. Jonathan Sydenham. New York: Viking, 1998.
Norton, Mary Beth. *In the Devil's Snare.* New York: Knopf, 2002.
Notman, Malkah. "Midlife Concerns of Women: Implications of the Menopause." *American Journal of Psychiatry,* vol. 136:10 (October 1979), pp. 1270–4.
Oakley, David. "Hypnosis and Conversion Hysteria: A Unifying Model." In *Conversion Hysteria.*
Oates, Caroline. "Cheese Gives You Nightmares: Old Hags and Heartburn." In *Folklore,* (August 2003), n.p. (online).
Occult and Scientific Mentalities in the Renaissance. Ed. Brian Vickers. Cambridge: Cambridge University Press, 1984.
O'Connor, Bonnie and David Hufford. "Understanding Folk Medicine." In *Healing Logics,* pp. 13–35.
Oesterreich, T. K. *Possession: Demoniacal & Other.* Secaucus, NJ: Citadel, 1974.
Of Mice and Women: Aspects of Female Aggression. Ed. Kaj Björkqvist and Pirkko Niemelä. San Diego: Academic Press, 1992.
Ogden, Daniel. "Binding Spells: Curse Tablets and Voodoo Dolls in the Greek and Roman Worlds." In *Witchcraft and Magic in Europe: Ancient Greece and Rome.*
Ogilvie, Sheilagh. *State Corporatism and Proto-Industry: The Württemberg Black Forest, 1580–1797.* Cambridge: Cambridge University Press, 1997.
Ohrt, F. *Herba, Gratia, Plena: Die Legenden der Alteren Segensprüche über der Göttlichen Ursprung der Heil-und Zauberkrauter.* FF Communications No. 82, Helsinki, 1929. Suomalainen Tiedeakatemia Academia Scientiarum Fennica.
Ohrt, F. *Fluchtafel und Wettersegen.* FF Communications No. 86, Helsinki, 1929. Suomalainen Tiedeakatemia Academia Scientiarum Fennica.
Old Age in Preindustrial Society. Ed. Peter Stearns. New York and London: Holmes and Meier, 1982.
Oldridge, Darren. *The Devil in Early Modern England.* Stroud: Sutton, 2000.
Oldridge, Darren. "General Introduction." In *Witchcraft Reader.*
Oliver, Reggie: "The Poisons Affair." *History Today,* vol 51:3 (March 2001), pp. 28–34.
Olli, Soili-Maria. "The Devil's Pact: A Male Strategy." In *Beyond the Witch Trials,* pp. 100–14.

Olsen, Dale. "Music Alone Can Alter a Shaman's Consciousness, Which Itself Can Destroy Tape Recorders." In *Shamans through Time*.
Olsen, Lea. "Charms in Medieval Memory." In *Charms and Charming*.
Ornstein, Robert and David Galin. "Physiological Studies of Consciousness." In *Symposium on Consciousness*.
Ortega, Maria. "Sorcery and Exoticism in Love Magic." In *Cultural Encounters*.
Osborne, Max. *Die Teufellitteratur des XVI Jahrhunderts*. Berlin: Mayer and Müller, 1893.
Oubré, Alondra Yvette. *Instinct and Revelation: Reflections on the Origins of Numinous Perception*. Australia: Gordon and Breach, 1997.
Out of the Ordinary: Folklore and the Supernatural. Ed. Barbara Walker. Logan, UT: Utah State University, 1995.
The Oxford Companion to Medicine. Ed. John Walton et al. Oxford: Oxford University Press, 1986).
The Oxford History of the Prison. Ed. Norval Morris and David Rothman. Oxford: Oxford University Press, 1995.
The Pagan Middle Ages. Ed. Ludo Milis. Trans. Tanis Guest. Rochester, NY: Boydell Press, 1998, trans. of 1991.
Pagels, Elaine. *The Origin of Satan*. New York: Vintage, 1995.
Palermo, George and Michele Del Re. *Satanism: Psychiatric and Legal Views*. Springfield, IL: Charles C. Thomas, 1999.
Pallikari, Fotini. "Must the 'Magic' of Psychokinesis Hinder Precise Scientific Measurement?" *Journal of Consciousness Studies*, vol. 10: 6–7 (June–July 2003), pp. 199–219.
Parapsychology: The Science of Unusual Experience. Ed. Ron Roberts and David Groome. London: Arnold; New York: Oxford University Press, 2001.
Parish, Helen and William Naphy. "Introduction." In *Religion and Superstition*.
Parker, Elizabeth. *The Seven Ages of Woman*. Ed. Evelyn Breck. Baltimore: Johns Hopkins, 1960.
Parker Jenifer and Susan Blackmore. "Comparing the Content of Sleep Paralysis and Dream Reports." *Dreaming*, vol. 12:1 (March 2002), pp. 45–59.
Parker, Adrian and Göran Brusewitz. "A Compendium of the Evidence for Psi." *European Journal of Parapsychology*, vol. 18 (2003), pp. 33–51.
Parsons, Jacquelynne. "Psychosexual Neutrality: Is Anatomy Destiny?" In *The Psychobiology of Sex Differences*.
"Passauer Schutzzauber." *Sagen.at: das Projekt des Sagensammelung*. Ed. Wolfgang Morscher, 2000–2006, http://www.sagen.at.
Patients and Practitioners: Lay Perceptions of Medicine in Pre-industrial Society. Ed. Roy Porter. Cambridge: Cambridge University Press, 1985.
Pattison, E. Mansell. "Psychosocial Interpretations of Exorcism." *Journal of Operational Psychiatry*, vol. 8:2 (1977), pp. 5–19.
Paulus, Nikolaus. "Die Rolle der Frau in der Geschichte der Hexenwahns." *Historische Jahrbuch*, vol. XXIX (1908), pp. 72–95.
Payaguaje, Fernando. "A Shaman Endures the Temptation of Sorcery (and Publishes a Book)." In *Shamans through Time*.
Peasant Society. Ed. Jack Potter et al. Boston: Little, Brown and Company, 1967.
Peleg, Gili et al. "Hereditary family signature of facial expression." *Proceedings of the National Academy of Sciences*, vol. 103:43 (October 4, 2006), pp. 15921–6.
"The Pendulum," Mid-Atlantic Geomancy, http://www.geomancy.org/dowsing/dowsing-3.html.

Perception without Awareness: Cognitive, Clinical, and Social Perspectives. Ed. Robert Bornstein and Thane Pittman. New York and London: The Guilford Press, 1992.

Perkins, Maureen. *The Reform of Time: Magic and Modernity.* London and Serling, VA: Pluto Press, 2001.

The Performance of Healing. Ed. Carol Laderman and Marina Reseman. New York and London: Routledge, 1996.

Perry, E. K. "Cholinergic Components of Dementia and Aging." In *Dementia and Normal Aging.*

Persinger, Michael. *Neuropsychological Bases of God Beliefs.* New York: Praeger, 1987.

Persinger, Michael and and Gyslaine Lafrenière. *Space-Time Transients and Unusual Events.* Chicago: Nelson Hall, 1977.

Perspectives on Human Memory and Cognitive Aging. Ed. Moshe Naveh-Benjamin et al. New York: Psychology Press, 2001.

Pert, Candace. "The Chemical Communicators." In *Healing and the Mind.*

Pert, Candace. *Molecules of Emotion.* New York: Touchstone, 1997.

Peters, Edward. "Destruction of the Flesh – Salvation of the Spirit: The Paradoxes of Torture in Medieval Christian Society." In *The Devil, Heresy, and Witchcraft.*

Peters, Edward. *The Magician, the Witch, and the Law.* Philadelphia: University of Pennsylvania Press, 1978.

Petzoldt, Leader. *Schwäbische Volkssagen.* Stuttgart: Kohlhammer, 1990.

Peuckert, Will-Erich. *Deutsche Volksglaube in Spätmittelalter.* Hildesheim: Georg Olms, 1978.

Pfeiffer, Eric. "Psychopathology and Social Pathology." In *Handbook of the Psychology of Aging.*

Phillips, M. L. et al. "Neural Responses to Facial and Vocal Expressions of Fear and Disgust." *Proceedings: Biological Sciences,* vol. 265:1408 (October 7, 1998), pp. 1809–17.

Pike, Jennifer et al. "Chronic Life Stress Alters Sympathetic, Neuroendocrine, and Immune Responsivity to an Acute Psychological Stressor in Humans." *Psychosomatic Medicine,* vol. 59 (1997), pp. 447–57.

Pinkard, Terry. *German Philosophy, 1760–1860: The Legacy of Idealism.* Cambridge: Cambridge Universtity Press, 2002.

Pinker, Steven. *How the Mind Works.* New York: Norton, 1997.

Place, Robert. *The Tarot: History, Symbolism, and Divination.* New York: Tarcher/Penguin, 2005.

Pócs, Éva. "The Alternative World of the Witches' Sabbat." In *Witchcraft Reader.*

Pócs, Éva. *Between the Living and the Dead: A Perspective on Witches and Seers in the Early Modern Age.* Trans. Szilvia Rédey and Michael Webb. Budapest: Central European University Press, 1999.

Pócs, Éva. "Curse, *Maleficium,* Divination: Witchcraft on the Borderline of Religion and Magic." In *Witchcraft Continued.*

Pócs, Éva. "Evil Eye in Hungary: Belief, Ritual, Incantation." In *Charms and Charming.*

Pócs, Éva. *Fairies and Witches at the Boundary of South-Eastern and Central Europe.* Folklore Fellows Communications 243. Helsinki, 1989.

Pócs, Éva. "Possession Phenomena, Possession Systems. Some East-Central European Examples." In *Communicating with the Spirits.*

Po-Chia Hsia, R. *Social Discipline in the Reformation.* London and New York: Routledge, 1989.

Politics and Society in Reformation Europe. Ed. E. I. Kouri and Tom Scott. New York: St. Martin's Press, 1987.

Pollock, Bruce. "Gender Differences in Psychotropic Drug Metabolism." In *Hormones, Gender, and the Aging Brain*.
Pool, Robert. *Eve's Rib: The Biological Roots of Sex Differences*. New York: Crown Publishers, 1994.
Pope, Geoffrey. *The Biological Bases of Human Behavior*. Boston: Allyn and Bacon, 2000.
Popkin, Beate. "Marriage, Social Discipline, and Identity in Eighteenth Century Württemberg." Ph.D. dissertation, University of Pittsburg, 1994.
Popkin, Beate. "Wives, Mothers, and Witches: The Learned Discouse about Women in Early Modern Europe," *Journal of Women's History*, vol. 9 (1997), pp. 193–202.
Popular Culture and Popular Movements in Reformation Germany. Ed. R. W. Scribner. London: Humbledon, 1987.
Popular Religion in Germany and Central Europe, 1400–1800. Ed. Bob Scribner and Trevor Johnson. New York: St. Martin's Press, 1996.
Porter, Roy. "Witchcraft and Magic in Enlightenment, Romantic, and Liberal Thought." In *Witchcraft and Magic in Europe: The Eighteenth and Nineteenth Centuries*.
Posner, Judith. "It's All in Your Head: Feminists and Medical Models of Menopause (Strange Bedfellows)." *Sex Roles*, vol. 5:2 (1979), pp. 179–90.
Pott, Martin. *Aufklärung und Aberglaube: Die deutsche Frühaufklärung im Spiegel ihrer Aberglaubenskritik*. Tübingen: Max Niemeyer, 1992.
Pott, Martin. "Aufklärung und Hexenaberglaube: Philosophische Ansätze zur Überwindung der Teufelspakttheorie in der deutschen Frühaufklärung." In *Das Ende der Hexenverfolgung*.
The Power of Belief: Psychosocial Influence on Illness, Disability and Medicine. Ed. Peter Halligan and Mansel Aylward. Oxford, New York: Oxford University Press, 2006.
Price, Neil. "An Archaeology of Altered States: Shamanism and Material Culture Studies." In *Archaeology of Shamanism*, pp. 3–15.
Priesner, Claus. "Phantastische Reisen: Über Hexenkräuter und Flugsalben," Teil I and II. *Kultur und Technik*, vol. 17 (March 1993 and April 1993), pp. 22–7, 34–9.
Problems in the Historical Anthropology of Early Modern Europe. Ed. R. Po-Chia Hsia and R. W. Scribner. Wiesbaden: Harrassowitz Verlag, 1997.
Probst, Christian. *Fuhrende Heiler und heilmittelhändler: Medizin von Marktplatz und Landstrasse*. Rosenheim, Germany: Rosenheimer, 1992.
Processes of Aging: Social and Psychological Perspectives, 2 vols. Ed. Richard Williams et al. New York: Atherton, 1963.
Psychadelic Drugs Reconsidered. Ed. Lester Greenspoon et al. New York: Basic Books, 1979.
Psychiatry in the Elderly, 3rd Edition. Ed. Robin Jacoby and Catharine Oppenheimer. Oxford: Oxford University Press, 2002.
The Psychobiology of Sex Differences and Sex Roles. Ed. Jacquelynne Parsons. Washington, DC: Hemisphere Publishing, 1980.
Psychogenic Movement Disorders: Neurology and Neuropsychiatry. Ed. Mark Hallett et al. Philadelphia: Lippincott, Williams & Wilkins, 2006.
The Psychology of Facial Expression. Ed. James A. Russell and José Fernández-Dols. Cambridge: Cambridge University Press, 1997.
Psychology of Women: A Handbook of Issues and Theories. Ed. Florence Denmark and Michele Paludi. Westport, CT: Greenwood Press, 1993.
Psychopharmacology: A Biological Approach. Ed. Robert Levitt. New York: Wiley; Washington, DC: Hemisphere Publishing, 1975.
Psychophysiological Disorders: Research and Clinical Applications. Ed. Robert Gatchel and Edward Blanchard. Washington, DC: American Psychological Association, 1993.

Psychosomatic Disorders: A Psychophysiological Approach to Etiology and Treatment. Ed. Stephen Haynes and Linda Gannon. New York: Praeger, 1981.
Psychosomatic Illness Review. Ed. Wilfred Dorfman and Leo Cristofar. New York: Macmillan, 1985.
Purkiss, Diane. "Sounds of Silence: Fairies and Incest in Scottish Witchcraft Stories." In *Languages of Witchcraft*.
Quaife, G.R. *Godly Zeal and Furious Rage: The Witch in Early Modern Europe*. New York: St. Martin's Press, 1987.
Questions of Consciousness. Ed. Anthony Cohen and Nigel Rapport. London: Routledge, 1995.
Rabb, Theodore. *The Struggle for Stability in Early Modern Europe*. New York: Oxford, 1975.
Rabbie, Jacob et al. "Sex Differences in Conflict and Aggression in Individual and Group Settings." In *Of Mice and Women*.
Radding, Charles. *A World Made by Men: Cognition and Society, 400–1200*. Chapel Hill and London: University of North Carolina Press, 1986.
Radin, D. I. "Event-Related Electroencephalographic Correlations between Isolated Human Subjects." *Journal of Alternative and Complementary Medicine* (2004), vol. 10, pp. 315–23.
Radin, Dean. *Entangled Minds*. New York: Paraview, 2006.
Raeff, Marc. *The Well Ordered Police State*. New Haven, 1983.
Raith, Anita. "Die Hexenprozesse in Tuttlingen." *Tuttlinger Heimatblätter 1994*, Neue Folge 57. Tuttlingen: Braun-Druck, 1994.
Raith, Anita. "Ein württembergischer Hexenprozeß des Jahres 1592. Eine Fallstudie." In *Hexenverfolgung: Beigräge*.
Raith, Anita. "Herzogtum Württemberg." In *Hexen und Hexenverfolgung im deutschen Südwesten*.
Raith, Anita. "Hexenprozesse beim württembergischen Oberrat." In *Hexenverfolgung: Beigräge*.
Raith, Anita. "Hexenverfolgungen: Württemberg, Herzogtum." At LMU, Historicum.Net, server frühe neuzeit, http://www.lrz-muenchen.de/~u9332br/webserver/webdata/hexenverfolgung/frame_lexikon.html?art853.htm.
Raith, Anita. "Von den bösen Weibern, die man nennt Hexen – Männerphantasie und Frauenverachtung in württembergischen Hexenprozess," unpublished paper delivered to the 91st Stitzung of the Arbeitskreis für Landes- und Ortsgeschichte, 3/28/98.
Raith, Anita. "Württemberg, Duchy of." Trans. Edward Bever. In *Encyclopedia of Witchcraft*.
Raith, Anita. "Württemberg – Witch Persecutions." *Encyclopedia of the History of Witch Persecutions*. Ed. Gudrun Gersmann, Katrin Moeller and Jürgen Michael Schmidt, at http://www.historicum.net/no_cache/persistent/artikel/1633/.
Rakover, Sam and Baruch Cahlin. *Face Recognition: Cognitive & Computational Processes*. Amsterdam: John Benjamin, 2001.
Ramsey, Clay. *The Ideology of the Great Fear: The Loissonvais in 1789*. Baltimore and London: Johns Hopkins University Press, 1992.
Ramsey, Matthew. *Professional and Popular Medicine in France, 1770–1830: The Social World of Medical Practice*. Cambridge: Cambridge University Press, 1988.
Rao, Ramakrishna. "Introduction: Reality, Replicability, and the Lawfulness of Psi." In *Basic Research in Parapsychology*, pp. 3–37.
Rapley, Robert. *A Case of Witchcraft: The Trial of Urbain Grandier*. Montreal and Kingston, London, Buffalo: McGill-Queen's University Press, 1998.

Rasmussen, Knud. "Seeking Knowledge in the Solitude of Nature." In *Shamans through Time*.
Ray, Oakley. *Drugs, Society, and Human Behavior*, 2nd Edition. St Louis, MO: Mosby, 1978.
Reed, Graham. *The Psychology of Anomalous Experience: A Cognitive Approach*, revised edition. Buffalo, NY: Prometheus Books, 1988.
Reichel-Dolmatoff, Gerardo. "Shamans are Intellectuals, Translators, and Shrewd Dealers." In *Shamans through Time*.
Reid, Pamela and Michele Paludi. "Developmental Psychology of Women: Conception to Adolescence." In *Psychology of Women*.
Reill, Peter. *The German Enlightenment and the Rise of Historicism*. Berkeley: University of California Press, 1975.
Reformed, "Strong Trip, but Long Lasting After-Effects." *Eorwid's Experience Vault*, http://www.erowid.org/experiences/exp.php?ID=34297.
Religion and Society in Early Modern Europe. Ed. Kaspar von Greyerz. London: German Historical Institute; Boston, MA: Allen & Unwin, 1984.
Religion and Superstition in Early Modern Europe. Ed. Helen Parish and William Naphy. Manchester: Manchester University Press, 2002.
Religion and the People. Ed. James Obelkavich. Chapel Hill: University of North Carolina Press, 1979.
Religion in Mind: Cognitive Perspectives on Religious Belief, Ritual, and Experience. Ed. Jensine Andressen. Cambridge: Cambridge University Press, 2001.
Restak, Richard. *The Brain*. Toronto and New York: Bantam Books, 1984.
Reyscher, August Ludwig. *Vollständige, historisch und kritisch bearbeitet Sammlung der württembergischen Gesetze*, 19 vols. Stuttgart and Tübingen: Cotta, 1828–51.
Rice, Eugene. *The Foundations of Early Modern Europe, 1460–1559*. New York: Norton, 1970.
Richard, John. "Shapes in the Clouds: Commentary on 'Information and Uncertainty in Remote Perception Research,'" http://www.skepticreport.com/psychics/shapesintheclouds.htm.
Richards, Todd et al. "Replicable Functional Magnetic Resonance Imaging Evidence of Correlated Brain Signals between Physically and Sensory Isolated Subjects." *Journal of the Association for Computing Machinery*, vol. 11:6 (2005), pp. 955–63.
Richardson, John. "Imagery and the Brain." In *Imagery and Cognition*.
Richardson, P. Mick. *The Encyclopedia of Psychoactive Drugs: Flowering Plants; Magic in Bloom*. New York: Chelsea House, 1986.
Richardson Deborah and Laura Green. "Circuitous Harm: Determinants and Consequences of Nondirect Aggression." In *Aversive Interpersonal Behaviors*.
Riches, David. "Dreaming as Social Process and Its Implications for Consciousness." In *Questions of Consciousness*.
Rief, Winfried and Wolfgang Hiller. "Somatization – Future Perspectives on a Common Phenomenon." *Journal of Psychosomatic Research*, vol. XLIV (1998), pp. 387–90.
Riley, James. *Sickness, Recovery, and Death: A History and Forecast of Ill Health*. Iowa City: University of Iowa Press, 1989.
Rinisch, June et al. "Sex Differences Emerge during the First Year of Life." In *Women, Men, and Gender*.
Rios, Marlene Doblin de. *Hallucinogens: Cross-Cultural Perspectives*. Albuquerque: University of New Mexico Press, 1984.
Rivera, Joseph de. "Relinquishing Believed-In Imaginings: Narratives of People Who Have Repudiated False Accusations." In *Believed-in Imaginings*.

Rivera, Joseph de and Theodore Sarbin. "Introduction." In *Believed-in Imaginings*.
Rivera, Joseph de. "Evaluating Believed-in Imaginings." In *Believed-in Imaginings*.
Roach, Mary. *Spook: Science Tackles the Afterlife*. New York: Norton, 2005.
Roberts, John. "Belief in the Evil Eye in World Perspective." In *The Evil Eye*.
Robischeaux, Thomas. *Rural Society and the Search for Order in Early Modern Germany*. Cambridge: Cambridge University Press, 1989.
Robischeaux, Thomas. "Witchcraft and Forensic Medicine in Seventeenth-century Germany." In *Languages of Witchcraft*.
Rochs, Sabine. *A Primer on the German Enlightenment*. Columbia, MO: University of Missouri Press, 1995.
Rock, Andrea. *The Mind at Night: The New Science of How and Why We Dream*. New York: Basic Books, 2004.
Roeck, Bernd. "Säkularisierung als Desensibilisierung: Der Hexenwahn aus der Perspektive der Sensibilitätsgeschichte." In *Das Ende der Hexenverfolgung*.
Rogge, Roswitha. "Schadenzauber, Hexerei, und die Waffen der Justiz in frühneuzeitlichen Hamburg." In *Hexerei, Magie, und Volksmedizin*.
Rogo, D. Scott. *The Poltergeist Experience*. Harmondsworth, UK: Penguin, 1979.
Röhrich, Lutz. *Folktales and Reality*. Trans. Peter Tokofsky. Bloomington and Indianaopolis: University of Indiana Press, 1979.
Roll, William. "Poltergeists, Electromagnetism, and Consciousness." *Journal of Scientific Exploration*, vol. 17:1 (2003), pp. 75–86.
Roodenburg, Herman. "Gestures." In *Encyclopedia of European Social History*, vol. 4.
Roos, Keith. *The Devil in Sixteenth Cenetury German Literature: The Teufelsbücher*. Bern: Herbert Lang; Frankfurt am Main: Peter Lang, 1972.
Roper, Jonathan. *English Verbal Charms*. Helsinki: Academia Scientiarum Fennica, Folklore Fellows Communication No. 288, 2005.
Roper, Johathan. "Introduction." In *Charms and Charming*.
Roper, Lyndal. "'Evil Imaginings and Fantasies': Child-Witches and the End of the Witch Craze." *Past and Present*, vol. 167, pp. 107–39.
Roper, Lyndal. "Magic and the Theology of the Body: Exorcism in Sixteenth-Century Augsburg." In *New*, vol. 1.
Roper, Lyndal. *Oedipus and the Devil: Witchcraft, Sexuality, and Religion in Early Modern Europe*. London: Routledge, 1994.
Roper, Lyndal. "Witchcraft and Fantasy in Early Modern Germany." *History Workshop Journal*, vol. 32 (1991), pp. 19–43.
Roper, Lyndal. *Witch Craze: Terror and Fantasy in Baroque Germany*. New Haven, CT: Yale University Press, 2004.
Rose, Ronald. "Clever Cords and Clever Men." In *Shamans through Time*.
Rosen, George. *Madness in Society: Chapters in the Historical Sociology of Mental Illness*. Chicago: University of Chicago Press, 1968.
Rösener, Werner. *The Peasantry of Europe*. Trans. Thomas M. Barten. Oxford: Blackwell, 1994.
Rosnow, Ralph. "Rumor as Communication: A Contextualist Approach." *Journal of Communications*, vol. 38:1 (Winter 1988), pp. 12–28.
Ross, Marc. *The Culture of Conflict: Interpretation and Interest in Camparative Perspective*. New Haven, CT: Yale University Press, 1993.
Rosser, Sue. *Biology and Feminism: A Dynamic Interpretation*. New York: Twayne Publishers, 1992.
Rowland, Robert. "'Fantastical and Devilishe Persons': The European Witch-Beliefs in Comparative Perspective." In *Early Modern European Witchcraft*.

Rowlands, Alison. "Witchcraft and Old Women in Early Modern Germany." In *Past and Present*, vol. 173 (November 2001), pp. 50–89.
Rowlands, Alison. "Witchcraft and Popular Religion Early Modern Rottenberg ob der Tauber." In *Popular Religion in Germany*.
Rowlands, Alison. *Witchcraft Narratives in Germany: Rothenburg 1561–1652*. Manchester: Manchester University Press, 2003.
Rublack, Hans-Christoph. "Luthertum und Aberglaube: Die *Theologische Abhandlund des Aberglaubens* des Georg Christoph Zimmerman." In *Problems in the Historical Anthropology of Early Modern Europe*.
Rublack, Ulinka. *The Crimes of Women in Early Modern Germany*. Oxford: Clarendon Press, 1999.
Rublack, Ulinka. "Gender in Early Modern German History." *German History*, vol. 17 (1999), pp. 1–8.
Rublack, Ulinka. "The Public Body: Policing Abortion in Early Modern Germany." In *Gender Relations*.
Ruble, Thomas and Joy Schneer. "Gender Differences in Conflict-Handling Styles: Less than Meets the Eye?" In *Conflict and Gender*.
Rudgley, Richard. *The Alchemy of Culture: Intoxicants in Society*. London: British Museum Press, 1993.
Rummel, Walter. "Die historische Hexenverfolgung – 'Vernichtung der weisen Frauen' oder Handlungsfeld der Volkskulten gegen Hexerei?" In *Alltagsleben und Magie*.
Rummel, Walter. "Exorbitantien und Ungerechtigten: Skandalerfahrung und ordnungspolitische Motive im Abbruch der kurtrierischen und sponheimischen Hexenprozesse 1653/1660." In *Das Ende der Hexenverfolgung*.
Rummel, Walter. "Verletzung von Körper, Ehre, und Eigentum. Varianten im Umang mit Gewalt in Dörfern der 17 Jahrhunderts." In *Mit den Waffen der Justiz*.
Rush, Jeffrey, *Witchcraft and Sorcery*. Springfield, IL: Charles C. Thomas, 1974.
Rushton, Peter. "Texts of Authority: Witchcraft Accusations and the Demonstration of Truth in Early Modern England." In *Languages of Witchcraft*.
Rushton, Peter. "Women, Witchcraft, and Slander in Early Modern England: Cases from the Church Courts of Durham, 1560–1675." *Northern History*, vol. XVIII (1982), pp. 116–32.
Russell, Jeffrey Burton. *Lucifer: The Devil in the Middle Ages*. Ithaca and London: Cornell University Press, 1984.
Russell, Jeffrey Burton. *Mephistopeles: The Devil in the Modern World*. Ithaca and London: Cornell University Press, 1986.
Russell, Jeffrey Burton. *The Prince of Darkness: Radical Evil and the Power of Good in History*. Ithaca, NY: Cornell University Press, 1988.
Russell, Jeffrey Burton. *Witchcraft in the Middle Ages*. Ithaca, NY: Cornell University Press, 1972.
Ryan, W. F. *The Bathhouse at Midnight: Magic in Russia*. University Park, PA: Pennsylvania State University Press, 1999.
Ryan, W. F. "Eclecticism in the Russian Charm Traditions." In *Charms and Charming*.
Ryan, Kenneth. "Conference Summary." In *Menopause and Aging*.
Saarni, Carolyn and Maria von Salisch. "The Socialization of Emotional Dissemblance." In *Lying and Deception*.
Sabean, David. "Aspects of Kinship Behavior and Property in Rural Western Europe before 1600." In *Family and Inheritance*.
Sabean, David. *Kinship in Neckarhausen, 1700–1870*. Cambridge: Cambridge University Press, 1998.

Sabean, David. "Production of the Self during the Age of Confessionalization." *Central European History*, vol. 29:1 (1996), pp. 1–18.
Sabean, David. *Power in the Blood: Popular Culture and Village Discourse in Early Modern Germany*. Cambridge: Cambridge Universtiy Press, 1984.
Sabean, David. *Property, Production, and Family in Neckarhausen, 1700–1870*. Cambridge: Cambridge University Press, 1990.
Safley, Thomas. *Let No Man Put Asunder: The Control of Marriage in the German Southwest: A Comparative Study, 1550–1600*. Kirksville, MO: Sixteenth Century Journal Publishers, Northeast Missouri State University, 1984.
Sallins, Marshall. *The Use and Abuse of Biology: An Anthropological Critique of Sociobiology*. Ann Arbor, MI: University of Michigan Press, 1976.
Samuel, Geoffrey. *Mind, Body, and Culture: Anthropology and the Biological Interface*. Cambridge: Cambridge University Press, 1990.
Sanders, Sabine. *Handwerkschirurgen: Socialgeschichte einer verdrangten Berufsgruppe*. Gottingen: Vandenhoeck & Ruprecht, 1989.
Santhouse, A. M. et al. "Visual Hallucinatory Syndrome and the Anatomy of the Visual Brain." *Brain*, vol. 123 (2000), pp. 2055–64.
Sarbin, Theodore. "Believed-in Imaginings: A Narrative Approach." In *Believed-in Imaginings*.
Sauer, Paul. *Herzog Friedrich I. von Württemberg*. Munich: Deutsche Verlags-Anstalt, 2003.
Sauer, Paul. "Not und Armut in den Dörfern des Mittleren Neckarraum in vorindustrieller Zeit." *Zeitschrift für Württembergische Landesgeschichte*, vol. 41 (1982), pp. 131–49.
Saur, Abraham. *Ein kurtze / treuwe Warnung / Anzeige und Underricht: Ob auch zu diser unser zeit unter uns Christen / Hexen / Zauberer / un Unholden vorhanden: Und was sie ausrichten Konnen*. n.p., 1582.
Saville-Troike, Muriel. *The Ethnography of Communication: An Introduction*. Baltimore, MD: University Park Press, 1982.
Scharfe, Martin. "The Distances between the Lower Classes and Official Religion: Examples from Eighteenth-Century Württemberg Protestantism." Trans. Deborah Monroe. In *Religion and Society in Early Modern Europe*.
Scharfe, Martin. "Soziale Kontrolle im Dorf Des Vorindustriellen Zeitalters." In *Aus der Heimatsgeschichte*.
Scheibe, Karl. "Replicas, Imitations, and the Question of Authenticity." In *Believed-in Imaginings*.
Schein, Sylvia. "Used and Abused: Gossip in Medieval Society." In *Good Gossip*.
Schiefenhövel, Wulf. "Universals in Interpersonal Interactions." In *Nonverbal Communication*.
Schindler, Norbert. *Rebellion, Community and Custom in Early Modern Germany*. Trans. Pamela E. Selwyn. Cambridge: Cambridge University Press, 2002.
Schnabel-Schüle, Helga. *Überwachen und Strafen im Territorialstaat: Bedingungen und Auswirkungen des Systems strafrechtlicer Sanktionen im frühneuzeitlichen Württemberg*. Köln, Weimar, Wein: Böhlau, 1997.
Schneidler, Gertrude. "Afterword." In *Hauntings and Poltergeists: Multidisciplinary Perspectives*. Ed. James Houran and Rense Large. Jefferson, N.C.: McFarland, 2001.
Schöck, Inge. "Das Ende der Hexenprozesse – das Ende der Hexenglaubens?" In *Hexenverfolgung: Beigräge*.
Schöck, Inge. *Hexenglaube in der Gegenwart*. Tübinger Vereinigung für Volkskunde, 1978.

Schofield, Phillip. "Peasants and the Manor Court: Gossip and Litigation in a Suffolk Village at the Close of the Thirteenth Century." *Past and Present*, vol. 159 (May 1998), pp. 3–42.
Schöpf, Hans. *Zauberkräuter*. Wiesbaden: VMA-Verlag, 1986.
Schormann, Gerhard. *Hexenprozesse in Deutschland*. Göttingen: Vandenhoeck & Ruprecht, 1981.
Schott, Heinz. "Imagination – Einbildungskraft – Suggestion: Zur 'Scharlatanerie' In der Neuzeitlichen Medizin." *Berichte zur Wissenschaftsgeschichte*, vol. 27:2 (2004), pp. 99–108.
Schrader, Abby. "Punishment." In *Encyclopedia of European Social History*, vol. 3.
Schrochliche Zeitung / Wahrhafftiger und gruntlicher Bericht / was sich zutragen hat mit einem armen Hirten / im Durmgerland / welcher mit mancherly anfechtung / und eusserlichen leiblichen plagen / biss aufft diesen tag / vom laidigen Teuffel angefochten wundt (1563); *Wahrafftige unnd Erschreckliche Thatten ud Handlungen der LXIII Hexen und Unholden / So zu Wisenstaig / mit dem Brandt gericht worden seindt* (1563).
Schultes, Richard. *Hallucinogenic Plants*. New York: Golden, 1976.
Schultes, Richard and Albert Hoffman. *The Botany and Chemistry of Hallucinogens*, 2nd Edition. Springfield, IL: Charles C. Thomas, 1980.
Schwäbische Sagen. Ed. Leander Petzoldt. Düsseldorf: Eugen Diedericke, 1975.
Schwäbische Spraechkunst. Ed. Wilhelm Moench. Stuttgart: Siberburg, 1937.
Schwartz, Gary. *The Afterlife Experiments*. New York: Pocket Books, 2002.
Schwartz, Jeffrey and Shanon Begley. *The Mind and the Brain: Neuroplasticity and the Power of Mental Force*. New York: Regan Books (HarperCollins), 2002.
Schwartz, Stephan. "NIH and the Harkin Directive: Subtle Energies and Social Policy," http://www.stehpanaschwartz.com/papers.htm.
The Science of Consciousness: Psychological, Neuropyschological and Clinical Reviews. Ed. Max Velmans. London: Routledge, 1996.
The Scottish Witch-Hunt in Context. Ed. Julian Goodare. Manchester, UK: Manchester University Press, 2002.
Scribner, Bob. "The *Mordbrenner* Fear in Sixteenth-Century Germany: Political Paranoia or the Revenge of the Outcast?" In *The German Underworld*.
Scribner, Bob. "Police and the Territorial State in Sixteenth-Century Württemberg." In *Politics and Society in Reformation Europe*.
Scribner, Bob. "Reformation and Desacralisation: From Sacramental World to Moralized Universe." In *Problems in the Historical Anthropology*.
Scribner, Robert. "The Reformation, Popular Magic, and the 'Disenchantment of the World.'" *The Journal of Interdisciplinary History*, vol. 23:3 (Winter 1993), pp. 475–94.
Scribner, R. W. "Sorcery, Superstition, and Society: The Witch of Urach, 1529." In *Popular Culture and Popular Movements in Reformation Germany*.
Sebald, H. "Franconian Witchcraft: The Demise of a Folk Magic." In *Anthropological Quarterly*, vol. 53:3 (July 1980), pp. 173–87.
Sebald, H. "Justice by Magic: Witchcraft as Social Control among Franconian Peasants." Reprinted in *New*, vol. 6.
Sebald, Hans. "Shaman, Healer, Witch: Comparing Shamanism and Franconian Folk Magic." Reprinted in *New*, vol. 5.
Sebald, Hans. *Witch-Children from the Salem Witch-Hunts to Modern Courtrooms*. Amherst, NY: Prometheus Books, 1995.
Secrets of Nature: Astrology and Alchemy in Early Modern Europe. Ed. William Newman and Anthony Grafton. Cambridge, MA: MIT Press, 2001.

Segall, Marshall et al. *Human Behavior in Global Perspective: An Introduction to Cross-cultural Psychology.* New York: Pergamon Press, 1990.
Segelmann, Kurt. Magic, Supernaturalism, and Religion. London: Penguin, 1971, rpt. of 1948.
Seidler, Eduard. "Abendländische Neuzeit." In *Krankheit, Heilkunst, Heilung.*
Sex and Gender Hierarchies. Ed. Barbara Miller. Cambridge: Cambridge University Press, 1993.
Sexual Underworlds. Ed. G. S. Rousseau and Roy Porter. Chapel Hill: University of North Carolina Press, 1988.
Shamanism: Past and Present, 2 vols. Ed. Mihâly Hoppâl and Otto von Sadovszky. Budapest: Ethnographic Institute, Hungarian Academy of Science, 1989.
Shamans through Time. Ed. Jeremy Narby and Francis Huxley. New York: Penguin, 2001.
Sharpe, J. A. "Witchcraft." In *Encylopedia of European Social History*, vol. 3, pp. 361–371.
Sharpe, J. A. "Witchcraft and Women in Seventeenth Century England: Some Northern Evidence." *Continuity and Change*, 6 (1991), pp. 179–99.
Sharpe, James. *The Bewitching of Anne Gunter.* New York: Routedge, 2001.
Sheikh, Anees A. et al. "Somatic Consequences of Consciousness." In *The Science of Consciousness.*
Shermer, Michael. *How We Believe: The Search for God in an Age of Science.* New York: W. H. Freeman, 2000.
Shermer, Michael. *Why People Believe Weird Things.* New York: Freeman, 1997.
Shibitani, Tamotsu. *Improvised News: A Sociological Study of Rumor.* Indianapolis, IN: Bobbs-Merril Educational Publishing, 1966.
Shore, Brad. *Culture in Mind: Cognition, Culture, and the Problem of Meaning.* Oxford: Oxford University Press, 1996.
Sidkey, H. *Witchcraft, Lycanthropy, Drugs, and Disease: An Anthropological Study of the European Witch-Hunts.* New York: Peter Lang, 1997.
Siebel, Friedrich. *Die Hexenverfolgung in Köln.* Bonn, 1959.
Siegel, James. *Naming the Witch.* Stanford: Standford University Press, 2006.
Sieroshevski, Wenceslas. "The-Man-Who-Fell-from-Heaven Shamanizes Despite Persection." In *Shamans through Time.*
Sierra, Mauricio and German Berrios. "Towards a Neuroscience of Conversion Hysteria." In *Conversion Hysteria.*
Sigel, Lisa. "The Body and Its Representations." In *Encyclopedia of European Social History*, vol. 4.
Signifying Animals: Human Meaning in the Natural World. Ed. Roy Willis. London: Unwin Hyman, 1989.
Simon, Gregory et al. "Somatic Symptoms of Distress: An International Primary Care Study." *Psychosomatic Medicine*, vol. 58 (1996), pp. 481–88.
Simon, Manual. *Heilige, Hexe, Mutter: Der Wandel des Frauenbildes durch die Medizin in sechzehnten Jahrhundert.* Berlin: Dietrich Reimer Verlag, 1993.
Simmons, Mark. "Interview with an Icon, Stuart R. Kaplan." Reprinted from *Games Quarterly Magazine*, Issue #3, 2004. Online at http://www.usgamesinc.com/pages.php?page=news/gamesquarterly_2004.html.
Singer, Stanley. "Ball Lightning – The Scientific Effort." *Philosophical Transactions: Mathematical, Physical and Engineering Sciences*, vol. 360:1790 (Jan 15, 2002), pp. 5–9.
Siraisi, Nancy. *Medieveal and Early Renaissance Medicine.* Chicago: University of Chicago Press, 1990.

Skafte, Peter. "Interview with a Killing Shaman." In *Shamans through Time*.
Slade, Peter and Richard Bentall: *Sensory Desception: A Scientific Analysis of Hallucination*. Baltimore: Johns Hopkins University Press, 1988.
Slutovsky, Moshe. "Discerning Spirits in Early Modern Europe." In *Communicating with the Spirits*.
Slutovsky, Moshe. "A Divine Apparition or Demonic Possession?" In *Witchcraft Reader*.
Smallwood, T. M. "The Transmission of Charms in England, Medieval and Modern." In *Charms and Charming*.
Smith, Moira. Review of Emma Wilby, *Cunning Folk and Familiar Spirits*. *Journal of Folklore Research* (posted November 21, 2006). At http://www.indiana.edu/%7Ejofr/review.php?id=324.
Smith, Peter and Michael Bond. *Social Psychology Across Cultures: Analysis and Perspectives*. Boston: Allyn and Bacon, 1994.
Smith, Timothy. "Marginal People." In *Encyclopedia of European Social History*, vol. 3.
The Social Construction of Illness. Ed. Jens Lachmund and Gunnar Stollberg. Stuttgart: Franz Steiner, 1992.
The Social Context of Nonverbal Behavior. Ed. Pierre Philippot et al. Cambridge: Cambridge University Press, 1999.
Social History and Issues in Human Consciousness: Some Interdisiplinary Connnections. Ed. Andrew Barnes and Peter Steams. New York: New York University Press, 1989.
The Sociobiological Imagination. Ed. Mary Maxwell. Albany, NY: SUNY Press, 1991.
Sökefeld, Martin. "Debating Self, Identity, and Culture in Anthropology." *Current Anthropology*, vol. 40:4 (August–October 1999), pp. 417–48.
Solms, Mark. *The Neuropsychology of Dreams: A Clinico-anatomical Study*. Mahwah, NJ: Lawrence Erlbaum Associates, 1997.
Soman, Alfred. "The Parliament of Paris and the Great Witch Hunt (1565–1640)." *Sixteenth Century Journal*, vol. IX:2 (1978), pp. 31–44.
Somé, Malidoma Patrice. "Invisible Projectiles in Africa." In *Shamans through Time*.
Somby-Borgstram et al. "Emotional Empathy as Related to Mimicry Reactions at Different Levels of Information Processing." *Journal of Nonverbal Behavior*, vol. 27:1 (Spring 2003), p. 3.
Spamer, Adolf. "Zauberbuch und Zauberspruch." *Deutsches Jahrbuch für Volkskunde*, vol. 1: 1/2 (1955), pp. 109–206.
Spanos, Nicholas and Cheryl Burgess. "Hypnosis and Multiple Personality Disorder: A Sociocognitive Perspective." In *Dissociation*.
Sparing, Margarthe. *The Perception of Reality in the Volksmärchen of Schleswig-Holstein: A Study of Interpersonal Relations and Worldview*. Lanham, MD: University Press of America, 1984.
The Spectrum of Ritual: A Biogenetic Structuralist Analysis. Ed. Eugene d'Aquili et al. New York: Columbia University Press, 1979.
Spence, Donald. "The Mythic Properties of Popular Explanations." In *Believed-in Imaginings*.
Spence, G. A. et al. "A PET Study of Voluntary Movement in Schizophrenic Patients Experiencing Passiviity Phenomena (Delusions of Alien Control)." *Brain*, vol. 120 (1997), pp. 1997–2011.
Spence, Sean. "The Cognitive Executive is Implicated in the Maintenance of Psychogenic Movement Disorders." In *Psychogenic Movement Disorders*.
Spence, Sean. "Hysterical Paralysis as Disorders of Action." In *Conversion Hysteria*.
Spence, Sean, et al. "Lying as an Executive Function." In *Malingering*.
Spiegel, David. "Therapeutic Support Groups." In *Healing and the Mind*.

Spierenberg, Pieter. "The Body and the State: Early Modern Europe." In *Oxford History of the Prison*.
Spierenberg, Pieter. *The Broken Spell: A Cultural and Anthropological History of Preindustrial Europe*. New Brunswick, NJ: Rutgers University Press, 1991.
Spierenburg, Pieter. "Crime." In *Encyclopedia of European Social History*, vol. 3.
Spierenberg, Pieter. *The Prison Experience: Disciplinary Institutions and Their Inmates in Early Modern Europe*. New Brunswick, NJ: Rutgers University Press, 1991.
Spirit vs. Scalpel: Traditional Healing and Modern Psychotherapy. Ed. Leonore Adler and B. Runi Mukherji. Westport, CT: Greenwood, 1995.
Spooner, Brian. "Anthropology and the Evil Eye." In *The Evil Eye*.
Sreenivasan, Govind. "The Social Origins of the Peasants' War of 1525 in Upper Swabia." *Past and Present*, vol. 171 (May 2001), pp. 30–65.
Stälin, Christop, *Württembergische Geschichte*, 4 vols. Stuttgart: J.G. Cottel, 1873.
Standish, L. J. et al. "Electroencephalographic Evidence of Correlated Event-Related Signals between the Brains of Spatially and Sensory Isolated Human Subjects." *Journal of Alternative and Complementary Medicine*, vol. 10 (2004), pp. 307–14.
Stanford, Peter. *The Devil: A Biography*. New York: Henry Holt, 1996.
Stannard, Jerry. "Magiferous Plants and Magic in Medieval Botany." In *Maryland Historian*, vol. 8:1 (Spring 1977), pp. 33–46.
Stark, Rodney and William Bainbridge. "Network of Faith: Interpersonal Bonds and Recruitment to Cults and Sects." In *The American Journal of Sociology*, vol. 85:6 (May 1980), pp. 1376–95.
Starker, Steven. *Fantastic Thought: All About Dreams, Daydreams, Hallucination and Hypnosis* Englewood Cliffs, NJ: Prentice Hall, 1982.
Stearns, Peter, "Old Women: Some Historical Observations." *Journal of Family History*, vol. V:1 (Spring 1980), pp. 44–57.
Stephens, Walter. *Demon Lovers: Witchcraft, Sex, and the Crisis of Belief*. Chicago and London: University of Chicago Press, 2002.
Stevens, Anthony. *Private Myths: Dreams and Dreaming*. Cambridge, MA: Harvard University Press, 1995.
Stewart, Charles. "Fields in Dreams: Anxiety, Experience, and the Limits of Social Constructionism in Modern Greek Dream Narratives." *American Ethnologist*, vol. 24:4 (November 1997), pp. 877–94.
Stewart, Neil and Sebastian Fairweather. "Delirium: The Physician's Perspective." In *Psychiatry in the Elderly*.
Steward, Pamela and Andrew Strathern. *Witchcraft, Sorcery, Rumors, and Gossip*. Cambridge: Cambridge University Press, 2004.
Stitziel, Judd. "God, the Devil, Medicine, and the Word: A Controversy over Ecstatic Women in Protestant Middle Germany, 1691–1693." In *Central European History*, vol. 29:3, pp. 309–38.
Stoeffler, Ernst. *German Pietism during the Eighteenth Century*. Leiden: E. J. Brill, 1973.
Strauss, Gerald. "Local Anticlericalism in Reformation Germany." In *Anticlericalism*.
Strauss, Gerald. *Luther's House of Learning: Indoctrination of the Young in Reformation Germany*. Baltimore: Johns Hopkins, 1978.
Stoddart, David. *The Scented Ape: The Biology and Culture of Human Odour*. Cambridge: Cambridge University Press, 1990.
Ströhmer, Michael. "Carolina (Constitutio Criminalis Carolina, CCC)." In *Lexikon zur Geschichte der Hexenverfolgung*. Ed. Gudrun Gersmann, Katrin Moeller, and Jürgen-Michael Schmidt. Created and last updated 15.2.2006, at http://www.historicum.net/no_cache/persistent/artikel/1586/.

Stuart, Kathy. *Defiled Trades and Social Outcasts: Honor and Ritual Pollution in Early Modern Germany*. Cambridge: Cambridge University Press, 1999.
Studies on Shamanism. Ed. Anna-Leena Sükala and Mihály Hoppál. Helsinki: Finnish Anthropological Society; Budapest: Akadémiai Kiadó, 1992.
Sturzbecher, Manfred. "The Physici in German-Speaking Countries from the Middle Ages to the Enlightenment." In *The Town and State Physician*.
Stutley, Margaret. *Shamanism: An Introduction*. London and New York: Routledge, 2003.
Sullivan, Margaret. "The Witches of Durer and Hans Baldung Grier." *Renaissance Quarterly*, vol. 53:2 (Summer 2000), pp. 333–401.
Sulzman, Patricia. "Charms and Blessings in Old High German." MA Thesis, SUNY, Stony Brook, 1972.
Sutter, Berthold. *Der Hexenprozeß gegen Katharina Kepler*. Weil der Stadt, 1979.
Styers, Randall. *Making Magic*. Oxford: Oxford University Press, 2004.
Sylwester, Robert. *How to Explain a Brain*. Thousand Oaks, CA: Corwin Press, 2005.
Symposium on Consciousness. Ed. Philip Lee et al. New York: Viking, 1976.
Tambiah, Stanley. "On the Magic Power of Words." *Man*, vol. 3, pp. 175–208.
Tangherlini, Timothy. "How Do You Know She's a Witch? Witches, Cunning Folk, and Competition in Denmark." *Western Folklore*, vol. 59: 3/4 (Summer 2000), Research Library, pp. 279–303.
Targ, Russell and Jane Katra. *Miracles of Mind*. Novato, CA: New World Library, 1999.
Tart, Charles. "The Psychophysiology of Some Altered States of Consciousness." *Altered States of Consciousness*. Ed. Charles Tart. New York: Wiley, 1969.
Tausiet, María. "From Illusion to Disenchantment: Feijoo Versus the 'Falsely Possessed' in Eighteenth-Century Spain." In *Beyond the Witch Trials*.
Tausiet, María. "Witchcraft as Metaphor: Infanticide and Its Tranlations in Aragón in the Sixteenth and Seventeenth Centuries." In *Languages of Witchcraft*.
Taussig, Michael. "Viscerality, Faith, and Skepticism." In *Magic and Modernity*, pp. 272–306.
Taves, Ann. *Fits, Trances, and Visions: Experiencing Religion and Explaining Experience from Wesley to James*. Princeton: Princeton University Press, 1999.
Tebbutt, Melanie. *Women's Talk? A Social History of 'Gossip' in Working-Class Neighborhoods, 1880–1960*. Aldershot: SCOLAR Press, 1995.
Tek22, "Dark and Hopeless Hell: Datura." *Eorwid's Experience Vault*, at http://www.erowid.org/experiences/exp.php?ID=11218.
Teresi, Scott. "The Current State of Parapsychology Research." Available at *SkepticReport.com*, (January 2004), http://www.skepticreport.com/psychics/teresi.htm.
Temoshek, Lydia and Clifford Attkisson. "Epidemiology of Hysterical Phenomena: Evidence for a Psychosocial Theory." In *Hysterical Personality*.
Theibault, John. "Jeremiah in the Village: Prophecy, Preaching, Pamphlets, and Penance in the Thirty Years' War." In *Central European History*, vol. 27 (1994), pp. 441–60.
Thiessen, Hillard von. *Das Verschwinden der Hexen aus Freiburg*. Freiburg im Breisgau: J. Haug, 1997.
Thomas, Keith. *Religion and the Decline of Magic*. New York: Scribner, 1971.
Thompson, Tok. "Hosting the Dead: Thanotopic Aspects of the Irish Sidhe." In *Communicating with the Spirits*.
Thomsen, Marie-Louise. "Witchcraft and Magic in Ancient Mesopotamia." In *Witchcraft and Magic in Early Modern Europe: Biblical and Pagan Societies*.

Thurn, Everard. "A White Man Goes to a Peaimar." In *Shamans through Time*.
Thurston, Robert. *Wtich, Wicce, Mother Goose*. London: Pearson, 2001.
Tiger, Lionel. *Optimism: The Biology of Hope*. New York: Simon and Schuster, 1979.
Tilly, Louise and Joan Scott. *Women, Work, and Family*. New York: Holt, Rinehart, & Winston, 1978.
Tolley, Bruce. *Pastors and Parishoners in Württemberg during the Late Reformation, 1581–1621*. Stanford, CA: Stanford University Press, 1995.
Tomasello, Michael. *The Cultural Origins of Human Cognition*. Cambridge, MA: Harvard University Press, 1999.
Totman, Richard. *Social Causes of Illness*. York: Pantheon, 1979.
Toward a General Theory of Social Control, vol. 1. Ed. Donald Black. Orlando: Academic Press, 1984.
Towell, Tony. "Unconscious Awareness." In *Parapsychology: The Science of Unusual Experience*.
The Town and State Physician in Europe from the Middle Ages to the Enlightenment. Ed. Andrew Russell. Wolfenbüttel: Herzog August Bibliotek, 1981.
Townsend, Joan. "Shamanism." In *The Anthropology of Religion*.
Transition and Revolution. Ed. Robert Kingdon. Minneapolis, MN: Burgess, 1974.
Trevor-Roper, Hugh *The European Witch Craze*. New York: Harper, 1969.
Tschaikner, Manfred. "Also schlecht ist das Weib von Natur: Grundsätzliches zur Rolle der Frau in den Vorarlberger Hexenverfolgungen." In *Hexe oder Hausfrau*.
Tschaikner, Manfred. *Magie und Hexerei in südlichen Vorarlberg zu Beginn der Neuzeit*. Konstanz: UVK, 1997.
Tuczay, Christa. "Holda." In *Encyclopedia of Witchcraft*.
Tuczay, Christa. "Incubus and Succubus." In *Encyclopedia of Witchcraft*.
Tuczay, Christa. "Trance Prophets and Diviners in the Middle Ages." In *Communicating with the Spirits*.
Turner, David. "The Missing Science of Ball Lightning." *Journal of Scientific Exploration*, vol. 17:3, pp. 435–96.
Turning Points: Historical and Sociological Essays on the Family. Ed. John Demos and Sarane Boocock. Chicago: University of Chicago Press, 1978.
Ullman, Montague. "Dreams and Society." In *The Variety of Dream Experience*.
Understanding the Immune System. US Department of Health and Human Services, NIH, National Cancer Institute. NIH Publication No. 03-5423, September 2003.
Understanding Popular Culture: Europe from the Middle Ages to the Nineteenth Century. Ed. Steven Kaplan. New York: Mouton, 1984.
Utts, Jessica. "Replacation and Meta-Analysis in Parapsychology." *Statistical Science*, vol. 6:4 (November 1991), pp. 363–78.
Vangelisti, Anita. "Messages that Hurt." In *The Dark Side of Interpersonal Communications*.
Vann, James. *The Making of a State: Württemberg, 1593–1793*. Ithaca, NY: Cornell University Press, 1984.
Varieties of Anomalous Experience: Examining the Scientific Evidence. Ed. Etzel Cardeña, et al. Washington, DC: American Psychological Association, 2000.
The Variety of Dream Experience, 2nd Edition. Ed. Montague Ullman and Claire Limmer. Albany, NY: SUNY Press, 1999.
Vasek, Marie E. 1986. "Lying as a Skill: The Development of Deception in Children." In *Deception*.
Vedfelt, Ole. *The Dimensions of Dreams*. Trans. Kenneth Tindall. London and Philadelphia: Jessice Kingsley Publishers, 2002.

Velmans, Max. "An Introduction to the Science of Consiousness." In *The Science of Consciousness.*
Velmans, Max. "A Natural Account of Phenomenal Consciousness." *NeuroQuantology,* vol. 3 (2005), pp. 164–79.
Verbrechen, Strafen, und soziale Kontrolle. Ed. Richard van Dülmen. Frankfurt am Main: Fischer, 1990.
Verdon, Jean. *Night in the Middle Ages.* Trans. George Holoch. Notre Dame, IN: University of Notre Dame Press, 2002.
Victor, Jeffrey. "Social Construction of Satanic Ritual Abuse and the Creation of False Memories." In *Believed-in Imaginings.*
Vinden, Peneope. "Imagination and True Belief: A Cross-Cultural Perspective." In *Believed-in Imaginings.*
Vines, Gail. *Raging Hormones: Do They Rule Our Lives?* Berkley: University of California Press, 1993.
Vitebsky, Piers. *Shamanism.* Norman, OK: University of Oklahoma Press, 2001.
Vitebsky, Piers. "Shamanism and the Rigged Marketplace." In *Shamans through Time.*
Vogel, Hubert. *Der große Schongauer Hexenprozeß und seine Opfer: 1589–1592.* Published by the city of Schongau, 1989.
Vogt, Evon and Ray Hyman. *Water Witching, USA.* Chicago: University of Chicago Press, 1959.
Vöhringer-Rubröder, Gisela. "Hexenverfolgungen in der Reichstadt Esslingen." In *Hexenverfolgung: Beiträge,* pp. 141–58.
Der Volksmund in Schwaben. Ed. August Laemmle. Stuttgart: Silberburg, 1924.
Volkstümliches aus Schwaben, 2 vols. Ed. Anton Birlinger. Freiburg: Herder'sche Verlagshandlung, 1861-2.
Voltmer, Rita. "Konflikt, Streit, Gewalt: Geschlectsverhältnis und Sexualität in der Dörfern des Luxemburger, Eifeler und Trierer Landes zur Zeit der Hexenvervolgungen." In *Alltagsleben und Magie.*
Vom Patriarchat zur Partnerschaft: Zum Strukturwandel der Familie. Ed. Michael Mitterauer and Reinhard Seidler. Munich: Beck, 1977.
Vos, George and Eric de. *Basic Dimensions in Conscious Thought: The Self and Socialization of Human Consciousness.* Lanham, MD: Rowman and Littlefield, 2004.
Vyse, Stuart. *Believing in Magic: The Psychology of Supersitition.* Oxford: Oxford University Press, 1997.
Waardt, Hans de. "From Cunning man to Natural Healer." In *Curing and Insuring.*
Wade, Nicholas and Michal Swanston. *Visual Perception: An Introduction.* Philadelphia: Taylor and Francis Psychology Press, 2001.
Wahrafftige unnd Erschreckliche Thatten ud Handlungen der LXIII Hexen und Unholden / So zu Wisenstaig / mit dem Brandt gericht worden seindt (1563).
Waite, Gary. *Heresy, Magic and Witchcraft in early modern Europe.* Houndmills, Basingstoke, Hampshire, UK: Palgrave Macmillan, 2003.
Wagman, Frederick. *Magic and Natural Science in German Baroque Literature.* New York: AMS Press, 1966.
Wagner, Kurt. *Aberglaube, Volksglaube und Erfahrung.* Halle: Max Niemeyer, 1941.
Wahl, Johannes. *Lebensplanung und Alltagserfahrung: Württembergische Pfarrfamilien im 17. Jahrundert.* Mainz: Philipp von Zabern, 2000.
Walinski-Kiehl, Robert. "The Devil's Children: Child Witch-Trials in Early Modern Germany." In *Continuity and Change,* vol. 11:2 (1996), pp. 171–89.
Walker Barbara and Curt Sandman. "Disregulation of the Gastrointestinal System." In *Psychosomatic Disorders.*

Walker, Timothy. *Doctors, Folk Medicine, and the Inquisition: The Repression of Magical Healing in Portugal during the Enlightenment.* Leiden: Brill, 2005.
Wall, Patrick. "The Placebo Effect." In *The Science of Consciousness.*
Walsh, Anthony. *Biosociology: An Emerging Paradigm.* Westport, CT: Praeger, 1995.
Walsham, Alexandra. "Frantick Hacket: Prophesy, Sorcery, Insanity, and the Elizabethan Puritan Movement." *Historical Journal,* vol. 41:1 (1998), pp. 27–66.
Walter, Rolf. *Die Kommerzialisieriung von Landwirtschaft und Gewerbe in Württemberg, 1750–1850.* St. Katharinen: Scripta Mercaturae, 1990.
Walther, Paul. *Schwäbische Volkskunde.* Leipzig: Quelle und Meyer, 1929.
Waltner-Kallfez, Isolde. *Die Schatzsuche als religiöses Motiv.* Wiesbaden: Harrassowitz, 1993.
Walz, Rainer. *Hexenglaube und Magische Kommunikation im Dorf der Frühen Neuzeit.* Paderborn: Ferdinand Schönurgh, 1993.
Walz, Reiner. "Schimpfende Weiber: Frauen in Lippischen Beleidigungsprozessen des Siebzehnten Jahrhunderts." In *Weiber, Menschen, Frauenzimmer.*
Warde, Paul. *Ecology, Economy, and State Formation in Early Modern Germany.* Cambridge: Cambridge University Press, 2006.
Wardell, Diane and Kathryn Weymouth. "Review of Studies of Healing Touch." *Journal of Nursing Scholarship,* vol. 36:2 (2004), pp. 147–54.
Wartenkin, Abraham. *The Devil in the German Traditional Story.* Chicago: University of Chicago Press, 1937.
The Watcher, "Datura Extraction and Effect." *Eorwid's Experience Vault,* http://www.erowid.org/experiences/exp.php?ID=11686.
Watson, Lyall. *Supernature.* New York: Bantam, 1974.
Watson, Patricia. "The 'Hidden Ones': Women and Healing in Colonial New England." In *Medicine and Healing.*
Watt, Caroline. "Paranormal Cognition." In *Parapsychology: The Science of Unusual Experience.*
Webb, William. "Chronic Pain: Psychosomatic Illness Review No. 14." *Psychosomatics,* vol. 24:12 (1983), pp. 1053–63.
Weber, Hartwig. *Kinderhexenprozesse.* Frankfurt am Main: Insel Verlag, 1991.
Weber, Hartwig. *"Von der verführten Kinder Zauberei": Hexenprozesse gegen Kinder im alten Württemberg.* Sigmaringen: Jan Thorbecke Verlag, 1996.
Weber-Kellerman, Ingeborg. *Die deutsche Familie: Versuch einer Sozialgeschichte.* Frankfurt am Main: Suhrkamp, 1974.
Weber-Unger, Heinrich. "Strafrecht und Volksglaube." Diss., University of Heidelberg, n.d.
Webster, Hutton. *Magic: A Sociological Study.* New York: Octagon, 1973, rpt. of 1948.
Weiber, Menschen, Frauenzimmer: Frauen in der ländlichen Gesellschaft, 1500–1800. Ed. Heide Wunder and Christina Varija. Göttingen: Vandenhoeck and Ruprecht, 1996.
Wegert, Karl. *Popular Culture, Crime, and Social Control in 18th-Century Württemberg.* Stuttgart: Franz Steiner, 1994.
Weideger, Paula. *Menstruation and Menopause: The Physiology and Psychology, the Myth and Reality.* New York: Knopf, 1976.
Weil, Andrew and Winifred Rosen. *From Chocolate to Morpine: Everything You Need to Know about Mind-Altering Drugs,* revised and updated. Boston and New York: Houghton Mifflin, 1993.
Weiler, Inge. *Giftmordwissen und Giftmörderinnen: Eine diskursgeschichte Studie.* Tübingen: Max Niemeyer, 1998.
Weiner, Herbert. *Psychobiology and Human Disease* (1977).

Weingart, Peter et al. "Shifting Boundaries between the Biological and the Social: The Social and Political Contexts." In *Human by Nature*.
Welborne, F. B. "Healing as a Psychosomatic Event." In *Witchcraft and Healing*.
Weller, Arnold. *Sozialgeschichte Südwestdeutschlands*. Stuttgart: Konrad Theiss, 1979.
Weller, Karl and Arnold Weller. *Württembergische Geschichte im Südwestdeutschen Raum*. Stuttgart: Konrad Theiss, 1972.
Wessel-Berg, Tore. "Ball Lightning and Atmospheric Light Phenomena: A Common Origin?" *Journal of Scientific Exploration*, vol. 18:3 (2004), pp. 439–81.
Werewolves, Witches, and Wandering Spirits: Traditional Belief and Folklore in Early Modern Europe. Ed. Kathryn Edwards. Kirksville, MO: Truman State University Press, 2002.
Wessling, Mary. "Medicine and Government in Early Modern Württemberg." Ph.D. Dissertation, University of Michigan, 1988.
"What is Psoriasis?" PsoriasisNet, American Academy of Dermatology, 2005. Last updated 8/31/05, http://www.skincarephysicians.com/psoriasisnet/whatis.html.
Whitbourne, Susan. *The Aging Individual: Physical and Psychological Perspectives*, 2nd Edition. New York: Springer Publishing, 2002.
Whiting, John. *Culture and Human Development*. Ed. Eleanor Chasdi. Cambridge University Press, 1994.
Whitney, Elspeth. "International Trends: The Witch 'She' / The Historian 'He.'" *Journal of Women's History*, vol. 7 (1995), pp. 77–101.
Why Language Matters for Theory of Mind. Ed. Janet Astington and Jodie Baird. Oxford: Oxford University Press, 2005.
Wickham, Chris. "Gossip and Resistance among the Medieval Peasantry." *Past and Present*, issue 160 (August 1998), pp. 3–25.
Widmann, Hans. *Tübingen als Verlagstadt*. (Tübingen: Mohr, 1971).
Wier, Dennis. *Trance: From Magic to Technology*. Ann Arbor, MI: TransMedia, 1996.
Wiercinski, Andrzej. "On the Origins of Shamanism." In *Shamanism: Past and Present*.
Wierzbicka, Anna. *Semantics, Culture, and Cognition: Human Concepts in Culture-Specific Configurations*. New York and Oxford: Oxford University Press, 1992.
Wiesner, Merry. *Gender, Church, and State in Early Modern Germany*. London and New York: Longman, 1997.
Wijngaard, Marianne van den. *Reinventing the Sexes: Feminism and Biomedical Construction of Femininity and Masculinity, 1959–1985*. Delft: Eburon, 1991.
Wilbey, Emma. "The Witch's Familiar and the Fairy in Early Modern England and Scotland." *Folklore* vol. 111:2 (October 2000), pp. 283–305.
Willburger, August. "Hexenverfolgungen in Württemberg." *Rottenburger Monatschrift für praktische Theologie*, vol. 13 (1929/30), pp. 135–45, 167–73.
Willis, Deborah. *Malevolent Nurture: Witch-Hunting and Maternal Power in Early Modern England*. Ithaca: Cornell University Press, 1995.
Willis, Roy. "New Shamanism." *Anthropology Today*, vol. 10:6 (December 1994), pp. 16–18.
Wilson, Stephen. *The Magical Universe: Everyday Ritual and Magic in Pre-modern Europe*. London: Hambledon and London, 2000.
Winkelman, Michael. "Altered States of Consciousness." In *Anthropology of Religion*, pp. 399–428.
Winkelman, Michael. "Magico-religious Practitioner Types and Socioeconomic Conditions." In *Behavioral Science Research*, vol. 20 (1986), pp. 17–46.
Winkelman, Michael. *Shamanism: The Neural Ecology of Consciousness and Healing*. Westport, CT and London: Bergin and Garvey, 2000.

Winkelman, Michael. "Shamans and Other 'Magico-religious' Healers: A Cross-Cultural Study of Their Origins, Nature, and Social Transformations." *Ethos*, vol. 18:3 (September 1990), pp. 308–52.
Winkelman, Michael. "Trance States: A Theoretical Model and Cross-Cultural Analysis." *Ethos*, vol. 14:2 (Summer 1986), pp. 174–203.
Winkelman, M. and Philip Peek. "Introduction: Divination and Healing Processes." In *Divination and Healing*, pp. 3–25.
Wintterlin, Friedrich. *Geschichte der Behördenorganisation in Württemberg*, vol. 1. Stuttgart: Kohlhammer, 1904.
Wirth, Jean. "Against the Acculturation Thesis." Trans. John Burke. In *Religion and Society*.
Wiseman, Richard. *Deception and Self-Deception: Investigating Psychics*. Amherst, NY: Prometheus, 1997.
Witchcraft and Healing. Centre of African Studies. Edinburgh: University of Edinburgh, 1969.
Witchcraft and Magic in Europe: Ancient Greece and Rome. Ed. Bengt Ankarloo and Stuart Clark. Philadelphia: University of Pennsylvania Press, 1999.
Witchcraft and Magic in Europe: Biblical and Pagan Societies. Ed. Bengt Ankarloo and Stuart Clark. Philadelphia: University of Pennsylvania Press, 2001.
Witchcraft and Magic in Europe: The Eighteenth and Nineteenth Centuries. Ed. Bengt Ankarloo and Stuart Clark. Philadelphia: University of Pennsylvania Press, 1999.
Witchcraft and Magic in Europe: The Middle Ages. Ed. Bengt Ankarloo and Stuart Clark. Philadelphia: University of Pennsylvania Press, 2002.
Witchcraft and Magic in Europe: The Period of the Witch Trials. Ed. Bengt Ankarloo and Stuart Clark. Philadelphia: University of Pennsylvania Press, 2002.
Witchcraft and Magic in Europe: The Twentieth Century. Ed. Bengt Ankarloo and Stuart Clark. Philadelphia: University of Pennsylvania Press, 1999.
Witchcraft and Sorcery. Ed. Max Marwick. Harmondsworth, UK: Penguin, 1970.
Witchcraft: Confessions and Accusations. Ed. Mary Douglas. London: Tavistock, 1970.
Witchcraft Continued: Popular Magic in Modern Europe. Ed. Willem de Blécourt and Owen Davies. Manchester: Manchester University Press, 2004.
Witchcraft in Early Modern Europe. Ed. Jonathan Barry et al. Cambridge: Cambridge University Press, 1996.
The Witchcraft Reader. Ed. Darren Oldridge. London and New York: Routledge; Taylor and Francis, 2002.
The Witch Figure. Ed. Venetia Newall. London: Routledge and Kegan Paul, 1973.
Wigzell, Faith. *Reading Russian Fortunes: Print Culture, Gender, and Divination in Russia from 1765*. Cambridge: Cambridge University Press, 1998.
Wolcock, John. "The use of dowsing for the location of caves, with some results from the first Royal Forest of Dean Caving Symposium, June 1994." Section INRIA de Spéléologie, http://www-sop.inria.fr/agos/sis/dowsing/dowsdean.html.
The Wolf and the Lamb: Popular Culture in France from the Old Regime to the Twentieth Century. Ed. Jacques Beauroy et al. Saratoga, CA: Anma Libri, 1977.
Wolman, Benjamin. *Psychosomatic Disorders*. New York: Plenum Medical Books 1988.
Women, Crime, and the Courts in Early Modern England. Ed. Jennifer Kermode and Garthine Walker. Chapel Hill: University of North Carolina Press, 1994.
Women, Culture, and Society. Ed. Michelle Rosaldo and Louise Lamphere. Stanford: Stanford University Press, 1974.
Women in German Yearbook 3: Feminist Studies and German Culture. Ed. Marianne Buckhard and Edith Waldstein. Lanham, MD: University Press of America, 1986.

Women in Their Speech Communities: New Perspectives on Language and Sex. Ed. Jennifer Coates and Deborah Cameron. London and New York: Longman, 1988.
Women, Men, and Gender: Ongoing Debates. Ed. Mary Walsh. New Haven, CT: Yale University Press, 1997.
Wonders of the Invisible World, 1600–1900. Ed. Peter Benes. The Dublin Seminar for New England Folklife, Annual Proceedings. Boston: Boston University, 1992.
Woody, Erik and Kenneth Bowers. "A Frontal Assault on Dissociated Control." In *Dissociation*.
Wortley, John. "Three Not-So-Miraculous Miracles." In *Health, Disease, and Healing*.
Wunder, Gerd. "Bauerliche Oberschichten im Alten Wirtemberg." In *Bauernschaft und Bauernstand*.
Wunder, Heidi. "Gender Norms and Their Enforcement in Early Modern Germany." In *Gender Relations*.
Wunder, Heidi. *He is the Sun, She is the Moon: Women in Early Modern Germany*. Trans. Thomas Dunlap. Cambridge, MA: Harvard University Press, 1998.
Wunderlei, Richard. *Peasant Fires: The Drummer of Niklashausen*. Bloomington: Indiana University Press, 1992.
Wyman, Walker. *Witching for Water, Oil, Pipes, and Precious Minerals*. Park Falls, WI: University of Wisconsin, River Falls Press, 1977.
Yarrow, Marian. "Appraising Environment." In *Processes of Aging*.
Yeoman, Louise. "The Devil as Doctor: Witchcraft, Wodrow and the Wider World." In *New*, vol. 1.
Yrizarry, Nathan et al. "Culture and Emotion." In *Cross-Cultural Topics in Psychology*.
Zagorin, Perez. *Ways of Lying: Dissimulation, Persection, and Conformity in Early Modern Europe*. Cambridge, MA: Harvard University Press, 1990.
Zaleski, Philip and Carol Zaleski. *Prayer: A History*. Boston and New York: Houghton Mifflin, 2005.
Zarit, Steven and Judy Zant. *Mental Disorders in Older Adults*. New York and London: The Guilford Press, 1998.
Zauberer – Selbstmörder – Schatzsucher: Magische Kultur und behördliche Kontrolle im frühneuzeitlichen Württemberg. Ed. Johannes Dillinger. Trier: Cliomedia, 2003.
Zeman, Adam. "Consciousness." In *Psychogenic Movement Disorders*.
Zilboorg, Gregory. *A History of Medical Psychology*. New York: Norton, 1941.
Zilka, Charles. "The Devil's Hoodwink: Seeing and Believing in the world of Sixteenth-Century Witchcraft." In *New*, vol. 1.
Zilka, Charles. *Exorcizing Our Demon: Magic, Witchcraft and Visual Culture in Early Modern Europe*. Leiden, Boston: Brill, 2003.
Zsindely, Endre. *Krankheit und Heilung im älteren Pietismus*. Stuttgart: Zwingli, 1962.
Zusne, Leonard and Warren Jones. *Anomalistic Psychology: A Study of Magical Thinking*, 2nd Edition. Hillsdale, NJ: Lawrence Erlbaum Associates, 1989.
Zwo schröckliche Newe Zeituung / Die erste Ist von dem Grewlichen Elend / so sich jetzund in der Churfurstlichen Stadt Aschenburck / am Maunstrom gelegen / und in den umbliegenden Flecken von einer grossen anzahl Hexen und Unholden (Stessen, 1612).

Index

A

Abduction experiences
　alien 74
　witch 22–3, 187
Aberglaube see Superstition
Abershausen 240
Ability, abnormal 337
Absorption 202
　see also Dissociation
Abuses 392
　clerical 356
　judicial 63
Accidents 2, 19–21, 43, 171, 273
　workplace 50
Acculturation 53, 412
　society's 118
Accusations xvi, 2, 6, 7, 13, 15, 27–9, 37, 46–9, 57, 59, 75, 97, 99, 103, 106–7, 116–18, 132, 158, 166, 229, 304, 307, 319, 350, 355, 386–7, 389, 392, 400, 404, 412
　divisive 231
　false 393
　formal 355, 386
　generating 387
　informal 355
　of maleficium 6
　secondary 6, 7, 22, 29, 46, 49, 57
　unfounded 433
Accusatory principle 355, 386
　see also Tübingen Contract
Accusatory symptoms see Conversion reaction
Accusers xvi, 7, 27, 37, 45–7, 152, 158, 167–8, 402, 412
Acetylcholine 11, 119, 143–4, 195–6
　deficiencies 119
　neurotransmitter 11, 143
　released 208
　see also Cholinergic
Acne 312
Activation, emergency 298
　see also Fight/flight response
Ada, Catharina 10, 13, 14, 17–19, 21, 23, 28, 37, 40, 56–7, 411

Ada, Margaretha 10, 14, 22, 306, 411
Adjurations 242, 276, 217
　see also Conjure
Administration
　civil 266
　governmental 394
　high 369
　judicial xiv
　local 386
　church 360
Administrators 369
　enlightened 354
　trained professional 351
　see also Bureaucracy, Ducal government, Government
Admonish 356, 383
Admonishments 358
　church's 358
　cultural 59
　government's 403
Admonitions 258, 260, 263
　see also Sermons, Pamphlet literature
Adolescents 312, 332
Adulterants, psychoactive 131, 142
Adultery 75, 133, 243, 261, 263
　committed 75, 244
Adults 31, 34, 111, 115–16, 118, 332, 346, 364, 412, 416
　middle-aged 46–7, 115, 117
　suspects 97
　young 14
Affliction 89, 126, 256, 307, 329
　complex symbolic 402
　see also Ailments, Misfortunes
Africa 186
African spiritual specialists 186
Age 3, 47, 57–60, 68, 72, 88, 90, 111, 116, 259, 312, 345–6, 370, 420, 422
　advanced 120
　profile 57
　recorded 346
　relative 46
　see also Children, Adults, Elderly suspects, Old age

558

Agents   20, 34, 319, 339, 398, 435
  active   70, 153, 373, 417
  causative   406
  chemical   11
  direct   67
  effective   163
  external   204
  extraordinary   205
  independent conscious   182
  infectious   299
  intermediate   399
  intoxicating   186
  intrusive   365
  local   356
  nefarious   440
  physical   287
  psychoactive   143
  social   105
  spiritual   237
  widely used as an aborting   135
  zealous   363
Aggress   52, 55
Aggression   44, 52–3, 117
  counter occult   335
  covert   53
  direct   52–3
  indirect   52, 54
  verbal   52
  women   54
Aggressive
  behaviors   53
  initiatives   406
  police effort   385
  reactions   60
Aggressiveness   47, 55, 58, 410–11
  see also Combativeness
Agnes   19, 158–9, 161, 329–32
Agricola, Georgius   233
Agrippa, Cornelius   155, 166, 224
Ahrendt-Schulte, Ingrid   xviii
Ailments   12, 16–19, 39, 40, 45, 159, 226, 275, 285–6, 289, 296, 304–5, 308, 342–3, 416
  bodily   119
  curing   281
  natural   343
  psychophysical   12, 33, 159
  somatic   15
  see also Afflictions, Delirium, Disorders, Distress, Disease, Maladies
Aitlingen   313

Alb, Noah   267
Alber, Matthew   70
Albrecht, Jacob's wife   295
Alchemy   246, 320
Alcohol   95, 131–2, 202, 279
  intoxication   131
Aldingen   231
Alemanni   96, 193
Alexen, Catharina   166
Alienation, process of   184–5
Alkaloids   9, 132, 135, 143
  atropine   11
  hallucinogenic   139
  lysergic acid   134
  of the peptide type   134
  see also Drugs
Allegations   3, 6, 7, 10–11, 13, 22, 37–8, 45, 48, 63, 99, 100, 103, 156, 168–9, 176, 243, 246, 317, 324, 329, 388, 395, 403
Alliette, Jean-Baptiste   see Etteilla
Allport and Postman   100–1
Alms   60, 415
Almshouse administrator   344
Almshouses   33, 60, 77, 356
  see also Hospitals, Orphan house, *Spitalen*
Alpirsbach   158, 240, 309, 328
Alps   67, 94, 96
Alsace   257
Altdorf   316
Altensteig   169, 193–4, 316
Altered states
  of consciousness   186, 195, 209, 295
  spontaneous   225
Aminergic neurotransmitters   110, 195–6, 203, 207
Aminita muscara   202
Amphetamines   202
Amtmann   351
  see also Constable
Amulets   191, 271, 274, 280, 282, 288, 306, 314, 319, 342
  protective   303, 215
  supplied   408
Amygdala   26, 292
Anabaptism   268
Anabaptists   95–6, 343
Analgesic   203, 274
Andreae, Johann Valentin   259, 265, 406
Androgens   53–4

Angel 72, 85–6, 200, 260–5, 269, 325, 439, 215
Anger 5, 8, 12, 20, 24–6, 29, 40, 45, 55, 111, 113, 117, 153, 155–6, 165, 176, 213, 237, 265, 309, 311, 317, 381, 410–12, 433
  bitter 44
  clear 18
  expressed 156
  expressions of xv, 29, 39, 153, 176, 213, 433
  person's 165, 430
  projecting 427
  speaker's 24
  violent 411
Angoulême 227
Angry 10, 25, 56, 58, 106–7, 116, 121, 181, 312
  display 433
  gaze 25
  interchanges 28
  people 65, 434
Animal
  forms 71
  husbandry 41
  hypnosis 294
  magnetism 301
  maladies 38
  metamorphosis 67
  reproduction 38, 83, 165
  sacrifices 382
Animals 6, 13, 25, 37–40, 45, 56, 73, 78, 82, 86–7, 95, 101, 111, 122, 137–8, 148, 152–3, 155, 164–5, 167, 175, 189–92, 200, 204–5, 207, 236, 250, 255, 272–3, 309, 343, 382
  bewitched 166
  dead 168
  domesticated 164–5
  dominant 38
  freeze 163
  harm people or 121
  harming 7, 419
  healing of 275
  injuring 37, 56
  sick 37
  spook 164, 173, 260
  startled 294
  transformation into 140
  unnatural power over 37
  young 111
  zoo 38
  see also Cattle maiming
Animate beings 436
Animosities 43, 269
Animosity 134
Anna Barbara from Hörterichshof 19, 20
Anna Maria from Wasserstetten 8–10, 133
Anoint, observed people 129, 131
  see also Salves
Anomalous
  cases 326
  deflections 333
  luminous phenomena 325
  physical phenomena 225
Anticholinergics 143–7, 149
  see also Drugs
Antichrist 258–9
Anticlericalism 95, 117
Antipathy 149, 179, 182, 233, 382
Antiquity 95, 107, 135, 152, 177, 224, 237, 240, 256, 280, 324, 328, 332, 350, 381, 425, 437
Antiwitch 284
  see also Countermeasures
Anxiety 20, 58, 210, 288, 300, 311, 315
  a continuing 58
  normal 134
  reducing 297
  relieve 209
Aphrodisiac 131–2
Apocalyptic character 258, 268
Apostasy 178, 392
Apostles, Acts of 263
Apothecaries 50, 279, 281, 305, 307, 345, 360–1, 363, 367–8, 404
  visitations 361
Apothecary Ordinances
  First 361
  Second 404
Apparitions 31, 86, 240, 243, 265, 267, 322, 328–32, 426
  fully realized 265
  hostile 329
Appeasement 1
  see Countermeasures
Apple 56, 71
  poisoned 9, 38, 49

Appten, Barbara   266-7
Apuleius   131-2
Aquili, Eugene d'   xx
Arabic scholarship   382
Arabs   255
Arcane
  symbols   171
  systems   251
Archer wizards   314-15
Aristocracy, international   370
Aristocrats   180, 368, 370
Arguments, bitter   390
Arms   10, 14, 19, 20, 22, 27, 50, 56, 169, 233, 266, 268, 281, 286, 324, 350, 356
  hurt   306, 400
  right   49
Arousal   32, 78, 144, 146
  cortical   126
  curses escalate   23
  endocrine structures mediating   160, 298
  intense   208
  stress-induced   32
Arrhythmias   *see* Cardiac arrhythmias
Arrow   314
Arson   6, 7, 44, 122, 353, 424
Artifacts
  linguistic   109
  literary   109
Artisans   41-2, 62, 345, 362, 367-8, 423
Arts, forbidden   228, 339, 426
Arznei *see* Healing
ASCs   146, 148, 195
  see also Consciousness
Assault   6-11, 14, 21, 27, 40, 48, 212, 329
  spiritual   175
Associational-imagic systems   376
Associations, visual and auditory   110
Astrologers   255-7, 259, 267
  professional   252
Astrology   254-9, 320
Astronomy   254, 256, 320
Atherosclerosis   18
Atropa belladonna   143
  see also Belladonna, Nightshade
Atropine   143-4
Attack   9, 11, 14, 22-3, 34, 37, 44-5, 65, 153, 155, 187, 312

  covert   52
  recognizable Old Hag   34
  spiritual   152
Augsburg   68, 81, 85, 115, 175, 314
Augsburg, League of   258
Aunts, old   190, 192, 343
Austerities   431
Austria   189
Authoritative pronouncements   94
Authorities   15, 28, 82, 138, 149, 151, 164, 167, 178, 192, 209, 232, 235, 242, 264, 281, 304-5, 342, 347, 353, 356-7, 365, 369, 382, 387, 397, 411, 414, 417
  civil   356
  enlightened   418
  highest   354
  judicial   221, 350
  moral   242
  religious   73, 215
  secular   150, 172, 293, 357
  spiritual   258
Auto-suggestion   18, 161, 288, 290-1
Autonomic
  adjustment   25
  balance   299
  damage-control systems   273
  systems   23, 146, 161
Autonomous
  conscious agency   235
  consciousnesses   87-8, 92, 207, 236, 287
  entities   205
  ideation   196
  intelligences   141-2, 260, 269, 431-2, 436
  rational actors   431
  see also Consciousness
Auvegne, Willilam of   188
Avarice   172, 238-9, 245, 261, 387
Awake   33, 110-11, 121, 128-9, 141, 149, 189, 197, 265, 330
  see also Consciousness, normal
Awareness   21, 54, 70, 72, 77, 87, 92, 113, 125-6, 161, 184, 197-8, 220, 226, 230, 315, 374-5, 425
  conscious   78, 87, 112, 185, 198, 290, 375
  heightened   72, 315
  increased   72
  people's   358

562   Index

Awareness (*Continued*)
  rational-linguistic   377
  real   230
  retrospective   373
  unacknowledged   226
  see also Consciousness
Ax   241, 250

B
Babylonians   255
Backnang   244–5, 280, 307, 310, 319
Bad
  person   47
  reputations   47, 90, 411
  very   120
The "bad spirit"   262
Bailey, Michael   xvi
Baitinger, Catharina   10, 14, 56, 61, 307, 389, 400
Balingen   7, 329, 387
Balkans   94, 180
Ball lightning   xv, 272, 325–6, 332
  existence of   325
  understanding   325
Balls, crystal   171, 220, 222, 236
Bandits   423
Banished suspects   47
Banishment   352–3, 358, 382–3, 405, 440
Baptism   410
Barber   19, 137, 147–8, 179, 305, 310, 343, 397, 416
Barber-surgeons   106, 360–1
  see also Surgeon
Bark   279, 284
Basal
  forebrain   195
  ganglia   199
    structures   297
Base metals, transmute   320, 216
Bastard   75–6, 106, 244
Bästlin, healer from Besigheim   280, 282–4, 286, 293, 300
Bathe   283, 293
Bather, town   222
Bathers   221–2, 281, 305, 344, 360
Baths   99, 286, 308
  herbal   286
  mineral   361

Bats   314
Battery   52, 309, 355
Bavaria   277, 314, 319, 321
Bavarian coin   313–14
Bean-casting   253
Beard, red   97
Beat   82, 85, 119, 132, 179, 267, 389
  her badly   174
Beaten
  to compel confession   245, 270, 427
  as punishment   79, 107, 138,
  see also Testimony, Torture
Bebenhausen   178, 316
Bebion, Johann   77, 410
Bebion, Johann's wife   77–9, 81, 86–7, 90, 186, 205, 400, 409–10
Bechtold, Anna   266–8, 270
Beck, Agnes   32–34, 348
Bed
  under   227
  woman's   166, 298
Bedside manner   209
Beelzebub   175–6, 180, 184
Beer   130–1, 135, 142, 192
  brewer's house   136–7
  cellars   139, 141, 145
    raided neighboring   434
  pilsner   130
Beggars   60–1, 117
Behavior-modification   412–13
Behaviors, women's   411, 415
Behringer, Wolfgang   xvii, xviii
Belladonna   11, 130, 140, 143
  see also Nightshade
Bells   271
Bempfingen   82
Benandanti   xvii, 36, 94, 97, 113, 120–3, 130, 161, 187, 201, 437
  female   122, 240
Benedict root   283–4
Benedictions   279
Benedict's day   283–4
Beneficent   303, 312, 319, 334–5, 383, 406, 437–8, 216–17
  magic   xiv, xix, 2, 178, 215–17, 221, 232, 249, 270, 303–4, 307, 334–5, 337, 339–41, 343, 346, 348, 358, 380–1, 406–8, 429

Index 563

magicians xvi, 7, 383, 405, 429
  punish 406
  practices xviii, 4, 213, 273, 383, 405–6, 438,
  traditions 213
Bengel, Johann Albrecht 420
Benne, Benedict 388
Berich 184
Bern 251
Bernhard, Georg and Chrisoph 237
Bertha 96
Bertschen, Catharina 21
Besigheim 75, 239
Besold, Christoph 392
Beta-endorphin 203–4
Beta wave activity 196
Beurlin, Frantz 321
Bewitch 166, 192
Bewitchings 10, 186, 349, 395, 401–2
Beyler, Anna 49, 50, 311, 400
Biases 3, 438
Biblical
  figures 381
  sayings 349
  and songs 275, 280, 296, 298
Bidembadr, Wilhelm 70
Biener, Hans 156
Bietigheim 88, 133, 173, 279
Bilfinger, Glaßer's wife 230, 309–10
Billfinger, George 420
Bilsenkraut 130
  see also Henbane
Binder, Hannß 283
Bioelectric activity 203–4, 206, 211
Bioenergy 301–2
Biological
  differences 53
  endowment, basic 34
Biology 52–3
Birch, Thomas 391
Birds 83–4, 109–10, 131, 409
Bite marks 85, 332
"Bitter almonds" 132
  arguments 390
  feuds 43
  see also Nightshade
Black
  arts 153, 140, 180
  figure 157, 385
  man 97, 106–7, 113
  markets 429

mustache 118
  numbers 154
Black Forest 41, 103, 241, 252
Blacksmith 173, 282, 313
Blaubeuern 7, 81, 311, 321
Blécourt, Willem xviii
Blencklen, Conrad 310–11, 322
Blessers 340, 361
Blessings 4, 216–17, 228, 250, 275–7, 279–86, 288–9, 292, 294–5, 298, 306–7, 309–10, 317–19, 321–2, 339–40, 342–3, 346–8, 359, 382, 407–8, 421, 424
  command form 276–7, 279, 318, 429
  comparative form 276–9
  illicit 250, 276, 318, 321, 427
  narrative form 277–9, 291
  nineteenth-century Swabian 277
  protective 303
  short 224, 280
  supplicative form 276–8, 291
  see also Charms, Incantation, Prayer
Blind spot 197
Blocking, neuropsychological
  cogitations 440
  information 377
Blood 38, 42, 75, 80, 137–9, 148, 158, 168, 176, 179, 256, 262–3, 276, 291, 293, 309, 329–30, 388, 400, 428
  glucose 291
  human 301
  innocent 318
  of Jesus Christ 238
  menstrual 168
  pressure 203, 291, 294, 298, 300, 302
    increased 160
    reduced 204
  pump 18
  staunching 273
  vessels 16, 290
    constricted 297
Bloodstream 11, 16, 145, 298
Blow (breath) 82, 174, 282, 284–5, 401, 408
Boach 173
Boarders 60, 82, 228, 362
Böblingen 173, 238–9, 248, 323–6, 334, 341, 348
Bocer, Heinrich 391
Bodin, Jean 129, 189

Body
  consciousness 436
  language 39, 164, 227
  parts 155
Body's defenses 299
Bohemia 244–5, 319
Böhmler, Agnes 281
Boils 262, 308
Bolingbroke, Roger 169
Bondorf 242
Bonds
  betrayal of communal 353
  social 297, 353
Bones 154–5, 157, 169, 192, 222, 273, 304, 306, 308, 314–15, 329
Book market 71, 73
Books 131, 137, 139, 148, 152, 155, 170–1, 179–80, 184, 193, 224, 236, 251, 253–4, 257, 281–3, 286–7, 309–10, 319–21, 337, 343, 369, 378, 382, 393, 407, 426
  Devil 71–2
  a "planet book" 281
  priest's 320
  a "witch book" 168
  see also Devil books
Bottwar 19, 79, 321
Bourbon, Etienne de 188
Boyle, Robert 233
Brackenheim 233, 248, 266–7
The brain 299
Brain 11, 13, 26, 30, 53–4, 74, 83, 85–6, 92, 101, 108–9, 111–12, 114, 125–6, 146–7, 149, 160–1, 182, 195, 199, 202–4, 207–8, 211, 223–5, 269, 292–5, 297, 299, 376–7, 432, 434
  activity 199, 293
    synchronizing 292
  ages 120
  centers 78, 110–12, 203, 225, 295
  frontal lobes 116, 147, 204, 299, 376
  left 374, 377
  men's 54
  models reality 30
  regions 374
  size 91
  stem 161, 195, 203–4, 206
  structures 86, 199, 203
  wave activity 198–9
  waves 109–10, 195, 298

  see also Cerebral Cortex, Integrative brain state
Brain's spatial sense 203
Braittingen, Maria 7, 81–2, 84–7, 90, 121–4, 127–9, 149, 161, 175–8, 205, 212, 264, 388, 400
Brand, Johannes 8, 15, 19, 21, 46, 133, 305, 307, 387, 406–7
Brandenburg 193, 257
Brands sister-in-law Susanna Catharina 8, 15, 21, 46
Brandy, burn 175
Bread 8, 9, 13, 15, 106, 133–5, 139, 141, 190, 192, 210, 238, 243, 250, 262, 270, 280, 310
  bake 11, 13, 45
  ergot-laced 15, 134, 167
  inspectors 363
  peculiar 134
  piece of 134
  stale 8
  tainted 134
Breitenberg 242
Brenz, Johann 69, 70, 72, 356, 391–2
Brenzfeld 244
Brenzian argument 398–9
Breull, Diell 191
Breüninger, Barbara 284, 342–3, 347–8
Brewers 147, 344
Bride 23, 28, 79, 81
  abandon his 80
  ex-boyfriend's 14, 46, 49, 222
Brien, Michael 19
Briggs, Robin xvi, xvii, 12
Broadsides 68, 261–2, 264
  see also Pamphlet literature
Bronchial asthma 15
Brückner, Hans 222, 226, 236, 281–3, 286, 289, 291, 293, 306–8
Buck, Georg 242–3, 270
Bucket 223, 227
Bullets 314, 318–19
Burchard of Worms 152
Burdock 190
Bureaucracy 350, 368, 371
Bureaucrats 367–70, 372, 378, 390, 396
  high 371
  professional 350, 370
  see also Elite, Government, Officials

Burial 75, 324
  live 353
  mounds, pre-Christian 188
Burning, for arson 353
Burns 70, 176, 212, 295, 316, 325
Business cycle 423
Butcher 119, 129, 148–9, 242, 309
Butter 166
Byzantine and Arab civilizations 152, 170

C

Cache
  hidden 249
  recover 232
  treasure 171, 235, 238, 242, 249, 427
Cadence 163–4
Calculations 225, 231, 257, 365, 373
Calf 38, 133, 141, 309
Calmbach 98
Calmbach, Barbara 281, 349, 418
Calvinist Isenburg-Büdinger 191
Calvinists 398
Calw 98–9, 258, 397–8
Cammer, Christian 22, 49, 56, 158–60, 212, 298, 306
Cancers 18, 292, 299
Cannibalism 434
Cannstatt 10, 29, 73, 168, 222, 243, 276, 279, 281–2, 317, 388
Capital
  cases 44, 354, 386, 394
  crimes, magistrates report 392
  shortages 423
Capuchin monk 180, 236, 324
Card
  decks 251–3
  divination 251–3
  games 251
Card-makers 252
Cardiac arrhythmias 16, 18, 19, 38
  see also Heart
Cards 251–3, 256
  trump 251
Carichter's Healing and Herb Book 281
Carolina *see Constitution Criminialis Carolina*

Carpenter, William 224
Cartomancy 252
Catalepy 122, 294, 414
Catechism 72, 359, 397
  classes 72
  large 359
  small 359
Cathars 95, 189
Cathartic release 279
  see also Ecstasy
Catholic
  ceremony 282
  Church 240, 371
  clergymen 339
  clerics 246
  elements 321
  ex- 321
  maid 232
  mass 322
  territories 339
Catholicism 240, 371
Catholics 68, 80, 398
Cats 111, 118, 129, 327, 329
  brains 168
  in REM sleep 207
Cattle maiming 44
  see also Animals
Caul 36, 176
Celestial
  conjunctions 259
  relationships, changing 255
Cell, white blood content and solar activity 256
Cells 143, 299
  cancer, and placebos 288
  immune, communication with brain 299
  killer, and loneliness 293
Cellular defenses and emotions 299
  see also Immune system
Celtic parts of Britain 94, 96–7
Cemetery, town 324
Cerebral cortex 26, 86, 199, 290
  left 376
  see also Brain
Ceremonies 17, 50, 169, 171–2, 227, 237, 245, 283, 285, 301, 306, 321–2, 342, 426, 434
  diabolical 128
  exacting 437
  intense 247

Cervantes, Fernando 85
Chain reactions 57, 93
  see also Witch persecutions
Chameleon-like phenomenon 194, 211
  see also Shamanism
Chanting 202, 297, 313
  incantations 157
Charfreytag 313
Charitable foundations, private 415
Charity 61
  denial model 23, 45
  refused 23, 45
Charivaries 365
Charlatans 137, 147, 252, 344, 361
  out-and-out 172
  rank 210
Charles, Military Order of St. 242
Charles V 384, 2
Charm
  forms 279
  formula 278
Charms 154–5, 176, 198, 276, 278, 280–2, 289, 294
  earliest 278
    German 277
    recorded 277
  early Middle Ages Germanic 278
  high medieval 277
  pagan 318
  single 342
  standardized narrative 291
Cheat 290, 366
Cheese 8, 15, 55, 304
  goat 222
  poisoned 8, 55
Chemicals 11, 110, 143, 145, 147, 172, 299
  mix of 146, 203, 208
  pain-reducing 297
  psychoactive 143
Chemistry 143, 320
Cherry pits 326, 328
Chest 88, 155, 190, 262, 282, 300, 309–10
Chevreul, Michel 224
Chickens 38, 45, 157, 165
Child 22, 49, 56, 73, 75, 77, 107, 113, 175, 190, 266, 280, 283, 285, 323, 326, 329, 342, 346, 349, 388–9, 408

accusers 117
confessions 118
witches 117
Childbirth 49, 57, 360
Children 10, 26, 29, 34, 45–7, 50, 52, 59, 72, 80, 97, 103, 113, 115–18, 126, 167, 174–5, 222, 231, 266, 280, 282, 285, 295, 321, 326, 331, 342, 347, 359–60, 364
  outcast 117
  surreptitious battery of 39, 40
  and witch allegations 50, 115
Children's
  involvement 116–17
  role in witch trials 117
  sabbaths 115
China 233, 251
Cholinergic
  neurotransmitters 110, 144
  system 144, 206
  see also Acetylcholine
Christ 68, 76, 96, 193, 238, 266–7, 277, 318, 414
Christian 7, 72, 82, 171, 182, 184, 242, 258, 274, 280, 359, 382, 388
  beliefs 410
  benedictions 278
  blessings 318
  commonwealth 72, 357, 434
  community 95, 383
  deity 238, 276
  ethics 242
  faith 377
    historic 420
  figures 278
  identity 187
  morality 180, 358–9, 413
  rituals 67, 271, 215
  sacraments 67, 93
  saints 381
  society 114, 183
  supernatural powers 95
  symbolism 193
  symbols 89, 168, 238
  theology 123, 382
  tradition 274, 420
  trinity 237
Christian/humanist morality 76
Christianity 68, 72, 94, 152, 171, 178–80, 182–3, 193, 219, 261, 284, 381
  renounce 179

Christianized 177, 271, 277, 382
  incantations 275
Christine, grenadier corporal's wife 252
Christmas 138, 239, 266, 426
Christoph, Duke 383, 391, 397
Christopher's Prayer
  see St. Christopher
Chrysanthemum vulgare 132
Church 42–3, 50, 73, 95, 123, 181, 184, 229, 232, 243, 246, 258, 270, 323, 327–8, 331, 349, 356, 358–61, 363, 365, 368, 377, 382–3, 397, 413, 440
  administrators 363–4
  attended 121, 167
  avoided 184
  bells 271, 293
  consistory 265, 267–8
  conventicles 271
  courts 363, 365–6, 399, 406
  membership 42
  sanctions 371
  stewards 356
  wardens 363
Church Council 351, 356, 359–60
Church's supervisory systems 406
Churchyard, village 173
Citizenry, assembled 352
Citizenship 76, 364–5
Civil servants, professional 350
  see also Bureaucrats
Civilizations 93, 273, 287
  agricultural 200
  classical 152
  earliest 170
  early 219, 274
  expansive 423
  modern industrial 219
Civilizing process 413
  see also Social disciplining
Clairvoyance 231–2, 247, 253
Clark, Stuart 91
Class, councilor's 396
  see also Bureaucrats
Classes 3, 47, 263, 362, 367, 423
  artisanal 414
  lower 344, 371
  lower middle 344
  ruling 431
  social 200
  upper 162, 371

Claviceps purpurea 134
  see also Ergot
Clavicula Salomonis 224
Clergy 225, 263, 266, 339, 350, 368, 383
Clergymen bless fields 382
Clerics 71–2, 93–4
Clientele 254, 340, 347
Clients
  female 154
  magical practitioners' 50, 70, 152, 156, 175, 178, 188, 226–8, 232, 245, 253–4, 256, 300, 304, 308, 341, 348, 383, 408, 436
Climacteric 58–9
Cloister schools 358, 368
Cockroaches 38, 273
Coercion
  effective 383
  noneconomic 364
  physical 427
Coercive approach 410
Cogitations 239, 374
  rational-linguistic 377
  unconscious 377
Cognition xv, xx, 30, 78, 87, 101, 114, 162, 206–8, 273, 339, 370, 375–6, 425
  conscious 26
  emotive 110
  integrative shamanic 208
Cognitive
  abilities 91, 185, 196
  capabilities, enhanced 183
  malfunctions 5, 48, 51, 63
  processes xiv, 79, 84, 92, 112, 130, 144, 248, 377
    common human 108
    unconscious 269
  revolution xx
  skills 86
  structures xx, 31, 78, 111–12, 116, 436
  systems, subordinate 87
  universe 77
Coin-hoards, a small number of 249
Coins 80, 171, 234, 240, 313–14, 328
  heathen silver 249
Cologne 408

Combative village culture 48
Combativeness 44
  magical 59
  see also Aggressiveness
Comet 254, 258–9
Command
  brief 291
  charm's 278, 284
  healer's 277
  shaman's 277
  see also Blessings
Commandment, second 359
Commission, poor 415
Commoners
  honor-conscious 367
  prosperous 43, 45, 60
  see also Peasants, Townspeople
Communal
  council 352
  councilors 42
  gatherings, regular 356
  interference 364
  leadership 349
  life 44
  norms 43
  opinion 365, 411
  participation 294
  relations 363
  sanctions 43
  standards, exacting 365
  status 353
  supervision, pervasive 365
  see also Animosity, Enemy, Neighborliness,
Communarchs 367
Communication 24–5, 71–2, 85, 88, 92, 100, 165, 237, 294, 373, 386, 420
  channel of 28–9, 231
  direct sensory 166
  non-verbal 27
  subliminal xix, 39, 40, 159, 290, 294–5, 433
  verbal 86
Communion 73, 80–1, 200, 267, 270, 357–9
Communities 9, 37, 40, 42–3, 60–1, 63, 76, 86, 90–3, 99, 100, 102–4, 115, 118, 151, 159, 162, 166–7, 183, 186–7, 189, 209, 229–30, 269–70, 293, 334, 344–5, 348–51, 355, 357–8, 361–7, 411–12
  circumscribed 104
  closely bound 37
  negligent 323
  small-scale 39
  strong 292
  village 365
Community
  offices 363
  participation 274
  standards 365
    informal 352
Community's viability 364
Competition for resources 389, 434
Confession, church 72–3, 357–8
  avoid 358
Confessional conflicts xvi, 43, 61, 68, 71
Confessions, criminal 5, 7, 51, 80–1, 118, 121, 138, 149, 157, 174, 179, 262–3, 271, 307, 354, 387–8, 412, 418
Confidence, bolster 315
Confinement 50, 106, 244, 352–3, 397
  dank 353
  solitary 270
  see also Incarceration
Confirmation 359, 418
Conflict strategies, women's 53–5
Conflicts 40, 42–4, 46–7, 53, 59, 61, 73, 87, 106, 156, 174, 179, 184, 268, 293, 364, 374
  bitter 318
  chronic 163
  class xviii, 38, 158
  communal 44–5
  economic 62
  intense 185
  intracommunal 40
  intrapsy-chic 13
  political 313, 317
  psychosocial 13, 20
  resolving 274
  social xix, 12, 117, 293
Conformity enforced 362, 365, 372, 392
Confrontations 53, 99, 107, 158, 263, 277, 396, 412
Conjure 177, 276, 319–20

A conjurer 349
Conjuring 170, 246
 a spirit, the art of 246
 spirits 170, 232, 239, 216
 see also Incantation
Connectedness, sense of 207, 297
Connection, visceral interpersonal 165
 see also Mirror neurons
Conquistadores, Catholic 183
Conrad, ghost of 243
Conscience 76, 407
 proactive 79
Conscious
 activities 375
 attention 374
 beings 204
 decision 359
 entity, independent 181–2
 facility 294
 formulation 377
 imaging 290
 mind 207, 269, 290, 294, 436
 practices 51, 62
 reasoning 112
 spirits 288
 suppression 374
 thought 290–1
Consciousness xv, 26, 78, 84–5, 87–9, 92, 109, 118, 125, 129, 132, 145–7, 151, 160–1, 186, 193–9, 201–3, 206–7, 209, 211–12, 224–6, 230, 236, 239, 245–7, 269–70, 294–5, 299, 335, 372–3, 375–7
 alteration of 135, 212, 296, 430, 435–6
 alterations of 195, 202, 211, 296, 436
 altered
  state of 89, 186, 210, 223, 226, 294
  states of 142, 144–5, 147–9, 185, 195, 197–8, 211, 213
 autonomous centers of 84, 86, 205;
  see also Autonomous
 distinct state of 128
 early modern 76
 foreign 87
 lost 189
 manipulating 201
 modes of 161, 195, 197, 211
 mold children's 118
 normal 89, 146, 150, 195, 375, 425, 438–9
 patient's 274
 practitioner's 223
 range 198
 redirect 375
 shamanic states of 195, 202–9
 state of 125, 135, 146–7, 197
 states of xv, xx, 148, 202–3
 see also Awake, Awareness, ASCs, Control
Consensus 256, 330, 399
 changing 440
 growing 398
 scientific 36, 209, 232, 288, 325
 skeptical 398
Consistories, village 357
Consistory 356–7
 ducal 242
 local 357
Conspiracy 93, 99, 434
 fears, ideology's 398
 mythical 412
 supposed witch 413
Constables 351, 356, 386, 393
 decree criticizing 393
 see also Government, Bureaucrats
Constitution Criminalis Carolina 2, 348, 352, 384
Constitutional document, basic 386
Constraints, cultural 339
Consubstantiation 82
Consultations 304, 308, 351
 legal 394
 theological 354
 see also Trials
Contact
 bodily 24, 45
 diabolic 113
 spontaneous 237, 241
Control, conscious 27, 198
 see also Consciousness
Conventicles 413
 separatist 414
 see also Pietism
Conversion reaction 17, 18, 50, 303
 accusatory 33
Conviction 63, 82, 99, 142, 177, 208, 260, 354, 392, 427–8, 430
Convulsions 9, 88–9, 135, 331
Copper 272, 319

Cornelius the Centurion   263
Cornish miners   179
Corporatist society   361
Corpus callosum   54, 377
Cortex   78, 147, 161
  frontal   147, 203–4; inhibitatory power   373
  human   78
  left anterior cingulate   199
  primary sensory   199
Cortical
  areas   127, 297
  structures   78, 160–1, 199, 298
Corvée officers   363
Cosmology, new   257, 419
Cosmopolitan   65
  French culture   419
  outlook   369
  policies   422
Cotters   42, 60, 362
Coué, Emile   290–2, 294
Council, privy   351, 371–2
Councilors
  ducal   240–2, 267, 330, 369–70, 396–7, 401, 416
  learned   368
  political   356
  privy   422
Counseling, spiritual   330
Counter witchcraft   307, 408, 419
Counteraction   1, 311
Countercharge   304
Countermagic   1, 7, 65, 70, 216, 303, 308–12, 321, 438
  aggressive   304
Countermagical ritual   311–12
Countermeasure, potent   382
Countermeasures   65, 310, 381
  active   308
  informal   308
  see also Antiwitch, Magic
Cours théoretique et pratique du liver de Thot   252
Court, judicial   48, 68, 105, 220, 271, 351–2, 367, 372
Court, ducal   367, 370, 372, 406, 415
  cosmopolitan   371
  extravagant   370
  nobility   371
  opulent   385

Courtiers   168, 370, 372, 390
Cow   7, 13, 37–8, 44–5, 155, 157, 165, 173–5, 222, 228, 231, 237, 260, 281, 306, 309–10, 408, 417
Craziness   286, 308
Crazy   10, 38, 133–4, 222, 282
Cream, stolen   7
Creative insights   206
Creativity, heightened   204
Crimes   1, 6, 7, 48, 51, 57, 63, 69, 149, 207, 229–30, 307, 352–3, 355, 390–1, 394, 403–4, 428
  malefic   435
  physical   391
  verifiable   398
  violent   52
Criminal
  act, specific   394
  behavior   48
  cases   351
  courts   406
  laws   352
  proceedings   390
Crisis   91–2, 298, 395, 419, 424, 426
  of confidence   390, 398, 415, 419
  economic   61
  existential   411
  personal   436
Crops   41, 137, 148, 152–3, 187, 257
Cross-fertilization, magical traditions   279, 437
Crosses, tracing   291, 308
Crucifixes   171, 238, 314
Cruelty, early moderns'   44
Crystal stone   280, 342
Cues   25
  cognitive   32
  social   198
Cult   68, 170, 185, 187–8, 270, 428
  activities, extra-Christian   179
  devilish   213
  diabolic   94, 435
    shamanic   213
  quasi-religious   172
Cults
  contemporary fairy   170
  formal pagan   382
Cultural
  artifacts   39, 125, 127, 182
  conceptions   240, 323

conditioning 160, 438
constructs xx
decoding rules, learned 26
expectations 16, 20, 26, 34, 49, 51–2, 55, 83, 113, 125, 127, 145, 210, 297
factors 91, 144, 204
features 371
forces 210
habits 72
idioms 91
meaning 114, 335
osmosis 194
prompting 30
rules 27, 31
script 32
shaping 27
ties 42
traditions 26, 28, 129, 194, 200, 202, 211, 437
values 84, 115
zones 194
Culture xiv, xv, xx, 13, 16, 25–7, 30–1, 33–4, 36, 39, 52–3, 58, 62, 76–7, 79, 80, 83–5, 91–2, 114, 120, 124–5, 142, 161, 194–5, 200–1, 248–9, 287, 339–40, 370–3, 400–1, 428–9, 431, 435
common 177
intellectual 185
linguistic 376
local 181, 193
official 193
provincial 378, 394, 402, 429, xiv, xv
traditional 198
Culture's expectations 55
Cunning
folk 70–1, 221, 226–7, 229, 269, 290, 306–9, 340, 342
folk/healer traditions, Europe's 279
men 50
person 226–8, 307–8, 311
see also Healers, Magicians, Practitioners
Cure 37, 50, 152, 157, 187, 209, 257, 274, 281–3, 285–6, 289, 301–4, 308, 348, 408
ailments 209, 225
diseases 188
forbidden 342

horses 276, 285
people 310, 343
superstitious 418
tumors 342
witchcraft 281
Cured people 310
Cures
herbal 286
natural 308
psychological 301
Curing 152, 275, 280, 304
goiter 342
magical 408
see also Healing
Curses 14, 18, 19, 21, 23–4, 32, 45, 48, 50, 73, 156, 166, 213, 308, 310–12, 359, 417
common 23
conscious 408
sorcerer inscribes 153
Cursing 23, 40, 45, 153, 261, 309
tablets 152, 154–5
Cusa, Nicholas of 179
Cycles 255, 298
normal daily 202
ultradian 196
Cysat, Renward 189

D

Dactyliomancy 220
Daggers 171, 244
looking 25
Damage 6, 12, 14, 16, 37, 44–5, 105, 165, 176, 273–4
fatal 45
ischemic heart 18
neurological 135
organic 12
psychological 111
punishing 38
unnatural 316
Dances 74, 80, 97–8, 102, 106–7, 113–14, 116, 118–19, 121–2, 128, 134, 137, 148–9, 151, 161, 384
country 145
diabolic 108
Daniel 12 267
Dannenritter, Barbara 10, 46, 56, 306
Danube River 137
Dark numbers 154

Datura 11, 139
  stramonium 139, 143
Davies, Owen xviii, xix
Daydreaming 84, 202
De Re Metallica 233
Dead
  man's head 237, 247
  people 314
  person 172, 238–9
Death 10, 11, 17–19, 28, 38, 44, 55–7, 96, 125, 155, 157, 159, 175–6, 187, 192, 204, 247, 273, 352–3, 361, 364, 385, 391–2, 405–6, 412, 422, 2
  animal's 176
  deserved 384, 391–2
  fiery 440
  penalty 384
  sudden 16, 18
  voodoo 18
Debt 8, 10, 14, 22, 60–1, 261, 389
Decapitation 353
Deception, therapeutic xix
Decker, Catharine 162, 167, 173
Delicti occultis 394
Delirium 9, 119–20, 135, 140, 144, 147
  persistent 149
  see also Ailments
Della Porta, Giambattista 129, 131, 142
Delusions 11, 119, 331
  collective 327
  devilish 391
  isolated pathological 185
  narcissistic 5
  waking 139
Demon incanters 340
Demonization of the world 72
Demonological
  accounts 132, 140
  fears 397, 435
  literature 122–3, 131, 140, 147
  theory 2, 151
Demonologists 1, 66, 70, 129, 141, 147, 168, 185, 208, 212–13, 437
  late Medieval 123
Demonology xvi, xix, 80, 123, 128, 132, 176, 212, 383, 390, 398, 402–3, 435
  early modern 212–13
  learned 113
  pan-European 113

Demonology's insistence 399
Demons xvi, 67, 70, 80, 85, 145, 153, 170, 172, 177–8, 184, 200, 205, 219, 237, 239, 291
  agency of 1, 381
  conjuring 170
  exercise supernatural power 381
  exorcize 191
  subservient to Devil 183
  summoning 152
  see also Devil Incantation, Exorcism, Incantation
Dengler, Jacob 97, 103–4
Dengler, Jacob's wife 103
Dengler, Judith 98, 103
Denglers 97, 103–4, 106
Denial of magic 200
  see also Repression
Denunciations of magic, early enlightenment 419
Depression, post-Thirty Years' War 423
Despondency 20, 113–14, 401, 409, 436
Destitute 60, 364
  paupers 60, 423
Destitution 44, 353
Deterrent effect 353, 405
  see also Repression
Devil 63, 71, 75, 134, 175, 177, 184, 314, 359
  books 71–3
  card 251
  conjuration 172
  held to 417–18
  incanters 223, 231, 240, 244, 352, 383
  incantation 384
  loathsome 68, 134
  and OBE 161
  pact with the 352
  used by magicians 391
  worship 67, 93, 148, 184
  see also Lucifer, Satan
Devilish
  behaviors 179
  features 84
Devilishness 46
Devil's
  activity 70
  aid 173, 183
  approaches 81
  attack 114

banner 118
blandishments 107, 121
conspiracy 70, 105, 123, 157, 181, 383–4
disciples 97
empire 316
evil cause 400
game 119–20
gifts 177
hand 71, 174
instigation 175
interest 176
involvement 71, 400
legions 70
machinations 116
malignant influence 399
manipulation 410
mark 75
mass 267
men 405
misrepresentation 425
name 32, 173, 175, 313
 in the 173–4, 388
path 180
power 184, 420
promptings 79, 81
role 71, 175, 399
service 118, 178
snare 92, 225
territory 238
tool 410
voice 120
woman's saying 178
work 405
Diabolic
 activities 75
 arts 153
 conspiracy 350, 386
 deceptions 220
 influence, supposed 51
 intervention 314
 obsession 283
 possession 88–90
 ritual 76
 stereotype 67–9, 74, 80, 94
 witch stereotype 72, 359
 witchcraft 50, 99, 65
Diabolical
 agency 399
 conspiracy 419
 illusions 69

intercourse 148
 sexual experiences 410
 stereotype 69
Diabolism xix, 50, 63, 65, 76, 89, 117, 157, 176, 307, 316, 337, 353, 383, 388, 430, 434
 stereotypical 354
Diagnoses 119–20, 152, 207, 209, 221, 256–7
 healer's 330
Diana 69, 96, 123, 170, 382
 see also Berta, Pechta, Venus
Dice, throwing 251
Dietersweiler 388
Dietsch, Christina 243
Dietscher, Hanns 190, 192, 228–9
Disbelief xiv, xix, 376, 392, 425, 431
 dogmatic 422, 424, 426
 enlightened 419–20
 hardening 419
Disciplined behaviors 411
 see Social Discipline, Women
Discourse, printed 70
Disdain, enlightened 419
Disease xv, xix, xx, 11, 15–20, 26, 37, 61–2, 71, 152, 159, 187, 210, 222, 273–4, 277, 280, 285–8, 291–2, 297, 299–301, 305, 312, 399, 401
 agents 297
 combat 299
 coronary artery 16
 countering 273
 gout or some other 401
 infectious 18, 19, 204
 organic 18, 39
 physical 16, 305
 skin 15
 see also Ailments
Dishonor 76, 355, 358, 363, 366
Disobedient 162, 172, 419
Disorders 15, 16, 18, 20, 62, 119, 212, 273
 autoimmune 18
 conversion 12, 13
 menstrual 15
 mental 91
 metabolic 119
 multiple-personality 198
 organic 12
 pathological 127

Index 573

Disorders (*Continued*)
  physical   20, 286, 297
  physiological   264
  psychogenic   298
  psychophysical   16, 18, 25, 39
  somatization   12
  somato-form   296
  somatoform   12–15, 17
  stress-related   20
  see also Ailments
Display rules   26
Disreputability   113
Disreputable
  behaviors   47
  people   365
Dissociate brain states   146
Dissociated
  activities   375
  brain states   146
  state   88, 92, 198–9, 331
Dissociation   87–8, 91–2, 127–8, 196–9, 201–2, 211, 223, 246, 294–5, 374, 431
  due to abuse   199
  hypnotic   278, 294
  neurological   127
  purported   198–9
  relaxed   300, 315
  somatic   126
  state
    of   89, 91, 253
    of relaxed   300, 315
  traumatized children   126
Dissociative
  ability   431
  skills   253
  states   148, 438
Distilled spirits, prescribed   279
Distress   13, 15, 17, 20, 50, 54, 74–5, 126, 260, 274, 294, 331, 396, 401–2
  gastrointestinal   12
  human   437
  psychological   16, 18, 33, 296
  somatic   15
  see also Ailments
District
  honorability   368
  seats   254, 351, 360, 362–3, 367–8
  supervisor   98
Districts, cloister   60
Divination   xv, xix, 7, 165, 186, 216, 219–21, 223, 225–33, 235, 237, 239, 241, 243, 245–7, 249–53, 255–7, 259, 261, 263, 265, 267, 269, 271–3, 303, 307, 310, 312, 319, 341–2, 438
  card-based   252
  clerical opinion of   225
  conducted   232
  deliberate   219
  fortune-telling   254
  harmless   153
  historical analyses of   230
  judicial   220
  practice   381
  process of   226
Divinatory
  activity   219
  powers   220
  practices   236
  rituals   226, 229, 250
  services   221, 436
  systems   253
  techniques   222, 225, 231, 235
  traditional systems   253
  see also Astrology, Scrying, Sieve and Shears, Cards
Divine
  inspiration   265
  retribution   154, 363
Diviners   70, 155, 187, 189, 220, 227, 230, 249, 256
Doctors   9, 10, 12, 19, 267, 290, 304–5, 307–8, 329–30, 359–61, 363, 397–9, 401, 404, 416, 418
  official   397
  professional   287
  university-trained   256–7, 279, 360, 397
Döffingen   246–7, 271
Donald, Merlin   xx
Donauworth   137
Donni di fuora   74, 121–2
Dornhan   387
Dornstetten   12, 233, 237, 245, 252, 426
Dosage   141, 143
Dottingen   8
Dowsers   233–5
  novice   235
  test   234
Dowsing   233–6, 246, 249, 342
  electromagnetic hypothesis   234
  instruments   171
  rod   233, 235–6, 238

Dream
  content   92, 111, 114, 120
  experiences   107, 113, 129, 144, 161, 185, 192
    understanding   108
  narratives   109
  researchers   112
  states   33, 123
Dreamers   112, 120, 126
  lucid, modern   161
Dreaming   108–10, 112, 126, 129, 144, 146, 148, 212
  micro-REM   197
  modes   146
  normal   202, 206
  practices lucid   161
  visual   144
Dreams   xx, 31, 33, 36–7, 77, 94, 107–16, 118–20, 123, 125–6, 128–9, 133–4, 136, 139–41, 149–50, 154, 180, 187, 189, 191, 197, 206, 210, 220, 401, 409, 412, 416, 435
  bad   89
  children's   115, 400
  coordinated   36
  drugged   141
  drunken   137, 140
  fantastic   147
  high   149
  historical   108
  inhibiting   144
  lucid   126, 129, 146, 202
  normal   118, 125, 141
  nREM   113
  in REM   110
  taking place in a   122
  vivid   116, 144, 148, 198, 202, 434
  waking   146
  see also Sleep, REM, nREM
Dreamy state   409
Drink   95–7, 132, 139, 166, 190, 222, 305
  alcoholic   135
Drinks, herbal   279, 286, 306, 308
Drivers, ANS   202–3
Droll, Michael   31
Drug
  experiences   149
    early modern, realness of   142
    reported   141
  use   130
  users   140–1; groups   134, 148

Drugs   xix, 131, 139–45, 148–9, 289–90, 431
  anticholinergic   141, 143–4, 147, 149
  hallucinogenic   xix, 68, 130, 143, 146, 203, 391, 417
  narcotic   297
  psychoactive   133
  see also Alkaloids, Anticholinergics, Consciousness, Hallucingens, Ointments, Potions
Ducal government   41, 50, 77, 107, 229, 254, 313, 324, 350, 352, 360–1, 370, 383–6, 392, 394, 406–7, 415
  see also Government
Dukes of Württemberg   162, 243, 264, 350–2, 356–7, 370–1, 386, 395–7, 420
Dumme, Christoph Ernst   223, 329
Dürrner, Gallus   243, 270, 428

E
Eberhard III, Duke   261–2, 264, 370, 395–7, 406
Eberhard Ludwig, Duke   170, 370–1
Eberlin, Anna   82–8, 90, 186, 205, 228, 231, 280, 283, 306, 342, 400, 409
Ebersbach   7, 81, 388
Ebingen   17
Economy   41, 62, 415, 423, 429
  agricultural   255
  capitalist   431
  duchy's   60
  improving   415
Ecstasies   xvii
Ecstasy   201, 208, 210, 306
  collective   180
Ecstatic
  experiences   187, 189, 191, 270, 278, 414
  forms   270
  spirit communication   277
  swooning   292
  traditions, vigorous   211
  see also Cathartic release, Simultaneous discharge, Tuning
Education   358, 360, 368–9, 420
  advanced   368–9
  elementary   359

Education (*Continued*)
  primary 420
  public 359–60
  traditional Württemberg 370
Educational
  process, stringent 358
  systems 351, 359
  see also School
Efficacy xix, 159, 165–6, 209, 211, 225, 248, 257, 287–90, 294, 302, 315, 372, 430, 438
Effringen 237
Eggs 22, 38, 49, 56, 158–61, 165–6, 212, 279, 284, 298, 306
Egypt, ancient 251
Ehrbarkeit 351, 362, 367, 371
  see also Elite, Honorability, Notability
Eighteenth century 60, 62, 76, 115, 171, 213, 248–9, 251–2, 301, 320, 323, 349, 354, 360, 366–7, 371, 378–9, 391–2, 395, 398, 402, 406, 408–9, 411, 415, 418–19, 423, 425, 427, 429
  communities, early 364
  early 135, 233, 361, 380, 415
  late 361, 425
  mid- 321, 415, 428
Elderly suspects 57, 355, 390
Electromagnetic
  field, weak 302
  theories 249, 255
Eleusis, Mysteries of 135
Elf-shot 188
Elisabeth, model for women 409, 414
Elite
  beliefs 339, 418, 424
  culture xvii, 71, 184–5, 323, 363, 370, 398, 402–3
  duchy's 213, 339, 422
  educated 170, 177, 373
  local urban 351
  provincial 62, 331, 362, 366, 371, 415
  rejection of magic 429
  ruling 419
  social 420
  see also Bureaucrats, Clergy, Ehrbarkeit, Honorability, Notability
Ellwein, Michael 50–1, 404
Elrich, Magdelena 414

Ember nights 96
Emmau 284, 308
Emotional 15, 20, 26–7, 79, 110, 126, 159–60, 297, 355, 371, 376, 434
  circumstances 19, 20
  cognition 206
  communication processes 225
  contagion 295
  culpability 22
  deception 27
  distress 32, 58
  expression 293
  impulses 195
  liability 58
  memory 292
  power, attack's 22
  processing 54
    low-level 112
    women's 54
  reactions 25, 158, 225, 299
  stress 311–12
  systems, brain's 112
Emotions xx, 13, 24–6, 34, 37, 54, 92, 101, 110, 126, 147, 160, 165, 207, 291–3, 298–9
  angry person's 213
  basic 26
  heightened 32
  personal 176
  spontaneous 435
  strong negative 20
  universal 25–6, 34
Employers 98, 103, 106, 164, 174–5, 349, 369, 408
Encountering ghosts 245
Enculturation 40, 73, 114, 118, 159, 359
  see also Internalization
Endersbach 77
Endocrine 160, 298, 300
  systems 15, 18, 161, 299
Endorphins 208–9, 297–8, 300
  release 297, 302
Endriss, Jakob 9, 46, 307, 404
Enemies 28, 33, 35, 37, 43–4, 51, 65, 152–3, 156, 161, 168, 175, 179, 182, 200, 212, 216, 353, 355, 391, 405, 435, 439
  harass 44
Energy, nonconscious 288

Enhanced
  accuracy 314
  ability 205
  dexterity 316–17
  endurance 308
  job skills 272, 313
  learning 207
  power 207, 430
  productivity 200, 328–9
  prowess 205, 208, 319
  skilled performance 430
  skills 348
Enhancements
  artificial 213
  personal 317
Eningen 309
Enkephalins 297
Enlightened
  culture 371
  moderns 270, 339
Enlightenment 337, 378, 415
  French 370
Enthusiasm 269
  quasi-religious 242
Entrainments 160–1, 207, 299, 300, 302
  interconnect 160
  nonconscious 295
  of organs 299
Environment, supportive interpersonal 209
Epidemics 256–7
Epilepsy 50, 126–7
Epinephrine 208
Epiphany 243
Episcopi, Canon 69, 70, 123, 382
Episcopi tradition 70, 142, 382–3, 390–1, 399
Erectile problems 17
  see also Impotence
Ergot 9, 134–5, 141, 144
  poisoning 9
    accidental 9
Ergotism 9, 134–5
Ergotropic 147, 196, 202, 223
  state 196
  systems 196, 202
Ergotropic-trophotropic balance 196
Error, job related 20
Esoteric traditions 171, 215
Esslingen 96, 227, 321, 384

Establishments, religious 95, 398–9
Estates
  provincial 406
  recalcitrant 420
Estates, Württemberg 370–1, 422
Estrogen 54, 58
Etteilla 252–3
Eucharist 89
Europe
  eastern 170
  late Medieval 430
  northeastern 187
  southeastern 131, 187
Europeans, earliest 289
Eve 71
Evil 12, 23, 68, 71–3, 76, 94, 113, 117, 172, 175, 177, 241, 258, 280, 283, 361, 411, 434, 439
  enemy 77, 82, 173, 238, 323–4, 410
  eye 25, 152
  forces 175
  master 97
  role 167
Evil Satan 73
Evil Spirit 75, 79, 80, 82, 89, 92, 121–2, 128, 154, 172, 175, 190, 237–8, 247, 381
Evolution, cultural 108, 279
Examination, theological 396–7
Exchanges
  face-to-face interpersonal 24
  hostile interpersonal 400
  interpersonal 28, 44, 104
  ugly 31
  verbal 48
Excommunication 357–8
Excrement 168
  see also Feces
Executioner 155, 305–6, 343, 417
Executions 7, 55, 153, 263, 352–3, 358, 375, 383–4, 393, 407
Exorcism 273, 303, 321, 341, 343, 427
Exorcists 191, 241, 321, 340
Exorcize 237, 241, 245, 343, 426
  bothersome spirits 343
  spirits 343
Exotic items 239
Experiences
  aural 235
  benign 35

Experiences (*Continued*)
  blissful 196
  collective 67
  common 200, 240
  conscious 78, 197, 225, 430, 439
  conversion 117
  cosmopolitan 369
  direct 92, 165–6, 434
  first-hand 192, 417
  imaginary 276, 278
  imagined 277, 66
  integrative 204
  life 160, 227
  lived 92, 434
  magical xix, 142, 390, 429
  mental 108
  nocturnal 121, 123
  real 116, 192, 434–5
  reported xix, 123, 146, 198, 439
  singular 210, 268
  subjective xiv, 220, 222, 224, 239
  traumatic 126
  vision xvii, 264
  witch-related 240
  women's 127
"Experiential" process or model 34, 194
Experients 124–5, 140–2, 144–5, 147
Expressions 3, 12, 25–6, 28, 54, 103, 165, 200, 226, 235, 273, 291, 294, 378, 424
  of anger, raw 55
  autonomic 25
  coded 108
  conscious 433
  displaced xvi
  innate 26
  nonverbal 27–8
  person's impulsive 433
  physiological 26
  practitioner's 165
  ritualized 153
  spontaneous 165, 213
  symbolic 20
  unconscious 290
  verbal 23
Expulsion of ideas 375
  see also Repression
Exteriorization 127
External
  spirit 87
  world 31, 210, 247, 335, 375

Eyes 24–6, 30, 75, 81, 84, 87, 130, 189, 195, 284, 314, 342
  see also Evil eye
Eÿsinger Hof 238

F
Fabrications 32, 158, 337
  imaginative 83
Face-to-face 166
  community 364
  interactions 25, 170
  placed 158
  societies 433
Faces 26, 32, 54, 126
  negative 26
  expressions 24, 26, 164, 293, 295
  recognizable 111
  features 26
Factions 366, 372
Faculty 81, 119
  legal 394
  theological 354
Fairies 94, 121–2, 170, 179–80, 187–8
Fairy beliefs, British 188
Fairy Queen 191
Faith 72, 163, 184, 219, 315, 326
Fake 27, 89, 263
  smiles 27
Familiars 29, 188
Families, dysfunctional 46
Fantasies xvi, 108, 115, 123, 131, 136–7, 140, 160, 166, 196, 212, 330, 412, 416
  illusions of a corrupt 329
  infantile 5
  lurid 168
  melancholic 391
  misogynist 93
  rooted xvi
  shared 103
Fantastical adventure 242
Fantasy mentation 125
Fantasy-proneness 126
Farm 42, 60, 344, 346, 424
  animals 38, 56, 73, 155
    harmed 37
  dairy 321
  hands 42, 60
  single 41
  see also Animals

Farmers   42, 60, 62, 236, 240, 344, 362, 426
  tenant   362
Fat
  cook   310
  human   168
Fate   122, 251, 257, 355
Father figure   113, 115
Faust   177, 261, 264
Fear, innate   26
Fears   xiv, 5, 6, 17, 18, 20–1, 24–6, 31, 34, 38, 46, 58, 62–3, 65–6, 76, 78, 94, 125, 149, 152, 157, 165, 179, 185, 231, 237, 245, 311, 324, 331, 363–4, 403, 433–4
  people's   324, 403
  psychological   31
Feasts   95, 97, 121–2, 128, 388
Feathers   89
Feces   168
  human   152, 168, 211
Fee   152, 244
Fees, standard   345
Feet
  cloven   71
  goat's   82–3, 409
Fehlen, Johanna   8, 55, 132, 305
Fehlen, Johanna   132, 389
Feind   43
Feldkirch   241
Fellbach   38, 156
Female
  aggression   52
  aggressiveness   410
  behavior   53, 411, 414
  figure   192
  followers   96
  groups   47
  healing spirit   211
  magicians   187
  sexuality   410
  suspects   49, 51, 406
  vanity   261
  violence   411
  virtues   105
Females   52–4, 105, 122, 186, 408
  see also Women
Ferdinand, Duke   170, 246, 385
Ferner, Hanß   106–9, 112–17, 118, 305, 400

Fertility   154, 187
Fest der Erscheinung   243
Festivities   68, 95, 107, 113, 122, 128–9, 141, 147, 187, 388
  illicit   97
  merry and happy   106
  nocturnal   96–7
  popular   42–3, 95
Feuds, bitter   43
Feuerbach meadow   74, 118, 384
Fever   91–2, 281, 283
Fiery   83, 190, 301, 323–4
  display   323, 334
  glow   82–3
  lights   323
  sparks   324
  spectacles   324
  specter   327
Fight/flight response   23, 26, 32, 147, 196, 294, 297–8
Fine-tuning   296, 306, 335, 436
  see also Tuning, Nervous system
Fines   352–3, 357–8, 397, 407, 428, 440
  levy   43
Fingernails   155
Finninger   156
Finnmark   135
Fire-fighting services   415
Fist-shaking   28
Fists   55, 267, 400
Fiume, Giovanna   xviii
Fleas   137, 148–9, 158, 179, 212
Flew   33, 36, 68–9, 94, 107, 118, 122–3, 127, 131, 149, 176, 212, 305, 319, 330, 382, 388, 417
  people   434
  to   36
  women's souls   305
Flight   62, 70, 113–14, 120, 123, 128–9, 139–40, 146, 149–50, 163, 186, 188, 204–5, 388, 391, 400, 434
  dreamy   388
  experiences   127
    early modern   128
  fantastic   123
  imaginal   291
  out-of-body   161
  shaman experiences   186
  soaring   128

Flight (*Continued*)
  soul 194
  spiritual 153
  stereotypical 388
Flight-fight systems 147
Flight, Slovenia sorcerers' 187
Flights
  experience 149, 191
  nocturnal 129, 161
Floating 124–5, 127
Flogging 353
  see also Torture
Florence 153, 180
Flour products 135
Flow state 315
Flowers 283
Flown 107, 128, 130, 148, 178, 212, 328
Fluctuations, geomagnetic 255
Fluid, magnetic 301
Flux, critical moment of 146
Fly 83, 95, 97, 127–9, 145, 148, 153, 170, 186, 200, 208, 244–5, 435
Flying 23, 113, 122, 125, 127, 132, 139, 146, 170
  dreams 434
  female spirits 188
  people 439
  reported 141
  sensation of 144, 147
  spirits 96
  see also Dreams, OBEs, Out-of-body experiences
Folk 171, 314, 321
  beliefs xvii, 430, 434
  culture 113, 210, 255, 284
    regional 113
  healers 274
  healing 275, 287, 289, 299
    early modern 302
  magic 184
  magicians 187
  medicine 292
  pharmacopoeia 130
  practices 274
  techniques 153
  traditions 73, 215
Folk-magical conceptions 315
Folklore 71, 74, 139, 167, 179
Followers 183, 189, 242–3, 253, 266, 268, 310, 439

Food 9, 10, 21, 41, 45, 96, 115, 128, 138–9
Forest
  ranger 88, 162–3, 173–4, 280, 296, 298, 344
  ducal 29
  regulation 162
  see also Poachers
Forester 162, 344, 349
Forests 41, 131, 162, 324, 215
Foretell 208, 220, 250
Forked twig 233
Fortune-telling 171, 180, 191, 250–1, 340, 383
France 154, 188–9, 258, 370, 420
Franck 284, 321, 405
Franck, Jakob ("Schafer J") 284, 308, 321, 343, 347, 405
Frankhen, Hanß Jacob 98
  children 98, 103
Franconia 277
  twentieth-century 167
Francophile orientation, ducal court's 370
Frankfurt 137
Fraud xix, 209, 231–2, 242–3, 245–7, 265, 290, 321, 328–9, 331–3, 381, 419, 425–8, 440
  committed 264
  conscious 35, 210, 228, 244–5, 268–9, 331, 427
  evidence of 261, 264
  and malice 418
  self-conscious 106
Fraudulence 242, 425
Fraudulent xix, 301, 425–7
  practices 427
  purposes 239
  self-interest 5
Fredrich, Johannes 241, 244
Fredrick the Great 422
Freestanding figures 84, 205
  see also Hallucinations
Freiburg, University of 333
French
  armies 257
  Cartesians 419
  culture 370, 406, 419
  raiders 258
  Wars 319, 406, 423
Freud, Sigmund 108, 112, 432

Freudenstadt 7, 387
Freudian psychology 12, 108, 409
Freyberger, Catharina 8, 15, 55, 304
Freyin, Anna Maria 242–3, 270, 318
Fridays 284, 322
Friedrich Karl, regent 170, 370, 420
Fritz, Agnes 7
Friuli region of northern Italy 36, 94, 97, 187, 437
Frogs 154–5, 220
Frost, create magically 137, 148, 155
Fuehrman, Johannes 38
Fugger, Anton 155, 220, 223, 236
Fühner, H. 140–1
Fumigation procedures 311
Fungus 9, 134
   see also Ergot
Furious Horde 170

G
Galenic medicine 256, 274
Gallows 75, 152
Gaming 261, 365
Gangrene, dry 9
Ganßer 31–2
Gansslen, Michel 11, 308
Garabonciás 190
Gärdnerin, Burga 98, 101, 103, 105
Gärtnerin, Anna 97, 101–6
Gaze 25, 223, 414
   bottle 231, 251
   patterns 25
   signal threat 25
Gébelin, Antoine Court de 251–2
Gebhard, Anna 17, 23, 56, 389, 408–9
Gehring, Paul 411
Geigler, Jacob 228, 230, 237, 281, 283, 309–10
Geiler, Gerg 133
Geisterbeschwörung 216
Gekin, Maria 164–7, 173, 178, 211–12, 388, 417–18
Geldmannlin 172
Geldt-mannlen 320
Gender 3, 47, 51–2, 105, 346–7, 407
   aggressive sexuality 409
   difference 53
   equation 52
   oppression xviii
   tensions 103
General Decree 393, 396

Generalists 343–5
   robust 343
Generalized magic 275, 307, 311, 329
Generalreskrept 361
Generational differences 46
Generations xviii, 13, 42, 47, 72, 95, 105, 111, 167, 170, 178, 183, 193, 204, 206, 220–1, 248, 258, 274, 334, 355, 363, 398–9, 412, 426, 437
Genetic 53, 199
   basis 199
Geological anomalies 234
Geomagnetic
   field, earth's 255, 320
   fields 234
   forces 332
Geradstetten 8, 46, 307, 387
Gerlingen 260–2, 264–5
German schools 359
German-speaking Alps 189
Germanic 96, 274, 386
   charms 278
   folklore 171
   invaders 152
   legend 191
   sagas 314
   successor states 382
   tribes 193
Germany xiv, xvi, 33, 41, 72, 115, 155, 187, 261, 263, 267, 333, 368–9, 419
   northern 189
   southern 96, 135, 180
   southwestern xiv, xvi, 55, 69, 123, 248, 261, 346, 384, 390–2
Gerstenmaier brothers 407
Gesner, Court Physician 361
Gessler, Barbara 9, 15, 38, 49, 56–7, 305, 348, 404–5, 411
Gestenmaier brothers 314–15
Gestenmaier, Jerg 313
Gestenmaier, Johannes 313
Gestenmaier, Ludwig 313, 385
Gestenmaier, Young Jerg 313
Gesture, hostile 56
Gestures 2, 24, 27, 45, 158, 165–6, 179, 226, 271, 273, 295
Ghost
   appearances 328
   cult 243, 260, 270, 318, 428

Ghost (*Continued*)
  dead wife's 244, 322
  experiences 248
  husband's 241
  random 249
  reported 321
  sightings 249, 323
  stories 242
Ghostlike creatures 240
Ghosts 84, 171, 215, 232, 236–49, 260, 269, 272, 310, 321–3, 327, 329–30, 426, 428
  lies about encountering 245
  in many forms 241
  in Protestant and Catholic doctrine 240
Gifts, suspected poisons 13, 45, 158, 166
Ginzburg, Carlo xvii, xviii, 36, 93–4, 113, 135,
Glass plate 222
Goat 121, 128, 191
God 14, 74, 76, 85, 113, 138, 177, 179, 182, 184, 193, 219–20, 224, 238, 242, 247, 259–61, 265–7, 269, 276, 279–80, 285, 300, 317–19, 322, 339, 359, 381–3, 399, 413–14, 439
  omnipotent 219
  renounced 65, 138, 179, 182, 418
  word of, rejected 77
Goddess, benign 96
Goddesses 96, 187, 193
Gödelmann, Johann Georg 391
Gold 234–5, 244, 319
Golden cups 118
Good
  company 96
  lady and her folk 187
  spirit, the 262
Good Friday 173
"good words" 308
Goods, cheaper manufactured 415
Göppingen 240–1, 249, 326–7, 413
Gossip 43, 52, 99, 100, 103–5, 365, 372
  local 357
  malicious 355
  village 118
  women's 105

Government 44, 50–1, 75, 99, 105, 108, 130, 134, 138, 153, 240, 242, 245–6, 257, 261–4, 270, 316, 322–4, 326, 331, 350, 356, 361, 378, 381, 390, 392, 397, 399–402, 419–21, 425, 428–9
  bureaucracy 397
  central 254, 261, 367–8, 378, 383, 385–6, 392–3, 397, 406
  decrees 100
  local 350, 415
  offices 362
  officials 321, 350, 359
  opposition to Pietism 243
  provincial 369, 337
  worldly 323
Governmental
  policy 402
  tyranny 261
Government's
  claim to treasure 248
  policy 400
  shift 397
  see also Administration, Bureaucracy, Constables, Ducal Government, Elite
Grabenstetten 249
Graeter, Jacob 414
Grain 9, 14, 134, 220, 399
  bleeding 261
  kernels of 220
  special 134
  stores 155
Grandmother 14, 50, 106–7, 113, 118, 136, 416–18
Granier, Urbaine 177
Grass 82, 162
  blessing 317
Grave xv, 37, 165, 243, 323
  child's 156
  digger 323
Graveyard 76, 173, 237, 283, 323–4, 326
  communal 323–4
Gravity 255, 419
  moon's 255
Greases 130
Great Church Ordinance 356, 359, 361, 397
  see also Provincial Ordinances

Greece 135, 152, 170, 187, 255, 274, 381
Grimm, Jacob 328
Grip 56, 311, 400
Gröningen 254, 257, 404
Grossman, Viet 19, 20, 50, 311, 400
Güglingen 164, 417
Guilt 5, 9, 12, 43, 48, 51, 76, 82, 220–1, 230, 311, 355, 358, 390, 399
Guilty
  conscience 312
  feelings 81
  secrets 230
Gültingen 363
Gunpowder 313–14
Gunzenhausen 138
Gut feelings 225
Gypsies 340

H

Haasen, Hans 189–94, 206, 209–11, 213, 250, 276, 279, 282–3, 293, 300, 318, 343–4, 437
Habsburg empire 258
Haeberlin, Georg Heinrich 398
Hahn, Conrad 316, 328–9
Hail 138, 154, 158, 410
  storms 76, 155, 324, 384
Hair 44, 155, 401
Hallucinations 8, 9, 30–4, 83–5, 91, 102, 119, 133–5, 140–1, 147, 150, 265, 325, 331
  audio 196
  auditory 31, 85, 205, 220
  aural 85, 87
  experience 31
    aural 85
  hypnogogic 128
  mass 324, 327
  visual 31, 84, 196, 223
  vivid tactile 34
Hallucinatory
  episodes 32
  experiences 31–3, 148
Hallucinogenic
  experiences 11, 143–5
  plants 143
  substances 202
  trips 138
Hallucinogenics 142
Hallucinogens 21, 131, 134–5, 140, 142, 144–5, 147–9, 198, 202, 434
  nonanticholinergic 144
  potent 139
  Solanaceous 140, 142
  see also Drugs
Hanau-Lichtenbeg, Count Philipp of 384
Hannß (the Devil) 118–19, 121, 179
Hannß, a barber 137, 148, 179
Hansen, Chadwick xviii
Hansen, Leonberger's widow 133–4, 167
Harassment 28, 43, 50, 413
Harm 1–3, 6, 11, 17, 23, 37, 48, 56, 62–3, 122, 134, 137–8, 148, 151, 153, 155–7, 165–7, 172, 174, 212, 303–4, 312, 343, 348, 352, 355, 381, 384, 388, 433, 435
  direct 312
  farm animals 2, 37–40
  inflict 21, 28, 33, 56, 63, 153, 168, 312, 391, 435
    occult 71
  inflicted 391
  inflicting 153
    interpersonal 33
  infliction of 39, 54
  magic without 394
  people 2, 137, 154
  perpetrating 62
  potential xiv
  real 435
  supposed 433
Harmful magic 1, 2, 66, 70, 114, 149, 151–4, 189, 352, 358, 384, 398
  proscribed 2
  people 137
  see also Maleficium
Harprecht, Johann 392, 398
Harvest 36, 121–2, 174
Hassles 16, 17
Hatreds 44, 387
Haufler, Johann Heinrich 231
Hauntings *see* Ghost
Hay inspector 364
Hazelnuts 326, 328
Headaches 17, 82, 89, 286, 297, 308
  migraine 126
  psychophysical tension 17

Heal 151, 186, 190–2, 205, 212, 272–3, 276, 280, 283, 287, 294–5, 342, 349, 435, 437
  burns 303, 342
  illnesses 180
  people 187
Healer stage 278, 292
Healers xvii, 19, 20, 50, 70, 157, 180, 188–9, 193, 222, 275–83, 285, 288–9, 293–5, 300–2, 304–7, 329, 345, 360–1, 406, 408–9, 418, 427
  activities of 341, 405
  female 348
  holy 187
  illicit 361
  itinerant 360
  licit 361
  local 437
  magical 50, 285
  male 347–8, 405
  popular 178, 276, 306
  public 408
  reputed magical 406
  sanctioned 307
  semi-professional 305
  trained 209
  unofficial 305
  village 307
Healer's hands 302
Healing xix, xx, 151–2, 165, 186–7, 190, 192, 198, 209, 213, 216, 272, 280, 282, 284–5, 287–8, 290–1, 294–5, 297, 301, 303, 308, 313, 321, 334, 340–1, 343, 348–9, 360–1, 384, 407, 421, 423–4
  accelerated 300
  activities 257, 275–6, 282, 286–7, 289, 292, 296, 303, 361, 406
    women's 348
  advice 349
  aid 287
  animals 283
  arts 190
  blessings 295
  ceremonies 281, 292
    shamanic 187
  effect 294
  experience, initial 192
  forbidden herbal 348
  and Herb book 281
  illicit 216, 250, 279, 307, 340, 346

  intent 302
  learned 190, 281
  magic 340
  measures 308
  mechanism 298
  methods 301–2
    traditional 290, 301
  natural mechanisms 274, 438
  organic 210, 303
  of people 189, 250, 341
  popular 274–5, 282
  powers 211, 282, 302
    claim 210
  practices 274, 281, 285–6, 288, 301–2, 342
    spiritual 435
  process 273–4, 293, 436
  propitious day for 284
  rituals 217, 281, 283–4, 294, 296–7, 300, 302, 312
    calming 298
    performing 281
  sessions 285
  skills 255
  spiritual 301
  stone 280, 347
  techniques 274–5, 298, 301
    classical shamanic 277
    most numerous 282
  touch therapies 300
  traditional 290, 297
  unsuccessful 157
  see also Cure
Heals people 308
Health xv, 17, 19–22, 26, 37–8, 152, 159, 165, 193, 272, 280, 283, 288, 292–4, 297, 299, 301, 312, 320, 334, 346–7, 375, 396–8, 412, 437
  behaviors, maladaptive 19
  bodily 16
  collective 257
  human 288
  mental 397
  people's 37, 275, 424
  physical 18, 183
  problem 304
  psychological xix
    factors influence 23
    processes influence 19
  psychosocial factors influence 15

public   360
restoring   273
somatic   16, 19
status   299
Heart
  attacks   18, 256
  disease   16, 18, 19, 292
  pains   282
  problems   19, 190, 293
  rate
    accelerated   204
    lowers   298
  see also Cardiac arrhythmias
Heaven   76, 106, 114–15, 240, 242, 255, 257–8, 260–1, 264, 270, 401
Hebrews, ancient   381
Heidenheim   115, 133, 240, 282, 322, 345
Heidleberg University   177
Heilbronn   266
Helfenstein   384
Hellebore   145
  black   132
Helleboreine   132
Helleborus niger   132
Hemisphere
  left cerebral   54, 110, 196, 291, 376
  right cerebral   54, 110, 196, 291–2, 376–7
Hemispheres
  brain switches between   196
  cerebral   54, 147, 296, 376; left 196, 376
  see also Brain, Cerebral cortex
Hemispheric
  activation reverses   196
  dominance   196
Henbane   11, 130–2, 143
Herb
  book   281
  gardens   131
Herbal
  concoctions   209, 279
  grasses   187
  lore   287
  remedies   209, 211, 302, 306, 347
Herbals   281, 306
Herber, Juliana   33
Herbs   28, 46, 132, 155, 190, 192, 239, 279, 282–3, 285, 306, 309
  a drink   280, 286
  local   279
  used   279, 285
  wholesome   279, 281
Herders   344, 362
  cow   13, 17, 28, 276, 342, 344, 362
Heretical movements   95
Heretics   67, 94, 96
  see also Anabaptists, Waldensians
Hermann, Hanns   313
"*Herr*"   367
Herrenberg   10, 33, 169, 233, 236, 309–10, 416, 426
Herrigel, Eugen   315
Herwick, Conrad   10
Herwick, Conrad's wife's lameness   11
Hesse   132
Hesse-Kassel   249
Heterodox
  rituals   381
  spirit   276
Heuberg   96, 133–5, 144, 434
Hexen   see Witch
Hexenman   see Healers, Witches
Hexentöpfe   155
Hexerei   394–5, 426
  see also Witchcraft
Hezler, Stoffel   46
High Council   3, 88, 119, 121, 190, 240–1, 266–7, 316, 324, 327, 329, 351, 354, 368, 387, 392–6, 400–1, 416–18, 426
  ducal   3, 137, 328
  inquiry   327
  records   3
  response   416
  vocabulary   395
  see also Government
High Councilors   330
Hiller, Jacob   244
Himmelreich, Christiane Catarina   252
Hippocampal-sepal areas   203
Hippocampus   204
Hirsau, Cloister   258
Hisler, card reader   252
Historians   xviii, xix, 5, 12, 19, 21, 27, 44, 48, 52, 63, 76, 92–4, 115, 117, 130, 140, 158, 165, 167, 181, 183, 225, 230, 340, 362, 440
  rationalist   32
  romantic   147
  traditional   119

Hit 22, 44–5, 56, 174–5, 308, 400, 410
Hoch, Johann Georg 33
Hofburg 370
Hofen, Georg Jacob 233–5, 342
Höfingen 262
Hogwarts 210
Hohen Karlschule 426
Hohenneuffen 262, 264, 267
Holda 69, 96, 170, 191, 305
Holle, Frau 191
Holstein 175
Horn, Magdelena 9, 21, 38, 40, 45, 56–7, 73, 76, 79, 81, 86–7, 90, 118, 175, 384, 388–9, 400, 411
Holy Roman Empire 2, 68, 384
Holy Spirit 156, 224, 275–6, 283, 286, 318, 321, 382
Homage 177, 314
  ritual 115
Home, nursing 321
Honor 104, 355, 363, 366–7, 396
  -bound culture 355
  -conscious society 73
  poor possessed 366
Honorability 367–9, 371, 415
  local 362
Honorable people 222, 396
Honorables 367–9
Honoratioren 367
  see also *Ehrbarkeit*, Elite, notability
Horb 282
Hormonal
  adjustment 59
  balance 58, 312
  changes 17
  difference 53
Hormones 58, 293, 299
  changes in some 291
  harmful stress 294
  male sex 53
  see also Androgens, Estrogen, Endorphin
Horse
  charm 276
  inspectors 363
  master 8
Horses 37, 99, 101–2, 105, 164–5, 174, 190, 244, 282, 285, 342, 353, 364
  bewitch 165
  spook 164–5, 173, 178, 212

Hörterichshof 19
Horticulture 41
Hospitals 88, 415
  see also Almshouses
Host, communion 29, 115, 169, 176, 179
Hostile 26–7, 32, 59, 191, 238–9, 254
  actions 40
  subtext 27
Hostility 65, 19, 23–5, 28, 39, 56, 168, 175, 381, 433
  person's 20
  witch's 157
  see also Anger
Huberinus, Kaspar 410
Human experiences, common 34
Humiliation 355, 357–8
Hungarian
  "abductions" by witches 122–3, 187
  culture 192, 201
  practitioners 187
  taltos flew 187
  witches 187
Hungary xvii, 6, 115, 122, 175–6, 180, 190, 437
Hunters 200, 320, 344–5
Hussites 95
Hutelerin, Jacobina 323–4, 326
Hyoscaymine 143
Hypercognitive 208
Hypertension 15, 16, 292, 297
Hypnagogic 30, 33–4, 110
  experiences 113
  phase 109
Hypnogogic state 125–6, 128
Hypnopompic 33
  experiences 30, 33
  phases 109–10, 114
  state 148
Hypnosis 158, 198–9, 202, 209, 223, 291, 294–5, 298, 301–2, 311
  classic 295
Hypnotherapy, a form of 295
Hypnotic
  capabilities 199
  effects, pronounced 211
  experiences 239
  inductions 198, 296, 300
  state 198–9
  subject 199

Hypnotizability 199, 296
Hypnotizable
  highly 436
  people 199, 296
    highly 148, 198
Hypochondria 286
Hypothalamus 53, 78, 195
Hysteria 12, 58, 414

I
Id 181–2
  collective 181–2
Ideomotor
  actions xv, 224–5, 235–6, 438
  -based instruments 236
  manifestations 249
  movements 235
  systems 253
Idolatry 382, 425
Ill 2, 3, 8, 9, 15, 19, 22–3, 28–9, 35, 38, 46–7, 49, 55–6, 122, 152, 158, 171, 205, 215, 269, 304, 340, 418
  effects 8, 15, 55
  person 312
  projection of 21
Ill-health 273, 292
Ill-will 12, 411
  expressions of 3, 21
  projecting 48
  witch's 157
Ill, wished 311
Illness xv, 2, 16, 17, 20–1, 23, 27, 29, 43, 155, 157–8, 176, 188, 190, 202, 207, 209, 212–13, 222, 292, 303, 397, 401, 411, 427, 433, 436
  diagnose 360–1
  handling 303
  inflict 151
  initiatory 191
  mental 92
  person's 430
Illogical thought 195
Illsfelden 316, 328
Illusion susceptibility 84
Illusions 30, 70, 123, 134, 137, 140, 166, 181, 324, 330, 381–2, 385, 431, 439
  aberrant 129
  multisensory 127
  optical 325

  satanic 265
  trivial 427
  vestibular 127
  see also Delusions, Hallucinations, Images, Misperceptions, Perceptions
Image magic 152–3, 175
Imagery 291–2, 431
  generated 223, 331
  self-generated 148
Images 30, 84, 86, 112, 124–5, 131, 149, 153, 170, 210, 223, 225, 227, 236, 243, 253, 291–2, 434, 438
  composite 435
  dreamy 30
  freestanding visual 84
  generated 223
  hallucinatory 125
  hypnogogic 125
  hypnopompic 34
  mutilate 153
  projecting 260
  reflected 223
  self-standing 83
  sustained moving 223
  wax 154–5
Imaginal world 278
Imaginative constructions 74
Immune function 298
  compromised 19
Immune-related problems 33
Immune system 18, 20, 291–2, 297–300, 312
  manipulate 299
  see also Cells, Cellular defenses and emotions
Immunoglobulin 16
Imperial cities 41, 119, 227, 387
Impiety 263, 265
"Impious and disobedient" 426
Impotence 2, 6, 17, 23, 56, 154–5, 389
Impression, fleeting 223
Imprisonment 156, 262, 358
Impulses 58, 79, 86, 197, 224, 377
  antisocial 412
  hormonal 78
  immoral 402
  nerve 13
  repressive 383
  witch-related 413

Incantational arts   235
Incantations   2, 29, 152–3, 155, 162–8, 170–1, 173–4, 178, 198, 209, 237–8, 242, 245, 250, 275–6, 278, 285, 287, 292, 294–6, 298, 300, 302, 308, 317–19, 341, 417
  collective   181
  diabolic   280, 388, 418
  forbidden   162
  formulaic   278
  illicit   50
  muttered   247
  protracted   285
  repetitive   164
  verbal   161
Incanting   156, 303
  blessings   360
  person   164
  see also Blessing, Conjure, Exorcize, Demons
Incarceration   353–5, 407, 412, 428, 440
  prolonged   428, 440
  see also Confinement, Jail, Penetentiary
Incense   172, 279, 330
Incubi   33, 80
Indecency   79–81
Indoctrinate   358, 371
Induction   296
  deliberate   200, 202, 213
Industrial society, modern   200, 415
Industry   41, 423
Infanticide   353
Infections   119, 299
  avert   280
  bacterial   299
  minor   286
Inflation   61, 423
Influence
  baleful   72
  behavior   79
  benign   216
  corrupting   407
  curative   301
  disruptive   147
  exerting   369
  indirect   415
  inducements   xv
  interpersonal   295, 433
  malign   405
  moderating   392, 394
  people's perceptions   83
  psycho-physical   334
  see Subliminal, Healing, Mirror neurons, Sorcery, Threat displays, Visceral
Information
  accessing   270, 439
  ambiguous   102
  bodily   126
  channels   225
  distorting   376
  emotional   24
  extraordinary   219
  hidden   220
  incomplete   32
  infrastructures   212
  interpersonal   26–7
  invalid   431
  leakage   36
  limited   23
  linguistic   32
  overt   227
  processing, multimodal sensory   297
  rejecting   375
  semantic   32
  sources of   281–2
  unconscious   198, 201, 204, 206, 226, 431, 438
  unknown   438
  unsubstantiated   100
  visual   31, 126
Information-processing systems   273
Ingolstadt   136, 139, 141
Inhibition
  bilateral   377
  reflexive   377
  systems   374
Initiation
  shamanic   151, 192, 209
  witch's   186–7
Initiations, attempted   133
Injure people   2
Injuring livestock   44
Injury   1–3, 6, 11, 14, 25, 37–8, 44, 48–9, 51, 55, 85, 157, 165, 173–5, 213, 244, 264, 274, 298, 304, 319, 331, 384, 388, 394, 411, 433
  covert   45
  inflict   89, 156, 176, 200, 310, 330

inflicted   49
limited   10
mechanical   38
perceived   85
physical   202
physiological   273
Inputs
  cognitive   126
  disallowed   377
  mysterious   78
  neural   203
  nonconscious   78
  real, excluded   375
  verbal   225
Inquiries, informal   352
Inquisitorial
  methods, illegal   418
  process   386
Inquisitors   67, 94, 157, 180, 194
Insects, poisonous   155
Insfeld   283
Inspectors, community   363–4
Instinctive reactions   78
Institutions, communal
  formal   372
  informal   42–3
Instructions
  conscious   372
  explicit   373
  informal   372
  moral   359
  religious   359, 420
Insults   44, 51, 73, 156, 244, 264, 365, 395
Integrability   372, 374
Integrated person   432
Integration   31, 83, 111, 126, 207–8
  interpersonal psychic   37
  personal   204
  psychophysical   292
Integrative brain state   207
  see also Brain, Consciousness
Intentionality   116, 160, 207, 375
Intentions, suppressing   372, 375
Interdependence, psychological   37, 151
Internalization   106, 374–5, 377, 400, 410, 413–14
  see also Enculturation
Interpersonal   16, 18, 19, 363, 402, 433
  aggression   412

altercation   19
  ugly   29
animosities   364
attitudes   24–5
bonds   381
  cementing   104
charisma   208
communications   20, 226
conflicts   20–1, 23, 60, 63, 175, 226, 292, 302, 386, 413, 415, 429, 433, 3
  normal   45
  sharp   43
contact   33
disputes   49
effect   39
  unconscious   51
integration   297
interactions   62, 159, 433
relations   20, 375
  disturbed   22, 402
tensions   33, 209, 297, 302
Interrogation   51, 123, 130, 174, 194, 222, 355, 412, 416–17, 426
Intoxication   xx, 119, 131, 135, 144
Intuition   204, 269
Intuitive skills   256
Inversion   113, 168–9, 183
Invisibility   317
Invocation   154, 178, 183, 201, 238, 275, 285, 341–2, 357, 382, 436
  deliberate   67
  ritual   237
  forbidden   246
  idolatrous   381
  open   246
  performed   343
  ritualized   153
  spiritual   249
  see also Conjure, Incantation
Invoking spirits   439
Invulnerability   272
Ireland   179, 188
Irish
  legends   188
  popular culture   188
Iron Century   61, 434
Iron spike   171, 239
Irregularities, judicial   394, 417–18
Isolation, social   292, 411

Istria 154
Italian Alps 191
Italy 74, 94, 97, 143, 154, 169, 175, 179, 181, 369
Itinerant
 charlatans 136, 289
 man's claim 419
 outsiders 191
 scholars 189–92, 201, 210–11, 250, 343, 437
 sorcerers 152, 315
Itinerants 147, 254, 340, 343–4, 405
Izelberg 322

J
Jäcklen, Peter 310
Jäger, Fuchs' wife 222, 226
Jail 14, 81, 98, 105, 121, 136–7, 141, 149, 244, 316, 355, 387, 418
 local 353
 sentences 357
 terms, short 428
 time 353
 see also Incarceration
James, William 224–5
Jausen, Agnes 281
Jealousy 103, 433
Jergle, Peter 281–2, 284–5, 289, 295–6, 298, 300, 303, 345
Jesuits 236, 254, 257, 392
Jimson Weed 139
Joan of Arc 86
John the Baptist 238, 260, 266, 275
Journeys 122, 134, 204, 210, 277
 ecstatic 191
 other world 189
 protracted 278
 see also Flying, OBEs, Shamanism
Judeo-Christian tradition 1, 71, 182, 267, 381
Judicial process 44, 341, 350, 378
 see also Trials
Jurisdictions, neighboring 386–7
Jurists 350–1, 394, 396, 398

K
Kählin, Othmar 222, 308
Karl Alexander, Duke 422
Karl Eugen, Duke 422, 426
 consultant in Paris 370

Kartenschlagen 251
Keil, Hans 260–8, 270, 354
Keisersberg, Johann Geiler of 96, 131
Keller, Christoph 233, 342
Kellern, Hans Rolf 8, 15, 55
Kepler, Johannes 255
Kerber, Albrecht 38
Kettener, Hans Jacob 97–9, 101–3
Kettlemoth House 98
Key, St. Hubert's 282
Kieffer 317
King David 266
Kirchekonvents 265
 see also Church's supervisor systems, Church courts
Kirchenrat 356
Kircher, Fr. A. 224, 233
Kirchheim 113, 317, 342
Kiss "in name of the Devil" 174
Klaniczay, Gábor xviii
Klein 29–31
Klein Ingersheim 88
Klein, Michaels wife 29, 31
Kliegstein, Anna 14
Klingen, Georg 19
Klingen, George 10
Knacker 305–6, 361
Knighthoods, independent 368
Knittlingen 177
Knödler, Johannes 282
Knötzlerin, Maria Juditha 236, 247, 319–21
Knowledge 9, 26, 29, 34–5, 74, 100, 102, 109–10, 112, 132, 139, 151, 154, 159, 167, 170, 174, 186, 193–4, 198, 205–8, 210–12, 222, 225, 269, 355, 358–9, 372, 376–7, 382–3, 430–1
 book-based 359
 collective 425
 common 35
 enhanced 208, 430
 esoteric 341
 extraordinary 186
 hidden 188
 learned 94
 magical 431
 occult 191, 305, 323
 prior 208, 232
 repressed 90

unexpressed 226
Kochen, Magdalena 11, 13, 45, 56–7, 59, 61, 306, 410
Koenbeckhen, Johann 11, 13
Kohler, Johannes 233
Köhlern, Heinrich 426–7
Köll, Hans 228–9, 231, 280, 283, 306, 342, 409
Körner, Wolf 11
Kramer, Catharina 162
Kramer, Heinrich 1, 69
Kramer, Michel 169
Kressich springs 190, 283
Krieger, Georg 49
Kugel, Hans Jerg 281, 283, 309
Kühler, Ludwig 244
Kurzen, Hanns Jacob 281, 317, 343, 418

L
Labor
  duties 365
  hard 353
Ladies
  nighttime 188, 437
  from outside 121, 187, 437
Lady Abundance 188
Laguna, Andrés de 129, 131–2, 143
Laichlin, Maria 8, 15, 19, 21, 46, 133, 387, 305, 307, 406–7
Laisslin, Johann 400
Lancashire witches 176
Landesordnung 385
Langen, Hanß Jacob 136–41, 147, 149, 157, 179, 206, 212, 344, 388
Langjahr, Agnes 10, 14, 19, 22, 28–9, 49, 56–7, 158–9, 161, 166, 212, 228, 308, 411
Language 23, 86, 109–10, 126, 145, 190, 192, 194, 291, 297
  centers 54
  foreign 89
  unknown 89
Lap 22, 49, 56, 158
Late seventeenth century 42, 212, 248, 251, 316, 359, 361, 370, 380, 400, 405–6, 411, 415
Lauffen 136–8, 222
Laughlin, Charles xx
Lavender water rub 306

Law
  code 1
    imperial 384
    government's model 352
    model 2
  codes, medieval 1
  faculty 252, 351, 394
Laws 1, 65, 81, 109, 230, 325, 333, 361, 368–9, 373, 382–4, 386, 390, 425, 428, 440
  adopted Imperial 382
  antidrug 130
  basic 101
  duchy's 351, 369
  secular 357
  see also Government, Provincial Ordinances
Lawsuits 223, 329, 365
Lawyers 69, 359, 394, 396–7
Laying on hands 301
Leader spirit 68
Learned
  associations 203
  culture 154, 337
  expectations 37, 302
  magical traditions 170
Left
  cerebral hemisphere 196, 376
  frontal lobe 374, 377
Leg, sore 295–6, 298
Legal
  forms 392
  procedures, systematic 387
  scrutiny 394
  terms 394
  training 368, 394
Legends 189, 192, 240
Leibniz, Gottfried 420
Leichten, Andrea 19, 28, 49, 56
Leipzig 252
Leonberg 11, 260–2
Lerchheimer, August 130, 391
Letters 70, 173, 261, 401
Lice 137, 148–9, 158, 179
Lilienskiold 135
Limbic
  activities 195
  component 39
  structures 26, 161, 207–8
    mediating sentiment 160, 298

Limbic (*Continued*)
  system 23, 26, 78, 110, 147, 161, 195, 206, 209, 225, 291–3, 296, 299, 376–7
Linguistic
  culture 376
  principles and dreams 109
  representations 377
  terms 431
  thought 206
  see also Psycholinguistic programming, Rational thought
Lipp, Matthew 321
Lippe 48
Literacy 358, 368, 420
"Little George" from Ladenberg 189–92, 210
Living arrangements controlled 352
Local
  communities 40, 77, 95, 162, 340, 349–50, 362–3, 373, 430, 440, 337
  elites 103, 330, 378, 337
  notability 158, 362, 366, 368
  traditions 2, 123, 210
Lord's Prayer 359
Lorraine xvi, 154
Lost objects 187, 219, 223, 231, 269, 341–2, 438
Lotions 130
  black-magic 135
Louis XIV 168, 257–8
Love magic 153, 155, 169, 175, 189, 416
  coercive 251
  learned 135
  manipulative 180
  recipes 154
Low Countries 194
LSD 9, 134, 141, 144–5, 149–50
Lucerne 249
Lucifer 173, 175–6
  see also Devil, Satan
Luciferan conspiracy 185
Ludwig, Duke 385
Ludwig, Margritha 222, 226
Ludwig William, Duke 370
Ludwigsburg 236, 241–2, 417–18, 426
  penitentiary 241, 418, 427–8
Lusts 58, 156
  insatiable 409–10
Luther, Martin 71, 108, 131, 233, 258–9, 267, 359, 399

Lutheran
  apocalyptic prophesy 258
  leaders 72
  mainstream 268
  orthodoxy 368, 371, 422
Lutheranism 43, 413
Lutherans 73, 259, 321, 356, 369, 398
Luzin, Agnes 281, 349, 418
Lye 9
Lying 229–30

M
MacFarlane, Alan 23
Madonna di Finemundo 179
Magia 1, 4, 216, 394, 398
Magiae Universalis Naturae 224
Magic xiv–xviii, 1, 2, 19, 20, 67, 95–6, 118, 152–5, 159, 162–7, 173, 178–81, 193–4, 231–2, 246–7, 271–2, 303, 309–10, 312–21, 327–9, 339–43, 345–53, 355–9, 373, 375–87, 391, 393–5, 397–9, 403–7, 415–17, 419–35, 438–40
  active 246
  arcane 228
  beliefs xix, 5
  black 50, 152, 155, 191, 394
  books 170, 191, 349, 407
  chest 155
  conjuration 276
  curing 284
  defensive 310, 437, 65
  employed routinely 429
  experience 431
  forbidden 240
  formulas 155, 278
  health-care-oriented 340
  illicit 167, 180, 304, 321
  learned 152, 167, 169–70, 191, 212, 252
    ceremonial 171, 176
  malevolent 155, 185, 359, 2
  manipulative 216, 273, 303, 313, 319–20, 334, 438
  marginalization of 378
  natural 383
  nonharmful 2
  nonmalefic 216
  pagan 170
  petty 148

potions   96, 152
practice   70, 212, 410
practiced   29, 176, 317, 340-1, 348, 405, 416-17, 429
practitioners of   440
protective   1, 271, 304, 319
rejection of   30, 381
repress   350, 381
ritual   175, 183, 315
  a healing   169
secret   28
skills, learned   68
spell   50
sympathetic   131, 314
Western   153
words   280
see also Beneficient, Countermagic, Cross-fertilization, Heal, Practitioners
Magical
  abilities   49, 95
  activities   240, 271, 337, 339, 342, 382, 407, 425, 427, 429, 440
    illicit   356
    participants in   xvi
    popular   219
  acts, forbidden   401
  affliction   307
  aggression   62
  amulets   152
  arts   189, 250
    devilish   405
  assault   312
  assumptions   152
  attacks   31, 33, 36, 65, 152, 159
  beliefs   xvi, xvii, 142, 375-7, 419-20, 429-30, 440
    understanding   376
  ceremonies   172, 308
  cognition   425
  connections   228
  counteraction   312
  countermeasures   273, 303-4, 313, 418
  crimes   7, 378, 394, 398, 402, 422
  culture, common   170, 211
  effects   273, 381, 425
  enhancements   303, 312-13
  events   120, 142
  feats   188
  fertility warriors, self-proclaimed   94
  flights   67, 94, 108, 123, 191, 437
  formulas   180, 278
  harm   149, 152
  healing   273, 302, 308, 319, 347-9, 406, 428, 438
    activities   347
    efficacy of   287
    practiced   342
    rituals   273, 341
  incantations   275, 318
  intensifier   175
  manipulations   312
  marksmanship   314
  mobilization, ritual   165
  objects   280
    hidden   45
  poisoning   134
  powers
    gain   181
    use   53
  practices   4, 33, 94, 135, 148, 179-80, 193, 271-2, 316, 341, 345-6, 348-9, 360, 370, 378, 381, 407, 418, 428-31
    ancient   153
    capital offenses   382
    novel   193
  practitioners   67, 180, 340, 344, 346, 378, 383, 408, 434-5
    marginalized   429
    public   343, 346
    Romans persecuted   1
    and sorcery   155
  rituals   175, 314, 320, 335
  soothsaying   384
  specialists   221, 321, 339
  techniques   153, 219, 303
  therapies, efficacy   287
  thinking, children   116
  traditions, popular   340; *see also* cross-fertilization
  treasure-hunting   245, 248, 282
  world view   142
Magicians   169-70, 187, 189, 227, 244, 278, 340, 359, 383, 391, 397, 428
  "cabals," Paris   180
  groups   67, 153, 172, 180
  learned   152, 178, 391
  natural   233, 382
  popular, and learned magic   170

Magicians (*Continued*)
  professional   177
  wandering   192
  white   175
Magnetic gradient changes   234
Magneus, Olaus   187
"magnificent people"   190–1
Magus, Simon   95
Maladies   11, 15, 16, 20, 23, 28, 56, 82, 209, 227, 286, 302, 304–5, 396, 402
  arthritic   329
  counteract   307
  cow's   309
  inexplicable   312
  physical   307
  physiological   17
  psychophysical   294, 297
  psychosphysical   21
  see also Ailments
Male   19, 47, 51–4, 80, 105, 405, 410
  magicians   391
  poisoners   352
  violence   53, 411
Malefic   1, 45, 50, 70, 174, 178, 180, 213, 357, 383
  behaviors   63
  magic   xiv, xviii, 20, 67, 105, 184, 350, 383, 394, 400
    popular   148
    practice   67
  materials   115
  practices   xviii, 63, 176
  witchcraft   26, 62, 176, 213
Maleficium   xix, 1–3, 5–7, 9–11, 20, 22, 24, 37, 39–43, 45–53, 55–63, 65–6, 99, 117, 138, 156–7, 159, 169, 172, 174–6, 179, 181, 186, 263, 312, 319, 348, 383–4, 386–9, 394, 433–4
  allegations of   3, 56, 117, 418, 433
  collective   180
  effects, 413, 415
  natural remedies against   343
  perpetrated   5, 65
  popular   176
  spontaneous   294, 312, 435, 438
  in Theodosius law code   1
  see also Harmful magic, Witchcraft
Malevolent clan shaman   176
Malice   104, 411

Malign
  spirits   71, 89, 184, 238
  substance   55
Malleus Maleficarum   xvi, 1, 46, 69, 70, 123, 155, 314, 409–10
Mandrake   130–1, 143, 155, 306
Mangelwurzel   309
Manipulations
  informal   372
  limited   212, 436
Manufacturing sector   41, 415, 423
Marbach   135, 173, 331, 417–18
Margaretha from Vöhringen   133–4, 141
Margrave of Baden-Durlach   371
Maria, to be emulated   310, 409, 414
Marital status   46–7
Marketplace, local magical   254
Marksmanship   272–3, 313–14, 349
  influence   315
Marriage   42, 79, 81, 219, 352, 365, 371
Martin, Christoph   316–17, 328, 348
Mass (religious ceremony)   117, 168–9, 179, 184, 266, 369, 371, 415
  black   93, 168, 180
  secret   169
Mass panics   55, 62–3, 119, 355, 387, 390, 398, 412–13, 3
  see also Witch persecutions
Masten, Katharina   10, 14, 22, 56–7, 61, 304, 307, 400, 410
Maulbronn, Cloister   50
Maurer, Barbara   279, 281
Mauritius, Erich   398
Mayer, Maria   38
Meat   106, 121–2, 154
Mechanisms
  physiological   13, 296–7, 300, 302
  psychophysical   311
  restorative   273, 288
Mechanistic model of world   377
Medical
  activities   257
  establishment   301
  hierarchy   397
  practices, illicit   361, 216
  practitioners   222, 257, 307, 360
    low-level   221
  professionals   159
  regulations   360–1
  response   304

sanctioned 306
services, charity 360
system, official 360–1
systems 274
testimony 396–7
Medical Ordinances, First and Second 361
Medicines 50, 222, 256, 273, 275, 279, 282, 285, 288, 290, 306–7, 341, 345, 360–1, 368, 397–8
 active 288–9
 herbal 342–3, 406, 408
 illicit 421, 424
 internal 279–80, 342, 397
 popular 287
 potency 306
 traditional 398
 unofficial 287
 see also Doctors, Herbs, Physical remedies, Potions
"Medico" 306–7
Medieval
 church 95, 382
 churchmen 96
 late 350, 409, 437
 people 131
 see also Middle Ages
Medieval Europe 95, 104
 early 278
 late 278
Medieval Europeans 65
Meditation 148, 202–3, 298
Mediterranean 194
Mediums 151, 186, 205–6, 247, 277
Megerler, Anton Fuggers cunning woman 220, 236
Melancholic 77, 186, 391, 416
 witch confessions 416
Melancholy 268, 392
 severe 266
Memes 182, 211
Memories 30–1, 35, 48–9, 54, 74, 76, 88, 101–2, 110, 116, 126, 147, 208, 223, 265, 277, 317, 332, 423, 434
 altered 439
 brain constructs 112
 constructing 74
 early 376
 false 326
 long-term 111
 ritualized 193
 social 102
 visual and auditory 81
Memory
 consolidation 111
 functions 144
 systems 376
Memory-bank 74
Menopause 57–9
Menstruation 59, 90
Mental
 activities 163, 196, 203, 223
 life 77
 preparation 156
 programming 290
 scaffolding 375
 structures 112
Mentation 87, 109–10, 112, 116
 agitated verbal 113
 unfocused interior 197
Merchants 41, 162, 193, 368
 large-scale 367
 wealthy 42, 390
Merlini Cocai Sonnets 251
Mesopotamia, ancient 152
Messmer, Franz Anton 301
Meth, Ezechiel 267
Metzingen 10
Meuse River 258
Meÿer, Catharina 283
Mice 37, 301
Middle Ages xviii, 71, 80, 94, 135, 152–3, 184, 193, 224, 258, 274, 278, 346, 360, 402
 early 71, 95, 170, 279, 353, 382
Middle Ages, High 71–2, 190, 382–3
Middle Ages, late 72, 96, 152–3, 170, 277
Midwives 135, 360–1, 363, 397
 handbook 361
Miembler, Endriss 79–81, 84–7, 90, 205, 264, 400
Miembler, Katharina 10, 79–81
Milan 187
Milk 2, 8, 45, 135, 165, 173, 175, 228, 281, 309–10, 322, 417
 hare 176
 steal 7, 176, 228, 230, 237, 309–11
Miller 98, 133, 244
Miller's helpers 244
Miners, German 233
Minister 76, 138, 243
Mirables 208, 319

Index

Miracles 96, 208, 242–3, 262–5, 382
  biblical 419
  fake 264, 268
  false 331
  manifesting God's power 381
  physical 264
Miraculous
  cures 191
  results 381
Mirror 171, 222–3, 236–7, 247, 281, 286, 307, 320, 342
  magic 424
  neurons 293, 295; *see also* Connection, visceral interpersonal
Mirror of Domestic Discipline 410
Mirror of Witches, A 391
Miscarriage 155
Misfortunes 5, 23, 28, 32, 48, 70–1, 106, 208, 213, 220, 226, 266, 391, 399
  common 303
  inexplicable 5, 32
  miserable 323
  unpredictable 198
  see also Afflictions
Misogyny, clerical 66
Misperceptions 51, 326, 332, 381, 439
  see also delusions, hallucinations, illusions, Perceptions
Misrepresentation 35, 49
Missing
  objects 208, 231
  people 250, 343
"Mistress of Ceremonies" 96
Mittel Scheuthal 244
Möckmühl 116
Modern
  educated psyche, traditional 375
  psychologists and Devil beliefs 76–7
  understanding 337, 370
Modules
  cognitive 205
  executive 224
  higher-order 87
  latent 92
  lower-level 86
  neurocognitive 86–7, 207
  quasi-independent 224
  unconscious neural 438
  see also Brain, Network
Moessinger 401

Monde Primitif 251
Money
  economy, rising 423
  seed 232, 319, 322
Montaillou 177, 240
Moon 253, 255–6, 275, 284–5, 317
Moral
  acceptance, subconscious 365
  advice 172
  being 73
  character 394
  frame, customary 76
  guides 72
  implications 400, 406, 425, 434
  improvement 259, 265
  lapses 1, 178, 402
  offenses 357
  orientation 172, 394, 434
  outrage 372
  spectrum 148–9
  strictures 200, 377, 440
  suasion 347
  supervision 405–6
  values 76, 372
Morality 76, 117, 179, 366
Morality, Manichean 117
Morality, official 360
Morals 350, 398
  regulations 162
  tribunals 265
Morning 283–4
Mortgages, cosigned 43
Morus, Barbara 322
Moselle River 258
Mother 9, 10, 50, 80, 97, 106–7, 113, 118, 138, 154, 167, 169, 186, 189, 348, 416
  spiritual 243
Mothers
  new 22, 158
  unmarried 361
Motor
  activities 197
  neurons, associated 293
  output systems 110
Mound 188
Mountain 96, 184, 189, 191–2, 194, 210, 212, 234
  Cosmic 191
  see also Venusberg

Mouse 83–4, 409
Movements
　inexplicable 325
　nonvolitional 224
　sieve's 224
　tiny muscle 226
　uncontrollable 89, 133
　see also Ideomotor
Mück, Christina 309, 311–12
Muhlmaÿer, Johann Josef Michael 241, 249
Muhlmaÿer, Michael 241
Müller, Thomas Walzen 243
Multisensory experiences 110, 434
Münsignen 313
Muoth 305–6
Murray, Margaret xviii, 93–4
Murrhardt 223, 228–9, 244, 319, 329, 345
Music, beautiful 96
Musician, local 106–7
Mutschler, Georg 240, 328
Mysteries of Eleusis 135
Mysterious
　barrages 327
　beings 215
　bombardment 326
　disappearance 229
　intruder 316–17
　noises 333
　see also Ball lightning, Poltergeists
Mystical
　gatherings 123
　merriments 170
　see also Good company, Dances, Sabbaths
Mysticism 72, 301
Mystics 186, 200
　learned 267
Mythomania 116
Myths 97, 129, 135, 181, 185, 192, 210, 277, 301

N

Nachtriben, Hans Jerg 311
Nagold 243, 343
Nails 310, 418
　finger 155
　horseshoe 29
　human 154–5

Naples 177, 191
Narratives 74, 109, 276–9
Natal predilections 257
Nativities 255
Nature vs. nurture 34, 52, 199
Near-death experiences 202, 433
　see also Shamanic experiences
Neck 75, 82, 241, 286, 311, 322, 342, 400
Neckar River 177, 257
Neckar Valley, upper 41
Neckargröningen 281
Neckarshausen 321
Necromancers 152, 177, 179
Necromancy 67, 152–3, 170, 172, 193, 212, 220, 238, 437
　see also Sorcery, Magic, Ritual
Needles 154–5, 233, 235–6, 329
　knitting 232–3, 236, 239, 342
Negative interactions 59
Neighborhood butcher 366
Neighborhoods 42–4, 96, 130, 162, 229
Neighboring
　ruler 384
　territory 339, 385
Neighborliness 42–3, 340
Neighborly snooping, formalized 363
Neighbors 8–10, 13, 30, 38, 40, 42–6, 48, 50, 55, 59, 61–3, 155, 157, 162, 166, 183, 185, 222, 226, 228, 281, 313, 327, 343, 347, 349–50, 357, 365–6, 388, 412, 414
　bonds 43
　estranged 44
　hired 43
　well-to-do 45, 306
　see also Communities, Conflicts, Enemies, Towns, Villages
Neocortex 147, 196, 293, 374
Nervous system 85, 92, 143–4, 146–7, 161, 163–6, 196, 201–3, 206, 208, 210–11, 223, 235, 246, 274, 291–3, 296, 298, 302, 306, 376, 430, 436–7
　autonomic 18, 144, 292, 298–9, 302, 376
　central 144, 299
　ergotropic 146, 296
　fine-tuning the 211
　human 143, 335

Nervous system (*Continued*)
  manipulating people's 212
  parasympathetic 145, 298–9
  peripheral 11, 143
  person's 161, 438
  practitioner's 162, 164
  sick people's 296
  sympathetic 202, 208, 298
  trophotrophic 223
  tuning the 202
  see also Autonomic, Brain, Consciousness, ergotropic, Fine-tuning, Neural, Tuning, Fight/flight response, trophotropic
Nethen, Christina 88, 401, 408
Networks, neurocognitive 86, 110, 146–9, 160, 291, 298
  conscious 377
  external 376
  functional 86
Networks, social 42, 94, 99, 180, 193, 341, 344
  active 167
  clientage 362
  external 376
  formed 67
  informal 215
Neuburg 137
Neuenburg 98, 101
Neuenstadt 395–6
Neuffen 141, 316
Neural
  activity, unconscious 235
  circuitry 30–1, 149
  hardware, shared basic 91
  networks 111, 126, 160–1, 298, 300, 374
  processing 111, 223
  see also Nervous system
Neurological fine-tuning 377
Neuromodulatory balance, shift 203
Neurons 11, 26, 54, 160, 290, 293, 376
  cholinergic 143–4
  groups 86
Neuropeptides 299, 302
Neurophysiological response 234
Neurophysiology 159, 198
  universal 91
Neuroscientists xx
Neurotransmitters 143–4, 203, 299

Neutral spirits 382
Neuweyler 98
New Testament 104
News 68, 70, 100–1, 231, 261, 268
Newton, Isaac 419
Nicholas of Cusa 179
Nider, Johann xvi, 96, 129, 131–2, 146
Niederhofen 266–7, 270
Night dance 121–2, 127–8, 388
Nightshade 11, 130, 132, 143
  berries 132
  family 202
  ordience concerning 130
  see also Atropa belladonna, Belladonna, Drugs
Niklashausen, drummer of 95
Nineteenth century 38, 140, 233, 252, 378, 424
  early 290
Nobility, national 370
Nobleman, minor 371
Nobles 168, 171, 351, 368, 415
  regional 350
Nocturnal lights 326
Nonconscious 78, 373
  interpersonal communication xv
  neural processing 236
  see also Subliminal, Unconscious
Nonverbal
  communication 24, 27–8, 225, 295
  implicit 37
  cues 24, 26–7
  signals 24, 26, 165
  signs 29
  see also Body language, Subliminal
Nordlingen 61, 257
Nordlingen, Battle of 61
Normandy 154, 169
Norms 26
  internalized 350, 356
  see also Enculturation, Internalization
Notability 69, 101, 367
Notables, local 45, 74, 367
  see also Elite, Government
Noxious
  items 22, 158
  materials 435
  remedies 406
Numerology 253
Nurnberg 138, 190

O

Oberstdorf xvii
OBEs *see* Out-of-body experiences
Objects
  buried enchanted 175, 303
  exotic 171
  potent 2, 281, 341
  religious 169
  secreted 153, 157
  special 275
  symbolic 302
Occult 1, 22, 62–3, 65, 135, 205, 208, 233, 235, 274, 319, 381, 419, 430, 433
  attacker 216
  attacks 5–7, 48, 65
  bonds 227
  countermeasures 309
  energy 301
  forces 287, 215
  healing traditions 288
  injury 11
  processes 219, 398
  see also Magic
Occupations 344, 367–9
Oceanic oneness 204
Offenses
  capital 221, 358
  repeated 358, 405
Officials 22, 98, 123, 130, 190, 261–2, 267–8, 304, 342, 344, 351, 356–7, 363–4, 369, 371, 387–8, 394, 396, 405–7, 416–18, 422, 425–8
  communal 363–4, 386
  district 351
  ducal 2, 162, 262, 367
  duke's forestry 163
  executive 352
  habits of thought 369
  high 351, 369, 371
  local 2, 45, 357, 378, 386, 416
  minor 344
  see also Bureaucrats, Elite, Government
Ointments 10, 11, 21, 129–30, 136–9, 148, 152, 155, 279, 282
  witches 119
  see also Drugs, Hallucinogens, Lotions, Salves

Old
  people and the Devil 58
  woman, deluded 391
"Old Hag" 34, 194, 309
  experience xix, 33–7, 194
Old age 57–8
Omens 220, 250, 258–9, 271
  bad 76
  natural 220
  see also Portents
Oneiroscopy 220
Onstmettingen 331
Opiates, natural 297
  see also Endorphin
Optimism 209, 294, 397
Ordeals, judicial 220
Ordered argument, learned 369
Ordinances *see* Provincial Ordinances
Orientation Association Areas 203–4, 207
Orphan house 415, 417–18
  see also Almshouses
Orthodoxy 182, 268, 398
  theological 259, 360
  see Lutheran
Osiander, Johann Adam 398
Ostracism 364–5, 372, 377–8
Oswald, Magdelena 157
Out-migration 415, 422
Out-of-body experiences 124–9, 146, 148, 202, 204, 434
Outbursts, spontaneous 156
Overpopulation 61, 386
Ovulation 78
Ox 22

P

Pact 2, 3, 65, 75, 157, 176–7, 179–81, 191, 263, 323, 348, 355, 358, 384, 388, 391–2, 394, 398, 405, 412
  adventurous students and 177
  diabolic 115, 329
  formal 176
  implicit 1, 70, 178, 235
  purported 177
  satanic 176
  signed 177
  see also Devil, Diabolism
Pagan
  beliefs, disguised 193

600 Index

Pagan (*Continued*)
  deities 382
  forms, unchanged 271
  philosophy 381
  rituals 271
  spirits 278
Paganism 94
  classical 215
Pagans 177, 382
Pain xiv, 8, 12–14, 17, 49, 56, 208, 234, 256, 284–5, 288–9, 297–8, 300, 308, 311, 329, 355, 374, 400–1, 412, 417
  disorder 12, 13
  experience 13, 374
  intense 14, 17
  network 199
  perceived 14
  perception 199, 208
  reduced 297
    by neuropeptides 302
  signal 199
  stomach 133
  suppression 300
  see also Ailment, Conversion reaction, Healing
Pain-reducing effects 297
Palatinate 257
Paleolithic 53, 151, 219, 319
Paleomammalian brain 207
Paleomentation 225
Pamphilë's transformation 131
Pamphlet literature 6, 70, 118, 132, 239, 261–2, 386, 391
  regional 2
  see also Broadsides, Tracts
Pamphleteer 70, 410
Panics 348, 412
  child-centered 397
  see also Mass panics
Paracelsus 23
Paradise, Waldensians and 189, 201
Paralysis 14, 38, 56, 132, 145
  conversion symptoms 17
  hypnopompic 34
  see also Conversion reaction, *Maleficium*, "Old Hag"
Paranormal 225, 234, 247, 319, 376
Parapsychology 36, 124, 209, 313, 430
Parasympathetic 144, 196, 202, 209, 298
  see also Nervous system, Quiescent, Relaxation response, Trophotropic
Parenting, bad 117
Parietal lobes 126
Paris 41
  medieval 437
Parishes, number of 420
Parody, religious 169
Passau 190, 319
Passauer Kunst 319
Passions xvi, 394, 409
  Emotions, Lusts
Pastoral societies 151, 186
Pastors 8, 73, 263, 266, 356–9, 387, 391, 405, 420
Paternosters 277
Pathology xix, 21, 83, 85, 124
Patients 13, 17, 85, 131, 209–10, 275–9, 282–5, 288–90, 292–5, 297, 300, 302, 306, 308, 345, 399, 436, 438
  see also Doctor, Healer, Sick person
Patient's spirit 291
Patricians 362, 367
  class-conscious 371
Patronage 42–3, 61, 385
Paupers, resident 61
  see also Destitute
Peace of Augsburg 68
Peasant
  rebelliousness xix
  uprising 259
Peasantries, rural 287
Peasantry 362, 367, 423
  seventeenth-century 77
Peasants 37, 39, 40, 42, 76, 95, 147, 152, 156, 165, 305, 371, 401, 428
  "stupid and uncouth" 419
  well-to-do 171
  see also Commoners, Farmers
Peasants, Most 38
Pechta 96
  see also Berta, Diana, Venus
Peer pressure, informal 384
Penalties 352, 355, 357–8, 406
Penance 72, 75, 156, 238
  preached 261
  prescribed 382
Pendulums 224, 232–3, 236, 246, 253

Penetrate   160–1
Penitentials, Early medieval   152
Penitentiary   353, 415, 426
    see also Incarceration, Jail, Ludwigsburg
Pentateuch   398
Pentecost evening   283
People
    bad   305, 322
    lonely   293
    magical   340
    night   96
    sick   296–7
Perceptions   xiv, xv, xix, xx, 9, 16, 21, 30–1, 82–4, 101, 105, 125–6, 139–40, 159–60, 162–3, 176, 197, 202, 204, 207–8, 236, 247–8, 291, 297, 321, 323, 339, 370, 376–8, 399, 402, 425, 429
    auditory   146
    aural   240
    content of   83
    direct   235
    extraordinary   83
    extrasensory   209
    generated   195
    illusory   440
    impaired   119
    misinterpret   375
    nonconscious   239
    olfactory   84
    sensory   196
    subliminal   377
    suppress   440
    visual   30, 83, 126, 240, 248
    see also Delusions, Images, Illusions, Misperceptions
Percepts   30, 160, 208, 248, 298, 425, 438
    symbolic   160, 298–9
Perceptual
    apparatuses   161
    experiences   30, 83, 66
    field   83, 160, 298
    processes   xx, 30
    systems   30
Performance, healer's   151, 294
Peripheral
    blood vessels   134
    nerve transmissions   143–4
    see also Blood, Nervous system
Persecutions   xvii–xix, 44, 96, 385–6, 390, 400, 402, 412–15
    intense witchcraft   378, 385–6
    see also Mass trials
Persian magu   381
Personal territory   28
Personalities
    integrated   366
    modern   77
Personality
    disorder
        histrionic   12
        multiple   87
    traits
        disagreeable   47
        negative   59
Perversions of Christianity   67, 93, 168
Perversity, functions   168
Pfalz   249
Pfüllingen   222
Pharmaceutical dabblings   132
Pharmacopoeia   135
Phenomena, extraordinary   209
Philosophy   382, 420
    mystical   251
Physicists   325, 333
Physics   256, 325, 333
Physiologic control systems   299
Physiological
    effects, direct   15, 287, 293, 306, 335
    patterns, new   146
    processes   13, 91, 264, 306, 333, 437
    systems   160, 298
Physiology   13, 31, 34, 91, 109, 124, 143, 203–4, 256
Piatte, Zuanue delle   191
Pietism   399
    German   399
    radical   268
    separatist movement   414
    Swabian   420
Pietist
    conventicle   413
    movement   391, 413–15
        radical   413
Pietistic groups   268, 413
Pietists   413–14, 422
    early   399
    radical   413

Pigs 37–8, 400
Pincers, hot 353
Pitchfork 118, 129, 136–7, 148, 168, 179, 212, 316, 417
  riding the 388
  travel on a 149, 344
Placebo effect 209, 288–92, 302
Placebos 149, 288–91, 297
  see also Cells
Planets 255–7, 259
Plants 131, 135, 139–40, 143, 255, 262, 283
  a narcotic ranunculaceous 132
  psychoactive 130, 306
  solenaceous 139
  solo-caneaes 11
Plantsch, Martin 69
Plasters 273, 279
Plochingen 249
Poaching 162–3, 361
Pócs xvii, xviii
Poetry, of blessings 277–8
Poisoners 21, 155, 391
  suspected 405
Poisoning 7–11, 15, 21–2, 39, 40, 46, 51, 117, 155–6, 352–3, 387, 395, 402–6
  accidental 130, 135
  alleged 403
  attempted 51
  suspected 9
Poisonous
  drinks and apples 51
  substances 404
Poisons xv, 6, 8, 9, 11, 15, 21, 38, 45–6, 49, 51–2, 55–6, 73, 135, 147, 152, 155–6, 165, 174, 180, 212, 307, 389, 395, 404, 410, 435
  affair of the 168
  deadly 130
  fly 50
  mixing 50
  synthetic 9
  use 405
  victim 8
  see also Drugs, Herbs, Maleficium, Ointments, Potions, Powders
Police 61, 171
  patrols 61
  systems, state's 406

Police Ordinance, First 352, 361
Policing 405–6
Polished thumbnails 223
Poltergeist
  case, modern 331 ff
  events, reported 333
  phenomena, combined 329
Poltergeists 223, 228, 316, 325, 327–9, 331–3
Popular
  activities 399
  beliefs xvi, xvii, 66, 94, 99, 166–7, 189, 213, 402, 414, 440
  celebrations 95
  culture xvi, xvii, 67, 71, 95–6, 105, 117–18, 167, 174, 185, 188, 212, 271, 339, 341, 347, 350, 362, 371, 402, 419–20, 426, 429, 437
  experiences 124
  magic 337
  magic's adaptability 382
  medical traditions 287
  practices 96, 170, 222, 274, 287, 357, 382, 406, 421–2, 428, 440
  practitioners, Most 438
  prophets 267–8
  traditions 67, 94, 115, 301
  see also Elite beliefs, Magic
Population 41, 60–2, 155, 162, 184, 339, 362, 366–7, 379, 415, 420, 422–3, 429
  floating 191
  itinerant 344
  marginal 210
Portents 259, 264
  singular 259
  see also Omens
Possession 42, 54, 87–92, 101, 154, 170, 193, 201–2, 206, 229, 315, 436
  cases 88–91
  cult 180
  demonic xix, 73, 89–90
  involuntary 205
  mediumistic 200
  societies 89
  young women 90
Postmodernism xviii, xix, 83–4, 108, 375,
Posture 24, 165
  bodily 28, 40

Pot   80, 168
Potency
  reproductive   57, 59
  spiritual   306
Potions   2, 65, 12, 56, 394
  hallucinogenic   135
  herbal   308
  toxic   152
  see also Drugs, Medicines, Poisons
Potter   223, 228, 329, 344
Poverty   167, 189, 349, 364, 423
  bitter   423
  endemic   62
  relative   210
  see also Destitute, Economy, Paupers
Powders   2, 10, 28, 132, 135, 171–2, 237, 247, 279, 305, 315
  a black   280
  fumigating   306
  "inheritance"   180
  noxious   152
  smoked   172
  white   8, 46
Power
  interpersonal   47, 183
  lethal   174
  magical   30, 68, 122, 157, 167, 186, 188, 192, 280–1, 327, 381, 436
  malefic   215
  malign   184, 215
  nonmalefic   29
  occult   11, 94, 280
  potent magical   280
  psychological   6, 211
  repressive   356, 428
  spiritual   169, 200, 285, 353, 435, 437
  unconscious   213
  see also Beneficent, Diabolism, Healing, Magic, Maleficic, Shamanism
Practices
  antisocial   168
  cunning   308
  full-service   152
  illicit   280, 361
  magico-religious   151
  men's   348
  pre-Christian   271
  preparatory   314
  public   342, 347, 352
  ritual   381
  semi-professional   250
  shamanistic   153, 202, 204, 211, 436–7
  thriving   408
  women's   347, 408
Practitioners   xviii, 94, 151, 166, 180, 186, 200, 211–12, 217, 222, 225, 232, 236, 274, 276, 305, 307, 339–45, 350, 360–1, 381, 405, 435–7, 440
  accused   346–7
  beneficent   405
  of beneficent magic   339
  casual   341
  female   346–7
  full service   346
  generalized   343, 345–6
  illicit   285, 361
  licit   307, 397
  local   193, 340
  official   361
  popular   339, 437
  professional   152
  public   340–3, 345–6, 408, 429
  sanctioned   305
  semi-speccialts   250
  single-service   342–3, 346
  skillful   278
  specialized   215, 221, 341, 344–5, 431
  suspected   346
  unlettered   193
  unofficial   361
  unsanctioned   361
  unscrupulous   223
  well-rounded generalized   342
  see also Diviners, Doctors, Healing, Magic, Shamanism, Sorcery
Pray   83, 138, 178, 184, 242, 267, 270, 275, 283, 293, 295, 322, 409, 413–14
Prayer
  book   262
  sessions, all night   426
Prayers   164, 169, 178, 181, 190, 198, 211, 239, 242, 260, 271, 275–6, 284, 286, 294–5, 298, 300, 302, 318, 418, 427
  collective   283

Prayers (*Continued*)
  defensive 247
  earnest 107
  grass 180
  intercessionary 302
  quiet 294
  religious 166
  silent 239
  special 190
  strong 80
Praying 120, 177, 184, 242, 260, 285
  see also Blessing, Incantation
Preacher 29, 38, 49, 70, 72, 74, 82–3, 88, 119–20, 179, 262–3, 267, 305, 316–17, 328–9, 358, 362, 365, 386–8, 397, 414, 417–18
Preaching 357
Precious metals 234, 236, 249, 320
Precognition 247, 253
Prediction, astrological 257–9
Predisposition, cultural 12, 13, 20–1
Preisen, Georg 279, 345
Pressing, magical 135, 161, 173, 212, 309, 439
  see also Out-of-body esperiences, "Old Hag," "Pushing" people
Pressures
  barometric 255
  psychological 15, 43, 225, 227, 331
  raw emotional 22
Pride 71, 355, 365, 420
  professional 254
Priests 72, 98, 132, 154, 169, 186, 242, 277–8, 319–20, 344, 381–2
  early Hebrew 381
  pagan 382
Priming, psychological 161
Prince, Devil as 113, 118–19, 177, 179, 183
Printers 68
Printing 68–9, 72, 170, 185
Prior suspicions 47, 405
Prison 80–1, 365, 428
Private practitioners 340–1, 348
Probation 353, 358, 397, 405–6, 428
Processions of the dead 96, 145, 170
Processor, serial 197
Professions 305, 361, 367–8, 398
Prognostication 250, 254–5, 257–8

Prohibitions 369, 373–4
Property 6, 42, 59, 61, 167, 176, 228, 230, 233, 237, 353, 364
Prophesies 172, 191, 219–20, 258–9, 262, 264, 268–70
  admonitory 259–60
  apocalyptic 259
  biblical 258–9
  discredited 268
  divine 260
  spiritual 260, 266
  spontaneous 219–20
Prophesy, Spontaneous forms of 270
Prophet, false 263
Prophets 267, 269
  see also Divination
Prosecutions xiv, 48, 55, 60, 192, 304, 307, 340, 350, 354–5, 357, 380, 382, 384–6, 390, 399, 400, 402, 405–7, 419, 421–2, 425, 428, 430
  changing pace of 339, 380
  criminal 44, 352
  declining 422
  falter 389
  formal 377
  frequent 405
  full-blown 261
  intense 392
  judicial 340
  legal 371
  pace of 62, 378–80, 384–5, 421
  renewed 353
    secular 358
  tide of 390, 422
  virulent xvi
Prosody 24, 39
Protoindustrial 364
Providential interpretations 391
Provincial intellectual traditions 398–9
  see also Episcipi tradition
Provincial Law Code 70
Provincial Ordinances 162, 248, 352, 357, 361, 367, 405
  anti-blessing (1643) 361
  First (1495) 162
  First Apothacary 361
  First Medical (1720) 361
  First Police (1549) 352, 361
  Fifth (1552) 352, 383
  Funeral 367

Great Church Ordinance (1569)   356, 359, 361, 397
Second Apothacary (1626)   404
Second Medical (1755)   361
Sixth (1567)   2, 352, 358, 383-4
Seventh (1621)   361
see also Laws
Pseudohallucinations   30
Psoriasis   312
Psychic performance   209
Psychoactive substances   133, 147
Psychoanalytic traditions   78
Psychodynamics   18, 91, 226
Psychogenic   127
Psychokinesis   36
see also Parapsychology
Psycholinguistic programming   163
see also Blessing, Incantation, Language, Linguistic, Spells, Sorcery
Psychological
  changes   409
  characteristics   22
  defenses   183
  dimensions   21, 375, 401
  etiology   15
  explanations   63, 91, 290
  factors   xix, 18-20, 38, 199, 286
  forces   15, 22
  influence   19, 26, 288
  integrity   185
  learning   112
  malfunctions   182
  manipulation and magic   54
  mechanisms   29, 65
    repressive   372
  phenomena   200
  problems   19-21, 296, 301
  processes   xix, 12, 15, 16, 18, 19, 63, 381, 435
    repressed   12
  state, marginal   168
Psychology   xix, 16, 34, 91, 124
  bedeviled   198
  cognitive   78
  modern depth   301
Psychoneuroimmunology   299
Psychophysical   15, 33
  benefits   312
  debilities   183

driving mechanism   292
dysfunction   124
endowments   55
manipulations   166
predisposition   60
problems   17, 20
reactions   159, 312, 401
Psychophysical process   12, 17, 226, 331
  analogue   206
  associational-imagic   377
  attentional   144
  autonomic   291, 335
  autonomous   110
  biochemical   255
  creative   112
  dowsing   235
  emotional   78, 86
  hidden   383
  hypnotic   298
  magical   271, 310
  mental   87, 103, 126
  neurobiological   59, 128
  neurocognitive   201-2
  neurological   373, 66
  neurophysiological   74
  novel challenges   110
  physical   84, 247, 260, 315, 320, 398, 419
  psychophysiological   437, 440
  right-brain   377
  storage   111
  symbolic   91
  top-down   350
  unconscious   274, 290-2
Psychophysical processes
  psychosomatic   12
  unconscious thought   269
Psychophysical processing   26, 32, 111-12, 234-5, 249, 373
  analogue   206
  bodily   127
  capacity   204
  cognitive   78, 114, 208, 290, 374, 438
  conscious   207, 373
  cortical   208
  emotion-based unconscious   225
  emotionally charged   369
  mental   372
  nonconscious   236, 375

Psychophysical processing (*Continued*)
 parallel distributed 86, 197
 perceptual 197, 374
 rational 206
 repeated 111
 sequential-temporal 110
 social-emotional 141
 special 373
 subconscious 232
 symbolic 206
 top-level 373
Psychophysiology 349, 372
Psychosocial 26
 dynamics 297
 factors in disease xv, 11ff
 influence 17
 stressors 17
Psychosomatic 15, 302
 factors 37
 problems 286
 reactions 12, 402
Ptolemaic astronomy 256–7
Ptolomaic astronomy and Galenic medicine 430
Pubic hair 168
Punishment 2, 44, 47–8, 115, 138, 149, 238, 261, 316, 323, 354–6, 358, 404–7, 411, 428, 440
Punitive experiences 354
 see also Fines, Incarceration, Prosecution, Social discipline, Trials, Torture
Pupils 25, 130, 143, 360
 constricted 25
Purgatory 240
Purposes, benign 1, 292
"push" people 33, 166, 239
 see also "Old Hag," "Pressing"
Pustules 309, 311–12

Q
Quacks 135, 191
Quarrels 43, 105, 174
 bitterness of 44
 see also Conflicts, Enemies, Interpersonal
Querulous tendencies 58
Quiescent
 functions, body's 294
 system 298
 see also Parasympathetic, Relaxation

R
Raitsen, Gertrudt 276, 286, 291, 295, 303, 342, 347
Random process 227, 438
Rangers, forest 162
Raster, George 309
Rat-catchers 191
"Ratchet effect" 68, 435
Rational
 calculation 350
  conscious 258
 control 440
Rational-linguistic systems 376
Rational thought 439
 processes 206
Rational-verbal representations 377
Rationalist 108, 147
 doubts 242
 interpretations 30
 materialism 326, 377
Rationalistic developments 420
Rationalists, traditional xviii, xix, 94
Rationality 439
Rationalization 126
Rationalize 185, 225
Rau, Maria 11, 19, 406
Rauschenberger, Maria Magdalena 156
Ravens 220
Reality discrimination 31–2
 see also Dreams, Nervous system
Receptor sites 11
 see also Cells, Neurons
Receptors 119, 299
 nerve-end 143
 opioid 297
 peptide 299
 sensory 300
Rechlin, Anna 31–2
Recipes 130, 132, 143, 145, 149, 279, 306, 308
 early modern 143
 salve 140
 standard 130
 see also Drugs, Herbs, Medicines, Ointments, Poisons, Potions
Reciprocity and fear 43, 363
Recognition 26, 54, 86, 153, 160
 conscious 27
 retroactive 179
 unconscious 53

Recovery   292, 295, 302, 312
  coincidental   301
  see also Healing, Medicine
Reflective surface   222–3, 232, 236
  see also Scrying
Reform   xvi, 117, 259–60, 362, 396, 406
  campaign   72, 117, 185, 213, 257, 349, 360, 380, 406
  moral   264
  orderly   266
  schools   415
  suggested   2
Reformation   68, 95, 259, 347
Reformers   72, 391
  Protestant   108
  sixteenth century   72
Reformist worldview   422
Refugees   19, 23, 62
Regensburg   136
Regulation, social   162, 360, 362, 364, 434
Regulation, physiological   297
  cholinergic   147
  increasing   162
  low-level homeostatic   78
Reichenbach   237, 387
Reid, Scottish sorcerer   175
Relaxation   144, 163, 196, 294, 296
  response   144, 298, 300, 302
  see also Parasympathetic, Quiescence
Religion   xx, 43, 72, 183, 193–4, 255, 269, 271, 274, 280, 318, 339, 413
  prehistoric   xvii, xix
Religious
  experience   270
    early modern   84
  rituals
    formal   95
    involved   169
  world   84
    early modern   85
REM   109–12, 125, 195–6, 202
  cats   111
  dream   113
  sleep   110–12, 114, 144, 148, 195, 202–3, 211
  see also Dreams, Sleep
Remedies, home   289, 340

Renaissance   255
  astrological theory   256
  intellectuals   131, 255–6
  state   383
Renaissance Florence   168, 175–6
Rencklern, Margretha   305, 348, 406, 408
Repatterning   146–7
Repetitions   238, 275, 284
Repetitive
  activities   236
  thoughts   290
Repress   xiv, 362, 365, 372, 440
Repression   95, 349, 356, 358, 363, 366, 370, 372–8, 406, 415, 428–9, 440, 337
  active   376
  directionality   376
  enlightened   429
  informal   371
  judicial   381
  of magic   350, 363, 372–3, 375–8, 422, 429, 431
  psychological   374
  reflexive   425
  socio-cultural   374
  systematic campaign of   339
  three centuries   440
Repressive mechanisms   339, 372
  see also Denial of magic, Deterrent effect, Expulsion of ideas,
Reproductive
  problems   20–1
  systems   58
  see also Impotence
Reputation   43, 47–8, 50, 55, 99, 104, 106, 183, 231, 243, 308, 327–8, 345, 355, 365–6, 371, 390, 406, 408, 411
  family's   327
  unsavory   371
  woman's   56
Resources   59–62, 363, 389, 434
  capital   424
  economic   307
  impacted material   363
Resurrection   192
Retaliation   23, 56, 168, 400
  extralegal   45
  righteous   179
Retina   83–4
  see also Eye, Evil eye

Retribution 61, 364
  informal 411
  spontaneous physical 1
  unnatural 329
Retroactive
  falsifications 48
  interpretations 400, 402
  reworking 434
Retrocognition 247
Retterstein 311
Rettnier, Margaretha 37
Reuss, court physician 361
Reutlingen 118–20, 129, 148–9, 344
Revelations 219, 267, 269
  spiritual 258
Revelry 43, 94, 122, 187
Revenge 116, 156, 309, 410, 424
Reverse-shamanism 377
Rewards for moral spies 363
Rhine River 41, 253, 257, 263
Rhine Valley 194
Rhineland 257
Rhodt 387
Rhythmic
  activities 202, 296
    repetitive 202
  activity, subdued 298
  group activities 292
  movements, gentle 300
  sounds 292
  stroking 300
  structure 292
Rib 157, 190–1, 222
"Richella" 179
Richenbach 311
Richter, Dorothea 75–6, 79, 86–7, 90
Ridicule 105, 372
Right hemisphere processes 376
Rippen, Anna Maria 133
Rites 95, 168–9
  arcane 170
  blasphemous 168
  obscene 93, 97
Ritual
  actions 170, 220, 274, 302, 311, 341, 430
  activities 172, 247, 279, 287, 298–9, 315, 382, 435
    illicit 382, 413
    intense 296
  acts 239
  behaviors, organized 181
  circles 171
  death 192
  experiences 187
  healing 297, 299
  incantation 165
  magic 1, 52, 156, 165, 172
    harmful outlawed 1
    learned 193
  magicians 186
  preparations 161, 315, 430
  procedures 240
  process 285
  systems 375
  training 210
Ritualistic activities 315
Ritualized mutilation 153
Rituals 29, 55, 70, 153, 155, 161–2, 165, 168, 170–1, 175, 180, 186, 193, 209–12, 224–8, 230, 232, 237–40, 246–7, 269, 271, 274, 277, 280, 283, 285, 293, 295–6, 300, 302, 310–16
  athletes use 198
  collective rhythmic 293
  complex 152, 170
  defensive 308
  deliberate 2
  empty 413
  extreme 437
  invocatory 249
  involved performing 227
  modifying 274
  prolonged rhythmic 297
  protective 272
  restrained 296
  sanctioned 276
  secret 45, 166
  shamanistic 437
  unspecified 315
Rivalries 105, 433
Röcklin, Hans 280, 282, 284–5, 289, 303, 342, 347
Rods 137–8, 171, 224, 232–3, 235, 246
  buried iron 234
  divining 235
  trips on the 138
Rogel, Bueschelin 400–1
Rolle, Johann Michael 33

Romania   187
Rommelshausen   243
Root, sack with a   280
Roots   46, 131, 155, 180, 279–80, 286, 321
Roper, Lyndal   xvi, 81, 85
Rosary   184
Rosenfeld   133, 174
Rosenheim   333–4
Rostock   391
Rothin, Anna Maria   10, 11, 14, 19, 21, 46, 56–7, 306, 308
Rottenberg   282
Rowlands, Alison   xvi
Ruchhinbrodt, Margretha   8
Rueff, Anna   13, 17, 18, 28
Rueff, Hans   14, 22, 28, 49, 50, 56–7, 169, 304, 400
Ruethandten, Philipp Jacob   321
Rumor, basic law of   100
Rumors   29, 97, 99–103, 106, 164, 262, 309, 324, 355, 357, 372, 386–7, 389
Rural areas   429
Rustic community spirit   43
   see also Communities, Farms, Peasants, Villages

S

Sabbaths   65, 93, 96–7, 117, 121–3, 129, 138, 140, 148–50, 168, 186–7, 205, 388, 391, 400, 412, 434–5
   children conducted   115
   diabolic   212
   see also Dances, Diabolism, Festivities, Fly, Night dance
Sabean   76–7, 79
Sabean, David   76
Sacher, Agatha   12, 28, 14, 23, 28–9, 46, 49, 56–7, 222, 305, 388, 411
Sacraments   89, 184, 121, 267, 327, 357, 381
Sacred
   grove   194
   objects, misappropriated   169
Sacrifices   314
Sacrilegious   162, 172, 176, 65
Sagittarius   254
Saints   186–7, 193, 277–8, 319, 382
St. Anthony's Fire   9

St. Boniface   382
St. Christopher   171–2, 236–9, 246, 248, 313, 319–20
St. Hubert's key   282
St. John the Evangelist   275
St. Killian   224
St. Marta   175
St. Peter   224, 259
Salinaro, Maria   180
Salt   50, 280, 309–10
Salves   2, 11, 14, 28, 80, 119, 129–32, 136, 144–6, 149, 161, 168, 210, 279, 282, 284, 417
   bogus   130
   datura-based   141
   hallucinogenic   131, 136, 141, 143, 148–9
   inert   130, 149
   see also Anoint, observed people; Drugs, Hallucingens, Medicines, Ointments, Potions, Remedies
Salz   240
Sami   187
Samples of cases explained
   beneficent magic   216–17
   general magic   4
   witch   3
Sanctions   352, 357–8, 440
   explicit legal   378
   external   365
   formal   372, 1
   informal   372, 428
   mildest   357
   public   381
   symbolic   358
   see also Communal, Repression
Sanskrit poetry   277
Sap   279, 284
Sarrith   173
Satan   2, 7, 70, 74–5, 77, 121, 175–7, 180, 227, 238, 323, 416
   abominable   82
   firm stand against   324
   an illusion of   417
   loathsome   82, 88, 388
   renouncing   324
   see also Devil, Lucifer
Satanic
   arts, use   359
   ritual abuse   74

Satanism 168
Satan's servants 65
Satirical polemics 419
SATOR talisman 280–1
Sattler, Sigfried 241–2, 322
Saüberlichin, Barbara 408
Sauer, Abraham 130
Sauerzapf, Jakob 231
Sauter, Sara 283–5, 342, 347
Saÿer, Bernhardt's wife 303
Scapegoat figure 12
Scapegoating process 49
Scapulomancy 220
Scepticism, pious 422
"Schäfer J" *see* Franck, Hans
"Schafer Jerg" 319
Schaff, "Wild Georg" 173, 313, 316, 349
Schäffer, Jacob 276, 279, 281–4, 286, 289, 291, 293, 295–6, 298, 303, 308, 343, 345, 347
Schatzgraberei 232, 216
Scheelkrautt 283
Schelling, Anna Maria 9, 15, 49, 56, 305, 404
Schiller, Hans Jacob 223, 228–31, 329, 345, 427
Schizophrenia 124
Schizophrenic patients 32
Schlenzer, Hans 243–4
Schlosser, Ursula 49
Schmettlin Konrad 38
Schmid, Magdelena 133–5, 141, 144, 167
Schmidt, Ursula 31–2
Schmied, Barbara 8, 55, 132, 305, 389
Schnabel, Anna 29–31, 162–3, 167
Schneeberger, Egidins 136
Schnedler, Ludwig 241
Schneider, Maria 9, 15, 37, 46, 56–7, 389, 404, 410
Scholasticism 93, 96, 66
Scholderer, Zimmerman 342
Schölhornin 156, 165
Scholl, Maria 426
Scholl, Maria Agnes 236
Schollen, Anna 45, 306
Schöllhornin 156
Schondorf 8, 77, 156, 169, 282, 305, 307
Schöntal 244

School
  inspectors 363
  ordinances 72
  system 359
Schooling, primary 420
Schoolmaster 362
Schools xviii, 191, 254, 356, 359–60, 364, 368, 420, 440
  cloister 358, 368
  high 359, 420
  Latin 348, 360, 368
Schoolteachers 357
  see also Education
Schott, Gaspard 224
Schu, Jacob 241, 244, 322, 427
Schulen, Christina Dorothea 231–2, 251
Schuten, Hannß 295
Schwandorf 243
Schweickhlen, Hans Conrad 14, 27, 38, 49
Schweickhlen, Christoph 14, 56, 400
Schweizer, Jacob 322
Schwendel, Anna 88
Schwieberdingen 254
Science, Christian 301
Scientific
  explanatory systems 326
  revolution 383, 430
Scopolamine 11, 143
  see also Drugs
Scot, Reginald 23
Scotland 6, 117, 154, 175, 188
Scribes 351, 362, 368
Scribner, Bob 412
Scripts 74, 114, 125
  cultural 113–14, 129, 225
  social 74
Scriptures 190, 243, 267, 414
Scrofula, cure 300
Scrying 222–7, 230–1, 236, 246, 251, 253, 286, 308, 426, 438
  see also Dissociation, Divination
Sebald, Hans xviii, 167
Second Apothecary Ordinance 404
Secret
  censors 357, 363, 366
  spies 406
Secular 268, 350, 356, 420
  administration 356–7
  intervention 142

magistrates 94
  order 258
  professionals 397
Seeds 145, 154–5
  henbane 145
  see also Drugs, Magic
Seeger, Catharina 51
Seeger, Georg's wife 13
Seers 240
  lay 265
Segen 276
Seizures 8, 132
Self 77, 85, 87–8, 92, 112, 127, 200, 203, 207–8, 299, 431, 440, 337
  autonomous 77
  -censorship 355, 365, 374
  -confidence, boost 208
  -consciousness 315
  -control 371; rational 432
  -definition 94, 415
  -delusion 30, 209, 247
  -destructive social role 159
  -directed identity 431
  -hypnosis 290–1
  -knowledge 256
  normal conscious 87
  -recognition 255
  -regulation 306
  -restraint 58; personal 40
Semiotic
  analysis 91
  idiom 374
Semioticians 92
Semiotics xviii, 91, 109
Sensations 9, 21, 34, 36, 124–5, 127, 136, 140, 144, 149, 196, 297, 301, 375, 434, 439
  coherent 125
  disembodied 204
  hypnopompic 35
  painful 12
  physical 86
  physiological 240
  real 297
  visceral 225
  see also Consciousness, Nervous system, Psychophysical processes
Sense
  data 248
  modalities 87, 160

Sensibility, elites changing 426
Sensitivity
  to elecromagnetic environment 234, 249
  to subliminal signals 208
Sensorimotor deprivation 146
Sensorium 247–8, 402, 434, 438–9
  see also Perception, Cognition, Nervous system
Sensory
  cues 249
    normal 234
  deprivation 148, 202–3
  experiences 225
  input 83, 146, 197, 434
    discrete 126
    multiple 83
    systems 110
  modalities 31
  organ, earliest 300
  systems 12, 26, 31
  transfers, cross-modal 160, 298
  see also Perception, Cognition, Nervous system
Sensory-filtering 59
Sentence, indefinite 418, 428
Separatists 413
  radical 413–14
  see also Pietism, Women
Sermons 70, 72, 76, 118, 121, 263, 265–6, 324, 327, 358, 373, 398–9
  church 100
  pious 261
  preacher's 268
  witch 358
  see also Enculturation, Demonology
Serotonin 144, 203
Serrin, Anna 8, 9, 15, 21, 133
Servant 75, 98, 167, 175, 281, 344, 349, 362, 367
  girl 10, 14, 22, 56, 97, 133, 164, 174, 239, 241, 244, 410
  woman 270
Servants, propertyless 42
Services
  basic Sunday morning 73
  beneficient 179, 211, 222, 237, 250, 322, 339, 341–5, 360–1, 429–30, 437–8
  casual neighborly 407

Services (*Continued*)
  obligatory communal labor 364
  regular 43
  see also Catchism, Enculturation, Repression
Seventeenth century 62, 114–15, 117, 123, 154, 162, 171, 181, 191, 267, 321, 354, 368, 370, 386, 390, 404–5, 411, 413, 416, 422, 429
  early 40, 63, 380, 388, 394, 397
  late 42, 180, 212, 248, 251, 316, 359, 361, 370–1, 380, 391, 400, 405–6, 411, 415
  mid- 129, 233
  mid-to-late 115, 118
  women in 411
Sex 7, 53, 58–9, 65, 77, 79–82, 85, 88–91, 97, 105, 121–2, 128, 148–9, 168, 176–7, 202, 228, 280, 306, 342, 365, 388, 401, 409, 417–18
  in early modern diabolic possession 90
  illicit xv, 135
  indiscriminate 168
  involved 115
  organs 12
Sexual 78–9, 115, 408–9
  activities 128
  acts 97
  anxieties 90
  assignations, semi-furtive 95
  dysfunction 15, 16
  experiences 435
  fear 401
  features 94
  gratification 206
  impurity 90
  misbehavior 46
  misconduct 90
  misdemeanor 365
  offenses 241
  problems 17
  relations 139
  transgressions 90
Sexuality 408, 410
  children's precocious 117
  excessive 412
  lurid 434
  unconscious 409
  women's 411

Shaman
  clan 154
  commands spirits 277
  healer stage 278
  healers 278, 293
  inspired 211
Shamanic 201, 204, 211–13, 274
  activity xvii, 246, 270
  attacks 154
  concept of disease 305
  cultures 191
  divinatory techniques 270
  ecstasy 296
  experiences 192, 204, 207, 436
    mediumistic 205
  healers 277, 292
  healing 277, 292, 295–6
    classic 436
    rituals 209
  initiation 185–7, 192, 206–7, 209, 211, 213, 301, 435
  journey 277
  northern Asia's 279
  performances 278
    classic 291
  practices 170, 187, 202, 206–7, 211, 277, 437
    archaic 170
    early modern 437
    local 211
    manifest 206
  practitioners 151, 206, 209, 211, 437
  societies 199
  sorcery 212
  soul travel 189
  states 208, 210
    entered 211
  stories 192
  traditions 191, 193
  trance 223
  tribal cultures 296
  visions 206
Shamanic ASCs 207
Shamanism xvii, 151, 185–9, 192–5, 197, 201, 209–13, 289, 335, 435–7
  beneficent 213
  classical 187, 210
  highlights 192

pristine archaic 210, 437
spontaneous initial experience 211, 437
Shamanist 201
Shamanistic 193, 201, 212–13, 246, 270, 274
  activities 339
  phenomena 194
Shamanizing 436
Shamans 151-3, 170, 185-7, 191-2, 197–201, 210, 245, 277–9, 290, 293, 436
  candidate 209
  classic 277, 291
  nineteenth century 186
Shaman's status 209
  see also Consciousness, Healing, Practitioners, Sabbaths, Simultaneous discharge, Tuning
Shame 365
Shapeshifting 140
Shards, pottery 80
Shared experience 37
  see Experiential model
Sheep 155, 266
Shelter, public 169, 397
Shenk, Gustav 145
Shepherds 50, 76, 169, 244, 343–5, 362, 404
  "ridiculous" 419
Shoot 313–15, 410
Shooting contests 181, 313, 407
Shore, Brad xx
Shot, free 169
Siberia 187
Siberian
  healers 289
  shamanism, classic 192
  shamans 187, 210
  tribes 186, 435
  see also Shamanism
Sicilian *donnas* 122–3
Sick person 227, 274, 305, 327
Sieve and shears 224–8, 230, 233, 253, 256, 269, 438
  see also Divination
Sign, natural 92
  see also Semiotics
Signals
  emotionally charged 409

friendly 27
unconscious 230
Silling, David 244, 319
Silver 234, 244, 314
Simultaneous discharge 223, 296, 298, 306, 436
  See also Ecstasy, Shamanism, Tuning
Sindelfingen 13, 275–6, 305, 342, 347, 406, 408
Sindlingen 241
Sinful
  activities 322
  disgrace 114
  folly 316
  highly 426
  life 242
  thoughts 358
Single-service providers 343–6
Sinners 239, 314, 324, 357, 363, 399
Sins 58, 68, 72, 75–6, 82, 114, 168–9, 238, 261, 265, 267, 310, 322–3, 329, 357, 363, 381, 399, 407, 420
  collective 90
  common 261
  human 71
  incestuous 428
Sixteenth century 38, 41, 44, 60–1, 68–9, 71, 73, 77, 96, 117, 162, 188–9, 191, 213, 220, 233, 251, 255, 347, 349, 351, 353, 358, 360, 366, 369, 378, 383, 386, 390, 409
  early 69, 71, 177, 383
  late 40, 60, 63, 73, 88, 115, 117, 251, 347, 352, 368, 386
  mid- 162, 378, 380
Sixth Provincial Ordinance (1567) 2, 352, 358, 383–4
Skeptical
  critique 439
  scientists 324
Skepticism 117, 398, 418–19
  elite 418
  pious 419, 422, 424, 426
Skeptics 36, 129, 225, 235, 259, 301, 334
Skills, linguistic 434
Skin 11, 21, 85, 145, 154, 157–8, 267, 300, 311
  human 29, 168

Skull 169, 173
Slanders 48, 98, 107, 317–18
  see also Conflicts, Enemies, Hatreds
Sleep 33, 77, 88, 107–9, 111–12, 121, 126, 129, 132, 139, 144, 146–9, 153, 161, 195–6, 198, 204, 206, 211, 295, 410
  deprivation 297
  normal 122
  nREM 109–10, 113–14, 195–6
  paralysis xix, 125, 128, 239
  rapid eye movement 109
Sleepwalking 114, 332
Sleigh-of-hand 290
Slutovsky, Moshe xix, 90
Small-holders 42
Small waves 73
Smallholders 42, 60
Smear 10, 11, 21, 136, 161, 168, 263, 284, 308, 417
  see also Maleficium, Ointment, Poison, Salve
Smells 54, 126, 295, 438
Smile 27, 111
Smith 10, 344–5, 347–9, 401
  apprentice 173, 313
Social
  bonding 300
  discipline 118, 363, 411–12
    confessionalized 117; see also Communal supervision, Enculturation, Punitive experiences, Regulation, Rewards for moral spies
  forces xviii, 53
  order 104, 183, 259
  relations, disrupted 20
  relationships 20–1, 38, 40, 46, 79, 104–5, 273, 397
  rules 373
  space, women's 52
  standing 428
  status 59, 74, 183, 307
    low 183
  stresses 13, 20
  structures 104, 159, 240
  superiority 371
  support 274, 292–3, 300
  tensions 158
    displaced 66
  weapon, effective 27

Socialization 13, 54, 296, 373
  see also Enculturation, Repression
Society
  provincial 344, 362, 370, 378, 337
  small-scale 168, 211
    tribal 287
  traditional 431
  see also Communities
Sociocultural 5, 52, 440
  challenges 60
  constraints 226
  expectations 53
  forces 52
  images 53
    internalized 53
  structures 53
  trends xv
  see also Enculturation, Repression
Socioeconomic 200, 264, 337
  change 415
  circumstances 248, 344
  conditions 402
  developments xiv, 422
  resentments, generalized 103
  situation 386
  threshold 422
  see also Conflict, Economy
Söhnstetten 156, 165
Solanaceae
  family 130, 143
  hallucinogens 141
  see also Anticholinergics, Drugs, Salves
Soles, a pair of 281
Solomon's seal 309
Somatic
  disorders 16
  symptoms 12, 13, 16, 88, 400
Somaticizations 402
  symbolic 12, 39, 296, 312, 433
  see also Conversion reaction
Somatization 13
  direct 311
Somatosensory stimulation 114
Songs 242–3, 246, 275, 349, 408, 414
Soothing activities 298
  see also Influence, Relaxation response
Soothsaying 250, 267, 284, 340, 352, 384
  see also Divination

Sorcerers   154, 166, 168, 175, 183, 215,
      345, 359, 382
   a colony of   180
   hired   175
   professional   152
   reputed   29
   wandering   190
Sorceresses   131, 154
Sorcery   1, 2, 28–9, 67, 151–9, 161,
      163–73, 175, 177, 179–81, 183–5,
      187, 189, 191, 193, 195, 197, 199,
      201, 203, 205, 207, 209, 211–13,
      215–16, 292, 303, 311–12, 319,
      335, 381–2, 435
   cases   175–6, 180
   diabolic   175, 270
   evidence of   2
   late medieval trials for   168
   malefic   158
   mechanistic   153
   new form of   67
   paraphernalia   28
   popular   157, 222
   practice of   153, 155, 180, 185
   ritual   212, 294
   shamanistic   153, 213
   suspected   440
   temptation to use   156
   trials
      Florence   175
      late medieval   152
   see also Consciousness, Conflict,
      Curses, Incantation, *Maleficium*,
      Mirror neurons, Poisons, Ritual,
      Shamanism, Witchcraft
Sortilegii   272
Soul
   flight   188, 200–2, 277
      replacing   153
   journeying   151
   journeys   187, 210
   travel   94, 189, 436
   see also Out-of-body experiences,
      Flying, Shamanism
Souls   76, 96, 125, 172, 177, 186–7,
      189, 238, 240, 247, 260, 314,
      420
   damned   171, 238
   departed   191
   lost   323
   redeemer of   243

sick
   people's   436
   person's   205
   trapped   172
   see Ghosts, Shamanic healing,
      Treasure-hunting
Soup   8, 9, 15, 49, 56, 307, 340
Space
   personal   28, 126
   temporary home   28
Spain, late medieval   265
Spanish America   183
Spanish Succession, War of   258
"Spar"   43
   see also Community, Quarrel
Spatial behavior   24
Specialists
   magical   95, 186, 222, 226, 245, 250,
      278, 304, 341–5
   practitioners   340
   religious   339
   sanctioned   361
   semi-professional   172
   spiritual   323, 339
   see also Healers, Practitioners,
      Shamans, Sorcerers
Spee, Friedrich von   392–3, 398–9
Speech   24, 109, 120
   calming effects of rhythmic   163
   inner   109
Spell   50, 156, 159, 162, 164–7, 173, 287,
      303–4, 308–9, 311–12, 319, 412
   casting
      overt   22
      ritual   21
   grass   162, 167, 173–4, 406
   harmful   29, 154
   impotence   154
   invincibility   319
   see also Blessing, Curse, Incantation,
      Love magic, Magic, Mirror
      neurons, Nervous system, Ritual,
      Sorcery
Spener, Johann   399, 413
Speyer   387
Sphere, domestic   349
Spinning bees   261
Spirit
   adjuration   246
      cases   248
   allies, enlisting   170

Spirit (*Continued*)
  contacts 246
  doubles 95
  flight 277
  guarding 238, 342
  helpers 153
    personal 153
  incantation 421, 424
  manifestations 80
  overarching 200
  prophesy 259
  queens, Celtic 194
  rambunctious 329
  traditions 185
  troublesome 236, 321
  world 88, 97, 151, 170, 185–7, 191–2, 194, 198, 200, 205, 207, 212, 245, 277, 291, 435–6
Spirits 68, 80, 85, 94–7, 123, 141–2, 150–3, 155, 162, 170–2, 176, 186–9, 192, 194, 200–2, 204–5, 207–9, 211–13, 235–43, 245–7, 259–60, 269–72, 274, 276–7, 287, 303, 305–6, 320–3, 381–2, 426–7, 436–7
  benign 191
  bothersome 273, 343
  chaotic 71
  contact 186
  ethereal 215
  in European popular culture 240
  helping 186
  neutral 382
  non-Christian 212, 276, 300
  obscure 170
  perceiving 201, 206
  sacred xvii
  summon 170, 437
  unidentified 241
  unseen 215
  water 171
  see also Autonomous, Consciousness, Dreams, Shamanism, Nervous system
Spiritual
  activity 381
    illicit 183
  agency 176, 227, 235
  apprenticeship 193, 236
  chameleon 82
  contacts 248–9
    illicit 212
  depravity 92
  entities, independent 235
  experiences 402, 413
  forces 193
  intervention, illicit 233, 235
  life 422
  phenomena 306
  practices 186, 194
    legitimate 383
  presences 247
  pretenses 267
  progress 92
  quests 170
  reality, alternate 142
  traditions 193
  trance 200
  universe 435
Spiritualist 224
Spirituality, popular 95
Spitalen 60
  see also Almshouses
Spör, Jacob 99, 101–2
Spreter, Johann 70
SSCs (Shamanic states of consciousness) 202
  see also Consciousness, Shamanism
St. Christopher *see* St. Christopher
Stadi, Hanns Jerg 236–7, 247, 281, 309, 342, 424
Standards 72, 90, 95, 366, 370, 372, 415
  enforcing 366
  moral 72
  multiple 366
  public 363
  strict 354
  see also Communal, Enculturation, Repression, Social discipline
Stars 258–60, 266–8
  bright 266
  fixed 255–6
Stattler, Sigfried 242
Stauffen 326–8, 330
Stealthiness 313, 316–17
Steinach 343
Steiner, Margaritha 174–5, 388, 408
Steinler, Barbara 309–10
Stephens, Walter xvi
Stereotyped
  assumption 167
  recruitment process 434

suspects 390
witch experience 139
Stereotypes 68, 74, 117
    cultural 409
    demonological 140
    gender 268
Stereotypical 128, 167
    suspects 55
Stick, forked 233
    see also Dowsing
Stiefel, Esaias 267
Stiekhels, Simen 189
Stier, Conrad 283, 308, 343
Stift 358
    see also Clergy, Tübingen University
Stigma 159, 365, 428
    see also Communal, Honor,
Stimulation, intense 147
Stimuli 24, 26, 32, 58, 146, 149, 160, 184, 197–8, 202–3, 211, 225, 268
    external 110, 120, 197–8
    internally generated 203
    perceived 374
    repetitive 294
    see also Drivers, Perception
Stimulus overload 146
    see also Consciousness, Ecstasy, Nervous system, Simultaneous discharge, Shamanism, Tuning
Stink 82–3, 244, 409
Stockhenhäuser, Gorg 169
Stocklin, Chonrad 189
Stockperson, emotional effect on animals 38
Stolen
    goods 81, 175, 310–12, 349
        recover 191
        return 312
    objects 188, 220
    things 219, 229–31, 243, 269, 310–11, 322
Stomachache 134, 286, 308
Stone 133, 174, 280–1, 284–5, 303, 322, 326, 328, 342
    curing 282, 284–5, 342
Storms 70–1, 127, 152, 386, 391, 410, 417
    arouse 155
    destructive 323
    raised 398

Stosser, Agatha 7, 14, 27, 38, 49, 56–7, 157, 186, 222, 306, 308, 400, 408
Strapado 354
Strasburg 69, 96, 132, 231, 237, 252, 257, 277, 322, 406
Strawberry patch 133–4
Streich, Konrad 17, 23, 56, 389, 401, 408
Strength, unusual 205, 272–3, 313, 316–17, 348
Stress 15, 16, 18–20, 24, 32, 37–8, 91–2, 126, 158–9, 226, 292–3, 297, 311–12, 401, 433
    chronic xix, 16, 18, 33, 297
    compounds indicating 203
    from countermagic 312
    curtails 16
    effect 16
    inducing 19, 165
    inescapable 12
    levels 300
    moderate 32
    personal 202
    physical 437
    psychological 16, 20, 202, 228, 296
    reaction 17, 32, 39, 298
        generalized 165
        suppresses 298
    reducing 300
Stress-related
    organic problems 120
    somatic disorders 16
Stress response 15, 16, 18, 23, 25, 32–4, 164–5, 298, 433
    see also Arousal, Drivers, Ergotropic system, Fight/Flight response, Psychophysical Processes, Nervous system, Psychosocial, Psychosomatic
Stressors 16
Strokes
    in healing 119, 276, 284–5
    with rod, coercive 428
    as witchcraft 14, 27, 35
Stroking 282, 289
    repeated 296, 298
    see also Healing, *Maleficium*, Rhythmic, Touch

Stuertzen, Margaretha   14, 22, 49, 56, 304, 400
Stuttgart   69, 88, 96, 106, 177, 227, 231, 236, 251–2, 254, 257–8, 261, 305–6, 319, 323, 362, 366, 370, 384, 390–1, 420
Subliminal   226, 437
  cues   227
  give-and-take   256
  interaction   227
    intricate   166
  sensitivity   249
  signals   208
  stimuli   374
  see also Communication, Perception, Unconscious
Submodules   86
  see also Networks, neurocognitive
Subordinate groups   54
Substances   105, 203, 239, 273–4, 288, 301, 314
Subvocalization   85–6, 227, 292, 294
Succubi   80–1
Suggestibility   xv, 126, 294
Suicide   11, 19, 71, 77, 256
Suicide's colon   314–15
Sulz   13, 134, 158, 284, 321, 405
Summers, Montague   93
Sun   255–6, 266, 268, 283, 317, 321
Sunday   138, 261, 263, 283, 285, 359
  morning   229
Sunspot activities   255, 257
Sunspots   255, 320
Superego   76–7
  see also Devil, Repression, Social discipline
Superintendent, district   29, 98, 266, 358
Superintendents   98–9, 101, 316, 356–7
  biannual reports   357
Supernatural   28, 227, 280, 285, 321, 383, 398, 401, 425
  aggression   273
  aid   171
  attacks   37
  bewitching   29
  causation   419
  delusions   xvi
  effect   319, 425

entity, presumed   321
  features   381
  forces   232, 215
  injury   343
  manipulation   321
  miracles   319, 420
  phenomena   323, 216
  powers   177, 208–9, 273, 318
    ascribing   209
  processes   313
  see also Anomalous, Magic, Miracles
Supersition, shameful   427
Superstition   240, 324, 420, 425
Superstitious   136, 282, 322, 420, 215
  art   310
  nonsense   xviii
  people   324
  preconceptions   22
  see also Enlightenment, Repression
Surgeon   329–30, 397, 400
  see also Barber-surgeons
Surgical procedures   282, 297
Surreptitious milking   7, 228
Surveillance, intrusive   399
Susanna Catharina, Johann Brand's sister-in-law,   8, 15, 133
Swabia   96, 190
  upper   179
Swabian Alb   41, 96
Swabian League   61
Swabian traditions, ancient   211
Swäbisch Gmünd   96
Swindle   241, 427
Swindlers   191, 232, 245, 322, 427, 429
Switzerland   69, 89, 97, 184, 194
Sword blades   223
  see also Scrying
Syllogistic reasoning, impared by belief   374
Symbol
  processing   159
  systems   5, 91
Symbolic
  actions   39, 159
  penetration   160, 166, 211, 236, 298–300, 437
Symbols   xx, 76, 91–2, 159–61, 193, 200, 203, 206, 212, 253, 256, 273–5, 280, 289, 294, 298–300, 374–5

cultural   39, 113–14, 161, 166, 182, 297
occult   280
system of   91, 125, 161
Sympathetic nervous system   147, 298
see also Arousal, Ergotropic, Nervous system, Stress
Sympathies, occult   233, 382
Symptoms   12, 14, 15, 17, 21, 50, 58, 88, 91, 119–20, 132, 145, 210, 286, 305, 307, 400, 402
   accusatory   12, 33, 400
   conversion   13, 19
   exaggerated   88
   hysterical   303
   see also Stress, Poison
Synchronistic spirituality   201
Synchronization, neurocognitive   147, 293, 296, 436
   see also Ecstasy, Shamanism, Simultaneous discharge, Tuning
Synod   266, 356–7
   church   266
   ducal   358

T
Tacitus   193
Talismans   280, 282, 289, 310, 314, 319, 321, 342, 407
Taltos   201, 437
Tansy   132, 145
Tares   390, 399
Tarot
   card production   252
   cards   251–3
      traditional   253
   see also Cards, Divination
Taverns   70, 98
   -keepers   147
   rumors   118
Tax-farming   261
Taxes   41, 61, 261, 264, 364–5, 371, 423
   excessive   261
Teach   137, 148, 157, 162, 179, 190, 206, 212
Teachers   356, 390
   see also Elite, Education, Enculturation, Enlightenment, Repression, Schools

Techniques
   bad childrearing   117
   a classical hypnotic induction   164
   dissociation Messmer's   301
   illicit   222
   magical   153, 156, 161, 171, 193–5, 220–1, 223–5, 228, 236, 246, 269, 274, 341, 343
      treasure-hunting   249
   modern forensic   230
   personal divination   220
   potent   161
   shared   344
   swapping   181
   therapeutic   275
Teeth   154
Telepathy   36, 247
Teleportation   332
   see also Parapsychology
Telocinobufagine   132
   see also Drugs
Temples   136, 191, 417
Temporal
   dislocation   120
   lobes   126, 292
Temporo-parietal junction   126
   see also Brain, Out-of-body experiences
Tension
   generational   46
   headaches   16
Terror   xvi, 117, 160, 330
   community of   44
   see also Community, Conflicts
Testimony   8, 9, 48–50, 75, 80–1, 102–3, 107, 123, 135–7, 157, 161, 167, 174–5, 192, 316, 326, 388, 416, 418, 423, 427
   coerced   130
   contested   393
   credible   xv
   generating   99
   tortured   xv, 55, 68, 174, 245, 270, 394, 427
Testosterone   16, 53
Texts   70, 94, 108–9, 170, 210
   ancient medical   301
   canonical   200
   narrative   109

Theft 6, 7, 48, 121, 229–30, 272, 303–4, 352, 387–8
  committed 311
  physical 310
  and witch accusations 7
  see also Counteraction, Divination, Lying, Magic
Theodosius 1
Theologians 69, 123, 179, 185, 259, 265, 268, 300, 356, 382–3, 390, 392, 397, 420, 435
  early modern 350
  late-Classical 381
  orthodox 398
  see also Demonology
Theology 71, 358, 420, 1
  evaluated traditional 399
Theory of mind 207
Therapeutic
  effect 289–90
  effects, inherent 306
Therapeutic Touch 301–2
Therapies 74, 209, 282, 288–9, 303
  direct physical 282
  near-touch 302
  spiritual 274, 306
  see also Healing
Theta waves 111
Thief 229, 310–12, 438
  detection 408, 427
  purported magical 316, 348
Thieves 187, 223, 228–30, 232, 250, 312, 341–3, 407
  identifying 229–30, 341
Thigh 10, 14, 19, 56, 158, 279
Thoma, Jakob 38
Thomas, Keith xviii
Thomasius, Christian 419
Thorn apple 130–1, 139, 143
Threat display 45
Threats xix, 23–4, 44, 48, 58, 121–2, 156, 165, 176, 180, 213, 365, 372, 417, 424
  explicit 50
  interpersonal 39
  mortal 147
  occult 339
  overt 433
  signal 25
  spiritual 271
  vicious 44
  see also Conflict, *Maleficium*, Psychophysical processes, Psychosomatic, Subliminal,
Thresholds 152–5, 157
Thumbscrews 354
Thumm, Theodore 391–2, 398
Thursday-to-Friday nights 284–5
Tipping point 386, 413
Toads 132
Tobacco 202
Tobacco-smoking 364
Tobacco, snorted like 171
Tolmayer, Barbara 7, 387
Torture xvii, 3, 7, 51, 57, 68, 80, 94, 97, 99, 117, 130, 138, 148, 157, 174, 179, 263, 354–5, 384, 387–8, 390, 392–4, 396–7, 405, 407, 410, 417, 427–8, 434,
  chamber 174, 354, 412
  contaminates evidence 181
  judicial 354
  magical crimes 393
  mock 262
  session 174
  use 188, 392
  wanton 63
  see also Beaten, Strappado, Thumbscrews
Tortured
  people 397, 437
  suspects 97, 157, 387
  see also Beaten, Flogging, Strapado, Thumbscrews
Torture's effect on self-conception 412
Touch 2, 14, 27, 140, 166, 174, 244, 300–2, 319, 322, 439
  effects of 300
  royal 300
  therapies 301
  witch's 11
Touching 45, 274, 282, 289, 301
  see also Maleficium, Therapeutic Touch
Town
  council 351
  councilors 362
  courts 351, 363
  doctor 307, 329, 360, 404, 417

Index 621

governments 351–2
leaders 367
officials 351, 367
scribe 351, 354
society 434
Towns 7, 31, 41–2, 44, 59, 70, 75, 77, 79, 92, 97, 99, 101, 103, 222, 241, 257–8, 276, 305, 307, 313, 331, 344–5, 349, 351–2, 358, 362–3, 366–8, 371, 384, 387
crowded 42
lesser 368
market 351, 371
secondary 367
small 41, 103, 106, 156, 229, 323, 363, 366, 372, 415
Townspeople 40, 95, 344, 371
see also Commoners, Community, Villagers
Tractatus Tehologius de Magia 398
Tracts 350, 373, 398
see also Pamphlet literature
Tradespeople 136, 147, 344–5, 362
Traditions
learned 67, 193, 314, 320
occult 171
literary 68
local theological 6
materialist-rationalist 288
positivist 288
psychological xvi
regional 193, 278
Tragan 249
Trall, Hanns Greg 169
Tramps 60, 191
see also Destitute, Itinerants, Paupers, Vagrants
Trance xx, 68, 118, 151, 180, 187–8, 192–3, 197–8, 201, 203, 210, 226, 265, 279, 295
battles 154
cataleptic 146
degrees of 200
ecstatic 246, 278
effective for inducing 164
experiences 200–1, 209
deliberate 200
hypnotic 85, 198, 202, 294–6, 311
lying in a 122
shaman's 295

states 128, 148, 151, 164, 172, 198–201, 295
healer's 295
hypnotic 295
therapeutic 295
see also Catalepsy, Consciousness, Ecstasy, Flight, Shamanism
Trance-flight experiences 187
Trances, mini- 197
Tranquilizer 132
a mild 145
Transactions, social 74, 102
see also Community, Face-to-face, Gossip, Interpersonal, *Maleficium*, Slander
Transgressions 73, 76–7, 81, 171, 180, 262, 355, 357, 363, 365, 412
collective 357
furtive 407
inconsequential 353
moral 118, 352, 357
Transgressive thoughts 79
Transmission 24–5, 102, 193, 340, 372
continuous 437
cultural 373
explicit 373
implicit 373
oral 278
Trauma 119, 126
mechanical 14
see also Injury, Stress
Traumatic life changes 32
Travel 119, 122–3, 133–4, 137, 151, 164, 185, 187–8, 261
on the pitchfork 148
Treasure 171–2, 187, 191, 232–3, 235–40, 242–8, 271–2, 281, 309, 320–2, 341–2, 426
actually located 249
buried 171, 232
cursed 238
gain 236, 303
hidden 237, 243, 260, 269, 321, 427
hunted 246
Treasure
locating 232, 239, 320
magic 340
Treasure-finders 171, 232, 237, 244–5, 426
professional 244–5

622   Index

Treasure-hunters   180, 236, 238–41, 244, 248–9, 319, 343, 346
Treasure-hunting   170, 172, 221, 235, 237, 241, 245–6, 248, 250, 319–20, 322, 328, 340–4, 346, 420–1, 423–7, 4, 216
Treasure-Hunting   424
  activities, sponsored   170
  conjurations   321
  divination   248
  fraud   428
  and ghosts   171
  group   247
  incidents   239
  rituals   239
  scandal   341
  trials   423
  see also Divination, Incantation, St. Christopher
Treasure-man   172, 236, 320–1, 323
Treasure-men   320
  procure   320
Treasure-seekers   180, 234
Treasure spirit   239
Treatises   68, 373, 386
Trial procedures   392, 417
  inquisitorial   99
  see also Consultations, Judicial process
Trials   2, 3, 5–9, 11, 12, 14, 25, 28, 31, 36, 47, 49, 52, 55, 57, 62–3, 69, 70, 115–18, 121, 132, 154–5, 157–8, 174–5, 221, 307, 354, 379–80, 383–7, 389–90, 392–7, 405–7, 412, 420–4
  adult   117
  capital, lawyers required   394
  chain reaction   390
  child-centered   115, 118
  children's   116–17
  earliest   173
  early   347, 385, 387, 392, 407
  mass   57, 96, 117, 384, 390, 395, 397, 406
  poison   402–4, 421
  "quick"   392
  rate, per capita   389
  spun out of control   63
  systematic   386
  unrecorded   385

  see also Mass panics, Punitive experiences, Torture
Tribute, extorted by magicians   152
Triggering mechanisms, physiological   288
Trinity   137, 139, 148, 179, 238, 275, 321, 388
Trophotropic   144, 196, 202, 296
  state   196
  see also Parasympathetic, Relaxation response
Tscholi, Hans   189
Tübingen, town and district   69, 118–19, 241, 346, 399
Tübingen University   2, 3, 69–70, 81, 119, 351, 354, 368, 391, 394, 397–9, 420, 426
  law faculty   81, 134, 351, 354, 392–4, 411
  medical faculty   397
  theologians   391, 398, 420
Tübingen Contract   350, 386
  see also Accusatory principle
Tumors   280, 282, 293, 303
Tuning   203, 211, 223, 225, 296, 335, 436–7
  autonomic   300
  effect, full-blown   306
  experiences   436
  see also Drivers, Ecstasy, Fine-tuning, Integrative brain state, Nervous system, Simultaneous discharge
Turenne, Henri   257
Turf   152
Turkey   118, 127–8, 261
Tuttlingen   31, 346
Twigs   156, 171, 280
Tyrol   390

U
Ulcers   16, 37
Ulm   61, 267, 321
Ulmer, Jerg   311
Ulrich, Duke   70
Ultradian
  high   196
  low   196
Unconscious
  behaviors   62
  bias   228
  calculations   53

feedback 253
knowledge 198, 201, 206, 223–4, 227, 230–1, 246, 256, 438
 elicited xv
 minds 78, 150
 misrecording 334
 movements 224, 253
 processing 224–5, 234, 249, 290–1, 294, 296
 re-configuration 35
 reactions 234, 269
 sub-vocalization 120
 thoughts 108
Unconsciousness 197
Underemployment 60–1
Underground xix, 95
 conspiracy 383, 397
 counterreligion 93
 diabolic sect 94
 diabolical counter-religion 181
 heretical
  movements 185; persistent 95
  sect, malevolent 65
 movement 213
  widespread 66
 organization 185
 sect 95, 181, 434–5
 secret 95
Unguents 130–1
 noxious 168
 see also Salves
"Unhold" 69, 305
"Unholden" 96, 410
Universals, biological 201
University 279, 301, 358–9, 368–9, 397
Untertürkheim 391
Urach 82, 173, 236, 248, 309, 313
Urban 429
 areas 429
 communities 3
 culture, developing 429
 elites 413
 guilds 366
 society 40
 see also Towns
Urine 154, 227–8, 237, 281, 309–10
 see also Scrying
Users, early modern 146
 see also Drugs, Network
Utterances 24, 120, 242, 276–7, 373

V

Vagrants 60–1, 117, 229, 348, 423
 see also Itinerants, Tramps
Vaihingen 50
Valens, emperor 382
Value systems 410
Veins 80, 136–7, 148, 417
 also opened a 305
 geological 233–4
Veltin, soothsayer in Richenbach 311
"Veneficium" 394–5, 426
Venice 154, 251
Venus, goddess 191
Venusberg 190–3, 201, 206, 210, 276, 301, 318, 343, 439
 see also Mountain, Shamanism
Verbal
 abuse 44
 activity 54
 curses 152
  public 2
 fluency 54
 thoughts 291
 threats 45
Verbalizations 24, 39, 109, 112
 protracted 239
 see also Blessings, Charms, Curses, Language, Prayers, Vocalizations
Versailles 370
Vervain 309
Vespasian, emperor 249
Victims 3, 5, 8, 10, 11, 14, 21–2, 29, 69, 89, 115, 123, 141, 154, 187, 229, 245, 269, 313, 388–9, 414, 418
Victim's experience 33
Village
 courts 43, 48, 351
 mayors 352
 officials 352, 358
Villagers 38, 40–1, 44, 76, 162, 167, 216, 263, 363–4, 366
 ignorant 419
 ordinary 128, 156, 357
 see also Peasants, Commoners
Villages 3, 18, 38, 41–2, 44, 59, 60, 65, 103, 105, 162, 167, 200, 229, 344–5, 348–9, 351–2, 358, 362–3, 366–8, 372, 390, 413, 415, 434
 overcrowded 41
 overgrown 362
 peasant 362

Villages (*Continued*)
  surrounding 351
  see also Communities
Villages, Württemberg's 363
Villingen 305–6
Vine tender 260–1, 263, 266, 362
Vines 41, 62, 261–5, 268
  bleeding 261–5
Vineyard 79–81, 260–5
Vintners 62, 309
Violence 44–5, 52–3, 55, 61, 180, 202, 389, 405, 410–11
  see also Community, Conflict, Harm, Hatreds
Virgil 191
Virgin Mary 382
Visceral 39, 225, 274, 369, 431
  interconnections 432
  level human connection 430
  reactions 112
  see also Interpersonal, Mirror neurons, Subliminal
Vision, normal 83
Visionaries, inspired 268
Visions 117, 163, 202, 207, 223, 237, 249, 260, 262–8, 331, 439
  angelic 262
  apocalyptic 413
  falsely reported 263
  melancholic 268
  pretended 331
Visitations
  annual 356
    church 386
  biannual 357
  conducted triennial 360
  regular 357
  spring 29
  see also Church courts, Church's supervision systems
Visual 81, 87, 110, 140, 146, 220, 222, 235
  cortex 331
  disorienting 139
  experiences 140, 223
    ambiguous 223
  field 31, 84–5, 197
  hallucinations, prompted 223
  imagery 84
  memories 54, 223
  overlay 224

  processing 126–7, 223
  representation 205
  scenes 86
Visualizations 110, 114, 125, 291–2, 434, 438
  episodic 113
  highly hypnotizable peoples' 198
  manifesting subconscious 232
  semi-conscious 112
  shaman's 292
  spontaneous 291
  strong 90
  vivid airborne 146
  see also Perception, Sensorium
Vita Vagorum 190
Viticulture 41
Vocalizations 274–5, 282, 292–3, 295–7
  primate 292
  quieter 294
  rhythmic 278, 292, 294
  see also Verbalizations
Vogel, Hannß 326
Vogels 326–8
Vogtgericht 386–7
  see also Constables
Vöhringen 133
Voices 24, 44, 76, 85–6, 205, 266–9, 350, 434, 439
  discarnate 260
  imagined 85
  raised 24
  tone of 24, 27, 165
  see also Autonomous, Dissociation
Volition, autonomous 182
Volitional activity 87
Vorarlberg region of Germany 28
Vulnerability 18, 39, 159, 273
  body's 297
  culturally induced 159
  psychophysical 433
  real 65

W

Wagenhals, Wolfgang 254–5, 257–9, 267
Wages, low 423
Wageworkers 41
Wagner, Johann Jakob 88, 401–2, 408–9
Wagner, Margaretha 33–5, 133–6, 166, 173–4, 186, 212, 416–18

Wahlheim 239
Wahnhaasen, Ursula 17
Waiblingen 156, 262
Waiblingen/Winnenden 311
Wakefulness 109–10
Waking-dream state 436
Waking-sleepwalking 88
  see also Dissociation, Shamanism
Waldensian brethren, activities of 193
Waldensians 95–6, 184, 189, 193, 201, 437
  and Paradise 189, 201
Walstettin 329
Walther, Apolonia 118–24, 127–9, 148–9, 177, 179, 206, 212, 318, 344, 424
Walther, Hannß' wife 118
Walz, Reiner xviii, 48
Walzen, Forest Ranger 408
War 41, 61–2, 102, 229, 257–8, 390, 404
Wasserstetten 8
Wasson, Gordon 135
Water 29, 154, 220, 223, 227–8, 233–4, 253, 262, 266, 270, 282
  holy 171, 238–9, 281
Wax figure 154
Weakness, personal 5, 65, 159, 245
Weather 2, 6, 164, 173–4, 220, 255, 257, 320
  magic 6, 67, 166, 193, 433
    hostile 180
Wedding 12, 17, 23, 28, 46, 55–6, 79–81, 84, 95, 132, 222, 305, 371, 388–9, 411
Wedlin, Joacherin 169
"Weiblin", a 306, 308, 340, 408
  see also Cunning folk
Weil, Agatha 10, 33–7, 169, 324, 416
Weilheim 242, 260, 317, 428
Weird trajectories 332
  see also Poltergeist
Weißinger, Weilheim Leonard 317–19, 407
Weyer 391–2, 398, 403, 416
Weyer, Johann 391
Weylandt, Barbara 285–6, 343, 345–8, 408
Weÿldorf 222
Weÿwadels, Georg 309–10
White witches 189

Widows 8, 46, 415
Wieland, Christoph 280–1, 283–4, 289, 310, 342, 346, 424
Wiesensteig 384
Wife 8–10, 15, 19, 50–1, 77, 80–2, 97, 156, 222, 240, 244, 252, 266, 308, 317, 327, 348–9, 371, 387, 404, 408
Wild celery 145
Wild Horde 240, 215
Wild Hunt 96, 240
Wild Ride 96
  see also Diana, *Episcopi*, Fly, Processions of the dead
Wildbad 97–103, 105–6, 304, 307
Wildberg 99, 237, 363
Wine 8, 41, 55, 115, 121–2, 131, 142, 169, 279
  cellars 388
  grower 254
  tender 254
Winnenden 106, 108
Winterbach 75–6
Wisdom 193, 382–3
Witch
  abductions 115, 122
  accusations 51, 62, 105, 415
  cult 93
  dances 46, 50, 74, 97, 99, 102–3, 106–8, 113–16, 118, 120–3, 128, 149, 166, 176, 178, 186, 212, 305, 387–8, 394, 403, 416–17
  demonology 128, 138, 176, 185, 350, 358, 383–4, 399, 400, 402, 409–10, 414, 418–19, 426, 435–7
    late medieval 383
    pan-European 123
  fears 9, 52, 400
  feast 164
  gatherings, purported 181
  identifications 221
  ideology 129, 177, 184–5, 397–8
  literature 51, 70
  mythology 116
  panics 9
  persecutions 62, 93, 170, 191, 340, 347–9, 354, 379, 385, 399, 406, 408, 411, 413–14, 423, 429, 337
    indiscriminate 5
    see also Chain reactions, Mass panics

Witch (*Continued*)
  prosecutions 40, 405, 407, 422
    intense 60
    opposed 391
  publication 69
  stereotype xvii, 354
  trials xvi, 1, 7, 41, 62, 73, 115, 117, 119, 135, 181, 221, 304, 329, 340, 347–9, 351, 354, 391–2, 395, 397, 405, 407–9, 411, 419, 421, 427–8
    child-centered 416
    late 115, 428, 216
    mass 96
Witch-doctor, wandering 191
  see also Itinerant
Witch Hunting 392
Witch-related activities 52
Witch Sabbath xiv, 96, 107
Witch Salves 80, 130, 168, 306
  ingredients 11, 130, 132, 139, 143, 145
Witchcraft
  accusations xvi, xviii, xix, 49, 51, 307, 396,
  activity 105
  allegations 403, 419
  beliefs xvi, xviii, 12, 17, 18, 25, 199
  diagnoses 308
  fears xviii, 20, 32, 47, 62, 413, 415
  new 184, 194
  spontaneous 437
  suspicions 27, 48, 221
    generating 15
  traditional village 434
  trials 63, 396, 402
  see also Conflict, Diabolism, Magic, Maleficium, Social discipline, Trials
Witches 10, 11, 14, 21–3, 28–9, 33, 46–8, 50–2, 55, 69, 70, 93, 96–9, 101–3, 105–7, 121–2, 129, 131, 137–40, 150–1, 166, 168, 172, 176, 180, 186–8, 220–3, 227–30, 307–10, 343, 390–2, 405, 416–17
  combat evil 122, 187
  confessed 123, 397
    considered insane 391
  dance 98, 113
  devil-worshipping 51, 139, 185, 66
  flew 93, 96, 123
  identifying 221, 228, 232, 308

  night-flying 123
  seduced 65
  village 179, 437
Witekind, Hermann 391
Wittenweiler 96
Wittenweiler, Heinrich von 96
Wittershaven 158
Wolff, Christian 420
Wolff, Hanß 99
Wolff, Jacob 33
Woltz, Jerg 98
Women 16, 28, 46–55, 57–60, 63, 69, 90, 92, 105, 117, 122–3, 133, 146, 149, 152, 168, 170, 177, 179–80, 185, 187–8, 312, 342, 346–9, 382, 384, 388, 391, 406–11, 434
  admonished 410
  as accusers 47
  changes in early modern 407–13
  and disciplined behavior 411
  discontented 213
  early modern 55, 58
  elderly 46, 59, 60, 63, 349, 416, 434
  evil 222, 286, 410
  and gossip 105
  healers 408
  holy 409
  learned 413
  malevolent 70
  morality 409
  practitioners 347
  and Pietism 413–15
  "seeing" 188
  sixteenth century 409
  unmarried 364
  wise 68
  and witchcraft suspicions 51
  see also Females, Pietism, Social discipline
Women, Molitors warning to 410
Women's
  brains 54
  conflict strategies 53–5
  weakness 410
  see also Female
Wood 29, 152, 279
Workhouses 61, 415
World, normal 94, 141, 151, 205–7, 436
Worship idols 180
Wound-dressers 397
Wrath, women's 410

Wurster, Maria 88–9
Wurt, Christopher 244–5, 319
Württemberg xiv, xvi, 2, 3, 5, 6, 23, 25, 28, 31, 33, 41–7, 60–1, 67, 69, 71–3, 88–90, 96–7, 120–3, 130, 132–3, 167–73, 175–81, 257–61, 284–5, 337, 345, 349, 351–2, 354–6, 360–1, 370, 390–1

Y
Youth gangs 117

Z
Zen archery 315
Ziegler, Philipp of Nurnberg 267
Ziegler from Dornstettn's bride 12, 23, 305–6

Printed by Printforce, United Kingdom